Green
Perspectives

Green Perspectives

Thinking and Writing About Nature and the Environment

Walter Levy
Pace University

Christopher Hallowell
Baruch College, City University of New York

HarperCollins*College*Publishers

Acquisitions Editor: Patricia Rossi
Developmental Editor: Marisa L. L'Heureux
Project Editor: Claire M. Caterer
Text and Cover Design: Heather A. Ziegler
Cover Photo: Galen Rowell, copyright 1990
Photo Researcher: Roberta Knauf
Production Administrator: Valerie Sawyer
Compositor: BookMasters, Inc.
Printer and Binder: R. R. Donnelley & Sons Company
Cover Printer: The Lehigh Press

Green Perspectives: Thinking and Writing About Nature and the Environment

Library of Congress Cataloging-in-Publication Data

Levy, Walter.
    Green perspectives : thinking and writing about nature and the environment / Walter Levy, Christopher Hallowell.
        p.   cm.
    ISBN 0-06-501500-2 (student edition)
    ISBN 0-06-501501-0 (instructor's edition)
        1. Readers —Nature.   2. Environmental protection—Problems, exercises, etc.
3. Readers—Environmental protection.   4. Nature—Problems, exercises, etc.
5. English language—Rhetoric.   6. College readers.   I. Hallowell, Christopher.
II. Title.
PE1127.S3G74   1994
363.7—dc20   93-28619
                                                                              CIP

93 94 95 96   9 8 7 6 5 4 3 2 1

 Contents

v

PART 2 ❋ 1915–1949: Spiritual, Symbolic, and Practical Responses to the Environment   103

PART 3 ✳ 1950–1975: Conflicting Attitudes Toward the Human and Natural Environments   213

When Mark Fortune sells his rural fields and forest for commercial gain, he says, "The people like you and me with heads on their shoulders know you can't stop the marcher time for a cow."

PART 4   ❋   1976–1993: The Quandary of Achieving Individual and Social Harmony with the Environment   333

Thematic Contents

❧ Observing Nature

❧ Arguments for Wise Use

✳ The Fight for Preservation

✳ People in Nature

❧ Harming the Environment

 # Preface

The way we treat our planet and regard its resources has never been under greater scrutiny. Right now the results of ethical, scientific, and aesthetic examination are beginning to emerge. A balance is in the offing. Governmental regulation against environmental degradation is increasing every year, as is a spontaneous willingness to clean up after ourselves, to recycle, to unite against air and water pollution, to fight to save endangered species. Contemplating the future of our relationship with the environment is very exciting, but we must be vigilant if the environment is to be protected, restored, and improved.

A look at U.S. history shows that periodic efforts to safeguard the environment have consistently clashed with drives to exploit natural resources and to tolerate environmental degradation. This debate still sounds in the 1990s as the advocates of "wise use" of resources attempt to portray preservationists and deep environmentalists as out of touch with economic and social realities. One of the aims of *Green Perspectives* is to allow readers to examine how this ongoing debate has played out over the past 150 years. The arguments that have prevailed, at least for a moment in history, are those articulated not only by strict preservationists like John Muir or by wise use advocates like Gifford Pinchot, but by essayists, fiction writers, journalists, and poets. If we are to consider wisely the merits of ongoing struggles over nature and the environment, knowledge about the past can only serve to alert us to the practical and spiritual importance inherent in present and future discussions.

ENVIRONMENTAL STANCE

We want it clearly understood that *Green Perspectives* is pro-environment. Despite our bias, we think that nature must be considered in its entirety, the use of one part weighed against any harm to another part. In order to achieve our end, we present many viewpoints and believe that the essays, fiction, poetry, and reporting included in *Green Perspectives* gives a reasonably balanced viewpoint of the history of environmental awareness in America.

HISTORICAL SCOPE

We begin with Susan Fenimore Cooper's *Rural Hours* (1850) and end with Charles C. Mann's "How Many Is Too Many?" (1993). These two texts alone reveal our own perspective. Cooper wrote her book when she lived in Cooperstown, a village in central New York State named for her grandfather, who settled there in the 1780s. The land then was wilderness. "Civilizing" it subsumed almost all the action and thought of the early farmers and villagers. Cooper lamented the civilizing process when it destroyed the very things it sought to enhance. Yet she understood, as we must, the paradox of felling forests to make farms. Without such destruction, America would not be what it is. The cleared land also signified an attitude that at times has run rampant across the United States: We can have our way with nature, which is a resource to be harvested and abused.

Only the opposition of a minority of thinkers and writers—constant burrs under the saddle of "progress"—has stemmed the environmental abuse. While poets have both glorified the growth of American power and disparaged its disregard for nature, there are those, such as Al Gore, a politician and power broker, John Muir or Bill McKibben, naturalists and moralists, who give us stern warnings. The argument that Al Gore presented in 1992 is in many ways the end result of the one that Susan Fenimore Cooper began. Perhaps guilty of naïve idealism, Gore offers a solution in his contention that balancing civilization and nature is the key to survival, both physical and spiritual. Gore believes that in what civilization has done to nature lies the key to a profound change that transcends intellectualizing or rhapsodizing.

USING *GREEN PERSPECTIVES*

Within the parameters established by Cooper and Gore, we present a variety of viewpoints about nature: direct observation, aesthetic observation, spiritual musing, philosophical reflection, preservation, conservation, reclamation, and so-called wise use. You may use *Green Perspectives,* however, to support whatever point of view you wish to teach. It is not our intention to make any course fit a predetermined model. We have provided you with materials, and we have refrained from "leading" beyond the point at which our selections inform teachers and students.

Selections, we expect, will provide impetus for critical thinking on a very important and timely issue. Our experience informs us that students are interested in environmental issues from both practical and intellectual perspectives. The point ought to be made that saving newspapers and collecting glass and cans to conserve natural resources is not the same as preserving nature and its resources. Nature appreciation has a profound effect on spiritual experience and quality of life though it is sometimes antithetical to the exigencies of daily living.

If questions are raised and thoughts provoked concerning this contradiction, positive and practical debate can be achieved that will transcend mere classroom rhetoric.

Organization

We have attempted to place the selections for *Green Perspectives* in a historical context so readers can follow the pattern of the environmental debate over time. There is a tendency, especially prevalent now, to look only to the present and the near future. The media too much accentuate the here and now. In order to make the historical context of environmentalism vivid, we have included an idiosyncratic chronology that shows some of the events, inventions, and legislation by which we now live. Examination of history encourages reflection, if only to acquaint readers with other experiences beyond themselves. Perhaps having readers make their own time line of events and of the environmental debate will serve to reinforce the important concept that literature exists in time, and that time has a direct influence over writer and reader alike.

The thematic table of contents organizes the selections of *Green Perspectives* into five themes—Observing Nature, Arguments for Wise Use, The Fight for Preservation, People in Nature, and Harming the Environment. The use of both historical and thematic organization reinforces an understanding that the issues presented in the book from a historical perspective also recur as similar subject matters. Attitudes and stances typical of one period resurface during another, often cloaked in a fresh guise.

Apparatus

Each part of the book is introduced by a comprehensive introductory essay that provides an economic, political, and social context for the selections that follow. Each selection in turn is introduced by a biographical sketch of the writer that places him or her historically and mentions predominant experiences and influences.

Our postreading questions ask for careful consideration on two basic levels. First, we ask that readers understand the facts of the selection. Second, we ask for critical thinking, based on an understanding of the implications of the text. Questions are formatted to begin with the text and then move out to considerations in the world of the readers, both what they have experienced and what they have thought.

Reading and understanding environmental literature requires a mind able to grasp subtle themes and interrelated ideas. We hope teachers will help lead students to a better understanding of why we must save the fragile balance of life on our planet. Some questions may appear simplistic only because they demand evidence that the reader understands the text. We know from experience that many readers claim greater comprehension than they actually have. We encourage careful and accurate reading with attention to sometimes difficult vocabulary. We have balanced basic questions with some that are complex and require deeper understanding and transference of information from other disciplines. We expect that many readers are already knowledgeable in areas of environmental literature. Some questions tap this information in order to encourage spirited classroom discussion or essay writing.

We conclude each part with a series of questions for thinking and writing designed with two ends in mind: First, we want readers to make links between selections both in that part and between that and preceding parts; second, we want readers to consider their own relationship to the immediate environment. We encourage students to carry what they have learned from the selections into their everyday lives.

A Word About Terminology

Increasingly, the terms *environment* and *ecology* are used interchangeably. We use the term *environment* because it provides for broad avenues of considering nature and our relationship to it. *Ecology* implies a technical and scientific study of relationships between living organisms and their environment. Our selections are nontechnical and relatively nonscientific.

ACKNOWLEDGMENTS

We thank the many people whose generous counsel, enthusiasm, time, and spirit have allowed *Green Perspectives* to become a reality. We particularly thank our acquisitions editor, Patricia Rossi, for believing in the idea of the book from its unfocused beginnings, for her gentle and cheerful nudging that so helped to sharpen our ambitions, and for her enormous enthusiasm during the book's research and writing. We also thank Marisa L. L'Heureux, our developmental editor, for her entirely appropriate attention to the book's organization, flow of ideas, and tenor of questions for thinking and writing during the preparatory stages. With her anchoring grasp of details, order evolved out of what at times appeared as utter chaos.

We would also like to thank Professors Roslyn Bernstein and John Todd of the Baruch College (CUNY) English Department for their unfailing interest in and support for this project. Thanks to Seymour H. Hutner, Michael Levandowsky, Gloria Cahill and Glory Mongin for their suggestions and advice, and to William A. Clary for listening critically. For library assistance, we thank the staffs at Pace University, New York City, and Baruch College (CUNY).

We also acknowledge the immensely helpful responses offered by the following people during various stages of the preparation of the manuscript: Chris Anderson, Oregon State University; Gary Cummins, Cornell University; Diana George, Michigan Technological University; M. Jimmie Killingsworth, Texas A & M University; Barbara Lounsberry, University of Northern Iowa; Janet Marting, University of Akron; Jeff Schiff, Columbia College; and Craig Smith, University of Northern Colorado. Without their enormously supportive criticism, *Green Perspectives* would be a very different book.

Last, but certainly not least, we wish to thank our families for tolerating our single-minded devotion to preparing this book over so many months and yet supporting us all the way. Christopher Hallowell in particular wishes to express his appreciation to his wife, Willa Zakin; their two children, Matthew and Maggie Hallowell; and to Willie, the dog, who spent so many days curled up at his master's feet, forgoing his rightful dose of exercise. Walter Levy owes his spiritual support to Gene L. Moncrief, his wife, and his drive to his sons, Alexander and Matthew Levy, and his daughters, Kathrine and Kristina Wronski. Preparing a book provides even more pleasure when it is read by people you know and love.

WALTER LEVY
CHRISTOPHER HALLOWELL

President Theodore Roosevelt (sixth from the right) and John Muir (fourth from the right) and their party at Mariposa Big Tree Grove in 1903.

1 1850–1914: Evolving Environmental Awareness

Even into the first half of the twentieth century, the idea that this country's wilderness was infinite ran strong. Few people really considered that we could ever run out of it or that America's great uninhabited spaces might vanish.

From our vantage at the end of the twentieth century, this inexhaustible wilderness has given way to shopping malls and subdivisions, leaving many people wondering if the loss of virgin land is worth the square miles of tract housing, strip developments, and polluted waterways.

It is hard to imagine what America must have looked and felt like when European settlers first landed here. The solitary Atlantic coast suggested nothing of the continent that lay beyond. Native Americans could provide only incomplete hints as to how far one might travel west. But European adventurers, settlers, traders, and merchants were undaunted. The precept took hold that wilderness was the antithesis of civilization, and all who lived in it or grew in it needed to be civilized. To the Europeans, wilderness was disorderly (nature out of control) and without morality. According to William Bradford, Pilgrim elder and governor of Plymouth, the New World as seen late in 1621 was forbidding: "They that know the winters of that country know them to be sharp and violent, and subject to cruel and fierce storms," he wrote in his journal. "Besides, what could they see but a hideous and desolate wilderness, full of wild beasts and wild men? . . . If they looked behind them, there was the mighty ocean . . . to separate them from all civil parts of the world."

The European response was to hack farms and gardens out of the forest and by so doing to civilize it. Thomas Jefferson remarked that "gardens may be made

1

without expense. We have only to cut out the superabundant plants." Michel-Guillaume Crèvecoeur, a Frenchman who lived extensively in colonial America, optimistically proclaimed in *Letters from an American Farmer* (1782) that

> He who would wish to see America in its proper light and have a true idea of its feeble beginnings and barbarous rudiments must visit the extended line of frontiers, where the last settlers dwell and where he may see the first labors of settlement, the mode of clearing the earth, in all their different appearances, where men are wholly dependent on their native tempers . . . and uncertain industry, which often fails when not sanctified by the efficacy of a few moral rules.

Few voices were heard in defense of the environment as the Europeans, caught up in their belief of the infinite space here, inexorably changed it. Yet it was evident early on that resources were finite. James Fenimore Cooper had called attention to the waste of resources such as the wanton killing of fish and birds and careless forestry in *The Pioneers* (1823), a novel set in central New York State. Cooper's ecological message was ignored, and 27 years later, Susan Fenimore Cooper, his daughter, lamented the loss of a grove of pines, the last of the stately trees she knew that once comprised great forests. Echoing her father, Cooper recorded the results of the destruction caused by agricultural settlement, economic greed, and the depletion of the landscape.

Early in the 1830s, George Catlin, an artist, traveled the western prairies painting a startling record of Native American life and expressing concern that it would disappear. He was so impressed by the land and its wildness that he wrote letters (published in 1841) advocating the creation of a national park designed to keep the land as it was then.

A pragmatic-spiritual understanding of Americans' relationship with the land was called for by Ralph Waldo Emerson in *Nature* (1836). Emerson asked for a distinctly American vision of nature and civilization: "At present, man applies to nature but half his force. . . . He lives in it, and masters it by penny-wisdom . . . whilst his arms are strong . . . his mind is imbruted and he is a selfish savage." Emerson's appeal to achieve a redemption of the human mind and soul through nature is a hallmark of Romanticism. But it was Henry David Thoreau, Emerson's protégé, who portrayed the delicate balance of living in nature with common sense and self-reliance in *Walden* (1854). Thoreau's idea, which seemed radical, got some Americans thinking that there was more to nature than farming, industrialization, and power. He taught that nature is a source of refuge from society, that learning about the world through direct observation and deep thinking leads to the consideration of higher ideals and moral certitude. Thoreau's one-room cabin on the shore of Walden Pond was an easy walk to his family home in Concord, Massachusetts. But the intellectual and aesthetic distance was immense, and Thoreau's *Walden* set a pattern for appreciating natural beauty and preserving it.

While the Civil War raged, George Perkins Marsh, a Vermont lawyer and career foreign diplomat, called for an end to careless depletion of resources and advocated a new sense of responsibility for the land in his *Man and Nature*

(1864). The hills of New England had been stripped of their primeval forests. Topsoil engorged streams and rivers, leaving ragged ravines and ravaged pastures unfit for cattle grazing. Marsh's argument was taken up mainly by Easterners, whose sense of losing the wilderness was tempered by rapid industrial and urban growth in the Northeast.

Such pragmatic environmental concerns were not so pronounced in the West with its huge openness. In 1862, the Homestead Act was enacted to provide free land in the Midwest and the Far West to anyone who wanted to farm it. The act was meant to implement the belief that America's destiny lay with small farms worked by independent men and women. However, more land was given to the railroad trusts and land speculators than was settled by farmers. The introduction of barbed wire in 1874 signaled the end of open range cattle grazing, and this initiated a period of range warfare between the cattlemen and the farmers, often homesteaders, whose smaller parcels of land, 640 acres, required a different kind of farming. Barbed wire reduced the great open spaces and made the landscape more human in scale. Thus began the rapid process of civilizing the West in a pattern similar to the one in the East.

Some established Easterners in the meantime gradually realized that without some efforts toward restriction, open wild spaces would forever disappear. However, national expansion was generally thought to be more important than national conservation. Eastern mercantile, industrial, and railroad interests set economic and legislative policy that was basically unconcerned with environmental issues. Nature was much admired, especially by the wealthy and the leisure class, but scarcely thought to be in need of conservation. Remarkably, due to the concerted efforts of Frederick Law Olmsted, architect of Central Park, among others, Yellowstone Park was created in 1872, the first national park. Olmsted believed that urban masses have the moral right to enjoy unspoiled nature. Olmsted and others were more concerned with the aesthetic values of wilderness and only peripherally concerned with ecology. Though the aesthetic attitude toward nature, an aspect of Romanticism, is open to criticism, it provided a powerful argument for future conservation and ecological issues, particularly the establishment of the National Park Service in 1916.

As western farmers and cattle ranchers fought over water rights, urban centers began to claim their rights to water resources, too. Rivers were dammed; valleys were flooded. From 1909 to 1913, John Muir protested vociferously but in vain to prevent the Hetch Hetchy Valley from being turned into a reservoir to provide water for San Francisco. He considered the valley a masterpiece of nature.

Ironically Muir was defeated in his efforts by two conservationists—Theodore Roosevelt and Gifford Pinchot—who supported pragmatic use of natural resources. While Pinchot in *The Fight for Conservation* (1910) appreciates wild and scenic beauty, he argued for the use of wilderness as a resource to be managed and harvested. He was an architect of the idea of wise use, which (in rank order) stresses combining management, use, and preservation of environmental resources. Going further, Frederick H. Newell, the first director of the U.S. Bureau of Reclamation, in "What May Be Accomplished by

Reclamation" (1910), advocated the need for massive irrigation projects to open arid western lands to intensive agricultural development. His assumption that the desert has no value unless it is usefully farmed contrasts sharply with Mary Hunter Austin's *The Land of Little Rain* (1903), which describes the desert's rich natural environment.

Other writers have taken complementary perspectives in the ongoing debate: Walt Whitman's "Song of the Redwood-Tree" (1874) celebrates the great redwood trees even as they are being cut down; Sarah Orne Jewett's "A White Heron" (1886) portrays a young farm girl's moral decision that her secret knowledge of a wild bird is worth more than money; and John Burroughs's *Ways of Nature* (1905) is a philosophical argument that humankind's ways are refined from nature's ways and our progress is a blind groping and endless experimentation.

HISTORICAL CHRONOLOGY AND CONTEXT

1824:   Cyrus McCormick invents a practical reaping machine

1832:   George Catlin, painter, proposes a national park

1836:   Arkansas becomes the 25th state

1837:   Martin Van Buren is elected president

Michigan becomes the 26th state

1845:   Florida becomes the 27th state

Texas becomes the 28th state

1846:   Famine in Ireland increases Irish immigration to United States

Elias Howe invents the sewing machine

John Deere invents a successful steel plow

Iowa becomes the 29th state

1846–48:   U.S.-Mexican War

1848:   Land acquired from Mexico in the Southwest and Great Britain in the Northwest

Wisconsin becomes the 30th state

1849:   California Gold Rush

U.S. Department of the Interior established

1850:   California becomes the 31st state

1853:   New Mexico and Arizona territory purchased from Mexico

1854:   Henry David Thoreau's *Walden* published

1858:   Minnesota becomes the 32nd state

Oregon becomes the 33rd state

1859:   First oil well drilled in Pennsylvania

1861: Abraham Lincoln elected president

Kansas becomes the 34th state

1861–65: Civil War

1862: Homestead Act—opens Western lands for settlement

1863: West Virginia becomes the 35th state

1864: U.S. Congress grants Yosemite Valley to California for use as a state park

Nevada becomes the 36th state

1867: Alaska is purchased from Russia

Nebraska becomes the 37th state

1869: Completion of the Transcontinental Railroad

1872: Yellowstone is the first national park created by Congress

1874: Barbed wire patented

1876: Alexander Graham Bell invents the telephone

Colorado becomes the 38th state

Crazy Horse defeats General Custer at the Little Big Horn

1878: Timber Culture Act—allows logging on public lands by residents of western states

1879: U.S. Geological Survey established

Thomas Edison invents a successful electric light bulb

1883: The Brooklyn Bridge is completed

1888: Electric trolley cars are introduced in Richmond, Virginia

1889: North Dakota, South Dakota, Montana, and Washington become the 39th to 42nd states

1890: Idaho and Wyoming become the 43rd and 44th states

1892: John Muir founds the Sierra Club

1893: Frederick Jackson Turner, historian, contends the West is no longer a frontier

1896: Utah becomes the 45th state

1897: Forest Management Act—authorizes commercial use of public forests

1898: Spanish-American War

1901: Theodore Roosevelt becomes president when William McKinley is assassinated

1902: Reclamation Act—finances federal irrigation projects

1903: Wilbur and Orville Wright fly the first airplane

1906: U.S. Forest Service is created

San Francisco is severely damaged by earthquake

Congress passes the Pure Food and Drug Act and Meat Inspection Act

1907: Oklahoma becomes the 46th state

1909: Robert E. Peary and Matthew Hanson reach the North Pole

1911: Weeks Act—expands public forest reserves by purchase of private lands

1912: New Mexico and Arizona become the 47th and 48th states

1913: Henry Ford introduces the assembly line to automobile manufacturing

1914: World War I begins in Europe

🦎 Susan Fenimore Cooper (1813–1894)
Summer, Monday, July 23rd (1850)

Susan Fenimore Cooper was a gentle, practical, environmentally keen observer of nature. In Rural Hours *(1850), written in the form of a country diary, she shows how the settlement of central New York State gradually eroded the frontier and made it tame.*

Cooper was born in Scarsdale, New York, but when still in infancy she moved with her father and mother, James Fenimore Cooper and Susan Cooper, to Cooperstown in central New York State. The village was named after her grandfather, who was its principal landowner and founder. The family had planned to remain in Cooperstown, but when Cooper was 4 they returned to Scarsdale where her father wrote The Spy *(1821), the first of his successful novels that made him America's most famous writer from then on into the 1840s. Susan Cooper was largely educated at home where her mother taught her to read, write, and study the Bible. She went to school in New York City, but in 1826 the family moved to Europe, traveled extensively, and settled in Paris, where Cooper completed her education in French schools. During these years, she began copyediting her father's writings, a task she pursued until his death in 1851. She never married.*

Cooper's earliest visit to Cooperstown and the surrounding country filled her with warm memories and a love of nature, which were renewed when the family returned to America in 1833. Cooper became a leading citizen of the town, worked as secretary for her father, and began writing for herself. Besides Rural Hours *she wrote a novel,* Elinor Wyllys; or, The Young Folk at Longbridge, *under the pseudonym* Amabel Penfeather, *and* Pages and Pictures, *a volume about her father's writings, as well as several pamphlets and prefaces to editions of her father's novels.*

Rural Hours, *for which she is best remembered, is a picture of the conflict between civilization and nature, providing us with a detailed look at how a wilderness was transformed into agrarian society. Cooper's commentary is filled with the practical, gentler aspects of rural life: how it looked, felt, and smelled. Cooper loved nature, the landscape, and rural living. Though she was genteel and did no heavy toiling, she understood the conflicting needs of the farmers and the nature lovers. The charm of her record of life in* Rural Hours *is that she provides a picture of a rural farming community which has supplanted and eroded the natural wilderness. Cooper is firm in her belief that the loss is virtually irreparable for practical and aesthetic reasons. In this sense she is linked with her father's environmental views and with*

Henry David Thoreau whose Walden *(1854) was published shortly after* Rural Hours. *Cooper is an astute and careful observer of nature.*

*M*onday, *23d.*—Just at the point where the village street becomes a road and turns to climb the hillside, there stands a group of pines, a remnant of the old forest. There are many trees like these among the woods; far and near such may be seen rising from the hills, now tossing their arms in the stormy winds, now drawn in still and dark relief against the glowing evening sky. Their gaunt, upright forms standing about the hill-tops, and the ragged gray stumps of those which have fallen, dotting the smooth fields, make up the sterner touches in a scene whose general aspect is smiling. But although these old trees are common upon the wooded heights, yet the group on the skirts of the village stands alone among the fields of the valley; their nearer brethren have all been swept away, and these are left in isolated company, differing in character from all about them, a monument of the past.

It is upon a narrow belt of land, a highway and a corn-field on one side, a brook and an orchard on the other, that these trees are rooted; a strip of woodland connected with the forest on the hills above, and suddenly cut off where it approaches the first buildings of the village. There they stand, silent spectators of the wonderful changes that have come over the valley. Hundreds of winters have passed since the cones which contained the seed of that grove fell from the parent tree; centuries have elapsed since their heads emerged from the topmost wave of the sea of verdure to meet the sunshine, and yet it is but yesterday that their shadows first fell, in full length, upon the sod at their feet.

Sixty years since, those trees belonged to a wilderness; the bear, the wolf, and the panther brushed their trunks, the ungainly moose and the agile deer browsed at their feet; the savage hunter crept stealthily about their roots, and painted braves passed noiselessly on the warpath beneath their shade. How many successive generations of the red man have trod the soil they overshadowed, and then sat down in their narrow graves—how many herds of wild creatures have chased each other through that wood, and left their bones to bleach among the fern and moss, there is no human voice can tell. We only know that the summer winds, when they filled the canvas of Columbus and Cabot, three hundred years ago, came sweeping over these forest pines, murmuring then as we hear them murmur to-day.

There is no record to teach us even the name of the first white man who saw this sequestered valley, with its limpid lake; it was probably some bold hunter from the Mohawk, chasing the deer, or in quest of the beaver. But while towns were rising on the St. Lawrence and upon the sea-board, this inland region lay still unexplored; long after trading-houses had been opened, and fields had been tilled, and battles had been fought to the north, south, east, ay, and even at many points westward, those pines stood in the heart of a silent wilderness. This, little lake lay embedded in a forest until after the great struggle of the Revolution was over. A few months after the war was brought to an honorable close, Washington made a journey of observation among the inland waters of this part of the country; writing to a friend in France, he names this little lake, the source of a river, which, four degrees farther south, flows into the Chesapeake in near neighborhood with his own Potomac. As he passed along through a half-wild region, where the few marks of civilization then existing bore the blight of war, he conceived the outline of many of those improvements which have since been carried out by others, and have yielded so rich a revenue of prosperity. It is a pleasing reflection to those who live here, that while many important places in the country were never honored by his presence, Washington has trod the soil about our lake. But even at that late day, when the great and good man came, the mountains were still clothed in wood to the water's edge, and mingled with giant oaks and ashes, those tall pines waved above the valley.

At length, nearly three long centuries after the Genoese had crossed the ocean, the white man came to plant a home on this spot, and it was then the great change began; the axe and the saw, the forge and the wheel, were busy from dawn to dusk, cows and swine fed in thickets whence the wild beasts had fled, while the ox and the horse drew away in chains the fallen trunks of the forest. The tenants of the wilderness shrunk deeper within its bounds with every changing moon; the wild creatures fled away within the receding shades of the forest, and the red man followed on their track; his day of power was gone, his hour of pitiless revenge had passed, and the last echoes of the war-whoop were dying away forever among these hills, when the pale-faces laid their hearth-stones by the lake shore. The red man, who for thousands of years had been lord of the land, no longer treads the soil; he exists here only in uncertain memories, and in forgotten graves.

Such has been the change in the last half century. Those who from childhood have known the cheerful dwellings of the village, the broad and fertile farms, the well beaten roads, such as they are to-day, can hardly credit that this has all been done so recently by a band of men, some of whom, white-headed and leaning on their staves, are still among us. Yet such is the simple truth. This village lies just on the borders of the tract of country which was opened and peopled immediately after the Revolution; it was among the earliest of those little colonies from the sea-board which struck into the wilderness at that favorable moment, and whose rapid growth and progress in civilization have become a byword. Other places, indeed, have far surpassed this quiet borough; Rochester, Buffalo, and others of a later date, have become great cities, while this remains a rural village; still, whenever we pause to recall what has been done in this secluded valley during the lifetime of one generation, we must needs be struck with new astonishment. And throughout every act of the work, those old pines were there. Unchanged themselves, they stand surrounded by objects over all of which a great change has passed. The open valley, the half-shorn hills, the paths, the flocks, the buildings, the woods in their second growth, even the waters in the different images they reflect on their bosom, the very race of men who come and go, all are different from what they were; and those calm old trees seem to heave the sigh of companionless age, as their coned heads rock slowly in the winds.

The aspect of the wood tells its own history, so widely does it differ in character from the younger groves waving in gay luxuriance over the valley. In the midst of smooth fields it speaks so clearly of the wilderness, that it is not the young orchard of yesterday's planting, but the aged native pines which seem the strangers on the ground. The pine of forest growth never fails to have a very marked character of its own; the gray shaft rises clear and unbroken by bend or bough, to more than half its great elevation, thence short horizontal limbs in successive fan-like growth surround the trunk to its summit, which is often crowned with a low crest of upright branches. The shaft is very fine from its great height and the noble simplicity of its lines; in coloring, it is a pure clear gray, having the lightest and the smoothest bark of all its tribe, and only occasionally mottled with patches of lichens. The white pine of this climate gather but few mosses, unless in very moist situations; the very oldest trees are often quite free from them. Indeed, this is a tree seldom seen with the symptoms of a half-dead and decaying condition about it, like so many others; the gray line of a naked branch may be observed here and there, perhaps, a sign of age, but it generally preserves to the very last an appearance of vigor, as though keeping death at bay until struck to the heart, or laid low from the roots. It is true, this appearance may often prove deceptive; still, it is a peculiarity of our pine, that it preserves its verdure until the very last, unlike many other trees which are seen in the forest, half green, half gray, and lifeless.

The pine of the lawns or open groves and the pine of the forest differ very strikingly in outline; the usual pyramidal or conical form of the evergreen is very faintly traced on the short, irregular limbs of the forest tree; but what is lost in luxuriance and elegance is more than replaced by a peculiar character of wild dignity, as it raises its stern head high above the lesser wood, far overtopping the proudest rank of oaks. And yet, in their rudest shapes, they are never harsh; as we approach them, we shall always find something of the calm of age and the sweetness of nature to soften their aspect; there is a grace in the slow waving of their limbs in the higher air, which never fails; there is a mysterious melody in their breezy murmurs; there is an emerald light in their beautiful verdure, which lies in unfading wreaths, fresh and clear, about the heads of those old trees. The effect of light and shade on the foliage of those older forest pines is indeed much finer than what we see among their younger neighbors; the tufted branches, in their horizontal growth, are beautifully touched with circlets of a clear light, which is broken up and lost amid the confused medley of branches in trees of more upright growth. The long brown cones are chiefly pendulous, in clusters, from the upper branches; some seasons they are so numerous on the younger trees as to give their heads a decided brown coloring.

The grove upon the skirts of the village numbers, perhaps, some forty trees, varying in their girth from five or six to twelve feet; and in height, from a hundred and twenty to a hundred and sixty feet. Owing to their unscreened position and their height, these trees may be clearly distinguished for miles, whether from the lake, the hills, or the roads about the country—a landmark overtopping the humble church-spires, and every object raised by man within the bounds of the valley. Their rude simplicity of outline, the erect, unbending trunks, their stern, changeless character, and their scanty drapery of foliage, unconsciously lead one to fancy them an image of some band of savage chiefs, emerging in a long, dark line from the glen in their rear, and gazing in wonder upon their former hunting-ground in its altered aspect.

It needs but a short minutes to bring one of these trees to the ground; the rudest boor passing along the highway may easily do the deed; but how many years must pass ere its equal stand on the same spot! Let us pause to count the days, the months, the years; let us number the generations that must come and go, the centuries that must roll onward, ere the seed sown from this year's cones shall produce a wood like that before us. The stout arm so ready to raise the axe to-day, must grow weak with age, it must drop into the grave; its bone and sinew must crumble into dust long before another tree, tall and great as those, shall have grown from the cone in our hand. Nay, more, all the united strength of sinew, added to all the powers of mind, and all the force of will, of millions of men, can do no more toward the work than the poor ability of a single arm; these are of the deeds which time alone can perform. But allowing even that hundreds of years hence other trees were at length to succeed these with the same dignity of height and age, no other younger wood can ever claim the same connection as this, with a state of things now passed away forever; they cannot have that wild, stern character of the aged forest pines. This little town itself must fall to decay and ruin; its streets must become choked with bushes and brambles; the farms of the valley must be anew buried within the shades of a wilderness; the wild deer and the wolf and the bear must return from beyond the great lakes; the bones of the savage men buried under our feet must arise and move again in the chase, ere trees like those, with the spirit of the forest in every line, can stand on the same ground in wild dignity of form like those old pines now looking down upon our homes.

Questions for Thinking and Writing

1. How does Cooper link the cycle of historical, social, and agricultural development of the land with the changes in its appearance and the abundance of natural resources?
2. Explain how Cooper avoids sentimentalizing the grove of pines.
3. Explain the symbolism of the pine tree grove. How does it suggest that the depletion of the environment may also represent a lessening of spiritual strength, which Americans often take for granted?

❧ Henry David Thoreau (1817–1862)

Where I Lived, and What I Lived For (1854)

Henry David Thoreau was virtually unknown to the reading public during his lifetime. It was not until the 1880s, two decades after his death, that his essays and poetry became popular and respected for their rebellious logic and accurate observations on life and nature. He is now considered by many to be the preeminent American nature writer.

Thoreau was born in Concord, Massachusetts, and it was his home virtually all of his life except for brief excursions to Canada and to Cape Cod. As soon as he graduated from Harvard University at 16, he returned home. Thoreau never trained for a profession but became a schoolteacher for a short time before entering his father's pencil manufacturing business. In 1841, while working as a gardener, he met Ralph Waldo Emerson, then the leader of the American Transcendental movement, and fell under his influence. For a time, he took over the editorship of Emerson's journal The Dial, and carried on the argument for a new American point of view stressing self-reliance and an understanding of nature as opposed to merely living in it.

An iconoclast on moral and social issues, Thoreau adamantly argued against the U.S.-Mexican War of 1846. He defied popular sentiment and spent a night in jail because he would not pay the poll tax, which he said financed both slavery and the Mexican War.

Thoreau is best known for the two years he spent in quasi-isolation in a small cabin he built for himself on the edge of Walden Pond in Concord. In an effort to prove that one could live in a state of rustic simplicity, Thoreau compiled Walden (1854), a refined journal of his life in the woods. Applying the notion of self-reliance to the material and spiritual frames of life, Thoreau attempted to show that a person could come to terms with nature by living in its midst and taking the time to understand it.

Walden chronicles the seasons of the year; its chapter headings such as "Economy," "Solitude," "The Bean-Field," "Winter Animals," and "Higher Laws" suggest that observation and reflection are important components of the book. The selection here from the second chapter "Where I Lived, and What I Lived For" keynotes Thoreau's idea that ownership is more potent in spirit than in fact. He says that owning real estate encumbers the life of the mind and the imagination. He argues that rustic life is cheerful, and that living close to nature encourages innocence unknown in urban life, which is hurried, wasteful, and filled with delusions. Thoreau's philosophy is in keeping with the romanticism of mid-nineteenth-century America but without its superficial veneer of nature loving.

At a certain season of our life we are accustomed to consider every spot as the possible site of a house. I have thus surveyed the country on every side within a dozen miles of where I live. In imagination I have bought all the farms in succession, for all were to be bought, and I knew their price. I walked over each farmer's premises, tasted his wild apples, discoursed on husbandry with him, took his farm at his price, at any price, mortgaging it to him in my mind; even put a higher price on it,—took every thing but a deed of it,—took his word for his deed, for I dearly love to talk,—cultivated it, and him too to some extent, I trust, and withdrew when I had enjoyed it long enough, leaving him to carry it on. This experience entitled me to be regarded as a sort of real-estate broker by my friends. Wherever I sat, there I might live, and the landscape radiated from me accordingly. What is a house but a *sedes*, a seat?—better if a country seat. I discovered many a site for a house not likely to be soon improved, which some might have thought too far from the village, but to my eyes the village was too far from it. Well, there I might live, I said; and there I did live, for an hour, a summer and a winter life; saw how I could let the years run off, buffet the winter through, and see the spring come in. The future inhabitants of this region, wherever they may place their houses, may be sure that they have been anticipated. An afternoon sufficed to lay out the land into orchard woodlot and pasture, and to decide what fine oaks or pines should be left to stand before the door, and whence each blasted tree could be seen to the best advantage; and then I let it lie, fallow perchance, for a man is rich in proportion to the number of things which he can afford to let alone.

My imagination carried me so far that I even had the refusal of several farms,—the refusal was all I wanted,—but I never got my fingers

burned by actual possession. The nearest that I came to actual possession was when I bought the Hollowell Place, and had begun to sort my
seeds, and collected materials with which to make a wheelbarrow to
carry it on or off with; but before the owner gave me a deed of it, his
wife—every man has such a wife—changed her mind and wished to
keep it, and he offered me ten dollars to release him. Now, to speak the
truth, I had but ten cents in the world, and it surpassed my arithmetic
to tell, if I was that man who had ten cents, or who had a farm, or ten
dollars, or all together. However, I let him keep the ten dollars and the
farm too, for I had carried it far enough; or rather, to be generous, I
sold him the farm for just what I gave for it, and, as he was not a rich
man, made him a present of ten dollars, and still had my ten cents, and
seeds, and materials for a wheelbarrow left. I found thus that I had been
a rich man without any damage to my poverty. But I retained the landscape, and I have since annually carried off what it yielded without a
wheelbarrow. With respect to landscapes,—

"I am monarch of all I *survey*,
  My right there is none to dispute."

I have frequently seen a poet withdraw, having enjoyed the most valuable part of a farm, while the crusty farmer supposed that he had got a
few wild apples only. Why, the owner does not know it for many years
when a poet has put his farm in rhyme, the most admirable kind of invisible fence, has fairly impounded it, milked it, skimmed it, and got all
the cream, and left the farmer only the skimmed milk.

The real attractions of the Hollowell farm, to me, were; its complete
retirement, being about two miles from the village, half a mile from the
nearest neighbor, and separated from the highway by a broad field; its
bounding on the river, which the owner said protected it by its fogs from
frosts in the spring, though that was nothing to me; the gray color and
ruinous state of the house and barn, and the dilapidated fences, which
put such an interval between me and the last occupant; the hollow and
lichen-covered apple trees, gnawed by rabbits, showing what kind of
neighbors I should have; but above all, the recollection I had of it from
my earliest voyages up the river, when the house was concealed behind
a dense grove of red maples, through which I heard the house-dog bark.
I was in haste to buy it, before the proprietor finished getting out some
rocks, cutting down the hollow apple trees, and grubbing up some
young birches which had sprung up in the pasture, or, in short, had
made any more of his improvements. To enjoy these advantages I was
ready to carry it on; like Atlas, to take the world on my shoulders,—I
never heard what compensation he received for that,—and do all those
things which had no other motive or excuse but that I might pay for it
and be unmolested in my possession of it; for I knew all the while that

it would yield the most abundant crop of the kind I wanted if I could only afford to let it alone. But it turned out as I have said.

All that I could say, then, with respect to farming on a large scale, (I have always cultivated a garden,) was, that I had had my seeds ready. Many think that seeds improve with age. I have no doubt that time discriminates between the good and the bad; and when at last I shall plant, I shall be less likely to be disappointed. But I would say to my fellows, once for all, As long as possible live free and uncommitted. It makes but little difference whether you are committed to a farm or the county jail.

Old Cato, whose "De Re Rusticâ" is my "Cultivator," says, and the only translation I have seen makes sheer nonsense of the passage, "When you think of getting a farm, turn it thus in your mind, not to buy greedily; nor spare your pains to look at it, and do not think it enough to go round it once. The oftener you go there the more it will please you, if it is good." I think I shall not buy greedily, but go round and round it as long as I live, and be buried in it first, that it may please me the more at last.

The present was my next experiment of this kind, which I purpose to describe more at length; for convenience, putting the experience of two years into one. As I have said, I do not propose to write an ode to dejection, but to brag as lustily as chanticleer in the morning, standing on his roost, if only to wake my neighbors up.

When first I took up my abode in the woods, that is, began to spend my nights as well as days there, which, by accident, was on Independence Day, or the fourth of July, 1845, my house was not finished for winter, but was merely a defence against the rain, without plastering or chimney, the walls being of rough weather-stained boards, with wide chinks, which made it cool at night. The upright white hewn studs and freshly planed door and window casings gave it a clean and airy look, especially in the morning, when its timbers were saturated with dew, so that I fancied that by noon some sweet gum would exude from them. To my imagination it retained throughout the day more or less of this auroral character, reminding me of a certain house on a mountain which I had visited the year before. This was an airy and unplastered cabin, fit to entertain a travelling god, and where a goddess might trail her garments. The winds which passed over my dwelling were such as sweep over the ridges of mountains, bearing the broken strains, or celestial parts only, of terrestrial music. The morning wind forever blows, the poem of creation is uninterrupted; but few are the ears that hear it. Olympus is but the outside of the earth every where.

The only house I had been the owner of before, if I except a boat, was a tent, which I used occasionally when making excursions in the summer, and this is still rolled up in my garret; but the boat, after passing from hand to hand, has gone down the stream of time. With this more substantial shelter about me, I had made some progress toward settling in the world. This frame, so slightly clad, was a sort of crystallization around me, and reacted on the builder. It was suggestive somewhat as a picture in outlines. I did not need to go out doors to take the air, for the atmosphere within had lost none of its freshness. It was not so much within doors as behind a door where I sat, even in the rainiest weather. The Harivansa says, "An abode without birds is like a meat without seasoning." Such was not my abode, for I found myself suddenly neighbor to the birds; not by having imprisoned one, but having caged myself near them. I was not only nearer to some of those which commonly frequent the garden and the orchard, but to those wilder and more thrilling songsters of the forest which never, or rarely, serenade a villager,—the wood-thrush, the veery, the scarlet tanager, the field-sparrow, the whippoorwill, and many others.

I was seated by the shore of a small pond, about a mile and a half south of the village of Concord and somewhat higher than it, in the midst of an extensive wood between that town and Lincoln, and about two miles south of that our only field known to fame, Concord Battle Ground; but I was so low in the woods that the opposite shore, half a mile off, like the rest, covered with wood, was my most distant horizon. For the first week, whenever I looked out on the pond it impressed me like a tarn high up on the side of a mountain, its bottom far above the surface of other lakes, and, as the sun arose, I saw it throwing off its nightly clothing of mist, and here and there, by degrees, its soft ripples of its smooth reflecting surface was revealed, while the mists, like ghosts, were stealthily withdrawing in every direction into the woods, as at the breaking up of some nocturnal conventicle. The very dew seemed to hang upon the trees later into the day than usual, as on the sides of mountains.

This small lake was of most value as a neighbor in the intervals of a gentle rain storm in August, when, both air and water being perfectly still, but the sky overcast, mid-afternoon had all the serenity of evening, and the wood-thrush sang around, and was heard from shore to shore. A lake like this is never smoother than at such a time; and the clear portion of the air above it being shallow and darkened by clouds, the water, full of light and reflections, becomes a lower heaven itself so much the more important. From a hill top near by, where the wood had been recently cut off, there was a pleasing vista southward across the pond, though a wide indentation in the hills which form the shore there, where their opposite sides sloping toward each other suggested a stream flowing out in that direction through a wooded valley, but stream there was none. That way I looked between and over the near green hills to some distant and higher ones in the horizon, tinged with blue. Indeed, by standing on tiptoe I could catch a glimpse of some of the peaks of the still bluer and more distant mountain ranges in the north-west those true-blue coins from heaven's own mint, and also of some portion of the village. But in other directions, even from this point, I could not see over or beyond the woods which surrounded me. It is well to have some water in your neighborhood, to give buoyancy to and float the earth. One value even of the smallest well is, that when you look into it you see that earth is not continent but insular. This is as important as that it keeps butter cool. When I looked across the pond from this peak toward the Sudbury meadows, which in time of flood I distinguished elevated perhaps by a mirage in their seething valley, like a coin in a basin, all the earth beyond the pond appeared like a thin crust insulated and floated even by this small sheet of intervening water, and I was reminded that this on which I dwelt was but *dry land.*

Though the view from my door was still more contracted, I did not feel crowded or confined in the least. There was pasture enough for my imagination. The low shrub-oak plateau to which the opposite shore arose, stretched away toward the prairies of the West and the steppes of Tartary, affording ample room for all the roving families of men. "There are none happy in the world but beings who enjoy freely a vast horizon,"—said Damodara, when his herds required new and larger pastures.

Both place and time were changed, and I dwelt nearer to those parts of the universe and to those eras in history which had most attracted me. Where I lived was as far off as many a region viewed nightly by astronomers. We are wont to imagine rare and delectable places in some remote and more celestial corner of the system, behind the constellation of Cassiopeia's Chair, far from noise and disturbance. I discovered that my house actually had its site in such a withdrawn, but forever new and unprofaned, part of the universe. If it were worth the while to settle in those parts near to the Pleiades or the Hyades, to Aldebaran or Altair, then I was really there, or at an equal remoteness from the life which I had left behind, dwindled and twinkling with as fine a ray to my nearest neighbor, and to be seen only in moonless nights by him. Such was that part of creation where I had squatted;—

> "There was a shepherd that did live,
>   And held his thoughts as high
> As were the mounts whereon his flocks
>   Did hourly feed him by."

What should we think of the shepherd's life if his flocks always wandered to higher pastures than his thoughts?

Every morning was a cheerful invitation to make my life of equal simplicity, and I may say innocence, with Nature herself. I have been as sincere a worshipper of Aurora as the Greeks. I got up early and bathed in the pond; that was a religious exercise, and one of the best things which I did. They say that characters were engraven on the bathing tub of king Tching-thang to this effect: "Renew thyself completely each day; do it again, and again, and forever again." I can understand that. Morning brings back the heroic ages. I was as much affected by the faint hum of a mosquito making its invisible and unimaginable tour through my apartment at earliest dawn, when I was sitting with door and windows open, as I could be by any trumpet that ever sang of fame. It was Homer's requiem; itself an Iliad and Odyssey in the air, singing its own wrath and wanderings. There was something cosmical about it; a standing advertisement, till forbidden, of the everlasting vigor and fertility of the world. The morning, which is the most memorable season of the day, is the awakening hour. Then there is least somnolence in us; and for an hour, at least, some part of us awakes which slumbers all the rest of the day and night. Little is to be expected of that day, if it can be called a day, to which we are not awakened by our Genius, but by the mechanical nudgings of some servitor, are not awakened by our own newly acquired force and aspirations from within, accompanied by the undulations of celestial music, instead of factory bells, and a fragrance filling the air—to a higher life than we fell asleep from; and thus the darkness bear its fruit, and prove itself to be good, no less than the light. That man who does not believe that each day contains an earlier, more sacred, and auroral hour than he has yet profaned, has despaired of life, and is pursuing a descending and darkening way. After a partial cessation of his sensuous life, the soul of man, of its organs rather, are reinvigorated each day, and his Genius tries again what noble life it can make. All memorable events, I should say, transpire in morning time and in a morning atmosphere. The Vedas say, "All intelligences awake with the morning." Poetry and art, and the fairest and most memorable of the actions of men, date from such an hour. All poets and heroes, like Memnon, are the children of Aurora, and emit their music at sunrise. To him whose elastic and vigorous thought keeps pace with the sun, the day is a perpetual morning. It matters not what the clocks say or the attitudes and labors of men. Morning is when I am awake and there is a dawn in me. Moral reform is the effort to throw off sleep. Why is it that men give so poor an account of their day if they have not been slumbering? They are not such poor calculators. If they had not been overcome with drowsiness they would have performed something. The millions are awake enough for physical labor; but only one in a million is awake enough for effective intellectual exertion, only one in a hundred millions to a poetic or divine life. To be awake is to be alive. I have never yet met a man who was quite awake. How could I have looked him in the face?

We must learn to reawaken and keep ourselves awake, not by mechanical aids, but by an infinite expectation of the dawn, which does not forsake us in our soundest sleep. I know of no more encouraging fact than the unquestionable ability of man to elevate his life by a conscious endeavor. It is something to be able to paint a particular picture, or to carve a statue, and so to make a few objects beautiful; but it is far more glorious to carve and paint the very atmosphere and medium through which we look, which morally we can do. To affect the quality of the day, that is the highest of arts. Every man is tasked to make his life, even in its details, worthy of the contemplation of his most elevated and critical hour. If we refused, or rather used up, such paltry information as we get, the oracles would distinctly inform us how this might be done.

I went to the woods because I wished to live deliberately, to front only the essential facts of life, and see if I could not learn what it had to teach, and not, when I came to die, discover that I had not lived. I did not wish to live what was not life, living is so dear; nor did I wish to practise resignation, unless it was quite necessary. I wanted to live deep and suck out all the marrow of life, to live so sturdily and Spartanlike as to put to rout all that was not life, to cut a broad swath and shave close, to drive life into a corner, and reduce it to its lowest terms, and, if it proved to be mean, why then to get the whole and genuine meanness of it, and publish its meanness to the world; or if it were sublime, to know it by experience, and be able to give a true account of it in my next excursion. For most men, it appears to me, are in a strange uncertainty about it, whether it is of the devil or of God, and have *somewhat hastily* concluded that it is the chief end of man here to "glorify God and enjoy him forever."

Still we live meanly, like ants; though the fable tells us that we were long ago changed into men; like pygmies we fight with cranes; it is error upon error, and clout upon clout, and our best virtue has for its occasion a superfluous and evitable wretchedness. Our life is frittered away by detail. An honest man has hardly need to count more than his ten fingers, or in extreme cases he may add his ten toes, and lump the rest. Simplicity, simplicity, simplicity! I say, let your affairs be as two or three, and not a hundred or a thousand; instead of a million count half a dozen, and keep your accounts on your thumb nail. In the midst of this chopping sea of civilized life, such are the clouds and storms and quicksands and thousand-and-one items to be allowed for, that a man has to live, if he would not founder and go to the bottom and not make his port at all, by dead reckoning, and he must be a great calculator indeed who succeeds. Simplify, simplify. Instead of three meals a day, if it be necessary eat but one; instead of a hundred dishes, five; and reduce other things in proportion. Our life is like a German Confederacy, made up of petty states, with its boundary forever fluctuating, so that even a German cannot tell you how it is bounded at any moment. The nation itself, with all its so called internal improvements, which, by the way, are all external and superficial, is just such an unwieldy and overgrown establishment, cluttered with furniture and tripped up by its own traps, ruined by luxury and heedless expense, by want of calculation and a worthy aim, as the million households in the land; and the only cure for it as for them is in a rigid economy, a stern and more than Spartan simplicity of life and elevation of purpose. It lives too fast. Men think that it is essential that the *Nation* have commerce, and export ice, and talk through a telegraph, and ride thirty miles an hour, without a doubt, whether *they* do or not; but whether we should live like baboons or like men, is a little uncertain. If we do not get out sleepers, and forge rails, and devote days and nights to the work, but go to tinkering upon our *lives* to improve *them,* who will build railroads? And if railroads are not built, how shall we get to heaven in season? But if we stay at home and mind our business, who will want railroads? We do not ride on the railroad; it rides upon us. Did you ever think what those sleepers are that underlie the railroad? Each one is a man, an Irish-man, or a Yankee man. The rails are laid on them, and they are covered with sand, and the cars run smoothly over them. They are sound sleepers, I assure you. And every few years a new lot is laid down and run over; so that, if some have the pleasure of riding on a rail, others have the misfortune to be ridden upon. And when they run over a man that is walking in his sleep, a supernumerary sleeper in the wrong position, and wake him up, they suddenly stop the cars, and make a hue and cry about it, as if this were an exception. I am glad to know that it takes a gang of men for every five miles to keep the sleepers down and level in their beds as it is, for this is a sign that they may sometime get up again.

Why should we live with such hurry and waste of life? We are determined to be starved before we are hungry. Men say that a stitch in time saves nine, and so they take a thousand stitches to-day to save nine to-morrow. As for *work,* we haven't any of any consequence. We have the Saint Vitus' dance, and cannot possibly keep our heads still. If I should only give a few pulls at the parish bell-rope, as for a fire, that is, without setting the bell, there is hardly a man on his farm in the outskirts of Concord, notwithstanding that press of engagements which was his excuse so many times this morning, nor a boy, nor a woman, I might almost say, but would forsake all and follow that sound, not mainly to save property from the flames, but, if we will confess the truth, much more to see it burn, since burn it must, and we, be it known, did not set it on fire,—or to see it put out, and have a hand in it, if that is done as handsomely; yes, even if it were the parish church itself. Hardly a man takes a half hour's nap after dinner, but when he wakes he holds up his head and asks, "What's the news?" as if the rest of mankind had stood his sentinels. Some give directions to be waked every half hour, doubtless for no other purpose; and then, to pay for it, they tell what they have dreamed. After a night's sleep the news is as indispensable as the breakfast. "Pray tell me any thing new that has happened to a man any where on this globe",—and he reads it over his coffee and rolls, that a man has had his eyes gouged out this morning on the Wachito River; never dreaming the while that he lives in the dark unfathomed mammoth cave of this world, and has but the rudiment of an eye himself.

For my part, I could easily do without the post-office. I think that there are very few important communications made through it. To speak critically, I never received more than one or two letters in my life—I wrote this some years ago—that were worth the postage. The penny-post is, commonly, an institution through which you seriously offer a man that penny for his thoughts which is so often safely offered in jest. And I am sure that I never read any memorable news in a newspaper. If we read of one man robbed, or murdered, or killed by accident, or one house burned, or one vessel wrecked, or one steamboat blown up, or one cow run over on the Western Railroad, or one mad dog killed, or one lot of grasshoppers in the winter,—we never need read of another. One is enough. If you are acquainted with the principle, what do you care for a myriad instances and applications? To a philosopher all *news*, as it is called, is gossip, and they who edit and read it are old women over their tea. Yet not a few are greedy after this gossip. There was such a rush, as I hear, the other day at one of the offices to learn the foreign news by the last arrival, that several large squares of plate glass belonging to the establishment were broken by the pressure,—news which I seriously think a ready wit might write a twelvemonth or twelve years beforehand with sufficient accuracy. As for Spain, for instance, if you know how to throw in Don Carlos and the Infanta, and Don Pedro and Seville and Granada, from time to time in the right proportions,—they may have changed the names a little since I saw the papers,—and serve up a bull-fight when other entertainments fail, it will be true to the letter, and give us as good an idea of the exact state or ruin of things in Spain as the most succinct and lucid report under this head in the newspapers: and as for England, almost the last significant scrap of news from that quarter was the revolution of 1649; and if you have learned the history of her crops for an average year, you never need attend to that thing again, unless your speculations are of a merely pecuniary character. If one may judge who rarely looks into the newspapers, nothing new does ever happen in foreign parts, a French revolution not excepted.

What news! how much more important to know what that is which was never old! "Kieou-pe-yu (great dignitary of the state of Wei) sent a man to Khoung-tseu to know his news. Khoung-tseu caused the messenger to be seated near him, and questioned him in these terms: What is your master doing? The messenger answered with respect: My master desires to diminish the number of his faults, but he cannot accomplish it. The messenger being gone, the philosopher remarked: What a worthy messenger! What a worthy messenger!" The preacher, instead of vexing the ears of drowsy farmers on their day of rest at the end of the week,—for Sunday is the fit conclusion of an ill-spent week, and not the fresh and brave beginning of a new one,—with this one other draggle-tail of a sermon, should shout with thundering voice,—"Pause! Avast! Why so seeming fast, but deadly slow?"

Shams and delusions are esteemed for soundest truths, while reality is fabulous. If men would steadily observe realities only, and not allow themselves to be deluded, life, to compare it with such things as we know, would be like a fairy tale and the Arabian Nights' Entertainments. If we respected only what is inevitable and has a right to be, music and poetry would resound along the streets. When we are unhurried and wise, we perceive that only great and worthy things have any permanent and absolute existence,—that petty fears and petty pleasures are but the shadow of the reality. This is always exhilarating and sublime. By closing the eyes and slumbering, and consenting to be deceived by shows, men establish and confirm their daily life of routine and habit every where, which still is built on purely illusory foundations. Children, who play life, discern its true law and relations more clearly than men, who fail to live it worthily, but who think that they are wiser by experience, that is, by failure. I have read in a Hindoo book, that "there was a king's son, who, being expelled in infancy from his native city, was brought up by a forester, and, growing up to maturity in that state, imagined himself to belong to the barbarous race with which he lived. One of his father's ministers having discovered him, revealed to him what he was, and the misconception of his character was removed, and he knew himself to be a prince. So soul," continues the Hindoo philosopher, "from the circumstances in which it is placed, mistakes its own character, until the truth is revealed to it by some holy teacher, and then it knows itself to be *Brahme*." I perceive that we inhabitants of New England live this mean life that we do because our vision does not penetrate the surface of things. We think that that *is* which *appears* to be. If a man should walk through this town and see only the reality, where, think you, would the "Mill-dam" go to? If he should give us an account of the realities he beheld there, we should not recognize the place in his description. Look at a meeting-house, or a court-house, or a jail, or a shop, or a dwelling-house, and say what that thing really is before a true gaze, and they would all go to pieces in your account of them. Men esteem truth remote, in the outskirts of the system, behind the farthest star, before Adam and after the last man. In eternity there is indeed something true and sublime. But all these times and places and occasions are now and here. God himself culminates in the present moment, and will never be more divine in the lapse of all the ages. And we are enabled to apprehend at all what is sublime and noble only by the perpetual instilling and drenching of the reality which surrounds us. The universe constantly and obediently answers to our conceptions; whether we travel fast or slow, the track is laid for us. Let us spend our lives in conceiving then. The poet or the artist never yet had so fair and noble a design but some of his posterity at least could accomplish it.

Let us spend one day as deliberately as Nature, and not be thrown off the track by every nutshell and mosquito's wing that falls on the rails.

Let us rise early and fast, or break fast, gently and without perturbation; let company come and let company go, let the bells ring and the children cry,—determined to make a day of it. Why should we knock under and go with the stream? Let us not be upset and overwhelmed in that terrible rapid and whirlpool called a dinner, situated in the meridian shallows. Weather this danger and you are safe, for the rest of the way is down hill. With unrelaxed nerves, with morning vigor, sail by it, looking another way, tied to the mast like Ulysses. If the engine whistles, let it whistle till it is hoarse for its pains. If the bell rings, why should we run? We will consider what kind of music they are like. Let us settle ourselves, and work and wedge our feet downward through the mud and slush of opinion, and prejudice, and tradition, and delusion, and appearance, that alluvion which covers the globe, through Paris and London, through New York and Boston and Concord, through church and state, through poetry and philosophy and religion, till we come to a hard bottom and rocks in place, which we can call *reality*, and say, This is, and no mistake; and then begin, having a *point d'appui*, below freshet and frost and fire, a place where you might found a wall or a state, or set a lamp-post safely, or perhaps a gauge, not a Nilometer, but a Realometer, that future ages might know how deep a freshet of shams and appearances had gathered from time to time. If you stand right fronting and face to face to a fact, you will see the sun glimmer on both its surfaces, as if it were a cimeter, and feel its sweet edge dividing you through the heart and marrow, and so you will happily conclude your mortal career. Be it life or death, we crave only reality. If we are really dying, let us hear the rattle in our throats and feel cold in the extremities; if we are alive, let us go about our business.

Time is but the stream I go a-fishing in. I drink at it; but while I drink I see the sandy bottom and detect how shallow it is. Its thin current slides away, but eternity remains. I would drink deeper; fish in the sky, whose bottom is pebbly with stars. I cannot count one. I know not the first letter of the alphabet. I have always been regretting that I was not as wise as the day I was born. The intellect is a cleaver; it discerns and rifts its way into the secret of things. I do not wish to be any more busy with my hands than is necessary. My head is hands and feet. I feel all my best faculties concentrated in it. My instinct tells me that my head is an organ for burrowing, as some creatures use their snout and fore-paws, and with it I would mine and burrow my way through these hills. I think that the richest vein is somewhere hereabouts; so by the divining rod and thin rising vapors I judge; and here I will begin to mine.

Questions for Thinking and Writing

1. According to Thoreau, what are the essential facts of life? Why does Thoreau explain that he does not need to own land, need a post office, or own a house that is anything more than a shelter?

2. Contrast Thoreau's quest for "Simplicity, simplicity, simplicity!" with the material needs of a growing country. If Thoreau had had a mass following, do you think society would be better or worse off today? Why do you think Thoreau's message is remembered today? How does it relate to contemporary lifestyles and contemporary attitudes toward land and material things?
3. Analyze and discuss the metaphor of time as a stream in the final paragraph. How does Thoreau attempt to link the life of the mind with nature and the universe? What role do imagination and intellect play in Thoreau's perspective on nature? How does it conflict with the way people lead their everyday lives?

🌿 Emily Dickinson (1830–1886)

The Wind Begun to Rock the Grass (1891)

Emily Dickinson devoted her life to self-exploration and simplicity. She had no profession and no set goals, but lived according to her own sense of time and place. She was able to do this because her family was affluent. She spent almost all of her time in the family home in Amherst, Massachusetts, becoming more reclusive each year until toward the end of her life, she finally lived only in her own room.

Dickinson attended Amherst Institute, then South Hadley Female Seminary (now Mount Holyoke College), where she remained for less than a year before returning to Amherst with her family's blessing. In her youth and middle years, Dickinson had many friends and was socially active. One of her Amherst friends was Helen Hunt Jackson (see p. 53), who encouraged her poetry writing.

Dickinson began writing during her childhood, and though she wrote almost 2,000 poems, only 6 were published before she died. Many poems were found scribbled on scrap paper and on the backs of envelopes in her room. She had bound groups of them into little booklets. The themes she followed say something about her inner thoughts—a mystic view of nature, preoccupation with death and immortality, and recurrent images of disaster ranging from imprisonment to storms. Neither a nature lover nor an environmentalist, her incisive intelligence and wit allowed her to see into the life of things. Yet she was a keen observer of the natural world, which paradoxically she viewed from the confines of her own home. Like Henry David Thoreau, her power of imagination and strength of spirit gave her access to the power of the universe.

After her death, Dickinson's poems were edited, many of them in-accurately, in 1890–1891 by Thomas Wentworth Higginson, a Boston critic and editor of The Atlantic Monthly. *Not until 1955 did Dickinson's poems appear as she wrote them.*

T he Wind begun to rock the Grass
With threatening Tunes and low—
He threw a Menace at the Earth—
A Menace at the Sky.

The Leaves unhooked themselves from Trees—
And started all abroad
The Dust did scoop itself like Hands
And threw away the Road.

The Wagons quickened on the Streets
The Thunder hurried slow—
The Lightning showed a Yellow Beak
And then a livid Claw.

The Birds put up the Bars to Nests—
The Cattle fled to Barns—
There came one drop of Giant Rain
And then as if the Hands

That held the Dams had parted hold
The Waters Wrecked the Sky,
But overlooked my Father's House—
Just quartering a Tree—

Questions for Thinking and Writing

1. Explain how Dickinson uses personification to make the description of the thunderstorm believable.
2. How does the mixture of natural destruction and familiar images blend to make the image whole?
3. What are some possible interpretations for the phrase "my Father's House" in the penultimate line?

🦎 George Perkins Marsh (1801–1882)

Man's Responsibility for the Land (1864)

Throughout his life, George Perkins Marsh demonstrated genius in an astonishing variety of ways. Though Marsh was a believer in the necessity of wise land use, Man and Nature *(1864), the work he is best remembered for, is but a small example of his accomplishments and influence.*

Marsh was born in Woodstock, Vermont, into New England aristocracy, which still held on to puritanical ideals. He entered Dartmouth College in 1816 with only a few months of schooling behind him, and while there discovered his gift for languages, learning French, German, Italian, and Portuguese. After graduating, he practiced law, was active in Vermont state government where he was Commissioner of Fisheries, and was elected to Congress in 1830. President Zachary Taylor appointed him U.S. minister to Turkey in 1849, and from then on he spent most of the rest of his life abroad in diplomatic and legal posts. In 1860, President Abraham Lincoln named him U.S. minister to Italy, a post he kept for 21 years. He died near Florence and is buried in Rome. Marsh was eclectic and energetic in his tastes and interests. His hobbies ranged from collecting species of reptiles, to engravings (the Smithsonian purchased his collection), to studying the grammar of Scandinavian languages. He was also interested in camels, about whose habits and uses he wrote a book.

Much of the material in Man and Nature *was gathered during Marsh's travels through Europe and the Middle East where he witnessed the devastating effects of overgrazing and land clearing. He convincingly argued that overuse of land had resulted in the downfall of civilizations.* Man and Nature *is unique in that it appeals to an international sense of ecology, though Marsh does not use the term. It was greeted with enormous interest at the time of publication and was influential among environmentalists such as John Muir (see p. 55) and John Burroughs (see p. 66).*

STABILITY OF NATURE

Nature, left undisturbed, so fashions her territory as to give it almost unchanging permanence of form, outline, and proportion, except when shattered by geologic convulsions; and in these comparatively rare cases of derangement, she sets herself at once to repair the superficial damage, and to restore, as nearly as practicable, the former aspect of her dominion. In new countries, the natural inclination of the ground, the self-formed slopes and levels, are generally such as best secure the stability of the soil. They have been graded and lowered or elevated by frost and chemical forces and gravitation and the flow of water and vegetable deposit and the action of the winds, until, by a general compensation of conflicting forces, a condition of equilibrium has been reached which, without the action of man, would remain, with little fluctuation, for countless ages.

We need not go far back to reach a period when, in all that portion of the North American continent which has been occupied by British colonization, the geographical elements very nearly balanced and compensated each other. At the commencement of the seventeenth century, the soil, with insignificant exceptions, was covered with forests; and whenever the Indian, in consequence of war or the exhaustion of the beasts of the chase, abandoned the narrow fields he had planted and the woods he had burned over, they speedily returned, by a succession of herbaceous, arborescent, and arboreal growths, to their original state. Even a single generation sufficed to restore them almost to their primitive luxuriance of forest vegetation. The unbroken forests had attained to their maximum density and strength of growth, and, as the older trees decayed and fell, they were succeeded by new shoots or seedlings, so that from century to century no perceptible change seems to have occurred in the wood, except the slow, spontaneous succession of crops. This succession involved no interruption of growth, and but little break in the "boundless contiguity of shade;" for, in the husbandry of nature, there are no fallows. Trees fall singly, not by square roods, and the tall pine is hardly prostrate, before the light and heat, admitted to the ground by the removal of the dense crown of foliage which had shut them out, stimulate the germination of the seeds of broad-leaved trees that had lain, waiting this kindly influence, perhaps for centuries. Two natural causes, destructive in character, were, indeed, in operation in the primitive American forests, though, in the Northern colonies, at least, there were sufficient compensations; for we do not discover that any considerable permanent change was produced by them. I refer to the action of beavers and of fallen trees in producing bogs, and of smaller animals, insects, and birds, in destroying the woods. Bogs are less numerous and extensive in the Northern States of the American union, because the natural inclination of the surface favors drainage; but they are more frequent, and cover more ground, in the Southern States, for the opposite reason. They generally originate in the checking of watercourses by the falling of timber, or of earth and rocks, across their channels. If the impediment thus created is sufficient to retain a permanent accumulation of water behind it, the trees whose roots are overflowed soon perish, and then by their fall increase the obstruction, and, of course, occasion a still wider spread of the stagnating stream.

This process goes on until the water finds a new outlet, at a higher level, not liable to similar interruption. The fallen trees not completely covered by water are soon overgrown with mosses; aquatic and semi-aquatic plants propagate themselves, and spread until they more or less completely fill up the space occupied by the water, and the surface is gradually converted from a pond to a quaking morass. The morass is slowly solidified by vegetable production and deposit, then very often restored to the forest condition by the growth of black ashes, cedars, or, in southern latitudes, cypresses, and other trees suited to such a soil, and thus the interrupted harmony of nature is at least reëstablished.

I am disposed to think that more bogs in the Northern States owe their origin to beavers than to accidental obstructions of rivulets by wind-fallen or naturally decayed trees; for there are few swamps in those States, at the outlets of which we may not, by careful search, find the remains of a beaver dam. The beaver sometimes inhabits natural lakelets, but he prefers to owe his pond to his own ingenuity and toil. The reservoir once constructed, its inhabitants rapidly multiply, and as its harvests of pond lilies, and other aquatic plants on which this quadruped feeds in winter, become too small for the growing population, the beaver metropolis sends out expeditions of discovery and colonization. The pond gradually fills up, by the operation of the same causes as when it owes its existence to an accidental obstruction, and when, at last, the original settlement is converted into a bog by the usual processes of vegetable life, the remaining inhabitants abandon it and build on some virgin brooklet a new city of the waters.

In countries somewhat further advanced in civilization than those occupied by the North American Indians, as in mediæval Ireland, the formation of bogs may be commenced by the neglect of man to remove, from the natural channels of superficial drainage, the tops and branches of trees felled for the various purposes to which wood is applicable in his rude industry; and, when the flow of the water is thus checked, nature goes on with the processes I have already described. In such half-civilized regions, too, windfalls are more frequent than in those where the forest is unbroken, because, when openings have been made in it, for agricultural or other purposes, the entrance thus afforded to the wind occasions the sudden overthrow of hundreds of trees which might otherwise have stood for generations, and thus have fallen to the ground, only one by one, as natural decay brought them down. Besides this, the flocks bred by man in the pastoral state, keep down the incipient growth of trees on the half-dried bogs, and prevent them from recovering their primitive condition.

Young trees in the native forest are sometimes girdled and killed by the smaller rodent quadrupeds, and their growth is checked by birds which feed on the terminal bud; but these animals, as we shall see, are generally found on the skirts of the wood only, not in its deeper recesses, and hence the mischief they do is not extensive. The insects which damage primitive forests by feeding upon products of trees essential to their growth, are not numerous, nor is their appearance, in destructive numbers, frequent; and those which perforate the stems and branches, to deposit and hatch their eggs, more commonly select dead trees for that purpose, though, unhappily, there are important exceptions to this latter remark. I do not know that we have any evidence of the destruction or serious injury of American forests by insects, before or even soon after the period of colonization; but since the white man has laid bare a vast proportion of the earth's surface, and thereby produced changes favorable, perhaps, to the multiplication of these pests, they have greatly increased in numbers, and, apparently, in voracity also. Not many years ago, the pines of thousands of acres of land in North Carolina, were destroyed by insects not known to have ever done serious injury to that tree before. In such cases as this and others of the like sort, there is good reason to believe that man is the indirect cause of an evil for which he pays so heavy a penalty. Insects increase whenever the birds which feed upon them disappear. Hence, in the wanton destruction of the robin and other insectivorous birds, the *bipes implumis,* the featherless biped, man, is not only exchanging the vocal orchestra which greets the rising sun for the drowsy beetle's evening drone, and depriving his groves and his fields of their fairest ornament, but he is waging a treacherous warfare on his natural allies.

In fine, in countries untrodden by man, the proportions and relative positions of land and water, the atmospheric precipitation and evaporation, the thermometric mean, and the distribution of vegetable and animal life, are subject to change only from geological influences so slow in their operation that the geographical conditions may be regarded as constant and immutable. These arrangements of nature it is, in most cases, highly desirable substantially to maintain, when such regions become the seat of organized commonwealths. It is, therefore, a matter of the first importance, that, in commencing the process of fitting them for permanent civilized occupation, the transforming operations should be so conducted as not unnecessarily to derange and destroy what, in too many cases, it is beyond the power of man to rectify or restore.

RESTORATION OF DISTURBED HARMONIES

In reclaiming and reoccupying lands laid waste by human improvidence or malice, and abandoned by man, or occupied only by a nomade or thinly scattered population, the task of the pioneer settler is of a very different character. He is to become a co-worker with nature in the reconstruction of the damaged fabric which the negligence or the wantonness of former lodgers has rendered untenantable. He must aid her in reclothing the mountain slopes with forests and vegetable mould,

thereby restoring the fountains which she provided to water them; in
checking the devastating fury of torrents, and bringing back the surface
drainage to its primitive narrow channels; and in drying deadly
morasses by opening the natural sluices which have been choked up,
and cutting new canals for drawing off their stagnant waters. He must
thus, on the one hand, create new reservoirs, and, on the other, remove
mischievous accumulations of moisture, thereby equalizing and regulating the sources of atmospheric humidity and of flowing water, both
which are so essential to all vegetable growth, and, of course, to human
and lower animal life.

DESTRUCTIVENESS OF MAN

Man has too long forgotten that the earth was given to him for
usufruct alone, not for consumption, still less for profligate waste. Nature has provided against the absolute destruction of any of her elementary matter, the raw material of her works; the thunderbolt and the
tornado, the most convulsive throes of even the volcano and the earthquake, being only phenomena of decomposion and recomposition. But
she has left it within the power of man irreparably to derange the combinations of inorganic matter and of organic life, which through the
night of æons she had been proportioning and balancing, to prepare
the earth for his habitation, when, in the fulness of time, his Creator
should call him forth to enter into its possession.

Apart from the hostile influence of man, the organic and the inorganic world are, as I have remarked, bound together by such mutual relations and adaptations as secure, if not the absolute permanence and
equilibrium of both, a long continuance of the established conditions
of each at any given time and place, or at least, a very slow and gradual
succession of changes in those conditions. But man is everywhere a disturbing agent. Wherever he plants his foot, the harmonies of nature are
turned to discords. The proportions and accommodations which in-
sured the stability of existing arrangements are overthrown. Indigenous
vegetable and animal species are extirpated, and supplanted by others
of foreign origin, spontaneous production is forbidden or restricted,
and the face of the earth is either laid bare or covered with a new and
reluctant growth of vegetable forms, and with alien tribes of animal life.
These intentional changes and substitutions constitute, indeed, great
revolutions; but vast as is their magnitude and importance, they are, as
we shall see, insignificant in comparison with the contingent and un-
sought results which have flowed from them.

The fact that, of all organic beings, man alone is to be regarded as essentially a destructive power, and that he wields energies to resist which,
nature—that nature whom all material life and all inorganic substance
obey—is wholly impotent, tends to prove that, though living in physical

nature, he is not of her, that he is of more exalted parentage, and belongs to a higher order of existences than those born of her womb and submissive to her dictates.

There are, indeed, brute destroyers, beasts and birds and insects of prey—all animal life feeds upon, and, of course, destroys other life,—but this destruction is balanced by compensations. It is, in fact, the very means by which the existence of one tribe of animals or of vegetables is secured against being smothered by the encroachments of another; and the reproductive powers of species, which serve as the food of others, are always proportioned to the demand they are destined to supply. Man pursues his victims with reckless destructiveness; and, while the sacrifice of life by the lower animals is limited by the cravings of appetite, he unsparingly persecutes, even to extirpation, thousands of organic forms which he cannot consume.

The earth was not, in its natural condition, completely adapted to the use of man, but only to the sustenance of wild animals and wild vegetation. These live, multiply their kind in just proportion, and attain their perfect measure of strength and beauty, without producing or requiring any change in the natural arrangements of surface, or in each other's spontaneous tendencies, except such mutual repression of excessive increase as may prevent the extirpation of one species by the encroachments of another. In short, without man, lower animal and spontaneous vegetable life would have been constant in type, distribution, and proportion, and the physical geography of the earth would have remained undisturbed for indefinite periods, and been subject to revolution only from possible, unknown cosmical causes, or from geological action.

But man, the domestic animals that serve him, the field and garden plants the products of which supply him with food and clothing, cannot subsist and rise to the full development of their higher properties, unless brute and unconscious nature be effectually combated, and, in a great degree, vanquished by human art. Hence, a certain measure of transformation of terrestrial surface, of suppression of natural, and stimulation of artificially modified productivity becomes necessary. This measure man has unfortunately exceeded. He has felled the forests whose network of fibrous roots bound the mould to the rocky skeleton of the earth; but had he allowed here and there a belt of woodland to reproduce itself by spontaneous propagation, most of the mischiefs which his reckless destruction of the natural protection of the soil has occasioned would have been averted. He has broken up the mountain reservoirs, the percolation of whose waters through unseen channels supplied the fountains that refreshed his cattle and fertilized his fields; but he has neglected to maintain the cisterns and the canals of irrigation which a wise antiquity had constructed to neutralize the consequences of its own imprudence. While he has torn the thin glebe which confined the light earth of extensive plains, and has destroyed the fringe of semi-aquatic plants which skirted the coast and checked the drifting of the sea sand, he has failed to prevent the spreading of the dunes by clothing them with artificially propagated vegetation. He has ruthlessly warred on all the tribes of animated nature whose spoil he could convert to his own uses, and he has not protected the birds which prey on the insects most destructive to his own harvests.

Purely untutored humanity, it is true, interferes comparatively little with the arrangements of nature, and the destructive agency of man becomes more and more energetic and unsparing as he advances in civilization, until the impoverishment, with which his exhaustion of the natural resources of the soil is threatening him, at last awakens him to the necessity of preserving what is left, if not of restoring what has been wantonly wasted. The wandering savage grows no cultivated vegetable, fells no forest, and extirpates no useful plant, no noxious weed. If his skill in the chase enables him to entrap numbers of the animals on which he feeds, he compensates this loss by destroying also the lion, the tiger, the wolf, the otter, the seal, and the eagle, thus indirectly protecting the feebler quadrupeds and fish and fowls, which would otherwise become the booty of beasts and birds of prey. But with stationary life, or rather with the pastoral state, man at once commences an almost indiscriminate warfare upon all the forms of animal and vegetable existence around him, and as he advances in civilization, he gradually eradicates or transforms every spontaneous product of the soil he occupies.

HUMAN AND BRUTE ACTION COMPARED

It has been maintained by authorities as high as any known to modern science, that the action of man upon nature, though greater in *degree*, does not differ in *kind*, from that of wild animals. It appears to me to differ in essential character, because, though it is often followed by unforeseen and undesired results, yet it is nevertheless guided by a self-conscious and intelligent will aiming as often at secondary and remote as at immediate objects. The wild animal, on the other hand, acts instinctively, and, so far as we are able to perceive, always with a view to single and direct purposes. The backwoodsman and the beaver alike fell trees; the man that he may convert the forest into an olive grove that will mature its fruit only for a succeeding generation, the beaver that he may feed upon their bark or use them in the construction of his habitation. Human differs from brute action, too, in its influence upon the material world, because it is not controlled by natural compensations and balances. Natural arrangements, once disturbed by man, are not restored until he retires from the field, and leaves free scope to spontaneous recuperative energies; the wounds he inflicts upon the material creation are not healed until he withdraws the arm that gave the blow. On the other hand, I am not aware of any evidence that wild animals have ever destroyed the smallest forest, extirpated any organic species, or modified its natural character, occasioned any permanent change of terrestrial surface, or produced any disturbance of physical conditions which nature has not, or herself, repaired without the expulsion of the animal that had caused it.

The form of geographical surface, and very probably the climate of a given country, depend much on the character of the vegetable life belonging to it. Man has, by domestication, greatly changed the habits and properties of the plants he rears; he has, by voluntary selection, immensely modified the forms and qualities of the animated creatures that serve him; and he has, at the same time, completely rooted out many forms of both vegetable and animal being. What is there, in the influence of brute life, that corresponds to this? We have no reason to believe that in that portion of the American continent which, though peopled by many tribes of quadruped and fowl, remained uninhabited by man, or only thinly occupied by purely savage tribes, any sensible geographical change had occurred within twenty centuries before the epoch of discovery and colonization while, during the same period, man had changed millions of square miles, in the fairest and most fertile regions of the Old World, into the barrenest deserts.

The ravages committed by man subvert the relations and destroy the balance which nature had established between her organized and her inorganic creations; and she avenges herself upon the intruder, by letting loose upon her defaced provinces destructive energies hitherto kept in check by organic forces destined to be his best auxiliaries, but which he has unwisely dispersed and driven from the field of action. When the forest is gone, the great reservoir of moisture stored up in its vegetable mould is evaporated, and returns only in deluges of rain to wash away the parched dust into which that mould has been converted. The well-wooded and humid hills are turned to ridges of dry rock, which encumbers the low grounds and chokes the watercourses with its debris, and—except in countries favored with an equable distribution of rain through the seasons, and a moderate and regular inclination of surface—the whole earth, unless rescued by human art from the physical degradation to which it tends, becomes an assemblage of bald mountains, of barren, turfless hills, and of swampy and malarious plains. There are parts of Asia Minor, of Northern Africa, of Greece, and even of Alpine Europe, where the operation of causes set in action by man has brought the face of the earth to a desolation almost as complete as that of the moon; and though, within that brief space of time which we call "the historical period," they are known to have been covered with luxuriant woods, verdant pastures, and fertile meadows, they are now too far deteriorated to be reclaimable by man, nor can they become again fitted for human use, except through great geological changes, or other mysterious influences or agencies of which we have no present knowledge, and over which we have no prospective control. The earth is fast becoming an unfit home for its noblest inhabitant, and another era of equal human crime and human improvidence, and of like duration with that through which traces of that crime and that improvidence extend, would reduce it to such a condition of impoverished productiveness, of shattered surface, of climatic excess, as to threaten the depravation, barbarism, and perhaps even extinction of the species.

Questions for Thinking and Writing

1. Explain Marsh's statement that "man is everywhere a disturbing agent." Show how he uses it as a rallying cry for motivating action. Discuss your feelings about this statement and whether or not you agree with it.
2. How does Marsh show sympathy for the human inclination for environmental destruction? What images does Marsh use to support his thesis?
3. What is your definition of "civilized man" with regard to use of the environment? To what extent does it agree or disagree with Marsh's concept?

🦎 Frederick Law Olmsted (1822–1903)

The Yosemite Valley and the Mariposa Big Trees (1865)

Frederick Law Olmsted was once toasted as the man who "paints with lakes and wooded slopes . . . mountainsides and ocean views." As the first professional landscape architect in the United States, Olmsted's ambition was to create landscapes that improved nature and to preserve wilderness oases to give city dwellers the opportunity for tranquility and rejuvenation.

Olmsted was born in Hartford, Connecticut, into a wealthy merchant family. He traveled widely with his family and was imbued with a love of natural landscape scenery from youth. He did not attend college, but instead spent time variously studying engineering, working for a dry goods importer, and sailing as a common seaman to China. For a time he was a working farmer on Staten Island, New York City.

Olmsted's writing career began when he went on a walking tour of Great Britain and composed Walks and Talks of an American Farmer in England *(1852). The same year he was commissioned by the* New

York Times *to write a series of articles on the South, particularly focusing on slavery and economic and social conditions. Three books resulted from this reportage, which were collectively titled* The Cotton Kingdom *(1860).*

Interest in landscape design and architecture developed over the years but became really important to him on a tour of Italy in 1857. On his return, Olmsted was appointed superintendent of Central Park, which was then under construction. The following year he and Calvert Vaux, an English architect who was his partner, won a competition for the park's design. What is now the most famous U.S. urban park took its shape and character during this time. Olmsted worked widely and later designed parks in Boston, Hartford, Chicago, and San Francisco, among other cities. In each instance, he applied standards of design that made the resulting landscape look natural though, in fact, it was artificial.

While recuperating from an accident during the construction of Central Park, Olmsted moved to California where he managed the estate of the Mariposa Mining Company. At this time he was instrumental in having Yosemite Valley named a state park, and he wrote The Yosemite Valley and the Mariposa Big Trees.

Olmsted's philosophy was to create parks in order to conserve natural landscapes for pleasure: aesthetic enjoyment, camping, and sightseeing. Whether he was designing an urban park or preserving a vast wilderness such as Yosemite Valley, Olmsted believed that human beings could control nature so people could have reasonable access to it. His was an Eastern-based upper-class view of class welfare prevalent in the United States during the nineteenth century. This point of view may seem condescending, but it is driven by a sense of public service and order. Eastern political and economic power dominated the environmental movement from the 1870s until the early 1940s.

It was during one of the darkest hours [of the Civil War] . . . that consideration was first given to the danger that [the Yosemite Valley and the neighboring Sequoia grove] might become private property and through the false taste, the caprice or the requirements of some industrial speculation of their holders, their value to posterity be injured. To secure them against this danger Congress passed an act providing that the premises should be segregated from the general domain of the public lands, and devoted forever to popular resort and recreation, under the administration of a Board of Commissioners, to serve without pecuniary compensation, to be appointed by the Executive of the State of California. . . .

It is the will of the nation as embodied in the act of Congress that this scenery shall never be private property, but that like certain defensive points upon our coast it shall be held solely for public purposes.

Two classes of considerations may be assumed to have influenced the action of Congress. The first and less important is the direct and obvious pecuniary advantage which comes to a commonwealth from the fact that it possesses objects which cannot be taken out of its domain, that are attractive to travellers and the enjoyment of which is open to all.

To illustrate this it is simply necessary to refer to certain cantons of the Republic of Switzerland, a commonwealth of the most industrious and frugal people in Europe. The results of all the ingenuity and labor of this people applied to the resources of wealth which they hold in common with the people of other lands have become of insignificant value compared with that which they derive from the price which travellers gladly pay for being allowed to share with them the enjoyment of the natural scenery of their mountains. These travellers alone have caused hundreds of the best inns in the world to be established and maintained among them, have given the farmers their best and almost the only market they have for their surplus products, have spread a network of railroads and superb carriage roads, steamboat routes and telegraphic lines over the country, have contributed directly and indirectly for many years the larger part of the state revenue and all this without the exportation or abstraction from the country of any thing of the slightest value to the people. . . .

A more important class of considerations, however, remains to be stated. These are considerations of a political duty of grave importance to which seldom if ever before has proper respect been paid by any government in the world but the grounds of which rest on the same eternal base of equity and benevolence with all other duties of republican government. It is the main duty of government, if it is not the sole duty of government, to provide means of protection for all its citizens in the pursuit of happiness against the obstacles, otherwise insurmountable, which the selfishness of individuals or combinations of individuals is liable to interpose to that pursuit.

It is a scientific fact that the occasional contemplation of natural scenes of an impressive character, particularly if this contemplation occurs in connection with relief from ordinary cares, change of air and change of habits, is favorable to the health and vigor of men and especially to the health and vigor of their intellect beyond any other conditions which can be offered them, that it not only gives pleasure for the time being but increases the subsequent capacity for happiness and the means of securing happiness. The want of such occasional recreation where men and women are habitually pressed by their business or household cares often results in a class of disorders the characteristic quality of which is mental disability, sometimes taking the severe forms of softening of the brain, paralysis, palsy, monomania, or insanity, but more frequently of mental and nervous excitability, moroseness, melancholy or irascibility, incapacitating the subject for the proper exercise of the intellectual and moral forces.

It is well established that where circumstances favor the use of such means of recreation as have been indicated, the reverse of this is true. For instance, it is a universal custom with the heads of the important departments of the British government to spend a certain period of every year on their parks and shooting grounds or in travelling among the Alps or other mountain regions. This custom is followed by the leading lawyers, bankers, merchants and the wealthy classes generally of the empire, among whom the average period of active business life is much greater than with the most nearly corresponding classes in our own or any other country where the same practice is not equally well established. . . .

But in this country at least it is not those who have the most important responsibilities in state affairs or in commerce, who suffer most from the lack of recreation; women suffer more than men, and the agricultural class is more largely represented in our insane asylums than the professional, and for this, and other reasons, it is these classes to which the opportunity for such recreation is the greatest blessing.

If we analyze the operation of scenes of beauty upon the mind, and consider the intimate relation of the mind upon the nervous system and the whole physical economy, the action and reaction which constantly occur between bodily and mental conditions, the reinvigoration which results from such scenes is readily comprehended. Few persons can see such scenery as that of the Yosemite and not be impressed by it in some slight degree. All not alike, all not perhaps consciously, and amongst all who are consciously impressed by it, few can give the least expression to that of which they are conscious. But there can be no doubt that all have this susceptibility, though with some it is much more dull and confused than with others.

The power of scenery to affect men is, in a large way, proportionate to the degree of their civilization and the degree in which their taste has been cultivated. Among a thousand savages there will be a much smaller number who will show the least sign of being so affected than among a thousand persons taken from a civilized community. This is only one of the many channels in which a similar distinction between civilized and savage men is to be generally observed. The whole body of the susceptibilities of civilized men and with their susceptibilities their powers, are on the whole enlarged.

But as with the bodily powers, if one group of muscles is developed by exercise exclusively, and all others neglected, the result is general feebleness, so it is with the mental faculties. And men who exercise those faculties or susceptibilities of the mind which are called in play by beautiful scenery so little that they seem to be inert with them, are either in a diseased condition from excessive devotion of the mind to a limited range of interests, or their whole minds are in a savage state; that is, a state of low development. The latter class need to be drawn out generally; the former need relief from their habitual matters of interest and to be drawn out in those parts of their mental nature which have been habitually left idle and inert.

But there is a special reason why the reinvigoration of those parts which are stirred into conscious activity by natural scenery is more effective upon the general development and health than that of any other, which is this: The severe and excessive exercise of the mind which leads to the greatest fatigue and is the most wearing upon the whole constitution is almost entirely caused by application to the removal of something to be apprehended in the future, or to interests beyond those of the moment, or of the individual; to the laying up of wealth, to the preparation of something, to accomplishing something in the mind of another, and especially to small and petty details which are uninteresting in themselves and which engage the attention at all only because of the bearing they have on some general end of more importance which is seen ahead.

In the interest which natural scenery inspires there is the strongest contrast to this. It is for itself and at the moment it is enjoyed. The attention is aroused and the mind occupied without purpose, without a continuation of the common process of relating the present action, thought or perception to some future end. There is little else that has this quality so purely. There are few enjoyments with which regard for something outside and beyond the enjoyment of the moment can ordinarily be so little mixed. The pleasures of the table are irresistibly associated with the care of hunger and the repair of the bodily waste. In all social pleasures and all pleasures which are usually enjoyed in association with the social pleasures, the care for the opinion of others, or the good of others largely mingles. In the pleasures of literature, the laying up of ideas and self-improvement are purposes which cannot be kept out of view.

This, however, is in very slight degree, if at all, the case with the enjoyment of the emotions caused by natural scenery. It therefore results that the enjoyment of scenery employs the mind without fatigue and yet exercises it; tranquilizers it and yet enlivens it; and thus, through the influence of the mind over the body, gives the effect of refreshing rest and reinvigoration to the whole system.

Questions for Thinking and Writing

1. How does Olmsted make use of the upper class in this essay with regard to its access to unspoiled nature? Explain whether Olmsted can be justified in

using social snobbery to further his argument. What sentiments might his attitude elicit in a modern audience versus a nineteenth-century audience?
2. Analyze Olmsted's concern for the preservation of wild places versus his concept of happiness for the masses.
3. Analyze how Olmsted and George Perkins Marsh in *Man in Nature* (p. 26) contrast one social group or class with another as a means of persuasion.

❧ Walt Whitman (1819–1892)

Song of the Redwood-Tree (1874)

Walt Whitman was a visionary who based his dream of America on the freedom to express the self and to respect all things common. In many ways, he freed American literature from the constrictions and formulas of both its European ancestry and New England puritanism. He communicated his beliefs principally through Leaves of Grass, *which first appeared in 1855 with 12 poems. He reworked it eight times, adding new poems with each edition. The only real recognition the first edition received came from Ralph Waldo Emerson, who upon reading it welcomed Whitman "at the beginning of a great career."*

Whitman was born in Huntington, Long Island, the second of eight children. His father was a farmer but moved to the city of Brooklyn to take up carpentry when his son was 4. He was a friend of Thomas Paine and the household rang with conversation about liberal politics, egalitarianism, and individual rights, all of which made a lasting impression on young Walt.

Though Whitman was an eager reader who consumed his father's political tracts as well as writings by Homer, Dante, John Milton, and Charles Dickens, he received only five years of formal education. At age 12, he became a printer's apprentice and at 19 founded his own weekly newspaper, the Long Islander, *and worked as an editor and reporter for several other papers. In 1846, he became editor of the* Brooklyn Eagle, *but left after two years as a result of a dispute with its publishers over a political position he did not believe in.*

During his years as a journalist, Whitman was composing poems for Leaves of Grass, *which he envisioned as an interpretation of democratic idealism. Expecting that his poetry would not sell well, he arranged to have it privately printed, and he sold only a few copies from his home. Whitman sent a copy of his book to Emerson, who*

*was impressed and visited Whitman in New York. Later, Henry David
Thoreau and John Burroughs paid him visits. As succeeding editions
came out, European critics took a liking to the poems, and Whitman
gained international stature.*

*In 1862, Whitman volunteered as a war nurse in Washington hos-
pitals and worked part time in the army paymaster's office, but he was
eventually fired because of what was considered the erotic nature of
his poetry. It was during these years that he became a mentor to John
Burroughs who was also living in Washington. Burroughs later wrote
the first biography of Whitman:* Notes on Walt Whitman as Poet and
Person *(1867).*

*Until he was 54, Whitman was robust. But a stroke diminished his
health and he never really recovered. "Song of the Redwood-Tree"
(1874) was written about a year after Whitman suffered the stroke,
and the giant redwoods became a personal symbol for him. He was the
tree and the embodiment of the American spirit, doomed to be cut and
become part of the building of the United States. His attitude was
partly bittersweet. On the other hand, it seems not to have occurred
to Whitman that the trees were finite, for nature is exhaustible. The
greatness of the United States, Whitman suggested, derives from its
great size and inexhaustible natural resources. Whitman was a keen
observer and indefatigable cataloger of the senses and people, but he
was an armchair naturalist.*

1
A California song,
A prophecy and indirection, a thought impalpable to breathe as air,
A chorus of dryads, fading, departing, or hamadryads departing,
A murmuring, fateful, giant voice, out of the earth and sky,
Voice of a mighty dying tree in the redwood forest dense.

Farewell my brethren,
Farewell O earth and sky, farewell ye neighboring waters,
My time has ended, my term has come.

Along the northern coast,
Just back from the rock-bound shore and the caves,
In the saline air from the sea in the Mendocino country,
With the surge for base and accompaniment low and hoarse,
With crackling blows of axes sounding musically driven by strong
    arms,
Riven deep by the sharp tongues of the axes, there in the redwood
    forest dense,
I heard the mighty tree its death-chant chanting.

The choppers heard not, the camp shanties echoed not,
The quick-ear'd teamsters and chain and jack-screw men heard not,
As the wood-spirits came from their haunts of a thousand years to
     join the refrain,
But in my soul I plainly heard.
Murmuring out of its myriad leaves,
Down from its lofty top rising two hundred feet high,
Out of its stalwart trunk and limbs, out of its foot-thick bark,
That chant of the seasons and time, chant not of the past only but
     the future.

You untold life of me,
And all you venerable and innocent joys,
Perennial hardy life of me with joys 'mid rain and many a summer sun,
And the white snows and night and the wild winds;
O the great patient rugged joys, my soul's strong joys unreck'd by man,
(For know I bear the soul befitting me, I too have consciousness, identity,
And all the rocks and mountains have, and all the earth,)
Joys of the life befitting me and brothers mine,
Our time, our term has come.

Nor yield we mournfully majestic brothers,
We who have grandly fill'd our time;
With Nature's calm content, with tacit huge delight,
We welcome what we wrought for through the past,
And leave the field for them.

For them predicted long,
For a superber race, they too to grandly fill their time,
For them we abdicate, in them ourselves ye forest kings!
In them these skies and airs, these mountain peaks, Shasta, Nevadas,
These huge precipitous cliffs, this amplitude, these valleys, far Yosemite,
To be in them absorb'd, assimilated.

Then to a loftier strain,
Still prouder, more ecstatic rose the chant,
As if the heirs, the deities of the West,
Joining with master-tongue bore part.

Not wan from Asia's fetiches,
Nor red from Europe's old dynastic slaughter-house,
(Area of murder-plots of thrones, with scent left yet of wars and scaffolds
     everywhere,)
But come from Nature's long and harmless throes, peacefully builded thence,
These virgin lands, lands of the Western shore,

To the new culminating man, to you, the empire new,
You promis'd long, we pledge, we dedicate.

You occult deep volitions,
You average spiritual manhood, purpose of all, pois'd on yourself, giving
    not taking law,
You womanhood divine, mistress and source of all, whence life and love
    and aught that comes from life and love,
You unseen moral essence of all the vast materials of America, (age upon
    age working in death the same as life,)
You that, sometimes known, oftener unknown, really shape and mould the
    New World, adjusting it to Time and Space,
You hidden national will lying in your abysms, conceal'd but ever alert,
You past and present purposes tenaciously pursued, may-be unconscious
    of yourselves,
Unswerv'd by all the passing errors, perturbations of the surface;
You vital, universal, deathless germs, beneath all creeds, arts, statutes,
    literatures,
Here build your homes for good, establish here, these areas entire, lands of
    the Western shore,
We pledge, we dedicate to you.

For man of you, your characteristic race,
Here may he hardy, sweet, gigantic grow, here tower proportionate to Nature,
Here climb the vast pure spaces unconfined, uncheck'd by wall or roof,
Here laugh with storm or sun, here joy, here patiently inure,
Here heed himself, unfold himself, (not others' formulas heed,) here fill
    his time,
To duly fall, to aid, unreck'd at last,
To disappear, to serve.

Thus on the northern coast,
In the echo of teamsters' calls and the clinking chains, and the
    music of choppers' axes,
The falling trunk and limbs, the crash, the muffled shriek, the
    groan,
Such words combined from the redwood-tree, as of voices ecstatic,
    ancient and rustling,
The century-lasting, unseen dryads, singing, withdrawing,
All their recesses of forests and mountains leaving,
From the Cascade range to the Wahsatch, or Idaho far, or Utah,
To the deities of the modern henceforth yielding,
The chorus and indications, the vistas of coming humanity, the
    settlements, features all,
In the Mendocino woods I caught.

2
The flashing and golden pageant of California,
The sudden and gorgeous drama, the sunny and ample lands,
The long and varied stretch from Puget sound to Colorado south,
Lands bathed in sweeter, rarer, healthier air, valleys and mountain
    cliffs,
The fields of Nature long prepared and fallow, the silent, cyclic
    chemistry,
The slow and steady ages plodding, the unoccupied surface ripen-
    ing, the rich ores forming beneath;
At last the New arriving, assuming, taking possession,
A swarming and busy race settling and organizing everywhere,
Ships coming in from the whole round world, and going out to the
    whole world,
To India and China and Australia and the thousand island para-
    dises of the Pacific,
Populous cities, the latest inventions, the steamers on the rivers, the
    railroads, with many a thrifty farm, with machinery,
And wool and wheat and the grape, and diggings of yellow gold.

3
But more in you than these, lands of the Western shore,
(These but the means, the implements, the standing-ground,)
I see in you, certain to come, the promise of thousands of years, till
    now deferr'd,
Promis'd to be fulfill'd, our common kind, the race.

The new society at last, proportionate to Nature,
In man of you, more than your mountain peaks or stalwart trees
    imperial,
In woman more, far more, than all your gold or vines, or even
    vital air.

Fresh come, to a new world indeed, yet long prepared,
I see the genius of the modern, child of the real and ideal,
Clearing the ground for broad humanity, the true America, heir
    of the past so grand,
To build a grander future.

Questions for Thinking and Writing

1. If the giant redwood is a symbol of the United States, how does Whitman
   expect you to understand it in relation to nature, civilization, and the democratic spirit?

2. Is there validity to Whitman's claim that the new American society of the 1870s was at least proportionate to nature? Comment on the argument that the economic power of the United States is due to the availability and use of natural resources. Do you think this remains a valid argument concerning conflicts over environmental issues?
3. When you see a magnificent tree, how does it affect you and what do you think of?

❦ Sarah Orne Jewett (1849–1909)

A White Heron (1886)

Sarah Orne Jewett, like Sylvia, the young girl in "A White Heron," opted for nature rather than material things, and independence rather than dependence. Her fiction is peopled with characters, particularly women, who live on their own and believe in themselves, very much like Jewett herself.

Jewett was born and lived most of her life in the same house in South Berwick, Maine, a depressed inland port. Afflicted by arthritis during her childhood, Jewett was not required to attend school regularly; instead, she often accompanied her physician father on his house calls to isolated fishing communities and farm islands off the coast. Jewett began writing seriously as a teenager and published stories frequently in The Atlantic Monthly. *In 1877, she published a collection of short stories entitled* Deephaven, *a fictional coastal town, the first of 13 volumes of fiction. Her best known,* The Country of the Pointed Firs *(1896), which her friend Willa Cather considered a masterpiece, is a collection of loosely related stories that forms a kind of novel. Her writing career was cut short by injuries sustained during a carriage accident. In 1909, she suffered a severe stroke and died in the house where was born.*

From her firsthand knowledge and observant eye, Jewett developed a highly specialized literary ability to depict local color: the description and characterization of people in a specific place—the way they talked and the landscape they inhabited. She is at her best when describing the landscape of Maine, the blue sky and water, the rocky coasts, the green firs. Nature for her is a place to live in. She accepts it as it is. "A White Heron" is only incidentally a hunting tale. More to the point, the story's essence embodies the conflict that little Sylvia must face in the world: money or enjoying the spirit and freedom of nature, innocence or experience. Though the action is local and the characters humble, the message is universal; such is Jewett's literary technique.

I.

The woods were already filled with shadows one June evening, just before eight o'clock, though a bright sunset still glimmered faintly among the trunks of the trees. A little girl was driving home her cow, a plodding, dilatory, provoking creature in her behavior, but a valued companion for all that. They were going away from the western light, and striking deep into the dark woods, but their feet were familiar with the path, and it was no matter whether their eyes could see it or not.

There was hardly a night the summer through when the old cow could be found waiting at the pasture bars; on the contrary, it was her greatest pleasure to hide herself away among the high huckleberry bushes, and though she wore a loud bell she had made the discovery that if one stood perfectly still it would not ring. So Sylvia had to hunt for her until she found her, and call Co'! Co'! with never an answering Moo, until her childish patience was quite spent. If the creature had not given good milk and plenty of it, the case would have seemed very different to her owners. Besides, Sylvia had all the time there was, and very little use to make of it. Sometimes in pleasant weather it was a consolation to look upon the cow's pranks as an intelligent attempt to play hide and seek, and as the child had no playmates she lent herself to this amusement with a good deal of zest. Though this chase had been so long that the wary animal herself had given an unusual signal of her whereabouts, Sylvia had only laughed when she came upon Mistress Moolly at the swamp-side, and urged her affectionately homeward with a twig of birch leaves. The old cow was not inclined to wander farther, she even turned in the right direction for once as they left the pasture, and stepped along the road at a good pace. She was quite ready to be milked now, and seldom stopped to browse. Sylvia wondered what her grandmother would say because they were so late. It was a great while since she had left home at half past five o'clock, but everybody knew the difficulty of making this errand a short one. Mrs. Tilley had chased the hornèd torment too many summer evenings herself to blame any one else for lingering, and was only thankful as she waited that she had Sylvia, nowadays, to give such valuable assistance. The good woman suspected that Sylvia loitered occasionally on her own account; there never was such a child for straying about out-of-doors since the world was made! Everybody said that it was a good change for a little maid who had tried to grow for eight years in a crowded manufacturing town, but, as for Sylvia herself, it seemed as if she never had been alive at all before she came to live at the farm. She thought often with wistful compassion of a wretched dry geranium that belonged to a town neighbor.

"'Afraid of folks,'" old Mrs. Tilley said to herself, with a smile, after she had made the unlikely choice of Sylvia from her daughter's houseful of children, and was returning to the farm. "'Afraid of folks,' they said! I guess she won't be troubled no great with 'em up to the old place!" When they reached the door of the lonely house and stopped to unlock it, and the cat came to purr loudly, and rub against them, a deserted pussy, indeed, but fat with young robins, Sylvia whispered that this was a beautiful place to live in, and she never should wish to go home.

The companions followed the shady wood-road, the cow taking slow steps, and the child very fast ones. The cow stopped long at the brook to drink, as if the pasture were not half a swamp, and Sylvia stood still and waited, letting her bare feet cool themselves in the shoal water, while the great twilight moths struck softly against her. She waded on through the brook as the cow moved away, and listening to the thrushes with a heart that beat fast with pleasure. There was a stirring in the great boughs overhead. They were full of little birds and beasts that seemed to be wide-awake, and going about their world, or else saying good-night to each other in sleepy twitters. Sylvia herself felt sleepy as she walked along. However, it was not much farther to the house, and the air was soft and sweet. She was not often in the woods so late as this, and it made her feel as if she were a part of the gray shadows and the moving leaves. She was just thinking how long it seemed since she first came to the farm a year ago, and wondering if everything went on in the noisy town just the same as when she was there; the thought of the great red-faced boy who used to chase and frighten her made her hurry along the path to escape from the shadow of the trees.

Suddenly this little woods-girl is horror-stricken to hear a clear whistle not very far away. Not a bird's whistle, which would have a sort of friendliness, but a boy's whistle, determined, and somewhat aggressive. Sylvia left the cow to whatever sad fate might await her, and stepped discreetly aside into the bushes, but she was just too late. The enemy had discovered her, and called out in a very cheerful and persuasive tone, "Halloa, little girl, how far is it to the road?" and trembling Sylvia answered almost inaudibly, "A good ways."

She did not dare to look boldly at the tall young man, who carried a gun over his shoulder, but she came out of her bush and again followed the cow, while he walked alongside.

"I have been hunting for some birds," the stranger said kindly, "and I have lost my way, and need a friend very much. Don't be afraid," he added gallantly. "Speak up and tell me what your name is, and whether you think I can spend the night at your house, and go out gunning early in the morning."

Sylvia was more alarmed than before. Would not her grandmother consider her much to blame? But who could have foreseen such an accident as this? It did not appear to be her fault, and she hung her head as if the stem of it were broken, but managed to answer, "Sylvy," with much effort when her companion again asked her name.

Mrs. Tilley was standing in the doorway when the trio came into view. The cow gave a loud moo by way of explanation.

"Yes, you'd better speak up for yourself, you old trial! Where'd she tucked herself away this time, Sylvy?" Sylvia kept an awed silence; she knew by instinct that her grandmother did not comprehend the gravity of the situation. She must be mistaking the stranger for one of the farmer-lads of the region.

The young man stood his gun beside the door, and dropped a heavy game-bag beside it; then he bade Mrs. Tilley good-evening, and repeated his wayfarer's story, and asked if he could have a night's lodging.

"Put me anywhere you like," he said. "I must be off early in the morning, before day; but I am very hungry, indeed. You can give me some milk at any rate, that's plain."

"Dear sakes, yes," responded the hostess, whose long slumbering hospitality seemed to be easily awakened. "You might fare better if you went out on the main road a mile or so, but you're welcome to what we've got. I'll milk right off, and you make yourself at home. You can sleep on husks or feathers," she proffered graciously. "I raised them all myself. There's good pasturing for geese just below here towards the ma'sh. Now step round and set a plate for the gentleman, Sylvy!" And Sylvia promptly stepped. She was glad to have something to do, and she was hungry herself.

It was a surprise to find so clean and comfortable a little dwelling in this New England wilderness. The young man had known the horrors of its most primitive housekeeping, and the dreary squalor of that level of society which does not rebel at the companionship of hens. This was the best thrift of an old-fashioned farmstead, though on such a small scale that it seemed like a hermitage. He listened eagerly to the old woman's quaint talk, he watched Sylvia's pale face and shining gray eyes with ever growing enthusiasm, and insisted that this was the best supper he had eaten for a month; then, afterward, the new-made friends sat down in the doorway together while the moon came up.

Soon it would be berry-time, and Sylvia was a great help at picking. The cow was a good milker, though a plaguy thing to keep track of, the hostess gossiped frankly, adding presently that she had buried four children, so that Sylvia's mother, and a son (who might be dead) in California were all the children she had left. "Dan, my boy, was a great hand to go gunning," she explained sadly. "I never wanted for pa'tridges or gray squer'ls while he was to home. He's been a great wand'rer, I expect, and he's no hand to write letters. There, I don't blame him, I'd ha' seen the world myself if it had been so I could.

"Sylvia takes after him," the grandmother continued affectionately, after a minute's pause. "There ain't a foot o' ground she don't know her way over, and the wild creatur's counts her one o' themselves. Squer'ls she'll tame to come an' feed right out o' her hands, and all sorts o' birds. Last winter she got the jay-birds to bangeing here, and I believe she'd 'a' scanted herself of her own meals to have plenty to throw out amongst 'em, if I had n't kep' watch. Anything but crows, I tell her, I'm willin' to help support,—though Dan he went an' tamed one o' them that did seem to have reason same as folks. It was round here a good spell after he went away. Dan an' his father they did n't hitch,—but he never held up his head ag'in after Dan had dared him an' gone off."

The guest did not notice this hint of family sorrows in his eager interest in something else.

"So Sylvy knows all about birds, does she?" he exclaimed, as he looked round at the little girl who sat, very demure but increasingly sleepy, in the moonlight. "I am making a collection of birds myself. I have been at it ever since I was a boy." (Mrs. Tilley smiled.) "There are two or three very rare ones I have been hunting for these five years. I mean to get them on my own ground if they can be found."

"Do you cage 'em up?" asked Mrs. Tilley doubtfully, in response to this enthusiastic announcement.

"Oh, no, they're stuffed and preserved, dozens and dozens of them," said the ornithologist, "and I have shot or snared every one myself. I caught a glimpse of a white heron three miles from here on Saturday, and I have followed it in this direction. They have never been found in this district at all. The little white heron, it is," and he turned again to look at Sylvia with the hope of discovering that the rare bird was one of her acquaintances.

But Sylvia was watching a hop-toad in the narrow footpath.

"You would know the heron if you saw it," the stranger continued eagerly. "A queer tall white bird with soft feathers and long thin legs. And it would have a nest perhaps in the top of a high tree, made of sticks, something like a hawk's nest."

Sylvia's heart gave a wild beat; she knew that strange white bird, and had once stolen softly near where it stood in some bright green swamp grass, away over at the other side of the woods. There was an open place where the sunshine always seemed strangely yellow and hot, where tall, nodding rushes grew, and her grandmother had warned her that she might sink in the soft black mud underneath and never be heard of more. Not far beyond were the salt marshes and beyond those was the sea, the sea which Sylvia wondered and dreamed about, but never had looked upon, though its great voice could often be heard above the noise of the woods on stormy nights.

"I can't think of anything I should like so much as to find that heron's nest," the handsome stranger was saying. "I would give ten dollars to anybody who could show it to me," he added desperately, "and I mean to spend my whole vacation hunting for it if need be. Perhaps it was only migrating, or had been chased of out its own region by some bird of prey."

Mrs. Tilley gave amazed attention to all this, but Sylvia still watched the toad, not divining, as she might have done at some calmer time, that the creature wished to get to its hole under the doorstep, and was much hindered by the unusual spectators at that hour of the evening. No amount of thought, that night, could decide how many wished-for treasures the ten dollars, so lightly spoken of, would buy.

The next day the young sportsman hovered about the woods, and Sylvia kept him company, having lost her first fear of the friendly lad, who proved to be most kind and sympathetic. He told her many things about the birds and what they knew and where they lived and what they did with themselves. And he gave her a jack-knife, which she thought as great a treasure as if she were a desert-islander. All day long he did not once make her troubled or afraid except when he brought down some unsuspecting singing creature from its bough. Sylvia would have liked him vastly better without his gun; she could not understand why he killed the very birds he seemed to like so much. But as the day waned, Sylvia still watched the young man with loving admiration. She had never seen anybody so charming and delightful; the woman's heart, asleep in the child, was vaguely thrilled by a dream of love. Some premonition of that great power stirred and swayed these young foresters who traversed the solemn woodlands with soft-footed silent care. They stopped to listen to a bird's song; they pressed forward again eagerly, parting the branches,—speaking to each other rarely and in whispers; the young man going first and Sylvia following, fascinated, a few steps behind, with her gray eyes dark with excitement.

She grieved because the longed-for white heron was elusive, but she did not lead the guest, she only followed, and there was no such thing as speaking first. The sound of her own unquestioned voice would have terrified her,—it was hard enough to answer yes or no when there was need of that. At last evening began to fall, and they drove the cow home together, and Sylvia smiled with pleasure when they came to the place where she heard the whistle and was afraid only the night before.

II.

Half a mile from home, at the farther edge of the woods, where the land was highest, a great pine-tree stood, the last of its generation. Whether it was left for a boundary mark, or for what reason, no one could say; the woodchoppers who had felled its mates were dead and gone long ago, and a whole forest of sturdy trees, pines and oaks and maples, had grown again. But the stately head of this old pine towered above them all and made a landmark for sea and shore miles and miles away. Sylvia knew it well. She had always believed that whoever climbed to the top of it could see the ocean; and the little girl had often laid her hand on the great rough trunk and looked up wistfully at those dark boughs that the wind always stirred, no matter how hot and still the air might be below. Now she thought of the tree with a new excitement, for why, if one climbed it at break of day, could not one see all the world, and easily discover whence the white heron flew, and mark the place, and find the hidden nest?

What a spirit of adventure, what wild ambition! What fancied triumph and delight and glory for the later morning when she could make known the secret! It was almost too real and too great for the childish heart to bear.

All night the door of the little house stood open, and the whippoorwills came and sang upon the very step. The young sportsman and his old hostess were sound asleep, but Sylvia's great design kept her broad awake and watching. She forgot to think of sleep. The short summer night seemed as long as the winter darkness, and at last when the whippoorwills ceased, and she was afraid the morning would after all come too soon, she stole out of the house and followed the pasture path through the woods, hastening toward the open ground beyond, listening with a sense of comfort and companionship to the drowsy twitter of a half-awakened bird, whose perch she had jarred in passing. Alas, if the great wave of human interest which flooded for the first time this dull little life should sweep away the satisfactions of an existence heart to heart with nature and the dumb life of the forest!

There was the huge tree asleep yet in the paling moonlight, and small and hopeful Sylvia began with utmost bravery to mount to the top of it, with tingling, eager blood coursing the channels of her whole frame, with her bare feet and fingers, that pinched and held like bird's claws to the monstrous ladder reaching up, up, almost to the sky itself. First she must mount the white oak tree that grew alongside, where she was almost lost among the dark branches and the green leaves heavy and wet with dew; a bird fluttered off its nest, and a red squirrel ran to and fro and scolded pettishly at the harmless housebreaker. Sylvia felt her way easily. She had often climbed there, and knew that higher still one of the oak's upper branches chafed against the pine trunk, just where its lower boughs were set close together. There, when she made the dangerous pass from one tree to the other, the great enterprise would really begin.

She crept out along the swaying oak limb at last, and took the daring step across into the old pine-tree. The way was harder than she thought; she must reach far and hold fast, the sharp dry twigs caught and held her and scratched her like angry talons, the pitch made her thin little fingers clumsy and stiff as she went round and round the tree's great stem, higher and higher upward. The sparrows and robins in the woods below were beginning to wake and twitter to the dawn, yet it seemed much lighter there aloft in the pine-tree, and the child knew that she must hurry if her project were to be of any use.

The tree seemed to lengthen itself out as she went up, and to reach farther and farther upward. It was like a great main-mast to the voyaging earth; it must truly have been amazed that morning through all its ponderous frame as it felt this determined spark of human spirit creeping and climbing from higher branch to branch. Who knows how steadily the least twigs held themselves to advantage this light, weak creature on her way! The old pine must have loved his new dependent. More than all the hawks, and bats, and moths, and even the sweet-voiced thrushes, was the brave, beating heart of the solitary gray-eyed child. And the tree stood still and held away the winds that June morning while the dawn grew bright in the east.

Sylvia's face was like a pale star, if one had seen it from the ground, when the last thorny bough was past, and she stood trembling and tired but wholly triumphant, high in the tree-top. Yes, there was the sea with the dawning sun making a golden dazzle over it, and toward that glorious east flew two hawks with slow-moving pinions. How low they looked in the air from that height when before one had only seen them far up, and dark against the blue sky. Their gray feathers were as soft as moths; they seemed only a little way from the tree, and Sylvia felt as if she too could go flying away among the clouds. Westward, the woodlands and farms reached miles and miles into the distance; here and there were church steeples, and white villages; truly it was a vast and awesome world.

The birds sang louder and louder. At last the sun came up bewilderingly bright. Sylvia could see the white sails of ships out at sea, and the clouds that were purple and rose-colored and yellow at first began to fade away. Where was the white heron's nest in the sea of green branches, and was this wonderful sight and pageant of the world the only reward for having climbed to such a giddy height? Now look down again, Sylvia, where the green marsh is set among the shining birches and dark hemlocks; there where you saw the white heron once you will see him again; look, look! a white spot of him like a single floating feather comes up from the dead hemlock and grows larger, and rises, and comes close at last, and goes by the landmark pine with steady sweep of wing and outstretched slender neck and crested head. And wait! wait! do not move a foot or a finger, little girl, do not send an arrow of light and consciousness from your two eager eyes, for the heron has perched on a pine bough not far beyond yours, and cries back to his mate on the nest, and plumes his feathers for the new day!

The child gives a long sigh a minute later when a company of shouting cat-birds comes also to the tree, and vexed by their fluttering and lawlessness the solemn heron goes away. She knows his secret now, the wild, light, slender bird that floats and wavers, and goes back like an arrow presently to his home in the green world beneath. Then Sylvia, well satisfied, makes her perilous way down again, not daring to look far below the branch she stands on, ready to cry sometimes because her fingers ache and her lamed feet slip. Wondering over and over again what the stranger would say to her, and what he would think when she told him how to find his way straight to the heron's nest.

"Sylvy, Sylvy!" called the busy old grandmother again and again, but nobody answered, and the small husk bed was empty and Sylvia had disappeared.

The guest waked from a dream, and remembering his day's pleasure hurried to dress himself that it might sooner begin. He was sure from the way the shy little girl looked once or twice yesterday that she had at least seen the white heron, and now she must really be persuaded to tell. Here she comes now, paler than ever, and her worn old frock is torn and tattered, and smeared with pine pitch. The grandmother and the sportsman stand in the door together and question her, and the splendid moment has come to speak of the dead hemlock-tree by the green marsh.

But Sylvia does not speak after all, though the old grandmother fretfully rebukes her, and the young man's kind appealing eyes are looking straight in her own. He can make them rich with money; he has promised it, and they are poor now. He is so well worth making happy, and he waits to hear the story she can tell.

No, she must keep silence! What is it that suddenly forbids her and makes her dumb? Has she been nine years growing, and now, when the great world for the first time puts out a hand to her, must she thrust it aside for a bird's sake? The murmur of the pine's green branches is in her ears, she remembers how the white heron came flying through the golden air and how they watched the sea and the morning together, and Sylvia cannot speak; she cannot tell the heron's secret and give its life away.

Dear loyalty, that suffered a sharp pang as the guest went away disappointed later in the day, that could have served and followed him and loved him as a dog loves! Many a night Sylvia heard the echo of his whistle haunting the pasture path as she came home with the loitering cow. She forgot even her sorrow at the sharp report of his gun and the piteous sight of thrushes and sparrows dropping silent to the ground, their songs hushed and their pretty feathers stained and wet with blood. Were the birds better friends than their hunter might have been,—who can tell? Whatever treasures were lost to her, woodlands and summertime, remember! Bring your gifts and graces and tell your secrets to this lonely country child!

Questions for Thinking and Writing

1. Explain Sylvia's identification with the heron. What is the significance of the bird's color, the times of day when Sylvia observes the bird, and the bird's physical characteristics?
2. Explain the social and spiritual roles that the girl, the aunt, and the hunter play in understanding our relationship with nature. Can you explain why the girl resists the offer of money?
3. If the redwood tree in Walt Whitman's poem "Song of the Redwood-Tree" (p. 39) is symbolic of the nation, what symbolic possibilities concerning the values of American life do the heron and Sylvia suggest in this story?

🦋 Helen Hunt Jackson (1830–1885)

My Tenants (1886)

Helen Hunt Jackson did not begin her literary career until tragedy transformed her life. She was born in Amherst, Massachusetts, the same year as Emily Dickinson, and the two were lifelong friends.

Though Jackson's father was a philosophy professor at Amherst College, his daughter received a mediocre education at two private schools before marrying an army lieutenant, Edward Bissell Hunt. The couple had two sons, one of whom died at 11 months. Her husband, an engineer as well as military man, was killed in 1863 while experimenting with an underwater mining device. Their second son died two years later.

In 1866, Jackson, still in mourning, met Thomas Wentworth Higginson, Emily Dickinson's critic and editor, who encouraged her to write. He untapped a creative well, and she revived her spirits. In the following years Jackson published over 300 articles in the New York Independent, *and most major magazines of the time published her stories and poems. Her first volume of poetry,* Verses, *came out in 1870. By then, she was a prolific poet and essayist.*

Several years later, Jackson went to Colorado and met and married William Sharpless Jackson, a financier and promoter. She lived in Colorado Springs from then on and wrote several novels. She also became interested in the extent of the mistreatment of Native Americans by the government and wrote a report on the subject, A Century of Dishonor *(1881), copies of which she distributed to each member of Congress. This resulted in her appointment as a commissioner to investigate the condition of the Mission Indians in California, an experience that led to her writing her best known novel,* Ramona *(1884).*

Jackson is a romantic and a nature lover. She has a good eye and ear, and her descriptions of landscapes are clear and direct. She generally resists probing or arguing the conflicts of wildness and civilization, though her experiences with the Mission Indians demonstrate the negative effects of civilizing indigenous peoples. "My Tenants" typically shows Jackson's technique of setting a scene and making a statement. She understood her strengths and resists philosophical or moral examination of the issue. In this instance, it is useful to compare her sense of ownership of nature with Henry David Thoreau's "Where I Lived, and What I Lived For" (p. 12).

I never had a title-deed
To my estate. But little heed
Eyes give to me, when I walk by
My fields, to see who occupy.
Some clumsy men who lease and hire
And cut my trees to feed their fire,
Own all the land that I possess,
And tax my tenants to distress.
And if I said I had been first,
And, reaping, left for them the worst,
That they were beggars at the hands
Of dwellers on my royal lands,
With idle laugh of passing scorn
As unto words of madness born,
They would reply.
                                  I do not care;
They cannot crowd the charmèd air;
They cannot touch the bonds I hold
On all that they have bought and sold.
They can waylay my faithful bees,
Who, lulled to sleep, with fatal ease,
Are robbed. Is one day's honey sweet
Thus snatched? All summer round my feet
In golden drifts from plumy wings,
In shining drops on fragrant things,
Free gift, it came to me. My corn,
With burnished banners, morn by morn,
Comes out to meet and honor me;
The glittering ranks spread royally
Far as I walk. When hasty greed
Tramples it down for food and seed,
I, with a certain veiled delight,

Hear half the crop is lost by blight.
Letter of law these may fulfil,
Plant where they like, slay what they will,
Count up their gains and make them great;
Nevertheless, the whole estate
Always belongs to me and mine.
We are the only royal line.
And though I have no title-deed
My tenants pay me loyal heed
When our sweet fields I wander by
To see what strangers occupy.

Questions for Thinking and Writing

1. Explain Jackson's notion of ownership. Why is this attitude a rebuttal of the law of ownership?
2. What kinds of imagery does Jackson rely on? How do you characterize it? What does her selection indicate about her way of looking at the natural world? What aspects are not present? Explain whether or not you would call Jackson a naturalist.

John Muir (1838–1914)

The American Forests (1901)

John Muir believed that nature was God's temple and its destruction was sacrilegious. Muir saw trees, mountains, glaciers, and wildlife as belonging to God. Human beings, he complained, did not seem fit to be part of this scheme. "Why should man value himself as more than a small part of the one great unit of creation?" he asked.

Muir was born in Dunbar, Scotland, and emigrated with his family to the central Wisconsin wilderness when he was 11. His Calvinistic father cleared acreage for a farm and set his son to long hours of splitting rails, plowing, and planting. Something of an inventor, young Muir devised an "early-rising machine" that lit lamps automatically. At a state fair he exhibited clocks he had made with wooden works. Realizing his technical proficiency, he decided to enroll at the University of Wisconsin where he was introduced to the thinking of the geologist and zoologist Louis Agassiz and to the works of Ralph Waldo Emerson and Henry David Thoreau, particularly Emerson's "Nature" and "Self-Reliance" and Thoreau's Walden.

Though he studied at the university for two years, Muir was impatient and left to take a job in 1866 as an efficiency expert with a carriage factory. An accident during this time nearly cost him his eyesight, and influenced his decision to spend the rest of his life as a naturalist and writer. An illustration he happened to see of Yosemite Valley, California, persuaded him to walk from Indianapolis, where he was living, to Yosemite, a six-month-long trek. Once there he found a job herding sheep.

At Yosemite, he became fascinated by the form of the land. Concluding that glaciers were responsible, he wrote numerous articles on the theory, which at the time was controversial. Muir saw in his long walks in the Sierra Mountains a harmony in nature and that alpine meadows and fiery volcanoes were all part of the same forces.

In 1871, Muir met Emerson, then 68, in California, and came away inspired with the idea of preserving the entire Yosemite Valley as a national park. With typical enthusiasm, he began a campaign to save nature, if only Yosemite Valley. First, he founded the Sierra Club in 1892 as a publicity vehicle. Second, he published Our National Parks *(1901), from which "The American Forests" is excerpted. Third, he impressed President Theodore Roosevelt, who was himself a naturalist. Under Roosevelt's auspices, legislation in 1916 created the National Park Service. At this time, Muir was allied in his cause with Gifford Pinchot, whose idea of conservation was to protect lands so that they could be used for multiple purposes including logging, mining, and pleasure. The alliance was short lived, for Muir was a nature lover who was intolerant of Pinchot's notion of "wise use" of land, especially wilderness. Muir wanted the wilderness to remain as it was forever. Ironically, this proved to be Muir's last battle. In poor health anyway, he died after losing the fight over the Hetch Hetchy Valley. Pinchot and Roosevelt, applying the policy of wise use, agreed that the valley should be flooded to provide a reservoir for San Francisco. Muir claimed the valley was beautiful beyond compare and that it was a national treasure not to be despoiled.*

The forests of America, however slighted by man, must have been a great delight to God; for they were the best he ever planted. The whole continent was a garden, and from the beginning it seemed to be favored above all the other wild parks and gardens of the globe. To prepare the ground, it was rolled and sifted in seas with infinite loving deliberation and forethought, lifted into the light, submerged and warmed over and over again, pressed and crumpled into folds and ridges, mountains, and hills, subsoiled with heaving volcanic fires, ploughed and ground and sculptured into scenery and soil with glaciers and rivers,—every feature growing and changing from beauty to beauty, higher and higher. And in the fullness of time it was planted in groves, and belts, and broad, exuberant, mantling forests, with the largest, most varied, most fruitful, and most beautiful trees in the world. Bright seas made its border, with wave embroidery and icebergs; gray deserts were outspread in the middle of it, mossy tundras on the north, savannas on the south, and blooming prairies and plains; while lakes and rivers shone through all the vast forests and openings, and happy birds and beasts gave delightful animation. Everywhere, everywhere over all the blessed continent, there were beauty and melody and kindly, wholesome, foodful abundance.

These forests were composed of about five hundred species of trees, all of them in some way useful to man, ranging in size from twenty-five feet in height and less than one foot in diameter at the ground to four hundred feet in height and more than twenty feet in diameter,—lordly monarchs proclaiming the gospel of beauty like apostles. For many a century after the ice-ploughs were melted, nature fed them and dressed them every day,—working like a man, a loving, devoted, painstaking gardener; fingering every leaf and flower and mossy furrowed bole; bending, trimming, modeling, balancing; painting them with the loveliest colors; bringing over them now clouds with cooling shadows and showers, now sunshine; fanning them with gentle winds and rustling their leaves; exercising them in every fibre with storms, and pruning them; loading them with flowers and fruit, loading them with snow, and ever making them more beautiful as the years rolled by. Wide-branching oak and elm in endless variety, walnut and maple, chestnut and beech, ilex and locust, touching limb to limb, spread a leafy translucent canopy along the coast of the Atlantic over the wrinkled folds and ridges of the Alleghanies,—a green billowy sea in summer, golden and purple in autumn, pearly gray like a steadfast frozen mist of interlacing branches and sprays in leafless, restful winter.

To the southward stretched dark, level-topped cypresses in knobby, tangled swamps, grassy savannas in the midst of them like lakes of light, groves of gay, sparkling spice-trees, magnolias and palms, glossy-leaved and blooming and shining continually. To the northward, over Maine and Ottawa, rose hosts of spiry, rosiny evergreens,—white pine and spruce, hemlock and cedar, shoulder to shoulder, laden with purple cones, their myriad needles sparkling and shimmering, covering hills and swamps, rocky headlands and domes, ever bravely aspiring and seeking the sky; the ground in their shade now snow-clad and frozen, now mossy and flowery; beaver meadows here and there, full of lilies and grass; lakes gleaming like eyes, and a silvery embroidery of rivers and creeks watering and brightening all the vast glad wilderness.

Thence westward were oak and elm, hickory and tupelo, gum and liriodendron, sassafras and ash, linden and laurel, spreading on ever wider in glorious exuberance over the great fertile basin of the Mississippi, over damp level bottoms, low dimpling hollows, and round dotting hills, embosoming sunny prairies and cheery park openings, half sunshine, half shade; while a dark wilderness of pines covered the region around the Great Lakes. Thence still westward swept the forests to right and left around grassy plains and deserts a thousand miles wide: irrepressible hosts of spruce and pine, aspen and willow, nut-pine and juniper, cactus and yucca, caring nothing for drought, extending undaunted from mountain to mountain, over mesa and desert, to join the darkening multitudes of pines that covered the high Rocky ranges and the glorious forests along the coast of the moist and balmy Pacific, where new species of pine, giant cedars and spruces, silver firs and Sequoias, kings of their race, growing close together like grass in a meadow, poised their brave domes and spires in the sky, three hundred feet above the ferns and the lilies that enameled the ground; towering serene through the long centuries, preaching God's forestry fresh from heaven.

Here the forests reached their highest development. Hence they went wavering northward over icy Alaska, brave spruce and fir, poplar and birch, by the coasts and the rivers, to within sight of the Arctic Ocean. American forests! the glory of the world! Surveyed thus from the east to the west, from the north to the south, they are rich beyond thought, immortal, immeasurable, enough and to spare for every feeding, sheltering beast and bird, insect and son of Adam; and nobody need have cared had there been no pines in Norway, no cedars and deodars on Lebanon and the Himalayas, no vine-clad selvas in the basin of the Amazon. With such variety, harmony, and triumphant exuberance, even nature, it would seem, might have rested content with the forests of North America, and planted no more.

So they appeared a few centuries ago when they were rejoicing in wildness. The Indians with stone axes could do them no more harm than could gnawing beavers and browsing moose. Even the fires of the Indians and the fierce shattering lightning seemed to work together only for good in clearing spots here and there for smooth garden prairies, and openings for sunflowers seeking the light. But when the steel axe of the white man rang out on the startled air their doom was sealed. Every tree heard the bodeful sound, and pillars of smoke gave the sign in the sky.

I suppose we need not go mourning the buffaloes. In the nature of things they had to give place to better cattle, though the change might have been made without barbarous wickedness. Likewise many of nature's five hundred kinds of wild trees had to make way for orchards and cornfields. In the settlement and civilization of the country, bread more than timber or beauty was wanted; and in the blindness of hunger, the early settlers, claiming Heaven as their guide, regarded God's trees as only a larger kind of pernicious weeds, extremely hard to get rid of. Accordingly, with no eye to the future, these pious destroyers waged interminable forest wars; chips flew thick and fast; trees in their beauty fell crashing by millions, smashed to confusion, and the smoke of their burning has been rising to heaven more than two hundred years. After the Atlantic coast from Maine to Georgia had been mostly cleared and scorched into melancholy ruins, the overflowing multitude of bread and money seekers poured over the Alleghanies into the fertile middle West, spreading ruthless devastation ever wider and farther over the rich valley of the Mississippi and the vast shadowy pine region about the Great Lakes. Thence still westward, the invading horde of destroyers called settlers made its fiery way over the broad Rocky Mountains, felling and burning more fiercely than ever, until at last it has reached the wild side of the continent, and entered the last of the great aboriginal forests on the shores of the Pacific.

Surely, then, it should not be wondered at that lovers of their country, bewailing its baldness, are now crying aloud, "Save what is left of the forests!" Clearing has surely now gone far enough; soon timber will be scarce, and not a grove will be left to rest in or pray in. The remnant protected will yield plenty of timber, a perennial harvest for every right use, without further diminution of its area, and will continue to cover the springs of the rivers that rise in the mountains and give irrigating waters to the dry valleys at their feet, prevent wasting floods and be a blessing to everybody forever.

. . . An exception would seem to be found in the case of our forests, which have been mismanaged rather long, and now come desperately near being like smashed eggs and spilt milk. Still, in the long run the world does not move backward. The wonderful advance made in the last few years, in creating four national parks in the West, and thirty forest reservations embracing nearly forty million acres; and in the planting of the borders of streets and highways and spacious parks in all the great cities, to satisfy the natural taste and hunger for landscape beauty and righteousness that God has put, in some measure, into every human being and animal, shows the trend of awakening public opinion. The making of the far-famed New York Central Park was opposed by even good men, with misguided pluck, perseverance, and ingenuity; but straight right won its way, and now that park is appreciated. So we confidently believe it will be with our great national parks and forest reservations. There will be a period of indifference on the part of the rich, sleepy with wealth, and of the toiling millions, sleepy with poverty, most of whom never saw a forest; a period of screaming protest and objection from the plunderers, who are as unconscionable and enterprising as Satan. But light is surely coming, and the friends of destruction will preach and bewail in vain.

The United States government has always been proud of the welcome it has extended to good men of every nation, seeking freedom and homes and bread. Let them be welcomed still as nature welcomes them, to the woods as well as to the prairies and plains. No place is too good for good men, and still there is room. They are invited to heaven, and may well be allowed in America. Every place is made better by them. Let them be as free to pick gold and gems from the hills, to cut and hew, dig and plant, for homes and bread, as the birds are to pick berries from the wild bushes, and moss and leaves for nests. The ground will be glad to feed them, and the pines will come down from the mountains for their homes as willingly as the cedars came from Lebanon for Solomon's temple. Nor will the woods be the worse for this use, or their benign influences be diminished any more than the sun is diminished by shining. Mere destroyers, however, tree-killers, wool and mutton men, spreading death and confusion in the fairest groves and gardens ever planted,—let the government hasten to cast them out and make an end of them. For it must be told again and again, and be burningly borne in mind, that just now, while protective measures are being deliberated languidly, destruction and use are speeding on faster and farther every day. The axe and saw are insanely busy, chips are flying thick as snowflakes, and every summer thousands of acres of priceless forests, with their underbrush, soil, springs, climate, scenery, and religion, are vanishing away in clouds of smoke, while except in the national parks, not one forest guard is employed.

All sorts of local laws and regulations have been tried and found wanting, and the costly lessons of our own experience, as well as that of every civilized nation, show conclusively that the fate of the remnant of our forests is in the hands of the federal government, and that if the remnant is to be saved at all, it must be saved quickly.

Any fool can destroy trees. They cannot run away; and if they could, they would still be destroyed,—chased and hunted down as long as fun or a dollar could be got out of their bark hides, branching horns, or magnificent bole backbones. Few that fell trees plant them; nor would planting avail much towards getting back anything like the noble primeval forests. During a man's life only saplings can be grown, in the place of the old trees—tens of centuries old—that have been destroyed. It took more than three thousand years to make some of the trees in these Western woods,—trees that are still standing in perfect strength and beauty, waving and singing in the mighty forests of the Sierra. Through all the wonderful, eventful centuries since Christ's time—and long before that—God has cared for these trees, saved them from drought, disease, avalanches, and a thousand straining, leveling tempests and floods; but he cannot save them from fools,—only Uncle Sam can do that.

Questions for Thinking and Writing

1. Explain Muir's contention that "Any fool can destroy trees" but that trees must be felled in order for the country to progress. Compare this view with Walt Whitman's in "Song of the Redwood-Tree" (p. 39).

2. Discuss whether or not Muir's argument for land and natural resource use is still valid today. Do you think more land should be preserved today? What about the people who need the land for their livelihood?

3. Compare Muir's idea of the American forest and its value with Frederick Law Olmsted's (p. 34). Comment on Muir's reference to God's creation of forests as a "garden" and whether you think it is as persuasive an argument for preservation as Olmsted's idea that parks encourage the "health and vigor of men."

❧ Mary Hunter Austin (1868–1934)

My Neighbor's Field (1903)

Mary Austin, an early writer on women's issues, was attracted to the physical and spiritual aspects of nature. Especially in her first and most memorable work, The Land of Little Rain, *she embraced the Southwest—its spaces, vegetation, native peoples, and the bravado of white settlers.*

Austin was born in Illinois and grew up in painful circumstances that affected her for her entire life. When she was 10, her father and her sister died. She forebore this, but was deeply hurt by her mother's frequent response to her sister's death: "Why couldn't it have been Mary?" Such rejection led to a lifelong struggle to gain her mother's affection, one that she never accomplished, though the mother and daughter appeared to develop a companionable relationship over the years.

When she was 20, Austin and her mother and brothers moved to southern California, largely unsettled then, to homestead. Austin was fascinated by the expanses and the emptiness and tried to understand it through unconventional means such as sitting out in the desert alone or talking to the local people—Native Americans, Chinese, and drifters—people looked upon with suspicion by the white settlers. She also grew to love the flora of the Southwest and went on long wanderings to collect specimens. She got to know local Native Americans and to understand something of how their culture and nature meshed.

In 1891, she married Wallace Stafford Austin, who also loved the desert, and she began writing steadily in the Overland Monthly. *Success came in a rush, and her stories and poems appeared in* Harper's, The Atlantic Monthly, *and* Century. The Land of Little Rain *(1903), was a success and broadened her life. She traveled to San Francisco where she joined the literary scene; she toured Europe; and settled for a time in New York. There she befriended Willa Cather, who was influenced by Austin's treatment of the Southwest.*

*Increasingly, Austin turned her attention to feminist writing and
the relations between the sexes. She wrote about the silencing that she
considered women had suffered at the hands of men, much of which
derived from her own unhappy marriage. However, the Southwest continued to attract her. She made a permanent move to Santa Fe, New
Mexico, in 1925, and with it, her writing turned to the relationship between land and culture, which still included feminist issues.*

*The Land of Little Rain is a series of descriptions about various
Southwest environs, written with a strong narrative voice and with a
main purpose of trying to understand the land. In structure it is very
like Sarah Orne Jewett's in* The Country of the Pointed Firs, *except that
Austin writes essays instead of stories. Austin's pattern is to write a
descriptive essay about an incident, describe a place, or explore its tex-
tures, and then offer a general observation of universal import. The
Land of Little Rain proved to be appealing because it described life in
the desert, which most people, especially Easterners, thought non-
existent. In fact, the desert Austin describes is teeming with life—
people, animals, plants—and its cycles and rhythms, which some might
have thought impossible, proved the vitality of nature even in a harsh
locale. "My Neighbor's Field" is typical of Austin's essay structure: It
combines the human history of the place with its natural history while
making the point that the intersection of the two is emblematic of the
human need not to want to let things be as nature wills them.*

I t is one of those places God must have meant for a field from all time,
lying very level at the foot of the slope that crowds up against Kearsarge,
falling slightly toward the town. North and south it is fenced by low old
glacial ridges, boulder strewn and untenable. Eastward it butts on orchard closes and the village gardens, brimming over into them by wild
brier and creeping grass. The village street, with its double row of unlike houses, breaks off abruptly at the edge of the field in a footpath that
goes up the streamside, beyond it, to the source of waters.

The field is not greatly esteemed of the town, not being put to the
plough nor affording firewood, but breeding all manner of wild seeds
that go down in the irrigating ditches to come up as weeds in the gardens and grass plots. But when I had no more than seen it in the charm
of its spring smiling, I knew I should have no peace until I had bought
ground and built me a house beside it, with a little wicket to go in and
out at all hours, as afterward came about.

Edswick, Roeder, Connor, and Ruffin owned the field before it fell
to my neighbor. But before that the Paiutes, mesne lords of the soil,
made a campoodie by the rill of Pine Creek; and after, contesting the
soil with them, cattle-men, who found its foodful pastures greatly to

their advantage; and bands of blethering flocks shepherded by wild, hairy men of little speech, who attested their rights to the feeding ground with their long staves upon each other's skulls. Edswick homesteaded the field about the time the wild tide of mining life was roaring and rioting up Kearsarge, and where the village now stands built a stone hut, with loopholes to make good his claim against cattle-men or Indians. But Edswick died and Roeder became master of the field. Roeder owned cattle on a thousand hills, and made it a recruiting ground for his bellowing herds before beginning the long drive to market across a shifty desert. He kept the field fifteen years, and afterward falling into difficulties, put it out as security against certain sums. Connor, who held the securities, was cleverer than Roeder and not so busy. The money fell due the winter of the Big Snow, when all the trails were forty feet under drifts, and Roeder was away in San Francisco selling his cattle. At the set time Connor took the law by the forelock and was adjudged possession of the field. Eighteen days later Roeder arrived on snowshoes, both feet frozen, and the money in his pack. In the long suit at law ensuing, the field fell to Ruffin, that clever one-armed lawyer with the tongue to wile a bird out of the bush, Connor's counsel, and was sold by him to my neighbor, whom from envying his possession I call Naboth.

Curiously, all this human occupancy of greed and mischief left no mark on the field, but the Indians did, and the unthinking sheep. Round its corners children pick up chipped arrow points of obsidian, scattered through it are kitchen middens and pits of old sweat-houses. By the south corner, where the campoodie stood, is a single shrub of "hoopee" (*Lycium Andersonii*), maintaining itself hardly among alien shrubs, and near by, three low rakish trees of hackberry, so far from home that no prying of mine has been able to find another in any cañon east or west. But the berries of both were food for the Paiutes, eagerly sought and traded for as far south as Shoshone Land. By the fork of the creek where the shepherds camp is a single clump of mesquite of the variety called "screw bean." The seed must have shaken there from some sheep's coat, for this is not the habitat of mesquite, and except for other single shrubs at sheep camps, none grows freely for a hundred and fifty miles south or east.

Naboth has put a fence about the best of the field, but neither the Indians nor the shepherds can quite forego it. They make camp and build their wattled huts about the borders of it, and no doubt they have some sense of home in its familiar aspect.

As I have said, it is a low-lying field, between the mesa and the town, with no hillocks in it, but a gentle swale where the waste water of the creek goes down to certain farms, and the hackberry-trees, of which the tallest might be three times the height of a man, are the tallest things in it. A mile up from the water gate that turns the creek into supply pipes for the town, begins a row of long-leaved pines, threading the watercourse to the foot of Kearsarge. These are the pines that puzzle the local botanist, not easily determined, and unrelated to other conifers of the Sierra slope; the same pines of which the Indians relate a legend mixed of brotherliness and the retribution of God. Once the pines possessed the field, as the worn stumps of them along the streamside show, and it would seem their secret purpose to regain their old footing. Now and then some seedling escapes the devastating sheep a rod or two down-stream. Since I came to live by the field one of these has tiptoed above the gully of the creek, beckoning the procession from the hills, as if in fact they would make back toward that skyward-pointing finger of granite on the opposite range, from which, according to the legend, when they were bad Indians and it a great chief, they ran away. This year the summer floods brought the round, brown, fruitful cones to my very door, and I look, if I live long enough, to see them come up greenly in my neighbor's field.

It is interesting to watch this retaking of old ground by the wild plants, banished by human use. Since Naboth drew his fence about the field and restricted it to a few wild-eyed steers, halting between the hills and the shambles, many old habitués of the field have come back to their haunts. The willow and brown birch, long ago cut off by the Indians for wattles, have come back to the streamside, slender and virginal in their spring greenness, and leaving long stretches of the brown water open to the sky. In stony places where no grass grows, wild olives sprawl; close-twigged, blue-gray patches in winter, more translucent greenish gold in spring than any aureole. Along with willow and birch and brier, the clematis, that shyest plant of water borders, slips down season by season to within a hundred yards of the village street. Convinced after three years that it would come no nearer, we spent time fruitlessly pulling up roots to plant in the garden. All this while, when no coaxing or care prevailed upon any transplanted slip to grow, one was coming up silently outside the fence near the wicket, coiling so secretly in the rabbit-brush that its presence was never suspected until it flowered delicately along its twining length. The horehound comes through the fence and under it, shouldering the pickets off the railings; the brier rose mines under the horehound; and no care, though I own I am not a close weeder, keeps the small pale moons of the primrose from rising to the night moth under my apple-trees. The first summer in the new place, a clump of cypripediums came up by the irrigating ditch at the bottom of the lawn. But the clematis will not come inside, nor the wild almond.

I have forgotten to find out, though I meant to, whether the wild almond grew in that country where Moses kept the flocks of his father-in-law, but if so one can account for the burning bush. It comes upon one with a flame-burst as of revelation; little hard red buds on leafless twigs, swelling unnoticeably, then one, two, or three strong suns, and from tip to tip one soft fiery glow, whispering with bees as a singing flame. A twig of finger size will be furred to the thickness of one's wrist by pink five-petaled bloom, so close that only the blunt-faced wild bees find their way in it. In this latitude late frosts cut off the hope of fruit too often for the wild almond to multiply greatly, but the spiny, tap-rooted shrubs are resistant to most plant evils.

It is not easy always to be attentive to the maturing of wild fruit. Plants are so unobtrusive in their material processes, and always at the significant moment some other bloom has reached its perfect hour. One can never fix the precise moment when the rosy tint the field has from the wild almond passes into the inspiring blue of lupines. One notices here and there a spike of bloom, and a day later the whole field royal and ruffling lightly to the wind. Part of the charm of the lupine is the continual stir of its plumes to airs not suspected otherwise. Go and stand by any crown of bloom and the tall stalks do but rock a little as for drowsiness, but look off across the field, and on the stillest days there is always a trepidation in the purple patches.

From midsummer until frost the prevailing note of the field is clear gold, passing into the rusty tone of bigelovia going into a decline, a succession of color schemes more admirably managed than the transformation scene at the theatre. Under my window a colony of cleome made a soft web of bloom that drew me every morning for a long still time; and one day I discovered that I was looking into a rare fretwork of fawn and straw colored twigs from which both bloom and leaf had gone, and I could not say if it had been for a matter of weeks or days. The time to plant cucumbers and set out cabbages may be set down in the almanac, but never seed-time nor blossom in Naboth's field.

Certain winged and mailed denizens of the field seem to reach their heyday along with the plants they most affect. In June the leaning towers of the white milkweed are jeweled over with red and gold beetles, climbing dizzily. This is that milkweed from whose stems the Indians flayed fibre to make snares for small game, but what use the beetles put it to except for a displaying ground for their gay coats, I could never discover. The white butterfly crop comes on with the bigelovia bloom, and on warm mornings makes an airy twinkling all across the field. In September young linnets grow out of the rabbit-brush in the night. All the nests discoverable in the neighboring orchards will not account for the numbers of them. Somewhere, by the same secret process by which the field matures a million more seeds than it needs, it is maturing red-hooded linnets for their devouring. All the purlieus of bigelovia and artemisia are noisy with them for a month. Suddenly as they come as suddenly go the fly-by-nights, that pitch and toss on dusky barred wings above the field of summer twilights. Never one of these nighthawks will you see after linnet time, though the hurtle of their wings makes a pleasant sound across the dusk in their season.

For two summers a great red-tailed hawk has visited the field every afternoon between three and four o'clock, swooping and soaring with

the airs of a gentleman adventurer. What he finds there is chiefly con-
jectured, so secretive are the little people of Naboth's field. Only when
leaves fall and the light is low and slant, one sees the long clean flanks
of the jackrabbits, leaping like small deer, and of late afternoons little
cotton-tails scamper in the runways. But the most one sees of the bur-
rowers, gophers and mice is the fresh earthwork of their newly opened
doors, or the pitiful small shreds the butcher-bird hangs on spiny
shrubs.

It is a still field, this of my neighbor's, though so busy, and admirably
compounded for variety and pleasantness,—a little sand, a little loam,
a grassy plot, a stony rise or two, a full brown stream, a little touch of humanness, a footpath trodden out by moccasins. Naboth expects to make
town lots of it and his fortune in one and the same day; but when I take
the trail to talk with old Seyavi at the campoodie, it occurs to me that
though the field may serve a good turn in those days it will hardly be
happier. No, certainly not happier.

Questions for Thinking and Writing

1. What is the natural and social history of Austin's neighbor's field? How do
   you react to a vacant field when you see one? Do you think of it as a home-
   site or as a place for nature?
2. Why does Austin covet this field? Why is she content not to own it, but to
   have a house built beside it? Compare her attitude with Henry David
   Thoreau's in "Where I Lived, and What I Lived For" (p. 12) and Helen Hunt
   Jackson's "My Tenants" (p. 53).
3. Describe the process by which nature is reclaiming the field. How does this
   demonstrate both Austin's knowledge as a naturalist and her understanding
   of the spiritual aspects of the ecological succession of life?

❧ John Burroughs (1837–1921)
Ways of Nature (1905)

*John Burroughs once said that he had inherited his passion for in-
tellectual pursuit from his father's side of the family and his passion
for nature from his mother's. Whatever the origins, his intellectual me-
andering into the ways of nature and human beings as part of nature
never exhausted his curiosity. Descended from 16th-century New England settlers, he was born on a farm in Roxbury, New York, in the
Catskills, the seventh of ten children. He spent his boyhood wandering*

the hills, apparently absorbing an early appreciation for the peace and solitude of nature that later would concern so much of his writing.

Burroughs began teaching in local schools when he was 17, but two years later took up studies at Cooperstown Seminary, where he was introduced to the writings of William Wordsworth and Ralph Waldo Emerson. His excitement over Emerson seemed boundless, and he said that he read him "in a sort of ecstasy." Around this time, he married and decided that he would spend the rest of his life writing. He began publishing Emersonian-like essays in the 1860s though he continued teaching.

Burroughs's interest in both nature and in writing nature essays quickened, but little came of it. In 1863, he went to Washington to work for the U.S. Treasury Department, a job he kept for ten years. There he met Walt Whitman, also living and working in Washington, and became devoted to him. "I loved him as I never loved any man," he said. "I owe more to him than to any other man in the world." Burroughs's first book, published in 1867, Notes on Walt Whitman as Poet and Person, *was the first biography of the poet. After the Whitman book, Burroughs slowly returned to writing about nature and to revisiting the Catskill Mountains. In 1873, he left Washington to return permanently to his native soil.*

On a ridge above the Hudson River, Burroughs built a cottage he called "Slabsides." Here in the mountains he observed nature and wrote. By the 1880s, he had become something of a cult figure with his bushy beard and his down-to-earth personality. Burroughs was an excellent naturalist who was at home in the woods, which he now preferred to all else. He knew the plants, animals, birds, and insects of the region, and wrote about them with such clarity that they seemed real to even the most sophisticated urban reader. The last decades of his life were spent in a heated inner debate with himself between the logic of science and the power of observation and subjective interpretation. As his dedication to rigorous natural observation hardened, he vehemently argued against anthropomorphism, or any personification of natural life. He believed in nature as nature and argued against tendencies to see life only through human eyes. Nature, Burroughs wrote, is the law of our universe, and humans must accept their part in this scheme of things.

In view, then, of the doubtful sense or intelligence of the wild creatures, what shall we say of the new school of nature writers or natural history romancers that has lately arisen, and that reads into the birds and animals almost the entire human psychology? This, surely: so far as these writers awaken an interest in the wild denizens of the field and wood, and foster a genuine love of them in the hearts of the young people, so far is their influence good; but so far as they pervert natural history and give false impressions of the intelligence of our animals, catering to a taste that prefers the fanciful to the true and the real, is their influence bad. Of course the great army of readers prefer this sugar-coated natural history to the real thing, but the danger always is that an indulgence of this taste will take away a liking for the real thing, or prevent its development. The knowing ones, those who can take these pretty tales with the pinch of salt of real knowledge, are not many; the great majority are simply entertained while they are being humbugged. There may be no very serious objection to the popular love of sweets being catered to in this field by serving up the life-history of our animals in a story, all the missing links supplied, and all their motives and acts humanized, provided it is not done covertly and under the guise of a real history. We are never at a loss how to take Kipling in his "Jungle Book"; we are pretty sure that this is fact dressed up as fiction, and that much of the real life of the jungle is in these stories. I remember reading his story of "The White Seal" shortly after I had visited the Seal Islands in Bering Sea, and I could not detect in the story one departure from the facts of the life-history of the seal, so far as it is known. Kipling takes no covert liberties with natural history, any more than he does with the facts of human history in his novels.

Unadulterated, unsweetened observations are what the real nature-lover craves. No man can invent incidents and traits as interesting as the reality. Then, to know that a thing is true gives it such a savor! The truth—how we do crave the truth! We cannot feed our minds on simulacra any more than we can our bodies. Do assure us that the thing you tell is true. If you must counterfeit the truth, do it so deftly that we shall never detect you. But in natural history there is no need to counterfeit the truth; the reality always suffices, if you have eyes to see it and ears to hear it. Behold what Maeterlinck makes out of the life of the bee, simply by getting at and portraying the facts—a true wonder-book, the enchantment of poetry wedded to the authority of science.

Works on animal intelligence, such as Romanes's, abound in incidents that show in the animals reason and forethought in their simpler forms; but in many cases the incidents related in these works are not well authenticated, nor told by trained observers. The observations of the great majority of people have no scientific value whatever. Romanes quotes from some person who alleges that he saw a pair of nightingales, during a flood in the river near which their nest was placed, pick up the nest bodily and carry it to a place of safety. This is incredible. If Romanes himself or Darwin himself said he saw this, one would have to believe it. Birds whose nests have been plundered sometimes pull the old nest to pieces and use the material, or parts of it, in building a new nest; but I cannot believe that any pair of birds ever picked up a nest containing eggs and carried it off to a new place. How could they do it? With one on each side, how could they fly with the nest between them? They could not carry it with their feet, and how could they manage it with their beaks?

My neighbor met in the woods a black snake that had just swallowed a red squirrel. Now your romance-naturalist may take such a fact as this and make as pretty a story of it as he can. He may ascribe to the snake and his victim all the human emotions he pleases. He may make the snake glide through the tree-tops from limb to limb, and from tree to tree, in pursuit of its prey: the main thing is, the snake got the squirrel. If our romancer makes the snake fascinate the squirrel, I shall object, because I don't believe that snakes have this power. People like to believe that they have. It would seem as if this subtle, gliding, hateful creature ought to have some such mysterious gift, but I have no proof that it has. Every year I see the black snake robbing birds'-nests, or pursued by birds whose nests it has just plundered, but I have yet to see it cast its fatal spell upon a grown bird. Or, if our romancer says that the black snake was drilled in the art of squirrel-catching by its mother, I shall know he is a pretender.

Speaking of snakes reminds me of an incident I have several times witnessed in our woods in connection with a snake commonly called the sissing or blowing adder. When I have teased this snake a few moments with my cane, it seems to be seized with an epileptic or cataleptic fit. It throws itself upon its back, coiled nearly in the form of a figure eight, and begins a series of writhings and twistings and convulsive movements astonishing to behold. Its mouth is open and presently full of leaf-mould, its eyes are covered with the same, its head is thrown back, its white belly up; now it is under the leaves, now out, the body all the while being rapidly drawn through this figure eight, so that the head and tail are constantly changing place. What does it mean? Is it fear? Is it a real fit? I do not know, but any one of our romance-naturalists could tell you at once. I can only suggest that it may be a ruse to baffle its enemy, the black snake, when he would attempt to crush it in his folds, or to seize its head when he would swallow it.

I am reminded of another mystery connected with a snake, or a snake-skin, and a bird. Why does our great crested flycatcher weave a snake-skin into its nest, or, in lieu of that, something that suggests a snake-skin, such as an onion-skin, or fish-scales, or a bit of oiled paper? It is thought by some persons that it uses the snake-skin as a kind of scarecrow, to frighten away its natural enemies. But think what this purpose in the use of it would imply. It would imply that the bird knew that there were among its enemies creatures that were afraid of snakes—so afraid of them that one of their faded and cast-off skins would keep these enemies away. How could the bird obtain this knowledge? It is not afraid of the skin itself; why should it infer that squirrels, for instance, are? I am convinced there is nothing in this notion. In all the nests that have come under my observation, the snake-skin was in faded fragments woven into the texture of the nest, and one would not be aware of its presence unless he pulled the nest to pieces. True, Mr. Frank Bolles reports finding a nest of this bird with a whole snake-skin coiled around a single egg; but it was the skin of a small garter-snake, six or seven inches long, and could not therefore have inspired much terror in the heart of the bird's natural enemies. Dallas Lore Sharp, author of that delightful book, "Wild Life Near Home," tells me he has seen a whole skin dangling nearly its entire length from the hole that contained the nest, just as he has seen strings hanging from the nest of the kingbird. The bird was too hurried or too careless to pull in the skin. Mr. Sharp adds that he cannot "give the bird credit for appreciating the attitude of the rest of the world toward snakes, and making use of the fear." Moreover, a cast-off snake-skin looks very little like a snake. It is thin, shrunken, faded, papery, and there is no terror in it. Then, too, it is dark in the cavity of the nest, consequently the skin could not serve as a scarecrow in any case. Hence, whatever its purpose may be, it surely is not that. It looks like a mere fancy or whim of the bird. There is that in its voice and ways that suggests something a little uncanny. Its call is more like the call of the toad than that of a bird. If the toad did not always swallow its own cast-off skin, the bird would probably use that too.

At the best we can only guess at the motives of the birds and beasts. As I have elsewhere said, they nearly all have reference in some way to the self-preservation of these creatures. But how the bits of an old snake-skin in a bird's nest can contribute specially to this end, I cannot see.

Nature is not always consistent; she does not always choose the best means to a given end. For instance, all the wrens except our house wren seem to use about the best material at hand for their nests. What can be more unsuitable, untractable, for a nest in a hole or cavity than the twigs the house wren uses? Dry grasses or bits of soft bark would bend and adapt themselves easily to the exigencies of the case; but stiff, unyielding twigs! What a contrast to the suitableness of the material the hummingbird uses—the down of some plant, which seems to have a poetic fitness!

Yesterday in my walk I saw where a red squirrel had stripped the soft outer bark off a group of red cedars to build its winter's nest with. This also seemed fit,—fit that such a creature of the trees should not go to the ground for its nest-material, and should choose something soft and pliable. Among the birches, it probably gathers the fine curling shreds of the birch bark.

Beside my path in the woods a downy woodpecker, late one fall, drilled a hole in the top of a small dead black birch for his winter quarters. My attention was first called to his doings by the white chips upon the ground. Every day as I passed I would rap upon his tree, and if he was in he would appear at his door and ask plainly enough what I wanted now. One day when I rapped, something else appeared at the door—I could not make out what. I continued my rapping, when out came two flying-squirrels. On the tree being given a vigorous shake, it broke off at the hole, and the squirrels went sliding down the air to the foot of a hemlock, up which they disappeared. They had dispossessed Downy of his house, had carried in some grass and leaves for a nest, and were as snug as a bug in a rug. Downy drilled another cell in a dead oak farther up the hill, and, I hope, passed the winter there unmolested. Such incidents, comic or tragic, as they chance to strike us, are happening all about us, if we have eyes to see them.

The next season, near sundown of a late November day, I saw Downy trying to get possession of a hole not his own. I chanced to be passing under a maple, when white chips upon the ground again caused me to scrutinize the branches overhead. Just then I saw Downy come to the tree, and, hopping around on the under side of a large dry limb, begin to make passes at something with his beak. Presently I made out a round hole there, with something in it returning Downy's thrusts. The sparring continued some moments. Downy would hop away a few feet, then return to the attack, each time to be met by the occupant of the hole. I suspected an English sparrow had taken possession of Downy's cell in his absence during the day, but I was wrong. Downy flew to another branch, and I tossed up a stone against the one that contained the hole, when, with a sharp, steely note, out came a hairy woodpecker and alighted on a near-by branch. Downy, then, had the "cheek" to try to turn his large rival out of doors—and it was Hairy's cell, too; one could see that by the size of the entrance. Thus loosely does the rule of *meum* and *tuum* obtain in the woods. There is no moral code in nature. Might reads right. Man in communities has evolved ethical standards of conduct, but nations, in their dealings with one another, are still largely in a state of savage nature, and seek to establish the right, as dogs do, by the appeal to battle.

One season a wood duck laid her eggs in a cavity in the top of a tall yellow birch near the spring that supplies my cabin with water. A bold climber "shinned" up the fifty or sixty feet of rough tree-trunk and looked in upon the eleven eggs. They were beyond the reach of his arm, in a well-like cavity over three feet deep. How would the mother duck get her young up out of that well and down to the ground? We watched, hoping to see her in the act. But we did not. She may have done it at night or very early in the morning. All we know is that when Amasa one morning passed that way, there sat eleven little tufts of black and yellow down in the spring, with the mother duck near by. It was a pretty sight. The feat of getting down from the tree-top cradle had been safely effected, probably by the young clambering up on the inside walls of the cavity and then tumbling out into the air and coming down gently like huge snowflakes. They are mostly down, and why should they not fall without any danger to life or limb? The notion that the mother duck takes the young one by one in her beak and carries them to the creek is doubtless erroneous. Mr. William Brewster once saw the golden-eye, whose habits of nesting are like those of the wood duck, get its young from the nest to the water in this manner: The mother bird alighted in the water under the nest, looked all around to see that the coast was clear, and then gave a peculiar call. Instantly the young shot out of the cavity that held them, as if the tree had taken an emetic, and came softly down to the water beside their mother. Another observer assures me that he once found a newly hatched duckling hung by the neck in the fork of a bush under a tree in which a brood of wood ducks had been hatched.

The ways of nature,—who can map them, or fathom them, or interpret them, or do much more than read a hint correctly here and there? Of one thing we may be pretty certain, namely, that the ways of wild nature may be studied in our human ways, inasmuch as the latter are an evolution from the former, till we come to the ethical code, to altruism and self-sacrifice. Here we seem to breathe another air, though probably this code differs no more from the animal standards of conduct than our physical atmosphere differs from that of early geologic time.

Our moral code must in some way have been evolved from our rude animal instincts. It came from within; its possibilities were all in nature. If not, where were they?

I have seen disinterested acts among the birds, or what looked like such, as when one bird feeds the young of another species when it hears them crying for food. But that a bird would feed a grown bird of another species, or even of its own, to keep it from starving, I have my doubts. I am quite positive that mice will try to pull one of their fellows out of a trap, but what the motive is, who shall say? Would the same mice share their last crumb with their fellow if he were starving? That, of course, would be a much nearer approach to the human code, and is too much to expect. Bees will clear their fellows of honey, but whether it be to help them, or to save the honey, is a question.

In my youth I saw a parent weasel seize one of its nearly grown young which I had wounded and carry it across an open barway, in spite of my efforts to hinder it. A friend of mine, who is a careful observer, says he once wounded a shrike so that it fell to the ground, but before he got to it, it recovered itself and flew with difficulty toward some near trees, calling to its mate the while; the mate came and seemed to get beneath the wounded bird and buoy it up, so aiding it that it gained the top of a tall tree, where my friend left it. But in neither instance can we call this helpfulness entirely disinterested, or pure altruism.

Emerson said that he was an endless experimenter with no past at his back. This is just what Nature is. She experiments endlessly, seeking new ways, new modes, new forms, and is ever intent upon breaking away from the past. In this way, as Darwin showed, she attains to new species. She is blind, she gropes her way, she trusts to luck; all her successes are chance hits. Whenever I look over my right shoulder, as I sit at my desk writing these sentences, I see a long shoot of a honeysuckle that came in through a crack of my imperfectly closed window last summer. It came in looking, or rather feeling, for something to cling to. It first dropped down upon a pile of books, then reached off till it struck the window-sill of another large window; along this it crept, its regular leaves standing up like so many pairs of green ears, looking very pretty. Coming to the end of the open way there, it turned to the left and reached out into vacancy, till it struck another window-sill running at right angles to the former; along this it traveled nearly half an inch a day, till it came to the end of that road. Then it ventured out into vacant space again, and pointed straight toward me at my desk, ten feet distant. Day by day it kept its seat upon the window-sill, and stretched out farther and farther, almost beckoning me to give it a lift or to bring it support. I could hardly resist its patient daily appeal. Late in October it had bridged about three feet of the distance that separated us, when, one day, the moment came when it could maintain itself outright in the air no longer, and it fell to the floor. "Poor thing," I said, "your faith was blind, but it was real. You knew there was a support somewhere, and you tried all ways to find it." This is Nature. She goes around the circle, she tries every direction, sure that she will find a way at some point. Animals in cages behave in a similar way, looking for a means of escape. In the vineyard I see the grape-vines reaching out blindly in all directions for some hold for their tendrils. The young arms seize upon one another and tighten their hold as if they had at last found what they were in search of. Stop long enough beside one of the vines, and it will cling to you and run all over you.

Behold the tumble-bug with her ball of dung by the roadside; where is she going with it? She is going anywhere and everywhere; she changes her direction, like the vine, whenever she encounters an obstacle. She only knows that somewhere there is a depression or a hole in which her ball with its egg can rest secure, and she keeps on tumbling about till she finds it, or maybe digs one, or comes to grief by the foot of some careless passer-by. This, again, is Nature's way, randomly and tirelessly seeking her ends. When we look over a large section of history, we see that it is man's way, too, or Nature's way in man. His progress has been a blind groping, the result of endless experimentation, and all his failures and mistakes could not be written in a book. How he has tumbled about with his ball, seeking the right place for it, and how many times has he come to grief! All his successes have been lucky hits: steam, electricity, representative government, printing—how long he groped for them before he found them! There is always and everywhere the Darwinian tendency to variation, to seek new forms, to improve upon the past; and man is under this law, the same as is the rest of nature. One generation of men, like one generation of leaves, becomes the fertilizer of the next; failures only enrich the soil or make smoother the way.

There are so many conflicting forces and interests, and the conditions of success are so complex! If the seed fall here, it will not germinate; if there, it will be drowned or washed away; if yonder, it will find too sharp competition. There are only a few places where it will find all the conditions favorable. Hence the prodigality of Nature in seeds, scattering a thousand for one plant or tree. She is like a hunter shooting at random into every tree or bush, hoping to bring down his game, which he does if his ammunition holds out long enough; or like the British soldier in the Boer War, firing vaguely at an enemy that he does not see. But Nature's ammunition always holds out, and she hits her mark in the end. Her ammunition on our planet is the heat of the sun. When this fails, she will no longer hit the mark or try to hit it.

Let there be a plum tree anywhere with the disease called the "blackknot" upon it, and presently every plum tree in its neighborhood will have black knots. Do you think the germs from the first knot knew where to find the other plum trees? No; the wind carried them in every direction, where the plum trees were not as well as where they were. It was a blind search and a chance hit. So with all seeds and germs. Nature covers all the space, and is bound to hit the mark sooner or later. The sun spills his light indiscriminately into space; a small fraction of his rays hit the earth, and we are warmed. Yet to all intents and purposes it is as if he shone for us alone.

Questions for Thinking and Writing

1. Why does Burroughs seek to dispel the notion of anthropomorphism and pathetic fallacy? Why do you think that many people tend to give inanimate objects and animals human characteristics? To what degree does this tendency facilitate our attempt to dominate nature?
2. What does Burroughs claim real nature lovers crave? Explain whether or not your accept his argument, or if you believe he is too dogmatic and obstinate.

🌿 Frederick H. Newell (1862–1932)

What May Be Accomplished by Reclamation (1909)

For over a decade Frederick H. Newell worked to organize the irrigating of arid lands in the West and Southwest. He succeeded in putting 1.5 million acres under irrigation, largely by fighting for the rights to drain wetlands, as he does in "What May Be Accomplished by Reclamation" (1909).

Newell was born in Bradford, Pennsylvania, and raised in Newton, Massachusetts. He graduated from the Massachusetts Institute of Technology in 1881 with a degree in mining engineering. In 1888, he joined the U.S. Geological Survey under Major John Wesley Powell, who became Newell's mentor. For the next 14 years, Newell surveyed reservoir sites and designed irrigation projects in the West for the Geological Survey. With passage of the Reclamation Act in 1902, Newell was made chief engineer of the Reclamation Service, and five years later became its director. During his tenure, the Service surveyed and constructed 25 irrigation projects involving dams, reservoirs, canals, and power plants.

As an architect of water conservation and use, Newell's work was important. In the arid regions of the United States, Newell worked mainly at making the desert fit for humans. He was a conservationist in the sense that he sought to seek water sources and conserve them for industry and farming. However, Newell was not interested in developing strategies for using less water for irrigation or efficient use of water for settlements. Above all, he was a practical engineer.

In the conservation of natural resources reclamation plays a very large part, both directly and indirectly. There is involved in the idea of reclamation not merely the better use of lands otherwise practically valueless, but in connection with this the creation of opportunities for homes; also, but secondary to this, is frequently brought in the storage or disposal of waters in such way as to render possible the use of these waters for power or other industrial purposes, including the manufacture of electricity for lighting, heating and transportation.

The word "reclamation" as now commonly employed involves the conception of regulating the water supply for a given area of land, which, under natural conditions, has an excess or deficiency of moisture so great that agricultural values are nearly or completely destroyed. We speak of reclaiming the swamp or overflowed lands by keeping the waters off them, or of reclaiming arid lands by bringing waters to them at the time and in the quantities best adapted for the development of plants useful to mankind.

The National Government has been and still is an owner of vast areas of reclaimable land. In the early history of the life of the nation, individuals initiated works for draining and reclaiming areas of low-lying but very fertile land. Later, to promote the reclamation of these, Congress passed laws which, in general terms, conveyed to the separate states the title of the swamp and overflowed lands within their borders in order that these lands might be reclaimed by the state through corporate as well as individual activities. The grants were not, however, sufficiently well guarded to secure the desired results, and although practically all of the states eagerly sought and acquired the swamp lands and passed them over to individuals and corporations, very little was ever done to reclaim and utilize these lands. They became objects of speculation, and vast areas still remain in the hands of men who are holding them for rise in prices. The experience of this kind of legislation had strong influence on subsequent debates in Congress on measures to promote the reclamation of arid lands. The failure of the states to secure reclamation of the swamp lands was a very powerful argument against giving the arid lands to the states in which they were situated, although very convincing pleas were advanced why this work should be confined to the state officials.

There remains yet to be worked out some feasible scheme by which the vast areas of swamp and overflowed lands whose title is now in private ownership may be reclaimed, subdivided, and put in the hands of men who will cultivate them. The soil of these swamp lands is extremely fertile and with effective systems of drainage the lands are capable not merely of supporting large and prosperous agricultural communities, but will be sources of strength to each commonwealth in which they are situated, instead of being, as now, breeding places of mosquitoes and other pests, centers of disease and a menace to land values in the neighborhood.

It may be possible after diffusing information and stimulating public interest to bring together the diverse interests and ultimately to reclaim the large tracts of the swamp land donated to the states, but this can come about on a broad scale only after careful study of the entire situation and the adoption of far-reaching plans. It is, of course, possible to take up one particular tract and build levees, dikes and drains, but it frequently happens that the plans made for one area are such as seriously to interfere with the development of another or more important piece of land; or the system proposed for several areas may be such as not to provide adequate waterways for tracts higher up, and thus disaster may follow the carrying out of schemes which are not sufficiently broad to take in all the surrounding conditions. Where, on the contrary, plans for reclamation start with a full knowledge of all the conditions as they exist and a comprehension of ideal results to be attained, it should result that with the execution of these plans, great tracts of fertile but water-clogged soil will be made available for agriculture.

The term "reclamation" has of late been popularly used with a somewhat restricted meaning, as applying to the irrigation of arid lands and the bringing on of a needed amount of water at proper seasons. Reclamation in this sense has been undertaken by the National Government under the terms of an act passed June 17, 1902, which creates a special fund in the treasury out of the proceeds of the disposal of public lands. This fund is entirely distinct from the general revenues of the Government, derived by imposts or taxation, and hence it is not subject to many of the constitutional limitations which are imposed upon acts of Congress. The expenditure of the reclamation fund has been placed by Congress in the hands of the Secretary of the Interior for the purpose of making surveys and examinations and later constructing feasible projects for the reclamation by irrigation of arid and semi-arid lands. He is also charged with the duty of maintaining and operating these projects until the charges for water for the major portions of the land have been repaid, when the burden of operation and maintenance passes to the owners of the lands.

The Reclamation Act is very general in character and imposes large discretion upon the secretary. In order to carry it out, he has organized what is known as the Reclamation Service, which is practically a bureau of the Department of the Interior. This service consists of men selected through competitive civil service examinations, based largely on practical experience, and who have made a record for efficiency each in his specialty. This organization has been in existence for a little over six years, and during that time, under the direction of the Secretary of the Interior, has made plans for many important works, and has erected a number of these, the estimated expenditures being in round numbers, fifty millions of dollars. Already nearly a million acres have been placed under irrigation, and a third of this has been actually watered. Large dams and other structures for conserving water have been built, so that additional areas can be brought under irrigation by completing other units.

The building of large structures for water conservation and for the reclamation of land is not, however, the ultimate object. These works in themselves are notable, but their importance to the nation comes from the fact that they make possible opportunities for the creation of small farms and building of homes for an independent citizenship. The question of prime interest to the general public is not so much that of how far these works may be extended, but what may be accomplished through them by the reclamation of lands otherwise valueless.

Throughout an extent of land, equalling fully two-fifths of the area of the entire United States, there is not enough rain, at least in the crop season, for the needs of useful plants, and for success in agriculture there must be a constant supply of water, artificially controlled and brought to the fields. Between the two extremes—on the east a humid region with occasional summer droughts, and on the west a truly arid region where all plants need irrigation—lies a broad and somewhat debatable belt of land known as sub-humid or semi-arid region, within which irrigation is valuable, but where the need is not so pressing as to render the practice always successful. In the arid region there is no question as to what may be accomplished by reclamation. The extent of the accomplishments are bounded simply by available water supply, and the acreage which will be reclaimed in the future can be given accurately when facts become available as to the quantity of water which may be stored or pumped to the dry lands.

In the semi-arid region, however, the question is a little more complicated, as the extent to which irrigation may be extended in the future is modified by the possibilities of finding useful drought-resisting plants which can be cultivated on the rich soil where the water supply is now somewhat deficient. Our present knowledge of the water supply available for use in both the arid and semi-arid regions is not sufficient to state accurately the limits which are set by nature to the irrigable areas.

There is more good land in the arid region than there is water for it. If all the run-off waters of this region could be conserved and employed in irrigation, the total reclaimed area might, perhaps, be brought to nearly 60,000,000 acres. This is uncertain, however, as our data on run-off are confined to a portion only of the streams, and are incomplete even for these; furthermore, such an estimate involves assumptions regarding the duty of water that may introduce large errors; that is to say, we do not know in all cases how much land can be irrigated by a given amount of water. It is known, moreover, that large portions of the water of the arid region can not be used in irrigation, as no irrigable land exists upon which it can be brought at feasible cost.

In general it may be stated that the value of irrigated land is increasing while improvements in machinery are tending to decrease costs of construction of reclamation works, so that it is impossible to draw an exact line between the probable and improbable schemes, even if we had full knowledge regarding present costs. This would require elaborate surveys, which have not been made. For these reasons any present estimate of the total irrigable area is necessarily little better than a guess. With present data, the closest statement is probably under 60,000,000 acres and between 40,000,000 and 50,000,000 acres, including the lands now under ditch.

The subjects of irrigation, forestry, power, domestic water supply, drainage and navigation are all closely interrelated and should be thoroughly studied together, not only in the arid, but in the humid regions. No one of these questions can be properly treated without full regard to all the others. Proper study of these comprehensive subjects should include more extended observations of rainfall and evaporation, especially in high altitudes, and of the annual flow of all streams. Topographic maps should be made showing the areas of drainage basin, the location of reservoir sites, and their relation in altitude and location to irrigable lands and to power and navigation resources. Such maps are the basic information most urgently needed for all land classification, and without them no wise policy can be adopted.

Both state and national laws are incomplete in permitting and encouraging settlement on lands which should be reserved for reservoir sites. Thorough surveys should be made and all feasible reservoir sites, when discovered, should be reserved for development.

The present laws in some states tend to promote irrigation, but in others they do not. The most primitive form of the regulation of water in irrigation is best exemplified by the present laws of the State of California. These declare the principles of priority and beneficial use, and provide that claims to the use of water shall be recorded in the form of a notice of appropriation, and shall be perfected by application to a beneficial use. At the same time they try to recognize as concurrent on the same stream, rights derived by prior appropriation and rights depending on riparian ownership. The riparian doctrine of water rights should be definitely and permanently abrogated in all arid regions. This has been done in some states by constitutional provision and in some by judicial decision. In all the states of the arid region where the riparian doctrine is recognized material modifications in the old common-law doctrine have been made and put into effect.

The progress of reclamation in many of the western states will be extremely slow until better laws are passed covering some of the important points above indicated. The uncertainties concerning rights to water are so great that no one would be justified in incurring large expenditures without better safeguards. The conditions are very much as though we had no system for describing or recording land titles, and every man could claim all of the land he desired, leaving it to the courts from time to time to determine how much land was actually used by each man. The litigation which results from this indefinite condition is endless, since it frequently determines only the relative rights of two men and leaves out of account the rights of third parties or of the public. The confusion which now exists with reference to water titles is indescribable, excepting in those states where a definite system of measuring and recording the amount of water has been adopted.

With larger knowledge of the subject, with better laws, and with skill in handling water, it will be possible to reclaim the vast areas above mentioned, and to make opportunities for at least a million farms and homes, supporting directly five millions of people, and indirectly enabling an equal or greater number of people to be supported through the transportation and manufacturing business which grows up incidental to farming. The yield per acre of the reclaimed land is so great that when completely utilized it is possible that it will support, directly or indirectly, a population averaging very nearly one to the acre. This means communities nearly independent of the effect of fluctuating trade conditions, or of wet or dry weather, and a people more nearly self-supporting than any other similar number in the country. It means a citizenship attached to the soil and with the incentives to the highest patriotism.

Questions for Thinking and Writing

1. Discuss Newell's interpretation of the word *reclamation*.
2. Comment on Newell's statement that swamps are "breeding places of mosquitoes and other pests, centers of disease and a menace to land values in the neighborhood."
3. What evidence does Newell present that he discriminates between "good" and "bad" reclamation projects? What criteria does he feel are important for beneficial projects?

Gifford Pinchot (1865–1946)

From *The Fight for Conservation* (1910)

Gifford Pinchot was groomed from childhood to be influential in adulthood. He was the son of James Wallace Pinchot, a wealthy New York merchant who surrounded himself and his family with important social, political, and artistic figures. Young Pinchot traveled widely, was sent to Phillips Exeter Academy, and then Yale where his father suggested he study forestry, a concentration that American universities had not yet developed.

Pinchot took related courses and after graduation studied at the French National Forestry School and toured the managed forests of France, Germany, and Switzerland. When he returned, he managed the Biltmore forest in North Carolina, on the estate of George W.

Vanderbilt. Later he became an independent forest consultant and traveled through the United States examining and surveying forests and planning harvests for both private concerns and state governments.

In 1896, he was appointed to the National Forest Commission, a part of the National Academy of Sciences, that pushed through the Forest Management Act of 1897, a boon to commercial logging on public lands. The following year, Pinchot became head of the Division of Forestry in the Department of Agriculture and succeeded, with the backing of President Theodore Roosevelt, to reorganize it as the more politically powerful U.S. Forest Service. Its designated purpose was to treat the nation's forests as renewable crops.

During the Roosevelt administration, Pinchot was a pioneer in the politically loaded arena of the use of natural resources and became one of Roosevelt's closest advisers. His influence with President William Howard Taft, who followed Roosevelt, was strained, and he was fired. In 1912, he worked with Roosevelt to establish the Progressive Party, a third political party, which was unsuccessful.

Though Pinchot was elected to the governorship of Pennsylvania for two terms, conservation was his first priority. In 1909, he founded the National Conservation Association, a powerful lobby that sought to increase federal regulation of forests and rivers. Pinchot, the educator, was a founder of the Yale School of Forestry. He served as a professor there from 1903 to 1930.

Pinchot's philosophy of life and nature led him to attempt to be both practical and a nature lover. In order to resolve the dilemma, he espoused a doctrine of wise use. This concept provides support for nature—maintaining wilderness, establishing national parks, restricting industrial exploitation of forests by loggers, miners, oil drillers, electric power utilities, and irrigation for cattle raising and agriculture. It balances conservation by permitting limited use of natural resources on federal lands otherwise held in trust for the public. The use of land, making it available to everyone, seeks to please by conserving and developing: hence wise use.

The first principle of conservation is development, the use of the natural resources now existing on this continent for the benefit of the people who live here now. There may be just as much waste in neglecting the development and use of certain natural resources as there is in their destruction. We have a limited supply of coal, and only a limited supply. Whether it is to last for a hundred or a hundred and fifty or a thousand years, the coal is limited in amount, unless through geological changes which we shall not live to see, there will never be any more of it than there is now. But coal is in a sense the vital essence of our civilization. If it can be preserved, if the life of the mines can be extended, if by preventing waste there can be more coal left in this country after we of this generation have made every needed use of this source of power, then we shall have deserved well of our descendants.

Conservation stands emphatically for the development and use of water-power now, without delay. It stands for the immediate construction of navigable waterways under a broad and comprehensive plan as assistants to the railroads. More coal and more iron are required to move a ton of freight by rail than by water, three to one. In every case and in every direction the conservation movement has development for its first principle, and at the very beginning of its work. The development of our natural resources and the fullest use of them for the present generation is the first duty of this generation. So much for development.

In the second place conservation stands for the prevention of waste. There has come gradually in this country an understanding that waste is not a good thing and that the attack on waste is an industrial necessity. I recall very well indeed how, in the early days of forest fires, they were considered simply and solely as acts of God, against which any opposition was hopeless and any attempt to control them not merely hopeless but childish. It was assumed that they came in the natural order of things, as inevitably as the seasons or the rising and setting of the sun. To-day we understand that forest fires are wholly within the control of men. So we are coming in like manner to understand that the prevention of waste in all other directions is a simple matter of good business. The first duty of the human race is to control the earth it lives upon.

We are in a position more and more completely to say how far the waste and destruction of natural resources are to be allowed to go on and where they are to stop. It is curious that the effort to stop waste, like the effort to stop forest fires, has often been considered as a matter controlled wholly by economic law. I think there could be no greater mistake. Forest fires were allowed to burn long after the people had means to stop them. The idea that men were helpless in the face of them held long after the time had passed when the means of control were fully within our reach. It was the old story that "as a man thinketh, so is he"; we came to see that we could stop forest fires, and we found that the means had long been at hand. When at length we came to see that the control of logging in certain directions was profitable, we found it had long been possible. In all these matters of waste of natural resources, the education of the people to understand that they can stop the leakage comes before the actual stopping and after the means of stopping it have long been ready at our hands.

In addition to the principles of development and preservation of our resources there is a third principle. It is this: The natural resources must be developed and preserved for the benefit of the many, and not merely for the profit of a few. We are coming to understand in this country that public action for public benefit has a very much wider field to cover and a much larger part to play than was the case when there were resources enough for every one, and before certain constitutional provisions had given so tremendously strong a position to vested rights and property in general. . . .

The people of the United States are on the verge of one of the great quiet decisions which determine national destinies. Crises happen in peace as well as in war, and a peaceful crisis may be as vital and controlling as any that comes with national uprising and the clash of arms. Such a crisis, at first uneventful and almost unperceived, is upon us now, and we are engaged in making the decision that is thus forced upon us. And, so far as it has gone, our decision is largely wrong. Fortunately it is not yet final.

The question we are deciding with so little consciousness of what it involves is this: What shall we do with our natural resources? Upon the final answer that we shall make to it hangs the success or failure of this Nation in accomplishing its manifest destiny.

Few Americans will deny that it is the manifest destiny of the United States to demonstrate that a democratic republic is the best form of government yet devised, and that the ideals and institutions of the great republic taken together must and do work out in a prosperous, contented, peaceful, and righteous people; and also to exercise, through precept and example, an influence for good among the nations of the world. That destiny seems to us brighter and more certain of realization to-day than ever before. It is true that in population, in wealth, in knowledge, in national efficiency generally, we have reached a place far beyond the farthest hopes of the founders of the Republic. Are the causes which have led to our marvellous development likely to be repeated indefinitely in the future, or is there a reasonable possibility, or even a probability, that conditions may arise which will check our growth?

Danger to a nation comes either from without or from within. In the first great crisis of our history, the Revolution, another people attempted from without to halt the march of our destiny by refusing to us liberty. With reasonable prudence and preparedness we need never fear another such attempt. If there be danger, it is not from an external source. In the second great crisis, the Civil War, a part of our own people strove for an end which would have checked the progress of development. Another such attempt has become forever impossible. If there be danger, it is not from a division of our people.

In the third great crisis of our history, which has now come squarely upon us, the special interests and the thoughtless citizens seem to have united together to deprive the Nation of the great natural resources without which it cannot endure. This is the pressing danger now, and it is not the least to which our National life has been exposed. A nation deprived of liberty may win it, a nation divided may reunite, but a nation whose natural resources are destroyed must inevitably pay the penalty of poverty, degradation, and decay.

At first blush this may seem like an unpardonable misconception and over-statement, and if it is not true it certainly is unpardonable. Let us consider the facts. Some of them are well known, and the salient ones can be put very briefly.

The five indispensably essential materials in our civilization are wood, water, coal, iron, and agricultural products.

We have timber for less than thirty years at the present rate of cutting. The figures indicate that our demands upon the forest have increased twice as fast as our population.

We have anthracite coal for but fifty years, and bituminous coal for less than two hundred.

Our supplies of iron ore, mineral oil, and natural gas are being rapidly depleted, and many of the great fields are already exhausted. Mineral resources such as these when once gone are gone forever.

We have allowed erosion, that great enemy of agriculture, to impoverish and, over thousands of square miles, to destroy our farms. The Mississippi alone carries yearly to the sea more than 400,000,000 tons of the richest soil within its drainage basin. If this soil is worth a dollar a ton, it is probable that the total loss of fertility from soil-wash to the farmers and forest-owners of the United States is not far from a billion dollars a year. Our streams, in spite of the millions of dollars spent upon them, are less navigable now than they were fifty years ago, and the soil lost by erosion from the farms and the deforested mountain sides, is the chief reason. The great cattle and sheep ranges of the West, because of overgrazing, are capable, in an average year, of carrying but half the stock they once could support and should still. Their condition affects the price of meat in practically every city of the United States.

These are but a few of the more striking examples. The diversion of great areas of our public lands from the home-maker to the landlord and the speculator; the national neglect of great water powers, which might well relieve, being perennially renewed, the drain upon our non-renewable coal; the fact that but half the coal has been taken from the mines which have already been abandoned as worked out and by caving-in have made the rest forever inaccessible; the disuse of the cheaper transportation of our waterways, which involves comparatively slight demand upon our non-renewable supplies of iron ore, and the use of the rail instead—these are other items in the huge bill of particulars of national waste.

We have a well-marked national tendency to disregard the future, and it has led us to look upon all our natural resources as inexhaustible. Even now that the actual exhaustion of some of them is forcing itself upon us in higher prices and the greater cost of living, we are still asserting, if not always in words, yet in the far stronger language of action, that nevertheless and in spite of it all, they still are inexhaustible.

It is this national attitude of exclusive attention to the present, this absence of foresight from among the springs of national action, which is directly responsible for the present condition of our natural resources. It was precisely the same attitude which brought Palestine, once rich and populous, to its present desert condition, and which destroyed the fertility and habitability of vast areas in northern Africa and elsewhere in so many of the older regions of the world.

The conservation of our natural resources is a question of primary importance on the economic side. It pays better to conserve our natural resources than to destroy them, and this is especially true when the national interest is considered. But the business reason, weighty and worthy though it be, is not the fundamental reason. In such matters, business is a poor master but a good servant. The law of self-preservation is higher than the law of business, and the duty of preserving the Nation is still higher than either.

The American Revolution had its origin in part in economic causes, and it produced economic results of tremendous reach and weight. The Civil War also arose in large part from economic conditions, and it has had the largest economic consequences. But in each case there was a higher and more compelling reason. So with the third great crisis of our history. It has an economic aspect of the largest and most permanent importance, and the motive for action along that line, once it is recognized, should be more than sufficient. But that is not all. In this case, too, there is a higher and more compelling reason. The question of the conservation of natural resources, or national resources, does not stop with being a question of profit. It is a vital question of profit, but what is still more vital, it is a question of national safety and patriotism also.

We have passed the inevitable stage of pioneer pillage of natural resources. The natural wealth we found upon this continent has made us rich. We have used it, as we had a right to do, but we have not stopped there. We have abused, and wasted, and exhausted it also, so that there is the gravest danger that our prosperity to-day will have been bought at the price of the suffering and poverty of our descendants. We may now fairly ask of ourselves a reasonable care for the future and a natural interest in those who are to come after us. No patriotic citizen expects this Nation to run its course and perish in a hundred or two hundred, or five hundred years; but, on the contrary, we expect it to grow in influence and power and, what is of vastly greater importance, in the happiness and prosperity of our people. But we have as little reason to expect that all this will happen of itself as there would have been for the men who established this Nation to expect that a United States would grow of itself without their efforts and sacrifices. It was their duty to found this Nation, and they did it. It is our duty to provide for its continuance in well-being and honor. That duty it seems as though we might neglect— not in wilfulness, not in any lack of patriotic devotion, when once our patriotism is aroused, but in mere thoughtlessness and inability or unwillingness to drop the interests of the moment long enough to realize that what we do now will decide the future of the Nation. For, if we do not take action to conserve the Nation's natural resources, and that soon, our descendants will suffer the penalty of our neglect.

Let me use a homely illustration: We have all known fathers and mothers, devoted to their children, whose attention was fixed and limited by the household routine of daily life. Such parents were actively concerned with the common needs and precautions and remedies entailed in bringing up a family, but blind to every threat that was at all unusual. Fathers and mothers such as these often remain serenely unaware while some dangerous malady or injurious habit is fastening itself upon a favorite child. Once the evil is discovered, there is no sacrifice too great to repair the damage which their unwitting neglect may have allowed to become irreparable. So it is, I think, with the people of the United States. Capable of every devotion in a recognized crisis, we have yet carelessly allowed the habit of improvidence and waste of resources to find lodgment. It is our great good fortune that the harm is not yet altogether beyond repair.

The profoundest duty that lies upon any father is to leave his son with a reasonable equipment for the struggle of life and an untarnished name. So the noblest task that confronts us all to-day is to leave this country unspotted in honor, and unexhausted in resources, to our descendants, who will be, not less than we, the children of the Founders of the Republic. I conceive this task to partake of the highest spirit of patriotism.

Questions for Thinking and Writing

1. Discuss Pinchot's belief that "the first duty of the human race is to control the earth it lives upon" and contrast it with Thoreau's belief that humankind is but one part of nature.
2. Analyze how Pinchot builds his case for conservation. Compare Muir's techniques with Pinchot's.
3. Discuss any connections between some of today's environmental problems and Pinchot's argument for the wise use of land and natural resources.

🌿 Theodore Roosevelt (1858–1919)

The Natural Resources of the Nation (1913)

"There are men," wrote Theodore Roosevelt in his autobiography, *"who love out-of-doors who yet never open a book; and other men who love books but to whom the great book of nature is a sealed volume . . . "* Roosevelt spent much of his seemingly boundless energy explaining both the beauty and economic value of *"the great book of nature"* to those who saw it only through greedy eyes. As president, his commitment to the public good propelled substantial environmental regulatory policies through Congress. Unfortunately, much of the legislation was reversed or watered down following his presidency, and succeeding years saw an increase of environmental abuse, particularly of forests, public lands, and waterways.

Some of Roosevelt's exuberance and dash probably resulted from his asthmatic condition during childhood, which did not allow him even to attend school. Private tutors inspired a love of reading, and the books he read were of heroic characters who, like himself, endured tremendous physical hardship and refused to become victims. Roosevelt was apparently instilled with the idea that he would not become a victim. Out of this realization began his lifelong passion for physical exercise and exertion.

A prolific writer, Roosevelt began his first book, Naval History of the War of 1812, while still an undergraduate at Harvard University. Another of his publications is the four-volume Winning of the West, published from 1889 to 1896, undoubtedly inspired by his two-year stint as owner of a cattle ranch in North Dakota.

Roosevelt entered politics in 1881, when he won a seat in the New York legislature. His political career appeared to be short-lived when he withdrew from politics after being defeated in a campaign for mayor of New York City. In 1889, however, President Benjamin Harrison appointed him a Civil Service Commissioner. During the Spanish-American War, Roosevelt formed a regiment of cowboys and athletes know as the Rough Riders to fight against Spanish colonialism in Cuba. It is this exploit that most people remember him for, and it brought new political prominence.

In 1898, he easily won the campaign for governor of New York state on the Republican ticket. Two years later, he was elected vice president under President William McKinley. Finding his duties restricted, he considered resigning, a decision he never had to make due to McKinley's assassination in 1901. At 42, Roosevelt became the youngest person to hold the country's highest political office.

The following selection from Roosevelt's Autobiography *testifies not only to his passion for "wise use" of resources but to the formation of a legal framework for conservation, which today is again being called for and redefined.*

When Governor of New York, as I have already described, I had been in consultation with Gifford Pinchot and F. H. Newell, and had shaped my recommendations about forestry largely in accordance with their suggestions. Like other men who had thought about the national future at all, I had been growing more and more concerned over the destruction of the forests.

. . .

The idea that our natural resources were inexhaustible still obtained, and there was as yet no real knowledge of their extent and condition. The relation of the conservation of natural resources to the problems of National welfare and National efficiency had not yet dawned on the public mind. The reclamation of arid public lands in the West was still a matter for private enterprise alone; and our magnificent river system, with its superb possibilities for public usefulness, was dealt with by the National Government not as a unit, but as a disconnected series of pork-barrel problems, whose only real interest was in their effect on the reëlection or defeat of a Congressman here and there—a theory which, I regret to say, still obtains.

All the forests which belonged to the United States were held and administered in one Department, and all the foresters in Government employ were in another Department. Forests and foresters had nothing whatever to do with each other. The National Forests in the West (then called forest reserves) were wholly inadequate in area to meet the purposes for which they were created, while the need for forest protection in the East had not yet begun to enter the public mind.

Such was the condition of things when Newell and Pinchot called on me. I was a warm believer in reclamation and in forestry, and, after listening to my two guests, I asked them to prepare material on the subject for me to use in my first message to Congress, of December 3, 1901. This message laid the foundation for the development of irrigation and forestry during the next seven and one-half years. It set forth the new attitude toward the natural resources in the words: "The Forest and water problems are perhaps the most vital internal problems of the United States."

On the day the message was read, a committee of Western Senators and Congressmen was organized to prepare a Reclamation Bill in accordance with the recommendations. By far the most effective of the Senators in drafting and pushing the bill, which became known by his name, was Newlands. The draft of the bill was worked over by me and others at several conferences and revised in important particulars; my active interference was necessary to prevent it from being made unworkable by an undue insistence upon States Rights, in accordance with the efforts of Mr. Mondell and other Congressmen, who consistently fought for local and private interests as against the interests of the people as a whole.

On June 17, 1902, the Reclamation Act was passed. It set aside the proceeds of the disposal of public lands for the purpose of reclaiming the waste areas of the arid West by irrigating lands otherwise worthless, and thus creating new homes upon the land. The money so appropriated was to be repaid to the Government by the settlers, and to be used again as a revolving fund continuously available for the work.

. . .

What the Reclamation Act has done for the country is by no means limited to its material accomplishment. This Act and the results flowing from it have helped powerfully to prove to the Nation that it can handle its own resources and exercise direct and business-like control over them. The population which the Reclamation Act has brought into the arid West, while comparatively small when compared with that in the more closely inhabited East, has been a most effective contribution to the National life, for it has gone far to transform the social aspect of the West, making for the stability of the institutions upon which the welfare of the whole country rests: it has substituted actual homemakers, who have settled on the land with their families, for huge, migratory bands of sheep herded by the hired shepherds of absentee owners.

When I became President, the Bureau of Forestry (since 1905 the United States Forest Service) was a small but growing organization, under Gifford Pinchot, occupied mainly with laying the foundation of American forestry by scientific study of the forests, and with the promotion of forestry on private lands. It contained all the trained foresters in the government service, but had charge of no public timberland whatsoever. The Government forest reserves of that day were in the care of a Division in the General Land Office, under the management of clerks wholly without knowledge of forestry, few if any of whom had ever seen a foot of the timberlands for which they were responsible. Thus the reserves were neither well protected nor well used. There were no foresters among the men who had charge of the National Forests, and no Government forests in charge of the Government foresters.

In my first message to Congress I strongly recommended the consolidation of the forest work in the hands of the trained men of the Bureau of Forestry. This recommendation was repeated in other messages, but Congress did not give effect to it until three years later. In the meantime, by thorough study of the Western public timberlands, the groundwork was laid for the responsibilities which were to fall upon the Bureau of Forestry when the care of the National Forests came to be transferred to it. It was evident that trained American foresters would be needed in considerable numbers, and a forest school was established at Yale to supply them.

In 1901, at my suggestion as President, the Secretary of the Interior, Mr. Hitchcock, made a formal request for technical advice from the Bureau of Forestry in handling the National Forests, and an extensive examination of their condition and needs was accordingly taken up. The same year a study was begun of the proposed Appalachian National Forest, the plan of which, already formulated at that time, has since been carried out. A year later experimental planting on the National Forests was also begun, and studies preparatory to the application of practical forestry to the Indian Reservations were undertaken. In 1903, so rapidly did the public work of the Bureau of Forestry increase, that the examination of land for new forest reserves was added to the study of those already created, the forest lands of the various States were studied, and coöperation with several of them in the examination and handling of their forest lands was undertaken. While these practical tasks were pushed forward, a technical knowledge of American Forests was rapidly accumulated. The special knowledge gained was made public in printed bulletins; and at the same time the Bureau undertook, through the newspaper and periodical press, to make all the people of the United States acquainted with the needs and the purposes of practical forestry. It is doubtful whether there has ever been elsewhere under the Government such effective publicity—publicity purely in the interest of the people—at so low a cost. Before the educational work of the Forest Service was stopped by the Taft Administration, it was securing the publication of facts about forestry in fifty million copies of newspapers a month at a total expense of $6000 a year. Not one cent has ever been paid by the Forest Service to any publication of any kind for the printing of this material. It was given out freely, and published without cost because it was news. Without this publicity the Forest Service could not have survived the attacks made upon it by the representatives of the great special interests in Congress; nor could forestry in America have made the rapid progress it has.

The result of all the work outlined above was to bring together in the Bureau of Forestry, by the end of 1904, the only body of forest experts under the Government, and practically all of the first-hand information about the public forests which was then in existence. In 1905, the obvious foolishness of continuing to separate the foresters and the forests, reënforced by the action of the First National Forest Congress, held in Washington, brought about the Act of February 1, 1905, which transferred the National Forests from the care of the Interior Department to the Department of Agriculture, and resulted in the creation of the present United States Forest Service.

The men upon whom the responsibility of handling some sixty million acres of National Forest lands was thus thrown were ready for the work, both in the office and in the field, because they had been preparing for it for more than five years. Without delay they proceeded, under the leadership of Pinchot, to apply to the new work the principles they had already formulated. One of these was to open all the resources of the National Forests to regulated use. Another was that of putting every part of the land to that use in which it would best serve the public. Following this principle, the Act of June 11, 1906, was drawn, and its passage was secured from Congress. This law throws open to settlement all land in the National Forests that is found, on examination, to be chiefly valuable for agriculture. Hitherto all such land had been closed to the settler.

The principles thus formulated and applied may be summed up in the statement that the rights of the public to the natural resources outweigh private rights, and must be given its first consideration. Until that time, in dealing with the National Forests, and the public lands generally, private rights had almost uniformly been allowed to over-balance public rights. The change we made was right, and was vitally necessary; but, of course, it created bitter opposition from private interests.

One of the principles whose application was the source of much hostility was this: It is better for the Government to help a poor man to make a living for his family than to help a rich man make more profit for his company. This principle was too sound to be fought openly. It is the kind of principle to which politicians delight to pay unctuous homage in words. But we translated the words into deeds, and when they found that this was the case, many rich men, especially sheep owners, were stirred to hostility, and they used the Congressmen they controlled to assault us—getting most aid from certain demagogues, who were equally glad improperly to denounce rich men in public and improperly to serve them in private. The Forest Service established and enforced regulations which favored the settler as against the large stock owner; required that necessary reductions in the stock grazed on any National Forest should bear first on the big man, before the few head of the small man, upon which the living of his family depended, were reduced; and made grazing in the National Forests a help, instead of a hindrance, to permanent settlement. As a result, the small settlers and their families became, on the whole, the best friends the Forest Service has; although in places their ignorance was played on by demagogues to influence them against the policy that was primarily for their own interest.

Another principle which led to the bitterest antagonism of all was this—whoever (except a bona-fide settler) takes public property for private profit should pay for what he gets. In the effort to apply this principle, the Forest Service obtained a decision from the Attorney-General that it was legal to make the men who grazed sheep and cattle on the National Forests pay for what they got. Accordingly, in the summer of 1906, for the first time, such a charge was made; and, in the face of the bitterest opposition, it was collected.

Up to the time the National Forests were put under the charge of the Forest Service, the Interior Department had made no effort to establish public regulation and control of water powers. Upon the transfer, the Service immediately began its fight to handle the power resources of the National Forests so as to prevent speculation and monopoly and to yield a fair return to the Government. On May 1, 1906, an Act was passed granting the use of certain power sites in Southern California to the Edison Electric Power Company, which Act, at the suggestion of the Service, limited the period of the permit to forty years, and required the payment of an annual rental by the company, the same conditions which were thereafter adopted by the Service as the basis for all permits for power development. Then began a vigorous fight against the position of the Service by the water-power interests. The right to charge for water-power development was, however, sustained by the Attorney-General.

In 1907, the area of the National Forests was increased by Presidential proclamation more than forty-three million acres; the plan necessary for the full use of the Forests, such as roads, trails, and telephone lines, began to be provided on a large scale; the interchange of field and office men, so as to prevent the antagonism between them, which is so destructive of efficiency in most great businesses, was established as a permanent policy; and the really effective management of the enormous area of the National Forests began to be secured.

With all this activity in the field, the progress of technical forestry and popular education was not neglected. In 1907, for example, sixty-one publications on various phases of forestry, with a total of more than a million copies, were issued, as against three publications, with a total of eighty-two thousand copies, in 1901. By this time, also, the opposition of the servants of the special interests in Congress to the Forest Service had become strongly developed, and more time appeared to be spent in the yearly attacks upon it during the passage of the appropriation bills than on all other Government Bureaus put together. Every year the Forest Service had to fight for its life.

One incident in these attacks is worth recording. While the Agricultural Appropriation Bill was passing through the Senate, in 1907, Senator Fulton, of Oregon, secured an amendment providing that the President could not set aside any additional National Forests in the six Northwestern States. This meant retaining some sixteen million of acres to be exploited by land grabbers and by the representatives of the great special interests, at the expense of the public interest. But for four years the Forest Service had been gathering field notes as to what forests ought to be set aside in these States, and so was prepared to act. It was equally undesirable to veto the whole agricultural bill, and to sign it with this amendment effective. Accordingly, a plan to create the necessary National Forest in these States before the Agricultural Bill could be passed and signed was laid before me by Mr. Pinchot. I approved it. The necessary papers were immediately prepared. I signed the last proclamation a couple of days before by my signature, the bill became law; and when the friends of the special interests in the Senate got their amendment through and woke up, they discovered that sixteen million acres of timberland had been saved for the people by putting them in the National Forests before the land grabbers could get at them. The opponents of the Forest Service turned handsprings in their wrath; and dire were their threats against the Executive; but the threats could not be carried out, and were really only a tribute to the efficiency of our action.

. . .

The idea that the Executive is the steward of the public welfare was first formulated and given practical effect in the Forest Service by its law officer, George Woodruff. The laws were often insufficient, and it became well nigh impossible to get them amended in the public interest when once the representatives of privilege in Congress grasped the fact that I would sign no amendment that contained anything not in the public interest. It was necessary to use what law was already in existence, and then further to supplement it by Executive action. The practice of examining every claim to public land before passing it into private ownership offers a good example of the policy in question. This practice, which has since become general, was first applied in the National Forests. Enormous areas of valuable public timberland were thereby saved from fraudulent acquisition; more than 250,000 acres were thus saved in a single case.

This theory of stewardship in the interest of the public was well illustrated by the establishment of a water-power policy. Until the Forest Service changed the plan, water-powers on the navigable streams, on the public domain, and in the National Forests were given away for nothing, and substantially without question, to whoever asked for them. At last, under the principle that public property should be paid for and should not be permanently granted away when such permanent grant is avoidable, the Forest Service established the policy of regulating the use of power in the National Forests in the public interest and making a charge for value received. This was the beginning of the water-power policy now substantially accepted by the public, and doubtless soon to be enacted into law. But there was at the outset violent opposition to it on the part of the water-power companies, and such representatives of their views in Congress as Messrs. Tawney and Bede.

Many bills were introduced in Congress aimed, in one way or another, at relieving the power companies of control and payment. When these bills reached me I refused to sign them; and the injury to the public interest which would follow their passage was brought sharply to public attention in my message of February 26, 1908. The bills made no further progress.

Under the same principle of stewardship, railroads and other corporations, which applied for and were given rights in the National Forests, were regulated in the use of those rights. In short, the public resources in charge of the Forest Service were handled frankly and openly for the public welfare under the clear-cut and clearly set forth principle that the public rights come first and private interest second.

. . .

In its administration of the National Forests, the Forest Service found that valuable coal lands were in danger of passing into private ownership without adequate money return to the Government and without safeguard against monopoly; and that existing legislation was insufficient to prevent this. When this condition was brought to my attention I withdrew from all forms of entry about sixty-eight million acres of coal land in the United States, including Alaska. The refusal of congress to act in the public interest was solely responsible for keeping these lands from entry.

The Conservation movement was a direct outgrowth of the forest movement. It was nothing more than the application to our other natural resources of the principles which had been worked out in connection with the forests. Without the basis of public sentiment which had been built up for the protection of the forests, and without the example of public foresight in the protection of this, one of the great natural resources, the Conservation movement would have been impossible. The first formal step was the creation of the Inland Waterways Commission, appointed on March 14, 1907. In my letter appointing the Commission, I called attention to the value of our streams as great natural resources, and to the need for a progressive plan for their development and control, and said: "It is not possible to properly frame so large a plan as this for the control of our rivers without taking account of the orderly development of other natural resources. Therefore I ask that the Inland Waterways Commission shall consider the relations of the streams to the use of all the great permanent natural resources and their conservation for the making and maintenance of prosperous homes."

. . .

The most striking incident in the history of the Commission was the trip down the Mississippi River in October, 1907, when, as President of the United States, I was the chief guest. This excursion, with the meetings which were held and the wide public attention it attracted, gave the development of our inland waterways a new standing in public estimation. During the trip a letter was prepared and presented to me asking me to summon a conference on the conservation of natural resources. My intention to call such a conference was publicly announced at a great meeting at Memphis, Tenn.

In the November following I wrote to each of the Governors of the several States and to the Presidents of various important National Societies concerned with natural resources, inviting them to attend the conference, which took place May 13 to 15, 1908, in the East Room of the White House. It is doubtful whether, except in time of war, any new idea of like importance has ever been presented to a Nation and accepted by it with such effectiveness and rapidity, as was the case with this Conservation movement when it was introduced to the American people by the Conference of Governors. The first result was the unanimous declaration of the Governors of all the states and Territories upon the subject of Conservation, a document which ought to be hung in every schoolhouse throughout the land. A further result was the appointment of thirty-six State Conservation Commissions and, on June 8, 1908, of the National Conservation Commission. The task of this Commission was to prepare an inventory, the first ever made for any nation, of all the natural resources which underlay its property. The making of this inventory was made possible by an Executive order which placed the resources of the Government Departments at the command of the Commission, and made possible the organization of subsidiary committees by which the actual facts for the inventory were prepared and digested. Gifford Pinchot was made chairman of the Commission.

The report of the National Conservation Commission was not only the first inventory of our resources, but was unique in the history of Government in the amount and variety of information brought together. It was completed in six months. It laid squarely before the American people the essential facts regarding our natural resources, when facts were greatly needed as the basis for constructive action. This report was presented to the Joint Conservation Congress in December, at which there were present Governors of twenty States, representatives of twenty-two State Conservation Commissions, and representatives of sixty National organizations previously represented at the White House conference. The report was unanimously approved, and transmitted to me, January 11, 1909. On January 22, 1909, I transmitted the report of the National Conservation Commission to Congress with a Special Message, in which it was accurately described as "one of the most fundamentally important documents ever laid before the American people."

. . .

Throughout the early part of my Administration the public land policy was chiefly directed to the defense of the public lands against fraud and theft. Secretary Hitchcock's efforts along this line resulted in the Oregon land fraud cases, which led to the conviction of Senator Mitchell, and which made Francis J. Heney known to the American people as one of the best and most effective servants. These land fraud prosecutions under Mr. Heney, together with the study of the public lands which preceded the passage of the Reclamation Act in 1902, and the investigation of land titles in the National Forests by the Forest Service, all combined to create a clearer understanding of the need of land law reform, and thus led to the appointment of the Public Lands Commission. This Commission, appointed by me on October 22, 1903, was directed to report to the President: "Upon the condition, operation, and effect of the present land laws, and to recommend such changes as are needed to effect the largest practicable disposition of the public lands to actual settlers who will build permanent homes upon them, and to secure in permanence the fullest and most effective use of the resources of the public lands." It proceeded without loss of time to make a personal study on the ground of public land problems throughout the West, to confer with the Governors and other public men most concerned, and to assemble the information concerning the public lands, the laws and decisions which governed them, and the methods of defeating or evading those laws, which was already in existence, but which remained unformulated in the records of the General Land Office and in the minds of its employees. The Public Lands Commission made its first preliminary report on March 7, 1904. It found "that the present land laws do not fit the conditions of the remaining public lands," and recommended specific changes to meet the public needs. A year later the second report of the Commission recommended still further changes, and said "The fundamental fact that characterizes the situation under the present land laws is this, that the number of patents issued is increasing out of all proportion to the number of new homes." This report laid the foundation of the movement for Government control of the open range, and included by far the most complete statement ever made of the disposition of the public domain.

Among the most difficult topics considered by the Public Land Commission was that of the mineral land laws. This subject was referred by the Commission to the American Institute of Mining Engineers, which reported upon it through a Committee. This Committee made the very important recommendation, among others, "that the Government of the United States should retain title to all minerals, including coal and oil, in the lands of unceded territory, and lease the same to individuals or corporations at a fixed rental." The necessity for this action has since come to be very generally recognized. Another recommendation, since partly carried into effect, was for the separation of the surface and the minerals in lands containing coal and oil.

Our land laws have of recent years proved inefficient; yet the land laws themselves have not been so much to blame as the lax, unintelligent, and often corrupt administration of these laws. The appointment on March 4, 1907, of James R. Garfield as Secretary of the Interior led to a new era in the interpretation and enforcement of the laws governing the public lands. His administration of the Interior Department was beyond comparison the best we have ever had. It was based primarily on the conception that it is as much the duty of public land officials to help the honest settler get title to his claim as it is to prevent the looting of the public lands. The essential fact about public land frauds is not merely that public property is stolen, but that every claim fraudulently acquired stands in the way of the making of a home or a livelihood by an honest man.

As the study of the public land laws proceeded and their administration improved, a public land policy was formulated in which the saving of the resources on the public domain for public use became the leading principle. There followed the withdrawal of coal lands as already described, of oil lands and phosphate lands, and finally, just at the end of the Administration, of water-power sites on the public domain. These withdrawals were made by the Executive in order to afford to Congress the necessary opportunity to pass wise laws dealing with their use and disposal; and the great crooked special interests fought them with incredible bitterness.

Among the men of this Nation interested in the vital problems affecting the welfare of the ordinary hand-working men and women of the Nation, there is none whose interest has been more intense, and more wholly free from taint of thought of self, than that of Thomas Watson, of Georgia. While President I often discussed with him the condition of women on the small farms, and on the frontier, the hardship of their lives as compared with those of the men, and the need for taking their welfare into consideration in whatever was done for the improvement of life on the land. I also went over the matter with C. S. Barrett, of Georgia, a leader in the Southern farmers' movement, and with other men, such as Henry Wallace, Dean L. H. Bailey, of Cornell, and Kenyon Butterfield. One man from whose advice I especially profited was not an American, but an Irishman, Sir Horace Plunkett. In various conversations he described to me and my close associates the reconstruction of farm life which had been accomplished by the Agricultural Organization Society of Ireland, of which he was the founder and the controlling force; and he discussed the application of similar methods to the improvements of farm life in the United States. In the spring of 1908, at my request, Plunkett conferred on the subject with Garfield and Pinchot, and the latter suggested to him the appointment of a Commission on Country Life as a means for directing the attention of the Nation to the problems of the farm, and for securing the necessary knowledge of the actual conditions of life in the open country. After long discussion a plan for a Country Life Commission was laid before me and approved. The appointment of the Commission followed in August, 1908. In the letter of appointment the reasons for creating the Commission were set forth as follows: "I doubt if any other nation can bear comparison with our own in the amount of attention given by the Government, both Federal and State, to agricultural matters. But practically the whole of this effort has hitherto been directed toward increasing the production of crops. Our attention has been concentrated almost exclusively on getting better farming. In the beginning this was unquestionably the right thing to do. The farmer must first of all grow good crops in order to support himself and his family. But when this has been secured, the effort for better farming should cease to stand alone, and should be accompanied by the effort for better business and better living on the farm. It is at least as important that the farmer should get the largest possible return in money, comfort, and social advantages from the crops he grows, as that he should get the largest possible return in crops from the land he farms. Agriculture is not the whole of country life. The great rural interests are human interests, and good crops are of little value to the farmer unless they open the door to a good kind of life on the farm."

The Commission on Country Life did work of capital importance. By means of a widely circulated set of questions the Commission informed itself upon the status of country life throughout the Nation. Its trip through the East, South, and West brought it into contact with large numbers of practical farmers and their wives, secured for the Commissioners a most valuable body of first-hand information, and laid the foundation for the remarkable awakening of interest in country life which has since taken place throughout the Nation.

One of the most illuminating—and incidentally one of the most interesting and amusing—series of answers sent to the Commission was from a farmer in Missouri. He stated that he had a wife and 11 living children, he and his wife being each 52 years old; and that they owned 520 acres of land without any mortgage hanging over their heads. He had himself done well, and his views as to why many of his neighbors had done less well are entitled to consideration. These views are expressed in terse and vigorous English; they cannot always be quoted in full. He states that the farm homes in his neighborhood are not as good as they should be because too many of them are encumbered by mortgages; that the schools do not train boys and girls satisfactorily for life on the farm, because they allow them to get an idea in their heads that city life is better, and that to remedy this practical farming should be taught. To the question whether the farmers and their wives in his neighborhood are satisfactorily organized, he answers: "Oh, there is a little one-horse grange gang in our locality, and every darned one thinks they ought to be a king." To the question, "Are the renters of farms in your neighborhood making a satisfactory living?" he answers: "No; because they move about so much hunting a better job." To the question, "Is the supply of farm labor in your neighborhood satisfactory?" the answer is: "No; because the people have gone out of the baby business"; and when asked as to the remedy, he answers, "Give a pension to every mother who gives birth to seven living boys on American soil." To the question, "Are the conditions surrounding hired labor on the farm in your neighborhood satisfactory to the hired men?" he answers: "Yes, unless he is a drunken cuss," adding that he would like to blow up the stillhouses and root out whisky and beer. To the question, "Are the sanitary conditions on the farms in your neighborhood satisfactory?" he answers: "No, too careless about chicken yards, and the like, and poorly covered wells. In one well on neighbor's farm I counted seven snakes in the wall of the well, and they used the water daily: his wife dead now and he is looking for another." He ends by stating that the most important single thing to be done for the betterment of country life is "good roads"; but in his answers he shows very clearly that most important of all is the individual equation of the man or woman.

. . .

The things accomplished that have been enumerated above were of immediate consequence to the economic wellbeing of our people. In addition certain things were done of which the economic bearing was more remote, but which bore directly upon our welfare, because they add to the beauty of living and therefore to the joy of life. Securing a great artist, Saint-Gaudens, to give us the most beautiful coinage since the decay of Hellenistic Greece was one such act. In this case I had power myself to direct the Mint to employ Saint-Gaudens. The first, and most beautiful, of his coins were issued in thousands before Congress assembled or could intervene; and a great and permanent improvement was made in the beauty of the coinage. In the same way, on the advice and suggestion of Frank Millet, we got some really capital medals by sculptors of the first rank. Similarly, the new buildings in Washington were erected and placed in proper relation to one another, on plans provided by the best architects and landscape architects. I also appointed a Fine Arts Council, an unpaid body of the best architects, painters, and sculptors in the country, to advise the Government as to the erection and decoration of all new buildings. The "pork-barrel" Senators and Congressmen felt for this body an instinctive, and perhaps from their standpoint a natural, hostility; and my successor a couple of months after taking office revoked the appointment and disbanded the Council.

Even more important was the taking of steps to preserve from destruction beautiful and wonderful wild creatures whose existence was threatened by greed and wantonness. During the seven and a half years closing on March 4, 1909, more was accomplished for the protection of wild life in the United States than during all the previous years, excepting only the creation of the Yellowstone National Park. The record includes the creation of five National Parks—Crater Lake, Oregon; Wind Cave, South Dakota; Platt, Oklahoma; Sully Hill, North Dakota, and Mesa Verde, Colorado; four big game refuges in Oklahoma, Arizona, Montana, and Washington; fifty-one bird reservations; and the enactment of laws for the protection of wild life in Alaska, the District of Columbia, and on National bird reserves. These measures may be briefly enumerated as follows:

The enactment of the first game laws for the Territory of Alaska in 1902 and 1908, resulting in the regulation of the export of heads and trophies of big game and putting an end to the slaughter of deer for hides along the southern coast of the Territory.

The securing in 1902 of the first appropriation for the preservation of buffalo and the establishment in the Yellowstone National Park of the first and now the largest herd of buffalo belonging to the Government.

The passage of the Act of January 24, 1905, creating the Wichita Game Preserves, the first of the National game preserves. In 1907, 12,000 acres of this preserve were inclosed with a woven wire fence for the reception of the herd of fifteen buffalo donated by the New York Zoölogical Society.

The passage of the Act of June 29, 1906, providing for the establishment of the Grand Cañon Game Preserve of Arizona, now comprising 1,492,928 acres.

The passage of the National Monuments Act of June 8, 1906, under which a number of objects of scientific interest have been preserved for all time. Among the Monuments created are Muir Woods, Pinnacles National Monument in California and the Mount Olympus National Monument, Washington, which form important refuges for game.

The passage of the Act of June 30, 1906, regulating shooting in the District of Columbia and making three-fourths of the environs of the National Capital within the District in effect a National Refuge.

The passage of the Act of May 23, 1908, providing for the establishment of the National Bison Range in Montana. This range comprises about 18,000 acres of land formerly in the Flathead Indian Reservation, on which is now established a herd of eighty buffalo, a nucleus of which was donated to the Government by the American Bison Society.

The issue of the Order protecting birds on the Niobrara Military Reservation, Nebraska, in 1908, making this entire reservation in effect a bird reservation.

The establishment by Executive Order between March 14, 1903, and March 4, 1909, of fifty-one National Bird Reservations distributed in seventeen States and Territories from Porto Rico to Hawaii and Alaska. The creation of these reservations at once placed the United States in the front rank in the world work of bird protection. Among these reservations are the celebrated Pelican Island rookery in Indian River, Florida; The Mosquito Inlet Reservation, Florida, the northernmost home of the manatee; the extensive marshes bordering Klamath and Malheur Lakes in Oregon, formerly the scene of slaughter of ducks for market and ruthless destruction of plume birds for the millinery trade; the Tortugas Key, Florida, where, in connection with the Carnegie Institute, experiments have been made on the homing instinct of birds; and the great bird colonies on Laysan and sister islets in Hawaii, some of the greatest colonies of sea birds in the world.

Questions for Thinking and Writing

1. Discuss Theodore Roosevelt's attitude in this essay regarding his administration and the country as a whole.
2. Describe Theodore Roosevelt's idea of "stewardship" and "for the public good." Do you think his vision of conservation as implied in this selection warrants the use of these terms?
3. Compare Roosevelt's ideas toward the conservation of western lands with those in circulation today. Pay particular attention to the irony that today the Clinton Administration is debating the same issues. What are some of the differences between the way they were handled then and the way they are being dealt with today?

Thinking and Writing About Part 1

1. How does direct observation of the natural world by writers in Part 1 lead to an understanding of (a) the human condition, (b) our beliefs, (c) the role of materialism and spirituality, and (d) the formulation and development of morality?
2. Discuss whether or not nature should be left as it is, or is it humankind's right to use nature? Is the act of civilizing wilderness ethical? How fragile is nature anyway? Does it seems that nature can be "killed," or will it always renew itself?
3. Consider whether Henry David Thoreau's actually living in a cabin in the woods conflicts with George Perkins Marsh's largely intellectual argument on the moral obligation to use nature and land intelligently. How do you think living in nature as Thoreau did might help you better understand Marsh's argument?
4. Several writers in this section—John Muir, Emily Dickinson, Frederick Law Olmsted, Frederick H. Newell, and Gifford Pinchot—play on readers' emotions as an important part of their argument to persuade readers to understand the natural world through their eyes and ideas. Discuss how powerful a force emotion can be when discussing the environment and whether or not you feel that the debate is more successfully carried by cool logic or by emotion.
5. Why do trees play such an important symbolic role in our moral, spiritual, and material lives? Contrast the grove of pine trees described in Susan Fenimore Cooper's "Summer, Monday, July 23rd" (p. 7) with Frederick Law Olmsted's plea for preserving the sequoia trees in "The Yosemite Valley and the Mariposa Big Trees" (p. 34) with Walt Whitman's joyous praise of the use of trees in "Song of the Redwood-Tree" (p. 39).
6. Outline the cycle of progress as mentioned by Susan Fenimore Cooper, Henry David Thoreau, Walt Whitman, Frederick H. Newell, and Gifford Pinchot that leads from wilderness to a civilized community. Relate this cycle to ethical questions of personal, social, and industrial development.
7. Discuss whether you believe that living in a wilderness makes a person good or more ethical than living in a city.
8. Give your reaction to the argument that one can be a naturalist or nature lover without going out into the field. In what ways can someone offer a philosophy of nature and yet not experience it in person?

A severe drought ravaged the Great Plains throughout the early 1930s, resulting in the sort of dust storm this farmer and his sons battled in April 1936 in Cimarron County, Oklahoma.

2 1915–1949: Spiritual, Symbolic, and Practical Responses to the Environment

The United States endured tumultuous periods during the 34 years from 1916 to 1950. The country fought World War I (1917–1918), expanded economically in the 1920s, endured the stock market crash of 1929, suffered through the Depression (1930s), fought World War II in Europe and in the Pacific (1941–1945), and became ensnared with the Soviet Communists in the Cold War (1946–1950s). Despite all, this time was also a period of romance with ideals and ingenuity, power, and technological advances, generally at the expense of the environment. The expansion in the name of progress, capitalism, and world peace superseded conservation and environmental preservation. For the most part, civilization and nature were headed on a collision course.

The policy of wise use of natural resources, land, and water was predicated on the belief that nature and the national economy are served best by conservation. As advocated by Theodore Roosevelt (1858–1919), Gifford Pinchot (1865–1946), and Frederick Newell (1862–1932), there was a moral and practical basis for extensive harvesting of forests, fish, wildlife, and mining. Congress was sympathetic to the issue and passed the National Park Service Act (1916) and the Mineral Leasing Act (1918). These acts set limits for industrial use of U.S. lands and were partial remedies for the excesses of unrestrained industrialization. They proved to be a kind of environmental spark, and once promulgated, persuaded environmentalists to relax their lobbying.

There followed a period of complacency, during which industry recouped most of its losses.

With World War I over, industrial development became unassailable. The rallying cry under the administrations of presidents Warren G. Harding (1921–1923) and Calvin Coolidge (1923–1929) was laissez-faire. Neither president cared for or really understood that the need for conservation stood at the other end of unregulated exploitation. Few really comprehended the vulnerability of the natural resources that fueled the burgeoning U.S. economy. In the heady world of power politics, increasing the gross national product left little room to call for a stop to strip mining, clear-cutting forests, or ruining habitats that resulted in the depletion of species or extinction. From an industrial point of view there was little sympathy for the fact that the snowy egret, its plumes coveted for women's hats, hovered at the edge of extinction, that American bison once numbering in the millions had been reduced to hundreds, or that the last passenger pigeon died in 1914.

The era of the 1920s was characterized by a hazy understanding of the unity of nature and the environment. President Coolidge is remembered for his insensitive reference to Muscle Shoals, the landscape designated as the future site of the TVA, as being a "first class battleship." The Teapot Dome Scandal in 1922 marked the Harding administration for its disregard of federal reserve land and the political expediency of trading natural resources, in this case oil rights, for political and personal gain. Without notice, the Department of the Interior leased the Teapot Dome (Wyoming) and Elk Hills (California) oil fields to independent oil companies. This proved to be a classic instance of laissez-faire environmentalism at the public's expense, for the oil fields were a national treasure.

The prevailing economic growth bubble of the 1920s reinforced the long-held optimism that nature in the United States was infinite and endlessly renewable. The heights of environmental exploitation may have occurred during President Herbert Hoover's administration (1929–1933) with the selling off of millions of acres of federal land to industrial speculators. Hoover claimed to be a conservationist, but in following the pathways of wise or multiple use of resources he sought to control nature, thereby making it accessible for industrial purposes. As secretary of the interior under Coolidge, Hoover regulated the Alaskan salmon fisheries and pushed forward wide-ranging flood control projects. As president during the early stages of the Great Depression in 1929, Hoover encouraged business recovery by selling off millions of acres of government land to industry and developers. This short-term economic gimmick had long-term environmental consequences, for it exemplified the peculiarly American concept that the environment is a disposable commodity.

Franklin Roosevelt, who succeeded Hoover to the presidency in 1932, began a radical and systematic plan for economic recovery. He closed the banks, set up stringent controls on the stock market, sought regulations of industrial, monetary, and manufacturing practices, and created enormous civilian works projects to provide jobs and renew industrial impetus. Social and economic necessity was rarely weighed, understandably, against ecological well-being. Under the rule of wise use, Roosevelt's New Deal produced the Tennessee Valley Authority (TVA), a massive decade-long waterworks project that changed the face of the Tennessee River Valley by building over 30 dams, scores of hydro-electric power plants, and thousands of miles of roads.

David E. Lilienthal, TVA's first director, praised the project. "Waters once wasted, and destructive," he wrote in *TVA: Democracy on the March* (1944), "have been controlled and now work, night and day, creating electric energy to lighten the burden of human drudgery." Lilienthal's enthusiasm was unchecked. It introduced a new motive for environmental exploitation in the pattern of wise use: The land was there to be manipulated so our lives could be made easier and more productive. Lakes for fishing now replaced useless shoals; hillsides of fruit trees grew where inaccessible forest had once stood; and small cities bustled on the sites of sleepy towns. Whether or not these changes represented wise use of the land or whether they gutted a way of life that would have changed of its own accord can be debated. Unfortunately this debate is more often than not conducted after the fact.

Key words for the New Deal were democracy, energy, and control, which in practice encouraged environmental exploitation. Nature could be controlled and made to improve civilization: That was what the United States was all about. Public works projects and agricultural projects were linchpins of the New Deal. There was the Agricultural Adjustment Administration (AAA), the Works Project Administration (WPA), the National Recovery Administration (NRA), the Tennessee Valley Authority (TVA), and the Civil Conservation Corps (CCC). Under the directorship of Harold Ickes, the CCC merged political and environmental concerns. It provided work for unemployed young men and women, primarily from urban areas, who might otherwise turn revolutionary. The work, another aspect of wise use, included making roads on federal land and parks, planting and reforesting, containing soil erosion, and electrification. This alteration of nature, however, had its down side, for it also meant that fertile river valleys were depopulated and made into reservoirs for cities; rural populations of people and animals were displaced; local climate was altered; and wild scenery was lost. In effect, civilizing the landscape changed nature's cycles.

The rapid alterations and depletion of nature were not entirely unnoticed. Wallace Stevens laments in "Anecdote of the Jar" (1923) that a simple jar placed in the wilderness changed the landscape and made it "slovenly," bare, and barren. Stevens's poem, which begins, "I placed a jar in Tennessee," predates the TVA by ten years. Robert Frost decries the loss of a farm and the agrarian way of life in "A Brook in the City" (1921). The brook, now buried under development, suggests not only the loss of nature but the loss of the possibility of learning from nature.

Certainly the idea of natural unity—combining animal and plant life, human life and history, has been expressed in a variety of ways by many writers. Willa Cather's "The Ancient People" (1915) describes the experience of an aspiring opera singer who finds spiritual renewal by spending time in the ruins of a Pueblo cliff dwelling. Robert Frost depicts the meeting of humans and animals in "Two Look at Two" (1923), in which a man and woman meet a buck and doe that ignore the human intrusion of their domain. Somehow the people come off for the better for this encounter.

In "Chee's Daughter" (1948), Juanita Platero and Siyowin Miller describe the conflict experienced by a Navajo man which leads him to understand that adherence to the land brings self-respect and success which is denied to those who commercialize their tribal heritage.

Both Caroline A. Henderson and John Steinbeck write about the great drought of the middle 1930s and its effects on the Midwest, especially in Oklahoma. Henderson, who with her husband ran a farmstead, tried to keep her spirits up while daily meeting the challenges of natural calamity. Steinbeck's *The Grapes of Wrath* (1939) is a searing tale about human trial and error. Steinbeck was a kind of literary ecologist who understood the interrelationship of humans and nature. In this, he complements Aldo Leopold's advocacy for ethical consideration of nature and land, and he foreshadows a sentiment that today is at the forefront of environmental considerations.

World War II affirmed that the United States was the leading political, economic, and industrial nation. Though ecology paid a price for winning the war against nazism and fascism, when the war was over, new voices were heard. Most prominently, Aldo Leopold argued that nature intertwines all forms of life on earth. Though he was writing before and during the war, it was not until the publication of *A Sand County Almanac* in 1949 that people heard him. In "Conservation Esthetic," first published in 1933 and reappearing in *A Sand County Almanac* as "The Land Ethic," he wrote that there is no ethic for dealing with land and nature, since society has not affirmed that despoiling land or nature is wrong. Society, he implies, has not yet reached the moral ground necessary for passing judgment on that issue.

HISTORICAL CHRONOLOGY AND CONTEXT

1916: National Park Service Act

First birth control clinic opened by Margaret Sanger

1917: United States declares war on Germany and enters World War I

1918: War in Europe ends

Migratory Bird Treaty with Canada restricts hunting of migratory species

Save-the-Redwoods League founded

1919: Eighteenth Amendment bans sale of alcoholic beverages

1920: Nineteenth Amendment gives women the right to vote

Mineral Leasing Act regulates mining on federal lands

1921: Warren G. Harding begins his presidency

1922: Izaak Walton League established

Teapot Dome Scandal

1923:   Calvin Coolidge begins his presidency

Robert Frost's *New Hampshire* published

Charles Birdseye introduces the idea of frozen food

1924:   Native Americans are officially designated U.S. citizens

First National Conference on Outdoor Recreation held

John Scopes is tried for teaching evolution in a Tennessee school

1927:   Charles A. Lindberg flies solo across the Atlantic Ocean

1928:   Walt Disney creates Mickey Mouse

1929:   Herbert Hoover begins his presidency

The stock market crashes

1930:   The planet Pluto is discovered

1931:   Hoover Dam on the Colorado River begun

"The Star Spangled Banner" is officially designated the national anthem

1933:   Franklin Roosevelt begins his presidency

Civilian Conservation Corp (CCC) established

Tennessee Valley Authority (TVA) established

Soil Erosion Service created

1934:   Taylor Grazing Act—regulates grazing on public lands

1935:   Soil Conservation Act passed

Soil Conservation Service becomes part of Department of Agriculture

Wilderness Society formed

Historic Sites Act

1936:   Hoover Dam completed

1937:   Pittman-Robertson Act gives states federal funding for wildlife protection

1938:   Nylon, the first synthetic fiber, is used commercially

1939:   Germany invades Poland; World War II begins

John Steinbeck's *The Grapes of Wrath* published

1940:   U.S. Fish and Wildlife Service established

1941:   Pearl Harbor attacked; U.S. declares war on Japan and Germany

1944:   Soil Conservation Society of America founded

World War II over in Europe; Germany capitulates

1945:   World War II over in the Pacific; Japan capitulates after atomic bombs are dropped on Hiroshima and Nagasaki

Harry S. Truman becomes president when Roosevelt dies

1946:   U.S. Bureau of Land Management created to oversee use of public lands

Atomic Energy Commission is established

1947:   Bell Laboratories scientists invent the transistor

1948:   Federal Water Pollution Control Act established

1949:   Aldo Leopold's *A Sand County Almanac* is published

First Sierra Club Biennial Wilderness Conference held

1950:   Korean War begins

❧ Willa Cather (1876–1947)

The Ancient People (1915)

Willa Cather first visited the Southwest as a young girl. The conflict between the region's human history on the land—of Native Americans and Spanish-descended peoples—and its stark and rejuvenating beauty fascinated her for years, culminating in The Song of the Lark *(1915) and her novel* Death Comes for the Archbishop *(1927).*

Cather was born in Virginia. She lived there until she was 9 and then moved with her family to the great prairies of the Midwest at Red Cloud, Nebraska. During these years, she met and befriended the immigrants, many of them Scandinavian, who populate her fiction. In Red Cloud, Cather received a rich education from local teachers and townspeople. At the University of Nebraska, she studied journalism and began working as a professional journalist when she graduated in 1895. She also began writing fiction, which she published in McClure's Magazine *and* Cosmopolitan.

Until 1903, Cather worked as a journalist and teacher. She then traveled to Europe and worked on a book of poems, April Twilights *(1903). In 1905, she published a book of short stories,* The Troll Garden, *and the following year settled in New York City, where she worked as an editor for* McClure's *until 1912. There, she met Edith Lewis who became her companion for the rest of her life. She also met Sarah Orne Jewett, who may have influenced Cather to begin writing in earnest about the landscape she knew best: the prairies of the West and the Southwest.*

Cather's novels O Pioneers *(1913),* The Song of the Lark, *and* My Antonia *(1918) are about the frontier in which the land becomes a character in itself and the people struggle to find a unity with it. Cather's landscapes, like Jewett's and Mary Austin's, have metaphorical meanings—spiritual, moral, material.*

The Song of the Lark, *from which "The Ancient People" comes, is about Thea Kronberg, an aspiring opera singer, and her trials that eventually enable her to achieve success. At a particularly low point in her career, Kronberg travels to the Southwest for a respite. Time spent at a ranch in northern Arizona restores both her body and spirit. "The Ancient People" describes the slow process by which Kronberg rebuilds her strength, demonstrating how one's physical senses can lead to higher and deeper states of mind and spirit. Kronberg's direct contact with the natural landscape and the cliff dwellings of the ancient people connects with the natural landscape and its spiritual presence, from which her physical and spiritual health renews, grows, and flourishes.*

I

The San Francisco Mountain lies in northern Arizona, above Flagstaff, and its blue slopes and snowy summit entice the eye for a hundred miles across the desert. About its base lie the pine forests of the Navajos, where the great red-trunked trees live out their peaceful centuries in that sparkling air. The *piñons* and scrub begin only where the forest ends, where the country breaks into open, stony clearings and the surface of the earth cracks into deep cañons. The great pines stand at a considerable distance from each other. Each tree grows alone, murmurs alone, thinks alone. They do not intrude upon each other. The Navajos are not much in the habit of giving or of asking help. Their language is not a communicative one, and they never attempt an interchange of personality in speech. Over their forests there is the same inexorable reserve. Each tree has its exalted power to bear.

That was the first thing Thea Kronberg felt about the forest, as she drove through it one May morning in Henry Biltmer's democrat wagon—and it was the first great forest she had ever seen. She had got off the train at Flagstaff that morning, rolled off into the high, chill air when all the pines on the mountain were fired by sunrise, so that she seemed to fall from sleep directly into the forest.

Old Biltmer followed a faint wagon-trail which ran southeast, and which, as they travelled, continually dipped lower, falling away from the high plateau on the slope of which Flagstaff sits. The white peak of the mountain, the snow gorges above the timber, now disappeared from time to time as the road dropped and dropped, and the forest closed behind the wagon. More than the mountain disappeared as the forest closed thus. Thea seemed to be taking very little through the wood with her. The personality of which she was so tired seemed to let go of her. The high, sparkling air drank it up like blotting-paper. It was lost in the thrilling blue of the new sky and the song of the thin wind in the *piñons.* The old, fretted lines which marked one off, which defined her—made her Thea Kronborg, Bowers's accompanist, a soprano with a faulty middle voice—were all erased.

So far she had failed. Her two years in Chicago had not resulted in anything. She had failed with Harsanyi, and she had made no great progress with her voice. She had come to believe that whatever Bowers had taught her was of secondary importance, and that in the essential things she had made no advance. Her student life closed behind her, like the forest, and she doubted whether she could go back to it if she tried. Probably she would teach music in little country towns all her life.

Failure was not so tragic as she would have supposed; she was tired enough not to care.

She was getting back to the earliest sources of gladness that she could remember. She had loved the sun, and the brilliant solitudes of sand and sun, long before these other things had come along to fasten themselves upon her and torment her. That night, when she clambered into her big German feather bed, she felt completely released from the enslaving desire to get on in the world. Darkness had once again the sweet wonder that it had in childhood.

II

Thea's life at the Ottenburg ranch was simple and full of light, like the days themselves. She awoke every morning when the first fierce shafts of sunlight darted through the curtainless windows of her room at the ranch-house. After breakfast she took her lunch-basket and went down to the cañon. Usually she did not return until sunset.

Panther Cañon was like a thousand others—one of those abrupt fissures with which the earth in the Southwest is riddled; so abrupt that you might walk over the edge of any one of them on a dark night and never know what had happened to you. This cañon headed on the Ottenburg ranch, about a mile from the ranch-house, and it was accessible only at its head. The cañon walls, for the first two hundred feet below the surface, were perpendicular cliffs, striped with even-running strata of rock. From there on to the bottom the sides were less abrupt, were shelving, and lightly fringed with *piñons* and dwarf cedars. The effect was that of a gentler cañon within a wilder one. The dead city lay at the point where the perpendicular outer wall ceased and the V-shaped inner gorge began. There a stratum of rock, softer than those above, had been hollowed out by the action of time until it was like a deep groove running along the sides of the cañon. In this hollow (like a great fold in the rock) the Ancient People had built their houses of yellowish stone and mortar. The overhanging cliff above made a roof two hundred feet thick. The hard stratum below was an everlasting floor. The houses stood along in a row, like the buildings in a city block, or like a barracks.

In both walls of the cañon the same streak of soft rock had been washed out, and the long horizontal groove had been built up with houses. The dead city had thus two streets, one set in either cliff, facing each other across the ravine, with a river of blue air between them.

The cañon twisted and wound like a snake, and these two streets went on for four miles or more, interrupted by the abrupt turnings of the gorge, but beginning again within each turn. The cañon had a dozen of these false endings near its head. Beyond, the windings were larger and less perceptible, and it went on for a hundred miles, too narrow, precipitous, and terrible for man to follow it. The Cliff-Dwellers liked wide cañons, where the great cliffs caught the sun. Panther Cañon had been deserted for hundreds of years when the first Spanish missionaries came into Arizona, but the masonry of the houses was still wonderfully firm; had crumbled only where a landslide or a rolling boulder had torn it.

All the houses in the cañon were clean with the cleanness of sunbaked, wind-swept places, and they all smelled of the tough little cedars that twisted themselves into the very doorways. One of these rock-rooms Thea took for her own. Fred had told her how to make it comfortable. The day after she came, old Henry brought over on one of the packponies a roll of Navajo blankets that belonged to Fred, and Thea lined her cave with them. The room was not more than eight by ten feet, and she could touch the stone roof with her finger-tips. This was her old idea: a nest in a high cliff, full of sun. All morning long the sun beat upon her cliff, while the ruins on the opposite side of the cañon were in shadow. In the afternoon, when she had the shade of two hundred feet of rock wall, the ruins on the other side of the gulf stood out in the blazing sunlight. Before her door ran the narrow, winding path that had been the street of the Ancient People. The yucca and niggerhead cactus grew everywhere. From her doorstep she looked out on the ochrecoloured slope that ran down several hundred feet to the stream, and this hot rock was sparsely grown with dwarf trees. Their colours were so pale that the shadows of the little trees on the rock stood out sharper than the trees themselves. When Thea first came, the chokecherry bushes were in blossom, and the scent of them was almost sickeningly sweet after a shower. At the very bottom of the cañon, along the stream, there was a thread of bright, flickering, golden-green—cottonwood seedlings. They made a living, chattering screen behind which she took her bath every morning.

Thea went down to the stream by the Indian water-trail. She had found a bathing-pool with a sand bottom, where the creek was dammed by fallen trees. The climb back was long and steep, and when she reached her little house in the cliff, she always felt fresh delight in its comfort and inaccessibility. By the time she got there, the woolly redand-grey blankets were saturated with sunlight, and she sometimes fell asleep as soon as she stretched her body on their warm surfaces. She used to wonder at her own inactivity. She could lie there hour after hour in the sun and listen to the strident whirr of the big locusts, and to the light, ironical laughter of the quaking asps. All her life she had been hurrying and sputtering, as if she had been born behind time and had been trying to catch up. Now, she reflected, as she drew herself out long upon the rugs, it was as if she were waiting for something to catch up with her. She had got to a place where she was out of the stream of meaningless activity and undirected effort.

Here she could lie for half a day undistracted, holding pleasant and incomplete conceptions in her mind—almost in her hands. They were scarcely clear enough to be called ideas. They had something to do with fragrance and colour and sound, but almost nothing to do with words. She was singing very little now, but a song would go through her head all morning, as a spring keeps welling up, and it was like a pleasant sensation indefinitely prolonged. It was much more like a sensation than like an idea, or an act of remembering.

Music had never before come to her in that sensuous form. It had always been a thing to be struggled with, had always brought anxiety and exaltation and chagrin—never content and indolence. Thea began to wonder whether people could not utterly lose the power to work, as they can lose their voice or their memory. She had always been a little drudge, hurrying from one task to another—as if it mattered! And now her power to think seemed converted into a power of sustained sensation. She could become a mere receptacle for heat, or become a colour, like the bright lizards that darted about on the hot stones outside her door; or she could become a continuous repetition of sound, like the cicadas.

III

The faculty of observation was never highly developed in Thea Kronborg. A great deal escaped her eye as she passed through the world. But the things which were for her, she saw; she experienced them physically and remembered them as if they had once been a part of herself. The roses she used to see in the florists' shops in Chicago were merely roses. But when she thought of the moonflowers that grew over Mrs. Tellamantez's door, it was as if she had been that vine and had opened up in white flowers every night. There were memories of light on the sand hills, of masses of prickly-pear blossoms she had found in the desert in early childhood, of the late afternoon sun pouring through the grape leaves and the mint bed in Mrs. Kohler's garden, which she would never lose. These recollections were a part of her mind and personality. In Chicago she had got almost nothing that went into her subconscious self and took root there. But here, in Panther Cañon, there were again things which seemed destined for her.

Panther Cañon was the home of innumerable swallows. They built nests in the wall far above the hollow groove in which Thea's own rockchamber lay. They seldom ventured above the rim of the cañon, to the flat, wind-swept tableland. Their world was the blue air-river between the cañon walls. In that blue gulf the arrow-shaped birds swam all day long, with only an occasional movement of the wings. The only sad thing about them was their timidity: the way in which they lived their lives between the echoing cliffs and never dared to rise out of the shadow of the cañon walls. As they swam past her door, Thea often felt how easy it would be to dream one's life out in some cleft in the world.

From the ancient dwelling there came always a dignified, unobtrusive sadness; now stronger, now fainter—like the aromatic smell which the dwarf cedars gave out in the sun—but always present, a part of the air one breathed. At night, when Thea dreamed about the cañon—or in the early morning when she hurried toward it, anticipating it—her conception of it was of yellow rocks baking in sunlight, the swallows, the cedar smell, and that peculiar sadness—a voice out of the past, not very loud, that went on saying a few simple things to the solitude eternally.

Standing up in her lodge, Thea with her thumbnail could dislodge flakes of carbon from the rock-roof—the cooking-smoke of the Ancient People. They were that near! A timid, nest-building folk, like the swallows. How often Thea remembered Ray Kennedy's moralizing about the cliff cities. He used to say that he never felt the hardness of the human struggle or the sadness of history as he felt it among those ruins. He used to say, too, that it made one feel an obligation to do one's best. On the first day that Thea climbed the water-trail, she began to have intuitions about the women who had worn the path, and who had spent so great a part of their lives going up and down it. She found herself trying to walk as they must have walked, with a feeling in her feet and knees and loins which she had never known before—which must have come up to her out of the accustomed dust of that rocky trail. She could feel the weight of an Indian baby hanging to her back as she climbed.

The empty houses, among which she wandered in the afternoon, the blanketed one in which she lay all morning, were haunted by certain fears and desires; feelings about warmth and cold and water and physical strength. It seemed to Thea that a certain understanding of those old people came up to her out of the rock-shelf on which she lay; that certain feelings were transmitted to her, suggestions that were simple, insistent, and monotonous, like the beating of Indian drums. They were not expressible in words, but seemed rather to translate themselves into attitudes of body, into degrees of muscular tension or relaxation; the naked strength of youth, sharp as the sun-shafts; the crouching timorousness of age, the sullenness of women who waited for their captors. At the first turning of the cañon there was a half-ruined tower of yellow masonry, a watch-tower upon which the young men used to entice eagles and snare them with nets. Sometimes for a whole morning Thea could see the coppery breast and shoulders of an Indian youth there against the sky: see him throw the net, and watch the struggle with the eagle.

Old Henry Biltmer, at the ranch, had been a great deal among the Pueblo Indians who are the descendants of the Cliff-Dwellers. After supper he used to sit and smoke his pipe by the kitchen stove and talk to Thea about them. He had never found anyone before who was interested in his ruins. Every Sunday the old man prowled about in the cañon, and he had come to know a good deal more about it than he could account for. He had gathered up a whole chestful of Cliff-Dweller relics which he meant to take back to Germany with him some day. He taught Thea how to find things among the ruins: grinding-stones, and drills and needles made of turkey-bones. There were fragments of pottery everywhere. Old Henry explained to her that the Ancient People had developed masonry and pottery far beyond any other crafts. After they had made houses for themselves, the next thing was to house the precious water. He explained to her how all their customs and ceremonies and their religion went back to water. The men provided the food, but water was the care of the women. The stupid women carried water for most of their lives; the cleverer ones made the vessels to hold it. Their pottery was their most direct appeal to water, the envelope and sheath of the precious element itself. The strongest Indian need was expressed in those graceful jars, fashioned slowly by hand, without the aid of a wheel.

When Thea took her bath at the bottom of the cañon, in the sunny pool behind the screen of cottonwoods, she sometimes felt as if the water must have sovereign qualities, from having been the object of so much service and desire. That stream was the only living thing left of the drama that had been played out in the cañon centuries ago. In the rapid, restless heart of it, flowing swifter than the rest, there was a continuity of life that reached back into the old time. The glittering thread of current had a kind of lightly worn, loosely knit personality, graceful and laughing. Thea's bath came to have a ceremonial gravity. The atmosphere of the cañon was ritualistic.

One morning, as she was standing upright in the pool, splashing water between her shoulder-blades with a big sponge, something flashed through her mind that made her draw herself up and stand still until the water had quite dried upon her flushed skin. The stream and the broken pottery: what was any art but an effort to make a sheath, a mould in which to imprison for a moment the shining, elusive element which is life itself—life hurrying past us and running away, too strong to stop, too sweet to lose? The Indian women had held it in their jars. In the sculpture she had seen in the Art Institute, it had been caught in a flash of arrested motion. In singing, one made a vessel of one's throat and nostrils and held it on one's breath, caught the stream in a scale of natural intervals.

IV

Thea had a superstitious feeling about the potsherds, and liked better to leave them in the dwellings where she found them. If she took a few bits back to her own lodge and hid them under the blankets, she did it guiltily, as if she were being watched. She was a guest in these houses, and ought to behave as such. Nearly every afternoon she went to the chambers which contained the most interesting fragments of pottery, sat and looked at them for a while. Some of them were beautifully decorated. This care, expended upon vessels that could not hold food or water any better for the additional labour put upon them, made her heart go out to those ancient potters. They had not only expressed their desire, but they had expressed it as beautifully as they could. Food, fire, water, and something else—even here, in this crack in the world, so far back in the night of the past! Down here at the beginning, that painful thing was already stirring; the seed of sorrow, and of so much delight.

There were jars done in a delicate overlay, like pine cones; and there were many patterns in a low relief, like basket-work. Some of the pottery was decorated in colour, red and brown, black and white, in graceful geometrical patterns. One day, on a fragment of a shallow bowl, she found a crested serpent's head, painted in red on terra-cotta. Again she found half a bowl with a broad band of white cliff-houses painted on a black ground. They were scarcely conventionalized at all; there they were in the black border, just as they stood in the rock before her. It brought her centuries nearer to these people to find that they saw their houses exactly as she saw them.

Yes, Ray Kennedy was right. All these things made one feel that one ought to do one's best, and help to fulfil some desire of the dust that slept there. A dream had been dreamed there long ago, in the night of ages, and the wind had whispered some promise to the sadness of the savage. In their own way, those people had felt the beginnings of what was to come. These potsherds were like fetters that bound one to a long chain of human endeavour.

Not only did the world seem older and richer to Thea now, but she herself seemed older. She had never been alone for so long before, or thought so much. Nothing had ever engrossed her so deeply as the daily contemplation of that line of pale-yellow houses tucked into the wrinkle of the cliff. Moonstone and Chicago had become vague. Here everything was simple and definite, as things had been in childhood. Her mind was like a ragbag into which she had been frantically thrusting whatever she could grab. And here she must throw this lumber away. The things that were really hers separated themselves from the rest. Her ideas were simplified, became sharper and clearer. She felt united and strong.

When Thea had been at the Ottenburg ranch for two months, she got a letter from Fred announcing that he 'might be along at almost any time now.' The letter came at night, and the next morning she took it down into the cañon with her. She was delighted that he was coming soon. She had never felt so grateful to anyone, and she wanted to tell him everything that had happened to her since she had been there—

more than had happened in all her life before. Certainly she liked Fred better than anyone else in the world. There was Harsanyi, of course—but Harsanyi was always tired. Just now, and here, she wanted someone who had never been tired, who could catch an idea and run with it.

She was ashamed to think what an apprehensive drudge she must always have seemed to Fred, and she wondered why he had concerned himself about her at all. Perhaps she would never be so happy or so good-looking again, and she would like Fred to see her, for once, at her best. She had not been singing much, but she knew that her voice was more interesting than it had ever been before. She had begun to understand that—with her, at least—voice was, first of all, vitality; a lightness in the body and a driving power in the blood. If she had that, she could sing. When she felt so keenly alive, lying on that insensible shelf of stone, when her body bounded like a rubber ball away from its hardness, then she could sing. This, too, she could explain to Fred. He would know what she meant.

Another week passed. Thea did the same things as before, felt the same influences, went over the same ideas; but there was a livelier movement in her thoughts, and a freshening of sensation, like the brightness which came over the underbrush after a shower. A persistent affirmation—or denial—was going on in her, like the tapping of the woodpecker in the one tall pine tree across the chasm. Musical phrases drove each other rapidly through her mind, and the song of the cicada was now too long and too sharp. Everything seemed suddenly to take the form of a desire for action.

It was while she was in this abstracted state, waiting for the clock to strike, that Thea at last made up her mind what she was going to try to do in the world, and that she was going to Germany to study without further loss of time. Only by the merest chance had she ever got to Panther Cañon. There was certainly no kindly Providence that directed one's life; and one's parents did not in the least care what became of one, so long as one did not misbehave and endanger their comfort. One's life was at the mercy of blind chance. She had better take it in her own hands and lose everything than meekly draw the plough under the rod of parental guidance. She had seen it when she was at home last summer—the hostility of comfortable, self-satisfied people toward any serious effort. Even to her father it seemed indecorous. Whenever she spoke seriously, he looked apologetic. Yet she had clung fast to whatever was left of Moonstone in her mind. No more of that! The Cliff-Dwellers had lengthened her past. She had older and higher obligations.

Questions for Thinking and Writing

1. What do you think Cather had in mind in setting up such a startling contrast between Kronberg's professional environment and the one she finds in northern Arizona? Why is this place so antithetical to her regular life?

2. How does Kronberg's first view of the mountain and the great pine forest of northern Arizona suggest her awakening to the power of the landscape and her developing sense of self? In what ways do Kronberg's experiences in the canyon change her faculty for observation?
3. Can you relate to Kronberg's experience in nature? Has some experience in the natural environment deeply affected the way that you think about yourself or others?

Liberty Hyde Bailey (1858–1954)
The Farmer's Relation (1919)

Liberty Hyde Bailey is remembered not only for his extraordinary collections of plants but also for his realization that the perpetuation of farming had the potential for unconsciously creating an environmental ethic throughout the country. He was a champion of farmers as he saw them fleeing the land for factories and offices in the hope that urban life would offer greater rewards.

Born in South Haven, Michigan, the son of a farmer and fruit-grower, Bailey attended local schools and Michigan Agricultural College. In 1883, he married Annette Smith, the daughter of a Lansing, Michigan, farmer. Two years later, while working on his master's degree at Michigan Agricultural College, he formed the Department of Horticulture and Landscape Gardening, the first in the country. For the next three years he taught horticulture at the college but in 1888 moved to Ithaca, New York, to assume the chair of general and experimental horticulture at Cornell University. In 1903, he was named director of Cornell's College of Agriculture. Bailey retired from teaching in 1913 but remained at Cornell as a dean and professor emeritus. During these years he traveled extensively, collecting plant specimens, particularly palms and blackberries, and became widely known as an expert in botany, horticulture, and agriculture. In 1935, he founded the Liberty Hyde Bailey Hortorium, which became an extensive herbarium with more than 250,000 plant specimens. He directed the Hortorium until 1952 and bequeathed it, along with buildings and library, to Cornell before he died in 1954.

Bailey was a prolific writer with over 100 books to his credit that he either wrote or edited. Among the best known are Plant-Breeding *(1897),* The Cylopedia of American Agriculture *(1907–1909),* Hortus *(1930), and* Hortus Second *(1941). He believed strongly that horticul-*

ture is an applied science, an argument that upset some naturalists but
that eventually prevailed.

The selection here, from The Holy Earth (1919), is a poignant argument in defense of the rural farmer of America, whom he calls the
"trustee" of the land. Given this responsibility, Bailey says it is our
"public duty" not only to train farmers in agriculture but to pay them
high regard.

The surface of the earth is particularly within the care of the farmer.
He keeps it for his own sustenance and gain, but his gain is also the gain
of all the rest of us. At the best, he accumulates little to himself. The successful farmer is the one who produces more than he needs for his support; and the overplus he does not keep; and, moreover, his own needs
are easily satisfied. It is of the utmost consequence that the man next
the earth shall lead a fair and simple life; for in riotous living he might
halt many good supplies that now go to his fellows.

It is a public duty so to train the farmer that he shall appreciate his
guardianship. He is engaged in a quasi-public business. He really does
not even own his land. He does not take his land with him, but only the
personal development that he gains from it. He cannot annihilate his
land, as another might destroy all his belongings. He is the agent or the
representative of society to guard and to subdue the surface of the
earth; and he is the agent of the divinity that made it. He must exercise
his dominion with due regard to all these obligations. He is a trustee.
The productiveness of the earth must increase from generation to generation: this also is his obligation. He must handle all his materials, remembering man and remembering God. A man cannot be a good
farmer unless he is a religious man.

If the farmer is engaged in a quasi-public business, shall we undertake to regulate him? This relationship carries a vast significance to the
social order, and it must color our attitude toward the man on the land.
We are now in that epoch of social development when we desire to regulate by law everything that is regulatable and the other things besides.
It is recently proposed that the Congress shall pass a law regulating the
cropping scheme of the farmer for the protection of soil fertility. This
follows the precedent of the regulation, by enactment, of trusts and
public utilities. It is fortunate that such a law cannot be passed, and
could not be enforced if it were passed; but this and related proposals
are crude expressions of the growing feeling that the farmer owes an
obligation to society, and that this obligation must be enforced and the
tiller of the soil be held to account.

We shall produce a much better and safer man when we make him
self-controlling by developing his sense of responsibility than when we
regulate him by exterior enactments.

In the realm of control of the farming occupation we shall invoke other than legal means, and perhaps these means will be suggestive for other situations. These means may be somewhat indefinite in the law-book sense, but they may attain to a better human result. We shall reach the question by surer ways than the crudities of legislation. We shall reach the man, in this field, rather than his business. We have begun it by accepting it as one part of our duty to the race to provide liberally at public expense for the special education of the man on the land. This is the reason, even if we have not formulated it to ourselves, why society is willing to go farther in the education of the farming people than in the popular education of other ranges of the people. This, of course, is the fundamental way; and if there are any governments that attempt to safeguard this range directly by laws rather than by education, then they have not arrived at a long view of the situation.

We invoke regulatory law for the control of the corporate activities; but we must not forget the other kinds of activities contributing to the making of society, nor attempt to apply to them the same methods of correction.

Into this secular and more or less technical education we are now to introduce the element of moral obligation, that the man may understand his peculiar contribution and responsibility to society; but this result cannot be attained until the farmer and every one of us recognize the holiness of the earth.

The farmer and every one of us: every citizen should be put right toward the planet, should be quicked to his relationship to his natural background. The whole body of public sentiment should be sympathetic with the man who works and administers the land for us; and this requires understanding. We have heard much about the "marginal man," but the first concern of society should be for the bottom man.

If this philosophy should really be translated into action, the farmer would nowhere be a peasant, forming merely a caste, and that a low one, among his fellows. He would be an independent co-operating citizen partaking fully of the fruits of his labor, enjoying the social rewards of his essential position, being sustained and protected by a body of responsive public opinion. The farmer cannot keep the earth for us without an enlightened and very active support from every other person, and without adequate safeguards from exploitation and from unessential commercial pressure.

This social support requires a ready response on the part of the farmer; and he must also be developed into his position by a kind of training that will make him quickly and naturally responsive to it. The social fascination of the town will always be greater than that of the open country. The movements are more rapid, more picturesque, have more color and more vivacity. It is not to be expected that we can overcome this fascination and safeguard the country boy and girl merely by introducing more showy or active enterprises into the open country. We must develop a new background for the country youth, establish new standards, and arouse a new point of view. The farmer will not need all the things that the city man thinks the farmer needs. We must stimulate his moral response, his appreciation of the worthiness of the things in which he lives, and increase his knowledge of all the objects and affairs amongst which he moves. The backbone of the rural question is at the bottom of a moral problem.

We do not yet know whether the race can permanently endure urban life, or whether it must be constantly renewed from the vitalities in the rear. We know that the farms and the back spaces have been the mother of the race. We know that the exigencies and frugalities of life in these backgrounds beget men and women to be serious and steady and to know the value of every hour and of every coin that they earn; and whenever they are properly trained, these folk recognize the holiness of the earth.

For some years I have had the satisfaction to speak to rural folk in many places on the holy earth and to make some of the necessary applications. Everywhere I have met the heartiest assent from these people. Specially do they respond to the suggestion that if the earth is hallowed; so are the native products of the earth hallowed; and they like to have the mystery—which is the essential sentiment—of these things brought home to them with frequency. I will here let my reader have a letter that one of these persons wrote me, and I print it without change. On inquiry, the writer of it told me that he is a farmer, has never followed any other occupation, was brought up "in the woods," and has had practically no education. I did not ask him, but I judge from the narrative style that he has been a reader or a hearer of the Old Testament; and here is the letter:

As you say, too many people confound farming, with that sordid, selfish, money-getting game, called "business," whereas, the farmer's position is administrative, being in a way a dispenser of the "Mysteries of God," for they are mysteries. Every apple is a mystery, and every potato is a mystery, and every ear of corn is a mystery, and every pound of butter is a mystery, and when a "farmer" is not able to understand these things he is out of place.

The farmer uses the soil and the rains and the snows and the frosts and the winds and the sun; these are also the implements of the Almighty, the only tools He uses, and while you were talking that day, it brought to mind the recollection of an account I once read of an occurrence which took place in the vicinity of Carlsruhe, in Germany, about thirty years ago, and I want to tell you about it. An old man and his two sons, who were laborers on a large farm there, went out one morning to mow peas, with scythes, as was the method in use at that time, and soon after they began work, they noticed a large active man coming along a pathway which bordered the field on one side, and when he came to where they were, he spoke to them, very pleasantly, and asked them some questions about their work and taking the scythe from the hands of the older man he mowed some with it and finally returned it and went his way. After a time when the owner of the farm came out to oversee the work they told him of the occurrence, and asked him if he could tell who the stranger might be, and he told them that he was Prince Bismarck, the Chancellor of the empire, who was staying at his country home at Carlsruhe, and was out for his morning walk, and they were astonished, and the old man was filled with a great pride, and he felt himself elevated above all his fellows, and he wouldn't have sold his scythe for half the money in Germany, and his descendants to this day boast of the fact that their father and Bismarck mowed with the same scythe. Now if it was sufficient to stimulate the pride of this old laborer, if it was sufficient to create for him a private aristocracy, if it was sufficient to convert that old rusty scythe into a priceless heirloom to be treasured up and transmitted from father to son, if it was sufficient for all these things that he had once held a momentarily unimportant association with the man of "blood and iron," how much more inconceivably and immeasurably high and exalted is the station of the farmer who is, in a measure, a fellow craftsman of the God of Nature, of the great First Cause of all things, and people don't know it. No wonder the boys leave the farm!

Questions for Thinking and Writing

1. What leads Bailey to say that "a man cannot be a good farmer unless he is a religious man"?
2. Discuss Bailey's attitude toward farmers. Why does he appear to feel sorry for them and to chastise them at the same time?
3. Explain whether you agree or disagree with Bailey that farmers are the "agent of the divinity that made [the land]." If you agree, why do you, considering the fact that farmers use pesticides, chemical fertilizers, and questionable tilling practices? If you disagree, explain the old saying that farmers are "the salt of the earth."

🌿 Robert Frost (1874–1963)

A Brook in the City (1921)

It is most people's perception that Robert Frost was New England's native sage. Yet he was born in San Francisco, grew up in a California factory town, and got his first literary recognition in England. Frost's family life was tough. His father was an alcoholic journalist and an abusive man who died at age 34. His mother returned to her native Massachusetts with her son and taught school. Though young Frost did not like studying, he eventually enjoyed the Classics and Romantic poetry. At graduation he shared valedictorian honors with Elinor White, whom he married in 1895.

Frost was impatient with formal education. He attended Dartmouth but withdrew before graduating. Then he went to Harvard but dropped out, this time due to ill heath. Later in his life, though, he enjoyed great success as a teacher, particularly at Amherst College. In 1901, he moved with his family to a farm in Derry, New Hampshire, which his grandfather had purchased for them, and they were able to live on a small annuity he had provided. Frost had five children by this time. He divided his time between farming and writing.

Until 1912, Frost's success was meager. At this time, he moved his family to England, hoping for a better reception, and published his first collection, A Boy's Will, *a month after his arrival, and* North of Boston *in 1914. When Frost returned to the United States in 1915, he had a solid reputation, though he did not earn much income. Great success soon followed: He was named Phi Beta Kappa poet at both Harvard and Tufts; began teaching at Amherst; and received the first of what would become 44 honorary degrees. He received the first of four Pulitzer Prizes with the publication of* New Hampshire *in 1923, in which "A Brook in the City" and "Two Look at Two" appeared.*

Frost's final years were marked by extensive public recognition. Vermont named a mountain after him. He read "The Gift Outright" at John F. Kennedy's presidential inauguration. He was named consultant in poetry to the Library of Congress. At age 88, he made an official visit to the Soviet Union as a representative of the U.S. Information Administration.

When Frost died at 89, he was America's best known poet, craggy as New England's mountains and with something to say to everyone. Yet this image concealed another side which was not revealed until his biography was published in 1966—that of a man with such a need to control his life and environment that he was haunted by feelings of despair and fear.

Frost is a poet of the country. He poses as a rustic but he has the wit, intelligence, and learning of a sophisticate. His depictions of New England cycles of nature, landscape, and life are clear, accurate, and fairly realistic. His counterpart in American art is the painter Andrew Wyeth, whose realistic paintings of the Northeast suggest feelings of loneliness and joy. Frost uses nature and landscape metaphorically, carefully creating tension between opposites. For example, "A Brook in the City," written in 1921, contrasts the rural with the urban but also the levels of human consciousness.

The farmhouse lingers, though averse to square
With the new city street it has to wear
A number in. But what about the brook
That held the house as in an elbow-crook?
I ask as one who knew the brook, its strength
And impulse, having dipped a finger length

And made it leap my knuckle, having tossed
A flower to try its currents where they crossed.
The meadow grass could be cemented down
From growing under pavements of a town;
The apple trees be sent to hearthstone flame.
Is water wood to serve a brook the same?
How else dispose of an immortal force
No longer needed? Staunch it at its source
With cinder loads dumped down? The brook was thrown
Deep in a sewer dungeon under stone
In fetid darkness still to live and run—
And all for nothing it had ever done,
Except forget to go in fear perhaps.
No one would know except for ancient maps
That such a brook ran water. But I wonder
If from its being kept forever under,
The thoughts may not have risen that so keep
This new-built city from both work and sleep.

Questions for Thinking and Writing

1. What does this poem suggest about the clash of rural and urban development? What is the significance of the farmhouse's need to have a number?
   What happens to the meadow? What happens to the brook?
2. Explain the connection between the brook and human thought. What do
   you think is the significance of the buried brook? What is Frost's feeling
   about the implications of humans tampering with nature?

Robert Frost (1874–1963)

Two Look at Two (1923)

*Frost's life and literary success are detailed in the headnote for "A
Brook in the City," page 123. "Two Look at Two" was written in 1921
and published in* New Hampshire *(1923).*

Love and forgetting might have carried them
A little further up the mountainside
With night so near, but not much further up.
They must have halted soon in any case
With thoughts of the path back, how rough it was

With rock and washout, and unsafe in darkness;
When they were halted by a tumbled wall
With barbed-wire binding. They stood facing this,
Spending what onward impulse they still had
In one last look the way they must not go,
On up the failing path, where, if a stone
Or earthslide moved at night, it moved itself;
No footstep moved it. "This is all," they sighed,
"Good-night to woods." But not so; there was more.
A doe from round a spruce stood looking at them
Across the wall, as near the wall as they.
She saw them in their field, they her in hers.
The difficulty of seeing what stood still,
Like some up-ended boulder split in two,
Was in her clouded eyes: they saw no fear there.
She seemed to think that, two thus, they were safe.
Then, as if they were something that, though strange,
She could not trouble her mind with too long,
She sighed and passed unscared along the wall,
"*This*, then, is all. What more is there to ask?"
But no, not yet. A snort to bid them wait.
A buck from round the spruce stood looking at them
Across the wall, as near the wall as they.
This was an antlered buck of lusty nostril,
Not the same doe come back into her place.
He viewed them quizzically with jerks of head,
As if to ask, "Why don't you make some motion?
Or give some sign of life? Because you can't.
I doubt if you're as living as you look."
Thus till he had them almost feeling dared
To stretch a proffering hand—and a spell-breaking.
Then he too passed unscared along the wall.
Two had seen two, whichever side you spoke from.
"This *must* be all." It was all. Still they stood,
A great wave from it going over them,
As if the earth in one unlooked-for favor
Had made them certain earth returned their love.

Questions for Thinking and Writing

1. What do you think is Frost's purpose for presenting the parallel of two humans meeting two deer in the forest? How does Frost avoid humanizing this situation?

2. In whose domain do the man and woman meet the doe and buck? What do you think accounts for the peculiarity that none of the quartet feels fear?

❧ Wallace Stevens (1879–1955)

Anecdote of the Jar (1923)

Wallace Stevens's early poems, which include "Anecdote of the Jar" (1923) are noted for their physical sensuousness, use of color, and celebration of the natural world, whereas his later ones tend toward an intellectuality. This change has much to do with the design of his life.

He was born in Reading, Pennsylvania, into a well-to-do religious family and attended Lutheran schools. Later at Harvard, he lost his belief in God. Some critics maintain that much of his poetry is an attempt to come to terms with agnosticism. While at Harvard, Stevens began his writing career with poems, stories, and essays published in the Harvard Advocate.

In 1900, Stevens left Harvard after three years without graduating, intending to go to law school. Instead, he changed his mind and decided he wanted to become a journalist in New York City. Once there, he found that reporting was ultimately dissatisfying. His father, a lawyer, directed him to enroll at New York University Law School, and Stevens obeyed, graduating in 1903. From that point he conducted two careers—one as a poet, the other as a lawyer. He worked at several New York law firms, and he remained for a number of years with the American Bonding Company. Eventually, he became vice president of the Hartford Accident and Indemnity Company and remained there until his death.

During his early days as a lawyer, Stevens made himself familiar with artists and writers in Greenwich Village, among them William Carlos Williams. In 1923, his first volume of poetry, Harmonium, *was published. After his daughter was born the following year, he decided to stop writing poetry, and he did not take it up again until 1930. A second volume of poetry was published in 1935, followed by many more. His Collected Works was awarded the Pulitzer Prize for poetry in 1955. Sadly, he died of cancer before he could accept the award. On his deathbed, he converted to Roman Catholicism.*

Stevens was always intrigued with the conflict of matter and spirit. "Anecdote of the Jar" is a kind of landscape painting showing the struggle between wilderness and civilization, even though that civilization is merely an insignificant jar. The defeat of the landscape, no longer wild, is commensurate with the loss of poetry, which signifies a loss of the human spirit. The poem is from Harmonium, *Stevens's first volume of poems. A harmonium is a small reed organ, and the name suggests harmony, something that is not evident in "Anecdote of the Jar."*

I placed a jar in Tennessee,
And round it was, upon a hill.
It made the slovenly wilderness
Surround that hill.

The wilderness rose up to it,
And sprawled around, no longer wild.
The jar was round upon the ground
And tall and of a port in air.

It took dominion everywhere.
The jar was gray and bare.
It did not give of bird or bush,
Like nothing else in Tennessee.

Questions for Thinking and Writing

1. Explain the metaphor in the poem. What is Stevens implying by saying that even an object as simple as a jar can drastically change the organic unity of the landscape?
2. Explain the phrase "slovenly wilderness." Discuss whether or not wilderness can be slovenly. How does this turn of phrase indicate a profound moral argument about the human relationship to landscape?

🌸 Ernest Hemingway

Big Two-Hearted River, Part I (1925)

"Big Two-Hearted River" is set in upper Michigan, where Ernest Hemingway spent his boyhood summers at the family cottage. Here his physician father taught him to fish and hunt and instilled in him a passion for these two sports, which he used so frequently as a background in his writing.

Hemingway never went to college. He went directly from high school to a job as a cub reporter for the Kansas City Star. *When World War I broke out, he tried to enlist, but an eye ailment prevented him. Anxious to participate in the war, he volunteered as an ambulance driver. In northern Italy, he was badly wounded and sent to the Red Cross Hospital in Milan, where he became something of a hero with the nurses.*

In 1919, Hemingway returned from Europe and immediately went to upper Michigan for further recuperation, noting with some anguish that as he limped off the train at Seney, a conductor referred to him as a "cripple." He also wrote for the Toronto Star *during this period. Two years later, he sailed for Paris in hopes of improving his journalism and fiction-writing techniques there. Paris at that time was full of what Gertrude Stein called "the lost generation"—expatriate American writers and artists—F. Scott Fitzgerald, Ezra Pound, and Sherwood Anderson among them. It was here during the early 1920s that Hemingway wrote "Big Two-Hearted River" (1925). This story and others were quickly accepted, and with the publication in 1926 of* The Sun Also Rises, *Hemingway was recognized by critics and the public as a writer possessing a unique voice and powerful ability to convey character.*

Publication over the next few years of Men Without Women *and* A Farewell to Arms *further established him as a writer with the courage to tackle sensitive and emotional issues. His popularity quickly waned during the 1930s, however. Critics said he had lost his novelty. Though he continued to write excellent short stories, it was not until 1954, with the publication of* The Old Man and the Sea, *that critics once again heaped praise on him.*

The subjects of his writing—blood sports, hunting, war, and sexuality—suggested an inner turmoil that boiled not far beneath Hemingway's charm and dashing romanticism. He was married four times, and he was an extravagant womanizer. Hemingway seemed obsessed with war, and though obviously too old, he desperately wanted to enlist during World War II. Instead, he served as a war correspondent. In 1961, in a deepening depression, he committed suicide by shooting himself in the head with a shotgun. The act was symbolic, for his father had committed suicide in the same way when Hemingway was verging on adolescence.

The character of Nick Adams appears in the stories collected in Our Time *(1925),* Men Without Women *(1927), and* Winner Take Nothing *(1930). The title of "Big Two-Hearted River" is obviously symbolic. Nick Adams, the only character, must overcome his traumatic war experiences, and this trip across the desolate landscape to the river marks the start of a process of restoration. Nick's immersion in the river is a kind of baptism. The river will not change, but Nick will. Hemingway confided to his friends, including F. Scott Fitzgerald, that he did not mean for this to be a mere fishing tale.*

The train went on up the track out of sight, around one of the hills of burnt timber. Nick sat down on the bundle of canvas and bedding the baggage man had pitched out of the door of the baggage car. There was no town, nothing but the rails and the burned-over country. The thirteen saloons that had lined the one street of Seney had not left a trace. The foundations of the Mansion House hotel stuck up above the ground. The stone was chipped and split by the fire. It was all that was left of the town of Seney. Even the surface had been burned off the ground.

Nick looked at the burned-over stretch of hillside, where he had expected to find the scattered houses of the town and then walked down the railroad track to the bridge over the river. The river was there. It swirled against the log spiles of the bridge. Nick looked down into the clear, brown water, colored from the pebbly bottom, and watched the trout keeping themselves steady in the current with wavering fins. As he watched them they changed their positions by quick angles, only to hold steady in the fast water again. Nick watched them a long time.

He watched them holding themselves with their noses into the current, many trout in deep, fast moving water, slightly distorted as he watched far down through the glassy convex surface of the pool, its surface pushing and swelling smooth against the resistance of the log-driven piles of the bridge. At the bottom of the pool were the big trout. Nick did not see them at first. Then he saw them at the bottom of the pool, big trout looking to hold themselves on the gravel bottom in a varying mist of gravel and sand, raised in spurts by the current.

Nick looked down into the pool from the bridge. It was a hot day. A kingfisher flew up the stream. It was a long time since Nick had looked into a stream and seen trout. They were very satisfactory. As the shadow of the kingfisher moved up the stream, a big trout shot upstream in a long angle, only his shadow marking the angle, then lost his shadow as he came through the surface of the water, caught the sun, and then, as he went back into the stream under the surface, his shadow seemed to float down the stream with the current, unresisting, to his post under the bridge where he tightened facing up into the current.

Nick's heart tightened as the trout moved. He felt all the old feeling.

He turned and looked down the stream. It stretched away, pebbly-bottomed with shallows and big boulders and a deep pool as it curved away around the foot of a bluff.

Nick walked back up the ties to where his pack lay in the cinders beside the railway track. He was happy. He adjusted the pack harness around the bundle, pulling straps tight, slung the pack on his back, got his arms through the shoulder straps and took some of the pull off his shoulders by leaning his forehead against the wide band of the tump-line. Still, it was too heavy. It was much too heavy. He had his leather rod-case in his hand and leaning forward to keep the weight of the pack high on his shoulders he walked along the road that paralleled the railway track, leaving the burned town behind in the heat, and then turned off around a hill with a high, fire-scarred hill on either side onto a road that went back into the country. He walked along the road feeling the ache from the pull of the heavy pack. The road climbed steadily. It was hard work walking up-hill. His muscles ached and the day was hot, but Nick felt happy. He felt he had left everything behind, the need for thinking, the need to write, other needs. It was all back of him.

From the time he had gotten down off the train and the baggage man had thrown his pack out of the open car door things had been different. Seney was burned, the country was burned over and changed, but it did not matter. It could not all be burned. He knew that. He hiked along the road, sweating in the sun, climbing to cross the range of hills that separated the railway from the pine plains.

The road ran on, dipping occasionally, but always climbing. Nick went on up. Finally the road after going parallel to the burnt hillside reached the top. Nick leaned back against a stump and slipped out of the pack harness. Ahead of him, as far as he could see, was the pine plain. The burned country stopped off at the left with the range of hills. On ahead islands of dark pine trees rose out of the plain. Far off to the left was the line of the river. Nick followed it with his eye and caught glints of the water in the sun.

There was nothing but the pine plain ahead of him, until the far blue hills that marked the Lake Superior height of land. He could hardly see them, faint and far away in the heat-light over the plain. If he looked too steadily they were gone. But if he only half-looked they were there, the far-off hills of the height of land.

Nick sat down against the charred stump and smoked a cigarette. His pack balanced on the top of the stump, harness holding ready, a hollow molded in it from his back. Nick sat smoking, looking out over the country. He did not need to get his map out. He knew where he was from the position of the river.

As he smoked, his legs stretched out in front of him, he noticed a grasshopper walk along the ground and up onto his woolen sock. The grasshopper was black. As he had walked along the road, climbing, he had started many grasshoppers from the dust. They were all black. They were not the big grasshoppers with yellow and black or red and black wings whirring out from their black wing sheathing as they fly up. These were just ordinary hoppers, but all a sooty black in color. Nick had wondered about them as he walked, without really thinking about them. Now, as he watched the black hopper that was nibbling at the wool of his sock with its fourway lip, he realized that they had all turned black from living in the burned-over land. He realized that the fire must have come the year before, but the grasshoppers were all black now. He wondered how long they would stay that way.

Carefully he reached his hand down and took hold of the hopper by the wings. He turned him up, all his legs walking in the air, and looked at his jointed belly. Yes, it was black too, iridescent where the back and head were dusty.

"Go on, hopper," Nick said, speaking out loud for the first time. "Fly away somewhere."

He tossed the grasshopper up into the air and watched him sail away to a charcoal stump across the road.

Nick stood up. He leaned his back against the weight of his pack where it rested upright on the stump and got his arms through the shoulder straps. He stood with the pack on his back on the brow of the hill looking out across the country toward the distant river and then struck down the hillside away from the road. Underfoot the ground was good walking. Two hundred yards down the hillside the fire line stopped. Then it was sweet fern, growing ankle high, to walk through, and clumps of jack pines; a long undulating country with frequent rises and descents, sandy underfoot and the country alive again.

Nick kept his direction by the sun. He knew where he wanted to strike the river and he kept on through the pine plain, mounting small rises to see other rises ahead of him and sometimes from the top of a rise a great solid island of pines off to his right or his left. He broke off some sprigs of the heathery sweet fern, and put them under his pack straps. The chafing crushed it and he smelled it as he walked.

He was tired and very hot, walking across the uneven, shadeless pine plain. At any time he knew he could strike the river by turning off to his left. It could not be more than a mile away. But he kept on toward the north to hit the river as far upstream as he could go in one days's walking.

For some time as he walked Nick had been in sight of one of the big islands of pine standing out above the rolling high ground he was crossing. He dipped down and then as he came slowly up to the crest of the bridge he turned and made toward the pine trees.

There was no underbrush in the island of pine trees. The trunks of the trees went straight up or slanted toward each other. The trunks were straight and brown without branches. The branches were high above. Some interlocked to make a solid shadow on the brown forest floor. Around the grove of trees was a bare space. It was brown and soft underfoot as Nick walked on it. This was the over-lapping of the pine needle floor, extending out beyond the width of the high branches. The trees had grown tall and the branches moved high, leaving in the sun this bare space they had once covered with shadow. Sharp at the edge of this extension of the forest floor commenced the sweet fern.

Nick slipped off his pack and lay down in the shade. He lay on his back and looked up into the pine trees. His neck and back and the small of his back rested as he stretched. The earth felt good against his back. He looked up at the sky, through the branches, and then shut his eyes. He opened them and looked up again. There was a wind high up in the branches. He shut his eyes again and went to sleep.

Nick woke stiff and cramped. The sun was nearly down. His pack was heavy and the straps painful as he lifted it on. He leaned over with the pack on and picked up the leather rod-case and started out from the pine trees across the sweet fern swale, toward the river. He knew it could not be more than a mile.

He came down a hillside covered with stumps into a meadow. At the edge of the meadow flowed the river. Nick was glad to get to the river. He walked upstream through the meadow. His trousers were soaked with the dew as he walked. After the hot day, the dew had come quickly and heavily. The river made no sound. It was too fast and smooth. At the edge of the meadow, before he mounted to a piece of high ground to make camp, Nick looked down the river at the trout rising. They were rising to insects come from the swamp on the other side of the stream when the sun went down. The trout jumped out of water to take them. While Nick walked through the little stretch of meadow alongside the stream, trout had jumped high out of water. Now as he looked down the river, the insects must be settling on the surface, for the trout were feeding steadily all down the stream. As far down the long stretch as he could see, the trout were rising, making circles all down the surface of the water, as though it were starting to rain.

The ground rose, wooded and sandy, to overlook the meadow, the stretch of river and the swamp. Nick dropped his pack and rod-case and looked for a level piece of ground. He was very hungry and he wanted to make his camp before he cooked. Between two jack pines, the ground was quite level. He took the ax out of the pack and chopped out two projecting roots. That leveled a piece of ground large enough to sleep on. He smoothed out the sandy soil with his hand and pulled all the sweet fern bushes by their roots. His hands smelled good from the sweet fern. He smoothed the uprooted earth. He did not want anything making lumps under the blankets. When he had the ground smooth, he spread his three blankets. One he folded double, next to the ground. The other two he spread on top.

With the ax he slit off a bright slab of pine from one of the stumps and split it into pegs for the tent. He wanted them long and solid to hold in the ground. With the tent unpacked and spread on the ground, the pack, leaning against a jackpine, looked much smaller. Nick tied the rope that served the tent for a ridge-pole to the trunk of one of the pine trees and pulled the tent up off the ground with the other end of the rope and tied it to the other pine. The tent hung on the rope like a canvas blanket on a clothesline. Nick poked a pole he had cut up under the back peak of the canvas and then made it a tent by pegging out the sides. He pegged the sides out taut and drove the pegs deep, hitting them down into the ground with the flat of the ax until the rope loops were buried and the canvas was drum tight.

Across the open mouth of the tent Nick fixed cheesecloth to keep out mosquitoes. He crawled inside under the mosquito bar with various things from the pack to put at the head of the bed under the slant of the canvas. Inside the tent the light came through the brown canvas. It smelled pleasantly of canvas. Already there was something mysterious and homelike. Nick was happy as he crawled inside the tent. He had not been unhappy all day. This was different though. Now things were done. There had been this to do. Now it was done. It had been a hard trip. He was very tired. That was done. He had made his camp. He was settled. Nothing could touch him. It was a good place to camp. He was there, in the good place. He was in his home where he had made it. Now he was hungry.

He came out, crawling under the cheesecloth. It was quite dark outside. It was lighter in the tent.

Nick went over to the pack and found, with his fingers, a long nail in a paper sack of nails, in the bottom of the pack. He drove it into the pine tree, holding it close and hitting it gently with the flat of the ax. He hung the pack up on the nail. All his supplies were in the pack. They were off the ground and sheltered now.

Nick was hungry. He did not believe he had ever been hungrier. He opened and emptied a can of pork and beans and a can of spaghetti into the frying pan.

"I've got a right to eat this stuff, if I'm willing to carry it," Nick said. His voice sounded strange in the darkening woods. He did not speak again.

He started a fire with some chunks of pine he got with the ax from a stump. Over the fire he stuck a wire grill, pushing the four legs down into the ground with his boot. Nick put the frying pan on the grill over the flames. He was hungrier. The beans and spaghetti warmed. Nick stirred them and mixed them together. They began to bubble, making little bubbles that rose with difficulty to the surface. There was a good smell. Nick got out a bottle of tomato catchup and cut four slices of bread. The little bubbles were coming faster now. Nick sat down beside the fire and lifted the frying pan off. He poured about half the contents out into the tin plate. It spread slowly on the plate. Nick knew it was too hot. He poured on some tomato catchup. He knew the beans and spaghetti were still too hot. He looked at the fire, then at the tent, he was not going to spoil it all by burning his tongue. For years he had never enjoyed fried bananas because he had never been able to wait for them to cool. His tongue was very sensitive. He was very hungry. Across the river in the swamp, in the almost dark, he saw a mist rising. He looked at the tent once more. All right. He took a full spoonful from the plate.

"Chrise," Nick said, "Geezus Chrise," he said happily.

He ate the whole plateful before he remembered the bread. Nick finished the second plateful with the bread, mopping the plate shiny. He had not eaten since a cup of coffee and a ham sandwich in the station restaurant at St. Ignace. It had been a very fine experience. He had been that hungry before, but had not been able to satisfy it. He could have made camp hours before if he had wanted to. There were plenty of good places to camp on the river. But this was good.

Nick tucked two big chips of pine under the grill. The fire flared up. He had forgotten to get water for the coffee. Out of the pack he got a folding canvas bucket and walked down the hill, across the edge of the meadow, to the stream. The other bank was in the white mist. The grass was wet and cold as he knelt on the bank and dipped the canvas bucket into the stream. It bellied and pulled hard in the current. The water was ice cold. Nick rinsed the bucket and carried it full up to the camp. Up away from the stream it was not so cold.

Nick drove another big nail and hung up the bucket full of water. He dipped the coffee pot half full, put some more chips under the grill onto the fire and put the pot on. He could not remember which way he made coffee. He could remember an argument about it with Hopkins, but not which side he had taken. He decided to bring it to a boil. He remembered now that was Hopkins's way. He had once argued about everything with Hopkins. While he waited for the coffee to boil, he opened a small can of apricots. He liked to open cans. He emptied the can of apricots out into a tin cup. While he watched the coffee on the fire, he drank the juice syrup of the apricots, carefully at first to keep from spilling, then meditatively, sucking the apricots down. They were better than fresh apricots.

The coffee boiled as he watched. The lid came up and coffee and grounds ran down the side of the pot. Nick took it off the grill. It was a triumph for Hopkins. He put sugar in the empty apricot cup and poured some of the coffee out to cool. It was too hot to pour and he used his hat to hold the handle of the coffee pot. He would not let it steep in the pot at all. Not the first cup. It should be straight Hopkins all the way. Hop deserved that. He was a very serious coffee drinker. He was the most serious man Nick had ever known. Not heavy, serious. That was a long time ago. Hopkins spoke without moving his lips. He had played polo. He made millions of dollars in Texas. He had borrowed carfare to go to Chicago, when the wire came that his first big well had come in. He could have wired for money. That would have been too slow. They called Hop's girl the Blonde Venus. Hop did not mind because she was not his real girl. Hopkins said very confidently that none of them would make fun of his real girl. He was right. Hopkins went away when the telegram came. That was on the Black River. It took eight days for the telegram to reach him. Hopkins gave away his .22 caliber Colt automatic pistol to Nick. He gave his camera to Bill. It was to remember him always by. They were all going fishing again next summer. The Hop Head was rich. He would get a yacht and they would all cruise along the north shore of Lake Superior. He was excited but serious. They said good-bye and all felt bad. It broke up the trip. They never saw Hopkins again. That was a long time ago on the Black River.

Nick drank the coffee, the coffee according to Hopkins. The coffee was bitter. Nick laughed. It made a good ending to the story. His mind was starting to work. He knew he could choke it because he was tired enough. He spilled the coffee out of the pot and shook the grounds loose into the fire. He lit a cigarette and went inside the tent. He took off his shoes and trousers, sitting on the blankets, rolled the shoes up inside the trousers for a pillow and got in between the blankets.

Out through the front of the tent he watched the glow of the fire, when the night wind blew on it. It was a quiet night. The swamp was perfectly quiet. Nick stretched under the blanket comfortably. A mosquito hummed close to his ear. Nick sat up and lit a match. The mosquito was on the canvas, over his head. Nick moved the match quickly up to it. The mosquito made a satisfactory hiss in the flame. The match went out. Nick lay down again under the blanket. He turned on his side and shut his eyes. He was sleepy. He felt sleep coming. He curled up under the blanket and went to sleep.

Questions for Thinking and Writing

1. What is the significance of the burned-out landscape and Nick Adams's state of mind? Why does Nick walk so far to get his campsite on the river? How would you judge Nick's woodlore and ability in the outdoors?
2. Discuss the various aspects of fire in this story. For example, contrast the deadened landscape at Seney with the verdant landscape upriver. What is so important about the deliberateness with which Nick makes his campfire?
3. Explain in what ways this story transcends a mere fishing tale.

❧ Henry Beston (1888–1968)

Night on the Great Beach (1928)

Asked why his book The Outermost House *(1928) continued to be a success, Henry Beston answered shortly before his death, "People see it's a kind of impossible world and they have to have something else. I wish people would get on more peaceably."*

In the book itself, he wrote, "The world today is sick to its thin blood for lack of elemental things, for fire before the hands, for water welling from the earth, for air, for the dear earth itself underfoot."

In these two quotes lies much of Beston's reverence for life that he claims we miss mostly because we are not paying attention. The excerpt here exclaims over the beauty of the night sky and questions our fear of such beauty. One of the reasons why Beston lived alone for a year on the beach was to give himself an opportunity to drink in nature. He said that one thing he learned after the year was "a sense that creation is still going on, that the creative forces are as great and as active today as they have ever been and that tomorrow's morning will be as heroic as any of the world."

The book came about almost accidentally. Beston planned to stay in the little house on the Cape Cod beach for only two weeks. At the end of that time, he found himself so possessed by the natural beauty there that he decided to remain. Beston donated the house to the National Audubon Society in 1964. It is now a national historical site.

Beston was born in Quincy, Massachusetts, the son of a physician. After graduating from Harvard College, he became a teacher. He served in both the army and navy during World War I. Following The Outermost House, *Beston published nine other books on nature, but none of them received the acclaim of the first. His year-long experience has often been compared to Thoreau's time by Walden Pond, but Beston disagreed. "I admire Thoreau," he told an interviewer, "but don't care much for him. He wasn't warm enough."*

Beston's denial is understandable: It is very difficult to withstand the comparison to a writer of genius.

I

Our fantastic civilization has fallen out of touch with many aspects of nature, and with none more completely than with night. Primitive folk, gathered at a cave mouth round a fire, do not fear night; they fear, rather, the energies and creatures to whom night gives power; we of the age of the machines, having delivered ourselves of nocturnal enemies, now have a dislike of night itself. With lights and ever more lights, we drive the holiness and beauty of night back to the forests and the sea; the little villages, the crossroads even, will have none of it. Are modern folk, perhaps, afraid of night? Do they fear that vast serenity, the mystery of infinite space, the austerity of stars? Having made themselves at home in a civilization obsessed with power, which explains its whole world in terms of energy, do they fear at night for their dull acquiescence and the pattern of their beliefs? Be the answer what it will, to-day's civilization is full of people who have not the slightest notion of the character or the poetry of night, who have never even seen night. Yet to live thus, to know only artificial night, is as absurd and evil as to know only artificial day.

Night is very beautiful on this great beach. It is the true other half of the day's tremendous wheel; no lights without meaning stab or trouble it; it is beauty, it is fulfilment, it is rest. Thin clouds float in these heavens, islands of obscurity in a splendour of space and stars: the Milky Way bridges earth and ocean; the beach resolves itself into a unity of form, its summer lagoons, its slopes and uplands merging; against the western sky and the falling bow of sun rise the silent and superb undulations of the dunes.

My nights are at their darkest when a dense fog streams in from the sea under a black, unbroken floor of cloud. Such nights are rare, but are most to be expected when fog gathers off the coast in early summer; this last Wednesday night was the darkest I have known. Between ten o'clock and two in the morning three vessels stranded on the outer beach—a fisherman, a four-masted schooner, and a beam trawler. The fisherman and the schooner have been towed off, but the trawler, they say, is still ashore.

I went down to the beach that night just after ten o'clock. So utterly black, pitch dark it was, and so thick with moisture and trailing showers, that there was no sign whatever of the beam of Nauset; the sea was only a sound, and when I reached the edge of the surf the dunes themselves had disappeared behind. I stood as isolate in that immensity of rain and night as I might have stood in interplanetary space. The sea was troubled and noisy, and when I opened the darkness with an outlined cone of light from my electric torch I saw that the waves were washing up green coils of sea grass, all coldly wet and bright in the motionless and unnatural radiance. Far off a single ship was groaning its way along the shoals. The fog was compact of the finest moisture; passing by, it spun itself into my lens of light like a kind of strange, aërial, and liquid silk. Effin Chalke, the new coast guard, passed me going north, and told me that he had had news at the halfway house of the schooner at Cahoon's.

It was dark, pitch dark to my eye, yet complete darkness, I imagine, is exceedingly rare, perhaps unknown in outer nature. The nearest natural approximation to it is probably the gloom of forest country buried in night and cloud. Dark as the night was here, there was still light on the surface of the planet. Standing on the shelving beach, with the surf breaking at my feet, I could see the endless wild uprush, slide, and withdrawal of the sea's white rim of foam. The men at Nauset tell me that on such nights they follow along this vague crawl of whiteness, trusting to habit and a sixth sense to warn them of their approach to the halfway house.

Animals descend by starlight to the beach. North, beyond the dunes, muskrats forsake the cliff and nose about in the driftwood and weed, leaving intricate trails and figure eights to be obliterated by the day; the lesser folk—the mice, the occasional small sand-coloured toads, the burrowing moles—keep to the upper beach and leave their tiny footprints under the overhanging wall. In autumn skunks, beset by a shrinking larder, go beach combing early in the night. The animal is by preference a clean feeder and turns up his nose at rankness. I almost stepped on a big fellow one night as I was walking north to meet the first man south from Nauset. There was a scamper, and the creature ran up the beach from under my feet; alarmed he certainly was, yet was he contained and continent. Deer are frequently seen, especially north of the light. I find their tracks upon the summer dunes.

Years ago, while camping on this beach north of Nauset, I went for a stroll along the top of the cliff at break of dawn. Though the path followed close enough along the edge, the beach below was often hidden, and I looked directly from the height to the flush of sunrise at sea. Presently the path, turning, approached the brink of the earth precipice, and on the beach below, in the cool, wet rosiness of dawn, I saw three deer playing. They frolicked, rose on their hind legs, scampered off, and returned again, and were merry. Just before sunrise they trotted off north together down the beach toward a hollow in the cliff and the path that climbs it.

Occasionally a sea creature visits the shore at night. Lone coast guardsmen, trudging the sand at some deserted hour, have been startled by seals. One man fell flat on a creature's back, and it drew away from under him, flippering toward the sea, with a sound "halfway between a squeal and a bark." I myself once had rather a start. It was long after sundown, the light dying and uncertain, and I was walking home on the top level of the beach and close along the slope descending to the ebbing tide. A little more than halfway to the Fo'castle a huge unexpected something suddenly writhed horribly in the darkness under my bare foot. I had stepped on a skate left stranded by some recent crest of surf, and my weight had momentarily annoyed it back to life.

Facing north, the beam of Nauset becomes part of the dune night. As I walk toward it, I see the lantern, now as a star of light which waxes and wanes three mathematic times, now as a lovely pale flare of light behind the rounded summits of the dunes. The changes in the atmosphere change the colour of the beam; it is now whitish, now flame golden, now golden red; it changes its form as well, from a star to a blare of light, from a blare of light to a cone of radiance sweeping a circumference of fog. To the west of Nauset I often see the apocalyptic flash of the great light at the Highland reflected on the clouds or even on the moisture in the starlit air, and, seeing it, I often think of the pleasant hours I have spent there when George and Mary Smith were at the light and I had the good fortune to visit as their guest. Instead of going to sleep in the room under the eaves, I would lie awake, looking out of a window to the great spokes of light revolving as solemnly as a part of the universe.

All night long the lights of coastwise vessels pass at sea, green lights going south, red lights moving north. Fishing schooners and flounder draggers anchor two or three miles out, and keep a bright riding light burning on the mast. I see them come to anchor at sundown, but I rarely see them go, for they are off at dawn. When busy at night, these fishermen illumine their decks with a scatter of oil flares. From shore, the ships might be thought afire. I have watched the scene through a night glass. I could see no smoke, only the waving flares, the reddish radiance on sail and rigging, an edge of reflection overside, and the enormous night and sea beyond.

One July night, as I returned at three o'clock from an expedition north, the whole night, in one strange, burning instant, turned into a phantom day. I stopped and, questioning, stared about. An enormous meteor, the largest I have ever seen, was consuming itself in an effulgence of light west of the zenith. Beach and dune and ocean appeared out of nothing, shadowless and motionless, a landscape whose every tremor and vibration were stilled, a landscape in a dream.

The beach at night has a voice all its own, a sound in fullest harmony with its spirit and mood—with its little, dry noise of sand forever moving, with its solemn, overspilling, rhythmic seas, with its eternity of stars that sometimes seem to hang down like lamps from the high heavens— and that sound the piping of a bird. As I walk the beach in early summer my solitary coming disturbs it on its nest, and it flies away, troubled, invisible, piping its sweet, plaintive cry. The bird I write of is the piping plover, *Charadrius melodus,* sometimes called the beach plover or the mourning bird. Its note is a whistled syllable, the loveliest musical note, I think, sounded by any North Atlantic bird.

Now that summer is here I often cook myself a camp supper on the beach. Beyond the crackling, salt-yellow driftwood flame, over the pyramid of barrel staves, broken boards, and old sticks all atwist with climbing fire, the unseen ocean thunders and booms, the breaker sounding hollow as it falls. The wall of the sand cliff behind, with its rim of grass and withering roots, its sandy crumblings and erosions, stands gilded with flame; wind cries over it; a covey of sandpipers pass between the ocean and the fire. There are stars, and to the south Scorpio hangs curving down the sky with ringed Saturn shining in his claw.

Learn to reverence night and to put away the vulgar fear of it, for, with the banishment of night from the experience of man, there vanishes as well a religious emotion, a poetic mood, which gives depth to the adventure of humanity. By day, space is one with the earth and with man— it is his sun that is shining, his clouds that are floating past; at night, space is his no more. When the great earth, abandoning day, rolls up the deeps of the heavens and the universe, a new door opens for the human spirit, and there are few so clownish that some awareness of the mystery of being does not touch them as they gaze. For a moment of night we have a glimpse of ourselves and of our world islanded in its stream of stars—pilgrims of mortality, voyaging between horizons across eternal seas of space and time. Fugitive though the instant be, the spirit of man is, during it, ennobled by a genuine moment of emotional dignity, and poetry makes its own both the human spirit and experience. . . .

III

All winter long I slept on a couch in my larger room, but with the coming of warm weather I have put my bedroom in order—I used it as a kind of storage space during the cold season—and returned to my old and rather rusty iron cot. Every once in a while, however, moved by some obscure mood, I lift off the bedclothing and make up the couch again for a few nights. I like the seven windows of the larger room, and the sense one may have there of being almost out-of-doors. My couch stands alongside the two front windows, and from my pillow I can look out to sea and watch the passing lights, the stars rising over ocean, the swaying lanterns of the anchored fishermen, and the white spill of the surf whose long sound fills the quiet of the dunes.

Ever since my coming I have wanted to see a thunderstorm bear down upon this elemental coast. A thunderstorm is a "tempest" on the Cape. The quoted word, as Shakespeare used it, means lightning and thunder, and it is in this old and beautiful Elizabethan sense that the word is used in Eastham. When a schoolboy in the Orleans or the Wellfleet High reads the Shakespearean play, its title means to him exactly what it meant to the man from Stratford; elsewhere in America, the terms seems to mean anything from a tornado to a blizzard. I imagine that this old significance of the word is now to be found only in certain parts of England and Cape Cod.

On the night of the June tempest, I was sleeping in my larger room, the windows were open, and the first low roll of thunder opened my eyes. It had been very still when I went to bed, but now a wind from the west-nor'west was blowing through the windows in a strong and steady current, and as I closed them there was lightning to the west and far away. I looked at my watch; it was just after one o'clock. Then came a time of waiting in the darkness, long minutes broken by more thunder, and intervals of quiet in which I heard a faintest sound of light surf upon the beach. Suddenly the heavens cracked open in an immense instant of pinkish-violet lightning. My seven windows filled with the violent, inhuman light, and I had a glimpse of the great, solitary dunes staringly empty of familiar shadows; a tremendous crash then mingled with the withdrawal of the light, and echoes of thunder rumbled away and grew faint in a returning rush of darkness. A moment after, rain began to fall gently as if someone had just released its flow, a blessed sound on a roof of wooden shingles, and one I have loved ever since I was a child. From a gentle patter the sound of the rain grew swiftly to a drumming roar, and with the rain came the chuckling of water from the eaves. The tempest was crossing the Cape, striking at the ancient land on its way to the heavens above the sea.

Now came flash after stabbing flash amid a roaring of rain, and heavy thunder that rolled on till its last echoes were swallowed up in vast detonations which jarred the walls. Houses were struck that night in Eastham village. My lonely world, full of lightning and rain, was strange to look upon. I do not share the usual fear of lightning, but that night there came over me, for the first and last time of all my solitary year, a sense of isolation and remoteness from my kind. I remember that I stood up, watching, in the middle of the room. On the great marshes the lightning surfaced the winding channels with a metallic splendour and arrest of motion, all very strange through windows blurred by rain. Under the violences of light the great dunes took on a kind of elemental passivity, the quiet of earth enchanted into stone, and as I watched them appear and plunge back into a darkness that had an intensity of its own I felt, as never before, a sense of the vast time, of the thousands of cyclic and uncounted years which had passed since these giants had risen from the dark ocean at their feet and given themselves to the wind and the bright day.

Fantastic things were visible at sea. Beaten down by the rain, and sheltered by the Cape itself from the river of west wind, the offshore brim of ocean remained unusually calm. The tide was about halfway up the beach, and rising, and long parallels of low waves, forming close inshore, were curling over and breaking placidly along the lonely, rain-drenched miles. The intense crackling flares and quiverings of the storm, moving out to sea, illumined every inch of the beach and the plain of the Atlantic, all save the hollow bellies of the little breakers, which were shielded from the light by their overcurling crests. The effect was dramatic and strangely beautiful, for what one saw was a bright ocean rimmed with parallel bands of blackest advancing darkness, each one melting back to light as the wave toppled down upon the beach in foam.

Stars came out after the storm, and when I woke again before sunrise I found the heavens and the earth rainwashed, cool, and clear. Saturn and the Scorpion were setting, but Jupiter was riding the zenith and paling on his throne. The tide was low in the marsh channels; the gulls had scarcely stirred upon their gravel banks and bars. Suddenly, thus wandering about, I disturbed a song sparrow on her nest. She flew to the roof of my house, grasped the ridgepole, and turned about, apprehensive, inquiring . . . *'tsi ped* her monosyllable of alarm. Then back toward her nest she flew, alighted in a plum bush, and, reassured at last, trilled out a morning song.

Questions for Thinking and Writing

1. The world of night that Beston presents is teeming with human and animal life. What moral does he derive from this? To what extent does he take a local experience and transform it to something universal?
2. Have you ever walked on a beach at night? What sensations did you feel? From your own experience, what makes walking or swimming at night an unusual experience?
3. Would you walk during the night through the streets of a city, the way that Beston walks the beach on Cape Cod? What is a city dweller to do about coming to terms with the world at night?

❧ Caroline A. Henderson (b. ca. 1880)

Letters from the Dust Bowl (1936)

Caroline A. Henderson moved to Eva, Oklahoma, in 1908 with her husband, Will, to homestead on 640 acres. She is quoted in the contributor's column of The Atlantic Monthly *as follows: "At the time of our marriage I was an exhausted school teacher, my husband an ex-cowboy, well-driller, and master of various arts of the big outdoors. . . .Only people like ourselves who have invested their lives in the 'short grass' country know the sorrow of seeing these hard-won acres 'all up in the air.' "*

Henderson's letters of 1935 and 1936 are more like notes in a diary, annotating the events of the hard times. "Evelyn" is a former neighbor from the Eastern seaboard. The letter of April 1937 shows a more sustained effort at explaining life in the dust bowl: The hyacinths in the window stand in contrast to the dust that covers everything else in the yard and fields.

Eva, Oklahoma, June 30, 1935

My Dear Evelyn:—

Your continued interest in our effort to 'tie a knot in the end of the rope and hang on' is most stimulating. Our recent transition from rain-soaked eastern Kansas with its green pastures, luxuriant foliage, abundance of flowers, and promise of a generous harvest, to the dust-covered desolation of No Man's Land was a difficult change to crowd into one short day's travel. Eleanor has laid aside the medical books for a time. Wearing our shade hats, with handkerchiefs tied over our faces and vaseline in our nostrils, we have been trying to rescue our home from the accumulations of wind-blown dust which penetrates wherever air can go. It is an almost hopeless task, for there is rarely a day when at some time the dust clouds do not roll over. 'Visibility' approaches zero and everything is covered again with a silt-like deposit which may vary in depth from a film to actual ripples on the kitchen floor. I keep oiled cloths on the window sills and between the upper and lower sashes. They help just a little to retard or collect the dust. Some seal the windows with the gummed-paper strips used in wrapping parcels, but no method is fully effective. We buy what appears to be red cedar sawdust with oil added to use in sweeping our floors, and do our best to avoid inhaling the irritating dust.

In telling you of these conditions I realize that I expose myself to charges of disloyalty to this western region. A good Kansas friend suggests that we should imitate the Californian attitude toward earthquakes and keep to ourselves what we know about dust storms. Since the very limited rains of May in this section gave some slight ground for renewed hope, optimism has been the approved policy. Printed articles or statements by journalists, railroad officials, and secretaries of small-town Chambers of Commerce have heralded too enthusiastically the return of prosperity to the drouth region. And in our part of the country that is the one durable basis for any prosperity whatever. There is nothing else to build upon. But you wished to know the truth, so I am telling you the actual situation, though I freely admit that the facts are themselves often contradictory and confusing.

Early in May, with no more grass or even weeds on our 640 acres than on your kitchen floor, and even the scanty remnants of dried grasses from last year cut off and blown away, we decided, like most of our neighbors, to ship our cattle to grass in the central part of the state. We sent 27 head, retaining here the heifers coming fresh this spring. The shipping charge on our part of the carload was $46. Pasture costs us $7.00 for a cow and calf for the season and $5.00 for a yearling. Whether this venture brings profit or loss depends on whether the cattle make satisfactory gains during the summer and whether prices remain reasonable or fall back to the level that most people would desire. We farmers here in the United States might as well recognize that we are a minority group, and that the prevailing interest of the nation as a whole is no longer agricultural. Hay for the horses and the heifers remaining here cost us $23 per ton, brought by truck from eastern Oklahoma.

The day after we shipped the cattle, the long drouth was temporarily broken by the first effective moisture in many months—about one and one-quarter inches in two or three gentle rains. All hope of a wheat crop had been abandoned by March or April.

Contrary to many published reports, a good many people had left this country either temporarily or permanently before any rains came. And they were not merely 'drifters,' as is frequently alleged. In May a friend in the southwestern county of Kansas voluntarily sent me a list of the people who had already left their immediate neighborhood or were packed up and ready to go. The list included 109 persons in 26 families, substantial people, most of whom had been in that locality over ten years, and some as long as forty years. In these families there had been two deaths from dust pneumonia. Others in the neighborhood were ill at that time. Fewer actual residents have left our neighborhood, but on a sixty-mile trip yesterday to procure tractor repairs we saw many pitiful reminders of broken hopes and apparently wasted effort. Little abandoned homes where people had drilled deep wells for the precious water, had set trees and vines, built reservoirs, and fenced in gardens,—with everything now walled in or half buried by banks of drifted soil,—told a painful story of loss and disappointment. I grieved especially over one lonely plum thicket buried to the tips of the twigs, and a garden with a fence closely built of boards for wind protection, now enclosing only a hillock of dust covered with the blue-flowered bull nettles which no winds or sands discourage.

It might give you some notion of our great 'open spaces' if I tell you that on the sixty-mile trip, going by a state road over which our mail comes from the railroad, and coming back by a Federal highway, we encountered only one car, and no other vehicles of any sort. And this was on Saturday, the farmers' marketing day!

The coming of the long-desired rain gave impetus to the Federal projects for erosion control. Plans were quickly made, submitted to groups of farmers in district gatherings, and put into operation without delay.

The proposition was that, in order to encourage the immediate listing of abandoned wheat ground and other acreage so as to cut down wind erosion, the Federal Government would contribute ten cents per acre toward the expense of fuel and oil for tractors or feed for horses, if the farmers would agree to list not less than one fourth of the acreage on contour lines. Surveys were made promptly for all farmers signing contracts for either contour listing or terracing. The latest report states that within the few weeks since the programme was begun in our county 299,986 acres have been ploughed or listed on these contour lines—that is, according to the lay of the land instead of on straight lines with right-angled turns as has been the usual custom.

The plan has been proposed and carried through here as a matter of public policy for the welfare of all without reproach or humiliation to anyone. It should be remembered that 1935 is the fourth successive year of drouth and crop failure through a great part of the high plains region, and the hopelessly low prices for the crop of 1931 gave no chance to build up reserves for future needs. If the severe critics of all who in any way join in government plans for the saving of homes and the restoration of farms to a productive basis could only understand how vital a human problem is here considered, possibly their censures might be less bitter and scornful.

At any rate the contour listing has been done over extensive areas. If rains come to carry forward the feed crops now just struggling up in the furrows, the value of the work can be appraised. The primary intention of the plan for contour listing is to distribute rainfall evenly over the fields and prevent its running off to one end of the field or down the road to some creek or drainage basin. It is hoped that the plan will indirectly tend to lessen wind erosion by promoting the growth of feed crops, restoration of humus to denuded surfaces, and some protection through standing stubbles and the natural coverage of weeds and unavoidable wastes. One great contributing cause of the terrible dust storms of the last two years has been the pitiful bareness of the fields resulting from the long drouth.

I am not wise enough to forecast the result. We have had two most welcome rains in June—three quarters of an inch and one-half inch. Normally these should have been of the utmost benefit, though they by no means guarantee an abundant feed crop from our now sprouting seeds as many editorial writers have decreed, and they do nothing toward restoring subsoil moisture. Actually the helpful effects of the rains have been for us and for other people largely destroyed by the drifting soil from abandoned, unworked lands around us. It fills the air and our eyes and noses and throats, and, worst of all, our furrows, where tender shoots are coming to the surface only to be buried by the smothering silt from the fields of rugged individualists who persist in their right to do nothing.

A fairly promising piece of barley has been destroyed for us by the merciless drift from the same field whose sands have practically buried the little mulberry hedge which has long sheltered our buildings from the northwest winds. Large spaces in our pastures are entirely bare in spite of the rains. Most of the green color, where there is any grazing, is due to the pestilent Russian thistles rather than to grass. Our little locust grove which we cherished for so many years has become a small pile of fence posts. With trees and vines and flowers all around you, you can't imagine how I miss that little green shaded spot in the midst of the desert glare.

Naturally you will wonder why we stay where conditions are so extremely disheartening. Why not pick up and leave as so many others have done? It is a fair question, but a hard one to answer.

Recently I talked with a young university graduate of very superior attainments. He took the ground that in such a case sentiment could and should be disregarded. He may be right. Yet I cannot act or feel or think as if the experiences of our twenty-seven years of life together had never been. And they are all bound up with the little corner to which we have given our continued and united efforts. To leave voluntarily—to break all these closely knit ties for the sake of a possibly greater comfort elsewhere—seems like defaulting on our task. We may *have* to leave. We can't hold out indefinitely without some return from the land, some source of income, however small. But I think I can never go willingly or without pain that as yet seems unendurable.

There are also practical considerations that serve to hold us here, for the present. Our soil is excellent. We need only a little rain—less than in most places—to make it productive. No one who remembers the wheat crops of 1926, 1929, 1931, can possibly regard this as permanently submarginal land. The newer methods of farming suggest possibilities of better control of moisture in the future. Our entire equipment is adapted to the type of farming suitable for this country and would have to be replaced at great expense with the tools needed in some other locality. We have spent so much in trying to keep our land from blowing away that it looks foolish to walk off and leave it, when somewhat more favorable conditions seem now to 'cast their shadows before.' I scarcely need to tell you that there is no use in thinking of either renting or selling farm property here at present. It is just a place to stand on—if we can keep the taxes paid—and work and hope for a better day. We could realize nothing whatever from all our years of struggle with which to make a fresh start.

We long for the garden and little chickens, the trees and birds and wild flowers of the years gone by. Perhaps if we do our part these good things may return some day, for others if not for ourselves.

Will joins me in earnest hopes for your recovery. The dust has been particularly aggravating to his bronchial trouble, but he keeps working on. A great reddish-brown dust cloud is rising now from the southeast, so we must get out and do our night work before it arrives. Our thoughts go with you.

August 11, 1935

My Dear Evelyn:—

On this blistering Sunday afternoon, I am, like Alexander Selkirk,

> . . . Monarch of all I survey;
> My right there is none to dispute.

There is no one within a mile and a half, and all day I've seen just one person pass by in an old stripped-down Ford.

Will and Eleanor went early this morning with a family of neighbors to visit the dinosaur pit in the next county to the westward—about seventy miles from here—where the State University is engaged in excavating the bones of some of these ancient monsters, reminders of a time when there was plenty of water even in the Panhandle.

It seemed impossible for us all to leave home at once, so I stayed here to care for a new Shorthorn brother, to keep the chickens' pails filled with fresh water, to turn the cattle and horses in to water at noon, and to keep them from straying to the extremely poisonous drouth-stricken cane. We spent the better part of a night during the week trying to save two of the best young cows from the effects of the prussic acid which develops in the stunted sorghum. We thought they would die and I am not sure yet whether they recovered because of the liberal doses of melted lard and molasses or whether the poison was not quite strong enough to be fatal. It produces a paralysis of the respiratory system, and when death occurs, as it frequently does, it is due to suffocation from lack of oxygen.

Ever since your letter came, I have been thinking how different are the causes of our personal difficulties. It is hard for us prodigals in this far country, in our scarcity of all things, not to feel envious of the Del Mar Va pigs luxuriating in potatoes, peaches (and cream?), and the delicious Younger-berries. But, as I started to say, our own problems are of a quite different sort. We cannot complain of laziness on the part of our citizens. Oklahoma is one of the first states to get away from direct relief. Official reports of the administrators here emphasize the eagerness with which people accept any sort of work to help themselves and to make unnecessary the acceptance of public aid. In our county the FERA force is being cut down. Three case workers and two from the office force have been dismissed during the past week.

This progress toward more nearly normal conditions of employment occurs in the face of the most critical farm situation that we have ever encountered. For over a month we have had *no* rain, and the two light local showers early in July had only a slight and temporary effect. All hope of an adequate forage crop has now followed into oblivion the earlier hopes of wheat and maize production. We have no native or cultivated hay crops. The cattle stay alive thus far on weeds, but the pastures are destitute of grass. Many think it can never be restored. The heat is intense and the drying winds are practically continuous, with a real 'duster' occurring every few days to keep us humble. After the government erosion control project was carried through there was, for a time, a partial cessation of the dust blowing. But as the freshly upturned earth is pulverizing under the influence of continued heat and wind and entire lack of moisture, it too is ready to blow. A recently established Oklahoma law permits the County Commissioners to require the working of the land that is being allowed to blow to the detriment of other farms, and I note that one such order has recently been issued in our county.

You asked about the soil erosion control programme and what could be done with an allowance of ten cents per acre. That amount just about covers actual expense of fuel and oil for listing with a large tractor. Possibly it leaves a slight margin if listing is done with a lighter outfit. In no case was any allowance made for a man's labor or the use of his farming equipment. The plan was proposed to encourage widespread and practically simultaneous working of the blowing fields, with a reasonable proportion on contour lines. Undoubtedly it has been of great benefit, and had rains followed, as everyone hoped, we should feel that we were approaching the turn in the long road. As a matter of fact, the complete absence of rain has given us no chance to test the effectiveness of the contour listing. A few people signed up for terracing as a more permanent method of conserving and distributing the longed-for moisture— if it ever comes! Will has been working early and late with one of the county terracing machines, laying up ridges on contour lines for every foot of fall. He hopes to be ready to-morrow to turn the machine over to a neighbor who will also make the experiment. Later on he would like to run the terrace lines across the pasture lands, but the future for us is most uncertain.

Everything now depends on whether a definite change of moisture conditions occurs in time for people to sow wheat for 1936. The 'suitcase farmers'—that is, insurance agents, preachers, real-estate men, and so forth, from cities near or far—have bet thousands of dollars upon *rain,* or, in other words, have hired the preparation of large areas of land all around us which no longer represent the idea of *homes* at all, but just parts of a potential factory for the low-cost production of wheat—*if it rains.*

A short time ago a big tractor, working for one of these absentee farmers across the road from our home, accidentally hooked on to the cornerstone of the original survey and dragged it off up the road. All these many years that stone has marked the corner of our homestead. I have walked past it hundreds of times as I have taken the cows to their pasture or brought them home again. Always it has suggested the beauty of the untouched prairie as it was when the surveyors set the stone, the luxuriant thick turf of native grasses,—grama grass, buffalo, and curly mesquite,—the pincushion cactuses, straw-color and rose, the other wild flowers which in their season fulfilled the thought of Shakespeare:—

> The summer's flower is to the summer sweet,
> Though to itself it only live and die.

The cornerstone has also suggested the preparation for human occupation—the little homes that were so hopefully established here, of which so very few remain. After twenty-nine years, eight places in our township, out of the possible 136 (excluding the two school sections), are still occupied by those who made the original homestead entry. And now the stone is gone and the manner of its removal seemed almost symbolic of the changes that appear inevitable.

We can't see why your wheat prices should be so hopelessly low. You may judge now a little of how we felt in 1931, with wheat at less than 'two bits' per bushel! The price here has recently been about a dollar a bushel, several cents above the Kansas City price. I suppose the idea is to discourage shipment, as there is not enough wheat in this area now to provide for fall sowing—if it rains—and seed wheat must be shipped in.

One morning at the store, being in a reckless mood, I invested a dime in five small tomatoes and wished you might be getting something like that price for your surplus. Potatoes cost us around thirty cents a peck. I hope the protest of the Maryland growers has been successful in giving them some return for their work. Peaches are priced at four pounds for a quarter, but are not for us. So count your mercies, lady. It may surprise you to see how numerous they are.

The last sack of flour cost $1.69, and twelve-ounce loaves of good bread are still to be had for a nickel, considerably *less* than the price we paid during the dear old days of reputed prosperity—before processing taxes were a subject for political debate and court consideration. We feel rather proud that the proprietor of the Elkhart flour mill which we have patronized for many years has withdrawn from the group of Kansas millers suing the government for recovery of the processing tax. He explained his position by stating that, as the benefits derived from these taxes had been an actual lifesaver for farming and general business interests in this section, he would not seek to embarrass the government in its attempt to collect the tax. His independent action in refusing to join in the raid seems worth mentioning in these days when individualism is supposed to be dead.

It's time to do the evening work, put the guinea pig to bed, and begin to watch for the return of our explorers. I do hope weather conditions are favoring the growth of your crops.

January 28, 1936

Dear Evelyn:—

As I have said before, our own problems seem of slight moment as compared with yours. Yet more than ever of late 'the day's journey' has indeed seemed to 'fill the whole long day.' As yet there are no decisive changes, no clear light on our way. Late in the summer, before Eleanor returned to her work in the medical school, she drove the tractor for her father, and with the help of the old header they worried down the scattering, scanty crop of sorghum cane and Sudan grass which had made all the growth it could through the hot, dry summer. That there was anything at all to harvest we attribute to the new planting methods encouraged by the Soil Erosion Control service, of listing on contour lines and laying up terraces to check the run-off in whatever rains might come. A shower the night they finished cutting and another about ten days later, conserved in the same way, gave us most fortunately a second cutting over the same fields, and a few loads of maize fodder from spots here and there on another part of the farm. These crops of roughage have little or no market value, but are indispensable if one plans to winter any cattle. The old, nutritious native grasses which used to provide winter pasturage are forever gone. Killing frosts happily came later than usual. In October, I drove the tractor myself and we two cut and hauled and put into the barn loft (including the earlier cutting) some twenty tons of fodder from two hundred acres, expensive feed when regarded as the entire outcome of a year's work and investment, yet essential to our attempt at carrying on.

As you know, however, wisely or otherwisely, this region has permitted wheat growing to become its main concern. The wheat situation around us is so varied and precarious as to be most difficult of appraisal. Our own acreage is fairly typical of the general condition. We have a little wheat that came up in September, made a fair start, and for a time furnished pasturage for the small calves. A part of it was early smothered out by the drift from near-by fields. Part of it would yet respond to abundant moisture if that were to come. Much of the early-sown wheat did not come up. Some of the seed sprouted and died before reaching the surface. Other portions remained dry until sprouted by a light rain in December. Most of that still lies dormant waiting for warmth to promote its growth. Large areas were drilled after the December rain, with varying results as to germination.

After the four-to-six-inch snow of early January, the editor of our county paper was asked by the United Press for a candid report of actual conditions. His estimate allowed the county as a whole a 25 per cent chance; not, if I understood him, a fair chance for a 25 per cent crop, but about one chance in four for anything at all. His statement showed that fall and winter precipitation so far had been a trifle over half the normal amount for that time of year. And you must try to remember that a failure this year would mean five in succession for a large part of the high plains region. So our great problem here is production, after all. You can readily see that the conditions I have so hastily outlined promise no protection against the ravages of dust storms if the spring winds rage as in previous years.

On the whole it is not surprising that here and there some bitterness should have been felt and expressed, perhaps immoderately, over the recent AAA decision in the Supreme Court. People here, business men as well as the farmers themselves, realize that the benefit payments under the AAA and the wage payments from Federal work projects are all that have saved a large territory here from abandonment. A December statement by the Soil Conservation service reports an area in five states, including part or all of sixty-eight counties and 87,900 square miles of territory, as in need of active measures for protection and control of the duststorm menace. Mr. Bennett, director of the service, regards this as the greatest 'physical problem facing the country to-day.' I was astonished to find by a little primary arithmetic that the area involved is equal to that of all the New England States, with New Jersey and Maryland and about half of Delaware added for good measure.

The desolation of the countryside would admittedly have meant the ruin of the small towns, entirely dependent as they are upon country patronage. It will also mean—if it must ever be abandoned through utter exhaustion of resources and sheer inability to hang on any longer— a creeping eastward into more settled and productive territory of the danger and losses originating in the arid wastelands. It is a problem now that no merely individual action can handle successfully.

But to return briefly to the Supreme Court decision. It has naturally been the cause of much regrettable confusion. It would probably have caused even more disturbance had there not been a background of hope that something may yet be done to compensate for the disappointments necessarily involved.

Farmers are not asking for special favors. They ask only an even chance as compared with other workers. But people don't understand.

Perhaps the many books on pioneer life with the usual successful and happy outcome have helped to give a wrong impression and perpetuate the idea that country people live on wild game and fish and fruits and in general on the free bounty of heaven. Many people have no idea of the cash expense of operating a farm to-day, or the work and planning required to keep the wheels going round, to say nothing of a decent living or suitable education for the children. This year we are keeping a separate account of expenses for car, truck, and tractor, all of which are old and frequently in need of repair. I fear we shall be horrified and discouraged by the close of the year. Not that I should willingly return to the long, slow trips of fifteen miles to town in a jolting wagon. Not that I want to take it out of the flesh and blood of horses in the hot heavy work of seed time and harvest—if they come again. But we can't combine the modern methods of work with the income of our early pioneering, when $200 used to cover all of a year's expense.

I think I told you of shipping our cattle to pasture. It proved to be a disastrous mistake. To keep in tune, I suppose we should blame Secretary Wallace or the broad-shouldered Mr. Tugwell, who likewise had nothing to do with it. Really the source of trouble was our own erroneous impression that grass is grass, and that our cattle would gain if they could have ample pasturage. Evidently other factors of acclimatization must be considered. Our experience was duplicated in that of many of our neighbors, most of whom, on finding their cattle in far worse condition in the fall than in the spring, decided to sell for whatever their stock would bring. Perhaps they were wise to do so. We shipped ours back, availing ourselves of the drouth rates for such shipments. In the spring we had paid 85 per cent of the regular rate. In the fall, to encourage reshipment and the restocking of the country if possible, the government rate was 15 per cent of the regular charge. I was quite alone here for a week while Will went after our little bunch. He had to unload them late at night ten miles from home.

That was November first, and most of our efforts and resources ever since have been devoted to trying to bring our cattle back to a normal condition. They are gaining slowly, but our home-grown feed is disappearing rapidly, and the grain feed of threshed maize which we must purchase, while about right in price for the seller at $1.10 per hundred, is piling up expenses. We have sold one mixed bunch of older cows and summer calves. That will help a little toward caring for the others, but there couldn't be much direct gain, as you will agree, in selling eleven head for $225. Still this is better than we could have done a year or two ago, when cattle were practically without value. In general, there has been an improvement in farm prices, both absolutely and relatively, which has given us courage to keep on working, and has kept alive our hope for some definite change in weather conditions that may once more make our acres fruitful and restore to us some sense of accomplishment.

At present this great southwestern plains region, most of which has been perseveringly tilled during the fall and winter so as to cut down the loss by wind erosion even if the wheat proves a disappointment, seems to be lying asleep like the princess in the fairy tale. Perhaps you can share with us the painful longing that soon the enchantment may be broken, that the deliverer may come with the soft footfalls of gentle rain and waken our homeland once more into gracious, generous life.

Perhaps it is a sin to parody anything as beautiful as *Ulysses*. Yet as we gray, lonely old people sit here by the fire to-night, planning for the year's work, my thoughts seem bound to fall into that pattern.

> It may be that the dust will choke us down;
> It may be we shall wake some happy morn
> And look again on fields of waving grain.

So good night, dear friend, and a happier to-morrow.

March 8, 1936

Dear Evelyn:—

Since I wrote to you, we have had several bad days of wind and dust. On the worst one recently, old sheets stretched over door and window openings, and sprayed with kerosene, quickly became black and helped a little to keep down the irritating dust in our living rooms. Nothing that you see or hear or read will be likely to exaggerate the physical discomfort or material losses due to these storms. Less emphasis is usually given to the mental effect, the confusion of mind resulting from the overthrow of all plans for improvement or normal farm work, and the difficulty of making other plans, even in a tentative way. To give just one specific example: the paint has been literally scoured from our buildings by the storms of this and previous years; we should by all means try to 'save the surface'; but who knows when we might safely undertake such a project? The pleasantest morning may be a prelude to an afternoon when the 'dust devils' all unite in one hideous onslaught. The combination of fresh paint with a real dust storm is not pleasing to contemplate.

The prospects for a wheat crop in 1936 still remain extremely doubtful. There has been no moisture of any kind since the light snow of early January. On a seventy-mile drive yesterday to arrange for hatchery chicks and to sell our week's cream and eggs, we saw more wheat that would still respond to immediate rainfall than I, with my stay-at-home habits, had expected to see. A few fields were refreshingly green and beautiful to look upon. There seems no doubt that improved methods of tillage and protection are already yielding some results in reducing wind erosion. But rain must come soon to encourage growth even on the best fields if there is to be any wheat harvest. Interspersed with the more hopeful areas are other tracts apparently abandoned to their fate. A field dotted thickly with shoulder-high hummocks of sand and soil bound together by the inevitable Russian thistles presents little encouragement to the most ardent conservationist. My own verdict in regard to plans for the reclaiming of such land would be, 'Too late.' Yet such fields are a menace to all the cultivated land or pasture ground around them and present a most difficult problem.

The two extremes I have just suggested—that is, the slight hope even yet for some production on carefully tilled fields, and the practically hopeless conditions on abandoned land—are indicative of the two conflicting tendencies now evident through an extensive section of the high plains. On the one hand we note a disposition to recognize a mistake, to turn aside from the undertaking with the least possible loss and direct one's time and energy to some new purpose. On the other hand we observe that many seem determined to use even the hard experiences of the past, their own mistakes and other people's, as warning signals, pointing the way to changes of method and more persistent and effective effort right where they stand.

The first attitude may be illustrated by an incident of the past week, the attempt of former neighbors to sell the pipe from the well on their now deserted homestead. This may not seem significant to you. But to old-timers in this deep-water country, so nearly destitute of flowing streams, the virtual destruction of a well of our excellent, life-nourishing water comes close to being the unpardonable sin against future generations.

The same disintegrating tendency is shown in a larger and more alarming way by the extent to which land once owned and occupied by farm families is now passing into ownership of banks, mortgage companies, assurance societies, and investment partnerships or corporations. The legal notices published in our county paper for the past week include two notices of foreclosure proceedings and nine notices of sheriff's sales to satisfy judgments previously rendered. These eleven legal actions involve the ownership of 3520 acres of land, the equivalent of twenty-two quarter sections, the original homestead allotment in this territory. In only two cases apparently had the loan been made from one person to another. Four life insurance companies, one investment company, and one joint-stock land bank are included among the plaintiffs.

These forced sales take place just outside of the window of the assessor's office, and we were told that they have now become merely a matter of routine. No one tries to redeem the property in question; no one even makes a bid on it; in fact, no one appears but the sheriff and the lawyer representing the plaintiff.

I am not questioning the legal right of these companies to take over the title of the farms for their own security or that of the people whose money they have invested. In a sense their action in pressing their claims may hold some encouragement for the rest of us, since it suggests that they look in time for a return of value to the acres which at present no one seeks to rescue. In addition to the large amount of land now owned by these corporate interests, very many farms belong to non-resident individuals. The 'quarters' north and south of our own place are so held, while the one on the west has recently been taken over by an investment company. Unquestionably this remote control stands in the way of constructive efforts toward recovery.

Yet there are numerous evidences of the persevering restoration of which I have written. The big road maintainers keep the highways in excellent condition. New license tags are appearing on cars and trucks. Churches, schools, and basket-ball tournaments continue much as usual. One village church reported forty people in attendance on one of the darkest and most dangerous of the recent dusty Sundays. The state agricultural college for this section has an increased enrollment this year. More people are managing in some way—we hardly see how— to keep in touch with the world of news and markets, politics and entertainment, through radio service. A local implement agency recently sent out invitations to a tractor entertainment with free moving pictures of factory operation and the like. The five hundred free lunches prepared for the occasion proved insufficient for the assembled crowd. Within a few succeeding days the company took orders for three tractors ranging in price from around $1200 to $1500. Some people must still have faith in the future!

More impressive to me was the Saturday rush of activity at the small produce house where we did our marketing. Cars kept driving up and people coming in with pails or crates or cases of eggs. Cream was delivered in containers of all sorts and sizes, including one heavy aluminum cooker! Eggs were bringing fifteen cents per dozen and cream thirty cents a pound of tested butterfat. No large sums of money were involved. In many cases the payments were pitifully small, but every such sale represents hard work and economy and the struggle to keep going.

At the hatchery they spoke of slow business through the extremely cold weather. The young man in charge also referred to the changes or postponements in people's plans because of their failure to receive the expected payments under the now extinct allotment plan. With spring in the dusty air, however, and renewed hope that the government contracts will later be fulfilled, orders were coming in encouragingly.

We plan ourselves for four hundred baby Leghorns about the middle of April. That will be an increase for us, but is about the safest small investment we can make to yield an all-the-year-round return. We shall have to put quite a bit of work and expense into the brooder house to keep out the dust, and the rain—if it ever comes. But we are happier to keep on trying.

This impressionistic account of conditions here and of our hope for the future would scarcely be complete without some mention of government assistance. We have had only slight contact with the Rehabilitation Service. We know that the man in charge here is taking his work seriously, trying to give definite aid and encouragement to those who have reached the end of their small resources and have lost hope and courage. He stopped here the other morning to see whether we really meant it when we promised the use of our tractor and other equipment to a young man in the neighborhood who is trying to make a new start for himself and wife and small daughter through a rehabilitation loan. In spite of seriously adverse conditions, this agent, who meets many people, spoke of a rather surprising general spirit of optimism. I suppose there is something of the gambler in all of us. We instinctively feel that the longer we travel on a straight road, the nearer we must be coming to a turn. People here can't quite believe yet in a hopeless climatic change which would deprive them permanently of the gracious gift of rain.

To me the most interesting and forward-looking government undertaking in the dust bowl centres about the group of erosion control experiments scattered over a wide area. The Pony Creek project, fifteen miles east of our home, includes all of one congressional township and parts of three others, seventy square miles altogether, or something over 42,000 acres. This is a pretty seriously damaged area, principally devoted to wheat growing, and even now blowing badly. If the methods employed succeed in checking the drift and in restoring productivity, much will have been accomplished, both of intrinsic value and of use as a stimulating object lesson. We hope some day to drive over and see how they are progressing.

We talked about this work with the young man who helped us last summer to run our terrace lines. At present they are employing 140 men from WPA rolls who would otherwise be idle and in need of relief. The work is frankly experimental. It includes such activities as surveying contour lines, laying up terraces, cleaning out fence rows piled high with drifted soil, filling gullies to prevent washing in that longed-for time of heavy rainfall, cutting down dead trees and brush, digging holes for the resetting of trees in favorable locations, testing the adaptability of different types of grass to the difficult task of reseeding wind-blown spaces, and so on. Altogether it is just such work as a provident farmer would like to get done if he had the time and means. It is done without expense to the farmers who agree to coöperate in the plan. Our young friend smiled when I asked about 'regimentation.' The farmers do promise to maintain for five years, I believe, the terraces built for them and to follow a system of crop rotation. But plans for planting and cultivation are worked out for each place in individual conferences, to suit the farm and the farmer. Don't worry about the stifling of individuality. 'It can't be did,' as one of our preachers used to say. Of course no one can predict yet the result of these experiments, but they seem to me abundantly worth while.

Our personal plans—like those of all the rest—are entirely dependent on whether or not rain comes to save a little of our wheat, to give grass or even weeds for pasturage, to permit the growing of roughage for the winter, and provide some cover on the surface and promote the intertwining of rootlets in the soil to reduce wind damage. Our terraces are in good condition to distribute whatever moisture may come. We hope we have learned a little about protecting the soil which is the basis of our physical life. In the house the poinsettia and Christmas cactus are blooming a second time and the geraniums blossom in spite of the dust. Eleanor has just sent us budded hyacinth and daffodil bulbs in little moss-filled nests. They will help us to look forward for a time at least.

March 13

We *must* try to get this mailed tomorrow. It has been a terrible week, with one day of almost complete obscurity, and others when only a part of the sun's rays struggled through the gloom with a strange bluish luminance. On such days each little wave of the troubled water in the stock tank glitters with a blue phosphorescent light. When I dip out a pail of water to carry to the henhouse, it looks almost as if it were covered with a film of oil. On days like this, when William Vaughn Moody's expression 'dust to eat' suggests a literal danger, we can't help questioning whether the traits we would rather think of as courage and perseverance are not actually recklessness and inertia. Who shall say?

❧ Caroline A. Henderson (b. ca. 1880)
Spring in the Dust Bowl (1937)

Caroline Henderson's experiences in Oklahoma and her submissions to The Atlantic Monthly *are discussed in the introduction to "Letters from the Dust Bowl," page 142.*

Eva, Oklahoma, April 6, 1937

Dear Atlantic:—

The kindness of your letter brought us definite encouragement. It is difficult to appraise our present situation with any exactitude, but some incidents and observations from our daily life may help you to judge of the prospects for 1937.

On our bleak Easter morning a jack rabbit sat crouched in the kindling pile by the kitchen door. He was, however, no frolicsome Easter bunny, but a starved, trembling creature with one eye battered out by the terrific dust storms of the preceding week. He made no effort to escape. I bathed his eye and put him into shelter with our guinea pig, hoping that he would live until showers might bring some tinge of green upon our dust-covered wasteland. Another blinded rabbit picked up in the yard had just died in spite of all my care. When these wild creatures, ordinarily so well able to take care of themselves, come seeking protection, their necessity indicates a cruel crisis for man and beast.

After another dry summer in 1936, with only the scantiest production, hope was revived by light rains in late September. This moisture was barely sufficient to encourage the sowing of wheat for the possibility of spring pasturage. Our acreage, like that of our neighbors, was materially reduced. The seed sprouted, but again the hope of a crop has vanished with the dry winter and the raging winds of spring. We are now reluctantly feeding the last small remainder of the crop of 1931.

High winds and consequent dust storms began early this year and still continue at frequent intervals. While perhaps no more violent than the storms of previous years, their effects, being cumulative, seem more disastrous and overwhelming. On some days the limit of vision has been a row of little elms about thirty feet from the front windows. No eye could penetrate any farther the swirling, blinding clouds of dust which made noonday as dark as late twilight of a clear evening. The worst storm thus far in 1937 occurred immediately after a slight snowfall which again roused delusive hopes. That snow melted on a Tuesday. Wednesday morning, with a rising wind, the dust began to move again, and until late Friday night there was little respite.

Almost as distressing are the more frequent days when the northward-creeping sun shines faintly above the dizzying drift of silt, ground to a fine whitish powder, which gives a ghastly appearance of unreality to the most familiar landscapes. On such days we suffer from a painful sense of helplessness and utter frustration. We need no calendar to tell us that planting time is here again. The cranes went north some time ago. Our hyacinths bloom fragrantly in the windows, and the Easter lily has a bud ready to open. The hardy yellow roses are struggling to put out a few green leaves on the tips of twigs rising above the dust. The other morning a solitary shrike trilled his spring song from the windmill tower. Yet any attempt to proceed with planting under present conditions would be stubborn and expensive folly.

During the winter and early spring, Will has rebuilt his terraces in anticipation of the rain that may not come. He has also done a considerable amount of listing to prepare the ground for possible moisture and to entrap blowing soil and humus from our own or other land.

The stripping of humus from the top soil is one of our most serious losses during these critical years. A striking evidence of this regrettable waste came to my notice last summer. I was herding our cattle near a temporary lake formed by the run-off in one rain which fell so fast that the unworked, wind-swept fields could not absorb more than a small portion of the precious moisture. Surrounding the lake were thick sheets of pure vegetable material, ground by the winds and washed away and deposited by the flowing waters. Both humus and rainfall should somehow have been saved to fill and fertilize the depleted subsoil. After a recent storm I brushed from one narrow window sill a cupful of pulverized soil. Putting this dust into a shallow dish and adding water, I was shocked by the thick scum of powdered vegetation which rose to the surface. Verily we are losing the 'cream' of our land.

Seeds for field crops are scarce and expensive, and their purchase requires the closest planning. Forage crops are all-important, as we can go no further with cattle or poultry unless we can provide them with home-grown feed. Our seed supplies include cowpeas, pie melons (for winter greens for chickens), sweet clover and crested wheat grass for experimental purposes, Indian corn, cane seed of different types, Sudan grass, Kafir corn, hegari, broomcorn, and millet. If rains come even by the middle of June, we must somehow secure seed of milo maize, our most dependable grain crop, which, under normal conditions, could still mature before frost.

In attacking the problem of erosion control, one great handicap lies in the scarcity of people left to do the essential work. On a recent drive to our county seat thirty miles away, we could count only sixteen occupied homes, including those within half a mile on either side of the federal highway.

Yet experienced people with ample opportunity for knowing the difficulty of the struggle are advising against general abandonment. As the dirt ploughed up here by the unrelenting winds darkens the sky in cities hundreds of miles away, there is a growing realization that the problem is not simply that of a few unsuccessful farmers who might be as well off in one place as another. People are beginning to understand that such conditions, if left unchecked, are progressive and threaten the welfare not only of other agricultural areas but of towns and cities dependent upon rural prosperity.

I am almost ashamed to remember that some years ago, when we first saw the extreme desolation in parts of New Mexico, I thought that surely our own locality could never experience such tragedy. The answer to that mood of unintentional pride is all around us today in barren fields, ruined pastures, buried fences, dead trees, abandoned wells, desolated homes.

We can easily understand the skepticism of those who ask what the government can do to help, since obviously it has no power to rule the winds or grant the blessing of rain. But other important things do come within its legitimate scope. In fact, to restore large areas to production and to prevent the increase of the seriously damaged acreage, rain alone no longer seems sufficient. We may say, as Robert Frost said to his young orchard trees, 'Something must be left to God,' and still recognize the need for human toil to counteract the damage already done. Rain and snow must be prepared for by special methods of tillage; all moisture must be conserved; cover of some sort must be procured to retard erosion.

When the entire root system of the hardy yuccas may be seen in places of special exposure, with their thick woody roots writhing on the surface and the finer rootlets extending like guy wires for perhaps twenty feet in different directions, the indications of serious erosion are too plain to be ignored. Often, while trailing the cattle around for scattered grazing, I have been dismayed to notice how tracks of cattle, horses, or tractors, made at some time of dampened surface, now project sharply several inches above the surrounding soil like rude cameos carved by the restless wind.

We cannot criticize the conservation plans of the Department of Agriculture. They embody many of the control measures that our own experience would recommend. They grant large individual liberty in working out contributions to the common welfare. The proposals seem practical and sufficiently generous.

A farmer willing to coöperate may select 15 per cent of his crop land, follow in cultivation any one of several soil-conserving methods, and agree to leave on the ground for protective purposes whatever crop is produced upon that acreage. For his labor, seed, and sacrifice of any harvested crop, he is offered $6.40 per acre for first-class land.

With the other 85 per cent of cultivated acreage one may do as he will, though in case of negligence which caused a piece of land to become a menace to surrounding farms any expected benefits would be forfeited. Should one desire to hasten measures for conservation and also augment his Class I payment, he may choose from thirty-three methods of procedure to be applied to his 85 per cent acreage, and so become eligible for payments of from twenty to seventy-five cents per acre. The combination of the two types of payment on a basis of one hundred acres of cultivation might amount to a maximum of $174.75. This sum hardly suggests idle affluence. It does mean distinct help in constructive efforts to accomplish together what no one can hope to do by himself.

We personally hope for the gradual success of these methods, because for the past two years we have had cane on terraced land. Though the crop was lighter than in normal years, enough stubble and roots remained on the ground to prevent appreciable erosion. Moreover, that particular plot still holds subsoil moisture. Dirt brought up with a post auger from a depth of over three feet retains sufficient moisture to be packed into a solid ball.

Naturally, all these plans must fail, at least for this year, unless rains come soon to settle the soil and prepare a normal seed bed. For that we must trust a government established in the nature of things beyond our utmost reach. It is good to remember that the laws of the universe recognize no favorites and cherish no hostility or small vindictiveness; that before sun and rain, stormy winds, or summer's kind beneficence, we all stand upon one common level.

Your interest and that of other friends have been to us a very real and present help.

Gratefully yours,

Caroline A. Henderson

Questions for Thinking and Writing

1. What is it in Henderson's voice and presentation of details that makes this a realistic account of the effects of the Dust Bowl?
2. What changes can be detected between the first letters of 1936 and the second letter of spring 1937? Can you notice any shifts in Henderson's attitude toward nature?
3. What are Henderson's views on individual responsibility toward the land? To what extent does she blame farmers for soil depletion and erosion? Explain the idea of contour plowing ("listing") and why it is an environmental improvement over traditional field plowing.

John Steinbeck (1902–1968)

Chapter Five, The Grapes of Wrath (1939)

John Steinbeck was born in Salinas, California, in Monterey County. From youth he seems to have been destined for a career as a writer, but it was not always smooth going. Early on, his mother encouraged him to read John Milton, Feodor Dostoevski, and Thomas Hardy, among other writers. In school, Steinbeck began writing his own stories and scribbled many of them on his father's accounting ledgers. As the treasurer of Monterey County, Steinbeck's father wanted his son to study law, but the young man would not do so.

As a high school student, Steinbeck wrote for the school newspaper, and he was elected president of his class. He attended Stanford University where he took 11 English courses but dropped out in 1925 to sign aboard a cattle freighter to New York City. There, he worked as a reporter. He returned to California after a short time and took odd jobs to support his writing. Tortilla Flat *(1935), his first critical success, is a novel consisting of a series of stories about the Mexican-Spanish-Native American mix of people in Monterey County living in great poverty. Steinbeck's style at this time has often been compared to Hemingway's for its crisp journalistic clarity. Where they differ is Steinbeck's deep sympathy for characters who have to fight it out in a cruel world. Much of Steinbeck's writing is about the disenfranchised, particularly migrant laborers, union laborers, and poor people who depend on the land. This is the subject of* In Dubious Battle *(1936) and* Of Mice and Men *(1937). His literary masterpiece is* The Grapes of Wrath *(1939) for which he received a Pulitzer Prize in 1940. Other novels include* The Moon Is Down *(1942),* Cannery Row *(1944),* The Wayward Bus *(1947),* East of Eden *(1952), and* The Winter of Our Discontent *(1961). For the significance of his literary work, Steinbeck was awarded the Nobel Prize for literature in 1962.*

A long friendship with Edward Rickets, a biologist in Monterey, California, provided Steinbeck with material for the character of Doc in Cannery Row. *It also brought him close to the science of biology. In 1940, Steinbeck accompanied Rickets on a specimen-collecting expedition in the Sea of Cortez. Steinbeck's* Sea of Cortez, *which he co-authored with Rickets in 1941, and* The Log of the Sea of Cortez *(1951) have become classics of their kind.*

Steinbeck's affinity for a fictional ecology is an important element of his technique for creating conflict. His characters flourish or fail according to their ability to master their environment. In The Grapes of Wrath, *the change in climate, the great drought of the 1930s, the economic disaster of the Great Depression, and heedless farming practices conflict head on with a people and their way of agrarian life. Steinbeck is not a strict Darwinian, but he shows that trying times lead people to attempt new strategies for surviving and prospering. He is always mindful that surviving includes the spiritual aspects of people and that their will to live is tempered by the strength of their inner lives. The episode excerpted here from Chapter 5 of* The Grapes of Wrath *depicts the destruction of a farmstead by a bulldozer, which has the characteristics of a monster. Dead as a result of the drought and poor farming practices, the farm is plowed under, house and all, when the bankers have foreclosed. The new fields, now part of a great farm of thousands of acres, obliterate the past, but are still unproductive. Forces far greater than any individual can control, or perhaps understand, are playing havoc with the natural and social environments. Wind and weather unsettle the land; commerce triumphs over humanity. There is no wise use of the environment here, according to Steinbeck.*

The owners of the land came onto the land, or more often a spokesman for the owners came. They came in closed cars, and they felt the dry earth with their fingers, and sometimes they drove big earth augers into the ground for soil tests. The tenants, from their sun-beaten dooryards, watched uneasily when the closed cars drove along the fields. And at last the owner men drove into the dooryards and sat in their cars to talk out of the windows. The tenant men stood beside the cars for a while, and then squatted on their hams and found sticks with which to mark the dust.

In the open doors the women stood looking out, and behind them the children—corn-headed children, with wide eyes, one bare foot on top of the other bare foot, and the toes working. The women and the children watched their men talking to the owner men. They were silent.

Some of the owner men were kind because they hated what they had to do, and some of them were angry because they hated to be cruel, and some of them were cold because they had long ago found that one could not be an owner unless one were cold. And all of them were caught in something larger than themselves. Some of them hated the mathematics that drove them, and some were afraid, and some worshiped the mathematics because it provided a refuge from thought and from feeling. If a bank or a finance company owned the land, the owner man said, The Bank—or the Company—needs—wants—insists—must have—as though the Bank or the Company were a monster, with thought and feeling, which had ensnared them. These last would take no responsibility for the banks or the companies because they were men and slaves, while the banks were machines and masters all at the same time. Some of the owner men were a little proud to be slaves to such cold and powerful masters. The owner men sat in the cars and explained. You know the land is poor. You've scrabbled at it long enough, God knows.

The squatting tenant men nodded and wondered and drew figures in the dust, and yes, they knew, God knows. If the dust only wouldn't fly. If the top would only stay on the soil, it might not be so bad.

The owner men went on leading to their point: You know the land's getting poorer. You know what cotton does to the land; robs it, sucks all the blood out of it.

The squatters nodded—they knew, God knew. If they could only rotate the crops they might pump blood back into the land.

Well, it's too late. And the owner men explained the workings and the thinkings of the monster that was stronger than they were. A man can hold land if he can just eat and pay taxes; he can do that.

Yes, he can do that until his crops fail one day and he has to borrow money from the bank.

But—you see, a bank or a company can't do that, because those creatures don't breathe air, don't eat side-meat. They breathe profits; they eat the interest on money. If they don't get it, they die the way you die without air, without side-meat. It is a sad thing, but it is so. It is just so.

The squatting men raised their eyes to understand. Can't we just hang on? Maybe the next year will be a good year. God knows how much cotton next year. And with all the wars—God knows what price cotton will bring. Don't they make explosives out of cotton? And uniforms? Get enough wars and cotton'll hit the ceiling. Next year, maybe. They looked up questioningly.

We can't depend on it. The bank—the monster has to have profits all the time. It can't wait. It'll die. No, taxes go on. When the monster stops growing, it dies. It can't stay one size.

Soft fingers began to tap the sill of the car window, and hard fingers tightened on the restless drawing sticks. In the doorways of the sun-beaten tenant houses, women sighed and then shifted feet so that the one that had been down was now on top, and the toes working. Dogs came sniffing near the owner cars and wetted on all four tires one after another. And chickens lay in the sunny dust and fluffed their feathers to get the cleansing dust down to the skin. In the little sties the pigs grunted inquiringly over the muddy remnants of the slops.

The squatting men looked down again. What do you want us to do? We can't take less share of the crop—we're half starved now. The kids are hungry all the time. We got no clothes, torn an' ragged. If all the neighbors weren't the same, we'd be ashamed to go to meeting.

And at last the owner men came to the point. The tenant system won't work any more. One man on a tractor can take the place of twelve or fourteen families. Pay him a wage and take all the crop. We have to do it. We don't like to do it. But the monster's sick. Something's happened to the monster.

But you'll kill the land with cotton.

We know. We've got to take cotton quick before the land dies. Then we'll sell the land. Lots of families in the East would like to own a piece of land.

The tenant men looked up alarmed. But what'll happen to us? How'll we eat?

You'll have to get off the land. The plows'll go through the dooryard.

And now the squatting men stood up angrily. Grampa took up the land, and he had to kill the Indians and drive them away. And Pa was born here, and he killed weeds and snakes. Then a bad year came and he had to borrow a little money. An' we was born here. There in the door—our children born here. And Pa had to borrow money. The bank owned the land then, but we stayed and we got a little bit of what we raised.

We know that—all that. It's not us, it's the bank. A bank isn't like a man. Or an owner with fifty thousand acres, he isn't like a man either. That's the monster.

Sure, cried the tenant men, but it's our land. We measured it and broke it up. We were born on it, and we got killed on it, died on it. Even if it's no good, it's still ours. That's what makes it ours—being born on it, working it, dying on it. That makes ownership, not a paper with numbers on it.

We're sorry. It's not us. It's the monster. The bank isn't like a man.

Yes, but the bank is only made of men.

No, you're wrong there—quite wrong there. The bank is something else than men. It happens that every man in a bank hates what the bank does, and yet the bank does it. The bank is something more than men, I tell you. It's the monster. Men made it, but they can't control it.

The tenants cried, Grampa killed Indians, Pa killed snakes for the land. Maybe we can kill banks—they're worse than Indians and snakes. Maybe we got to fight to keep our land, like Pa and Grampa did.

And now the owner men grew angry. You'll have to go.

But it's ours, the tenant men cried. We—

No. The bank, the monster owns it. You'll have to go.

We'll get our guns, like Grampa when the Indians came. What then?

Well—first the sheriff, and then the troops. You'll be stealing if you try to stay, you'll be murderers if you kill to stay. The monster isn't men, but it can make men do what it wants.

But if we go, where'll we go? How'll we go? We got no money.

We're sorry, said the owner men. The bank, the fifty-thousand-acre owner can't be responsible. You're on land that isn't yours. Once over the line maybe you can pick cotton in the fall. Maybe you can go on relief. Why don't you go on west to California? There's work there, and it never gets cold. Why, you can reach out anywhere and pick an orange. Why, there's always some kind of crop to work in. Why don't you go there? And the owner men started their cars and rolled away.

The tenant men squatted down on their hams again to mark the dust with a stick, to figure, to wonder. Their sunburned faces were dark, and their sun-whipped eyes were light. The women moved cautiously out of the doorways toward their men, and the children crept behind the women, cautiously, ready to run. The bigger boys squatted beside their fathers, because that made them men. After a time the women asked, What did he want?

And the men looked up for a second, and the smolder of pain was in their eyes. We got to get off. A tractor and a superintendent. Like factories.

Where'll we go? the women asked.

We don't know. We don't know.

And the women went quickly, quietly back into the houses and herded the children ahead of them. They knew that a man so hurt and so perplexed may turn in anger, even on people he loves. They left the men alone to figure and to wonder in the dust.

After a time perhaps the tenant man looked about—at the pump put in ten years ago, with a goose-neck handle and iron flowers on the spout, at the chopping block where a thousand chickens had been killed, at the hand plow lying in the shed, and the patent crib hanging in the rafters over it.

The children crowded about the women in the houses. What we going to do, Ma? Where we going to go?

The women said, We don't know, yet. Go out and play. But don't go near your father. He might whale you if you go near him. And the women went on with the work, but all the time they watched the men squatting in the dust—perplexed and figuring.

The tractors came over the roads and into the fields, great crawlers moving like insects, having the incredible strength of insects. They crawled over the ground, laying the track and rolling on it and picking it up. Diesel tractors, puttering while they stood idle; they thundered when they moved, and then settled down to a droning roar. Snub-nosed monsters, raising the dust and sticking their snouts into it, straight down the country, across the country, through fences, through dooryards, in and out of gullies in straight lines. They did not run on the ground, but on their own roadbeds. They ignored hills and gulches, water courses, fences, houses.

The man sitting in the iron seat did not look like a man; gloved, goggled, rubber dust mask over nose and mouth, he was a part of the monster, a robot in the seat. The thunder of the cylinders sounded through the country, became one with the air and the earth, so that earth and air muttered in sympathetic vibration. The driver could not control it—straight across country it went, cutting through a dozen farms and straight back. A twitch at the controls could swerve the cat', but the driver's hands could not twitch because the monster that built the tractor, the monster that sent the tractor out, had somehow got into the driver's hands, into his brain and muscle, had goggled him and muzzled him—goggled his mind, muzzled his speech, goggled his perception, muzzled his protest. He could not see the land as it was, he could not smell the land as it smelled; his feet did not stamp the clods or feel the warmth and power of the earth. He sat in an iron seat and stepped on iron pedals. He could not cheer or beat or curse or encourage the extension of his power, and because of this he could not cheer or whip or curse or encourage himself. He did not know or own or trust or beseech the land. If a seed dropped did not germinate, it was nothing. If the young thrusting plant withered in drought or drowned in a flood of rain, it was no more to the driver than to the tractor.

He loved the land no more than the bank loved the land. He could admire the tractor—its machined surfaces, its surge of power, the roar of its detonating cylinders; but it was not his tractor. Behind the tractor rolled the shining disks, cutting the earth with blades—not plowing but surgery, pushing the cut earth to the right where the second row of disks cut it and pushed it to the left; slicing blades shining, polished by the cut earth. And pulled behind the disks, the harrows combing with iron teeth so that the little clods broke up and the earth lay smooth. Behind the harrows, the long seeders—twelve curved iron penes erected in the foundry, orgasms set by gears, raping methodically, raping without passion. The driver sat in his iron seat and he was proud of the straight lines he did not will, proud of the tractor he did not own or love, proud of the power he could not control. And when that crop grew, and was harvested, no man had crumbled a hot clod in his fingers and let the earth sift past his fingertips. No man had touched the seed, or lusted for the growth. Men ate what they had not raised, had no connection with the bread. The land bore under iron, and under iron gradually died; for it was not loved or hated, it had no prayers or curses.

At noon the tractor driver stopped sometimes near a tenant house and opened his lunch: sandwiches wrapped in waxed paper, white bread, pickle, cheese, Spam, a piece of pie branded like an engine part. He ate without relish. And tenants not yet moved away came out to see him, looked curiously while the goggles were taken off, and the rubber dust mask, leaving white circles around the eyes and a large white circle around nose and mouth. The exhaust of the tractor puttered on, for fuel is so cheap it is more efficient to leave the engine running than to heat the Diesel nose for a new start. Curious children crowded close, ragged children who ate their fried dough as they watched. They watched hungrily the unwrapping of the sandwiches, and their hunger-sharpened noses smelled the pickle, cheese, and Spam. They didn't speak to the driver. They watched his hand as it carried food to his mouth. They did not watch him chewing; their eyes followed the hand that held the sandwich. After a while the tenant who could not leave the place came out and squatted in the shade beside the tractor.

"Why, you're Joe Davis's boy!"

"Sure," the driver said.

"Well, what you doing this kind of work for—against your own people?"

"Three dollars a day. I got damn sick of creeping for my dinner—and not getting it. I got a wife and kids. We got to eat. Three dollars a day, and it comes every day."

"That's right," the tenant said. "But for your three dollars a day fifteen or twenty families can't eat at all. Nearly a hundred people have to go out and wander on the roads for your three dollars a day. Is that right?"

And the driver said, "Can't think of that. Got to think of my own kids. Three dollars a day, and it comes every day. Times are changing, mister, don't you know? Can't make a living on the land unless you've got two, five, ten thousand acres and a tractor. Crop land isn't for little guys like us any more. You don't kick up a howl because you can't make Fords, or because you're not the telephone company. Well, crops are like that now. Nothing to do about it. You try to get three dollars a day someplace. That's the only way."

The tenant pondered. "Funny thing how it is. If a man owns a little property, that property is him, it's part of him, and it's like him. If he owns property only so he can walk on it and handle it and be sad when it isn't doing well, and feel fine when the rain falls on it, that property is him, and some way he's bigger because he owns it. Even if he isn't successful he's big with his property. That is so."

And the tenant pondered more. "But let a man get property he doesn't see, or can't take time to get his fingers in, or can't be there to walk on it—why, then the property is the man. He can't do what he wants, he can't think what he wants. The property is the man, stronger than he is. And he is small, not big. Only his possessions are big—and he's the servant of his property. That is so, too."

The driver munched the branded pie and threw the crust away. "Times are changed, don't you know? Thinking about stuff like that don't feed the kids. Get your three dollars a day, feed your kids. You got no call to worry about anybody's kids but your own. You get a reputation for talking like that, and you'll never get three dollars a day. Big shots won't give you three dollars a day if you worry about anything but your three dollars a day."

"Nearly a hundred people on the road for your three dollars. Where will we go?"

"And that reminds me," the driver said, "you better get out soon. I'm going through the dooryard after dinner."

"You filled in the well this morning."

"I know. Had to keep the line straight. But I'm going through the dooryard after dinner. Got to keep the lines straight. And—well, you know Joe Davis, my old man, so I'll tell you this. I got orders wherever there's a family not moved out—if I have an accident—you know, get too close and cave the house in a little—well, I might get a couple of dollars. And my youngest kid never had no shoes yet."

"I built it with my hands. Straightened old nails to put the sheathing on. Rafters are wired to the stringers with baling wire. It's mine. I built it. You bump it down—I'll be in the window with a rifle. You even come too close and I'll pot you like a rabbit."

"It's not me. There's nothing I can do. I'll lose my job if I don't do it. And look—suppose you kill me? They'll just hang you, but long before you're hung there'll be another guy on the tractor, and he'll bump the house down. You're not killing the right guy."

"That's so," the tenant said. "Who gave you orders? I'll go after him. He's the one to kill."

"You're wrong. He got his order from the bank. The bank told him, 'Clear those people out or it's your job.' "

"Well, there's a president of the bank. There's a board of directors. I'll fill up the magazine of the rifle and go into the bank."

The driver said, "Fellow was telling me the bank gets orders from the East. The orders were, 'Make the land show profit or we'll close you up.' "

"But where does it stop? Who can we shoot? I don't aim to starve to death before I kill the man that's starving me."

"I don't know. Maybe there's nobody to shoot. Maybe the thing isn't men at all. Maybe, like you said, the property's doing it. Anyway I told you my orders."

"I got to figure," the tenant said. "We all got to figure. There's some way to stop this. It's not like lightning or earthquakes. We've got a bad thing made by men, and by God that's something we can change." The tenant sat in his doorway, and the driver thundered his engine and started off, tracks falling and curving, harrows combing, and the phalli of the seeder slipping into the ground. Across the dooryard the tractor cut, and the hard, foot-beaten ground was seeded field, and the tractor cut through again; the uncut space was ten feet wide. And back he came. The iron guard bit into the house-corner, crumbled the wall, and wrenched the little house from its foundation so that it fell sideways, crushed like a bug. And the driver was goggled and a rubber mask covered his nose and mouth. The tractor cut a straight line on, and the air and the ground vibrated with its thunder. The tenant man stared after it, his rifle in his hand. His wife was beside him, and the quiet children behind. And all of them stared after the tractor.

Questions for Thinking and Writing

1. What is Steinbeck's attitude toward the farmers? Toward the bankers? What indications are there, if any, that Steinbeck is angry with nature for bringing on the drought? Or, are there indications that he accepts this element as a part of the natural cycle of things?

2. Explain what Steinbeck suggests about the Oklahoma farmers' practical and spiritual relationship with the environment when he says, "all of them were caught in something larger than themselves." How does this apply universally?

3. Compare "Letters from the Dust Bowl" (p. 142) with the excerpt here from Steinbeck's *The Grapes of Wrath*. What details do Henderson and Steinbeck give prominence to? What differences in detail and point of view tend to make Henderson's description more personal? Discuss whether or not the depiction of dust bowl conditions is more powerful coming from Steinbeck as a novelist or Henderson as a farmer.

✤ David E. Lilienthal (1899–1981)

One Valley—and a Thousand (1944)

David E. Lilienthal believed enthusiastically in public service and wise use of the environment. He was a prime mover for environmental transformations constructed by the Tennessee Valley Authority (TVA), which was designed to improve the lot of rural common people. Though not raised in a rural environment, Lilienthal was a first-generation American who achieved success in business and then entered public service.

The son of a Czech storekeeper in Morton, Illinois, Lilienthal graduated from Harvard Law School, after which he was hired as counsel for the city of Chicago. One of Lilienthal's triumphs during this time was winning a reduction in telephone rates and returning $20 million to subscribers. His specialty in public utility regulation led to his appointment to the Illinois Public Service Commission. In 1933, President Franklin D. Roosevelt heard of his talents and asked him to be on the first board of directors of the TVA, a position he held for 12 years, including its chairmanship in 1941.

The merits of damming the Tennessee River had been debated since the 1920s, but the project had been defeated because of its huge engineering, funding, and staffing requirements. Ironically, the Depression created a favorable economic and political climate because such an undertaking would provide jobs and help to improve the regional economy. TVA was authorized in 1933.

The metamorphosis of the wild and rural Tennessee River Valley into a civilized landscape that looked natural inspired Lilienthal. He thought other rivers and regions could be engineered to benefit both humans and nature. "I believe men may learn to work in harmony with the forces of nature," he wrote, "neither despoiling what God has given nor helpless to put them to use."

Following completion of the TVA, Lilienthal was appointed chairman of the Atomic Energy Commission (AEC) by President Truman, a post he held until 1950. His work involved overseeing the buildup of nuclear weapons, and Lilienthal played an important role in the development of nuclear power for commercial purposes. In 1955, he became chairman of the private Development and Research Corporation, which designed water control projects in developing countries.

Lilienthal's public spirit and dedication to public good, while beyond question, leaves unanswered his ruthless application of the doctrine of wise use. There is always the concern of how far one can apply the practical notion of what is best for society or whether or not progress is always for the best. "One Valley—and a Thousand" is excerpted from TVA: Democracy on the March *(1944).*

This book was written in the valley of a great American river, the Tennessee. It is about that river, and that valley; about the soil of its farms, the white oak and pine on its mountain slopes, the ores and minerals that lie buried in its hills. It is about the rain that falls so violently upon its fields, and the course the water follows as it seeks out first the streams and then the river itself. This book is about the people of this valley region, the men who work the land, the men who roll the silver sheets of aluminum, who run the cotton gins, and stand behind the counter in the general stores. It is about the women who tend the spindles or stir the kettles or teach the children in the schools.

This is the story of a great change. It is an account of what has happened in this valley since 1933 when Congress set the Tennessee Valley Authority to the task of developing the resources of this region. It is a tale of a wandering and inconstant river now become a chain of broad and lovely lakes which people enjoy, and on which they can depend, in all seasons, for the movement of the barges of commerce that now nourish their business enterprises. It is a story of how waters once wasted and destructive have been controlled and now work, night and day, creating electric energy to lighten the burden of human drudgery. Here is a tale of fields grown old and barren with the years, which now are vigorous with new fertility, lying green to the sun; of forests that were hacked and despoiled, now protected and refreshed with strong young trees just starting on their slow road to maturity. It is a story of the people and how they have worked to create a new valley.

I write of the Tennessee Valley, but all this could have happened in almost any of a thousand other valleys where rivers run from the hills to the sea. For the valleys of the earth have these things in common: the waters, the air, the land, the minerals, the forests. In Missouri and in Arkansas, in Brazil and in the Argentine, in China and in India there are just such rivers, rivers flowing through mountain canyons, through canebrake and palmetto, through barren wastes—rivers that in the violence of flood menace the land and the people, then sulk in idleness and drought—rivers all over the world waiting to be controlled by men—the Yangtze, the Ganges, the Ob, the Parana, the Amazon, the Nile. In a thousand valleys in America and the world over there are fields that need to be made strong and productive, land steep and rugged, land flat as a man's hand; on the slopes, forests—and in the hills, minerals—that can be made to yield a better living for people.

And in foreign but no longer distant lands, in the cities and the villages in those thousand valleys, live men of a hundred different tongues and many racial strains. As you move across the boundaries men have drawn upon their maps, you find that their laws are different, as are their courts and passport regulations, and what they use for money. Different too are the words you hear, the color of men's skin, the customs in the home and in the market. But the things the people live by are the same; the soil and the water, the rivers in their valleys, the minerals within the earth. It is upon these everywhere that men must build, in California or Morocco, the Ukraine or Tennessee. These are the things they dig for and hew and process and contrive. These are the foundation of all their hopes for relief from hunger, from cold, from drudgery, for an end to want and constant insecurity. A thousand valleys over the globe and our valley here are in this way the same: everywhere what happens to the land, the forests, and the water determines what happens to the people.

The Tennessee River had always been an idle giant and a destructive one. Today its boundless energy works for the people who live in this valley. This is true of but few of the thousands of rivers the world over. But it can be true of many, perhaps most. The job will be begun in our time, can be well along toward fulfillment within the life of men now living. There is almost nothing, however fantastic, that (given competent organization) a team of engineers, scientists, and administrators cannot do today. Impossible things can be done, are being done in this mid-twentieth century.

Today it is builders and technicians that we turn to: men armed not with the ax, rifle, and bowie knife, but with the Diesel engine, the bulldozer, the giant electric shovel, the retort—and most of all, with an emerging kind of skill, a modern knack of organization and execution. When these men have imagination and faith, they can move mountains; out of their skills they can create new jobs, relieve human drudgery, give new life and fruitfulness to worn-out lands, put yokes upon the streams, and transmute the minerals of the earth and the plants of the field into machines of wizardry to spin out the stuff of a way of life new to this world.

Such are the things that have happened in the Tennessee Valley. Here men and science and organizing skills applied to the resources of waters, land, forests, and minerals have yielded great benefits for the people. And it is just such fruits of technology and resources that people all over the world will, more and more, demand for themselves. That people believe these things can be theirs—this it is that constitutes the real revolution of our time, the dominant political fact of the generation that lies ahead. No longer do men look upon poverty as inevitable, or think that drudgery, disease, filth, famine, floods, and physical exhaustion are visitations of the devil or punishment by a deity.

Here is the central fact with which today's statesmanship must contend. The political promises that will be made and the great popular movements that have come into being deal with the demands of people for the ever larger harvest that science and nature, devoted to a common purpose, can be made to yield. The terms under which the people of the world receive the products of technical advance, such as those that have come to this valley, are at the vortex of the cyclonic forces of our century.

This is the right time for telling of such things. In the desperation of war, miracles were wrought in laboratories and with machines. Seeing the reality of things they had never dreamed could happen, men the world over were deeply stirred; they began to think of tomorrow, to think of it with longing tinged with fear and uncertainty, livened with hopes for the future.

A great restlessness and acute dissatisfaction with their present lot have seized large areas of the world; peoples who for centuries were without hope now demand an earnest of good faith as to their future—things that they can see, can themselves experience. As even the more obtuse conventional politicians are beginning to learn people seem less and less beguiled by abstractions and vague eloquence; their thinking is less complicated but closer to life than that of the intellectual on the lecture platform or the political leader drafting a manifesto.

In the recesses of men's thoughts they seem not so concerned with generalizations and exhortations as with quite concrete desires: sixty acres of land, how it can be brought back to fertility; how to get the crop to the best kind of market; how to get a job at a new kind of factory machine at good pay; about a pleasant town where the kids can have bicycles; about electric lights and heated schools and churches and hospitals for the ill; no more flooding out every spring; long Diesel barges on the river to carry off the warehoused wheat; refrigerators and irrigation canals and an end to the malaria mosquitoes. The word spreads that these and many other such things can be theirs; that the inventors and engineers and chemists can make them happen. The word has spread to the crossroad towns in the Ozarks, the trailer camps in Detroit, the boarding houses in Fall River; to men in the oil fields across the Rio Grande, the collieries in Wales, the shops of Leeds and Manchester; even to the villages on the Ganges and the caves beneath Chungking.

Our faith is sustained by the inspiring words of great leadership, by the pledges of freedom and prosperity and democracy. But it is when the words unbend—when they come into men's homes, to their farms, their shops—that they come alive to men. Do the words mean that a livelihood will not always be won at the cost of such drudgery for men and women, will not always be so skimpy and bitter? What of the soil of their land—will it always be so starved? What of the metal that could be made of the minerals, and the houses of the forests; what of the gadgets to pump the water that for so long the women have carried in buckets day after day? What of the river that flows through the valley— what great things would happen if its flow could turn the wheels of new factories? This is a job of building for the new skills of young engineers and chemists and the Army-trained mechanics; a job for the architects and engineers with ideas about new kinds of cities, for the physicians with ideas for new kinds of hospitals and revolutions in nutrition.

The inspiring principles—is this what they mean? To give them such a meaning takes more than words and promises, however eloquent and honestly uttered. This is a job of work to be done, a job for which there is already some experience and more than enough talent and skill. The words of promise can be made to come true. Here is the Grand Job of This Century.

But everything depends upon *how* this job is done.

The spirit in which the task is undertaken; its purpose, whether for the welfare of the many or the few; the methods chosen—these will determine whether men will live in freedom and peace, whether their resources will be speedily exhausted or will be sustained, nourished, made solid beneath their feet not only for themselves but for the generations to come.

The physical achievements that science and technology now make possible *may bring no benefits,* may indeed be evil, unless they have a moral purpose, unless they are conceived and carried out for the benefit of the people themselves. Without such a purpose, advances in technology may be disastrous to the human spirit; the industrialization of a raw material area may bring to the average man only a new kind of slavery and the destruction of democratic institutions.

But such a moral purpose alone is not enough to insure that resource development will be a blessing and not a curse. Out of TVA experience in this valley I am persuaded that to make such a purpose effective two other principles are essential.

First, that resource development must be governed by the unity of nature herself.

Second, that the people must participate actively in that development.

The physical job is going to be done; of that I think we can be sure. But if, in the doing, the unity of nature's resources is disregarded, the price will be paid in exhausted land, butchered forests, polluted streams, and industrial ugliness. And, if the people are denied an active part in this great task, then they may be poor or they may be prosperous but they will not be free.

Is it inescapable that such a task of resource development be carried on only by highly centralized government direction? Must it inevitably be run by a privileged élite of managers or experts or politicians? Yes, say the defeatists about democracy, the cynics, the disillusioned and frustrated liberals, the believers in force, the disbelievers in men. Can it be done in no other way than by gutting the resources of nature, by making the countryside hideous, by maiming the forests, fouling the streams, ignoring the unity of land and water and men? Yes, that is "the way things are," say the greedy, the short-sighted, the unperceptive.

The experience in this valley gives the lie to such answers and to those who utter them. The whole point of the TVA experience that I shall seek to make plain in this book is that the best way, perhaps the only way the job can be done effectively, is by observing the unity of nature, by following democratic methods, by the active daily participation of the people themselves.

What is going on in the Tennessee Valley and what I shall describe in this book is specific, graphic, particular, something that can be seen, appraised, analyzed. One demonstration is worth much generalized discussion and tall talk. TVA was initiated frankly as an experiment; it has been administered in the spirit of exploration and innovation. But it is no utopian Brook Farm experiment; no endeavor to escape into a simpler past or a more romantic future TVA and this valley face the facts of the present with all its complexities and difficulties.

The methods of democratic development represented by the TVA are distinctive, but their roots lie deep in the soil of American tradition and common experience. They are methods that differ from those customarily employed both by private enterprisers and public agencies. Nevertheless the TVA experiment has been carried on under the existing rules of the game of American life. It required no change in the Constitution of the United States. Congress has maintained full control. Property rights and social institutions have undergone no drastic amendment. In short, the valley's change has gone forward under typical and traditional American conditions rather than under non-existent "ideal" conditions that would not or could not be duplicated.

The breadth of purpose and the distinctive methods of the TVA— these it is that constitute the most important part of the enterprise. It is these that will have the greatest usefulness to other Americans and to the increasingly large number of responsible men in other nations who are concerned with problems essentially similar to those that faced this valley in 1933.

It is upon such purposes and methods that our answers to issues of peace and freedom will turn. All else—"principles" of economics and finance, dollars and pounds sterling, tariffs and taxation, unemployment insurance, health programs, new gadgets and plastics and chemicals and electronic devices, democratic government, even essential international arrangements—will depend upon the decisions we make and the course we follow tomorrow in the fundamental activity of developing the resources in the soil, the air, the water, and within the earth, through modern skills of science and organization.

Questions for Thinking and Writing

1. Explain what Lilienthal means when he says that any massive project like the TVA must "be governed by the unity of nature herself." How does Lilienthal reconcile this abstract concept with the actual fact of damming rivers and literally changing the contour, flora, and fauna of the land? Does the creation of the TVA prove George Perkins Marsh's contention that humans are destructive to the environment? (p. 26)
2. What philosophical point of view seems to be at the source of Lilienthal's social, political, and economic optimism? Explain Lilienthal's belief that without human intervention the Tennessee River was idle and destructive.
3. Compare Lilienthal's *"One Valley—and a Thousand"* with Walt Whitman's "Song of the Redwood-Tree" (p. 39) and Aldo Leopold's "The Land Ethic" (p. 195).

🌿 Elizabeth Bishop (1911–1974)

The Fish (1946)

As crisp and clear as Elizabeth Bishop's writing may appear, her poetry forces the exploration of inner motivation and self. Her detailed observation and description bring into focus questions of universal appeal.

She was born in Worcester, Massachusetts, but spent much of her early childhood in Nova Scotia with her maternal grandparents and later in Boston with her paternal grandparents. While growing up,

Bishop never had a home of her own. Her father died soon after she was born, and her mother was committed to a mental hospital when she was only 5. Such a devastating family life compelled Biship to carefully mask her deep emotional pain.

As a school-age girl, she was sent away to boarding school, after which she attended Vassar College. Bishop once said, "I was always sort of a guest, and I think I've always felt that way." This revealing statement about her inner life shows an insecurity that took great effort to overcome. Triumph over adversity was an important aspect of her life and a constant source of subjects in her poems.

After graduating, Bishop became a lifelong traveler, spending time first in Europe, North Africa, Mexico, and later dividing her time between Key West, Florida, and Rio de Janiero, Brazil. Her poems, which she wrote during her travels, reflect her various physical locations, though they never lose a New England quality of sparseness. In the early 1970s, Bishop returned from Brazil for good to live in Boston where she taught part time at several universities. She died suddenly in 1974.

"The Fish," an early poem, suggests Bishop's need to overcome adversity, whether it is illness, loss of love, or inability to create new poems. The poem suggests that the experience of beauty may be found where it is not expected. Here the natural environment is keenly observed. Bishop's fisherman sees something new in the ordinary world, and what seems to be plain changes before his eyes, and the eyes of the reader, as the old battered fish takes on the aspects of the rainbow. Overall, the details of the poem—the old boat, the rusted bailer, the oil-stained bilge—unexpectedly give way to a feeling of joy and victory. Water for Bishop is a source of knowledge, and when this fish is caught, it gives the fisherman knowledge of self. This unusual fish story becomes something else again when the fish is set free. Why the fisherman finds victory in letting it go poses the chief question of the poem. Perhaps, the fish may represent ego. If so, it is an ego symbolized by a common animal in the natural world.

I caught a tremendous fish
and held him beside the boat
half out of water, with my hook
fast in a corner of his mouth.
He didn't fight.
He hadn't fought at all.
He hung a grunting weight,
battered and venerable
and homely. Here and there

his brown skin hung in strips
like ancient wallpaper,
and its pattern of darker brown
was like wallpaper:
shapes like full-blown roses
stained and lost through age.
He was speckled with barnacles,
fine rosettes of lime,
and infested
with tiny white sea-lice,
and underneath two or three
rags of green weed hung down.
While his gills were breathing in
the terrible oxygen
—the frightening gills,
fresh and crisp with blood,
that can cut so badly—
I thought of the coarse white flesh
packed in like feathers,
the big bones and the little bones,
the dramatic reds and blacks
of his shiny entrails,
and the pink swim-bladder
like a big peony.
I looked into his eyes
which were far larger than mine
but shallower, and yellowed,
the irises backed and packed
with tarnished tinfoil
seen through the lenses
of old scratched isinglass.
They shifted a little, but not
to return my stare.
—It was more like the tipping
of an object toward the light.
I admired his sullen face,
the mechanism of his jaw,
and then I saw
that from his lower lip
—if you could call it a lip—
grim, wet, and weaponlike,
hung five old pieces of fish-line,
or four and a wire leader
with the swivel still attached,
with all their five big hooks

grown firmly in his mouth.
A green line, frayed at the end
where he broke it, two heavier lines,
and a fine black thread
still crimped from the strain and snap
when it broke and he got away.
Like medals with their ribbons
frayed and wavering,
a five-haired beard of wisdom
trailing from his aching jaw.
I stared and stared
and victory filled up
the little rented boat,
from the pool of bilge
where oil had spread a rainbow
around the rusted engine
to the bailer rusted orange,
the sun-cracked thwarts,
the oarlocks on their strings,
the gunnels—until everything
was rainbow, rainbow, rainbow!
And I let the fish go.

Questions for Thinking and Writing

1. Why does the fisherman achieve victory by setting the fish free? To what extent is letting the fish go a victory of humans over nature? Or a victory over self-doubt and instability?
2. Explain the symbolic meanings of the rainbow. Why does this naturally occurring phenomenon hold such fascination for humans?
3. Compare the relationship of character and setting in "The Fish" and Hemingway's story "Big Two-Hearted River" (p. 127). How does the fisherman in each benefit spiritually from the experience of dealing with nature directly without any mediators?

🌿 Marjory Stoneman Douglas (b. 1890)

Boom, Blow, Bust, and Recovery (1947)

Already a centenarian, Marjory Stoneman Douglas is one of the staunchest defenders of Florida's Everglades and wisest critics of south Florida development. These are positions she was thrown into and adopted by accident.

Born in Minnesota, reared in New England, and educated at Wellesley College, Douglas came to Miami in 1915 seeking a divorce from her husband of two years. Her estranged father, then editor of the Miami Herald, *offered his daughter, who had always wanted to write, a job on the newspaper as a society reporter. The newspaper then was very small, allowing Douglas the freedom to report and write many varied stories. She was given her own column in which she often wrote about the establishment of Everglades National Park.*

In 1941, an editor friend asked Douglas to contribute a chapter to a book being planned on rivers in America. Accepting the offer, she decided to write about the Everglades by construing it in a unique way—as a sheet of water, inches deep, flowing from Lake Okeechobee to the Gulf of Mexico. She called it a river of grass, a name that stuck. She spent the next five years on the project. The chapter she had set out to do evolved into a book.

Published in 1947, The Everglades *was immediately successful and has sold 10,000 copies every year since then. Douglas has also written an autobiography,* Marjory Stoneman Douglas: Voice of the River, *and is completing a biography of W. H. Hudson, the British writer who was a close observer of nature.*

The excerpt taken from The Everglades *describes the severity of the hurricane of 1926 that nearly ruined Miami. "Boom, Blow, Bust, and Recovery" serves to memorialize humankind's effort to live and prosper in a natural environment that has no interest in human preoccupations.*

Building in Miami, like the prices of lots, had its own boom. Railroads could not begin to handle the southbound freight in lumber, plumbing fixtures, wallboard, nails, roofing, window frames, everything. Railroad yards all the way north were congested. Carefully iced vegetable cars moved south full of brick. Tracks were too crowded for passenger trains. The Florida Coast and the newly extended Seaboard declared a freight embargo. Fleets of trucks then moved south with building supplies. Sailing vessels from as far away as Portland, Oregon, barks, barkentines, even one full-rigged ship were chartered, crammed full of building materials and pushed down to Biscayne Bay. A forest of masts lay along the bay-front. The narrow channel to the cut was filled with old wind-jammers, coming and going with their tugs.

The long four-masted *Prinz Valdemar* broke her towlines and slued across the channel and sank. The ship channel was locked shut. More windjammers let go their anchors on the reef outside the beach where in the nights they looked like a long lighted town. For two months, while salvage men dredged and pushed and dug, the *Prinz Valdemar* lay where she was. The rigged ships along the bayfront grew barnacles. Building in Miami stopped for the summer.

Lots were still selling. People said the embargo gave everybody a chance to get caught up so that the boom could begin again in the fall. Full-page announcements of new subdivisions, Opa-Locka with its lovely minarets, and new towns with nothing but gateways weighted the newspapers. Forty miles of waterfront were advertised for Coral Gables as the dredges cut canals in the rock south of Coconut Grove and moved a deep trail of salt water inland.

The physical appearance of Miami was already much changed, although a dozen elaborate new buildings still bristled with scaffolding. The Venetian Causeway to Miami Beach took the place of the old Collins Bridge. The Miami Woman's Club and many downtown churches on land Mr. Flagler had given them sold and built elsewhere. The old trees were torn down and tall buildings that might have stood anywhere were raised flush with the sidewalks, dwarfing the already narrow streets.

The yellow-and-white Royal Palm Hotel, among its fine gardens by the river, held its old charm and dignity. The crowded streets were overhung with signs. Only over the downtown roofs thrusting higher, in that late summer of 1926, against the remoter loveliness of the skies, pearly and violet and white frothed with the mountains of dazzling summer clouds, the night hawks in their unbelievable flight still slid and dived and tumbled and skated. Their fine twitterings, the deep thrum of wings, as they dived and sharply recovered, were never heard over the city's traffic. But they had their freedom of it still.

The sickle wings of the night hawks began the long beat southward in their fall migration. In their skyey courses they may have been the first to feel that vast shape of air spinning up from the equator along the line of the Bahamas. The word reached Miami on the morning of Friday, September 17, that a hurricane moved there somewhere. A fine gray rain began and blew and stopped and blew again. The sky darkened with a greenish light southeastward. The fine rain blew white against it and stopped. A dark sudden gale gathered. There was more rain. Then none, and for a while no wind. Old-timers, remembering hurricanes, felt their skins prickle and began to board up.

Most people knew nothing of hurricanes at all. It was reported from Nassau that hurricane winds higher than a hundred miles an hour had hit them. The center had curved before that, turning across the Gulf Stream. It moved directly on Miami.

Late that night, in absolute darkness, it hit, with the far shrieking scream, the queer rumbling of a vast and irresistible freight train.

The wind instruments blew away at a hundred twenty-five miles. The leaves went, branches, the bark off the trees. In the slashing assault people found their roofs had blown off, unheard in the tumult. The water of the bay was lifted and blown inland, in streaming sheets of salt, with boats, scows, ships, the *Rose Mahoney*, coconuts, debris of all sorts, up on the highest ridge of the mainland. Miami Beach was isolated in a sea of raving white water. Far out to the Everglades shacks, garages, sheds, barns, were smashed flat by the wind and trampled into mud by the machine-gunning of the steely rain.

At eight o'clock next morning the gray light lifted. The roaring stopped. There was no wind. Blue sky stood overhead. People opened their doors and ran, still a little dazed, into the ruined streets. They shouted and climbed up on collapsed walls, and walked and stared. A few people complained that their ears clicked or hummed, as if they were going down in an elevator. Only a few remembered or had ever heard that in the center of a spinning hurricane there is that bright deathly stillness.

It passed. The light darkened. The high shrieking came from the other direction as the opposite whirling thickness of the cyclonic cone moved on over the darkened city.

People died then in the streets, drowned, blown against walls, injured by bricks, planks, corrugated iron, blown and smashed down on them. For hours the screaming blowing terror of the storm went by. The center passed through the Everglades in a great swath, crushing the stiff saw grass, dwarfing the lake. The water was blown across the southwest rim, smashing the muck dikes that had been built to keep Moorehaven dry. The white foaming water poured out for miles back into the saw grass. Three hundred twenty Moorehaven people and people on remote farms along the canals, people huddled in boats, and on the roofs of floating houses were killed or drowned.

By sunset that same night in Miami the wind was gone. Two thousand houses were down, three thousand badly damaged. In Fort Lauderdale twelve hundred houses were smashed. Streets, bayfronts, rivers were obliterated with debris. Relief workers made their way to Hialeah rescuing people trapped under houses, women giving birth to babies among ruins, picking up people bleeding to death or dead. There were no lights, hardly any food or water. The relief trains began to come in.

Yet in the ruined city the cheapness, the flimsiness, the real estate shacks, the billboards, the garish swinging signs, the houses badly built, the dizzy ideas, the boom itself, was blown away. What was left were such foundations of buildings or ideas as had been well and truly laid. There was the sea and the bay, tranquil and innocent already as blue flowers. There was the rock below, the sun, the fine exuberant air. And the courage, the fundamental character, of a sobered people. Hundreds left. Those who stayed, newcomers or old-timers, worked together at last. When relief was no longer necessary and the city cleaned and patched, the days of mourning over, they saw that the place was real again.

Men, doubly ruined by boom and blow, went to work at anything they could get. Many who had been paper millionaires remembered that they had been bakers. "Men of vision" saw that they were still lawyers or printers. Those who had come here because they were promoters and had not yet learned to care for any place they could not exploit had left long before. Men stayed, operating elevators, working in grocery stores, going back to reporting or selling hurricane insurance or searching for clear titles through the vast layers of worthless paper mortgages. They learned that they had come because they loved the unique country, and they were not changed. There was still fish in the unharmed sea. A man could plant a sapling and watch its quick tropical growth and eat its fruit.

For years to come Florida real estate would be a laughing matter.

Questions for Thinking and Writing

1. What does this episode say about the power of a violent storm and the economic boom of south Florida in the 1920s? What does it suggest about human helplessness in nature?
2. Why does Douglas contrast the flight of the nighthawks with the building of Miami? How does this characterize the conflict of nature and the city?

Juanita Platero and Siyowin Miller
Chee's Daughter (1948)

Little is known about Juanita Platero and Siyowin Miller. Both are Navajo, and were friends and writing collaborators in 1929 when Chief Standing Bear of the Teton Sioux encouraged them to write about their Native American heritage. "Chee's Daughter" first appeared in Common Ground *magazine. The story was given wider distribution when Natachee Scott Momaday published it in her anthology*

American Indian Authors (*1971*). *A collaborative book of poetry,* Winds Erase Your Footprints, *was in progress, according to Momaday, but no record exists of it having been published.*

The dominant theme of "Chee's Daughter" portrays the difficulty that Navajos have experienced fitting their ancient beliefs and customs into white culture. Chee's daughter is recovered because Chee follows the old ways. Old Man Fat and his wife pay lip service to the old ways but really have given in to greed and materialism. When the highway bypasses their trading post, they have no inner resources to help them. The scared couple trade the girl for food, the lowest denominator of life, which Chee obtained through successful farming and propitiation of the Navajo spirits.

The hat told the story, the big, black, drooping Stetson. It was not at the proper angle, the proper rakish angle for so young a Navaho. There was no song, and that was not in keeping either. There should have been at least a humming, a faint, all-to-himself "he he he heya," for it was a good horse he was riding, a slender-legged, high-stepping buckskin that would race the wind with light knee-urging. This was a day for singing, a warm winter day, when the touch of the sun upon the back belied the snow high on distant mountains.

Wind warmed by the sun touched his high-boned cheeks like flicker feathers, and still he rode on silently, deeper into Little Canyon, until the red rock walls rose straight upward from the stream bed and only a narrow piece of blue sky hung above. Abruptly the sky widened where the canyon walls were pushed back to make a wide place, as though in ancient times an angry stream had tried to go all ways at once.

This was home—this wide place in the canyon—levels of jagged rock and levels of rich red earth. This was home to Chee, the rider of the buckskin, as it had been to many generations before him.

He stopped his horse at the stream and sat looking across the narrow ribbon of water to the bare-branched peach trees. He was seeing them each springtime with their age-gnarled limbs transfigured beneath veils of blossom pink; he was seeing them in autumn laden with their yellow fruit, small and sweet. Then his eyes searched out the indistinct furrows of the fields beside the stream, where each year the corn and beans and squash drank thirstily of the overflow from summer rains. Chee was trying to outweigh today's bitter betrayal of hope by gathering to himself these reminders of the integrity of the land. Land did not cheat! His mind lingered deliberately on all the days spent here in the sun caring for the young plants, his songs to the earth and to the life springing from it—". . . In the middle of the wide field . . . Yellow Corn Boy . . . He has started both ways . . . ," then the harvest and repayment in full measure. Here was the old feeling of wholeness and of oneness with the sun and earth and growing things.

Chee urged the buckskin toward the family compound where, secure in a recess of overhanging rock, was his mother's dome-shaped hogan, red rock and red adobe like the ground on which it nestled. Not far from the hogan was the half-circle of brush like a dark shadow against the canyon wall—corral for sheep and goats. Farther from the hogan, in full circle, stood the horse corral made of heavy cedar branches sternly interlocked. Chee's long thin lips curved into a smile as he passed his daughter's tiny hogan squatted like a round Pueblo oven be- side the corral. He remembered the summer day when together they sat back on their heels and plastered wet adobe all about the circling wall of rock and the woven dome of piñon twigs. How his family laughed when the Little One herded the bewildered chickens into her tiny hogan as the first snow fell.

Then the smile faded from Chee's lips and his eyes darkened as he tied his horse to a corral post and turned to the strangely empty com- pound. "Someone has told them," he thought, "and they are inside weeping." He passed his mother's deserted loom on the south side of the hogan and pulled the rude wooden door toward him, bowing his head, hunching his shoulders to get inside.

His mother sat sideways by the center fire, her feet drawn up under her full skirts. Her hands were busy kneading dough in the chipped white basin. With her head down, her voice was muffled when she said, "The meal will soon be ready, son."

Chee passed his father sitting against the wall, hat over his eyes as though asleep. He passed his older sister, who sat turning mutton ribs on a crude wire grill over the coals, noticed tears dropping on her hands. "She cared more for my wife than I realized," he thought.

Then because something must be said sometime, he tossed the black Stetson upon a bulging sack of wool and said, "You have heard, then." He could not shut from his mind how confidently he had set the hand- some new hat on his head that very morning, slanting the wide brim over one eye: he was going to see his wife, and today he would ask the doctors about bringing her home; last week she had looked so much better.

His sister nodded but did not speak. His mother sniffled and passed her velveteen sleeve beneath her nose. Chee sat down, leaning against the wall. "I suppose I was a fool for hoping all the time. I should have expected this. Few of our people get well from the coughing sickness. But *she* seemed to be getting better."

His mother was crying aloud now and blowing her nose noisily on her skirt. His father sat up, speaking gently to her.

Chee shifted his position and started a cigarette. His mind turned back to the Little One. At least she was too small to understand what had happened, the Little One who had been born three years before in the sanitarium where his wife was being treated for the coughing sickness, the Little One he had brought home to his mother's hogan to be nursed by his sister, whose baby was a few months older. As she grew fat-cheeked and sturdy-legged, she followed him about like a shadow; somehow her baby mind had grasped that of all those at the hogan who cared for her and played with her, he—Chee—belonged most to her. She sat cross-legged at his elbow when he worked silver at the forge; she rode before him in the saddle when he drove the horses to water; often she lay wakeful on her sheep pelts until he stretched out for the night in the darkened hogan and she could snuggle warm against him.

Chee blew smoke slowly, and some of the sadness left his dark eyes as he said, "It is not as bad as it might be. It is not as though we are left with nothing."

Chee's sister arose, sobs catching in her throat, and rushed past him out the doorway. Chee sat upright, a terrible fear possessing him. For a moment his mouth could make no sound. Then: "The Little One! Mother, where is she?"

His mother turned her stricken face to him. "Your wife's people came after her this morning. They heard yesterday of their daughter's death through the trader at Red Sands."

Chee started to protest, but his mother shook her head slowly. "I didn't expect they would want the Little One either. But there is nothing you can do. She is a girl child and belongs to her mother's people; it is custom."

Frowning, Chee got to his feet, grinding his cigarette into the dirt floor. "Custom! When did my wife's parents begin thinking about custom? Why, the hogan where they live doesn't even face the East!" He started toward the door. "Perhaps I can overtake them. Perhaps they don't realize how much we want her here with us. I'll ask them to give my daughter back to me. Surely, they won't refuse."

His mother stopped him gently with her outstretched hand. "You couldn't overtake them now. They were in the trader's car. Eat and rest, and think more about this."

"Have you forgotten how things have always been between you and your wife's people?" his father said.

That night, Chee's thoughts were troubled—half-forgotten incidents became disturbingly vivid—but early the next morning he saddled the buckskin and set out for the settlement of Red Sands. Even though his father-in-law, Old Man Fat, might laugh, Chee knew that he must talk to him. There were some things to which Old Man Fat might listen.

Chee rode the first part of the fifteen miles to Red Sands expectantly. The sight of sandstone buttes near Cottonwood Spring reddening in the morning sun brought a song almost to his lips. He twirled his reins in salute to the small boy herding sheep toward many-colored Butterfly Mountain, watched with pleasure the feathers of smoke rising against tree-darkened western mesas from the hogans sheltered there. But as he approached the familiar settlement sprawled in mushroom growth along the highway, he began to feel as though a scene from a bad dream was becoming real.

Several cars were parked around the trading store, which was built like two log hogans side by side, with red gas pumps in front and a sign across the tar-paper roofs: *Red Sands Trading Post—Groceries Gasoline Cold Drinks Sandwiches Indian Curios.* Back of the trading post an un-painted frame house and outbuildings squatted on the drab, treeless land. Chee and the Little One's mother had lived there when they stayed with his wife's people. That was according to custom—living with one's wife's people—but Chee had never been convinced that it was custom alone which prompted Old Man Fat and his wife to insist that their daughter bring her husband to live at the trading post.

Beside the Post was a large hogan of logs, with brightly painted pseudo-Navaho designs on the roof—a hogan with smoke-smudged windows and a garish blue door which faced north to the highway. Old Man Fat had offered Chee a hogan like this one. The trader would build it if he and his wife would live there and Chee would work at his forge making silver jewelry where tourists could watch him. But Chee had asked instead for a piece of land for a cornfield and help in building a hogan far back from the highway and a corral for the sheep he had brought to this marriage.

A cold wind blowing down from the mountains began to whistle about Chee's ears. It flapped the gaudy Navaho rugs which were hung in one long bright line to attract tourists. It swayed the sign *Navaho Weaver at Work* beside the loom where Old Man Fat's wife sat hunched in her striped blanket, patting the colored thread of a design into place with a wooden comb. Tourists stood watching the weaver. More tourists stood in a knot before the hogan where the sign said: *See Inside a Real Navaho Home 25¢.*

Then the knot seemed to unravel as a few people returned to their cars; some had cameras; and there against the blue door Chee saw the Little One standing uncertainly. The wind was plucking at her new pur-ple blouse and wide green skirt; it freed truant strands of soft dark hair from the meager queue into which it had been tied with white yarn.

"Isn't she cunning!" one of the women tourists was saying as she turned away.

Chee's lips tightened as he began to look around for Old Man Fat. Finally he saw him passing among the tourists collecting coins.

Then the Little One saw Chee. The uncertainty left her face, and she darted through the crowd as her father swung down from his horse. Chee lifted her in his arms, hugging her tight. While he listened to her breathless chatter, he watched Old Man Fat bearing down on them, scowling.

As his father-in-law walked heavily across the graveled lot, Chee was reminded of a statement his mother sometimes made: "When you see a fat Navaho, you see one who hasn't worked for what he has."

Old Man Fat was fattest in the middle. There was indolence in his walk even though he seemed to hurry, indolence in his cheeks so plump they made his eyes squint, eyes now smoldering with anger.

Some of the tourists were getting into their cars and driving away. The old man said belligerently to Chee, "Why do you come here? To spoil our business? To drive people away?"

"I came to talk with you," Chee answered, trying to keep his voice steady as he faced the old man.

"We have nothing to talk about," Old Man Fat blustered and did not offer to touch Chee's extended hand.

"It's about the Little One." Chee settled his daughter more comfortably against his hip as he weighed carefully all the words he had planned to say. "We are going to miss her very much. It wouldn't be so bad if we knew that *part* of each year she could be with us. That might help you too. You and your wife are no longer young people and you have no young ones here to depend upon." Chee chose his next words remembering the thriftlessness of his wife's parents, and their greed. "Perhaps we could share the care of this little one. Things are good with us. So much snow this year will make lots of grass for the sheep. We have good land for corn and melons."

Chee's words did not have the expected effect. Old Man Fat was enraged. "Farmers, all of you! Long-haired farmers! Do you think everyone must bend his back over the shorthandled hoe in order to have food to eat?" His tone changed as he began to brag a little. "We not only have all the things from cans at the trader's, but when the Pueblos come past here on their way to town, we buy their salty jerked mutton, young corn for roasting, dried sweet peaches."

Chee's dark eyes surveyed the land along the highway as the old man continued to brag about being "progressive." *He* no longer was tied to the land. He and his wife made money easily and could *buy* all the things they wanted. Chee realized too late that he had stumbled into the old argument between himself and his wife's parents. They had never understood his feeling about the land—that a man took care of his land and it in turn took care of him. Old Man Fat and his wife scoffed at him, called him a Pueblo farmer, all during that summer when he planted and weeded and harvested. Yet they ate the green corn in their mutton stews, and the chili paste from the fresh ripe chilis, and the tortillas from the cornmeal his wife ground. None of this working and sweating in the sun for Old Man Fat, who talked proudly of his easy way of living—collecting money from the trader who rented this strip of land beside the highway, collecting from the tourists.

Yet Chee had once won that argument. His wife had shared his belief in the integrity of the earth, that jobs and people might fail one, but the earth never would. After that first year she had turned from her own people and gone with Chee to Little Canyon.

Old Man Fat was reaching for the Little One. "Don't be coming here with plans for my daughter's daughter," he warned. "If you try to make trouble, I'll take the case to the government man in town."

The impulse was strong in Chee to turn and ride off while he still had the Little One in his arms. But he knew his time of victory would be short. His own family would uphold the old custom of children, especially girl children, belonging to the mother's people. He would have to give his daughter up if the case were brought before the headman of Little Canyon, and certainly he would have no better chance before a strange white man in town.

He handed the bewildered Little One to her grandfather who stood watching every movement suspiciously. Chee asked, "If I brought you a few things for the Little One, would that be making trouble? Some velvet for a blouse, or some of the jerky she likes so well . . . this summer's melon?"

Old Man Fat backed away from him. "Well," he hesitated, as some of the anger disappeared from his face and beads of greed shone in his eyes. "Well," he repeated. Then as the Little One began to squirm in his arms and cry, he said, "No! No! Stay away from here, you and all your family."

The sense of his failure deepened as Chee rode back to Little Canyon. But it was not until he sat with his family that evening in the hogan, while the familiar bustle of meal preparing went on about him, that he began to doubt the wisdom of the things he'd always believed. He smelled the coffee boiling and the oily fragrance of chili powder dusted into the bubbling pot of stew; he watched his mother turning round crusty fried bread in the small black skillet. All around him was plenty—a half of mutton hanging near the door, bright strings of chili drying, corn hanging by the braided husks, cloth bags of dried peaches. Yet in his heart was nothing.

He heard the familiar sounds of the sheep outside the hogan, the splash of water as his father filled the long drinking trough from the water barrel. When his father came in, Chee could not bring himself to tell a second time of the day's happenings. He watched his wiry, soft-spoken father while his mother told the story, saw his father's queue of graying hair quiver as he nodded his head with sympathetic exclamations.

Chee's doubting, acrid thoughts kept forming: Was it wisdom his father had passed on to him, or was his inheritance only the stubbornness of a long-haired Navaho resisting change? Take care of the land and it will take care of you. True, the land had always given him food, but now food was not enough. Perhaps if he had gone to school, he would have learned a different kind of wisdom, something to help him now. A schoolboy might even be able to speak convincingly to this government man whom Old Man Fat threatened to call, instead of sitting here like a clod of earth itself—Pueblo farmer indeed. What had the land to give that would restore his daughter?

In the days that followed, Chee herded sheep. He got up in the half-light, drank the hot coffee his mother had ready, then started the flock moving. It was necessary to drive the sheep a long way from the hogan to find good winter forage. Sometimes Chee met friends or relatives who were on their way to town or to the road camp where they hoped to get work; then there was friendly banter and an exchange of news. But most of the days seemed endless; he could not walk far enough or fast enough from his memories of the Little One or from his bitter thoughts. Sometimes it seemed his daughter trudged beside him, so real he could almost hear her footsteps—the muffled pad-pad of little feet clad in deerhide. In the glare of a snowbank he would see her vivid face, brown eyes sparkling. Mingling with the tinkle of sheep bells he heard her laughter.

When, weary of following the small sharp hoof marks that crossed and recrossed in the snow, he sat down in the shelter of a rock, it was only to be reminded that in his thoughts he had forsaken his brother-hood with the earth and sun and growing things. If he remembered times when he had flung himself against the earth to rest, to lie there in the sun until he could no longer feel where he left off and the earth began, it was to remember also that now he sat like an alien against the same earth; the belonging-together was gone. The earth was one thing and he was another.

It was during the days when he herded sheep that Chee decided he must leave Little Canyon. Perhaps he would take a job silversmithing for one of the traders in town. Perhaps, even though he spoke little English, he could get a job at the road camp with his cousins; he would ask them about it.

Springtime transformed the mesas. The peach trees in the canyon were shedding fragrance and pink blossoms on the gentled wind. The sheep no longer foraged for the yellow seeds of chamiso but ranged near the hogan with the long-legged new lambs, eating tender young grass.

Chee was near the hogan on the day his cousins rode up with the message for which he waited. He had been watching with mixed emotions while his father and his sister's husband cleared the fields beside the stream.

"The boss at the camp says he needs an extra hand, but he wants to know if you'll be willing to go with the camp when they move it to the other side of the town?" The tall cousin shifted his weight in the saddle.

The other cousin took up the explanation. "The work near here will last only until the new cutoff beyond Red Sands is finished. After that, the work will be too far away for you to get back here often."

That was what Chee had wanted—to get away from Little Canyon— yet he found himself not so interested in the job beyond town as in this new cutoff which was almost finished. He pulled a blade of grass, split it thoughtfully down the center, as he asked questions of his cousins. Finally he said: "I need to think more about this. If I decide on this job, I'll ride over."

Before his cousins were out of sight down the canyon, Chee was walking toward the fields, a bold plan shaping in his mind. As the plan began to flourish, wild and hardy as young tumbleweed, Chee added his own voice softly to the song his father was singing: ". . . In the middle of the wide field . . . Yellow Corn Boy . . . I wish to put in."

Chee walked slowly around the field, the rich red earth yielding to his footsteps. His plan depended upon this land and upon the things he remembered most about his wife's people.

Through planting time Chee worked zealously and tirelessly. He spoke little of the large new field he was planting, because he felt so strongly that just now this was something between himself and the land. The first days he was ever stooping, piercing the ground with the pointed stick, placing the corn kernels there, walking around the field and through it, singing, ". . . His track leads into the ground . . . Yellow Corn Boy . . . his track leads into the ground." After that, each day Chee walked through his field watching for the tips of green to break through; first a few spikes in the center and then more and more, until the corn in all parts of the field was above ground. Surely, Chee thought, if he sang the proper songs, if he cared for this land faithfully, it would not forsake him now, even though through the lonely days of winter he had betrayed the goodness of the earth in his thoughts.

Through the summer Chee worked long days, the sun hot upon his back, pulling weeds from around young corn plants; he planted squash and pumpkin; he terraced a small piece of land near his mother's hogan and planted carrots and onions and the moisture-loving chili. He was increasingly restless. Finally he told his family what he hoped the harvest from this land would bring him. Then the whole family waited with him, watching the corn: the slender graceful plants that waved green arms and bent to embrace each other as young winds wandered through the field, the maturing plants flaunting their pollen-laden tassels in the sun, the tall and sturdy parent corn with new-formed ears and a froth of purple, red, and yellow corn-beards against the dusty emerald of broad leaves.

Summer was almost over when Chee slung the bulging packs across two pack ponies. His mother helped him tie the heavy rolled pack behind the saddle of the buckskin. Chee knotted the new yellow kerchief about his neck a little tighter, gave the broad black hat brim an extra tug, but these were only gestures of assurance and he knew it. The land had not failed him. That part was done. But this he was riding into? Who could tell?

When Chee arrived at Red Sands, it was as he had expected to find it—no cars on the highway. His cousins had told him that even the Pueblo farmers were using the new cutoff to town. The barren gravel around the Red Sands Trading Post was deserted. A sign banged against the dismantled gas pumps: *Closed until further notice.*

Old Man Fat came from the crude summer shelter built beside the log hogan from a few branches of scrub cedar and the sides of wooden crates. He seemed almost friendly when he saw Chee.

"Get down, my son," he said, eyeing the bulging packs. There was no bluster in his voice today, and his face sagged, looking somewhat saddened, perhaps because his cheeks were no longer quite full enough to push his eyes upward at the corners. "You are going on a journey?"

Chee shook his head. "Our fields gave us so much this year, I thought to sell or trade this to the trader. I didn't know he was no longer here."

Old Man Fat sighed, his voice dropping to an injured tone. "He says he and his wife are going to rest this winter; then after that he'll build a place up on the new highway."

Chee moved as though to be traveling on, then jerked his head toward the pack ponies. "Anything you need?"

"I'll ask my wife," Old Man Fat said as he led the way to the shelter. "Maybe she has a little money. Things have not been too good with us since the trader closed. Only a few tourists come this way." He shrugged his shoulders. "And with the trader gone—no credit."

Chee was not deceived by his father-in-law's unexpected confidences. He recognized them as a hopeful bid for sympathy and, if possible, something for nothing. Chee made no answer. He was thinking that so far he had been right about his wife's parents: their thriftlessness had left them with no resources to last until Old Man Fat found another easy way of making a living.

Old Man Fat's wife was in the shelter working at her loom. She turned rather wearily when her husband asked with noticeable deference if she would give him money to buy supplies. Chee surmised that the only income here was from his mother-in-law's weaving.

She peered around the corner of the shelter at the laden ponies, and then she looked at Chee. "What do you have there, my son?"

Chee smiled to himself as he turned to pull the pack from one of the ponies, dragged it to the shelter where he untied the ropes. Pumpkins and hardshelled squash tumbled out, and the ears of corn—pale yellow husks fitting firmly over plump ripe kernels, blue corn, red corn, yellow corn, many-colored corn, ears and ears of it—tumbled into every corner of the shelter.

"Yooooh," Old Man Fat's wife exclaimed as she took some of the ears in her hands. Then she glanced up at her son-in-law. "But we have no money for all this. We have sold almost everything we own—even the brass bed that stood in the hogan."

Old Man Fat's brass bed. Chee concealed his amusement as he started back for another pack. That must have been a hard parting. Then he stopped, for, coming from the cool darkness of the hogan was the Little One, rubbing her eyes as though she had been asleep. She stood for a moment in the doorway, and Chee saw that she was dirty, barefoot, her hair uncombed, her little blouse shorn of all its silver buttons. Then she ran toward Chee, her arms outstretched. Heedless of Old Man Fat and his wife, her father caught her in his arms, her hair falling in a dark cloud across his face, the sweetness of her laughter warm against his shoulder.

It was the haste within him to get this slow waiting game played through to the finish that made Chee speak unwisely. It was the desire to swing her before him in the saddle and ride fast to Little Canyon that prompted his words. "The money doesn't matter. You still have something. . . ."

Chee knew immediately that he had overspoken. The old woman looked from him to the corn spread before her. Unfriendliness began to harden in his father-in-law's face. All the old arguments between himself and his wife's people came pushing and crowding in between them now.

Old Man Fat began kicking the ears of corn back onto the canvas as he eyed Chee angrily. "And you rode all the way over here thinking that for a little food we would give up our daughter's daughter?"

Chee did not wait for the old man to reach for the Little One. He walked dazedly to the shelter, rubbing his cheek against her soft dark hair, and put her gently into her grandmother's lap. Then he turned back to the horses. He had failed. By his own haste he had failed. He swung into the saddle, his hand touching the roll behind it. Should he ride on into town?

Then he dismounted, scarcely glancing at Old Man Fat, who stood uncertainly at the corner of the shelter, listening to his wife. "Give me a hand with this other pack of corn, grandfather," Chee said, carefully keeping the small bit of hope from his voice.

Puzzled, but willing, Old Man Fat helped carry the other pack to the shelter, opening it to find more corn as well as carrots and round, pale yellow onions. Chee went back for the roll behind the buckskin's saddle and carried it to the entrance of the shelter, where he cut the ropes and gave the canvas a nudge with his toe. Tins of coffee rolled out, small plump cloth bags; jerked meat from several butcherings spilled from a flour sack; and bright red chilis splashed like flames against the dust.

"I will leave all this anyhow," Chee told them. "I would not want my daughter nor even you old people to go hungry."

Old Man Fat picked up a shiny tin of coffee, then put it down. With trembling hands he began to untie one of the cloth bags—dried sweet peaches.

The Little One had wriggled from her grandmother's lap, unheeded, and was on her knees, digging her hands into the jerked meat.

"There is almost enough food here to last all winter," Old Man Fat's wife sought the eyes of her husband.

Chee said, "I meant it to be enough. But that was when I thought you might send the Little One back with me." He looked down at his daughter noisily sucking jerky. Her mouth, both fists, were full of it. "I am sorry that you feel you cannot bear to part with her."

Old Man Fat's wife brushed a straggly wisp of gray hair from her forehead as she turned to look at the Little One. Old Man Fat was looking too. And it was not a thing to see. For in that moment the Little One ceased to be their daughter's daughter and became just another mouth to feed.

"And why not?" the old woman asked wearily.

Chee was settled in the saddle, the barefooted Little One before him. He urged the buckskin faster, and his daughter clutched his shirt-front. The purpling mesas flung back the echo: ". . . . My corn embrace each other. In the middle of the wide field . . . Yellow Corn Boy embrace each other."

Questions for Thinking and Writing

1. What are Chee's sources of strength? How does he integrate his sense of self and Navajo obligation to the land? Why does Chee succeed and Old Man Fat and his wife fail?
2. Chee believes that if "you take care of the land it will take care of you." Explain how this could be so. How does this Navajo concept compare with Henderson's attitude in "Letters from the Dust Bowl" (p. 142), or David Lilienthal's in "One Valley—and a Thousand" (p. 170)?

🌿 Aldo Leopold (1887–1948)
The Land Ethic (1933)

Aldo Leopold became a voice of reason in the controversy between land use and conservation. When the practices of game management and unrestricted harvesting of forest resources and mining dominated, he expressed his views after considerable soul searching and practical experience as a forester?

Born in Burlington, Iowa, Leopold graduated from the Yale School of Forestry in 1909 and joined the U.S. Forest Service. He was assigned to Arizona and New Mexico. At the time, national forests were under the control of Gifford Pinchot's concept of controlled use. Leopold, a young man, fell right in with it, advocating the establishment of game refuges in which game animals could roam free of predators that, he advised, should be wiped out.

This surprising attitude may have come out of Leopold's academic training, however, rather than from his heart. During the two decades he spent in the Southwest, he came to realize the value of setting aside vast tracts of land that would remain undisturbed, though they might be surrounded by lumbering and mining operations. The change in philosophy came out of Leopold's gradual awakening to the unity of nature and the need for a balance best achieved by nature itself rather than through an invariably faulty human decision-making process.

The unspoiled area that Leopold had in mind became the Gila Wilderness, but before he could administer its half-million acres the way he envisioned it, he was transferred to the Forest Service's office in Madison, Wisconsin, an emotional letdown because Leopold had come to love the Southwest. In 1924, Leopold left the Forest Service and became associate director of the Forest Products Laboratory in Madison. In 1933, he became a professor of game management at the University of Wisconsin where a chair was endowed for him. The same year he published his Game Management, *a text that outlined his philosophy of natural unity. In it, he espoused his views that the environment deserves respect and protection because of its mere existence, rather than because some aspect of it could benefit humanity. Yet he maintained that due to the exalted position of humans, it was their responsibility to take care of the environment. Ironically, Leopold died in 1948 fighting a brushfire on a neighbor's farm. In 1965, he was named to the National Wildlife Federation's Conservation Hall of Fame. A Sand County Almanac, published posthumously in 1949, provides an intensive perspective of Leopold's life and thought. It is arranged in three parts. The first part is the Sand County almanac, a series of sketches arranged by season in which Leopold describes life on the sand farm he owned. The second part, "Sketches Here and There," is a collection of various writings on the theme of conservation published over the years. Most importantly, the third part includes "The Land Ethic," first delivered as a speech before the American Association for the Advancement of Science in 1933, and for which he is best known.*

W hen god-like Odysseus returned from the wars in Troy, he hanged all on one rope a dozen slave-girls of his house-hold whom he suspected of misbehavior during his absence.

This hanging involved no question of propriety. The girls were property. The disposal of property was then, as now, a matter of expediency, not of right and wrong.

Concepts of right and wrong were not lacking from Odysseus' Greece: witness the fidelity of his wife through the long years before at last his black-prowed galleys clove the wine-dark seas for home. The ethical structure of that day covered wives, but had not yet been extended to human chattels. During the three thousand years which have since elapsed, ethical criteria have been extended to many fields of conduct, with corresponding shrinkages in those judged by expediency only.

THE ETHICAL SEQUENCE

This extension of ethics, so far studied only by philosophers, is actually a process in ecological evolution. Its sequences may be described in ecological as well as in philosophical terms. An ethic, ecologically, is a limitation on freedom of action in the struggle for existence. An ethic, philosophically, is a differentiation of social from anti-social conduct. These are two definitions of one thing. The thing has its origin in the tendency of interdependent individuals or groups to evolve modes of co-operation. The ecologist calls these symbioses. Politics and economics are advanced symbioses in which the original free-for-all competition has been replaced, in part, by co-operative mechanisms with an ethical content.

The complexity of co-operative mechanisms has increased with population density, and with the efficiency of tools. It was simpler, for example, to define the anti-social uses of sticks and stones in the days of the mastodons than of bullets and billboards in the age of motors.

The first ethics dealt with the relation between individuals; the Mosaic Decalogue is an example. Later accretions dealt with the relation between the individual and society. The Golden Rule tries to integrate the individual to society; democracy to integrate social organization to the individual.

There is as yet no ethic dealing with man's relation to land and to the animals and plants which grow upon it. Land, like Odysseus' slave-girls, is still property. The land-relation is still strictly economic, entailing privileges but not obligations.

The extension of ethics to this third element in human environment is, if I read the evidence correctly, an evolutionary possibility and an ecological necessity. It is the third step in a sequence. The first two have already been taken. Individual thinkers since the days of Ezekiel and Isaiah have asserted that the despoliation of land is not only inexpedient but wrong. Society, however, has not yet affirmed their belief. I regard the present conversation movement as the embryo of such an affirmation.

An ethic may be regarded as a mode of guidance for meeting ecological situations so new or intricate, or involving such deferred reactions, that the path of social expediency is not discernible to the average individual. Animal instincts are modes of guidance for the individual in meeting such situations. Ethics are possibly a kind of community instinct in-the-making.

THE COMMUNITY CONCEPT

All ethics so far evolved rest upon a single premise: that the individual is a member of a community of interdependent parts. His instincts prompt him to compete for his place in that community, but his ethics prompt him also to co-operate (perhaps in order that there may be a place to compete for).

The land ethic simply enlarges the boundaries of the community to include soils, waters, plants, and animals, or collectively: the land.

This sounds simple: do we not already sing our love for and obligation to the land of the free and the home of the brave? Yes, but just what and whom do we love? Certainly not the soil, which we are sending helter-skelter downriver. Certainly not the waters, which we assume have no function except to turn turbines, float barges, and carry off sewage. Certainly not the plants, of which we exterminate whole communities without batting an eye. Certainly not the animals, of which we have already extirpated many of the largest and most beautiful species. A land ethic of course cannot prevent the alteration, management, and use of these 'resources,' but it does affirm their right to continued existence, and, at least in spots, their continued existence in a natural state.

In short, a land ethic changes the role of *Homo sapiens* from conqueror of the land-community to plain member and citizen of it. It implies respect for his fellow-members, and also respect for the community as such.

In human history, we have learned (I hope) that the conqueror role is eventually self-defeating. Why? Because it is implicit in such a role that the conqueror knows, *ex cathedra,* just what makes the community clock tick, and just what and who is valuable, and what and who is worthless, in community life. It always turns out that he knows neither, and this is why his conquests eventually defeat themselves.

In the biotic community, a parallel situation exists. Abraham knew exactly what the land was for: it was to drip milk and honey into Abraham's mouth. At the present moment, the assurance with which we regard this assumption is inverse to the degree of our education.

The ordinary citizen today assumes that science knows what makes the community clock tick; the scientist is equally sure that he does not. He knows that the biotic mechanism is so complex that its workings may never be fully understood.

That man is, in fact, only a member of a biotic team is shown by an ecological interpretation of history. Many historical events, hitherto explained solely in terms of human enterprise, were actually biotic interactions between people and land. The characteristics of the land determined the facts quite as potently as the characteristics of the men who lived on it.

Consider, for example, the settlement of the Mississippi valley. In the years following the Revolution, three groups were contending for its control: the native Indian, the French and English traders, and the American settlers. Historians wonder what would have happened if the English at Detroit had thrown a little more weight into the Indian side of those tipsy scales which decided the outcome of the colonial migration into the cane-lands of Kentucky. It is time now to ponder the fact that the cane-lands, when subjected to the particular mixture of forces represented by the cow, plow, fire, and axe of the pioneer, became bluegrass. What if the plant succession inherent in this dark and bloody ground had, under the impact of these forces, given us some worthless sedge, shrub, or weed? Would Boone and Kenton have held out? Would there have been any overflow into Ohio, Indiana, Illinois, and Missouri? Any Louisiana Purchase? Any transcontinental union of new states? Any Civil War?

Kentucky was one sentence in the drama of history. We are commonly told what the human actors in this drama tried to do, but we are seldom told that their success, or the lack of it, hung in large degree on the reaction of particular soils to the impact of the particular forces exerted by their occupancy. In the case of Kentucky, we do not even know where the bluegrass came from—whether it is a native species, or a stowaway from Europe.

Contrast the cane-lands with what hindsight tells us about the Southwest, where the pioneers were equally brave, resourceful, and persevering. The impact of occupancy here brought no bluegrass, or other plant fitted to withstand the bumps and buffetings of hard use. This region, when grazed by livestock, reverted through a series of more and more

worthless grasses, shrubs, and weeds to a condition of unstable equilibrium. Each recession of plant types bred erosion; each increment to
erosion bred a further recession of plants. The result today is a progressive and mutual deterioration, not only of plants and soils, but of
the animal community subsisting thereon. The early settlers did not expect this: on the ciénegas of New Mexico some even cut ditches to hasten it. So subtle has been its progress that few residents of the region
are aware of it. It is quite invisible to the tourist who finds this wrecked
landscape colorful and charming (as indeed it is, but it bears scant resemblance to what it was in 1848).

This same landscape was 'developed' once before, but with quite different results. The Pueblo Indians settled the Southwest in pre-
Columbian times, but they happened *not* to be equipped with range
livestock. Their civilization expired, but not because their land expired.

In India, regions devoid of any sod-forming grass have been settled,
apparently without wrecking the land, by the simple expedient of carrying the grass to the cow, rather than vice versa. (Was this the result of
some deep wisdom, or was it just good luck? I do not know.)

In short, the plant succession steered the course of history; the pioneer simply demonstrated, for good or ill, what successions inhered in
the land. Is history taught in this spirit? It will be, once the concept of
land as a community really penetrates our intellectual life.

THE ECOLOGICAL CONSCIENCE

Conservation is a state of harmony between men and land. Despite
nearly a century of propaganda, conservation still proceeds at a snail's
pace; progress still consists largely of letterhead pieties and convention
oratory. On the back forty we still slip two steps backward for each forward stride.

The usual answer to this dilemma is 'more conservation education.'
No one will debate this, but is it certain that only the *volume* of education needs stepping up? Is something lacking in the *content* as well?

It is difficult to give a fair summary of its content in brief form, but,
as I understand it, the content is substantially this: obey the law, vote
right, join some organizations, and practice what conservation is profitable on your own land; the government will do the rest.

Is not this formula too easy to accomplish anything worth-while? It
defines no right or wrong, assigns no obligation, calls for no sacrifice,
implies no change in the current philosophy of values. In respect of
land-use, it urges only enlightened self-interest. Just how far will such
education take us? An example will perhaps yield a partial answer.

By 1930 it had become clear to all except the ecologically blind that
southwestern Wisconsin's topsoil was slipping seaward. In 1933 the

farmers were told that if they would adopt certain remedial practices for five years, the public would donate CCC labor to install them, plus the necessary machinery and materials. The offer was widely accepted, but the practices were widely forgotten when the five-year contract period was up. The farmers continued only those practices that yielded an immediate and visible economic gain for themselves.

This led to the idea that maybe farmers would learn more quickly if they themselves wrote the rules. Accordingly the Wisconsin Legislature in 1937 passed the Soil Conservation District Law. This said to farmers, in effect: *We, the public, will furnish you free technical service and loan you specialized machinery, if you will write your own rules for land-use. Each county may write its own rules, and these will have the force of law.* Nearly all the counties promptly organized to accept the proferred help, but after a decade of operation, *no county has yet written a single rule.* There has been visible progress in such practices as strip-cropping, pasture renovation, and soil liming, but none in fencing woodlots against grazing, and none in excluding plow and cow from steep slopes. The farmers, in short, have selected those remedial practices which were profitable anyhow, and ignored those which were profitable to the community, but not clearly profitable to themselves.

When one asks why no rules have been written, one is told that the community is not yet ready to support them; education must precede rules. But the education actually in progress makes no mention of obligations to land over and above those dictated by self-interest. The net result is that we have more education but less soil, fewer healthy woods, and as many floods as in 1937.

The puzzling aspect of such situations is that the existence of obligations over and above self-interest is taken for granted in such rural community enterprises as the betterment of roads, schools, churches, and baseball teams. Their existence is not taken for granted, nor as yet seriously discussed, in bettering the behavior of the water that falls on the land, or in the preserving of the beauty or diversity of the farm landscape. Land-use ethics are still governed wholly by economic self-interest, just as social ethics were a century ago.

To sum up: we asked the farmer to do what he conveniently could to save his soil, and he has done just that, and only that. The farmer who clears the woods off a 75 per cent slope, turns his cows into the clearing, and dumps its rainfall, rocks, and soil into the community creek, is still (if otherwise decent) a respected member of society. If he puts lime on his fields and plants his crops on contour, he is still entitled to all the privileges and emoluments of his Soil Conservation District. The District is a beautiful piece of social machinery, but it is coughing along on two cylinders because we have been too timid, and too anxious for quick success, to tell the farmer the true magnitude of his obligations. Obligations have no meaning without conscience, and the problem we face is the extension of the social conscience from people to land.

No important change in ethics was ever accomplished without an internal change in our intellectual emphasis, loyalties, affections, and convictions. The proof that conservation has not yet touched these foundations of conduct lies in the fact that philosophy and religion have not yet heard of it. In our attempt to make conservation easy, we have made it trivial.

SUBSTITUTES FOR A LAND ETHIC

When the logic of history hungers for bread and we hand out a stone, we are at pains to explain how much the stone resembles bread. I now describe some of the stones which serve in lieu of a land ethic.

One basic weakness in a conservation system based wholly on economic motives is that most members of the land community have no economic value. Wildflowers and songbirds are examples. Of the 22,000 higher plants and animals native to Wisconsin, it is doubtful whether more than 5 per cent can be sold, fed, eaten, or otherwise put to economic use. Yet these creatures are members of the biotic community, and if (as I believe) its stability depends on its integrity, they are entitled to continuance.

When one of these non-economic categories is threatened, and if we happen to love it, we invent subterfuges to give it economic importance. At the beginning of the century songbirds were supposed to be disappearing. Ornithologists jumped to the rescue with some distinctly shaky evidence to the effect that insects would eat us up if birds failed to control them. The evidence had to be economic in order to be valid.

It is painful to read these circumlocutions today. We have no land ethic yet, but we have at least drawn nearer the point of admitting that birds should continue as a matter of biotic right, regardless of the presence or absence of economic advantage to us.

A parallel situation exists in respect of predatory mammals, raptorial birds, and fish-eating birds. Time was when biologists somewhat overworked the evidence that these creatures preserve the health of game by killing weaklings, or that they control rodents for the farmer, or that they prey only on 'worthless' species. Here again, the evidence had to be economic in order to be valid. It is only in recent years that we hear the more honest argument that predators are members of the community, and that no special interest has the right to exterminate them for the sake of a benefit, real or fancied, to itself. Unfortunately this enlightened view is still in the talk stage. In the field the extermination of predators goes merrily on: witness the impending erasure of the timber wolf by fiat of Congress, the Conservation Bureaus, and many state legislatures.

Some species of trees have been 'read out of the party' by economics-minded foresters because they grow too slowly, or have too low a sale value to pay as timber crops: white cedar, tamarack, cypress, beech, and hemlock are examples. In Europe, where forestry is ecologically more advanced, the non-commercial tree species are recognized as members of the native forest community, to be preserved as such, within reason. Moreover some (like beech) have been found to have a valuable function in building up soil fertility. The interdependence of the forest and its constituent tree species, ground flora, and fauna is taken for granted.

Lack of economic value is sometimes a character not only of species or groups, but of entire biotic communities: marshes, bogs, dunes, and 'deserts' are examples. Our formula in such cases is to relegate their conservation to government as refuges, monuments, or parks. The difficulty is that these communities are usually interspersed with more valuable private lands; the government cannot possibly own or control such scattered parcels. The net effect is that we have relegated some of them to ultimate extinction over large areas. If the private owner were ecologically minded, he would be proud to be the custodian of a reasonable proportion of such areas, which add diversity and beauty to his farm and to his community.

In some instances, the assumed lack of profit in these 'waste' areas has proved to be wrong, but only after most of them had been done away with. The present scramble to reflood muskrat marshes is a case in point.

There is a clear tendency in American conservation to relegate to government all necessary jobs that private landowners fail to perform. Government ownership, operation, subsidy, or regulation is now widely prevalent in forestry, range management, soil and watershed management, park and wilderness conservation, fisheries management, and migratory bird management, with more to come. Most of this growth in governmental conservation is proper and logical, some of it is inevitable. That I imply no disapproval of it is implicit in the fact that I have spent most of my life working for it. Nevertheless the question arises: What is the ultimate magnitude of the enterprise? Will the tax base carry its eventual ramifications? At what point will governmental conservation, like the mastodon, become handicapped by its own dimensions? The answer, if there is any, seems to be in a land ethic, or some other force which assigns more obligation to the private landowner.

Industrial landowners and users, especially lumbermen and stockmen, are inclined to wail long and loudly about the extension of government ownership and regulation to land, but (with notable exceptions) they show little disposition to develop the only visible alternative: the voluntary practice of conservation on their own lands.

When the private landowner is asked to perform some unprofitable act for the good of the community, he today assents only with outstretched palm. If the act costs him cash this is fair and proper, but when it costs only forethought, open-mindedness, or time, the issue is at least debatable. The overwhelming growth of land-use subsidies in recent years must be ascribed, in large part, to the government's own agencies for conservation education: the land bureaus, the agricultural colleges, and the extension services. As far as I can detect, no ethical obligation toward land is taught in these institutions.

To sum up: a system of conservation based solely on economic self-interest is hopelessly lopsided. It tends to ignore, and thus eventually to eliminate, many elements in the land community that lack commercial value, but that are (as far as we know) essential to its healthy functioning. It assumes, falsely, I think, that the economic parts of the biotic clock will function without the uneconomic parts. It tends to relegate to government many functions eventually too large, too complex, or too widely dispersed to be performed by government.

An ethical obligation on the part of the private owner is the only visible remedy for these situations.

THE LAND PYRAMID

An ethic to supplement and guide the economic relation to land presupposes the existence of some mental image of land as a biotic mechanism. We can be ethical only in relation to something we can see, feel, understand, love, or otherwise have faith in.

The image commonly employed in conservation education is 'the balance of nature.' For reasons too lengthy to detail here, this figure of speech fails to describe accurately what little we know about the land mechanism. A much truer image is the one employed in ecology: the biotic pyramid. I shall first sketch the pyramid as a symbol of land, and later develop some of its implications in terms of land-use.

Plants absorb energy from the sun. This energy flows through a circuit called the biota, which may be represented by a pyramid consisting of layers. The bottom layer is the soil. A plant layer rests on the soil, an insect layer on the plants, a bird and rodent layer on the insects, and so on up through various animal groups to the apex layer, which consists of the larger carnivores.

The species of a layer are alike not in where they came from, or in what they look like, but rather in what they eat. Each successive layer depends on those below it for food and often for other services, and each in turn furnishes food and services to those above. Proceeding upward, each successive layer decreases in numerical abundance. Thus, for every carnivore there are hundreds of his prey, thousands of their prey, millions of insects, uncountable plants. The pyramidal form of the system reflects this numerical progression from apex to base. Man shares an intermediate layer with the bears, raccoons, and squirrels which eat both meat and vegetables.

The lines of dependency for food and other services are called food chains. Thus soil-oak-deer-Indian is a chain that has now been largely converted to soil-corn-cow-farmer. Each species, including ourselves, is a link in many chains. The deer eats a hundred plants other than oak, and the cow a hundred plants other than corn. Both, then, are links in a hundred chains. The pyramid is a tangle of chains so complex as to seem disorderly, yet the stability of the system proves it to be a highly organized structure. Its functioning depends on the co-operation and competition of its diverse parts.

In the beginning, the pyramid of life was low and squat; the food chains short and simple. Evolution has added layer after layer, link after link. Man is one of thousands of accretions to the height and complexity of the pyramid. Science has given us many doubts, but it has given us at least one certainty: the trend of evolution is to elaborate and diversify the biota.

Land, then, is not merely soil; it is a fountain of energy flowing through a circuit of soils, plants, and animals. Food chains are the living channels which conduct energy upward; death and decay return it to the soil. The circuit is not closed; some energy is dissipated in decay, some is added by absorption from the air, some is stored in soils, peats, and long-lived forests; but it is a sustained circuit, like a slowly augmented revolving fund of life. There is always a net loss by downhill wash, but this is normally small and offset by the decay of rocks. It is deposited in the ocean and, in the course of geological time, raised to form new lands and new pyramids.

The velocity and character of the upward flow of energy depend on the complex structure of the plant and animal community, much as the upward flow of sap in a tree depends on its complex cellular organization. Without this complexity, normal circulation would presumably not occur. Structure means the characteristic numbers, as well as the characteristic kinds and functions, of the component species. This interdependence between the complex structure of the land and its smooth functioning as an energy unit is one of its basic attributes.

When a change occurs in one part of the circuit, many other parts must adjust themselves to it. Change does not necessarily obstruct or divert the flow of energy; evolution is a long series of self-induced changes, the net result of which has been to elaborate the flow mechanism and to lengthen the circuit. Evolutionary changes, however, are usually slow and local. Man's invention of tools has enabled him to make changes of unprecedented violence, rapidity, and scope.

One change is in the composition of floras and faunas. The larger predators are lopped off the apex of the pyramid; food chains, for the first time in history, become shorter rather than longer. Domesticated species from other lands are substituted for wild ones, and wild ones are moved to new habitats. In this world-wide pooling of faunas and floras, some species get out of bounds as pests and diseases, others are extinguished. Such effects are seldom intended or foreseen; they represent unpredicted and often untraceable readjustments in the structure. Agricultural science is largely a race between the emergence of new pests and the emergence of new techniques for their control.

Another change touches the flow of energy through plants and animals and its return to the soil. Fertility is the ability of soil to receive, store, and release energy. Agriculture, by overdrafts on the soil, or by too radical a substitution of domestic for native species in the superstructure, may derange the channels of flow or deplete storage. Soils depleted of their storage, or of the organic matter which anchors it, wash away faster than they form. This is erosion.

Waters, like soil, are part of the energy circuit. Industry, by polluting waters or obstructing them with dams, may exclude the plants and animals necessary to keep energy in circulation.

Transportation brings about another basic change: the plants or animals grown in one region are now consumed and returned to the soil in another. Transportation taps the energy stored in rocks, and in the air, and uses it elsewhere; thus we fertilize the garden with nitrogen gleaned by the guano birds from the fishes of seas on the other side of the Equator. Thus the formerly localized and self-contained circuits are pooled on a world-wide scale.

The process of altering the pyramid for human occupation releases stored energy, and this often gives rise, during the pioneering period, to a deceptive exuberance of plant and animal life, both wild and tame. These releases of biotic capital tend to becloud or postpone the penalties of violence.

This thumbnail sketch of land as an energy circuit conveys three basic ideas:

(1) That land is not merely soil.

(2) That the native plants and animals kept the energy circuit open; others may or may not.

(3) That man-made changes are of a different order than evolutionary changes, and have effects more comprehensive than is intended or foreseen.

These ideas, collectively, raise two basic issues: Can the land adjust itself to the new order? Can the desired alterations be accomplished with less violence?

Biotas seem to differ in their capacity to sustain violent conversion. Western Europe, for example, carries a far different pyramid than Caesar found there. Some large animals are lost; swampy forests have become meadows or plowland; many new plants and animals are introduced, some of which escape as pests; the remaining natives are greatly changed in distribution and abundance. Yet the soil is still there and, with the help of imported nutrients, still fertile; the waters flow normally; the new structure seems to function and to persist. There is no visible stoppage or derangement of the circuit.

Western Europe, then, has a resistant biota. Its inner processes are tough, elastic, resistant to strain. No matter how violent the alterations, the pyramid, so far, has developed some new *modus vivendi* which preserves its habitability for man, and for most of the other natives.

Japan seems to present another instance of radical conversion without disorganization.

Most other civilized regions, and some as yet barely touched by civilization, display various stages of disorganization, varying from initial symptoms to advanced wastage. In Asia Minor and North Africa diagnosis is confused by climatic changes, which may have been either the cause or the effect of advanced wastage. In the United States the degree of disorganization varies locally; it is worst in the Southwest, the Ozarks, and parts of the South, and least in New England and the Northwest. Better land-uses may still arrest it in the less advanced regions. In parts of Mexico, South America, South Africa, and Australia a violent and accelerating wastage is in progress, but I cannot assess the prospects.

This almost world-wide display of disorganization in the land seems to be similar to disease in an animal, except that it never culminates in complete disorganization or death. The land recovers, but at some reduced level of complexity, and with a reduced carrying capacity for people, plants, and animals. Many biotas currently regarded as 'lands of opportunity' are in fact already subsisting on exploitative agriculture, i.e. they have already exceeded their sustained carrying capacity. Most of South America is overpopulated in this sense.

In arid regions we attempt to offset the process of wastage by reclamation, but it is only too evident that the prospective longevity of reclamation projects is often short. In our own West, the best of them may not last a century.

The combined evidence of history and ecology seems to support one general deduction: the less violent the man-made changes, the greater the probability of successful readjustment in the pyramid. Violence, in turn, varies with human population density; a dense population requires a more violent conversion. In this respect, North America has a better chance for permanence than Europe, if she can contrive to limit her density.

This deduction runs counter to our current philosophy, which assumes that because a small increase in density enriched human life, that an indefinite increase will enrich it indefinitely. Ecology knows of no density relationship that holds for indefinitely wide limits. All gains from density are subject to a law of diminishing returns.

Whatever may be the equation for men and land, it is improbable that we as yet know all its terms. Recent discoveries in mineral and vitamin nutrition reveal unsuspected dependencies in the up-circuit: incredibly minute quantities of certain substances determine the value of soils to plants, of plants to animals. What of the down-circuit? What of the vanishing species, the preservation of which we now regard as an esthetic luxury? They helped build the soil; in what unsuspected ways may they be essential to its maintenance? Professor Weaver proposes that we use prairie flowers to reflocculate the wasting soils of the dust bowl; who knows for what purpose cranes and condors, otters and grizzlies may some day be used?

LAND HEALTH AND THE A-B CLEAVAGE

A land ethic, then, reflects the existence of an ecological conscience, and this in turn reflects a conviction of individual responsibility for the health of the land. Health is the capacity of the land for self-renewal. Conservation is our effort to understand and preserve this capacity.

Conservationists are notorious for their dissensions. Superficially these seem to add up to mere confusion, but a more careful scrutiny reveals a single plane of cleavage common to many specialized fields. In each field one group (A) regards the land as soil, and its function as commodity-production; another group (B) regards the land as a biota, and its function as something broader. How much broader is admittedly in a state of doubt and confusion.

In my own field, forestry, group A is quite content to grow trees like cabbages, with cellulose as the basic forest commodity. It feels no inhibition against violence; its ideology is agronomic. Group B, on the other hand, sees forestry as fundamentally different from agronomy because it employs natural species, and manages a natural environment rather than creating an artificial one. Group B prefers natural reproduction on principle. It worries on biotic as well as economic grounds about the loss of species like chestnut, and the threatened loss of the white pines. It worries about a whole series of secondary forest functions: wildlife, recreation, watersheds, wilderness areas. To my mind, Group B feels the stirrings of an ecological conscience.

In the wildlife field, a parallel cleavage exists. For Group A the basic commodities are sport and meat; the yardsticks of production are ciphers of take in pheasants and trout. Artificial propagation is acceptable as a permanent as well as a temporary recourse—if its unit costs permit. Group B, on the other hand, worries about a whole series of biotic side-issues. What is the cost in predators of producing a game crop? Should we have further recourse to exotics? How can management restore the shrinking species, like prairie grouse, already hopeless as shootable game? How can management restore the threatened rarities, like trumpeter swan and whooping crane? Can management principles be extended to wildflowers? Here again it is clear to me that we have the same A-B cleavage as in forestry.

In the larger field of agriculture I am less competent to speak, but there seem to be somewhat parallel cleavages. Scientific agriculture was actively developing before ecology was born, hence a slower penetration of ecological concepts might be expected. Moreover the farmer, by the very nature of his techniques, must modify the biota more radically than the forester or the wildlife manager. Nevertheless, there are many discontents in agriculture which seem to add up to a new vision of 'biotic farming.'

Perhaps the most important of these is the new evidence that poundage or tonnage is no measure of the food-value of farm crops; the products of fertile soil may be qualitatively as well as quantitatively superior. We can bolster poundage from depleted soils by pouring on imported fertility, but we are not necessarily bolstering food-value. The possible ultimate ramifications of this idea are so immense that I must leave their exposition to abler pens.

The discontent that labels itself 'organic farming,' while bearing some of the earmarks of a cult, it is nevertheless biotic in its direction, particularly in its insistence on the importance of soil flora and fauna.

The ecological fundamentals of agriculture are just as poorly known to the public as in other fields of land-use. For example, few educated people realize that the marvelous advances in technique made during recent decades are improvements in the pump, rather than the well. Acre for acre, they have barely sufficed to offset the sinking level of fertility.

In all of these cleavages, we see repeated the same basic paradoxes: man the conqueror *versus* man the biotic citizen; science the sharpener of his sword *versus* science the searchlight on his universe; land the slave and servant *versus* land the collective organism. Robinson's injunction to Tristram may well be applied, at this juncture, to *Homo sapiens* as a species in geological time:

> Whether you will or not
> You are a King, Tristram, for you are one
> Of the time-tested few that leave the world,
> When they are gone, not the same place it was.
> Mark what you leave.

THE OUTLOOK

It is inconceivable to me that an ethical relation to land can exist without love, respect, and admiration for land, and a high regard for its value. By value, I of course mean something far broader than mere economic value; I mean value in the philosophical sense.

Perhaps the most serious obstacle impeding the evolution of a land ethic is the fact that our educational and economic system is headed away from, rather than toward, an intense consciousness of land. Your true modern is separated from the land by many middlemen, and by innumerable physical gadgets. He has no vital relation to it; to him it is the space between cities on which crops grow. Turn him loose for a day on the land, and if the spot does not happen to be a golf links or a 'scenic' area, he is bored stiff. If crops could be raised by hydroponics instead of farming, it would suit him very well. Synthetic substitutes for wood, leather, wool, and other natural land products suit him better than the originals. In short, land is something he has 'outgrown.'

Almost equally serious as an obstacle to a land ethic is the attitude of the farmer for whom the land is still an adversary, or a taskmaster that keeps him in slavery. Theoretically, the mechanization of farming ought to cut the farmer's chains, but whether it really does is debatable.

One of the requisites for an ecological comprehension of land is an understanding of ecology, and this is by no means co-extensive with 'education'; in fact, much higher education seems deliberately to avoid ecological concepts. An understanding of ecology does not necessarily originate in courses bearing ecological labels; it is quite as likely to be labeled geography, botany, agronomy, history, or economics. This is as it should be, but whatever the label, ecological training is scarce.

The case for a land ethic would appear hopeless but for the minority which is in obvious revolt against these 'modern' trends.

The 'key-log' which must be moved to release the evolutionary process for an ethic is simply this: quit thinking about decent land-use as solely an economic problem. Examine each question in terms of what is ethically and esthetically right, as well as what is economically expedient. A thing is right when it tends to preserve the integrity, stability, and beauty of the biotic community. It is wrong when it tends otherwise.

It of course goes without saying that economic feasibility limits the tether of what can or cannot be done for land. It always has and it always will. The fallacy the economic determinists have tied around our collective neck, and which we now need to cast off, is the belief that economics determines *all* land-use. This is simply not true. An innumerable host of actions and attitudes, comprising perhaps the bulk of all land relations, is determined by the land-users' tastes and predilections, rather than by his purse. The bulk of all land relations hinges on investments of time, forethought, skill, and faith rather than on investments of cash. As a land-user thinketh, so is he.

I have purposely presented the land ethic as a product of social evolution because nothing so important as an ethic is ever 'written.' Only the most superficial student of history supposes that Moses 'wrote' the Decalogue; it evolved in the minds of a thinking community, and Moses wrote a tentative summary of it for a 'seminar.' I say tentative because evolution never stops.

The evolution of a land ethic is an intellectual as well as emotional process. Conservation is paved with good intentions which prove to be futile, or even dangerous, because they are devoid of critical understanding either of the land, or of economic land-use. I think it is a truism that as the ethical frontier advances from the individual to the community, its intellectual content increases.

The mechanism of operation is the same for any ethic: social approbation for right actions: social disapproval for wrong actions.

By and large, our present problem is one of attitudes and implements. We are remodeling the Alhambra with a steam-shovel, and we are proud of our yardage. We shall hardly relinquish the shovel, which after all has many good points, but we are in need of gentler and more objective criteria for its successful use.

Questions for Thinking and Writing

1. What does Leopold mean when he says that "land . . . is a fountain of energy"? How does he use this thesis as a platform on which to build a new definition of conservation? What is his land ethic? How can one have an ethical relationship with the land? How does the land ethic relate to the land pyramid?
2. Explain the land pyramid. How does it relate to the condition of the Dust Bowl? To what extent do agricultural practices defeat the natural cycle?
3. Why do you think Leopold maintains that humans resist understanding the environment and that conservation represents more than an economic problem?

Thinking and Writing About Part 2

1. Compare the feeling that Thea Kronberg, the heroine of Willa Cather's "The Ancient People" (p. 109), expresses for the landscape and nature's sparseness with those of Henry David Thoreau in "Where I Lived, and What I Lived For" (p. 12) and John Burroughs in "Ways of Nature" (p. 66), or Nick Adams in Ernest Hemingway's "Big Two-Hearted River" (p. 127). Why does Kronberg's readiness to leave Panther Canyon reflect a change in her psyche, and does it suggest that her feeling for the ancient people has diminished and she will lose the feeling when she returns to the urban world?

2. Compare the epiphany, or moment of enlightenment, that occurs in Robert Frost's "Two Look at Two" (p. 124) with Elizabeth Bishop's "The Fish" (p. 176). Consider the distinctions of the setting and activity of the humans and the animals. Explain how Frost and Bishop give you a realistic and spiritual sense of the animals without actually personifying them. You might want to compare their treatment of animals with the Walt Disney versions of Bambi or Cinderella.

4. Prepare an argument pro or con on this subject: Hunting is antithetical to an environmental ethic. Include in your argument whether or not hunting has a place in the scheme of wise use and land management.

5. Explain why wilderness or natural landscape is so often considered the antithesis of civilization. Compare Ernest Hemingway's sense of the wilderness in "Big Two-Hearted River" (p. 127) with Wallace Stevens's vision of wilderness in "Anecdote of the Jar" (p. 126). How does their point of view match up with Walt Whitman's vision of the new United States in "Song of the Redwood-Tree" (p. 39) or David E. Lilienthal's "One Valley—and a Thousand" (p. 170)?

6. How ingrained are metaphors of gardens and gardening in our culture? How does the story of the expulsion from the Garden of Eden (see Genesis 1–3) relate to the formulation of a land ethic? Having been expelled from the original garden and made to live in a world where it is necessary to farm and work, have humans lost their original connection with the natural world? To what extent does Aldo Leopold's call for a land ethic pose a practical and spiritual return of the human consciousness to the Garden of Eden?

7. What does Aldo Leopold suggest by his notion of the "derangement of the energy circuit" in "The Land Ethic" (p. 195)? How does this compare with the alterations in the environment described by Wallace Stevens in "Anecdote of the Jar" (p. 126), Robert Frost in "A Brook in the City" (p. 122), Caroline A. Henderson in "Letters from the Dust Bowl" (p. 142), and John Steinbeck in the excerpt from The Grapes of Wrath (p. 161)? Identify and explain how these works speak to the spiritual, symbolic, and practical aspects of our understanding of the environment.

Steel plants in Pittsburgh in the early 1960s were primarily responsible for the terrible air pollution that plagued the city for decades. The city has since instituted strict pollution controls that have vastly improved air quality.

3 1950–1975: Conflicting Attitudes Toward the Human and Natural Environments

Midcentury began as a sobering time for those concerned with the question of environmental use versus environmental protection. World War II had sapped the country of natural resources, or so many people thought. The cost of oil, coal, metals, and lumber rose steeply. Environmentalists like Fairfield Osborn (1887–1969), scientist and president of the New York Zoological Society in New York City, and author of *The Plundered Planet* (1948) and *The Limits of the Earth,* warned of impending dire shortages of raw materials, especially in light of the coming postwar baby boom that would create even more pressure on resources. Governmental policy still focused primarily on productivity and the availability of raw materials. Pro-environmentalists were becoming a powerful lobbying force, however. The natural environment, what remained of wilderness, was becoming a cause célèbre.

In the 1950s, aesthetic, spiritual, and moral values were no longer perceived as mere romanticism. Conservation, preservation, and efficient land use became issues not to be subsumed by economic interest alone. Prompted by Aldo Leopold's questioning of the morality of economic and industrial development at the expense of nature, Americans raised environmental issues— preservation, conservation, harvesting, mining, water purity—worthy of serious debate. Leopold advocated an environmental ethic that transcended the idea of conservation of resources promulgated by Gifford Pinchot, David Lilienthal, and others.

This new ethic replaced the idea that conservation meant civilizing nature to make the human environment more efficient. We can see its influence in Loren Eiseley's "The Bird and the Machine" (1950), which contrasts the capture of a sparrow hawk and the abstractness of machines; Gary Snyder's "Front Lines" (1972), which is an angry poem about land seekers, loggers, and bulldozers; and John McPhee's "Profiles: Carol Ruckdeschel" (1973), in which is depicted the devastation of a local stream in the name of flood control.

The debate over the proposed damming of the Green River at Echo Park, a part of Dinosaur National Monument straddling the Utah and Colorado border, crystallized the issue in 1950. The Bureau of Reclamation insisted that the dam was essential for water storage on the upper Colorado River. The preservationists fought bitterly, arguing that construction of the dam would violate the sanctity of all national parks and monuments. The preservationists' triumph marked a change in the national attitude, and a vindication of John Muir's struggle four decades earlier when he vainly tried to save the Hetch Hetchy valley from being dammed.

In the 1960s, relative prosperity and more leisure time supported the use of the natural environment as an outlet for urban tension, which added significant momentum toward preservation for the sake of preservation. As never before, due to the automobile and air travel, Americans enjoyed easier access to parks and wilderness areas: the ability to get there and return to the usual pattern of work life. Passage of the Wilderness Act (1964) and the Wild and Scenic Rivers Act (1968) were efforts to ensure the perpetuation of wilderness areas and the preservation and restoration of scenic rivers. Both acts were passed during the administration of Lyndon B. Johnson (1963–1969), whose goals for a Great Society included the beautification of America. Lady Bird Johnson, the president's wife, led a drive to plant native wildflowers along highways and other vacant land.

Congressional and White House support for protecting wilderness had the ironic effect of dismaying radical preservationists who wanted to keep nature pristine. They recoiled at the notion that wilderness was being treated as a commodity—a managed resource—and opposed those who wanted to open up the wilderness to tourism. Edward Abbey's "A Walk in the Park" (1972) is an argument for limited access to the natural environment. Abbey's hard-line approach to environmentalism foreshadowed the philosophical tenets of deep ecology, which crystalized in the mid-1980s. Deep ecologists believe that human-centered environmentalism is shallow and cannot work. This position is countered by René Dubos in "The Wooing of the Earth" (1968), which suggests that human involvement with the environment requires compromise and wise use. Dubos raises this question: Is use of the land merely for our economic convenience, or is there something deep within us that needs to see an imposed order?

Rachel Carson's *Silent Spring* (1962) brought to the surface the fear that environmental degradation had not stopped, and despite lobbying to the contrary, abuse had gone much further than imagined. It seemed that rivers and lakes everywhere were dying under the burden of chemical pollution. The air was becoming more foul with industrial smog. Carson raised the issue that insecticides and pesticides, which were killing agricultural pests and wildlife, perhaps were also harming, if not killing, humans. Particularly, she sought to ban the use of DDT, which was eventually accomplished in 1973. In reaction to all the controversy, Congress became active and enacted legislation aimed at maintaining and improving the air, water, soil, and forests. From the middle 1960s through the 1970s, most of the major legislation affecting the environment, which still has profound importance in the 1990s, was set in place.

The rapidly increasing population and the decline of urban centers and growth of suburbs began to blur the line between city and country. Cornfields were transformed into subdivisions, and small towns lost their identities, smothered under the expansion of larger neighboring cities. Flannery O'Connor describes the rural loss of innocence in "A View of the Woods" (1965). Mark Fortune, the story's antagonist, sells his land to a developer who wants to build a gas station and convenience store. Fortune contends that it is his right to be an entrepreneur and do whatever he wishes in the name of progress. In 1968, Garrett Hardin published "The Tragedy of the Commons" in *Science*, which reminded Americans that we are a different country now than we were in colonial times when the village green served as pastureland for everyone's cows. Hardin pointed out that now there are too many cows and not enough grass. He wrote that our resources are dwindling and greed is manifest as the scramble for limited resources intensifies.

Acquisitive and expansion-minded, Americans also became self-conscious and questioning during the 1960s. There was a shift in the moral sensibility and a concern that material growth and greed were throttling nature. President John F. Kennedy (term 1961–1963) acted on this new consciousness by establishing the Peace Corps and Vista, both indicative of a search for a national and an individual identity. There was a strong response to his famous statement at his inauguration: "Ask not what your country can do for you but what you can do for your country." In the South, momentum was gaining for equal civil rights and an end to segregation. Martin Luther King, Jr. (1929–1968) was leading the way to a new sense of American self based on the notion of civil disobedience conceived by Henry David Thoreau and Mohandas K. Gandhi (1869–1948). Despite these changes in the national temper, Kennedy was ominously permitting the United States to drift into full-scale war in order to prevent a communist regime from governing Vietnam. Over all was a deep fear of nuclear war with the Soviet Union. There was a virtual nuclear showdown between Kennedy and the Soviets in 1962 over missiles in Cuba. War was averted, but the incipient fear of the madness of planetary destruction and nuclear holocaust had already been explored in Walter Miller's *A Canticle for Leibowitz* (1959), which previewed the cultural, social, and spiritual results of nuclear devastation.

The expenditure of national emotional energy and self-questioning over the environment and our place in the environment intensified. Writings about the environment began to reexamine the importance of nature in our emotional depths. While some have raised the issue that humankind has lost touch with the natural world, others have reaffirmed the connection. Leonard Crow Dog's "Remaking the World" (1974) gives the Native American version of the cycle of growth and destruction. When the world gets to the point where people no longer know how to behave themselves, the Creating Power remakes the world.

On April 22, 1970, the doubt, the anger, the hope that we had not irreversibly damaged the environment erupted in the first celebration of Earth Day. It was a massively orchestrated appeal to our senses, enhanced by startling views of the planet from space that jolted the public into a fresh awareness of its beauty and fragility. Though Earth Day was rife with self-serving hype, it marked the beginning of public awareness of the need to temper our hell-bent consumerism and greed. Though the ethic of conservation of natural resources became more pronounced over the next two decades, the struggle to accept that we human beings are part of the environment rather than surrounded by the environment is ongoing. This is the message of Jack Kerouac's "Desolation Peak" (1958), Maxine Kumin's "Morning Swim" (1965), and May Sarton's "Death and the Maple" (1968).

HISTORICAL CHRONOLOGY AND CONTEXT

1950:   United States defends South Korea after an attack by North Korea
United States starts work on a hydrogen bomb

1951:   22nd Amendment passed (limits the president to two terms)
Color TV introduced

1952:   Jonas Salk develops an effective polio vaccine
United States detonates an H-bomb in the Pacific Ocean

1953:   Dwight David Eisenhower begins his presidency
Korean War ends

1954:   Sen. Joseph McCarthy of Wisconsin rebuked by U.S. Senate
U.S. Supreme Court orders desegregation of public schools

1955:   Disneyland opens in California
First McDonald's restaurant opens

1956:   Eisenhower reelected president

1957:   Soviet Union launches Sputnik, the first space satellite

1958:   First U.S. orbiting satellite is launched

1959:   Hawaii and Alaska are admitted to the Union as the 49th and 50th states

1960:   Laser is developed
U.S. advisers are sent to Vietnam

1961: John F. Kennedy begins his presidency
Bay of Pigs invasion of Cuba is a failure
Alan Shepard is the first American in space

1962: Rachel Carson's *Silent Spring* is published
John Glenn, American astronaut, orbits the Earth
Supreme Court bans prayer in public schools

1963: John F. Kennedy assassinated in Dallas
Lyndon B. Johnson sworn in as president
Martin Luther King, Jr., gives his speech "I Have a Dream"
Clean Air Act passed

1964: Lyndon Johnson reelected president
National Wilderness Preservation System (Wilderness Act) passed
Martin Luther King, Jr., receives the Nobel Peace Prize

1965: War in Vietnam escalates; antiwar rallies begin
Blacks riot in the Watts section of Los Angeles
The Northeast suffers a major electrical blackout
Water Quality Act passed
Noise Control Act passed
Solid Waste Disposal Act passed

1966: National Organization for Women is founded

1968: Vietnam peace talks begin in Paris
Martin Luther King, Jr., assassinated in Memphis
Robert F. Kennedy assassinated in Los Angeles
City police riot at the Democratic National Convention
in Chicago
Wild and Scenic Rivers Act passed

1969: Richard Nixon begins his presidency
Neal Armstrong walks on the moon
National Environmental Policy Act passed

1970: Environmental Protection Agency established
National Guard soldiers kill student antiwar demonstrators in
Kent, Ohio
First Earth Day is celebrated

1971: Twenty-sixth Amendment gives vote to 18-year-olds
Cigarette ads are banned on TV
Mariner 9 orbits Mars

1972: Watergate coverup begins
Marine Mammal Protection Act passed
U.N. Conference on the Human Environment in Stockholm
Clean Water Act passed

1973: OPEC oil embargo creates an energy crisis
U.S. Supreme Court strikes down antiabortion laws

Native Americans renew uprising at Wounded Knee,
   South Dakota
Endangered Species Act passed

1974:   Nixon is brought up on impeachment charges, but resigns
Safe Drinking Water Act passed

1975:   U.S. troops leave Vietnam; the war is over
New York City barely avoids financial default
Hazardous Materials Transportation Act passed

Loren Eiseley (1907–1977)
The Bird and the Machine (1950)

Combine the analytical mind of the scientist and the reflective in-clination of the poet, and you would have Loren Eiseley. In his poems and essays, he reminds the reader of the enormity of life in its bio-logical complexity and eons-long evolutionary process. Our daily con-cerns, he seems to be saying, pale beside the incredible magnificence and mystery of life.

Eiseley was born in Lincoln, Nebraska, and entered the University of Nebraska planning to major in zoology. He dropped out after a time to wander the country, mostly the West, uncertain about what to do with himself. He traveled by hopping freight trains and slept beside campfires ringed by hoboes. In one of his essays, Eiseley writes about his decision to end this period of his life and return to his studies. He tells that he made his decision while standing in the door of a moving freight car: "Time. Either you ride away inexorably upon its back, or, if you stop, it goes by you with someone else waving farewell whom you will never meet. I left the airport on the first morning flight to the East."

In 1933, Eiseley graduated from the University of Nebraska with a double major in anthropology and English. In 1947, he joined the graduate faculty in anthropology at the University of Pennsylvania where he remained for the next 30 years.

"The Bird and the Machine" was written in 1950 and collected in The Immense Journey, *Eiseley's first book published in 1957. He wrote four others and a volume of poems.* The Immense Journey, *a mix of scientific speculation and narrative concerning Eiseley's experiences in the field as an anthropologist, immediately established him as an accomplished writer as well as a scholar. A review in the* New York

Times *exclaimed at a scientist who "can also write with poetic sensibility and with a fine sense of wonder and of reverence before the mysteries of life and nature. In one sense of the word this book about evolution is a religious book."*

In most of his writing, Eiseley praises the observant eye of the naturalist and laments that the pressures of contemporary science do not permit mere wondering and contemplation. He feels that imagination is thwarted, and that when science is used only to rationalize or to fulfill practical purposes, it marks the end of the human spirit.

I suppose their little bones have years ago been lost among the stones and winds of those high glacial pastures. I suppose their feathers blew eventually into the piles of tumbleweed beneath the straggling cattle fences and rotted there in the mountain snows, along with dead steers and all the other things that drift to an end in the corners of the wire. I do not quite know why I should be thinking of birds over the *New York Times* at breakfast, particularly the birds of my youth half a continent away. It is a funny thing what the brain will do with memories and how it will treasure them and finally bring them into odd juxtapositions with other things, as though it wanted to make a design, or get some meaning out of them, whether you want it or not, or even see it.

It used to seem marvelous to me, but I read now that there are machines that can do these things in a small way, machines that can crawl about like animals, and that it may not be long until they do more things—maybe even make themselves—I saw that piece in the *Times* just now. And then they will, maybe—well, who knows—but you read about it more and more with no one making any protest, and already they can add better than we and reach up and hear things through the dark and finger the guns over the night sky.

This is the new world that I read about at breakfast. This is the world that confronts me in my biological books and journals, until there are times when I sit quietly in my chair and try to hear the little purr of the cogs in my head and the tubes flaring and dying as the messages go through them and the circuits snap shut or open. This is the great age, make no mistake about it; the robot has been born somewhat appropriately along with the atom bomb, and the brain they say now is just another type of more complicated feedback system. The engineers have its basic principles worked out; it's mechanical, you know; nothing to get superstitious about; the man can always improve on nature once he gets the idea. Well, he's got it all right and that's why, I guess, that I sit here in my chair, with the article crunched in my hand, remembering those two birds and that blue mountain sunlight. There is another magazine article on my desk that reads "Machines Are Getting Smarter Every

Day" I don't deny it, but I'll still stick with the birds. It's life I believe in, not machines.

Maybe you don't believe there is any difference. A skeleton is all joints and pulleys, I'll admit. And when man was in his simpler stages of machine building in the eighteenth century, he quickly saw the resemblances. "What," wrote Hobbes, "is the heart but a spring, and the nerves but so many strings, and the joints but so many wheels, giving motion to the whole body?" Tinkering about in their shops it was inevitable in the end that men would see the world as a huge machine "subdivided into an infinite number of lesser machines."

The idea took on with a vengeance. Little automatons toured the country—dolls controlled by clockwork. Clocks described as little worlds were taken on tours by their designers. They were made up of moving figures, shifting scenes and other remarkable devices. The life of the cell was unknown. Man, whether he was conceived as possessing a soul or not, moved and jerked about like these tiny puppets. A human being thought of himself in terms of his own tools and implements. He had been fashioned like the puppets he produced and was only a more clever model made by a greater designer.

Then in the nineteenth century, the cell was discovered, and the single machine in its turn was found to be the product of millions of infinitesimal machines—the cells. Now, finally, the cell itself dissolves away into an abstract chemical machine—and that into some intangible, inexpressible flow of energy. The secret seems to lurk all about, the wheels get smaller and smaller, and they turn more rapidly, but when you try to seize it the life is gone—and so, by popular definition, some would say that life was never there in the first place. The wheels and the cogs are the secret and we can make them better in time—machines that will run faster and more accurately than real mice to real cheese.

I have no doubt it can be done, though a mouse harvesting seeds on an autumn thistle is to me a fine sight and more complicated, I think, in his multiform activity, than a machine "mouse" running a maze. Also, I like to think of the possible shape of the future brooding in mice, just as it brooded once in a rather ordinary mousy insectivore who became a man. It leaves a nice fine indeterminate sense of wonder that even an electronic brain hasn't got, because you know perfectly well that if the electronic brain changes, it will be because of something man has done to it. But what man will do to himself he doesn't really know. A certain scale of time and a ghostly intangible thing called change are ticking in him. Powers and potentialities like the oak in the seed, or a red and awful ruin. Either way, it's impressive; and the mouse has it, too. Or those birds, I'll never forget those birds—yet before I measured their significance, I learned the lesson of time first of all. I was young then and left alone in a great desert—part of an expedition that had scattered its men over several hundred miles in order to carry on research more effectively. I learned there that time is a series of planes existing superficially in the same universe. The tempo is a human illusion, a subjective clock ticking in our own kind of protoplasm.

As the long months passed, I began to live on the slower planes and to observe more readily what passed for life there. I sauntered, I passed more and more slowly up and down the canyons in the dry baking heat of midsummer. I slumbered for long hours in the shade of huge brown boulders that had gathered in tilted companies out on the flats. I had forgotten the world of men and the world had forgotten me. Now and then I found a skull in the canyons, and these justified my remaining there. I took a serene cold interest in these discoveries. I had come, like many a naturalist before me, to view life with a wary and subdued attention. I had grown to take pleasure in the divested bone.

I sat once on a high ridge that fell away before me into a waste of sand dunes. I sat through hours of a long afternoon. Finally, as I glanced beside my boot an indistinct configuration caught my eye. It was a coiled rattlesnake, a big one. How long he had sat with me I do not know. I had not frightened him. We were both locked in the sleep-walking tempo of the earlier world, baking in the same high air and sunshine. Perhaps he had been there when I came. He slept on as I left, his coils, so ill discerned by me, dissolving once more among the stones and gravel from which I had barely made him out.

Another time I got on a higher ridge, among some tough little wind-warped pines half covered over with sand in a basin-like depression that caught everything carried by the air up to those heights. There were a few thin bones of birds, some cracked shells of indeterminable age, and the knotty fingers of pine roots bulged out of shape from their long and agonizing grasp upon the crevices of the rock. I lay under the pines in the sparse shade and went to sleep once more.

It grew cold finally, for autumn was in the air by then, and the few things that lived thereabouts were sinking down into an even chillier scale of time. In the moments between sleeping and waking I saw the roots about me and slowly, slowly, a foot in what seemed many centuries, I moved my sleep-stiffened hands over the scaling bark and lifted my numbed face after the vanishing sun. I was a great awkward thing of knots and aching limbs, trapped up there in some long, patient endurance that involved the necessity of putting living fingers into rock and by slow, aching expansion bursting those rocks asunder. I suppose, so thin and slow was the time of my pulse by then, that I might have stayed on to drift still deeper into the lower cadences of the frost, or the crystalline life that glisters in pebbles, or shines in a snowflake, or dreams in the meteoric iron between the worlds.

It was a dim descent, but time was present in it. Somewhere far down in that scale the notion struck me that one might come the other way. Not many months thereafter I joined some colleagues heading higher into a remote windy tableland where huge bones were reputed to protrude like boulders from the turf. I had drowsed with reptiles and moved with the century-long pulse of trees; now, lethargically, I was climbing back up some invisible ladder of quickening hours. There had been talk of birds in connection with my duties. Birds are intense, fast-living creatures—reptiles, I suppose one might say, that have escaped out of the heavy sleep of time, transformed fairy creatures dancing over sunlit meadows. It is a youthful fancy, no doubt, but because of something that happened up there among the escarpments of that range, it remains with me a lifelong impression. I can never bear to see a bird imprisoned.

We came into that valley through the trailing mists of a spring night. It was a place that looked as though it might never have known the foot of man, but our scouts had been ahead of us and we knew all about the abandoned cabin of stone that lay far up on one hillside. It had been built in the land rush of the last century and then lost to the cattlemen again as the marginal soils failed to take to the plow.

There were spots like this all over that country. Lost graves marked by unlettered stones and old corroding rim-fire cartridge cases lying where somebody had made a stand among the boulders that rimmed the valley. They are all that remain of the range wars; the men are under the stones now. I could see our cavalcade winding in and out through the mist below us: torches, the reflection of the truck lights on our collecting tins, and the far-off bumping of a loose dinosaur thigh bone in the bottom of a trailer. I stood on a rock a moment looking down and thinking what it cost in money and equipment to capture the past.

We had, in addition, instructions to lay hands on the present. The word had come through to get them alive—birds, reptiles, anything. A zoo somewhere abroad needed restocking. It was one of those reciprocal matters in which science involves itself. Maybe our museum needed a stray ostrich egg and this was the payoff. Anyhow, my job was to help capture some birds and that was why I was there before the trucks.

The cabin had not been occupied for years. We intended to clean it out and live in it, but there were holes in the roof and the birds had come in and were roosting in the rafters. You could depend on it in a place like this where everything blew away, and even a bird needed some place out of the weather and away from coyotes. A cabin going back to nature in a wild place draws them till they come in, listening at the eaves, I imagine, pecking softly among the shingles till they find a hole and then suddenly the place is theirs and man is forgotten.

Sometimes of late years I find myself thinking the most beautiful sight in the world might be the birds taking over New York after the last man has run away to the hills. I will never live to see it, of course, but I know just how it will sound because I've lived up high and I know the sort of watch birds keep on us. I've listened to sparrows tapping tentatively on the outside of air conditioners when they thought no one was listening, and I know how other birds test the vibrations that come up to them through the television aerials.

"Is he gone?" they ask, and the vibrations come up from below, "Not yet, not yet."

Well, to come back, I got the door open softly and I had the spotlight all ready to turn on and blind whatever birds there were so they couldn't see to get out through the roof. I had a short piece of ladder to put against the far wall where there was a shelf on which I expected to make the biggest haul. I had all the information I needed just like any skilled assassin. I pushed the door open, the hinges squeaking only a little. A bird or two stirred—I could hear them—but nothing flew and there was a faint starlight through the holes in the roof.

I padded across the floor, got the ladder up and the light ready, and slithered up the ladder till my head and arms were over the shelf. Everything was dark as pitch except for the starlight at the little place back of the shelf near the eaves. With the light to blind them, they'd never make it. I had them. I reached my arm carefully over in order to be ready to seize whatever was there and I put the flash on the edge of the shelf where it would stand by itself when I turned it on. That way I'd be able to use both hands.

Everything worked perfectly except for one detail—I didn't know what kind of birds were there. I never thought about it at all, and it wouldn't have mattered if I had. My orders were to get something interesting. I snapped on the flash and sure enough there was a great beating and feathers flying, but instead of my having them, they, or rather he, had me. He had my hand, that is, and for a small hawk not much bigger than my fist he was doing all right. I heard him give one short metallic cry when the light went on and my hand descended on the bird beside him; after that he was busy with his claws and his beak was sunk in my thumb. In the struggle I knocked the lamp over on the shelf, and his mate got her sight back and whisked neatly through the hole in the roof and off among the stars outside. It all happened in fifteen seconds and you might think I would have fallen down the ladder, but no, I had a professional assassin's reputation to keep up, and the bird, of course, made the mistake of thinking the hand was the enemy and not the eyes behind it. He chewed my thumb up pretty effectively and lacerated my hand with his claws, but in the end I got him, having two hands to work with.

He was a sparrow hawk and a fine young male in the prime of life. I was sorry not to catch the pair of them, but as I dripped blood and folded his wings carefully, holding him by the back so that he couldn't strike again, I had to admit the two of them might have been more than I could have handled under the circumstances. The little fellow had saved his mate by diverting me, and that was that. He was born to it, and made no outcry now, resting in my hand hopelessly, but peering toward me in the shadows behind the lamp with a fierce, almost indifferent glance. He neither gave nor expected mercy and something out of the high air passed from him to me, stirring a faint embarrassment.

I quit looking into that eye and managed to get my huge carcass with its fist full of prey back down the ladder. I put the bird in a box too small to allow him to injure himself by struggle and walked out to welcome the arriving trucks. It had been a long day, and camp still to make in the darkness. In the morning that bird would be just another episode. He would go back with the bones in the truck to a small cage in a city where he would spend the rest of his life. And a good thing, too. I sucked my aching thumb and spat out some blood. An assassin has to get used to these things. I had a professional reputation to keep up.

In the morning, with the change that comes on suddenly in that high country, the mist that had hovered below us in the valley was gone. The sky was a deep blue, and one could see for miles over the high outcroppings of stone. I was up early and brought the box in which the little hawk was imprisoned out onto the grass where I was building a cage. A wind as cool as a mountain spring ran over the grass and stirred my hair. It was a fine day to be alive. I looked up and all around and at the hole in the cabin roof out of which the other little hawk had fled. There was no sign of her anywhere that I could see.

"Probably in the next county by now," I thought cynically, but before beginning work I decided I'd have a look at my last night's capture.

Secretively, I looked again all around the camp and up and down and opened the box. I got him right out in my hand with his wings folded properly and I was careful not to startle him. He lay limp in my grasp and I could feel his heart pound under the feathers but he only looked beyond me and up.

I saw him look that last look away beyond me into a sky so full of light that I could not follow his gaze. The little breeze flowed over me again, and nearby a mountain aspen shook all its tiny leaves. I suppose I must have had an idea then of what I was going to do, but I never let it come up into consciousness. I just reached over and laid the hawk on the grass.

He lay there a long minute without hope, unmoving, his eyes still fixed on that blue vault above him. It must have been that he was already so far away in heart that he never felt the release from my hand. He never even stood. He just lay with his breast against the grass.

In the next second after that long minute he was gone. Like a flicker of light, he had vanished with my eyes full on him, but without actually seeing even a premonitory wing beat. He was gone straight into that towering emptiness of light and crystal that my eyes could scarcely bear to penetrate. For another long moment there was silence. I could not see him. The light was too intense. Then from far up somewhere a cry came ringing down.

I was young then and had seen little of the world, but when I heard that cry my heart turned over. It was not the cry of the hawk I had captured; for, by shifting my position against the sun, I was now seeing further up. Straight out of the sun's eye, where she must have been soaring restlessly above us for untold hours, hurtled his mate. And from far up, ringing from peak to peak of the summits over us, came a cry of such unutterable and ecstatic joy that it sounds down across the years and tingles among the cups on my quiet breakfast table.

I saw them both now. He was rising fast to meet her. They met in a great soaring gyre that turned to a whirling circle and a dance of wings. Once more, just once, their two voices, joined in a harsh wild medley of question and response, struck and echoed against the pinnacles of the valley. Then they were gone forever somewhere into those upper regions beyond the eyes of men.

I am older now, and sleep less, and have seen most of what there is to see and am not very much impressed any more, I suppose, by anything. "What Next in the Attributes of Machines?" my morning headline runs. "It Might Be the Power to Reproduce Themselves."

I lay the paper down and across my mind a phrase floats insinuatingly: "It does not seem that there is anything in the construction, constituents, or behavior of the human being which it is essentially impossible for science to duplicate and synthesize. On the other hand . . . "

All over the city the cogs in the hard, bright mechanisms have begun to turn. Figures move through computers, names are spelled out, a thoughtful machine selects the fingerprints of a wanted criminal from an array of thousands. In the laboratory an electronic mouse runs swiftly through a maze toward the cheese it can neither taste nor enjoy. On the second run it does better than a living mouse.

"On the other hand . . . " Ah, my mind takes up, on the other hand the machines does not bleed, ache, hang for hours in the empty sky in a torment of hope to learn the fate of another machine, nor does it cry out with joy nor dance in the air with the fierce passion of a bird. Far off, over a distance greater than space, that remote cry from the heart of heaven makes a faint buzzing among my breakfast dishes and passes on and away.

Questions for Thinking and Writing

1. Why is Eiseley so opposed to machines and to believing that they can solve problems? What does he imply are the dangers of a mechanistic point of view? How does he contrast these dangers with natural life?
2. What did Eiseley learn in the desert? What is the lesson of the rattlesnake? Of the tree roots and bark? Of the sparrow hawks? How does Eiseley relate animals to his personal sense of self?
3. In some instances, writers so closely identify with animals and innate objects that they give them human attributes. How does Eiseley avoid this technique of anthropomorphism? How does he avoid sentimentality in this essay?

❧ Flannery O'Connor (1925–1964)

A View of the Woods (1957)

Flannery O'Connor was fascinated by what she termed "the mystery of existence," and often the characters in her fiction act out horribly evil and unexpected deeds. This macabre sensibility expressed in her stories and characters, but not in her personal life, is linked to her deep commitment to Catholicism and her belief in the Fall, Redemption, and the Judgment. Nature in her writing, often simply described as woods or forests, acts as a brooding presence in which human beings are tested in ways that are beyond their immediate awareness or comprehension.

Born in Savannah, Georgia, as Mary Flannery O'Connor, she preferred not to use her given name. She was educated at Georgia State College for Women, and then studied at the University of Iowa where she received a master's degree in fine arts in 1947. From Iowa, O'Connor went to Yaddo, the writer's colony in Saratoga Springs, New York, then to New York City and Connecticut, where she wrote and worked as a sitter for the children of Robert and Sally Fitzgerald, who became her editors. Her first novel, Wise Blood, *was published in 1952. Except for her brief forays into the Midwest and the Northeast, O'Connor lived most of her life in Georgia.*

O'Connor's life changed markedly when she was only 25 and diagnosed with lupus, an autoimmune disease that had killed her father. She returned to Georgia to live on her mother's farm in Midgeville where she remained for the rest of her life, becoming progressively sicker until she died at 39.

Wise Blood *received sufficient acclaim to establish her literary career. A Kenyon Fellowship following the novel's publication provided O'Connor with enough money to help pay some medical expenses and to continue writing. In 1955, her collection of short stories,* A Good Man Is Hard to Find, *was published and, in 1960, her second novel,* The Violent Bear It Away.

After her death, a second collection of short stories, Everything That Rises Must Converge, *appeared in 1965. "A View of the Woods," part of this collection, shows how O'Connor frequently uses nature as a backdrop to the sometimes grotesque and violent behavior of her characters for whom hatred sometimes replaces love. In "A View of the Woods," Mark Fortune equates the natural landscape with money. His greed, which deprives his family of their meadow and a view of the woods, provokes his favorite granddaughter to renounce him. This act of childish hatred so provokes Fortune that he kills the girl. O'Connor's respect for the strength of nature to shape human behavior is very evident. Nature is the scene of humankind's temptation and fall from grace.*

The week before, Mary Fortune and the old man had spent every morning watching the machine that lifted out dirt and threw it in a pile. The construction was going on by the new lakeside on one of the lots that the old man had sold to somebody who was going to put up a fishing club. He and Mary Fortune drove down there every morning about ten o'clock and he parked his car, a battered mulberry-colored Cadillac, on the embankment that overlooked the spot where the work was going on. The red corrugated lake eased up to within fifty feet of the construction and was bordered on the other side by a black line of woods which appeared at both ends of the view to walk across the water and continue along the edge of the fields.

He sat on the bumper and Mary Fortune straddled the hood and they watched, sometimes for hours, while the machine systematically ate a square red hole in what had once been a cow pasture. It happened to be the only pasture that Pitts had succeeded in getting the bitterweed off and when the old man had sold it, Pitts had nearly had a stroke; and as far as Mr. Fortune was concerned, he could have gone on and had it.

"Any fool that would let a cow pasture interfere with progress is not on my books," he had said to Mary Fortune several times from his seat on the bumper, but the child did not have eyes for anything but the machine. She sat on the hood, looking down into the red pit, watching the big disembodied gullet gorge itself on the clay, then, with the sound of a deep sustained nausea and a slow mechanical revulsion, turn and spit it up. Her pale eyes behind her spectacles followed the repeated

motion of it again and again and her face—a small replica of the old
man's—never lost its look of complete absorption.

No one was particularly glad that Mary Fortune looked like her
grandfather except the old man himself. He thought it added greatly to
her attractiveness. He thought she was the smartest and the prettiest
child he had ever seen and he let the rest of them know that if, IF that
was, he left anything to anybody, it would be Mary Fortune he left it to.
She was now nine, short and broad like himself, with his very light blue
eyes, his wide prominent forehead, his steady penetrating scowl and his
rich florid complexion; but she was like him on the inside too. She had,
to a singular degree, his intelligence, his strong will, and his push and
drive. Though there was seventy years' difference in their ages, the spiritual distance between them was slight. She was the only member of the
family he had any respect for.

He didn't have any use for her mother, his third or fourth daughter
(he could never remember which), though she considered that she
took care of him. She considered—being careful not to say it, only to
look it—that she was the one putting up with him in his old age and that
she was the one he should leave the place to. She had married an idiot
named Pitts and had had seven children, likewise idiots except the
youngest, Mary Fortune, who was a throwback to him. Pitts was the kind
who couldn't keep his hands on a nickel and Mr. Fortune had allowed
them, ten years ago, to move onto his place and farm it. What Pitts made
went to Pitts but the land belonged to Fortune and he was careful to
keep the fact before them. When the well had gone dry, he had not allowed Pitts to have a deep well drilled but had insisted that they pipe
their water from the spring. He did not intend to pay for a drilled well
himself and he knew that if he let Pitts pay for it, whenever he had occasion to say to Pitts, "It's my land you're sitting on," Pitts would be able
to say to him, "Well, it's my pump that's pumping the water you're
drinking."

Being there ten years, the Pittses had got to feel as if they owned the
place. The daughter had been born and raised on it but the old man
considered that when she married Pitts she showed that she preferred
Pitts to home; and when she came back, she came back like any other
tenant, though he would not allow them to pay rent for the same reason he would not allow them to drill a well. Anyone over sixty years of
age is in an uneasy position unless he controls the greater interest and
every now and then he gave the Pittses a practical lesson by selling off
a lot. Nothing infuriated Pitts more than to see him sell off a piece of
the property to an outsider, because Pitts wanted to buy it himself.

Pitts was a thin, long-jawed, irascible, sullen, sulking individual and
his wife was the duty-proud kind: It's my duty to stay here and take care
of Papa. Who would do it if I didn't? I do it knowing full well I'll get no
reward for it. I do it because it's my duty.

The old man was not taken in by this for a minute. He knew they were waiting impatiently for the day when they could put him in a hole eight feet deep and cover him up with dirt. Then, even if he did not leave the place to them, they figured they would be able to buy it. Secretly he had made his will and left everything in trust to Mary Fortune, naming his lawyer and not Pitts as executor. When he died Mary Fortune could make the rest of them jump; and he didn't doubt for a minute that she would be able to do it.

Ten years ago they had announced that they were going to name the new baby Mark Fortune Pitts, after him, if it were a boy, and he had not delayed in telling them that if they coupled his name with the name Pitts he would put them off the place. When the baby came, a girl, and he had seen that even at the age of one day she bore his unmistakable likeness, he had relented and suggested himself that they name her Mary Fortune, after his beloved mother, who had died seventy years ago, bringing him into the world.

The Fortune place was in the country on a clay road that left the paved road fifteen miles away and he would never have been able to sell off any lots if it had not been for progress, which had always been his ally. He was not one of these old people who fight improvement, who object to everything new and cringe at every change. He wanted to see a paved highway in front of his house with plenty of new-model cars on it, he wanted to see a supermarket store across the road from him, he wanted to see a gas station, a motel, a drive-in picture-show within easy distance. Progress had suddenly set all this in motion. The electric power company had built a dam on the river and flooded great areas of the surrounding country and the lake that resulted touched his land along a half-mile stretch. Every Tom, Dick and Harry, every dog and his brother, wanted a lot on the lake. There was talk of their getting a telephone line. There was talk of paving the road that ran in front of the Fortune place. There was talk of an eventual town. He thought this should be called Fortune, Georgia. He was a man of advanced vision, even if he was seventy-nine years old.

The machine that drew up the dirt had stopped the day before and today they were watching the hole being smoothed out by two huge yellow bulldozers. His property had amounted to eight hundred acres before he began selling lots. He had sold five twenty-acre lots on the back of the place and every time he sold one, Pitts's blood pressure had gone up twenty points. "The Pittses are the kind that would let a cow pasture interfere with the future," he said to Mary Fortune, "but not you and me." The fact that Mary Fortune was a Pitts too was something he ignored, in a gentlemanly fashion, as if it were an affliction the child was not responsible for. He liked to think of her as being thoroughly of his clay. He sat on the bumper and she sat on the hood with her bare feet on his shoulders. One of the bulldozers had moved under them to shave the side of the embankment they were parked on. If he had moved his feet a few inches out, the old man could have dangled them over the edge.

"If you don't watch him," Mary Fortune shouted above the noise of the machine, "he'll cut off some of your dirt!"

"Yonder's the stob," the old man yelled. "He hasn't gone beyond the stob."

"Not YET he hasn't," she roared.

The bulldozer passed beneath them and went on to the far side. "Well you watch," he said. "Keep your eyes open and if he knocks that stob, I'll stop him. The Pittses are the kind that would let a cow pasture or a mule lot or a row of beans interfere with progress," he continued. "The people like you and me with heads on their shoulders know you can't stop the marcher time for a cow. . . ."

"He's shaking the stob on the other side!" she screamed and before he could stop her, she had jumped down from the hood and was running along the edge of the embankment, her little yellow dress billowing out behind.

"Don't run so near the edge," he yelled but she had already reached the stob and was squatting down by it to see how much it had been shaken. She leaned over the embankment and shook her fist at the man on the bulldozer. He waved at her and went on about his business. More sense in her little finger than all the rest of that tribe in their heads put together, the old man said to himself, and watched with pride as she started back to him.

She had a head of thick, very fine, sand-colored hair—the exact kind he had had when he had had any—that grew straight and was cut just above her eyes and down the sides of her cheeks to the tips of her ears so that it formed a kind of door opening onto the central part of her face. Her glasses were silver-rimmed like his and she even walked the way he did, stomach forward, with a careful abrupt gait, something between a rock and a shuffle. She was walking so close to the edge of the embankment that the outside of her right foot was flush with it.

"I said don't walk so close to the edge," he called; "you fall off there and you won't live to see the day this place gets built up." He was always very careful to see that she avoided dangers. He would not allow her to sit in snakey places or put her hands on bushes that might hide hornets.

She didn't move an inch. She had a habit of his of not hearing what she didn't want to hear and since this was a little trick he had taught her himself, he had to admire the way she practiced it. He foresaw that in her own old age it would serve her well. She reached the car and climbed back onto the hood without a word and put her feet back on his shoulders where she had had them before, as if he were no more than a part of the automobile. Her attention returned to the far bulldozer.

"Remember what you won't get if you don't mind," her grandfather remarked.

He was a strict disciplinarian but he had never whipped her. There were some children, like the first six Pittses, whom he thought should be whipped once a week on principle, but there were other ways to control intelligent children and he had never laid a rough hand on Mary Fortune. Furthermore, he had never allowed her mother or her brothers and sisters so much as to slap her. The elder Pitts was a different matter.

He was a man of nasty temper and of ugly unreasonable resentments. Time and again, Mr. Fortune's heart had pounded to see him rise slowly from his place at the table—not the head, Mr. Fortune sat there, but from his place at the side—and abruptly, for no reason, with no explanation, jerk his head at Mary Fortune and say, "Come with me," and leave the room, unfastening his belt as he went. A look that was completely foreign to the child's face would appear on it. The old man could not define the look but it infuriated him. It was a look that was part terror and part respect and part something else, something very like cooperation. This look would appear on her face and she would get up and follow Pitts out. They would get in his truck and drive down the road out of earshot, where he would beat her.

Mr. Fortune knew for a fact that he beat her because he had followed them in his car and had seen it happen. He had watched from behind a boulder about a hundred feet away while the child clung to a pine tree and Pitts, as methodically as if he were whacking a bush with a sling blade, beat her around the ankles with his belt. All she had done was jump up and down as if she were standing on a hot stove and make a whimpering noise like a dog that was being peppered. Pitts had kept at it for about three minutes and then he had turned, without a word, and got back in his truck and left her there, and she had slid down under the tree and taken both feet in her hands and rocked back and forth. The old man had crept forward to catch her. Her face was contorted into a puzzle of small red lumps and her nose and eyes were running. He sprang on her and sputtered, "Why didn't you hit him back? Where's your spirit? Do you think I'd a let him beat me?"

She had jumped up and started backing away from him with her jaw stuck out. "Nobody beat me," she said.

"Didn't I see it with my own eyes?" he exploded.

"Nobody is here and nobody beat me," she said. "Nobody's ever beat me in my life and if anybody did, I'd kill him. You can see for yourself nobody is here."

"Do you call me a liar or a blindman!" he shouted. "I saw him with my own two eyes and you never did a thing but let him do it, you never did a thing but hang onto that tree and dance up and down a little and blubber and if it had been me, I'd a swung my fist in his face and . . ."

"Nobody was here and nobody beat me and if anybody did I'd kill him!" she yelled and then turned and dashed off through the woods.

"And I'm a Poland china pig and black is white!" he had roared after her and he had sat down on a small rock under the tree, disgusted and furious. This was Pitts's revenge on him. It was as if it were *he* that Pitts was driving down the road to beat and it was as if *he* were the one submitting to it. He had thought at first that he could stop him by saying that if he beat her, he would put them off the place but when he had tried that, Pitts had said, "Put me off and you put her off too. Go right ahead. She's mine to whip and I'll whip her every day of the year if it suits me."

Any time he could make Pitts feel his hand he was determined to do it and at present he had a little scheme up his sleeve that was going to be a considerable blow to Pitts. He was thinking of it with relish when he told Mary Fortune to remember what she wouldn't get if she didn't mind, and he added, without waiting for an answer, that he might be selling another lot soon and that if he did, he might give her a bonus but not if she gave him any sass. He had frequent little verbal tilts with her but this was a sport like putting a mirror up in front of a rooster and watching him fight his reflection.

"I don't want no bonus," Mary Fortune said.

"I ain't ever seen you refuse one."

"You ain't ever seen me ask for one neither," she said.

"How much have you laid by?" he asked.

"Noner yer bidnis," she said and stamped his shoulders with her feet. "Don't be buttin into my bidnis."

"I bet you got it sewed up in your mattress," he said, "just like an old nigger woman. You ought to put it in the bank. I'm going to start you an account just as soon as I complete this deal. Won't anybody be able to check on it but me and you."

The bulldozer moved under them again and drowned out the rest of what he wanted to say. He waited and when the noise had passed, he could hold it in no longer. "I'm going to sell the lot right in front of the house for a gas station," he said. "Then we won't have to go down the road to get the car filled up, just step out the front door."

The Fortune house was set back about two hundred feet from the road and it was this two hundred feet that he intended to sell. It was the part that his daughter airily called "the lawn" though it was nothing but a field of weeds.

"You mean," Mary Fortune said after a minute, "the lawn?"

"Yes mam!" he said. "I mean the lawn," and he slapped his knee.

She did not say anything and he turned and looked up at her. There in the little rectangular opening of hair was his face looking back at him, but it was a reflection not of his present expression but of the darker one that indicated his displeasure. "That's where we play," she muttered.

"Well there's plenty of other places you can play," he said, irked by this lack of enthusiasm.

"We won't be able to see the woods across the road," she said.

The old man stared at her. "The woods across the road?" he repeated.

"We won't be able to see the view," she said.

"The view?" he repeated.

"The woods," she said; "we won't be able to see the woods from the porch."

"The woods from the porch?" he repeated.

Then she said, "My daddy grazes his calves on that lot."

The old man's wrath was delayed an instant by shock. Then it exploded in a roar. He jumped up and turned and slammed his fist on the hood of the car. "He can graze them somewheres else!"

"You fall off that embankment and you'll wish you hadn't," she said.

He moved from in front of the car around to the side, keeping his eye on her all the time. "Do you think I care where he grazes his calves! Do you think I'll let a calf interfere with my bidnis? Do you think I give a damn hoot where that fool grazes his calves?"

She sat, her red face darker than her hair, exactly reflecting his expression now. "He who calls his brother a fool is subject to hell fire," she said.

"Jedge not," he shouted, "lest ye be not jedged!" The tinge of his face was a shade more purple than hers. "You!" he said. "You let him beat you any time he wants to and don't do a thing but blubber a little and jump up and down!"

"He nor nobody else has ever touched me," she said, measuring off each word in a deadly flat tone. "Nobody's ever put a hand on me and if anybody did, I'd kill him."

"And black is white," the old man piped, "and night is day!"

The bulldozer passed below them. With their faces about a foot apart, each held the same expression until the noise had receded. Then the old man said, "Walk home by yourself. I refuse to ride a Jezebel!"

"And I refuse to ride with the Whore of Babylon," she said and slid off the other side of the car and started off through the pasture.

"A whore is a woman!" he roared. "That's how much you know!" But she did not deign to turn around and answer him back, and as he watched the small robust figure stalk across the yellow-dotted field toward the woods, his pride in her, as if it couldn't help itself, returned like the gentle little tide on the new lake—all except that part of it that had to do with her refusal to stand up to Pitts; that pulled back like an undertow. If he could have taught her to stand up to Pitts the way she stood up to him, she would have been a perfect child, as fearless and sturdy-minded as anyone could want; but it was her one failure of character. It was the one point on which she did not resemble him. He turned and looked away over the lake to the woods across it and told himself that in five years, instead of woods, there would be houses and stores and parking places, and that the credit for it could go largely to him.

He meant to teach the child spirit by example and since he had definitely made up his mind, he announced that noon at the dinner table that he was negotiating with a man named Tilman to sell the lot in front of the house for a gas station.

His daughter, sitting with her worn-out air at the foot of the table, let out a moan as if a dull knife were being turned slowly in her chest. "You mean the lawn!" she moaned and fell back in her chair and repeated in an almost inaudible voice, "He means the lawn."

The other six Pitts children began to bawl and pipe, "Where we play!" "Don't let him do that, Pa!" "We won't be able to see the road!" and similar idiocies. Mary Fortune did not say anything. She had a mulish reserved look as if she were planning some business of her own. Pitts had stopped eating and was staring in front of him. His plate was full but his fists sat motionless like two dark quartz stones on either side of it. His eyes began to move from child to child around the table as if he were hunting for one particular one of them. Finally they stopped on Mary Fortune sitting next to her grandfather. "You done this to us," he muttered.

"I didn't," she said but there was no assurance in her voice. It was only a quaver, the voice of a frightened child.

Pitts got up and said, "Come with me," and turned and walked out, loosening his belt as he went, and to the old man's complete despair, she slid away from the table and followed him, almost ran after him, out the door and into the truck behind him, and they drove off.

This cowardice affected Mr. Fortune as if it were his own. It made him physically sick. "He beats an innocent child," he said to his daughter, who was apparently still prostrate at the end of the table, "and not one of you lifts a hand to stop him."

"You ain't lifted yours neither," one of the boys said in an undertone and there was a general mutter from that chorus of frogs.

"I'm an old man with a heart condition," he said. "I can't stop an ox."

"She put you up to it," his daughter murmured in a languid listless tone, her head rolling back and forth on the rim of her chair. "She puts you up to everything."

"No child never put me up to nothing!" he yelled. "You're no kind of a mother! You're a disgrace! That child is an angel! A saint!" he shouted in a voice so high that it broke and he had to scurry out of the room.

The rest of the afternoon he had to lie on his bed. His heart, whenever he knew the child had been beaten, felt as if it were slightly too large for the space that was supposed to hold it. But now he was more determined than ever to see the filling station go up in front of the house, and if it gave Pitts a stroke, so much the better. If it gave him a stroke and paralyzed him, he would be served right and he would never be able to beat her again.

Mary Fortune was never angry with him for long, or seriously, and though he did not see her the rest of that day, when he woke up the next morning, she was sitting astride his chest ordering him to make haste so that they would not miss the concrete mixer.

The workmen were laying the foundation for the fishing club when they arrived and the concrete mixer was already in operation. It was about the size and color of a circus elephant; they stood and watched it churn for a half-hour or so. At eleven-thirty, the old man had an appointment with Tilman to discuss his transaction and they had to leave. He did not tell Mary Fortune where they were going but only that he had to see a man.

Tilman operated a combination country store, filling station, scrap-metal dump, used-car lot and dance hall five miles down the highway that connected with the dirt road that passed in front of the Fortune place. Since the dirt road would soon be paved, he wanted a good location on it for another such enterprise. He was an up-and-coming man—the kind, Mr. Fortune thought, who was never just in line with progress but always a little ahead of it so that he could be there to meet it when it arrived. Signs up and down the highway announced that Tilman's was only five miles away, only four, only three, only two, only one; then "Watch out for Tilman's, Around this bend!" and finally, "Here it is, Friends, Tilman's!" in dazzling red letters.

Tilman's was bordered on either side by a field of old used-car bodies, a kind of ward for incurable automobiles. He also sold outdoor ornaments, such as stone cranes and chickens, urns, jardinieres, whirligigs, and farther back from the road, so as not to depress his dance-hall customers, a line of tombstones and monuments. Most of his businesses went on out-of-doors, so that his store building itself had not involved excessive expense. It was a one-room wooden structure onto which he had added, behind, a long tin hall equipped for dancing. This was divided into two sections, Colored and White, each with its private nickelodeon. He had a barbecue pit and sold barbecued sandwiches and soft drinks.

As they drove up under the shed of Tilman's place, the old man glanced at the child sitting with her feet drawn up on the seat and her chin resting on her knees. He didn't know if she would remember that it was Tilman he was going to sell the lot to or not.

"What you going in here for?" she asked suddenly, with a sniffing look as if she scented an enemy.

"Noner yer bidnis," he said. "You just sit in the car and when I come out, I'll bring you something."

"Don'tcher bring me nothing," she said darkly, "because I won't be here."

"Haw!" he said. "Now you're here, it's nothing for you to do but wait," and he got out and without paying her any further attention, he entered the dark store where Tilman was waiting for him.

When he came out in half an hour, she was not in the car. Hiding, he decided. He started walking around the store to see if she was in the back. He looked in the doors of the two sections of the dance hall and walked on around by the tombstones. Then his eye roved over the field of sinking automobiles and he realized that she could be in or behind any one of two hundred of them. He came back out in front of the store. A Negro boy, drinking a purple drink, was sitting on the ground with his back against the sweating ice cooler.

"Where did that little girl go to, boy?" he asked.

"I ain't seen nair little girl," the boy said.

The old man irritably fished in his pocket and handed him a nickel and said, "A pretty little girl in a yeller cotton dress."

"If you speakin about a stout chile look lak you," the boy said, "she gone off in a truck with a white man."

"What kind of a truck, what kind of a white man?" he yelled.

"It were a green pick-up truck," the boy said smacking his lips, "and a white man she call 'daddy.' They gone thataway some time ago."

The old man, trembling, got in his car and started home. His feelings raced back and forth between fury and mortification. She had never left him before and certainly never for Pitts. Pitts had ordered her to get in the truck and she was afraid not to. But when he reached this conclusion he was more furious than ever. What was the matter with her that she couldn't stand up to Pitts? Why was there this one flaw in her character when he had trained her so well in everything else? It was an ugly mystery.

When he reached the house and climbed the front steps, there she was sitting in the swing, looking glum-faced in front of her across the field he was going to sell. Her eyes were puffy and pink-rimmed but he didn't see any red marks on her legs. He sat down in the swing beside her. He meant to make his voice severe but instead it came out crushed, as if it belonged to a suitor trying to reinstate himself.

"What did you leave me for? You ain't ever left me before," he said.

"Because I wanted to," she said, looking straight ahead.

"You never wanted to," he said. "He made you."

"I toljer I was going and I went," she said in a slow emphatic voice, not looking at him, "and now you can go on and lemme alone." There was something very final, in the sound of this, a tone that had not come up before in their disputes. She stared across the lot where there was nothing but a profusion of pink and yellow and purple weeds, and on across the red road, to the sullen line of black pine woods fringed on top with green. Behind that line was a narrow gray-blue line of more distant woods and beyond that nothing but the sky, entirely blank except for one or two threadbare clouds. She looked into this scene as if it were a person that she preferred to him.

"It's my lot, ain't it?" he asked. "Why are you so up-in-the-air about me selling my own lot?"

"Because it's the lawn," she said. Her nose and eyes began to run horribly but she held her face rigid and licked the water off as soon as it was in reach of her tongue. "We won't be able to see across the road," she said.

The old man looked across the road to assure himself again that there was nothing over there to see. "I never have seen you act in such a way before," he said in an incredulous voice. "There's not a thing over there but the woods."

"We won't be able to see 'um," she said, "and that's the *lawn* and my daddy grazes his calves on it."

At that the old man stood up. "You act more like a Pitts than a Fortune," he said. He had never made such an ugly remark to her before and he was sorry the instant he had said it. It hurt him more than it did her. He turned and went in the house and upstairs to his room.

Several times during the afternoon, he got up from his bed and looked out the window across the "lawn" to the line of woods she said they wouldn't be able to see any more. Every time he saw the same thing: woods—not a mountain, not a waterfall, not any kind of planted bush or flower, just woods. The sunlight was woven through them at that particular time of the afternoon so that every thin pine trunk stood out in all its nakedness. A pine trunk is a pine trunk, he said to himself, and anybody that wants to see one don't have to go far in this neighborhood. Every time he got up and looked out, he was reconvinced of his wisdom in selling the lot. The dissatisfaction it caused Pitts would be permanent, but he could make it up to Mary Fortune by buying her something. With grown people, a road led either to heaven or hell, but with children there were always stops along the way where their attention could be turned with a trifle.

The third time he got up to look at the woods, it was almost six o'clock and the gaunt trunks appeared to be raised in a pool of red light that gushed from the almost hidden sun setting behind them. The old man stared for some time, as if for a prolonged instant he were caught up out of the rattle of everything that led to the future and were held there in the midst of an uncomfortable mystery that he had not apprehended before. He saw it, in his hallucination, as if someone were wounded behind the woods and the trees were bathed in blood. After a few minutes this unpleasant vision was broken by the presence of Pitts's pick-up truck grinding to a halt below the window. He returned to his bed and shut his eyes and against the closed lids hellish red trunks rose up in a black wood.

At the supper table nobody addressed a word to him, including Mary Fortune. He ate quickly and returned again to his room and spent the evening pointing out to himself the advantages for the future of having an establishment like Tilman's so near. They would not have to go any distance for gas. Anytime they needed a loaf of bread, all they would have to do would be step out their front door into Tilman's back door. They could sell milk to Tilman. Tilman was a likable fellow. Tilman would draw other business. The road would soon be paved. Travelers from all over the country would stop at Tilman's. If his daughter thought she was better than Tilman, it would be well to take her down a little. All men were created free and equal. When this phrase sounded in his head, his patriotic sense triumphed and he realized that it was his duty to sell the lot, that he must insure the future. He looked out the window at the moon shining over the woods across the road and listened for a while to the hum of crickets and treefrogs, and beneath their racket, he could hear the throb of the future town of Fortune.

He went to bed certain that just as usual, he would wake up in the morning looking into a little red mirror framed in a door of fine hair. She would have forgotten all about the sale and after breakfast they would drive into town and get the legal papers from the courthouse. On the way back he would stop at Tilman's and close the deal.

When he opened his eyes in the morning, he opened them on the empty ceiling. He pulled himself up and looked around the room but she was not there. He hung over the edge of the bed and looked beneath it but she was not there either. He got up and dressed and went outside. She was sitting in the swing on the front porch, exactly the way she had been yesterday, looking across the lawn into the woods. The old man was very much irritated. Every morning since she had been able to climb, he had waked up to find her either on his bed or underneath it. It was apparent that this morning she preferred the sight of the woods. He decided to ignore her behavior for the present and then bring it up later when she was over her pique. He sat down in the swing beside her but she continued to look at the woods. "I thought you and me'd go into town and have us a look at the boats in the new boat store," he said.

She didn't turn her head but she asked suspiciously, in a loud voice, "What else are you going for?"

"Nothing else," he said.

After a pause she said, "If that's all, I'll go," but she did not bother to look at him.

"Well put on your shoes," he said. "I ain't going to the city with a barefoot woman." She did not bother to laugh at this joke.

The weather was as indifferent as her disposition. The sky did not look as if it were going to rain or as if it were not going to rain. It was an unpleasant gray and the sun had not troubled to come out. All the way into town, she sat looking at her feet, which stuck out in front of her, encased in heavy brown school shoes. The old man had often sneaked up on her and found her alone in conversation with her feet and he thought she was speaking with them silently now. Every now and then her lips moved but she said nothing to him and let all his remarks pass as if she had not heard them. He decided it was going to cost him considerable to buy her good humor again and that he had better do it with a boat, since he wanted one too. She had been talking boats ever since the water backed up onto his place. They went first to the boat store. "Show us the yachts for po' folks!" he shouted jovially to the clerk as they entered.

"They're all for po' folks!" the clerk said. "You'll be po' when you finish buying one!" He was a stout youth in a yellow shirt and blue pants and he had a ready wit. They exchanged several clever remarks in rapid-fire succession. Mr. Fortune looked at Mary Fortune to see if her face had brightened. She stood staring absently over the side of an outboard motor boat at the opposite wall.

"Ain't the lady interested in boats?" the clerk asked.

She turned and wandered back out onto the sidewalk and got in the car again. The old man looked after her with amazement. He could not believe that a child of her intelligence could be acting this way over the mere sale of a field. "I think she must be coming down with something," he said. "We'll come back again," and he returned to the car.

"Let's go get us an ice-cream cone," he suggested, looking at her with concern.

"I don't want no ice-cream cone," she said.

His actual destination was the courthouse but he did not want to make this apparent. "How'd you like to visit the ten-cent store while I tend to a little bidnis of mine?" he asked. "You can buy yourself something with a quarter I brought along."

"I ain't got nothing to do in no ten-cent store," she said. "I don't want no quarter of yours."

If a boat was of no interest, he should not have thought a quarter would be and reproved himself for that stupidity. "Well what's the matter, sister?" he asked kindly. "Don't you feel good?"

She turned and looked him straight in the face and said with a slow concentrated ferocity, "It's the lawn. My daddy grazes his calves there. We won't be able to see the woods any more."

The old man had held his fury in as long as he could. "He beats you!" he shouted. "And you worry about where he's going to graze his calves!"

"Nobody's ever beat me in my life," she said, "and if anybody did, I'd kill him."

A man seventy-nine years of age cannot let himself be run over by a child of nine. His face set in a look that was just as determined as hers. "Are you a Fortune," he said, "or are you a Pitts? Make up your mind."

Her voice was loud and positive and belligerent. "I'm Mary—Fortune—Pitts," she said.

"Well I," he shouted, "am PURE Fortune!"

There was nothing she could say to this and she showed it. For an instant she looked completely defeated, and the old man saw with a disturbing clearness that this was the Pitts look. What he saw was the Pitts look, pure and simple, and he felt personally stained by it, as if it had been found on his own face. He turned in disgust and backed the car out and drove straight to the courthouse.

The courthouse was a red and white blaze-faced building set in the center of a square from which most of the grass had been worn off. He parked in front of it and said, "Stay here," in an imperious tone and got out and slammed the car door.

It took him a half-hour to get the deed and have the sale paper drawn up and when he returned to the car, she was sitting on the back seat in the corner. The expression on that part of her face that he could see was foreboding and withdrawn. The sky had darkened also and there was a hot sluggish tide in the air, the kind felt when a tornado is possible.

"We better get on before we get caught in a storm," he said and added emphatically, "because I got one more place to stop at on the way home," but he might have been chauffeuring a small dead body for all the answer he got.

On the way to Tilman's he reviewed once more the many just reasons that were leading him to his present action and he could not locate a flaw in any of them. He decided that while this attitude of hers would not be permanent, he was permanently disappointed in her and that when she came around she would have to apologize; and that there would be no boat. He was coming to realize slowly that his trouble with her had always been that he had not shown enough firmness. He had been too generous. He was so occupied with these thoughts that he did not notice the signs that said how many miles to Tilman's until the last one exploded joyfully in his face: "Here it is, Friends, Tilman's!" He pulled in under the shed.

He got out without so much as looking at Mary Fortune and entered the dark store where Tilman, leaning on the counter in front of a triple shelf of canned goods, was waiting for him.

Tilman was a man of quick action and few words. He sat habitually with his arms folded on the counter and his insignificant head weaving snake-fashion above them. He had a triangular-shaped face with the point at the bottom and the top of his skull was covered with a cap of freckles. His eyes were green and very narrow and his tongue was always exposed in his partly opened mouth. He had his checkbook handy and they got down to business at once. It did not take him long to look at the deed and sign the bill of sale. Then Mr. Fortune signed it and they grasped hands over the counter.

Mr. Fortune's sense of relief as he grasped Tilman's hand was extreme. What was done, he felt, was done and there could be no more argument, with her or with himself. He felt that he had acted on principle and that the future was assured.

Just as their hands loosened, an instant's change came over Tilman's face and he disappeared completely under the counter as if he had been snatched by the feet from below. A bottle crashed against the line of tinned goods behind where he had been. The old man whirled around. Mary Fortune was in the door, red-faced and wild-looking, with another bottle lifted to hurl. As he ducked, it broke behind him on the counter and she grabbed another from the crate. He sprang at her but she tore to the other side of the store, screaming something unintelligible and throwing everything within her reach. The old man pounced again and this time he caught her by the tail of her dress and pulled her backward out of the store. Then he got a better grip and lifted her, wheezing and whimpering but suddenly limp in his arms, the few feet to the car. He managed to get the door open and dump her inside. Then he ran around to the other side and got in himself and drove away as fast as he could.

His heart felt as if it were the size of the car and was racing forward, carrying him to some inevitable destination faster than he had ever been carried before. For the first five minutes he did not think but only sped forward as if he were being driven inside his own fury. Gradually the power of thought returned to him. Mary Fortune, rolled into a ball in the corner of the seat, was snuffling and heaving.

He had never seen a child behave in such a way in his life. Neither his own children nor anyone else's had ever displayed such temper in his presence, and he had never for an instant imagined that the child he had trained himself, the child who had been his constant companion for nine years, would embarrass him like this. The child he had never lifted a hand to!

Then he saw, with the sudden vision that sometimes comes with delayed recognition, that that had been his mistake.

She respected Pitts because, even with no just cause, he beat her; and if he—with his just cause—did not beat her now, he would have nobody to blame but himself if she turned out a hellion. He saw that the time had come, that he could no longer avoid whipping her, and as he turned off the highway onto the dirt road leading to home, he told himself that when he finished with her, she would never throw another bottle again.

He raced along the clay road until he came to the line where his own property began and then he turned off onto a side path, just wide enough for the automobile and bounced for a half a mile through the woods. He stopped the car at the exact spot where he had seen Pitts take his belt to her. It was a place where the road widened so that two cars could pass or one could turn around, an ugly red bald spot surrounded by long thin pines that appeared to be gathered there to witness anything that would take place in such a clearing. A few stones protruded from the clay.

"Get out," he said and reached across her and opened the door.

She got out without looking at him or asking what they were going to do and he got out on his side and came around the front of the car.

"Now I'm going to whip you!" he said and his voice was extra loud and hollow and had a vibrating quality that appeared to be taken up and passed through the tops of the pines. He did not want to get caught in a downpour while he was whipping her and he said, "Hurry up and get ready against that tree," and began to take off his belt.

What he had in mind to do appeared to come very slowly as if it had to penetrate a fog in her head. She did not move but gradually her confused expression began to clear. Where a few seconds before her face had been red and distorted and unorganized, it drained now of every vague line until nothing was left on it but positiveness, a look that went slowly past determination and reached certainty. "Nobody has ever beat me," she said, "and if anybody tries it, I'll kill him."

"I don't want no sass," he said and started toward her. His knees felt very unsteady, as if they might turn either backward or forward.

She moved exactly one step back and, keeping her eye on him steadily, removed her glasses and dropped them behind a small rock near the tree he had told her to get ready against. "Take off your glasses," she said.

"Don't give me orders!" he said in a high voice and slapped awkwardly at her ankles with his belt.

She was on him so quickly that he could not have recalled which blow he felt first, whether the weight of her whole solid body or the jabs of her feet or the pummeling of her fist on his chest. He flailed the belt in the air, not knowing where to hit but trying to get her off him until he could decide where to get a grip on her.

"Leggo!" he shouted. "Leggo I tell you!" But she seemed to be everywhere, coming at him from all directions at once. It was as if he were being attacked not by one child but by a pack of small demons all with stout brown school shoes and small rocklike fists. His glasses flew to the side.

"I toljer to take them off," she growled without pausing.

He caught his knee and danced on one foot and a rain of blows fell on his stomach. He felt five claws in the flesh of his upper arm where she was hanging from while her feet mechanically battered his knees and her free fist pounded him again and again in the chest. Then with horror he saw her face rise up in front of his, teeth exposed, and he roared like a bull as she bit the side of his jaw. He seemed to see his own face coming to bite him from several sides at once but he could not attend to it for he was being kicked indiscriminately, in the stomach and then in the crotch. Suddenly he threw himself on the ground and began to roll like a man on fire. She was on top of him at once, rolling with him and still kicking, and now with both fists free to batter his chest.

"I'm an old man!" he piped. "Leave me alone!" But she did not stop. She began a fresh assault on his jaw.

"Stop stop!" he wheezed. "I'm your grandfather!"

She paused, her face exactly on top of his. Pale identical eye looked into pale identical eye. "Have you had enough?" she asked.

The old man looked up into his own image. It was triumphant and hostile. "You been whipped," it said, "by me," and then it added, bearing down on each word, "and I'm PURE Pitts."

In the pause she loosened her grip and he got hold of her throat. With a sudden surge of strength, he managed to roll over and reverse their positions so that he was looking down into the face that was his own but had dared to call itself Pitts. With his hands still tight around her neck, he lifted her head and brought it down once hard against the rock that happened to be under it. Then he brought it down twice more. Then looking into the face in which the eyes, slowly rolling back, appeared to pay him not the slightest attention, he said, "There's not an ounce of Pitts in me."

He continued to stare at his conquered image until he perceived that though it was absolutely silent, there was no look of remorse on it. The eyes had rolled back down and were set in a fixed glare that did not take him in. "This ought to teach you a good lesson," he said in a voice that was edged with doubt.

He managed painfully to get up on his unsteady kicked legs and to take two steps, but the enlargement of his heart which had begun in the car was still going on. He turned his head and looked behind him for a long time at the little motionless figure with its head on the rock.

Then he fell on his back and looked up helplessly along the bare trunks into the tops of the pines and his heart expanded once more with a convulsive motion. It expanded so fast that the old man felt as if he were being pulled after it through the woods, felt as if he were running as fast as he could with the ugly pines toward the lake. He perceived that there would be a little opening there, a little place where he could escape and leave the woods behind him. He could see it in the distance already, a little opening where the white sky was reflected in the water. It grew as he ran toward it until suddenly the whole lake opened up before him, riding majestically in little corrugated folds toward his feet. He realized suddenly that he could not swim and that he had not bought the boat. On both sides of him he saw that the gaunt trees had thickened into mysterious dark files that were marching across the water and away into the distance. He looked around desperately for someone to help him but the place was deserted except for one huge yellow monster which sat to the side, as stationary as he was, gorging itself on clay.

Questions for Thinking and Writing

1. Explain what you think Mark Fortune means when he says, "Any fool that would let a cow pasture interfere with progress is not on my books." What does this story say about the notion of progress with regard to vision, money, farming, and pleasure? Consider the surnames of the families, Fortune and Pitts, in your answers.
2. What is O'Connor's attitude toward machines in this story? To the natural environment? What is the significance of the story's title? What is the old man's view of the woods? What is the Pitts's view?
3. Explain whether or not you would sell your land for profit. Discuss the various possibilities: selling all of the land, developing a plan for multiple use, or keeping the land as it is.

🌺 E. B. White (1899–1985)

A Report in Spring (1957)

Elwyn Brooks White, though not a dedicated environmentalist or even a professed lover of natural wildness, viewed nature as a presence he could always count on. For White, nature is to be complimented when cooperative with human plans and goals, and tolerated when displaying a will of its own.

White was born in Mount Vernon, New York, went to high school there, and then attended Cornell University. One of his professors at Cornell was William S. Strunk, Jr., whose textbook on writing White later revised. The Elements of Style (1959), co-authored by Strunk and White, has sold millions of copies over the years.

At Cornell, White was editor in chief of the campus newspaper, the first of several positions with newspapers. After graduating he worked briefly for United Press, the American Legion News Service, and as a reporter and columnist for the Seattle Times.

In 1923, he moved to New York and worked as a copywriter and production assistant for several advertising firms. Later, he wrote about the brainwashing effect of advertising on the American public.

Two years later Harold Ross, founder of the New Yorker, *published one of White's essays, "Defense of the Bronx River." In 1927, Ross offered White a part-time position as a staff writer, which he immediately accepted. It was a job he kept for the rest of his life. During those years, he produced hundreds of essays for the magazine, many of which have been anthologized.*

Several years after joining the New Yorker, *White married Katharine S. Angell, the magazine's fiction editor, and in 1938, the couple moved with their son, Joel, to a farm in Brooklin, Maine, a small coastal town that became the center of the family's existence. Turtle Bay in this essay is actually Allen Cove, the area of Brooklin where White lived.*

In 1963, White was awarded the Presidential Medal of Freedom by President John F. Kennedy. In 1971, he won the National Medal for Literature, and in 1978, he was elected to the American Academy of Arts and Letters. Despite these accolades, his heart was very much tied to his farm, to the animals on it that became characters in his children's book Charlotte's Web *(1952), and to the people who lived near him in Maine. A private man who shunned publicity, he took measures not to reveal the location of his home for fear it would be overrun by schoolchildren following the publication of such classics as* Stuart Little, Charlotte's Web, *and* The Trumpet of the Swan. *Indeed, thousands of children wrote to White wondering if Stuart Little ever found Margalo, the bird, and what happened to Wilbur, the pig. White remained reticent to the end.*

I bought a puppy last week in the outskirts of Boston and drove him to Maine in a rented Ford that looked like a sculpin. There had been talk in our family of getting a "sensible" dog this time, and my wife and I had gone over the list of sensible dogs, and had even ventured once or twice into the company of sensible dogs. A friend had a litter of Labradors, and there were other opportunities. But after a period of uncertainty and waste motion my wife suddenly exclaimed one evening, "Oh, let's just get a dachshund!" She had had a glass of wine, and I could see that the truth was coming out. Her tone was one of exasperation laced with affection. So I engaged a black male without further ado.

For the long ordeal of owning another dachshund we prepared ourselves by putting up for a night at the Boston Ritz in a room overlooking the Public Garden, where from our window we could gaze, perhaps for the last time, on a world of order and peace. I say "for the last time" because it occurred to me early in the proceedings that this was our first adoption case in which there was a strong likelihood that the dog would survive the man. It had always been the other way around. The Garden had never seemed so beautiful. We were both up early the next morning for a final look at the fresh, untroubled scene; then we checked out hastily, sped to the kennel, and claimed our prize, who is the grandson of an animal named Direct Stretch of the Walls. He turned out to be a good traveller, and except for an interruption caused by my wife's falling out of the car in Gardiner, the journey went very well. At present, I am a sojourner in the city again, but here in the green warmth of Turtle Bay I see only the countenance of spring in the country. No matter what changes take place in the world, or in me, nothing ever seems to disturb the face of spring.

The smelts are running in the brooks. We had a mess for Monday lunch, brought to us by our son, who was fishing at two in the morning. At this season, a smelt brook is the night club of the town, and when the tide is a late one, smelting is for the young, who like small hours and late society.

No rain has fallen in several weeks. The gardens are dry, the road to the shore is dusty. The ditches, which in May are usually swollen to bursting, are no more than a summer trickle. Trout fishermen are not allowed on the streams; pond fishing from a boat is still permissible. The landscape is lovely to behold, but the hot, dry wind carries the smell of trouble. The other day we saw the smoke of a fire over in the direction of the mountain.

Mice have eaten the crowns of the Canterbury bells, my white-faced steer has warts on his neck (I'm told it's a virus, like everything else these days), and the dwarf pear has bark trouble. My puppy has no bark trouble. He arises at three, for tennis. The puppy's health, in fact, is exceptionally good. When my wife and I took him from the kennel, a week ago today, his mother kissed all three of us goodbye, and the lady who ran the establishment presented me with complete feeding instructions, which included a mineral supplement called Pervinal and some vitamin drops called Vi-syneral. But I knew that as soon as the puppy reached home and got his sea legs he would switch to the supplement *du jour*—a flake of well-rotted cow manure from my boot, a dead crocus bulb from the lawn, a shingle from the kindling box, a bloody feather from the execution block behind the barn. Time has borne me out; the puppy was not long discovering the delicious supplements of the farm, and he now knows where every vitamin hides, under its stone, under its loose board. I even introduced him to the tonic smell of coon.

On Tuesday, in broad daylight, the coon arrived, heavy with young, to take possession of the hole in the tree, but she found another coon in possession, and there was a grim fight high in the branches. The new tenant won, or so it appeared to me, and our old coon came down the tree in defeat and hustled off into the woods to examine her wounds and make other plans for her confinement. I was sorry for her, as I am for any who are evicted from their haunts by the younger and stronger—always a sad occasion for man or beast.

The stalks of rhubarb show red, the asparagus has broken through. Peas and potatoes are in, but it is not much use putting seeds in the ground the way things are. The bittern spent a day at the pond, creeping slowly around the shores like a little round-shouldered peddler. A setting of goose eggs has arrived by parcel post from Vermont, my goose having been taken by the fox last fall. I carried the package into the barn and sat down to unpack the eggs. They came out of the box in perfect condition, each one wrapped in a page torn from the *New England Homestead*. Clustered around me on the floor, they looked as though I had been hard at it. There is no one to sit on them but me, and I had to return to New York, so I ordered a trio of Muscovies from a man in New Hampshire, in the hope of persuading a Muscovy duck to give me a Toulouse gosling. (The theme of my life is complexity-through-joy.) In reply to my order, the duck-farm man wrote saying there would be a slight delay in the shipment of Muscovies, as he was "in the midst of a forest-fire scare." I did not know from this whether he was too scared to drive to the post office with a duck or too worried to fit a duck into a crate.

By day the goldfinches dip in yellow flight, by night the frogs sing the song that never goes out of favor. We opened the lower sash of the window in the barn loft, and the swallows are already building, but mud for their nests is not so easy to come by as in most springtimes. One afternoon, I found my wife kneeling at the edge of her perennial border on the north side, trying to disengage Achillea-the-Pearl from Coral Bell. "If I could afford it," she said bitterly, "I would take every damn bit of Achillea out of this border." She is a woman in comfortable circumstances, arrived at through her own hard labor, and this sudden burst of poverty, and her inability to indulge herself in a horticultural purge, startled me. I was so moved by her plight and her unhappiness that I went to the barn and returned with an edger, and we spent a fine, peaceable hour in the pretty twilight, rapping Achillea over the knuckles and saving Coral Bell.

One never knows what images one is going to hold in memory, returning to the city after a brief orgy in the country. I find this morning that what I most vividly and longingly recall is the sight of my grandson and his little sunburnt sister returning to their kitchen door from an excursion, with trophies of the meadow clutched in their hands—she with a couple of violets, and smiling, he serious and holding dandelions, strangling them in a responsible grip. Children hold spring so tightly in their brown fists—just as grownups, who are less sure of it, hold it in their hearts.

Questions for Thinking and Writing

1. How does country living in Turtle Bay support White's contention that "The theme of my life is complexity-through-joy"?
2. White's bias for country living is evident, but how does he hold the memory of his life in Maine when he is back in the city? Explain whether or not you think that Henry David Thoreau would approve of White's double life.
3. Discuss whether you have an attraction for living in the country as opposed to the city. If you live in a rural area, discuss the notion commonly held by city people that country life is restorative and more pure.

🌺 Jack Kerouac (1922–1969)

Desolation Peak (1958)

A disciple of American individuality in the vein of Henry David Thoreau and Walt Whitman, Jack Kerouac is known as the pioneer of the post-World War II Beat Generation. Its members, he said, "espouse mystical detachment and relaxation of social and sexual tensions, supposedly as a result of disillusionment stemming from the Cold War." Kerouac's 18 published books are field experiences and reflections on this loose philosophy. Despite their fictionalization, they are really an expansive and roaming autobiography.

Kerouac was born in Lowell, Massachusetts, attended Catholic schools there, and went to Columbia University on a football and track scholarship. A leg injury during his sophomore year forced him to stop playing football, and he left college in 1941 to join the merchant marine. After a short time, he returned to New York City, having been discharged as a "schizoid personality."

While at Columbia, he had met the poet Allen Ginsburg and author William Burroughs. Now he renewed his relationship with them in Greenwich Village and began to write. His first novel, The Town & The City *(1950), was well received, but Kerouac did not consider it to be in his voice. His second,* On the Road, *written intensely in the space of three weeks, exemplified what he called "spontaneous prose." Publishers were leery of the novel's story, however, and it took seven years before Viking took the risk and brought the book out. On the Road (1957) proved to be such a success that it marked Kerouac as the leader of what was perceived to be a social rebellion strewn with drugs, sexual excess, and nonconformity.*

During the years before On the Road *appeared, Kerouac wandered the country, taking odd jobs. One of them was as a railroad brakeman, another was as a fire lookout, the experience described in the portion of* The Dharma Bums *(1958) excerpted here. During this time he befriended Gary Snyder (see p. 307) who taught him how to survive living outdoors in the Rocky Mountains. In fact, Snyder is the protagonist of* The Dharma Bums, *given the name Japhy Ryder. As a fire lookout, Kerouac was able to literally sit on top of the natural world and experience what nature might deal him. During this lonely, and at times frightening ordeal, he learned to accept nature on its terms. This was what he learned from practicing Zen.*

When contemporary and established writers and critics parodied and attacked his work, Kerouac increasingly isolated himself. By age 57, he had severed all his ties to members of the Beat Generation that he had fostered. He died of heart disease and alcoholism, a lonely man in St. Petersburg, Florida, where he had moved to care for his elderly mother.

Finally came the gray rainy day of my departure to Desolation Peak. The assistant ranger was with us, the three of us were going up and it wasn't going to be a pleasant day's horseback riding in all that downpour. "Boy, you shoulda put a couple quarts of brandy in your grocery list, you're gonna need it up there in the cold," said Happy looking at me with his big red nose. We were standing by the corral, Happy was giving the animals bags of feed and tying it around their necks and they were chomping away unmindful of the rain. We came plowing to the log gate and bumped through and went around under the immense shrouds of Sourdough and Ruby mountains. The waves were crashing up and spraying back at us. We went inside to the pilot's cabin and he had a pot of coffee ready. Firs on steep banks you could barely see on the lake shore were like ranged ghosts in the mist. It was the real Northwest grim and bitter misery.

"Where's Desolation?" I asked.

"You ain't about to see it today till you're practically on top of it," said Happy, "and then you won't like it much. It's snowin and hailin up there right now. Boy, ain't you sure you didn't sneak a little bottle of brandy in your pack somewheres?" We'd already downed a quart of blackberry wine he'd bought in Marblemount.

"Happy when I get down from this mountain in September I'll buy you a whole quart of scotch." I was going to be paid good money for finding the mountain I wanted.

"That's a promise and don't you forget it." Japhy had told me a lot about Happy the Packer, he was called. Happy was a good man; he and old Burnie Byers were the best oldtimers on the scene. They knew the mountains and they knew pack animals and they weren't ambitious to become forestry supervisors either.

Happy remembered Japhy too, wistfully. "That boy used to know an awful lot of funny songs and stuff. He shore loved to go out loggin out trails. He had himself a Chinee girlfriend one time down in Seattle, I seen her in his hotel room, that Japhy I'm tellin you he shore was a grunge-jumper with the women." I could hear Japhy's voice singing gay songs with his guitar as the wind howled around our barge and the gray waves plashed up against the windows of the pilot house.

"And this is Japhy's lake, and these are Japhy's mountains," I thought, and wished Japhy were there to see me doing everything he wanted me to do.

In two hours we eased over to the steep timbered shore eight miles uplake and jumped off and lashed the float to old stumps and Happy whacked the first mule, and she scampered off the wood with her doublesided load and charged up the slippery bank, legs thrashing and almost falling back in the lake with all my groceries, but made it and went off clomping in the mist to wait on the trail for her master. Then the other mules with batteries and various equipment, then finally Happy leading the way on his horse and then myself on the mare Mabel and then Wally the assistant ranger.

We waved goodbye to the tugboat man and started up a sad and dripping party in a hard Arctic climb in heavy foggy rain up narrow rocky trails with trees and underbrush wetting us clean to the skin when we brushed by. I had my nylon poncho tied around the pommel of the saddle and soon took it out and put it over me, a shroudy monk on a horse. Happy and Wally didn't put on anything and just rode wet with heads bowed. The horse slipped occasionally in the rocks of the trail. We went on and on, up and up, and finally we came to a snag that had fallen across the trail and Happy dismounted and took out his doublebitted ax and went to work cursing and sweating and hacking out a new shortcut trail around it with Wally while I was delegated to watch the animals, which I did in a rather comfortable way sitting under a bush and rolling a cigarette. The mules were afraid of the steepness and roughness of the shortcut trail and Happy cursed at me "God-dammit it grab 'im by the hair and drag 'im up here." Then the mare was afraid. "Bring up that mare! You expect me to do everything around here by myself?"

We finally got out of there and climbed on up, soon leaving the shrubbery and entering a new alpine height of rocky meadow with blue lupine and red poppy feathering the gray mist with lovely vaguenesses of color and the wind blowing hard now and with sleet. "Five thousand feet now!" yelled Happy from up front, turning in the saddle with his old hat furling in the wind, rolling himself a cigarette, sitting easy in his saddle from a whole lifetime on horses. The heather wildflower drizzly meadows wound up and up, on switchback trails, the wind getting harder all the time, finally Happy yelled: "See that big rock face up thar?" I looked up and saw a goopy shroud of gray rock in the fog, just above. "That's another thousand feet though you might think you can reach up and touch it. When we get there we're almost in. Only another half hour after that."

"You sure you didn't bring just a *little* extry bottle of brandy boy?" he yelled back a minute later. He was wet and miserable but he didn't care and I could hear him singing in the wind. By and by we were up above timberline practically, the meadow gave way to grim rocks and suddenly there was snow on the ground to the right and to the left, the horses were slowshing in a sleety foot of it, you could see the water holes their hoofs left, we were really way up there now. Yet on all sides I could see nothing but fog and white snow and blowing mists. On a clear day I would have been able to see the sheer drops from the side of the trail and would have been scared for my horse's slips of hoof; but now all I saw were vague intimations of treetops way below that looked like little clumps of grasses. "O Japhy," I thought, "and there you are sailing across the ocean safe on a ship, warm in a cabin, writing letters to Psyche and Sean and Christine."

The snow deepened and hail began to pelt our red weather-beaten faces and finally Happy yelled from up ahead "We're almost there now." I was cold and wet: I got off the horse and simply led her up the trail, she grunted a kind of groan of relief to be rid of the weight and followed me obediently. She already had quite a load of supplies, anyway. "There she is!" yelled Happy and in the swirled-across top-of-the-world fog I saw a funny little peaked almost Chinese cabin among little pointy firs and boulders standing on a bald rock top surrounded by snowbanks and patches of wet grass with tiny flowers.

I gulped. It was too dark and dismal to like it. "This will be my home and restingplace all summer?"

We trudged on to the log corral built by some old lookout of the thirties and tethered the animals and took down the packs. Happy went up and took the weather door off and got the keys and opened her up and inside it was all gray dank gloomy muddy floor with rain-stained walls and a dismal wooden bunk with a mattress made of ropes (so as not to attract lightning) and the windows completely impenetrable with dust and worst of all the floor littered with magazines torn and chewed up by mice and pieces of groceries too and uncountable little black balls of rat turd.

"Well," said Wally showing his long teeth at me, "it's gonna take you a long time to clean up this mess, hey? Start in right now by taking all those leftover canned goods off the shelf and running a wet soapy rag over that filthy shelf." Which I did, and I had to do, I was getting paid.

But good old Happy got a roaring woodfire going in the potbelly stove and put on a pot of water and dumped half a can of coffee in it and yelled "Ain't nothing like real strong coffee, up in this country boy we want coffee that'll make your hair stand on end."

I looked out the windows: fog. "How high are we?"

"Six thousand an a half feet."

"Well how can I see any fires? There's nothing but fog out there."

"In a couple of days it'll all blow away and you'll be able to see for a hundred miles in every direction, don't worry."

But I didn't believe it. I remembered Han Shan talking about the fog on Cold Mountain, how it never went away; I began to appreciate Han Shan's hardihood. Happy and Wally went out with me and we spent some time putting up the anemometer pole and doing other chores, then Happy went in and started a crackling supper on the stove frying Spam with eggs. We drank coffee deep, and had a rich good meal. Wally unpacked the two-way battery radio and contacted Ross Float. Then they curled up in their sleeping bags for a night's rest, on the floor, while I slept on the damp bunk in my own bag.

In the morning it was still gray fog and wind. They got the animals ready and before leaving turned and said to me, "Well, do you still like Desolation Peak?"

And Happy: "Don't forget what I told ya about answerin your own questions now. And if a bar comes by and looks in your window just close your eyes."

The windows howled as they rode out of sight in the mist among the gnarled rock-top trees and pretty soon I couldn't see them any more and I was alone on Desolation Peak for all I knew for eternity, I was sure I wasn't going to come out of there alive anyway. I was trying to see the mountains but only occasional gaps in the blowing fog would reveal distant dim shapes. I gave up and went in and spent a whole day cleaning out the mess in the cabin.

At night I put on my poncho over my rain jacket and warm clothing and went out to meditate on the foggy top of the world. Here indeed was the Great Truth Cloud, Dharmamega, the ultimate goal. I began to see my first star at ten, and suddenly some of the white mist parted and I thought I saw mountains, immense black gooky shapes across the way, stark black and white with snow on top, so near, suddenly, I almost jumped. At eleven I could see the evening star over Canada, north way, and thought I could detect an orange sash of sunset behind the fog but all this was taken out of my mind by the sound of pack rats scratching at my cellar door. In the attic little diamond mice skittered on black feet among oats and bits of rice and old rigs left up there by a generation of Desolation losers. "Ugh, ow," I thought, "will I get to like this? And if I don't, how do I get to leave?" The only thing was to go to bed and stick my head under the down.

In the middle of the night while half asleep I had apparently opened my eyes a bit, and then suddenly I woke up with my hair standing on end, I had just seen a huge black monster standing in my window, and I looked, and it had a star over it, and it was Mount Hozomeen miles away by Canada leaning over my backyard and staring in my window. The fog had all blown away and it was perfect starry night. What a mountain! It had that same unmistakable witches' tower shape Japhy had given it in his brush drawing of it that used to hang on the burlap wall in the flowery shack in Corte Madera. It was built with a kind of winding rock-ledge road going around and around, spiraling to the very top where a perfect witches' tower peakied up and pointed to all infinity. Hozomeen, Hozomeen, the most mournful mountain I ever seen, and the most beautiful as soon as I got to know it and saw the Northern Lights behind it reflecting all the ice of the North Pole from the other side of the world.

33

Lo, in the morning I woke up and it was beautiful blue sunshine sky and I went out in my alpine yard and there it was, everything Japhy said it was, hundreds of miles of pure snow-covered rocks and virgin lakes and high timber, and below, instead of the world, I saw a sea of marshmallow clouds flat as a roof and extending miles and miles in every direction, creaming all the valleys, what they call low-level clouds, on my 6600-foot pinnacle it was all far below me. I brewed coffee on the stove and came out and warmed my mist-drenched bones in the hot sun of my little woodsteps. I said "Tee tee" to a big furry cony and he calmly enjoyed a minute with me gazing at the sea of clouds. I made bacon and eggs, dug a garbage pit a hundred yards down the trail, hauled wood and identified landmarks with my panoramic and firefinder and named all the magic rocks and clefts, names Japhy had sung to me so often: Jack Mountain, Mount Terror, Mount Fury, Mount Challenger, Mount Despair, Golden Horn, Sourdough, Crater Peak, Ruby, Mount Baker bigger than the world in the western distance, Jackass Mountain, Crooked Thumb Peak, and the fabulous names of the creeks: Three Fools, Cinnamon, Trouble, Lightning and Freezeout. And it was all mine, not another human pair of eyes in the world were looking at this immense cycloramic universe of matter. I had a tremendous sensation of its dreamlikeness which never left me all that summer and in fact grew and grew, especially when I stood on my head to circulate my blood, right on top of the mountain, using a burlap bag for a head mat, and then the mountains looked like little bubbles hanging in the void upside-down. In fact I realized they were upsidedown and I was upsidedown! There was nothing here to hide the fact of gravity holding us all intact upsidedown against a surface globe of earth in infinite empty space. And suddenly I realized I was truly alone and had nothing to do but feed myself and rest and amuse myself, and nobody could criticize. The little flowers grew everywhere around the rocks, and no one had asked them to grow, or me to grow.

In the afternoon the marshmallow roof of clouds blew away in patches and Ross Lake was open to my sight, a beautiful cerulean pool far below with tiny toy boats of vacationists, the boats themselves too far to see, just the pitiful little tracks they left rilling in the mirror lake. You could see pines reflected upsidedown in the lake pointing to infinity. Late afternoon I lay in the grass with all that glory before me and grew a little bored and thought "There's nothing there because I don't care." Then I jumped up and began singing and dancing and whistling through my teeth far across Lightning Gorge and it was too immense for an echo. Behind the shack was a huge snowfield that would provide me with fresh drinking water till September, just a bucket a day let melt in the house, to dip into with a tin cup, cold ice water. I was feeling happier than in years and years, since childhood, I felt deliberate and glad and solitary. "Buddy-o, yiddam, diddam dee," I sang, walking around kicking rocks. Then my first sunset came and it was unbelievable. The mountains were covered with pink snow, the clouds were distant and frilly and like ancient remote cities of Buddhaland splendor, the wind worked incessantly, whish, whish, booming at times, rattling my ship. The new moon disk was prognathic and secretly funny in the pale plank of blue over the monstrous shoulders of haze that rose from Ross Lake. Sharp jags popped up from behind slopes, like childhood mountains I grayly drew. Somewhere, it seemed, a golden festival of rejoicement was taking place. In my diary I wrote, "Oh I'm happy!" In the late day peaks I saw the hope. Japhy had been right.

As darkness enveloped my mountain and soon it would be night again and stars and Abominable Snowman stalking on Hozomeen, I started a cracking fire in the stove and baked delicious rye muffins and mixed up a good beef stew. A high west wind buffeted the shack, it was well built with steel rods going down into concrete pourings, it wouldn't blow away. I was satisfied. Every time I'd look out the windows I'd see alpine firs with snowcapped backgrounds, blinding mists, or the lake below all riffled and moony like a toy bathtub lake. I made myself a little bouquet of lupine and mountain posies and put them in a coffee cup with water. The top of Jack Mountain was done in by silver clouds. Sometimes I'd see flashes of lightning far away, illuminating suddenly the unbelievable horizons. Some mornings there was fog and my ridge, Starvation Ridge, would be milkied over completely.

On the dot the following Sunday morning, just like the first, daybreak revealed the sea of flat shining clouds a thousand feet below me. Every time I felt bored I rolled another cigarette out of my can of Prince

Albert; there's nothing better in the world than a roll-your-own deeply enjoyed without hurry. I paced in the bright silver stillness with pink horizons in the west, and all the insects ceased in honor of the moon. There were days that were hot and miserable with locusts of plagues of insects, winged ants, heat, no air, no clouds, I couldn't understand how the top of a mountain in the North could be so hot. At noon the only sound in the world was the symphonic hum of a million insects, my friends. But night would come and with it the mountain moon and the lake would be moon-laned and I'd go out and sit in the grass and meditate facing west, wishing there were a Personal God in all this impersonal matter. I'd go out to my snowfield and dig out my jar of purple Jello and look at the white moon through it. I could feel the world rolling toward the moon. At night while I was in my bag, the deer would come up from the lower timber and nibble at leftovers in tin plates in the yard: bucks with wide antlers, does, and cute little fawns looking like otherworldly mammals on another planet with all that moonlight rock behind them.

Then would come wild lyrical drizzling rain, from the south, in the wind, and I'd say "The taste of rain, why kneel?" and I'd say "Time for hot coffee and a cigarette, boys," addressing my imaginary bhikkus. The moon became full and huge and with it came Aurora Borealis over Mount Hozomeen ("Look at the void and it is even stiller," Han Shan had said in Japhy's translation); and in fact I was so still all I had to do was shift my crossed legs in the alpine grass and I could hear the hoofs of deers running away somewhere. Standing on my head before bedtime on that rock roof of the moonlight I could indeed see that the earth was truly upsidedown and man a weird vain beetle full of strange ideas walking around upsidedown and boasting, and I could realize that man remembered why this dream of planets and plants and Plantagenets was built out of the primordial essence. Sometimes I'd get mad because things didn't work out well, I'd spoil a flapjack, or slip in the snowfield while getting water, or one time my shovel went sailing down into the gorge, and I'd be so mad I'd want to bite the mountaintops and would come in the shack and kick the cupboard and hurt my toe. But let the mind beware, that though the flesh be bugged, the circumstances of existence are pretty glorious.

All I had to do was keep an eye on all horizons for smoke and run the two-way radio and sweep the floor. The radio didn't bother me much; there were no fires close enough for me to report ahead of anybody else and I didn't participate in the lookout chats. They dropped me a couple of radio batteries by parachute but my own batteries were still in good shape.

One night in a meditation vision Avalokitesvara the Hearer and Answerer of Prayer said to me "You are empowered to remind people that they are utterly free" so I laid my hand on myself to remind myself first and then felt gay, yelled "Ta," opened my eyes, and a shooting star shot. The innumerable worlds in the Milky Way, *words*. I ate my soup in little doleful bowlfuls and it tasted much better than in some vast tureen . . . my Japhy pea-and-bacon soup. I took two-hour naps every afternoon, waking up and realizing "none of this ever happened" as I looked around my mountaintop. The world was upsidedown hanging in an ocean of endless space and here were all these people sitting in theaters watching movies, down there in the world to which I would return. . . . Pacing in the yard at dusk, singing "Wee Small Hours," when I came to the lines "when the whole wide world is fast asleep" my eyes filled with tears. "Okay world," I said, "I'll love ya." In bed at night, warm and happy in my bag on the good hemp bunk, I'd see my table and my clothes in the moonlight and feel, "Poor Raymond boy, his day is so sorrowful and worried, his reasons are so ephemeral, it's such a haunted and pitiful thing to have to live" and on this I'd go to sleep like a lamb. Are we fallen angels who didn't want to believe that nothing *is* nothing and so were born to lose our loved ones and dear friends one by one and finally our own life, to see it proved? . . . But cold morning would return, with clouds billowing out of Lightning Gorge like giant smoke, the lake below still cerulean neutral, and empty space the same as ever. O gnashing teeth of earth, where would it all lead to but some sweet golden eternity, to prove that we've all been wrong, to prove that the proving itself was nil . . .

34

August finally came in with a blast that shook my house and augured little augusticity. I made raspberry Jello the color of rubies in the setting sun. Mad raging sunsets poured in seafoams of cloud through unimaginable crags, with every rose tint of hope beyond, I felt just like it, brilliant and bleak beyond words. Everywhere awful ice fields and snow straws; one blade of grass jiggling in the winds of infinity, anchored to a rock. To the east, it was gray; to the north, awful; to the west, raging mad, hard iron fools wrestling in the groomian gloom; to the south, my father's mist. Jack Mountain, his thousand-foot rock hat overlooked a hundred football fields of snow. Cinnamon Creek was an eyrie of Scottish fog. Shull lost itself in the Golden Horn of Bleak. My oil lamp burned in infinity. "Poor gentle flesh," I realized, "there is no answer." I didn't know anything any more, I didn't care, and it didn't matter, and suddenly I felt really free. Then would come really freezing mornings, cracking fire, I'd chop wood with my hat on (earmuff cap), and would feel lazy and wonderful indoors, fogged in by icy clouds. Rain, thunder in the mountains, but in front of the stove I read my Western magazines. Everywhere snowy air and woodsmoke. Finally the snow came, in a whirling shroud from Hozomeen by Canada, it came surling my way sending radiant white heralds through which I saw the angel of light peep, and the wind rose, dark low clouds rushed up as out of a forge, Canada was a sea of meaningless mist; it came in a general fanning attack advertised by the sing in my stovepipe; it rammed it, to absorb my old blue sky view which had been all thoughtful clouds of gold; far, the rum dum dum of Canadian thunder; and to the south another vaster darker storm closing in like a pincer; but Hozomeen mountain stood there returning the attack with a surl of silence. And nothing could induce the gay golden horizons far northeast where there was no storm, to change places with Desolation. Suddenly a green and rose rainbow shafted right down into Starvation Ridge not three hundred yards away from my door; like a bolt, like a pillar: it came among steaming clouds and orange sun turmoiling.

> What is a rainbow, Lord?
> A hoop
> For the lowly.

It hooped right into Lightning Creek, rain and snow fell simultaneous, the lake was milkwhite a mile below, it was just too crazy. I went outside and suddenly my shadow was ringed by the rainbow as I walked on the hilltop, a lovely-haloed mystery making me want to pray. "O Ray, the career of your life is like a raindrop in the illimitable ocean which is eternal awakenerhood. Why worry ever any more? Write and tell Japhy that." The storm went away as swiftly as it came and the late afternoon lake-sparkle blinded me. Late afternoon, my mop drying on the rock. Late afternoon, my bare back cold as I stood above the world in a snow-field digging shovelsful into a pail. Late afternoon, it was I not the void that changed. Warm rose dusk, I meditated in the yellow half moon of August. Whenever I heard thunder in the mountains it was like the iron of my mother's love. "Thunder and snow, how we shall go!" I'd sing. Suddenly came the drenching fall rains, all-night rain, millions of acres of Bo-trees being washed and washed, and in my attic millennial rats wisely sleeping.

Morning, the definite feel of autumn coming, the end of my job coming, wild windy cloud-crazed days now, a definite golden look in the high noon haze. Night, made hot cocoa and sang by the woodfire. I called Han Shan in the mountains: there was no answer. I called Han Shan in the morning fog: silence, it said. I called: Dipankara instructed me by saying nothing. Mists blew by, I closed my eyes, the stove did the talking. "Woo!" I yelled, and the bird of perfect balance on the fir point just moved his tail; then he was gone and distance grew immensely white. Dark wild nights with hint of bears: down in my garbage pit old soured solidified cans of evaporated milk bitten into and torn apart by mighty behemoth paws: Avalokitesvara the Bear. Wild cold fogs with awesome holes. On my calendar I ringed off the fifty-fifth day.

My hair was long, my eyes pure blue in the mirror, my skin tanned and happy. All night gales of soaking rain again, autumn rain, but I warm as toast in my bag dreaming of long infantry-scouting movements in the mountains; cold wild morning with high wind, racing fogs, racing clouds, sudden bright suns, the pristine light on hill patches and my fire roaring with three big logs as I exulted to hear Burnie Byers over the radio telling all his lookouts to come down that very day. The season was over. I paced in the windy yard with cup of coffee forked in my thumb singing "Blubbery dubbery the chipmunk's in the grass." There he was, my chipmunk, in the bright clear windy sunny air staring on the rock; hands clasping he sat up straight, some little oat between his paws; he nibbled, he darted away, the little nutty lord of all he surveyed. At dusk, big wall of clouds from the north coming in. "Brrr," I said. And I'd sing "Yar, but my she was yar!" meaning my shack all summer, how the wind hadn't blown it away, and I said "Pass pass pass, that which passes through everything!" Sixty sunsets had I seen revolve on that perpendicular hill. The vision of the freedom of eternity was mine forever. The chipmunk ran into the rocks and a butterfly came out. It was as simple as that. Birds flew over the shack rejoicing; they had a mile-long patch of sweet blueberries all the way down to the timberline. For the last time I went out to the edge of Lightning Gorge where the little outhouse was built right on the precipice of a steep gulch. Here, sitting every day for sixty days, in fog or in moonlight or in sunny day or in darkest night, I had always seen the little twisted gnarly trees that seemed to grow right out of the midair rock.

And suddenly it seemed I saw that unimaginable little Chinese bum standing there, in the fog, with that expressionless humor on his seamed face. It wasn't the real-life Japhy of rucksacks and Buddhism studies and big mad parties at Corte Madera, it was the realer-than-life Japhy of my dreams, and he stood there saying nothing. "Go away, thieves of the mind!" he cried down the hollows of the unbelievable Cascades. It was Japhy who had advised me to come here and now though he was seven thousand miles away in Japan answering the meditation bell (a little bell he later sent to my mother in the mail, just because she was my mother, a gift to please her) he seemed to be standing on Desolation Peak by the gnarled old rocky trees certifying and justifying all that was here. "Japhy," I said out loud, "I don't know when we'll meet again or what'll happen in the future, but Desolation, Desolation, I owe so much to Desolation, thank you forever for guiding me to the place where I learned all. Now comes the sadness of coming back to cities and I've grown two months older and there's all that humanity of bars and burlesque shows and gritty love, all upsidedown in the void God bless them, but Japhy you and me forever we know, O ever youthful, O ever weeping." Down on the lake rosy reflections of celestial vapor appeared, and I said "God, I love you" and looked up to the sky and really meant it. "I have fallen in love with you, God. Take care of us all, one way or the other."

To the children and the innocent it's all the same.

And in keeping with Japhy's habit of always getting down on one knee and delivering a little prayer to the camp we left, to the one in the Sierra, and the others in Marin, and the little prayer of gratitude he had delivered to Sean's shack the day he sailed away, as I was hiking down the mountain with my pack I turned and knelt on the trail and said "Thank you, shack." Then I added "Blah," with a little grin, because I knew that shack and that mountain would understand what that meant, and turned and went on down the trail back to this world.

Questions for Thinking and Writing

1. Do you think that Raymond's projections of his feelings for the landscape are justified? Is this just anthropomorphism or a deep understanding of his situation?

2. Compare Raymond's feelings at the beginning of the text and at the end. Does the climax show that Kerouac has a different sense of the environment or nature and his place in the universe? Dharma means "truth" in Hindi. Do you think he finds it?

3. Explain how Desolation Peak got its name. Is the peak an appropriate place for Raymond to connect with his soul? Have you ever experienced a revelation in a natural setting?

❧ Walter M. Miller, Jr. (b. 1923)
Fiat Lux (1959)

It has been long debated whether Walter M. Miller, Jr., views humankind's future as unending eons of despair or violence-laden cycles leading toward a higher evolutionary ground. This debate was inspired by A Canticle for Leibowitz, *which originally appeared as a three-part series in the* Magazine of Fantasy and Science Fiction, *and as a novel in 1959. Since then, it has sold over a million copies and has achieved the status of a cult book. Despite its success, Miller became a recluse after the novel appeared and still remains in seclusion.*

Miller was born in New Smyrna Beach, Florida, but left there at 17 to attend the University of Tennessee. At the start of World War II, he enlisted in the U.S. Army Air Corps and flew over 50 combat missions. On one of his sorties, he bombed the German-held town of Cassino in central Italy, the site of the Benedictine abbey and reputed to be the burial place of St. Benedict, the founder of the Benedictine Order. This event, a conflation of war and religion, death and destruction to save humanity from Nazi domination, may have been the germ for Canticle *and its antiwar theme. Miller converted to Catholicism two years after the war ended, and his newfound religious and spiritual sensitivity must have provided impetus for his agonized appraisal of the human condition.*

After the war, Miller began writing fiction. "MacDoughal's Wife" was his first published story. During the next ten years, he wrote dozens of short stories for science fiction magazines and screenplays for the television show, Captain Video.

Miller's favorite theme, recurrent in Canticle, *is that the process of human evolution is painfully slow and destructive, and ultimate human destiny is under the control of a nameless force. A* Canticle for Leibowitz *takes place far in the future and tells the story of members of the Order of Leibowitz who dedicate their lives to keeping books and knowledge during an interregnum that recalls the Dark Ages of European history. In their obscure abbey, located in the Southwest, the order venerates Emmanuel Leibowitz, an American electrical engineer who died in an atomic apocalypse that took place about 1950.*

The passage here, taken from the Canticle, *describes a reading of a rendition of the Book of Job, telling how the Earth was destroyed by war. The mixture of biblical allusion, the recent history of World War I and World War II, and the impending threat of nuclear holocaust brought on by the United States and the former Soviet Union provides a rich complexity to Miller's vision.*

" 'Now even as in the time of Job,' " Brother Reader began from the refectory lectern:

"When the sons of God came to stand before the Lord, Satan also was present among them.

"And the Lord said to him: 'Whence comest thou, Satan?'

"And Satan answering said, as of old: 'I have gone round about the earth, and have walked through it.'

"And the Lord said to him: 'Hast thou considered that simple and upright prince, my servant *Name*, hating evil and loving peace?'

"And Satan answering said: 'Doth *Name* fear God in vain? For hast Thou not blessed his land with great wealth and made him mighty among the nations? But stretch forth Thy hand a little and decrease what he hath, and let his enemy be strengthened; then see if he blasphemeth Thee not to Thy face.'

"And the Lord said to Satan: 'Behold what he hath, and lessen it. See thou to it.'

"And Satan went forth from the presence of God and returned into the world.

"Now the Prince *Name* was not as Holy Job, for when his land was afflicted with trouble and his people less rich than before, when he saw his enemy become mightier, he grew fearful and ceased to trust in God, thinking unto himself: I must strike before the enemy overwhelmeth me without taking his sword in hand.

" 'And so it was in those days,' " said Brother Reader:

"that the princes of Earth had hardened their hearts against the Law of the Lord, and of their pride there was no end. And each of them thought within himself that it was better for all to be destroyed than for the will of other princes to prevail over his. For the mighty of the Earth did contend among themselves for supreme power over all; by stealth, treachery, and deceit they did seek to rule, and of war they feared greatly and did tremble; for the Lord God had suffered the wise men of those times to learn the means by which the world itself might be destroyed, and into their hands was given the sword of the Archangel wherewith Lucifer had been cast down, that men and princes might fear God and humble themselves before the Most High. But they were not humbled.

"And Satan spoke unto a certain prince, saying: 'Fear not to use the sword, for the wise men have deceived you in saying that the world would be destroyed thereby. Listen not to the counsel of weaklings, for they fear you exceedingly, and they serve your enemies by staying your hand against them. Strike, and know that you shall be king over all.'

"And the prince did heed the word of Satan, and he summoned all of the wise men of that realm and called upon them to give him counsel as to the ways in which the enemy might be destroyed without bringing down the wrath upon his own kingdom. But most of the wise men said, 'Lord, it is not possible, for your enemies also have the sword which we have given you, and the fieriness of it is as the flame of Hell and as the fury of the sun-star from whence it was kindled.'

" 'Then thou shalt make me yet another which is yet seven times hotter than Hell itself,' commanded the prince, whose arrogance had come to surpass that of Pharaoh.

"And many of them said: 'Nay, Lord, ask not this thing of us; for even the smoke of such a fire, if we were to kindle it for thee, would cause many to perish.'

"Now the prince was angry because of their answer, and he suspected them of betraying him, and he sent his spies among them to tempt them and to challenge them; whereupon the wise men became afraid. Some among them changed their answers, that his wrath be not invoked against them. Three times he asked them, and three times they answered: 'Nay, Lord, even your own people will perish if you do this thing.' But one of the magi was like unto Judas Iscariot, and his testimony was crafty, and having betrayed his brothers, he lied to all the people, advising them not to fear the demon Fallout. The prince heeded this false wise man, whose name was Blackeneth, and he caused spies to accuse many of the magi before the people. Being afraid, the less wise among the magi counseled the prince according to his pleasure, saying: 'The weapons may be used, only do not exceed such-and-such a limit, or all will surely perish.'

"And the prince smote the cities of his enemies with the new fire, and for three days and nights did his great catapults and metal birds rain wrath upon them. Over each city a sun appeared and was brighter than the sun of heaven, and immediately that city withered and melted as wax under the torch, and the people thereof did stop in the streets and their skins smoked and they became as fagots thrown on the coals. And when the fury of the sun had faded, the city was in flames; and a great thunder came out of the sky, like the great battering-ram PIK-A-DON, to crush it utterly. Poisonous fumes fell over all the land, and the land was aglow by night with the afterfire and the curse of the afterfire which caused a scurf on the skin and made the hair to fall and the blood to die in the veins.

"And a great stink went up from Earth even unto Heaven. Like unto Sodom and Gomorrah was the Earth and the ruins thereof, even in the land of that certain prince, for his enemies did not withhold their vengeance, sending fire in turn to engulf his cities as their own. The stink of the carnage was exceedingly offensive to the Lord, Who spoke unto the prince, *Name*, saying: 'WHAT BURNT OFFERING IS THIS THAT YOU HAVE PREPARED BEFORE ME? WHAT IS THIS SAVOR THAT ARISES FROM THE PLACE OF HOLOCAUST? HAVE YOU MADE ME A HOLOCAUST OF SHEEP OR GOATS, OR OFFERED A CALF UNTO GOD?'

"But the prince answered him not, and God said: 'YOU HAVE MADE ME A HOLOCAUST OF MY SONS.'

"And the Lord slew him together with Blackeneth, the betrayer, and there was pestilence in the Earth, and madness was upon mankind, who stoned the wise together with the powerful, those who remained.

"But there was in that time a man whose name was Leibowitz, who, in his youth like the holy Augustine, had loved the wisdom of the world more than the wisdom of God. But now seeing that great knowledge, while good, had not saved the world, he turned in penance to the Lord, crying:"

The abbot rapped sharply on the table and the monk who had been reading the ancient account was immediately silent.

"And that is your only account of it?" asked Thon Taddeo, smiling tightly at the abbot across the study.

"Oh, there are several versions. They differ in minor details. No one is certain which nation launched the first attack—not that it matters anymore. The text Brother Reader was just reading was written a few decades after the death of Saint Leibowitz—probably one of the first accounts—after it became safe to write again. The author was a young monk who had not lived through the destruction himself: he got it second hand from Saint Leibowitz' followers, the original memorizers and bookleggers, and he had a liking for scriptural mimicry. I doubt if a single *completely* accurate account of the Flame Deluge exists anywhere. Once it started, it was apparently too immense for any one person to see the whole picture."

"In what land was this prince called Name, and this man Blackeneth?"

Abbot Paulo shook his head. "Not even the author of that account was certain. We've pieced enough together since that was written to know that even some of the *lesser* rulers of that time had got their hands on such weapons before the holocaust came. The situation he described prevailed in more than one nation. Name and Blackeneth were probably Legion."

"Of course I've heard similar legends. It's obvious that something rather hideous came to pass," the thon stated; and then abruptly: "But when may I begin to examine—what do you call it?"

"The Memorabilia."

"Of course." He sighed and smiled absently at the image of the saint in the corner. "Would tomorrow be too soon?"

"You may begin at once, if you like," said the abbot. "Feel free to come and go as you please."

Questions for Thinking and Writing

1. What does Prince Name represent? What is the sword of the Archangel? Who is Blackeneth? Why do you think that God permits the humans of the Earth to possess "the sword"?
2. What does this retelling of apocalypse tell about human arrogance, desire for power, cupidity, and the fate of the Earth?
3. What does the word *holocaust* mean? How is the word used in this text? To what extent do you think that the threat of nuclear holocaust is real?

❦ Rachel Carson (1907–1964)

The Human Price (1962)

Soft-spoken and shy, Rachel Carson became a household name when Silent Spring *was published in September 1962. The book's warnings that all life suffers under the indiscriminate use of insecticides jolted the chemical industry into launching a national publicity campaign to discredit her. Carson's scientific findings were termed "gross distortions of the actual facts, completely unsupported by scientific, experimental evidence . . . ," according to an industry spokesman. The Monsanto Company retaliated by parodying her gentle prose style, arguing that without pesticides the world would be overrun by plagues of insects. Nevertheless,* Silent Spring, *a bestseller even before publication, was praised by a presidential science advisory committee.*

Carson, an only child, was born in Springdale, Pennsylvania. She attributed her love of nature to her mother who introduced her to the cycles of nature in woods and streams when she was a small girl. After graduating from Parnassus High School, she went to the Pennsylvania College for Women at Pittsburgh to study writing. However, biology caught her interest and became the focus of her graduate education at Johns Hopkins. Carson did postgraduate research at the Woods Hole Oceanographic Institute in Massachusetts, but she never received a doctorate.

In 1936, Carson took a job as an aquatic biologist with the Bureau of Fisheries, the predecessor of the Fish and Wildlife Service. Five years later, in 1941, she published her first book, Under the Sea Wind. *As a result, she was appointed editor-in-chief of the Fish and Wildlife Service. Ten years later, she published* The Sea Around Us, *which established her as a writer able to explain scientific complexity to the public. The book was an enormous success. It was a bestseller for 86 weeks, and won the National Book Award and the John Burroughs Medal. Carson resigned from the government in 1952 to write full time, and published* The Edge of the Sea *three years later, in 1955.*

The idea for Silent Spring, *long in her mind, was propelled by a letter she received from two friends describing the toll that aerial spraying had taken on the flora and fauna of their two-acre property in Massachusetts. "We still talk in terms of conquest," she said in a television interview after the book's publication. "We still haven't become mature enough to think of ourselves as only a tiny part of a vast and incredible universe. Man's attitude towards nature is today critically important simply because we have now acquired a fateful power to alter and destroy nature. But man is part of nature and his war against nature is inevitably a war against himself."*

As the tide of chemicals born of the Industrial Age has arisen to engulf our environment, a drastic change has come about in the nature of the most serious public health problems. Only yesterday mankind lived in fear of the scourges of smallpox, cholera, and plague that once swept nations before them. Now our major concern is no longer with the disease organisms that once were omnipresent; sanitation, better living conditions, and new drugs have given us a high degree of control over infectious disease. Today we are concerned with a different kind of hazard that lurks in our environment—a hazard we ourselves have introduced into our world as our modern way of life has evolved.

The new environmental health problems are multiple—created by radiation in all its forms, born of the never-ending stream of chemicals of which pesticides are a part, chemicals now pervading the world in which we live, acting upon us directly and indirectly, separately and collectively. Their presence casts a shadow that is no less ominous because it is formless and obscure, no less frightening because it is simply impossible to predict the effects of lifetime exposure to chemical and physical agents that are not part of the biological experience of man.

"We all live under the haunting fear that something may corrupt the environment to the point where man joins the dinosaurs as an obsolete form of life," says Dr. David Price of the United States Public Health Service. "And what makes these thoughts all the more disturbing is the knowledge that our fate could perhaps be sealed twenty or more years before the development of symptoms."

Where do pesticides fit into the picture of environmental disease? We have seen that they now contaminate soil, water, and food, that they have the power to make our streams fishless and our gardens and woodlands silent and birdless. Man, however much he may like to pretend the contrary, is part of nature. Can he escape a pollution that is now so thoroughly distributed throughout our world?

We know that even single exposures to these chemicals, if the amount is large enough, can precipitate acute poisoning. But this is not the major problem. The sudden illness or death of farmers, spraymen, pilots, and others exposed to appreciable quantities of pesticides are tragic and should not occur. For the population as a whole, we must be more concerned with the delayed effects of absorbing small amounts of the pesticides that invisibly contaminate our world.

Responsible public health officials have pointed out that the biological effects of chemicals are cumulative over long periods of time, and that the hazard to the individual may depend on the sum of exposures received throughout his lifetime. For these very reasons the danger is easily ignored. It is human nature to shrug off what may seem to us a vague threat of future disaster. "Men are naturally most impressed by diseases which have obvious manifestations," says a wise physician, Dr. René Dubos, "yet some of their worst enemies creep on them unobtrusively."

For each of us, as for the robin in Michigan or the salmon in the Miramichi, this is a problem of ecology, of interrelationships, of interdependence. We poison the caddis flies in a stream and the salmon runs dwindle and die. We poison the gnats in a lake and the poison travels from link to link of the food chain and soon the birds of the lake margins become its victims. We spray our elms and the following springs are silent of robin song, not because we sprayed the robins directly but because the poison traveled, step by step, through the now familiar elm leaf–earthworm–robin cycle. These are matters of record, observable, part of the visible world around us. They reflect the web of life—or death—that scientists know as ecology.

But there is also an ecology of the world within our bodies. In this unseen world minute causes produce mighty effects; the effect, moreover, is often seemingly unrelated to the cause, appearing in a part of the body remote from the area where the original injury was sustained. "A change at one point, in one molecule even, may reverberate throughout the entire system to initiate changes in seemingly unrelated organs and tissues," says a recent summary of the present status of medical research. When one is concerned with the mysterious and wonderful functioning of the human body, cause and effect are seldom simple and easily demonstrated relationships. They may be widely separated both in space and time. To discover the agent of disease and death depends on a patient piecing together of many seemingly distinct and unrelated facts developed through a vast amount of research in widely separated fields.

We are accustomed to look for the gross and immediate effect and to ignore all else. Unless this appears promptly and in such obvious form that it cannot be ignored, we deny the existence of hazard. Even research men suffer from the handicap of inadequate methods of detecting the beginnings of injury. The lack of sufficiently delicate methods to detect injury before symptoms appear is one of the great unsolved problems in medicine.

"But," someone will object, "I have used dieldrin sprays on the lawn many times but I have never had convulsions like the World Health Organization spraymen—so it hasn't harmed me." It is not that simple. Despite the absence of sudden and dramatic symptoms, one who handles such materials is unquestionably storing up toxic materials in his body. Storage of the chlorinated hydrocarbons, as we have seen, is cumulative, beginning with the smallest intake. The toxic materials become lodged in all the fatty tissues of the body. When these reserves of fat are drawn upon the poison may then strike quickly. A New Zealand medical journal recently provided an example. A man under treatment for obesity suddenly developed symptoms of poisoning. On examination his fat was found to contain stored dieldrin, which had been metabolized as he lost weight. The same thing could happen with loss of weight in illness.

The results of storage, on the other hand, could be even less obvious. Several years ago the *Journal* of the American Medical Association warned strongly of the hazards of insecticide storage in adipose tissue, pointing out that drugs or chemicals that are cumulative require greater caution than those having no tendency to be stored in the tissues. The adipose tissue, we are warned, is not merely a place for the deposition of fat (which makes up about 18 per cent of the body weight), but has many important functions with which the stored poisons may interfere. Furthermore, fats are very widely distributed in the organs and tissues of the whole body, even being constituents of cell membranes. It is important to remember, therefore, that the fat-soluble insecticides become stored in individual cells, where they are in position to interfere with the most vital and necessary functions of oxidation and energy production. . . .

One of the most significant facts about the chlorinated hydrocarbon insecticides is their effect on the liver. Of all organs in the body the liver is most extraordinary. In its versatility and in the indispensable nature of its functions it has no equal. It presides over so many vital activities that even the slightest damage to it is fraught with serious consequences. Not only does it provide bile for the digestion of fats, but because of its location and the special circulatory pathways that converge upon it the liver receives blood directly from the digestive tract and is deeply involved in the metabolism of all the principal foodstuffs. It stores sugar in the form of glycogen and releases it as glucose in carefully measured quantities to keep the blood sugar at a normal level. It builds body proteins, including some essential elements of blood plasma concerned with blood-clotting. It maintains cholesterol at its proper level in the blood plasma, and inactivates the male and female hormones when they reach excessive levels. It is a storehouse of many vitamins, some of which in turn contribute to its own proper functioning.

Without a normally functioning liver the body would be disarmed—defenseless against the great variety of poisons that continually invade it. Some of these are normal by-products of metabolism, which the liver swiftly and efficiently makes harmless by withdrawing their nitrogen. But poisons that have no normal place in the body may also be detoxified. The "harmless" insecticides malathion and methoxychlor are less poisonous than their relatives only because a liver enzyme deals with them, altering their molecules in such a way that their capacity for harm is lessened. In similar ways the liver deals with the majority of the toxic materials to which we are exposed.

Our line of defense against invading poisons or poisons from within is now weakened and crumbling. A liver damaged by pesticides is not only incapable of protecting us from poisons, the whole wide range of its activities may be interfered with. Not only are the consequences far-reaching, but because of their variety and the fact that they may not immediately appear they may not be attributed to their true cause.

In connection with the nearly universal use of insecticides that are liver poisons, it is interesting to note the sharp rise in hepatitis that began during the 1950's and is continuing a fluctuating climb. Cirrhosis also is said to be increasing. While it is admittedly difficult, in dealing with human beings rather than laboratory animals, to "prove" that cause A produces effect B, plain common sense suggests that the relation between a soaring rate of liver disease and the prevalence of liver poisons in the environment is no coincidence. Whether or not the chlorinated hydrocarbons are the primary cause, it seems hardly sensible under the circumstances to expose ourselves to poisons that have a proven ability to damage the liver and so presumably to make it less resistant to disease.

Both major types of insecticides, the chlorinated hydrocarbons and the organic phosphates, directly affect the nervous system, although in somewhat different ways. This has been made clear by an infinite number of experiments on animals and by observations on human subjects as well. As for DDT, the first of the new organic insecticides to be widely used, its action is primarily on the central nervous system of man; the cerebellum and the higher motor cortex are thought to be the areas chiefly affected. Abnormal sensations as of prickling, burning, or itching, as well as tremors or even convulsions may follow exposure to appreciable amounts, according to a standard textbook of toxicology.

Our first knowledge of the symptoms of acute poisoning by DDT was furnished by several British investigators, who deliberately exposed themselves in order to learn the consequences. Two scientists at the British Royal Navy Physiological Laboratory invited absorption of DDT through the skin by direct contact with walls covered with a water-soluble paint containing 2 per cent DDT, overlaid with a thin film of oil. The direct effect on the nervous system is apparent in their eloquent description of their symptoms: "The tiredness, heaviness, and aching of limbs were very real things, and the mental state was also most distressing . . . [there was] extreme irritability . . . great distaste for work of any sort . . . a feeling of mental incompetence in tackling the simplest mental task. The joint pains were quite violent at times."

Another British experimenter who applied DDT in acetone solution to his skin reported heaviness and aching of limbs, muscular weakness, and "spasms of extreme nervous tension." He took a holiday and improved, but on return to work his condition deteriorated. He then spent three weeks in bed, made miserable by constant aching in limbs, insomnia, nervous tension, and feelings of acute anxiety. On occasion tremors shook his whole body—tremors of the sort now made all too familiar by the sight of birds poisoned by DDT. The experimenter lost 10 weeks from his work, and at the end of a year, when his case was reported in a British medical journal, recovery was not complete.

(Despite this evidence, several American investigators conducting an experiment with DDT on volunteer subjects dismissed the complaint of headache and "pain in every bone" as "obviously of psychoneurotic origin.")

There are now many cases on record in which both the symptoms and the whole course of the illness point to insecticides as the cause. Typically, such a victim has had a known exposure to one of the insecticides, his symptoms have subsided under treatment which included the exclusion of all insecticides from his environment, and most significantly *have returned with each renewed contact* with the offending chemicals. This sort of evidence—and no more—forms the basis of a vast amount of medical therapy in many other disorders. There is no reason why it should not serve as a warning that it is no longer sensible to take the "calculated risk" of saturating our environment with pesticides.

Why does not everyone handling and using insecticides develop the same symptoms? Here the matter of individual sensitivity enters in. There is some evidence that women are more susceptible than men, the very young more than adults, those who lead sedentary, indoor lives more than those leading a rugged life of work or exercise in the open. Beyond these differences are others that are no less real because they are intangible. What makes one person allergic to dust or pollen, sensitive to a poison, or susceptible to an infection whereas another is not is a medical mystery for which there is at present no explanation. The problem nevertheless exists and it affects significant numbers of the population. Some physicians estimate that a third or more of their patients show signs of some form of sensitivity, and that the number is growing. And unfortunately, sensitivity may suddenly develop in a person previously insensitive. In fact, some medical men believe that intermittent exposures to chemicals may produce just such sensitivity. If this is true, it may explain why some studies on men subjected to continuous occupational exposure find little evidence of toxic effects. By their constant contact with the chemicals these men keep themselves desensitized—as an allergist keeps his patients desensitized by repeated small injections of the allergen.

The whole problem of pesticide poisoning is enormously complicated by the fact that a human being, unlike a laboratory animal living under rigidly controlled conditions, is never exposed to one chemical alone. Between the major groups of insecticides, and between them and other chemicals, there are interactions that have serious potentials. Whether released into soil or water or a man's blood, these unrelated chemicals do not remain segregated; there are mysterious and unseen changes by which one alters the power of another for harm.

There is interaction even between the two major groups of insecticides usually thought to be completely distinct in their action. The power of the organic phosphates, those poisoners of the nerve-protective enzyme cholinesterase, may become greater if the body has first been exposed to a chlorinated hydrocarbon which injures the liver. This is because, when liver function is disturbed, the cholinesterase level drops below normal. The added depressive effect of the organic phosphate may then be enough to precipitate acute symptoms. And as we have seen, pairs of the organic phosphates themselves may interact in such a way as to increase their toxicity a hundredfold. Or the organic phosphates may interact with various drugs, or with synthetic materials, food additives—who can say what else of the infinite number of man-made substances that now pervade our world?

The effect of a chemical of supposedly innocuous nature can be drastically changed by the action of another; one of the best examples is a close relative of DDT called methoxychlor. (Actually, methoxychlor may not be as free from dangerous qualities as it is generally said to be, for recent work on experimental animals shows a direct action on the uterus and a blocking effect on some of the powerful pituitary hormones—reminding us again that these are chemicals with enormous biologic effect. Other work shows that methoxychlor has a potential ability to damage the kidneys.) Because it is not stored to any great extent when given alone, we are told that methoxychlor is a safe chemical. But this is not necessarily true. If the liver has been damaged by another agent, methoxychlor is stored in the body at *100 times* its normal rate, and will then imitate the effects of DDT with long-lasting effects on the nervous system. Yet the liver damage that brings this about might be so slight as to pass unnoticed. It might have been the result of any of a number of commonplace situations—using another insecticide, using a cleaning fluid containing carbon tetrachloride, or taking one of the so-called tranquilizing drugs, a number (but not all) of which are chlorinated hydrocarbons and possess power to damage the liver.

Damage to the nervous system is not confined to acute poisoning; there may also be delayed effects from exposure. Long-lasting damage to brain or nerves has been reported for methoxychlor and others. Dieldrin, besides its immediate consequences, can have long delayed effects ranging from "loss of memory, insomnia, and nightmares to mania." Lindane, according to medical findings, is stored in significant amounts in the brain and functioning liver tissue and may induce "profound and long-lasting effects on the central nervous system." Yet this chemical, a form of benzene hexachloride, is much used in vaporizers, devices that pour a stream of volatilized insecticide vapor into homes, offices, restaurants.

The organic phosphates, usually considered only in relation to their more violent manifestations in acute poisoning, also have the power to produce lasting physical damage to nerve tissues and, according to recent findings, to induce mental disorders. Various cases of delayed paralysis have followed use of one or another of these insecticides. A bizarre happening in the United States during the prohibition era about 1930 was an omen of things to come. It was caused not by an insecticide but by a substance belonging chemically to the same group as the organic phosphate insecticides. During that period some medicinal substances were being pressed into service as substitutes for liquor, being exempt from the prohibition law. One of these was Jamaica ginger. But the *United States Pharmacopeia* product was expensive, and boot-leggers conceived the idea of making a substitute Jamaica ginger. They succeeded so well that their spurious product responded to the appropriate chemical tests and deceived the government chemists. To give their false ginger the necessary tang they had introduced a chemical known as triorthocresyl phosphate. This chemical, like parathion and its relatives, destroys the protective enzyme cholinesterase. As a consequence of drinking the boot-leggers' product some 15,000 people developed a permanently crippling type of paralysis of the leg muscles, a condition now called "ginger paralysis." The paralysis was accompanied by destruction of the nerve sheaths and by degeneration of the cells of the anterior horns of the spinal cord.

About two decades later various other organic phosphates came into use as insecticides, as we have seen, and soon cases reminiscent of the ginger paralysis episode began to occur. One was a greenhouse worker in Germany who became paralyzed several months after experiencing mild symptoms of poisoning on a few occasions after using parathion. Then a group of three chemical plant workers developed acute poisoning from exposure to other insecticides of this group. They recovered under treatment, but ten days later two of them developed muscular weakness in the legs. This persisted for 10 months in one; the other, a young woman chemist, was more severely affected, with paralysis in both legs and some involvement of the hands and arms. Two years later when her case was reported in a medical journal she was still unable to walk.

The insecticide responsible for these cases has been withdrawn from the market, but some of those now in use may be capable of like harm. Malathion (beloved of gardeners) has induced severe muscular weakness in experiments on chickens. This was attended (as in ginger paralysis) by destruction of the sheaths of the sciatic and spinal nerves.

All these consequences of organic phosphate poisoning, if survived, may be a prelude to worse. In view of the severe damage they inflict upon the nervous system, it was perhaps inevitable that these insecticides would eventually be linked with mental disease. That link has recently been supplied by investigators at the University of Melbourne and Prince Henry's Hospital in Melbourne, who reported on 16 cases of mental disease. All had a history of prolonged exposure to organic phosphorus insecticides. Three were scientists checking the efficacy of sprays; 8 worked in greenhouses; 5 were farm workers. Their symptoms ranged from impairment of memory to schizophrenic and depressive reactions. All had normal medical histories before the chemicals they were using boomeranged and struck them down.

Echoes of this sort of thing are to be found, as we have seen, widely scattered throughout medical literature, sometimes involving the chlorinated hydrocarbons, sometimes the organic phosphates. Confusion, delusions, loss of memory, mania—a heavy price to pay for the temporary destruction of a few insects, but a price that will continue to be exacted as long as we insist upon using chemicals that strike directly at the nervous system.

Questions for Thinking and Writing

1. What, according to Carson, is the human price for the indiscriminate use of insecticides? Must there be such a price to begin with? What does it pay for?
2. Where does Carson place human beings in the order of the natural world? Why does Carson separate natural ecology from inner ecology? How does this way of thinking challenge the usual way that most people determine cause and effect?

3. Do you think that Carson's approach to her subject is scientifically sound, or does it appear to be a shrill reaction to modern agricultural practices? Besides DDT, which is now banned in the United States, do you know of any substances used to control pests that have adverse effects on animals or humans? Are there household products that may cause illness which you knowingly use? If so, why do you continue to use them?

❦ Maxine Kumin (b. 1925)

Morning Swim (1965)

One of Kumin's principal subjects is the relationship between a woman and nature, which is at the heart of her poem "Morning Swim." She emphasizes the necessity of fitting into nature's complexities and subtleties, similar to the need of women to negotiate the complex roles society has molded for them—as mothers, daughters, lovers, and survivors. Life, like nature, says Kumin, is unforgiving. Kumin's poetic mission is to create order out of what nature has presented to her. In an interview, she once said, "I think that there is an order to be discovered—that's very often true in the natural world—but there is also an order that a human can impose on the chaos of his emotions and the chaos of events." While nature may not be particularly comforting, Kumin takes the position that it is up to us to make peace with it.

Born in Philadelphia, Pennsylvania, Kumin received her bachelor's and master's degrees from Radcliffe College. She is the author of 4 novels, 9 volumes of poetry, 2 collections of essays, and over 20 children's books. She received a Pulitzer Prize for Up Country *(1972), a volume of poetry that focuses on the New England landscape and which critics note are reminiscent of the images used by Robert Frost and Henry David Thoreau. She has taught at Tufts, Columbia, and Princeton universities, and at the University of Massachusetts.*

"Morning Swim" commemorates love of swimming with deep feeling for nature. The immersion in water, a kind of baptism, brings pleasure and well-being, a rare moment in a busy world.

Into my empty head there come
a cotton beach, a dock wherefrom

I set out, oily and nude
through mist, in chilly solitude.

There was no line, no roof or floor
to tell the water from the air.

Night fog thick as terry cloth
closed me in its fuzzy growth.

I hung my bathrobe on two pegs.
I took the lake between my legs.

Invaded and invader, I
went overhand on that flat sky.

Fish twitched beneath me, quick and tame.
In their green zone they sang my name

and in the rhythm of the swim
I hummed a two-four-time slow hymn.

I hummed "Abide With Me." The beat
rose in the fine thrash of my feet,

rose in the bubbles I put out
slantwise, trailing through my mouth.

My bones drank water; water fell
through all my doors. I was the well

that fed the lake that met my sea
in which I sang "Abide With Me."

Questions for Thinking and Writing

1. What is the swimmer's sense of the natural world as she swims? How deep is her identification with the environment? Can you describe an experience similar to Kumin's?
2. Comment on the relationship between swimming and baptism. Why does swimming in a pond or lake increase the spiritual awareness of the swimmer?
3. Explain the contrasts in the swimmer's spiritual experience in nature with her decision to sing the Christian hymn "Abide with Me."

🌿 René Dubos (1901–1982)

The Wooing of the Earth (1968)

One of René Dubos's greatest concerns was the dangerous influence of technology on humankind. He warned that we must not let it dominate us. Air and water pollution, he felt, were evidence that we have lost a sense of balance with nature. He worried particularly that pollution would become accepted as part of the landscape. "This constant exposure [to pollution] conditions children," he said in an interview, "to accept public squalor as the normal state of affairs and thereby handicaps them mentally at the beginning of their lives."

Dubos was born in France and went to high school in his native Saint-Brice followed by attendance at the National Institute of Agronomy in Paris. In 1927, he received his doctorate from Rutgers University and remained in the United States for the rest of his life. He became a citizen in 1938.

Before becoming involved in environmental issues, Dubos was a respected bacteriologist who pioneered research in immunology by obtaining germ-fighting drugs from microbes. He also researched soil bacteria and human fungal infections. He spent most of his professional career at The Rockefeller University in New York City except for a stint at Harvard Medical School from 1942 to 1944 where he taught tropical medicine.

Dubos was the author of 20 books. The best known is So Human an Animal, *for which he received a Pulitzer Prize in 1969, and from which this selection is excerpted. Another book,* Only One Earth, *which he co-authored, served as the basis for the 1972 U.N. Conference on the Human Environment in Stockholm.*

Dubos was a rare sort of scientist, one who had the ability to see the connections between his specialty and life in general, especially as it related to the human condition. He often noted the similarities in the behavior of microbes and humans in their responses to stimuli and their relationships to other living things. Dubos also found it necessary to communicate his findings to the lay community. He tirelessly gave lectures, seminars, and interviews to get his beliefs before a wide audience. Just before his death, Dubos was engaged in organizing an environmental conference to commemorate the tenth anniversary of the Stockholm conference.

I live in mid-Manhattan and, like most of my contemporaries, experience a love-hate relationship with technological civilization. The whole world is accessible to me, but the unobstructed view from my 26th-floor windows reveals only a confusion of concrete and steel bathed in a dirty light; smog is a euphemism for the mud that constantly befouls the sky and blots out its blueness. Night and day, the roar of the city provides an unstructured background for the shrieking world news endlessly transmitted by the radio.

Everything I eat, drink, and use comes from far away, or at least from an unknown somewhere. It has been treated chemically, controlled electronically, and handled by countless anonymous devices before reaching me. New York could not survive a week if accident or sabotage should interrupt the water supply during the summer or the electric current during midwinter. My life depends on a technology that I do not really understand, and on social forces that are beyond my control. While I am aware of the dangers this dependence implies, I accept them as a matter of expediency. I spend my days in the midst of noise, dirt, ugliness, and absurdity, in order to have easier access to well equipped laboratories, libraries, museums, and to a few sophisticated colleagues whose material existence is as absurd as mine.

Our ancestors' lives were sustained by physical work and direct associations with human beings. We receive our livelihood in the form of anonymously computerized paper documents that we exchange for food, clothing, or gadgets. We have learned to enjoy stress instead of peace, excitement in lieu of rest, and to extract from the confusion of day-to-day life a small core of exhilarating experiences. I doubt that mankind can tolerate our absurd way of life much longer without losing what is best in humanness. Western man will either choose a new society or a new society will abolish him; this means in practice that we shall have to change our technological environment or it will change us.

The following remarks made during a discussion held at Massachusetts Institute of Technology bring out the problems posed by the adaptation of human values to technological development.

Harvey Cox: " . . . there are components of the situation which allow themselves to be addressed by technological answers. But I think there is this other one which I don't think the technological answers get to, and it has a little bit to do with a question about our basic philosophical assumptions about man, and what it means to be fulfilled."

Question from the floor: "But our basic philosophical assumptions may be pretechnological in nature, and *one of the main problems of man today may be to readjust philosophical perspective to modern technology*" [italics mine—R.D.].

Adjusting man's philosophical perspective to modern technology seems to me at best a dangerous enterprise. In any case, the technological conditions under which we now live have evolved in a haphazard way and few persons if any really like them. So far, we have followed technologists wherever their techniques have taken them, on murderous highways or toward the moon, under the threat of nuclear bombs or of supersonic booms. But this does not mean that we shall continue forever on this mindless and suicidal course. At heart, we often wish we had the courage to drop out and recapture our real selves. The impulse to withdraw from a way of life we know to be inhuman is probably so widespread that it will become a dominant social force in the future.

To long for a human situation not subservient to the technological order is not a regressive or escapist attitude but rather one that requires a progressive outlook and heroic efforts. Since we now rarely experience anything directly and spontaneously, to achieve such a situation would require the courage to free ourselves from the constraints that prevent most of us from discovering or expressing our true nature.

Sensitive persons have always experienced a biological and emotional need for an harmonious accord with nature. "Sometimes as I drift idly along Walden Pond," Thoreau noted in his *Journal,* "I cease to live and begin to be." By this he meant that he then achieved identification with the New England landscape.

The passive identification with nature expressed by Thoreau's phrase is congenial to Oriental thought but almost antithetical to Western civilization. Oddly enough, Tagore, a Hindu, came much closer than Thoreau to a typical Occidental attitude when he wrote that the great love adventure of European civilization had been what he called the active wooing of the earth.

"I remember how in my youth, in the course of a railway journey across Europe from Brindisi to Calais, I watched with keen delight and wonder that continent flowing with richness under the age-long attention of her chivalrous lover, western humanity. . . .

"Robinson Crusoe's island comes to my mind when I think of an institution where the first great lesson in the perfect union of man and nature, not only through love but through active communication, may be learnt unobstructed. We have to keep in mind the fact that love and action are the only media through which perfect knowledge can be obtained."

The immense and continued success among adults as well as among children of *Le Petit Prince* by the French writer Antoine de Saint Exupéry (1900–1944) also reflects a widespread desire for intimate relationships with the rest of creation.

"On ne connait que les choses que l'on apprivoise, dit le renard. Les hommes n'ont plus le temps de rien connaître. Ils achètent des choses toutes faites chez les marchands. Mais comme il n'existe point de marchands d'amis, les hommes n'ont plus d'amis. Si tu veux un ami, apprivoise-moi!"

In the popular English translation of *The Little Prince*, this passage reads as follows:

" 'One only understands the things that one tames,' said the fox. 'Men have no more time to understand anything. They buy things already made at the shops. But there is no shop anywhere where one can buy friendship, and so men have no friends any more. If you want a friend, tame me.' "

The French verb *apprivoiser* as used by Saint Exupéry is not adequately rendered by "tame." *Apprivoiser* implies here, not mastery of one participant over the other, but rather a shared experience of understanding and appreciation.

Poetical statements do not suffice to create conditions in which man no longer feels alienated from nature and from other men. But they are important nevertheless, because literary expressions often precede or at least sharpen social awareness. Poets, novelists, and artists commonly anticipate what is to be achieved one or two generations later by technological and social means. The poet is the conscience of humanity and at his best he carries high the torch illuminating the way to a more significant life.

Tagore wrote of man's active wooing of the earth, and stated that "love and action are the only media through which perfect knowledge can be obtained." Saint Exupéry urged that we can know and enjoy only that which we tame through love. Both have thus propounded a philosophical basis for conservation policies.

From a sense of guilt at seeing man-made ugliness, and also for reasons that must reach deep into man's origins, most people believe that Nature should be preserved. The exact meaning of this belief, however, has not been defined. There is much know-how concerning conservation practices but little understanding of what should be conserved and why.

Conservation certainly implies a balance among multiple components of Nature. This is a doctrine difficult to reconcile with Western civilization, built as it is on the Faustian concept that man should recognize no limit to his power. Faustian man finds satisfaction in the mastery of the external world and in the endless pursuit of the unattainable. No chance for a stable equilibrium here.

To be compatible with the spirit of Western culture, conservation cannot be exclusively or even primarily concerned with saving man-made artifacts or parts of the natural world for the sake of preserving isolated specimens of beauty here and there. Its goal should be the maintenance of conditions under which man can develop his highest potentialities. Balance involves man's relating to his total environment. Conservation therefore implies a creative interplay between man and animals, plants, and other aspects of Nature, as well as between man and his fellows. The total environment, including the remains of the past, acquires human significance only harmoniously incorporated into the elements of man's life.

The confusion over the meaning of the word Nature compounds the difficulty of formulating a philosophical basis for conservation. If we mean by Nature the world as it would exist in the absence of man, then very little of it survives. Not even the strictest conservation policies would restore the primeval environment, nor would this be necessarily desirable or even meaningful if it could be done.

Nature is never static. Men alter it continuously and so do animals. In fact, men have long recognized that they play a creative role in shaping Nature. In his *Concerning the Nature of the Gods,* written during the last century of the pre-Christian era, Cicero boasted: "We are absolute masters of what the earth produces. We enjoy the mountains and the plains. The rivers are ours. We sow the seed and plant the trees. We fertilize the earth. . . . We stop, direct, and turn the rivers; in short, by our hands we endeavor by our various operations in this world to make it as it were another Nature."

For animals as well as for men, the kind of environment which is most satisfactory is one that they have shaped to fit their needs. More exactly, the ideal conditions imply a complementary cybernetic relationship between a particular environment and a particular living thing. From man's point of view, civilized Nature should be regarded not as an object to be preserved unchanged, not as one to be dominated and exploited, but rather as a kind of garden to be developed according to its own potentialities, in which human beings become what they want to be according to their own genius. Ideally, man and Nature should be joined in a nonrepressive and creative functioning order.

Nature can be tamed without being destroyed. Unfortunately, taming has come to imply subjugating animals and Nature to such an extent as to render them spiritless. Men tamed in this manner lose their real essence in the process of taming. Taming demands the establishment of a relationship that does not deprive the tamed organism— man, animal, or nature—of the individuality that is the *sine qua non* of survival. When used in the sense of the French *apprivoiser,* taming is compatible with the spirit of conservation.

There are two kinds of satisfactory landscape. One is Nature undisturbed by human intervention. We shall have less and less of this as the world population increases. We must make a strenuous effort to preserve what we can of primeval Nature, lest we lose the opportunity to reestablish contact now and then with our biological origins. A sense of continuity with the past and with the rest of creation is a form of religious experience essential to sanity.

The other kind of satisfactory landscape is one created by human toil, in which, through progressive adjustments based on feeling and thought, as well as on trial and error, man has achieved a kind of harmony between himself and natural forces. What we long for is rarely Nature in the raw; more often it is a landscape suited to human limitations and shaped by the efforts and aspirations that have created civilized life. The charm of New England or of the Pennsylvania Dutch countryside is not a product of chance, nor did it result from man's "conquest" of nature. Rather it is the expression of a subtle process through which the natural environment was humanized in accordance with its own individual genius. This constitutes the wooing or the taming of nature as defined by Tagore and Saint Exupéry.

Among people of Western civilization, the English are commonly regarded as having a highly developed appreciation of Nature. But in fact, the English landscape at its best is so polished and humanized that it might be regarded as a vast ornamental farm or park. River banks and roadsides are trimmed and grass-verged; trees do not obscure the view but seem to be within the horizon; foregrounds contrast with middle distances and backgrounds. The parklands with their clumps of trees on shaven lawns, their streams and stretches of ornamental waters achieve a formula of scenery designed for visual pleasure in the spirit of the natural conditions.

The highland zone of western Britain constitutes a vast and remote area, not yet occupied by factories and settlements, offering open space for enjoyment and relative solitude. Conservation groups are struggling to protect its moors not only from industry and farming but also from reforestation. Yet the moors which are now almost treeless were once covered with an abundant growth of forest. The replacement of trees by heath and moor was not a "natural" event but one caused by the continued activities of man and his domesticated animals. Deforestation probably began as far back as the Bronze Age; the process was accelerated during the Middle Ages by the Cistercian monks and their flocks of sheep; then the exploitation of mines took a large toll of trees needed for smelting fires. In brief, the pristine ecological systems of the oak forest that once covered the highlands were eliminated by human action, leaving as relics only a few herd of deer. For nineteenth- and twentieth-century man, highland nature means sheepwalk, the hill peat bog, and the grouse moor. But this landscape is not necessarily the natural and right landscape, only a familiar one.

Public attitude toward the moors is now conditioned by literary associations. This type of landscape, which exists in other parts of England, evokes *Wuthering Heights* and the Brontë sisters. Since the wild moors are identified with passionate and romantic human traits, to reforest the highlands seems to show disrespect for an essential element of English literary tradition. Similarly, the garrets of Paris, sordid as they are physically, are associated with bohemian life, Mimi in *La Bohème*, and the tunes and romance of *Sous les Toits de Paris*. Art and literature have become significant factors in the landscape ecology of the civilized world.

The effects of history on nature are as deeply formative and as lasting as are those of early influences on individual persons and human societies. Much of what we regard today as the natural environment in England was in reality modified by the school of landscape painting in the seventeenth century. Under the guidance of landscape architects, a literary and artistic formula of naturalism transformed many of the great estates and then brought about secondarily similar modifications in large sectors of the English countryside and even of the cities. The effects of esthetic perceptions that first existed in the minds of the seventeenth-century painters thus became incorporated into the English landscape and will certainly long persist, irrespective of social changes. Less fortunately, the future development of American cities is bound to be oriented and constrained by the gridiron pattern and the network of highways which have shaped their early growth.

Profound transformations of nature by human activities have occurred during historical times over most of the world. Such changes are not all necessarily desirable, but the criteria of desirability are poorly defined. Since nature as it exists now is largely a creation of man, and in turn shapes him and his societies, its quality must be evaluated in terms not of primeval wilderness but of its relation to civilized life.

In his illuminating book *The Machine in the Garden,* Leo Marx has richly illustrated the contradictory attitudes toward Nature that have characterized American culture from its very beginning. The eighteenth-century Europeans saw America as a kind of utopian garden in which they could vicariously place their dreams of abundance, leisure, freedom, and harmony of existence. In contrast, most nineteenth-century immigrants regarded the forests, the plains, and the mountains as a hideous wilderness to be conquered by the exercise of power and harnessed for the creation of material wealth.

For most people all over the world today, the American landscape still has a grandeur and an ugliness uniquely its own. Above and beyond their geologic interest and intrinsic beauty, the Rocky Mountains and the Grand Canyon of the Colorado, for example, have acquired in world consciousness a cultural significance even greater than that of the highland moors or of the Mediterranean Riviera. The beauty of America is in those parts of the land that have not yet been spoiled because they have not been found useful for economic exploitation. The ugliness of America is in practically all its urban and industrial areas.

The American landscape thus means today either the vast romantic and unspoiled wilderness, or billboards and neon signs among dump heaps. Urban and industrial ugliness is the price that America and other technological societies seem to be willing to pay for the creation of material wealth. From the wilderness to the dump appears at present to symbolize the course of technological civilization. But this need not be so, or at least we must act in the faith that technological civilization does not necessarily imply the raping of nature. Just as the primeval European wilderness progressively evolved into a humanized creation through the continuous wooing of the earth by peasants, monks, and princes, so we must hope that the present technological wilderness will be converted into a new kind of urbanized and industrialized nature worthy of being called civilized. Our material wealth will not be worth having if we do not learn to integrate the machine, the city, and the garden.

Questions for Thinking and Writing

1. What does Dubos mean when he says, "Western man will either choose a new society or a new society will abolish him"?
2. Explain whether or not you agree with Dubos that we tend not to experience things directly anymore. What is the term *Faustian nature of man* allude to?
3. What does Dubos mean by nature? What are the two kinds of satisfactory nature that he defines? Can these aspects of nature be tamed without being destroyed? What does Dubos consider the paradox of the American landscape? Do you agree with him?

❦ May Sarton (b. 1912)

Death and the Maple (1968)

May Sarton's poems and novels explore the inner life's reaction to the outer life's observations and thoughts. In the excerpt here, the death of a maple tree causes her to reflect on the universality of death. She is a writer who contemplates individual loneliness and vulnerability in the immensity of life. By extension, our place in nature is a theme at the heart of her writing.

Sarton was born in Belgium, the only daughter of George Sarton, a well-known Belgian historian and philosopher, and Mabel Elwes Sarton, an English furniture designer. When she was only 4, her family moved to America to escape World War I and settled in Cambridge, Massachusetts, where George Sarton took a part-time teaching position at Harvard University. The girl attended Shady Hill School in Cambridge where she began writing poetry at age 9. She continued her schooling at the Institut Belge de Culture Française and at the Cambridge High and Latin School. Her first poems were published when she was 17 in the journal Poetry.

When she refused a scholarship to Vassar, Sarton moved to New York City to work as an apprentice in a repertory theater company. In 1933, she started her own theater company based at New York's New School for Social Research. Three years later, the company broke up and Sarton began writing full time, publishing a year later, in 1937, her first volume of poetry, Encounter in April*, a selection rich in observations about human relationships. Her novel,* The Single Hound, *was published in 1938, the first of 18 novels.*

Over the next 30 years Sarton divided her life between writing and teaching in a string of colleges and universities in the East and Midwest. During World War II, she worked for the U.S. Office of War Information, writing scripts for a series of films on life in the United States. The war over, she took a position at Harvard teaching freshman English composition. In 1953, her selection of poetry, The Land of Silence, *was acclaimed for its reflections on the permanence of landscapes and nature.*

In 1958, Sarton moved to a little house on the village green in Nelson, New Hampshire, where she wrote As Does New Hampshire *(1967), a book of poems focused on rural life and the ordinary examples of nature that one might observe there—animals and birds, flowers, and weather. (The volume's title recalls Robert Frost's* New Hampshire *of 1923.)* Plant Dreaming Deep *(1968), from which this excerpt comes, is about the cycle of life and how the inevitability of death is something to be put off. In her understated manner, Sarton suggests that it is easier to look away when her maple tree is cut down and stacked for firewood.*

It had not occurred to me until lately that a house is warmed by death as well as by life. But one day an English friend of mine, brought up in a house that had held many births and many deaths within its sheltering walls, and who had married an American and come to live in his exquisite new house, said, "Yes, it is beautiful. But I shall never feel at home in this house because no one has died here." My walls hold the death of "Aunt Cora." I do not brood about it, but I am not unaware that she died here in my study, a frail hunchback who had never been "downed" by a very hard life, and that death is a part of the human richness, the truth of the house for me.

We can accept death. It is dying that is not and never will be acceptable. For us who have to witness dying, it must always feel as if the very fabric of life were being torn apart. I was to experience that cruel tearing two years after I moved in, and in a strange way.

The great maple where the oriole had burst into song on that first day in May was beginning to show the signs of extreme old age. Standing between the house and the wide meadow that separates my grounds from the churchyard, it had looked at first as if it would live forever. It was such a staunch tree, wide at the base, branching low, so it rose up in amplitude, making a wide arc against the sky, "the great tree" of the place. But spring by spring a few more branches failed to leaf out, and in winter it had begun to groan when the icy north winds tore at it. More than once I got up in the night and paced the floor to shut out that sound, the wrenching, long creak and shudder, so much like suffering. What if the huge trunk did crack and the tree crash against the house? I was not alone in my anxiety. Neighbors looked up at it and shook their heads. "Sooner or later that tree will have to come down. It's a risk." Yes, sooner or later. . . . I put off the decision because it felt like murder.

But one summer day a truck stopped in the road, two young men got out, knocked at my door, and offered to take it down and cut and stack the wood for fifty dollars. Well, they had come, the messengers of fate, and I made the decision on the spot. But I was not going to watch. I went back to my desk to work, or to try to work. I had not imagined what that day would be like.

The men first got busy with a buzz saw, cutting into the enormous trunk, four feet across at least, representing over a hundred years of growth. Is there a more nerve-racking sound than the hideous, mechanistic screech of a buzz saw at work? It is an anti-sound. It does not fit in with any landscape or with any state of mind, except possibly hatred in its most dehumanized form. Under any circumstances I find the sound hard to bear; that day it was worse, for the saw was slicing into the living trunk of my tree. I could not look.

But when at last there was silence again, a long silence, I turned around to find out what was happening behind my back. I watched the men drive their truck far out into the meadow, then come back on foot to attach a heavy rope, first around the massive trunk of the tree, and then around the truck, for the *coup de grace*. I had to go outside. Quig was there, watching from his front yard, but we did not call or even wave to each other. It was a moment filled with awe. We watched in silence as the two men, for whom no doubt this was just "another job," got into the truck, started the motor, and inched forward until the rope was taut.

The saw had cut into the trunk more than halfway, and it should have been a simple matter now to pull that towering strength down. But we had to stand and watch the truck struggle, in short lunges, give up, and then start again, over and over. I felt the sweat on my face, for it was clear that the tree was not going to make it easy for anyone. The struggle was silent, and that made it all the worse. The tree was fighting for its life; it did not want to go.

After repeated attempts the men shut off the motor, got down from the truck, and soon the angry saw started up again. It had become a grim business. I went indoors, finding the suspense unbearable. But the end had to come soon, and it did. When the trunk tore apart, I was not watching. I heard a harsh crack, and then a kind of sigh as the branches sank through the air, and it was over. At last it was over.

There is no comfort when a great tree goes. There is no comfort in the dying struggle. For many months I missed something in the air over my head . . . that branch high up where once the oriole sang. But when winter came, I found comfort in those maple logs burning on a hearth. There are worse ways to die. . . .

Questions for Thinking and Writing

1. What does Sarton mean when she says, "We can accept death. It is dying that is not and never will be acceptable"? How does this notion fit in with our human sense of nature's cycle of growth and decay?
2. Does the maple tree really struggle for life, or is Sarton projecting her feelings of life and death onto the situation? Why can't Sarton watch the tree finally be cut down? Have you ever cut down a tree? Did you have feelings similar to Sarton's? Explain whether or not you consider it silly to have such feelings about nonhuman things like trees.
3. What is ironic about the comfort Sarton gets from her fireplace in the winter? How does this reflect the cycle of nature that is described by Eleanor Perenyi in "Compost" in such a different way (p. 368)?

🦡 Garrett Hardin (b. 1915)

The Tragedy of the Commons (1968)

A controversial thinker and writer, Garrett Hardin has long been concerned with limits—of economic growth, of population, of the utilization of natural resources. In fact, his theories have flown in the face of the American dream of endless bounty for all. His essay "The Tragedy of the Commons" articulated for the first time, in quasi-economic terms, the idea that natural resources, whether grazing space on a village green or the wealth of the oceans, are finite. If individuals grab more and more for themselves, little is left for the whole.

Hardin was born in Dallas, Texas, the son of a businessman. He attended the University of Chicago and received a doctorate in biology from Stanford University in 1941. The following year he began teaching at the University of California at Santa Barbara where he remains a professor emeritus of human ecology. He has also been a visiting professor or lecturer at numerous other colleges and universities and was the executive officer of The Environmental Fund in Washington, D.C., in 1980–1981.

As a child, Hardin realized he had an ability to write clearly. " . . . but I early concluded that it was important to have something to write about," he once said in an interview. "When I became inter-

ested in science, I saw this as an area in which I could exercise my writing abilities to good effect, because the level of competence in explaining science to the public was, and is, low."

Hardin is the author of a number of biology textbooks as well as collections of essays, among them Stalking the Wild Taboo (*1973*), The Limits of Altruism (*1977*), *and* Promethean Ethics: Living with Death, Competition, and Triage (*1980*). *He has also written over 200 articles for an array of publications.*

His most controversial theories revolve around population growth, the subject of his most recent book, Living Within Limits (*1993*). *A believer in strict limits to population in accordance with available resources, he argues that the country's lenient immigration policies are taxing cities and urban resources beyond their capacities. In the past he has raised the ire of many for advocating a triage system as a means of limiting population, whereby a higher authority would decide which groups of people could have access to certain areas or resources.*

But Hardin does offer a theoretical solution for halting the threat of diminishing resources. He is a thinker of a time in American history when the realization has set in that human beings are running out of control in their use of the environment and that something has to be done to stem their growing needs.

At the end of a thoughtful article on the future of nuclear war, Wiesner and York concluded that: "Both sides in the arms race are . . . confronted by the dilemma of steadily increasing military power and steadily decreasing national security. *It is our considered professional judgment that this dilemma has no technical solution.* If the great powers continue to look for solutions in the area of science and technology only, the result will be to worsen the situation."

I would like to focus your attention not on the subject of the article (national security in a nuclear world) but on the kind of conclusion they reached, namely that there is no technical solution to the problem. An implicit and almost universal assumption of discussions published in professional and semipopular scientific journals is that the problem under discussion has a technical solution. A technical solution may be defined as one that requires a change only in the techniques of the natural sciences, demanding little or nothing in the way of change in human values or ideas of morality.

In our day (though not in earlier times) technical solutions are always welcome. Because of previous failures in prophecy, it takes courage to assert that a desired technical solution is not possible. Wiesner and York exhibited this courage; publishing in a science journal, they insisted that the solution to the problem was not to be found in the natural sciences.

They cautiously qualified their statement with the phrase, "It is our considered professional judgment. . . . " Whether they were right or not is not the concern of the present article. Rather, the concern here is with the important concept of a class of human problems which can be called "no technical solution problems," and, more specifically, with the identification and discussion of one of these.

It is easy to show that the class is not a null class. Recall the game of tick-tack-toe. Consider the problem, "How can I win the game of tick-tack-toe?" It is well known that I cannot, if I assume (in keeping with the conventions of game theory) that my opponent understands the game perfectly. Put another way, there is no "technical solution" to the problem. I can win only by giving a radical meaning to the word "win." I can hit my opponent over the head; or I can drug him; or I can falsify the records. Every way in which I "win" involves, in some sense, an abandonment of the game, as we intuitively understand it. (I can also, of course, openly abandon the game—refuse to play it. This is what most adults do.)

The class of "No technical solution problems" has members. My thesis is that the "population problem," as conventionally conceived, is a member of this class. How it is conventionally conceived needs some comment. It is fair to say that most people who anguish over the population problem are trying to find a way to avoid the evils of overpopulation without relinquishing any of the privileges they now enjoy. They think that farming the seas or developing new strains of wheat will solve the problem—technologically. I try to show here that the solution they seek cannot be found. The population problem cannot be solved in a technical way, any more than can the problem of winning the game of tick-tack-toe.

WHAT SHALL WE MAXIMIZE?

Population, as Malthus said, naturally tends to grow "geometrically," or, as we would now say, exponentially. In a finite world this means that the per capita share of the world's goods must steadily decrease. Is ours a finite world?

A fair defense can be put forward for the view that the world is infinite; or that we do not know that it is not. But, in terms of the practical problems that we must face in the next few generations with the foreseeable technology, it is clear that we will greatly increase human misery if we do not, during the immediate future, assume that the world available to the terrestrial human population is finite. "Space" is no escape.

A finite world can support only a finite population; therefore, population growth must eventually equal zero. (The case of perpetual wide fluctuations above and below zero is a trivial variant that need not be discussed.) When this condition is met, what will be the situation of mankind? Specifically, can Bentham's goal of "the greatest good for the greatest number" be realized?

No—for two reasons, each sufficient by itself. The first is a theoretical one. It is not mathematically possible to maximize for two (or more) variables at the same time. This was clearly stated by von Neumann and Morgenstern, but the principle is implicit in the theory of partial differential equations, dating back at least to D'Alembert (1717–1783).

The second reason springs directly from biological facts. To live, any organism must have a source of energy (for example, food). This energy is utilized for two purposes: mere maintenance and work. For man, maintenance of life requires about 1600 kilocalories a day ("maintenance calories"). Anything that he does over and above merely staying alive will be defined as work, and is supported by "work calories" which he takes in. Work calories are used not only for what we call work in common speech; they are also required for all forms of enjoyment, from swimming and automobile racing to playing music and writing poetry. If our goal is to maximize population it is obvious what we must do: We must make the work calories per person approach as close to zero as possible. No gourmet meals, no vacations, no sports, no music, no literature, no art . . . I think that everyone will grant, without argument or proof, that maximizing population does not maximize goods. Bentham's goal is impossible.

In reaching this conclusion I have made the usual assumption that it is the acquisition of energy that is the problem. The appearance of atomic energy has led some to question this assumption. However, given an infinite source of energy, population growth still produces an inescapable problem. The problem of the acquisition of energy is replaced by the problem of its dissipation, as J. H. Fremlin has so wittily shown. The arithmetic signs in the analysis are, as it were, reversed; but Bentham's goal is still unobtainable.

The optimum population is, then, less than the maximum. The difficulty of defining the optimum is enormous; so far as I know, no one has seriously tackled this problem. Reaching an acceptable and stable solution will surely require more than one generation of hard analytical work—and much persuasion.

We want the maximum good per person; but what is good? To one person it is wilderness, to another it is ski lodges for thousands. To one it is estuaries to nourish ducks for hunters to shoot; to another it is factory land. Comparing one good with another is, we usually say, impossible because goods are incommensurable. Incommensurables cannot be compared.

Theoretically this may be true; but in real life incommensurables *are* commensurable. Only a criterion of judgment and a system of weighting are needed. In nature the criterion is survival. Is it better for a species to be small and hideable, or large and powerful? Natural selection commensurates the incommensurables. The compromise achieved depends on a natural weighting of the values of the variables.

Man must imitate this process. There is no doubt that in fact he already does, but unconsciously. It is when the hidden decisions are made explicit that the arguments begin. The problem for the years ahead is to work out an acceptable theory of weighting. Synergistic effects, non-linear variation, and difficulties in discounting the future make the intellectual problem difficult, but not (in principle) insoluble.

Has any cultural group solved this practical problem at the present time, even on an intuitive level? One simple fact proves that none has: there is no prosperous population in the world today that has, and has had for some time, a growth rate of zero. Any people that has intuitively identified its optimum point will soon reach it, after which its growth rate becomes and remains zero.

Of course, a positive growth rate might be taken as evidence that a population is below its optimum. However, by any reasonable standards, the most rapidly growing populations on earth today are (in general) the most miserable. This association (which need not be invariable) casts doubt on the optimistic assumption that the positive growth rate of a population is evidence that it has yet to reach its optimum.

We can make little progress in working toward optimum population size until we explicitly exorcize the spirit of Adam Smith in the field of practical demography. In economic affairs, *The Wealth of Nations* (1776) popularized the "invisible hand," the idea that an individual who "intends only his own gain," is, as it were, "led by an invisible hand to promote . . . the public interest." Adam Smith did not assert that this was invariably true, and perhaps neither did any of his followers. But he contributed to a dominant tendency of thought that has ever since interfered with positive action based on rational analysis, namely, the tendency to assume that decisions reached individually will, in fact, be the best decisions for an entire society. If this assumption is correct it justifies the continuance of our present policy of laissez-faire in reproduction. If it is correct we can assume that men will control their individual fecundity so as to produce the optimum population. If the assumption is not correct, we need to reexamine our individual freedoms to see which ones are defensible.

TRAGEDY OF FREEDOM IN A COMMONS

The rebuttal to the invisible hand in population control is to be found in a scenario first sketched in a little-known pamphlet in 1833 by a mathematical amateur named William Forster Lloyd (1794–1852). We may well call it, "the tragedy of the commons," using the word "tragedy" as the philosopher Whitehead used it: "The essence of dramatic tragedy is not unhappiness. It resides in the solemnity of the remorseless working of things." He then goes on to say, "This inevitableness of destiny can only be illustrated in terms of human life by incidents which in fact involve unhappiness. For it is only by them that the futility of escape can be made evident in the drama."

The tragedy of the commons develops in this way. Picture a pasture *narrative* open to all. It is to be expected that each herdsman will try to keep as many cattle as possible on the commons. Such an arrangement may work reasonably satisfactory for centuries because the tribal wars, poaching, and disease keep the numbers of both man and beast well below the carrying capacity of the land. Finally, however, comes the day of reckoning, that is, the day when the long-desired goal of social stability becomes a reality. At this point, the inherent logic of the commons remorselessly generates tragedy.

As a rational being, each herdsman seeks to maximize his gain. Explicitly or implicitly, more or less consciously, he asks, "What is the utility *to me* of adding one more animal to my herd?" This utility has one negative and one positive component.

1) The positive component is a function of the increment of one animal. Since the herdsman receives all the proceeds from the sale of the additional animal, the positive utility is nearly +1.

2) The negative component is a function of the additional overgrazing created by one more animal. Since, however, the effects of overgrazing are shared by all the herdsmen, the negative utility for any particular decision-making herdsmen is only a fraction of –1.

Adding together the component partial utilities, the rational herdsman concludes that the only sensible course for him to pursue is to add another animal to his herd. And another; and another . . . But this is the conclusion reached by each and every rational herdsmen sharing a commons. Therein is the tragedy. Each man is locked into a system that compels him to increase his herd without limit—in a world that is limited. Ruin is the destination toward which all men rush, each pursuing his own best interest in a society that believes in the freedom of the commons. Freedom in a commons brings ruin to all.

Some would say that this is a platitude. Would that it were! In a sense, it was learned thousands of years ago, but natural selection favors the forces of psychological denial. The individual benefits as an individual from his ability to deny the truth even though society as a whole, of which he is a part, suffers. Education can counteract the natural tendency to do the wrong thing, but the inexorable succession of generations requires that the basis for this knowledge be constantly refreshed.

A simple incident that occurred a few years ago in Leominster, Massachusetts, shows how perishable the knowledge is. During the Christmas shopping season the parking meters downtown were covered with plastic bags that bore tags reading: "Do not open until after Christmas. Free parking courtesy of the mayor and city council." In other words, facing the prospect of an increased demand for already scarce space, the city fathers reinstituted the system of the commons. (Cynically, we suspect that they gained more votes than they lost by this retrogressive act.)

In an approximate way, the logic of the commons has been understood for a long time, perhaps since the discovery of agriculture or the invention of private property in real estate. But it is understood mostly only in special cases which are not sufficiently generalized. Even at this late date, cattlemen leasing national land on the western ranges demonstrate no more than an ambivalent understanding, in constantly pressuring federal authorities to increase the head count to the point where overgrazing produces erosion and weed-dominance. Likewise, the oceans of the world continue to suffer from the survival of the philosophy of the commons. Maritime nations still respond automatically to the shibboleth of the "freedom of the seas." Professing to believe in the "inexhaustible resources of the oceans," they bring species after species of fish and whales closer to extinction.

The National Parks present another instance of the working out of the tragedy of the commons. At present, they are open to all, without limit. The parks themselves are limited in extent—there is only one Yosemite Valley—whereas population seems to grow without limit. The values that visitors seek in the parks are steadily eroded. Plainly, we must soon cease to treat the parks as commons or they will be of no value to anyone.

What shall we do? We have several options. We might sell them off as private property. We might keep them as public property, but allocate the right to enter them. The allocation might be on the basis of wealth, by the use of an auction system. It might be on the basis of merit, as defined by some agreed-upon standards. It might be by lottery. Or it might be on a first-come, first-served basis, administered to long queues. Those, I think, are all the reasonable possibilities. They are all objectionable. But we must choose—or acquiesce in the destruction of the commons that we call our National Parks.

POLLUTION

In a reverse way, the tragedy of the commons reappears in problems of pollution. Here it is not a question of taking something out of the commons, but of putting something in—sewage, or chemical, radioactive, and heat wastes into water: noxious and dangerous fumes into the air; and distracting and unpleasant advertising signs into the line of sight. The calculations of utility are much the same as before. The rational man finds that his share of the cost of the wastes he discharges into the commons is less than the cost of purifying his wastes before releasing them. Since this is true for everyone, we are locked into a system of "fouling our own nest," so long as we behave only as independent, rational, free-enterprisers.

The tragedy of the commons as a food basket is averted by private property, or something formally like it. But the air and waters surrounding us cannot readily be fenced, and so the tragedy of the commons as a cesspool must be prevented by different means, by coercive laws or taxing devices that make it cheaper for the polluter to treat his pollutants than to discharge them untreated. We have not progressed as far with the solution of this problem as we have with the first. Indeed, our particular concept of private property, which deters us from exhausting the positive resources of the earth, favors pollution. The owner of a factory on the bank of a stream—whose property extends to the middle of the stream—often has difficulty seeing why it is not his natural right to muddy the waters flowing past his door. The law, always behind the times, requires elaborate stitching and fitting to adapt it to this newly perceived aspect of the commons.

The pollution problem is a consequence of population. It did not much matter how a lonely American frontiersman disposed of his waste. "Flowing water purifies itself every 10 miles," my grandfather used to say, and the myth was near enough to the truth when he was a boy, for there were not too many people. But as population became denser, the natural chemical and biological recycling process became overloaded, calling for a redefinition of property rights.

HOW TO LEGISLATE TEMPERANCE?

Analysis of the pollution problem as a function of population density uncovers a not generally recognized principle of morality, namely: *the morality of an act is a function of the state of the system at the time it is performed.* Using the commons as a cesspool does not harm the general public under frontier conditions, because there is no public; the same behavior in a metropolis is unbearable. A hundred and fifty years ago a plainsman could kill an American bison, cut out only the tongue for his dinner, and discard the rest of the animal. He was not in any important sense being wasteful. Today, with only a few thousand bison left, we would be appalled at such behavior.

In passing, it is worth noting that the morality of an act cannot be determined from a photograph. One does not know whether a man killing an elephant or setting fire to the grassland is harming others until one knows the total system in which his act appears. "One picture is worth a thousand words," said an ancient Chinese; but it may take

10,000 words to validate it. It is as tempting to ecologists as it is to reformers in general to try to persuade others by way of the photographic shortcut. But the essence of an argument cannot be photographed: it must be presented rationally—in words.

That morality is system-sensitive escaped the attention of most codifiers of ethics in the past. "Thou shalt not . . . " is the form of traditional ethical directives which make no allowance for particular circumstances. The laws of our society follow the pattern of ancient ethics, and therefore are poorly suited to governing a complex, crowded, changeable world. Our epicyclic solution is to augment statutory law with administrative law. Since it is practically impossible to spell out all the conditions under which it is safe to burn trash in the back yard or to run an automobile without smog-control, by law we delegate the details to bureaus. The result is administrative law, which is rightly feared for an ancient reason—*Quis custodiet ipsos custodes?*—"Who shall watch the watchers themselves?" John Adams said that we must have "a government of laws and not men." Bureau administrators, trying to evaluate the morality of acts in the total system, are singularly liable to corruption, producing a government by men, not laws.

Prohibition is easy to legislate (though not necessarily to enforce); but how do we legislate temperance? Experience indicates that it can be accomplished best through the mediation of administrative law. We limit possibilities unnecessarily if we suppose that the sentiment of *Quis custodiet* denies us the use of administrative law. We should rather retain the phrase as a perpetual reminder of fearful dangers we cannot avoid. The great challenge facing us now is to invent the corrective feedbacks that are needed to keep custodians honest. We must find ways to legitimate the needed authority of both the custodians and the corrective feedbacks.

FREEDOM TO BREED IS INTOLERABLE

The tragedy of the commons is involved in population problems in another way. In a world governed solely by the principle of "dog eat dog"—if indeed there ever was such a world—how many children a family had would not be a matter of public concern. Parents who bred too exuberantly would leave fewer descendants, not more, because they would be unable to care adequately for their children. David Lack and others have found that such a negative feedback demonstrably controls the fecundity of birds. But men are not birds, and have not acted like them for millenniums, at least.

If each human family were dependent only on its own resources; *if* the children of improvident parents starved to death; *if,* thus, overbreeding brought its own "punishment" to the germ line—*then* there would be no public interest in controlling the breeding of families. But our society is deeply committed to the welfare state, and hence is confronted with another aspect of the tragedy of the commons.

In a welfare state, how shall we deal with the family, the religion, the race, or the class (or indeed any distinguishable and cohesive group) that adopts overbreeding as a policy to secure its own aggrandizement? To couple the concept of freedom to breed with the belief that everyone born has an equal right to the commons is to lock the world into a tragic course of action.

Unfortunately this is just the course of action that is being pursued by the United Nations. In late 1967, some 30 nations agreed to the following:

> The Universal Declaration of Human Rights describes the family as the natural and fundamental unit of society. It follows that any choice and decision with regard to the size of the family must irrevocably rest with the family itself, and cannot be made by anyone else.

It is painful to have to deny categorically the validity of this right; denying it, one feels as uncomfortable as a resident of Salem, Massachusetts, who denied the reality of witches in the 17th century. At the present time, in liberal quarters, something like a taboo acts to inhibit criticism of the United Nations. There is a feeling that the United Nations is "our last and best hope," that we shouldn't find fault with it; we shouldn't play into the hands of the archconservatives. However, let us not forget what Robert Louis Stevenson said: "The truth that is suppressed by friends is the readiest weapon of the enemy." If we love the truth we must openly deny the validity of the Universal Declaration of Human Rights, even though it is promoted by the United Nations. We should also join with Kingsley Davis in attempting to get Planned Parenthood-World Population to see the error of its ways in embracing the same tragic ideal.

CONSCIENCE IS SELF-ELIMINATING

It is a mistake to think that we can control the breeding of mankind in the long run by an appeal to conscience. Charles Galton Darwin made this point when he spoke on the centennial of the publication of his grandfather's great book. The argument is straightforward and Darwinian.

People vary. Confronted with appeals to limit breeding, some people will undoubtedly respond to the plea more than others. Those who have more children will produce a larger fraction of the next generation than those with more susceptible consciences. The differences will be accentuated, generation by generation.

In C. G. Darwin's words: "It may well be that it would take hundreds of generations for the progenitive instinct to develop in this way, but if it should do so, nature would have taken her revenge, and the variety *Homo contracipiens* would become extinct and would be replaced by the variety *Homo progenitivus*".

The argument assumes that conscience or the desire for children (no matter which) is hereditary—but hereditary only in the most general formal sense. The result will be the same whether the attitude is transmitted through germ cells, or exosomatically, to use A. J. Lotka's term. (If one denies the latter possibility as well as the former, then what's the point of education?) The argument has here been stated in the context of the population problem, but it applies equally well to any instance in which society appeals to an individual exploiting a commons to restrain himself for the general good—by means of his conscience. To make such an appeal is to set up a selective system that works toward the elimination of conscience from the race.

PATHOGENIC EFFECTS OF CONSCIENCE

The long-term disadvantage of an appeal to conscience should be enough to condemn it; but has serious short-term disadvantages as well. If we ask a man who is exploiting a commons to desist "in the name of conscience," what are we saying to him? What does he hear?—not only at the moment but also in the wee small hours of the night when, half asleep, he remembers not merely the words we used but also the non-verbal communication cues we gave him unawares? Sooner or later, consciously or subconsciously, he senses that he has received two communications and that they are contradictory: (i) (intended communication) "If you don't do as we ask, we will openly condemn you for not acting like a responsible citizen"; (ii) (the unintended communication) "If you *do* behave as we ask, we will secretly condemn you for a simpleton who can be shamed into standing aside while the rest of us exploit the commons."

Everyman then is caught in what Bateson has called a "double bind." Bateson and his co-workers have made a plausible case for viewing the double bind as an important causative factor in the genesis of schizophrenia. The double bind may not always be so damaging, but it always endangers the mental health of anyone to whom it is applied. "A bad conscience," said Nietzsche, "is a kind of illness."

To conjure up a conscience in others is tempting to anyone who wishes to extend his control beyond the legal limits. Leaders at the highest level succumb to this temptation. Has any President during the past generation failed to call on labor unions to moderate voluntarily their demands for higher wages, or to steel companies to honor voluntary guidelines on prices? I can recall none. The rhetoric used on such occasions is designed to produce feelings of guilt in noncooperators.

For centuries it was assumed without proof that guilt was a valuable, perhaps even an indispensable, ingredient of the civilized life. Now, in this post-Freudian world, we doubt it.

Paul Goodman speaks from the modern point of view when he says: "No good has ever come from feeling guilty, neither intelligence, policy, nor compassion. The guilty do not pay attention to the object but only to themselves, and not even to their own interests, which might make sense, but to their anxieties."

One does not have to be a professional psychiatrist to see the consequences of anxiety. We in the Western world are just emerging from a dreadful two-centuries-long Dark Ages of Eros that was sustained partly by prohibition laws, but perhaps more effectively by the anxiety-generating mechanisms of education. Alex Comfort has told the story well in *The Anxiety Makers*: it is not a pretty one.

Since proof is difficult, we may even concede that the results of anxiety may sometimes, from certain points of view, be desirable. The larger question we should ask is whether, as a matter of policy, we should ever encourage the use of a technique the tendency (if not the intention) of which is psychologically pathogenic. We hear much talk these days of responsible parenthood: the coupled words are incorporated into the titles of some organizations devoted to birth control. Some people have proposed massive propaganda campaigns to instill responsibility into the nation's (or the world's) breeders. But what is the meaning of the word responsibility in this context? It is not merely a synonym for the word conscience? When we use the word responsibility in the absence of substantial sanctions are we not trying to browbeat a free man in a commons into acting against his own interest? Responsibility is a verbal counterfeit for a substantial *quid pro quo*. It is an attempt to get something for nothing.

If the word responsibility is to be used at all, I suggest that it be in the sense Charles Frankel uses it. "Responsibility," says this philosopher, "is the product of definite social arrangements." Notice that Frankel calls for social arrangements—not propaganda.

MUTUAL COERCION MUTUALLY AGREED UPON

The social arrangements that produce responsibility are arrangements that create coercion, of some sort. Consider bank-robbing. The man who takes money from a bank acts as if the bank were a commons.

How do we prevent such action? Certainly not by trying to control his behavior solely by a verbal appeal to his sense of responsibility. Rather than rely on propaganda we follow Frankel's lead and insist that a bank is not a commons; we seek the definite social arrangements that will keep it from becoming a commons. That we thereby infringe on the freedom of would-be robbers we neither deny nor regret.

The morality of bank-robbing is particularly easy to understand because we accept complete prohibition of this activity. We are willing to say "Thou shalt not rob banks," without providing for exceptions. But temperance also can be created by coercion. Taxing is a good coercive device. To keep downtown shoppers temperate in their use of parking space we introduce parking meters for short periods, and traffic fines for longer ones. We need not actually forbid a citizen to park as long as he wants to; we need merely make it increasingly expensive for him to do so. Not prohibition, but carefully biased options are what we offer him. A Madison Avenue man might call this persuasion; I prefer the greater candor of the word coercion.

Coercion is a dirty word to most liberals now, but it need not forever be so. As with the four-letter words, its dirtiness can be cleansed away by exposure to the light, by saying it over and over without apology or embarrassment. To many, the word coercion implies arbitrary decisions of distant and irresponsible bureaucrats; but this is not a necessary part of its meaning. The only kind of coercion I recommend is mutual coercion, mutually agreed upon by the majority of the people affected.

To say that we mutually agree to coercion is not to say that we are required to enjoy it, or even to pretend we enjoy it. Who enjoys taxes? We all grumble about them. But we accept compulsory taxes because we recognize that voluntary taxes would favor the conscienceless. We institute and (grumblingly) support taxes and other coercive devices to escape the horror of the commons.

An alternative to the commons need not be perfectly just to be preferable. With real estate and other material goods, the alternative we have chosen is the institution of private property coupled with legal inheritance. Is this system perfectly just? As a genetically trained biologist I deny that it is. It seems to me that, if there are to be differences in individual inheritance, legal possession should be perfectly correlated with biological inheritance—that those who are biologically more fit to be the custodians of property and power should legally inherit more. But genetic recombination continually makes a mockery of the doctrine of "like father, like son" implicit in our laws of legal inheritance. An idiot can inherit millions, and a trust fund can keep his estate intact. We must admit that our legal system of private property plus inheritance is unjust—but we put up with it because we are not convinced, at the moment, that anyone has invented a better system. The alternative of the commons is too horrifying to contemplate. Injustice is preferable to total ruin.

It is one of the peculiarities of the warfare between reform and the status quo that it is thoughtlessly governed by a double standard. Whenever a reform measure is proposed it is often defeated when its opponents triumphantly discover a flaw in it. As Kingsley Davis has pointed out, worshippers of the status quo sometimes imply that no reform is possible without unanimous agreement, an implication contrary to historical fact. As nearly as I can make out, automatic rejection of proposed reforms is based on one of two unconscious assumptions: (i) that the status quo is perfect; or (ii) that the choice we face is between reform and no action; if the proposed reform is imperfect, we presumably should take no action at all, while we wait for a perfect proposal.

But we can never do nothing. That which we have done for thousands of years is also action. It also produces evils. Once we are aware that the status quo is action, we can then compare its discoverable advantages and disadvantages with the predicted advantages and disadvantages of the proposed reform, discounting as best we can for our lack of experience. On the basis of such a comparison, we can make a rational decision which will not involve the unworkable assumption that only perfect systems are tolerable.

RECOGNITION OF NECESSITY

Perhaps the simplest summary of this analysis of man's population problems is this: the commons, if justifiable at all, is justifiable only under conditions of low-population density. As the human population has increased, the commons has had to be abandoned in one aspect after another.

First we abandoned the commons in food gathering, enclosing farm land and restricting pastures and hunting and fishing areas. These restrictions are still not complete throughout the world.

Somewhat later we saw that the commons as a place for waste disposal would also have to be abandoned. Restrictions on the disposal of domestic sewage are widely accepted in the Western world; we are still struggling to close the commons to pollution by automobiles, factories, insecticide sprayers, fertilizing operations, and atomic energy installations.

In a still more embryonic state is our recognition of the evils of the commons in matters of pleasure. There is almost no restriction on the propagation of sound waves in the public medium. The shopping public is assaulted with mindless music, without its consent. Our government is paying out billions of dollars to create supersonic transport which will disturb 50,000 people for every one person who is whisked from coast to coast 3 hours faster. Advertisers muddy the airwaves of radio and television and pollute the view of travelers. We are a long way from outlawing the commons in matters of pleasure. Is this because our Puritan inheritance makes us view pleasure as something of a sin, and pain (that is, the pollution of advertising) as the sign of virtue?

Every new enclosure of the commons involves the infringement of somebody's personal liberty. Infringements made in the distant past are accepted because no contemporary complains of a loss. It is the newly proposed infringements that we vigorously oppose; cries of "rights" and "freedom" fill the air. But what does "freedom" mean? When men mutually agree to pass laws against robbing, mankind became more free, not less so. Individuals locked into the logic of the commons are free only to bring on universal ruin; once they see the necessity of mutual coercion, they become free to pursue other goals. I believe it was Hegel who said, "Freedom is the recognition of necessity."

The most important aspect of necessity that we must now recognize, is the necessity of abandoning the commons in breeding. No technical solution can rescue us from the misery of overpopulation. Freedom to breed will bring ruin to all. At the moment, to avoid hard decisions many of us are tempted to propagandize for conscience and responsible parenthood. The temptation must be resisted, because an appeal to independently acting consciences selects for the disappearance of all conscience in the long run, and an increase in anxiety in the short.

The only way we can preserve and nurture other and more precious freedoms is by relinquishing the freedom to breed, and that very soon. "Freedom is the recognition of necessity"—and it is the role of education to reveal to all the necessity of abandoning the freedom to breed. Only so, can we put an end to this aspect of the tragedy of the commons.

Questions for Thinking and Writing

1. Why does Hardin believe that the goal of the greatest good for the greatest number cannot be reached? What does Hardin mean when he says that "in real life incommensurables *are* commensurable"? And how does this relate to humankind's place in the environment and to population control?

2. Explain whether you believe that Hardin is optimistic or pessimistic. Do you agree with his logic or do you find him too harshly Darwinian in his approach to developing a philosophy of ecology?

3. Why does Hardin advocate limiting access to national parks? Why does he suggest redefining property rights? Can a human ecological program work without coercion as Hardin suggests?

🌿 Edward Abbey (1927–1989)
A Walk in the Park (1972)

Edward Abbey was a churlish loner who was fond of saying about nature, "Let's keep things the way they were." He fought the status quo, and was angrier than John Muir at what he considered to be the greedy ravaging of the country. He seemed to care not a hoot who he alienated and how he mired land-grabbing development schemes.

Abbey was born in Appalachia, the son of a fence post splitter, but hitchhiked out west when he was 17 and never really returned home. Instead, he fell in love with the Southwest and remained there for the rest of his life, making his home in Oracle, Arizona. He was married four times and had five children. Like Jack Kerouac, he worked for a time as a fire lookout in several national parks. He also taught at the University of Arizona and called himself a "fool professor" for doing it. The position gave him a base for his writing, some of which has become the philosophical foundation for environmental radical groups, particularly Earth First! Desert Solitaire *(1968) and* The Monkey Wrench Gang *(1975), the two most rebellious of his books, are not only indictments against development for the sake of development but also instruction manuals for halting the machines that scar the earth.* Desert Solitaire *has had 18 printings and* The Monkey Wrench Gang *has sold half a million copies.*

Abbey rarely left the Southwest and when he did, pleaded homesickness and soon returned. Nevertheless, he somehow felt the pulse of a growing resentment in America toward those who abused the environment. With wicked humor and irreverence, he tapped an audience that has come to admire him not only for his words but for his ability to turn his back on the traditional powers. He refused an award offered by the American Academy of Arts and Letters. He walked around with an unkempt beard. He was red-eyed and slow spoken. He liked cowboys and people who swore and spoke their mind.

Abbey died at age 62 of internal bleeding from a circulatory disorder. When he knew he was going to die, he decided to leave the hospital and head for the desert. He wanted to die in a sleeping bag in front of a campfire. Taken to the designated spot, he changed his mind and told his friends that he wanted to die on a mattress on the floor of his writing cabin. He died there and according to his written instructions was buried in his sleeping bag under a pile of rocks so the coyotes and buzzards could not get at him.

"A Walk in the Park" is a relatively mellow essay for the contentious Abbey. It describes the struggle to thwart a greedy, simple-minded road-building project through a park.

Canyonlands National Park in southeast Utah is one of the nation's newest national parks. Established in 1964 by Act of Congress, carved out of public lands formerly under the administration of the Bureau of Land Management, the park has been a source of controversy and hard feelings, regionally anyhow, since the Year One of its official existence.

Maybe we should have left the place to the cows, the coyotes, the turkey vultures, and the uranium miners. The miners—ah yes, there's the catch. With the Southwest plagued by another uranium rush, we can easily imagine what those Texas oil companies and Oklahoma drilling outfits would be doing to the Canyonlands if they had there, as they have most everywhere else, a free hand. One definition of happiness: watching a Texan headed home with an Okie under each arm. Undesirable elements, like plutonium and strontium.

Well, the "undesirable elements" are everywhere. We're all undesirable elements from somebody's point of view.

What really rankles the Utah business community, as it calls itself, is this: Having grudgingly consented—through their privately owned state politicians—to the creation of the new national park, the businessmen are embittered by the fact that Canyonlands, so far, has not been developed in the intensive, comprehensive style of Grand Canyon or Yellowstone. There is only one paved highway into the park, and it expires, near a place called Squaw Flat, into a forbidding jeep road. Nothing beyond but rock and sand, whiptail lizards, and skid plate grooves on the sandstone. For mass motorized traffic this is no better than a dead end. Unacceptable.

Furthermore, it now appears that back in the fifties and early sixties, when negotiations for the park were under way, the Interior Department made some kind of deal or "understanding" with the Utah congressional delegation—then as now the most primitive in America—that Canyonlands National Park would be fully developed for automobile tourism in the traditional grand manner, with hotels, motels, and visitor centers on panoramic headlands and a system of paved highways leading into and out of the park at different points. There is something in our automated American souls that cannot abide the dead-end drive; we demand that our scenic roads curve across the landscape in great winding loops, freeing us from the detestable necessity of motoring through the same scene twice.

Such roads have not been built—so far—at Canyonlands National Park. As a result the tourism business has not been nearly so expansive as local businessmen had expected. Remembering the promises made back in the sixties, they regard the failure to build the roads as a double cross by the Park Service. They are understandably outraged. The walkers, meanwhile, and the trail bikers and jeep herders continue to enjoy the park in their own relatively modest fashion, noisy enough at times, but on a scale of numbers too small to satisfy the great expectations of the Utah Chamber of Commerce.

This situation simmered along for a decade or so, changing little, the Park Service apparently ignoring its road-building promises, the commercial natives growing ever more restless. In the fall of 1977—after extensive public hearings—the Park Service released its Draft Management Plan for Canyonlands National Park. The plan makes no provision for the building of new roads within the park, although it does suggest an upgrading of at least one existent road. Citing a change in public attitudes to road building in the parks, the need for conservation of natural resources, and "irreversible environmental damage," the plan dropped completely a long-time pet project of Utah tourism developers: the proposed Confluence Overlook road.

The Confluence Overlook is a pile of sunburnt sandstone and limestone some 1,000 feet above a point in the heart of Canyonlands where the Green River from the north meets the Colorado River from the east. Here the two rivers merge to form the augmented master stream that used to be known as the Grand River. (At the insistence of Colorado politicians the Grand River became the Colorado River.) The point of the road proposal is this: If the Park Service could be persuaded to build a paved road to the Confluence Overlook, it would then be feasible, politically and economically, to continue the paved road south through the park to a junction with Utah State Highway 95 near Natural Bridges National Monument, thus completing the grand loop drive design so dear to the heart of its Utah promoters. A group that includes, naturally, not only the Chamber of Commerce but also the Utah State Highway Department. With a through-highway bisecting the park, the developers could hope to see an unbroken torrent of gas-guzzling Detroit machinery pouring through the Canyonlands. A river of gold. Waterfalls of money pooling behind the eager-beaver dams of commerce.

This great vision has been stalled, however, by public opposition to more road building in Canyonlands National Park. When the Park Service management plan became known, the tourism developers in Utah set their congressmen on the bureaucrats, with Representative Gunn McKay leading the pack. His insistent complaints led to a personal appearance in the town of Moab, Utah, heart of the heart of the canyon country, by William Whalen, President Carter's newly appointed director of the National Park Service.

After a briefing by local Park Service officials and a quick survey of the Canyonlands scene, the new director presented himself at a public meeting in Moab. Carefully noncommittal, promising only to reevaluate the road-building controversy, Whalen asked for comment from the crowd. He was followed by other officials and by Sam Taylor, editor of the local newspaper, all of them asking for thoughtful, reasonable, "nonemotional" suggestions for Whalen's consideration. (Those who

get emotional about money are considered "practical.") These repeated requests for public opinion used up the first half hour of the
one-and-a-half-hour meeting. When the men in business suits finally
sat down to listen, it became apparent immediately that old rifts had
not healed.

First to speak from the floor was Ray Tibbetts, a former cattleman,
now a Moab realtor, uranium prospector, and clothing store owner, and
a proud, outspoken conservative. ("What's wrong with being right?") As
expected, he demanded more and better roads in the park. "We want
the people of the world to see this beautiful country. . . . The present
roads out there are a disgrace. . . . The working taxpayer [deliberate dig
at nonworking eco freaks in the audience] is on a tight schedule and
should be able to drive his car into his national park. He shouldn't have
to put on a backpack to do it. I've lived here all my life and still haven't
seen all the park." (Rude voice from the back of the hall: "That's because you never get out of your car." *Crude laughter.*) "The Park Service,"
Tibbetts went on, "is being infiltrated by the worst kind of radical environmentalists." (*Delighted laughter.*) "Let's put the parks back on a paying business basis. . . . We want everybody to visit them, not just the
welfare backpackers." (Tibbetts sat down to a sitting ovation, mingled
with hoots, jeers, and laughter from the grungy crew in the rear of
the hall.)

Sam Taylor, acting as moderator, stood up to quiet the crowd, chid-
ing certain elements for indecorous behavior. He then advanced his
compromise solution to the problem of environmental damage. The
Confluence Overlook road would necessitate a multi-million-dollar
bridge over what is called Big Spring Canyon. Taylor proposed that the
bridge be redesigned and lowered so it could not be seen from a distance. He also suggested that paved roads do less damage to a national
park than foot trails, since motorists tend to buzz quickly through a park
while hikers stray all over the place, lingering for days and polluting the
countryside. (Unstructured activity.) This led to a demand by another
pro-development speaker that backpackers be required by law to carry
chemical toilets. The same man complained of too much "wilder-
nessization" in southern Utah. Somebody read a letter from former
Utah senator Frank Moss advocating more and better roads. (It was a
different Utah senator—Orrin Hatch—who once said to a friend of
this reporter: "But Miss McElhenny, you're much too pretty to be an
environmentalist.")

After a while the road opponents got in their say. The burden of their
argument was that, since neighboring parks like Arches, Deadhorse
Point, Natural Bridges, all in southeast Utah, have already been developed for motorized sightseeing it might be wise to let Canyonlands National Park remain in its relatively primitive condition. One little old
blue-haired lady in heavy boots stood up to say that she no longer took

friends to see Deadhorse Point, since the State Parks Commission had "ruined" it. Wild cheering from the rear.

Joe Stocks, a small miner (five foot eight), independent operator, and mining claims speculator, friend of the road builders, made a brief but moving plea. (Many moved out of the hall during his talk.) "When I was in the army," he said, "I carried an eighty-pound pack all over Georgia and Vietnam. I can't see much in this backpacking. . . . I've got a Mom and Dad in their seventies, and they don't have their health and they want to see Canyonlands. This confluence road is their only chance to see the confluence. . . . My ten- and twelve-year-old kids want to see it too, and they can't carry these backpacks. . . . "

So it went. The assembly broke up in total disarray. As usual, no minds were changed; many were hardened. William Whalen went back to his Park Service office in Washington presumably enlightened but less anxious than ever to make a decision. Either way he'll make a few friends but plenty of hearty enemies. The bureaucrat's lot is not an easy one.

One thing positive emerged from the meeting. Joe Stocks's concluding remarks reminded my daughter Suzie and me that we had never seen the confluence of the Green and Colorado either and that if we were going to get there before Joe Stocks *en famille* we'd have to walk it. But could we do it? After the talk about the hardships of desert hiking, we were a little uncertain. My daughter Suzie is nine years old, a child by profession, slightly built, not the rugged outdoor type. I am forty-nine and a half years old (and will be for the next decade or two), beer-bellied, broken-nosed, overweight, shakily put together, with a bad knee—lost the cartilage years ago.

Could we do it? It's a good five miles from trailhead to trail's end. The same coming back. I put the question to this kid of mine.

"Isn't there a road?" she said. "Why do we have to walk?"

"Shut up," I explained, "and tie your shoes."

We climbed in our friend Frank Mendonca's pickup—he would photograph the exploit—and drove out to the end of the Squaw Flat "scenic drive." Drove a hundred miles in order to walk ten. Anything to make a point.

The paved road ends abruptly on the very rim of Big Spring Canyon; giant red and white warning barriers alert the motorist to the terminus of the asphalt roadway. You see at a glance that the road builders never meant to stop here. The foot trail begins a few steps beyond. The sign says: Confluence Overlook 5.1 Miles, 8.1 Kilometers.

"Which is shorter?" I asked Suzie.

"Kilometers are shorter," she explained, "but there's more of them."

We walked down into the canyon. A pretty place, cottonwoods leafing out in April greenery, the great red walls of sandstone standing vertically beyond them. Would take a lot of blasting to ram a highway through here. The trail is a winding path among the boulders, stepping down from ledge to ledge, crossing beds of sand. Where the route looks doubtful, the way is marked by small cairns.

We reached the bottom of the canyon, a few hundred feet down from the parking lot. "How much farther?" Suzie wanted to know. I guessed we had come about one-twentieth of a mile, leaving 5.05 yet to go. "Yuck," she said. We started up the trail on the other side. "This is the part I hate," she said, "this uphill stuff."

We topped out on the rim beyond. Looking back, we could see Frank's truck and a couple of other vehicles parked in the circle at the end of the pavement. Beyond were the sandstone monoliths of nearby buttes, then the mesas and plateaus, then the snow-covered La Sal Mountains fifty miles away by line of sight, twice that distance by road. Frank set up his tripod and camera to make some pictures. Once again I gave thanks to my good sense in never getting hooked on photography. While he prepared his heavy, expensive, and elaborate equipment, I took a pen and notebook from my shirt pocket. As I say to my friends Eliot Porter, Ansel Adams, and Philip Hyde, one word is worth a thousand pictures. If it's the right word. The good word.

Two young hikers climbed past us, heavy-laden, panting too hard to do more than nod in greeting. A man and a woman, both wearing nylon track shorts. We watched them go on and out of sight. I made an unkind remark. "New Yorkers," I said.

"How do you know?" Frank asked.

"They both had hairy legs."

Suzie was kicking a bush. "What kind of bush is this?"

"Just an ordinary bush," I explained. "Stop kicking it around."

"But what do you call it?"

"We call it—single-leaf ash. But what it really *is* no man knows. No, nor woman either. Leave it alone."

"I think it's yucky."

I pointed to a small, green, spiky plant nearby. "*That* is a yucca."

The sun came out of the morning clouds. Feeling gay as the day was bright, we marched on. We reached a high point on a stone ridge. An unobstructed view in all directions. We could see three separate mountain ranges, sublime with distance and snow and the patient grandeur of high, lonely places. In the middle ground, south, stood the labyrinth of sandstone spires called the Needles. Suzie thought they looked more like noodles. They have that coloring, we agreed. Close by, growing out of cracks in the rock, glowing under blackbrush and from behind hedgehog cactus, were clumps of Indian paintbrush. We tried to pin down their color. "Fiery orange," I suggested. "Day-Glo cadmium," said Frank, "with here and there a shade of burnt magenta." "Paintbrush red," said Suzie.

Onward. The footpath, maintained only by the feet of many walkers before us, as a national park trail should be maintained, followed little sandy drainages among patches of sand. Untrod by cattle for many years, the sand bore on its surface a type of dark primitive moss called cryptogam. Dry, crunchy, but alive, this humble plant is one of the first to begin the transformation of bare sand into organic soil. (Don't step on the cryptogams!) Growing on top of the cryptogams, carrying the earth-making process forward, were clumps of gray and bluish lichens.

"Why do lichens always grow in bunches?" asked Suzie.

"Lichen attracts lichen. Symbiosis." We covered another half mile trying to explain that term to her. I think she understood it better than I do. We stopped in the shade of a juniper for water and a snack. In her pack Suzie carried a quart of water, an orange, a hunk of cheese, a jar of soy nuts, a chocolate bar, spare socks, a sweater. I carried a gallon of water and more food. Frank carried food, water, and the technology.

We went on, descending from the high rock into the first of a series of grabens—long, narrow, parallel sinks in the ground big as canyons, some of them with no outlet to the river only a few miles away. The grabens are hot, dry, with little plant life, rather dismal places compared with the slickrock gardens of flowers and trees above. A century of overgrazing has not helped.

Our footpath intersects the old jeep road leading to the Confluence Overlook. One mile to go. The trail brought us to the rimrock above the rivers. We passed a Park Service warning sign: Unfenced Overlook Ahead. Use Extreme Caution. Parents, Control Your Children.

Suzie yelled with delight and sprinted forward. When Frank and I arrived at the overlook point, we found Suzie waiting in the shade of a boulder, her toes six inches from the edge of a 500-foot drop-off. It's all right; I'm used to it; we are both incurable acrophiliacs.

Down past the drop-off and a talus slope, 1,000 feet below, are the two rivers confluencing. The Colorado comes in from the great canyon on the right, the Green from the left. The Colorado is chocolate brown today, the Green a muddy yellow. The colors do not blend at the meeting point, but flow on for several miles before becoming wholly a watery one. The division between the two is marked not only by the different colors but also by a thin line of floating driftwood. The rivers are high, in flood; a large beach near the confluence is completely under water.

Frank takes pictures. Suzie and I eat lunch. The rivers make no sound, sliding gently around the bend, flowing along side by side. I hear ravens croak on the rim over yonder, on the other side, near that high point of rock that leads to the Maze, the Standing Rocks, Candlestick Spire, the Fins, the Black Ledge, the Orange Cliffs, Land's End.

North of us stands Junction Butte and Grandview Point. Far off are the snowy mountains. Above is the same imperial blue sky that Major John Wesley Powell saw when he explored these canyons from the river in 1869. The same sky that sheltered one Captain J. N. Macomb over a century ago, when he stood where we are standing and wrote in his diary: "A more profitless locality than this can scarcely be imagined."

A sound of yodeling far below, echoing off the canyon walls. Two rubber rafts float into sunlight from the deep shade of the Green River's Stillwater Canyon, drift toward the confluence. We watch them pass slowly by until they go out of sight below the rimrock. Naked boat people floating with the stream, half-asleep in their reverie. Cataract Canyon, not far downriver, will wake them up.

After a long siesta under another comfortable juniper tree, we begin the walk back. "How far now?" asks Suzie. Still 5.1 miles, 8.1 kilometers. We make the return an easy stroll, with many stops for pictures and side explorations over the slickrock humps and into narrow corridors of stone where nothing grows but your sense of stillness. The enchantment of late afternoon in the desert retards our steps. We are loth, *loth to depart*—as old Walt Whitman said of his life.

"Maybe we should stay out here," I suggest to Suzie.

"But there's nothing to do."

"You're right. There's absolutely nothing that has to be done."

We were back at the road and Frank's truck before sundown. We drank a couple of cold beers while Suzie climbed up and down the barrier signs and practiced her cartwheels. Still bored and restless, that child. Next time I'll make *her* carry the big pack.

On the long drive home we interrogated the kid. "Look here, Suzie," we said, "should we let them build that bridge? Should we let them build their paved highway to the Confluence Overlook?"

"No," she said.

"But why not? What are you, some kind of elitist? How do you expect people to get in there if they don't have a good road?"

"They can walk."

"Suppose they're too old to walk? Too young? Too fat, thin, arthritic, decrepit, scared, ignorant, lazy, rich, poor, dumb? How about crippled war veterans who fought for their country—are you going to deny them the right to see the Confluence Overlook from the comfort and convenience of their Ford LTDs?"

"Everybody can't have everything."

"Is that so? You think you should have anything *you* want. If you can get it. Who do you think you are? Do you think you're better than most people?"

Suzie thought that one over for a moment. "Well," she said, "a little better."

Questions for Thinking and Writing

1. Explain whether or not you believe that Abbey is fairly presenting the conflict between the environmentalists and the developers. What is implied by the idea that wilderness is not profitable?
2. Why do you think that Abbey really takes this walk in the canyon with his daughter Suzie? Why does he contrast Suzie's vision with the photographer's?
3. Compare Abbey's real-life attitude toward improving the landscape with Mark Fortune's attitude—Flannery O'Connor's fictional character who insists on putting a gas station and convenience store in the Pitts's meadow (p. 226).

 # Gary Snyder (b. 1930)
Front Lines (1972)

Gary Snyder has turned the rejection of Western values into poetry. He was employed at various times as a forest ranger, a logger, and a merchant seaman, jobs which reflect his disdain for material possessions. Much of his denial of American materialism has been fostered, as was Jack Kerouac's, by a lifelong study of Zen and Oriental poetry. However, in Snyder's study of Native American cultures and their myths, he saw an accordance with Eastern philosophy, the subject of one of his earlier volumes of poetry, Myths and Texts *(1960).*

He was born in San Francisco but was raised on a small farm near Seattle. He graduated from Reed College in 1951 after studying anthropology and attended the University of California at Berkeley to study Chinese and Japanese culture. Receiving a Bollingen Grant for Buddhist Studies, Snyder spent a great deal of the 1950s living and writing in Japan. What emerged from these years was an awareness of the interrelationship of life's facets, typical of Eastern thought, rather than the accumulation of knowledge, much more common in Western thought. Snyder's poetry brims with the difference: His images are simple and pure and thoughts are expressed seemingly without effort.

Snyder was a member of the West Coast Beat movement which, unlike its Eastern counterpart centered in Greenwich Village, adopted a philosophy of awe for the natural world, an attitude which is reflected in much of his poetry. While most of Snyder's poetry during the 1960s dealt with nature and the human relationship to the environment, his volume entitled Regarding Wave *(1969) took a sharp turn toward domestic life, precipitated by the birth of his first child, Kai, by his third wife. His first two marriages ended in divorce. The poems of this volume are about the wonders of birth and parental responsibility, which he shares with his Japanese wife, Masa.*

Snyder's family is also prominent in Turtle Island (1974), the selection of poetry for which he won a Pulitzer Prize, and in which "Front Lines" was published. The title refers to the Native American name for North America. (See Leonard Crow Dog's "Remaking the World," page 309, for a myth demonstrating the importance of the turtle.) Of all Snyder's poems, the ones appearing in this volume are by far the most blatantly political. Sometimes poetic spirit gives way to pragmatic action. In "Front Lines," Snyder calls directly for action to stop the technology that destroys nature.

The edge of the cancer
Swells against the hill—we feel
            a foul breeze—
And it sinks back down.
The deer winter here
A chainsaw growls in the gorge.

Ten wet days and the log trucks stop,
The trees breathe.
Sunday the 4-wheel jeep of the
Realty Company brings in
Landseekers, lookers, they say
To the land,
Spread your legs.

The jets crack sound overhead, it's OK here;
Every pulse of the rot at the heart
In the sick fat veins of Amerika
Pushes the edge up closer—

A bulldozer grinding and slobbering
Sideslipping and belching on top of
The skinned-up bodies of still-live bushes
In the pay of a man
From town.

Behind is a forest that goes to the Arctic
And a desert that still belongs to the Piute
And here we must draw
Our line.

Questions for Thinking and Writing

1. What are *front lines* usually a reference to? Why do you think that Snyder uses this term to draw attention to humankind's use of the natural environment?

2. In how many ways does Snyder make technology the culprit for desecrating the landscape? Is it the technology and the machines that devastate the natural environment, or is it the people who use the technology and the machines?

3. Comment on your own attitude toward technology and machines. Do you consider the automobile an environmental menace? Would you give up your automobile for a cleaner, safer environment? Consider how many other facets of technology you use that adversely affect the natural environment.

❦ Leonard Crow Dog (b. 1942)

Remaking the World (1974)

Leonard Crow Dog, a full-blooded Sioux of the Brule Sioux tribe, was born on the Rosebud, South Dakota, Indian reservation into a family of historical prominence. His great-grandfather Crow Dog, a friend of Crazy Horse, chief of the Oglala Sioux, was instrumental in keeping the Brule Sioux out of the conflict at Little Bighorn in 1876 that resulted in the defeat and death of General George Custer.

His grandfather Crow Dog, strongly influenced by the Mormon church, helped create the Ghost Dance, which he adapted from a Mormon round dance. The performance of the Ghost Dance at Wounded Knee, South Dakota, in 1890, precipitated the massacre there of the Sioux by U.S. troops.

Henry Crow, Leonard's father, was active in the Native American Church in South Dakota. Its rituals included extensive use of peyote, a substance derived from a spineless cactus that contains mescaline, a hallucinogenic drug.

At an early age, Leonard Crow Dog was deemed special and was selected as a medicine man. Trained to retain tribal lore and old tradition, he was also taught the use of herbs and how to exploit their healing properties. In order to keep his learning and spirit pure, his contact with Western learning was kept to a minimum: He cannot read or write English. Crow Dog is also a Roadman, that is, a spiritual leader who helps others along the road of life. He conducts vision quests and is a Sun Dance leader.

Crow Dog's political life is complex, and he has taken part in many radical Native American activities. For example, in 1973, he was the official medicine man for the Sioux when 200 of them occupied Wounded Knee for 69 days in order to force an investigation into the treatment of Native Americans by the U.S. government. Though Crow Dog had clergy status and was not a combatant, he was harassed, arrested, and jailed for his participation. Later, he was part of a group that occupied the Bureau of Indian Affairs building in Washington, D.C. Much information about Crow Dog is available in Lakota Woman *(1990), the autobiography of Mary Crow Dog, his former wife.*

Richard Erdoes, scholar of Native American life and literature, says the stories that Crow Dog tells are a mixture of the traditional and the new. Crow Dog relates the traditional story but embellishes it with his own vision, as a medicine man is expected to do. In this way the stories and myths of Native Americans change and are adapted to new times and situations. This story was told to and recorded by Erdoes at Grass Mountain, Rosebud Indian Reservation, in 1974.

There was a world before this world, but the people in it did not know how to behave themselves or how to act human. The creating power was not pleased with that earlier world. He said to himself: "I will make a new world." He had the pipe bag and the chief pipe, which he put on the pipe rack that he had made in the sacred manner. He took four dry buffalo chips, placed three of them under the three sticks, and saved the fourth one to light the pipe.

The Creating Power said to himself: "I will sing three songs, which will bring a heavy rain. Then I'll sing a fourth song and stamp four times on the earth, and the earth will crack wide open. Water will come out of the cracks and cover all the land." When he sang the first song, it started to rain. When he sang the second, it poured. When he sang the third, the rain-swollen rivers overflowed their beds. But when he sang the fourth song and stamped on the earth, it split open in many places like a shattered gourd, and water flowed from the cracks until it covered everything.

The Creating Power floated on the sacred pipe and on his huge pipe bag. He let himself be carried by waves and wind this way and that, drifting for a long time. At last the rain stopped, and by then all the people and animals had drowned. Only Kangi, the crow, survived, though it had no place to rest and was very tired. Flying above the pipe, "Tunkashila, Grandfather, I must soon rest"; and three times the crow asked him to make a place for it to light.

The Creating Power thought: "It's time to unwrap the pipe and open the pipe bag." The wrapping and the pipe bag contained all manner of animals and birds, from which he selected four animals known for their ability to stay under water for a long time. First he sang a song and took the loon out of the bag. He commanded the loon to dive and bring up a lump of mud. The loon did dive, but it brought up nothing. "I dived and dived but couldn't reach bottom," the loon said. "I almost died. The water is too deep."

The Creating Power sang a second song and took the otter out of the bag. He ordered the otter to dive and bring up some mud. The sleek otter at once dived into the water, using its strong webbed feet to go down, down, down. It was submerged for a long time, but when it finally came to the surface, it brought nothing.

Taking the beaver out of the pipe's wrapping, the Creating Power sang a third song. He commanded the beaver to go down deep below the water and bring some mud. The beaver thrust itself into the water, using its great flat tail to propel itself downward. It stayed under water longer than the others, but when it finally came up again, it too brought nothing.

At last the Creating Power sang the fourth song and took the turtle out of the bag. The turtle is very strong. Among our people it stands for long life and endurance and the power to survive. A turtle heart is great medicine, for it keeps on beating a long time after the turtle is dead. "You must bring the mud," the Creating Power told the turtle. It dove into the water and stayed below so long that the other three animals shouted: "The turtle is dead; it will never come up again!"

All the time, the crow was flying around and begging for a place to light.

After what seemed to be eons, the turtle broke the surface of the water and paddled to the Creating Power. "I got to the bottom!" the turtle cried. "I brought some earth!" And sure enough, its feet and claws— even the space in the cracks on its sides between its upper and lower shell—were filled with mud.

Scooping mud from the turtle's feet and sides, the Creating Power began to sing. He sang all the while that he shaped the mud in his hands and spread it on the water to make a spot of dry land for himself. When he had sung the fourth song, there was enough land for the Creating Power and for the crow.

"Come down and rest," said the Creating Power to the crow, and the bird was glad to.

Then the Creating Power took from his bag two long wing feathers of the eagle. He waved them over his plot of ground and commanded it to spread until it covered everything. Soon all the water was replaced by earth. "Water without earth is not good," thought the Creating Power, "but land without water is not good either." Feeling pity for the land, he wept for the earth and the creatures he would put upon it, and his tears became oceans, streams, and lakes. "That's better," he thought.

Out of his pipe bag the Creating Power took all kinds of animals, birds, plants and scattered them over the land. When he stamped on the earth, they all came alive.

From the earth the Creating Power formed the shapes of men and women. He used red earth and white earth, black earth and yellow earth, and made as many as he thought would do for a start. He stamped on the earth and the shapes came alive, each taking the color of the earth out of which it was made. The Creating Power gave all of them understanding and speech and told them what tribes they belonged to.

The Creating Power said to them: "The first world I made was bad; the creatures on it were bad. So I burned it up. The second world I made was bad too, so I drowned it. This is the third world I have made. Look: I have created a rainbow for you as a sign that there will be no more Great Flood. Whenever you see a rainbow, you will know that it has stopped raining."

The Creating Power continued: "Now, if you have learned how to behave like human beings and how to live in peace with each other and with the other living things—the two-legged, the four- legged, the many-legged, the fliers, the no-legs, the green plants of this universe—then all will be well. But if you make this world bad and ugly, then I will destroy this world too. It's up to you."

The Creating Power gave the people the pipe. "Live by it," he said. He named this land the Turtle Continent because it was there that the turtle came up with the mud out of which the third world was made.

"Someday there might be a fourth world," the Creating Power thought. Then he rested.

Questions for Thinking and Writing

1. What are the natural elements that the Creating Power uses to remake the world?
2. What does Crow Dog's story share with the creation and destruction of the earth by flood as written in the Old Testament?
3. Does Crow Dog's story imply that the earth is infinite and that the Creating Power will also serve to remake the world when things get too bad? Do you believe that this is the case? Would Garrett Hardin (see p. 284) agree with Crow Dog on this issue?

🌿 Annie Dillard (b. 1945)
Seeing (1974)

Annie Dillard is a pilgrim. Through minute examination and description of the everyday bits and pieces of the natural world—an insect, a stream, a meadow—Dillard hopes to discover an essence to life that she likens to knowing God. Pilgrim at Tinker Creek, *from which this excerpt is taken, is a full-blown effort to unravel deep truths about nature, God, and the universe. The effort falls short, Dillard fully acknowledges, but the search does not because this is the mystery of the pilgrimage of life. For her the search continues.*

Annie Dillard was born Annie Doak in Pittsburgh, Pennsylvania, the daughter of a family affluent enough to send their eldest daughter to private schools. As a child, she was a voracious reader. One of the books she discovered in her local library was The Field Book of Ponds and Streams *by Ann Haven Morgan, a volume that may have triggered her lifelong affinity with nature.*

Dillard was determined to become a writer, and she entered Hollins College in Virginia in 1963 because she was attracted to its strong creative writing program led by the novelist William Golding. During her sophomore year, she married her creative writing teacher, Richard Henry Dillard. She was elected to Phi Beta Kappa in her junior year, earning her bachelor's degree in 1967 and her master's the following year. Her master's thesis was on Thoreau. She remained in the Hollins community and began to write poems and stories for publication. Some of them appeared in American Scholar *and the* Atlantic. *Her first volume of poems,* Tickets for a Prayer Wheel, *was published in 1974. But it was the publication of* Pilgrim at Tinker Creek *later that same year that gave her national recognition as well as a Pulitzer Prize in 1975.*

While at Hollins, Dillard lived in a little cabin on Tinker Creek in Virginia's Blue Ridge mountains. In the manner of her literary mentor, Thoreau, Tinker Creek is Dillard's Walden. *It is a journal of a year she spent there, jotting down observations on the natural world, thoughts and miscellaneous information, all of which contribute to her quest for truth about creation and life. Tinker Creek also has affinities to Henry Beston's "Night on the Great Beach" (p. 135).*

In 1975, Dillard became a scholar-in-residence at Western Washington University where she lived part time in a log cabin on Puget Sound and began writing Holy the Firm, *the book in which she attempts to reconcile pain and suffering with the presence of God. A book of essays followed,* Teaching a Stone to Talk: Expeditions and

Encounters (*1982*), *which focuses on her travels in the natural world. In 1979, she began teaching at Wesleyan University in Connecticut as a distinguished visiting professor. Her latest book,* The Living (*1992*), *is a novel about settlement in the Pacific Northwest.*

When I was six or seven years old, growing up in Pittsburgh, I used to take a precious penny of my own and hide it for someone else to find. It was a curious compulsion; sadly, I've never been seized by it since. For some reason I always "hid" the penny along the same stretch of sidewalk up the street. I would cradle it at the roots of a sycamore, say, or in a hole left by a chipped-off piece of sidewalk. Then I would take a piece of chalk, and, starting at either end of the block, draw huge arrows leading up to the penny from both directions. After I learned to write I labeled the arrows: SURPRISE AHEAD or MONEY THIS WAY. I was greatly excited, during all this arrow-drawing, at the thought of the first lucky passer-by who would receive in this way, regardless of merit, a free gift from the universe. But I never lurked about. I would go straight home and not give the matter another thought, until, some months later, I would be gripped again by the impulse to hide another penny.

It is still the first week in January, and I've got great plans. I've been thinking about seeing. There are lots of things to see, unwrapped gifts and free surprises. The world is fairly studded and strewn with pennies cast broadside from a generous hand. But—and this is the point—who gets excited by a mere penny? If you follow one arrow, if you crouch motionless on a bank to watch a tremulous ripple thrill on the water and are rewarded by the sight of a muskrat kit paddling from its den, will you count that sight a chip of copper only, and go your rueful way? It is dire poverty indeed when a man is so malnourished and fatigued that he won't stoop to pick up a penny. But if you cultivate a healthy poverty and simplicity, so that finding a penny will literally make your day, then, since the world is in fact planted in pennies, you have with your poverty bought a lifetime of days. It is that simple. What you see is what you get.

I used to be able to see flying insects in the air. I'd look ahead and see, not the row of hemlocks across the road, but the air in front of it. My eyes would focus along that column of air, picking out flying insects. But I lost interest, I guess, for I dropped the habit. Now I can see birds. Probably some people can look at the grass at their feet and discover all the crawling creatures. I would like to know grasses and sedges—and care. Then my least journey into the world would be a field trip, a series of happy recognitions. Thoreau, in an expansive mood, exulted, "What a rich book might be made about buds, including, perhaps, sprouts!" It would be nice to think so. I cherish mental images I have of three perfectly happy people. One collects stones. Another—an Englishman, say—watches clouds. The third lives on a coast and collects drops of seawater which he examines microscopically and mounts. But I don't see what the specialist sees, and so I cut myself off, not only from the total picture, but from the various forms of happiness.

Unfortunately, nature is very much a now-you-see-it, now-you-don't affair. A fish flashes, then dissolves in the water before my eyes like so much salt. Deer apparently ascend bodily into heaven; the brightest oriole fades into leaves. These disappearances stun me into stillness and concentration; they say of nature that it conceals with a grand nonchalance, and they say of vision that it is a deliberate gift, the revelation of a dancer who for my eyes only flings away her seven veils. For nature does reveal as well as conceal: now-you-don't-see-it, now-you-do. For a week last September migrating red-winged blackbirds were feeding heavily down by the creek at the back of the house. One day I went out to investigate the racket; I walked up to a tree, an Osage orange, and a hundred birds flew away. They simply materialized out of the tree. I saw a tree, then a whisk of color, then a tree again. I walked closer and another hundred blackbirds took flight. Not a branch, not a twig budged: the birds were apparently weightless as well as invisible. Or, it was as if the leaves of the Osage orange had been freed from a spell in the form of red-winged blackbirds; they flew from the tree, caught my eye in the sky, and vanished. When I looked again at the tree the leaves had reassembled as if nothing had happened. Finally I walked directly to the trunk of the tree and a final hundred, the real diehards, appeared, spread, and vanished. How could so many hide in the tree without my seeing them? The Osage orange, unruffled, looked just as it had looked from the house, when three hundred red-winged blackbirds cried from its crown. I looked downstream where they flew, and they were gone. Searching, I couldn't spot one. I wandered downstream to force them to play their hand, but they'd crossed the creek and scattered. One show to a customer. These appearances catch at my throat; they are the free gifts, the bright coppers at the roots of trees.

It's all a matter of keeping my eyes open. Nature is like one of those line drawings of a tree that are puzzles for children: Can you find hidden in the leaves a duck, a house, a boy, a bucket, a zebra, and a boot? Specialists can find the most incredibly well-hidden things. A book I read when I was young recommended an easy way to find caterpillars to rear: you simply find some fresh caterpillar droppings, look up, and there's your caterpillar. More recently an author advised me to set my mind at ease about those piles of cut stems on the ground in grassy fields. Field mice make them; they cut the grass down by degrees to reach the seeds at the head. It seems that when the grass is tightly packed, as in a field of ripe grain, the blade won't topple at a single cut through the stem; instead, the cut stem simply drops vertically, held in the crush of grain. The mouse severs the bottom again and again, the stem keeps dropping an inch at a time, and finally the head is low enough for the mouse to reach the seeds. Meanwhile, the mouse is positively littering the field with its little piles of cut stems into which, presumably, the author of the book is constantly stumbling.

If I can't see these minutiae, I still try to keep my eyes open. I'm always on the lookout for antlion traps in sandy soil, monarch pupae near milkweed, skipper larvae in locust leaves. These things are utterly common, and I've not seen one. I bang on hollow trees near water, but so far no flying squirrels have appeared. In flat country I watch every sunset in hopes of seeing the green ray. The green ray is a seldom-seen streak of light that rises from the sun like a spurting fountain at the moment of sunset; it throbs into the sky for two seconds and disappears. One more reason to keep my eyes open. A photography professor at the University of Florida just happened to see a bird die in midflight; it jerked, died, dropped, and smashed on the ground. I squint at the wind because I read Stewart Edward White: "I have always maintained that if you looked closely enough you could *see* the wind—the dim, hardly-made-out, fine débris fleeing high in the air." White was an excellent observer, and devoted an entire chapter of *The Mountains* to the subject of seeing deer: "As soon as you can forget the naturally obvious and construct an artificial obvious, then you too will see deer."

But the artificial obvious is hard to see. My eyes account for less than one percent of the weight of my head; I'm bony and dense; I see what I expect. I once spent a full three minutes looking at a bullfrog that was so unexpectedly large I couldn't see it even though a dozen enthusiastic campers were shouting directions. Finally I asked, "What color am I looking for?" and a fellow said, "Green." When at last I picked out the frog, I saw what painters are up against: the thing wasn't green at all, but the color of wet hickory bark.

The lover can see, and the knowledgeable. I visited an aunt and uncle at a quarter-horse ranch in Cody, Wyoming. I couldn't do much of anything useful, but I could, I thought, draw. So, as we all sat around the kitchen table after supper, I produced a sheet of paper and drew a horse. "That's one lame horse," my aunt volunteered. The rest of the family joined in: "Only place to saddle that one is his neck"; "Looks like we better shoot the poor thing, on account of those terrible growths." Meekly, I slid the pencil and paper down the table. Everyone in that family, including my three young cousins, could draw a horse. Beautifully. When the paper came back it looked as though five shining, real quarter horses had been corraled by mistake with a papier-mâché moose; the real horses seemed to gaze at the monster with a steady, puzzled air. I stay away from horses now, but I can do a creditable goldfish. The point is that I just don't know what the lover knows; I just can't see the artificial obvious that those in the know construct. The herpetologist asks the native, "Are there snakes in that ravine?" "Nosir." And the herpetologist comes home with, yessir, three bags full. Are there butterflies on that mountain? Are the bluets in bloom, are there arrowheads here, or fossil shells in the shale?

Peeping through my keyhole I see within the range of only about thirty percent of the light that comes from the sun; the rest is infrared and some little ultraviolet, perfectly apparent to many animals, but invisible to me. A nightmare network of ganglia, charged and firing without my knowledge, cuts and splices what I do see, editing it for my brain. Donald E. Carr points out that the sense impressions of one-celled animals are *not* edited for the brain: "This is philosophically interesting in a rather mournful way, since it means that only the simplest animals perceive the universe as it is."

A fog that won't burn away drifts and flows across my field of vision. When you see fog move against a backdrop of deep pines, you don't see the fog itself, but streaks of clearness floating across the air in dark shreds. So I see only tatters of clearness through a pervading obscurity. I can't distinguish the fog from the overcast sky; I can't be sure if the light is direct or reflected. Everywhere darkness and the presence of the unseen appalls. We estimate now that only one atom dances alone in every cubic meter of intergalactic space. I blink and squint. What planet or power yanks Halley's Comet out of orbit? We haven't seen that force yet; it's a question of distance, density, and the pallor of reflected light. We rock, cradled in the swaddling band of darkness. Even the simple darkness of night whispers suggestions to the mind. Last summer, in August, I stayed at the creek too late.

Where Tinker Creek flows under the sycamore log bridge to the tear-shaped island, it is slow and shallow, fringed thinly in cattail marsh. At this spot an astonishing bloom of life supports vast breeding populations of insects, fish, reptiles, birds, and mammals. On windless summer evenings I stalk along the creek bank or straddle the sycamore log in absolute stillness, watching for muskrats. The night I stayed too late I was hunched on the log staring spellbound at spreading, reflected stains of lilac on the water. A cloud in the sky suddenly lighted as if turned on by a switch; its reflection just as suddenly materialized on the water upstream, flat and floating, so that I couldn't see the creek bottom, or life in the water under the cloud. Downstream, away from the cloud on the water, water turtles smooth as beans were gliding down with the current in a series of easy, weightless push-offs, as men bound on the moon. I didn't know whether to trace the progress of one turtle I was sure of, risking sticking my face in one of the bridge's spider webs made invisible by the gathering dark, or take a chance on seeing the carp, or scan the mudbank in hope of seeing a muskrat, or follow the last of the swallows who caught at my heart and trailed it after them like streamers as they appeared from directly below, under the log, flying upstream with their tails forked, so fast.

But shadows spread, and deepened, and stayed. After thousands of years we're still strangers to darkness, fearful aliens in an enemy camp with our arms crossed over our chests. I stirred. A land turtle on the bank, startled, hissed the air from its lungs and withdrew into its shell. An uneasy pink here, an unfathomable blue there, gave great suggestion of lurking beings. Things were going on. I couldn't see whether that sere rustle I heard was a distant rattlesnake, slit-eyed, or a nearby sparrow kicking in the dry flood debris slung at the foot of a willow. Tremendous action roiled the water everywhere I looked, big action, inexplicable. A tremor welled up beside the gaping muskrat burrow in the bank and I caught my breath, but no muskrat appeared. The ripples continued to fan upstream with a steady, powerful thrust. Night was knitting over my face an eyeless mask, and I still sat transfixed. A distant airplane, a delta wing out of nightmare, made a gliding shadow on the creek's bottom that looked like a stingray cruising upstream. At once a black fin slit the pink cloud on the water, shearing it in two. The two halves merged together and seemed to dissolve before my eyes. Darkness pooled in the cleft of the creek and rose, as water collects in a well. Untamed, dreaming lights flickered over the sky. I saw hints of hulking underwater shadows, two pale splashes out of the water, and round ripples rolling close together from a blackened center.

At last I stared upstream where only the deepest violet remained of the cloud, a cloud so high its underbelly still glowed feeble color reflected from a hidden sky lighted in turn by a sun halfway to China. And out of that violet, a sudden enormous black body arced over the water. I saw only a cylindrical sleekness. Head and tail, if there was a head and tail, were both submerged in cloud. I saw only one ebony fling, a headlong dive to darkness; then the waters closed, and the lights went out.

I walked home in a shivering daze, up hill and down. Later I lay openmouthed in bed, my arms flung wide at my sides to steady the whirling darkness. At this latitude I'm spinning 836 miles an hour round the earth's axis; I often fancy I feel my sweeping fall as a breakneck arc like the dive of dolphins, and the hollow rushing of wind raises hair on my neck and the side of my face. In orbit around the sun I'm moving 64,800 miles an hour. The solar system as a whole, like a merry-go-round unhinged, spins, bobs, and blinks at the speed of 43,200 miles an hour along a course set east of Hercules. Someone has piped, and we are dancing a tarantella until the sweat pours. I open my eyes and I see dark, muscled forms curl out of water, with flapping gills and flattened eyes. I close my eyes and I see stars, deep stars giving way to deeper stars, deeper stars bowing to deepest stars at the crown of an infinite cone.

Questions for Thinking and Writing

1. What levels of meaning—personal, social, natural—can be ascribed to "seeing" in this essay? What do you think Dillard is trying to get across?

2. Dillard uses the penny and her childhood compulsion with an ulterior motive in mind. She's not really discussing a penny or money; what kind of currency is she referring to? How does this relate to the human presence in the natural environment?

3. What does Dillard learn from her experience at the creek in darkness? How does she relate her personal local experience to something that is universal? How does Dillard's experience compare with Maxine Kumin's in "Morning Swim" (p. 272)? Comment on the fact that Dillard's experience takes place in darkness while Kumin's occurs in the morning light.

 # John McPhee (b. 1931)

Profiles: Carol Ruckdeschel (1975)

John McPhee is known as a writer's writer. He is a master at arranging the contents of his writing to bring his diverse subjects, from hydroelectric energy to the Florida orange industry, to the best light. Despite being a meticulous interviewer, researcher, and organizer of his material, he calls writing a "wretched process."

He was born in Princeton, New Jersey, where he still lives. His father, Harry Roemer McPhee, was a physician, a sports medicine specialist, who attended to Princeton University's athletic teams as well as various U.S. Olympic teams. McPhee spent time as a boy hanging around his father and the Princeton teams. It may have been this experience that gave him a lifelong love of basketball and tennis. He is an expert canoeist, a skill he learned during summers at Keewaydin, a camp in Vermont. One of his best known books, The Survival of the Birchbark Canoe *(1975), was inspired by a birchbark canoe suspended from the rafters of the camp's dining hall.*

McPhee attended Princeton High School where one of his English teachers, Olive McKee, made her students hand in three compositions per week including outlines. McPhee attributes his writing's well-honed structure to his teacher's rigorous regime. After graduating from high school, his parents sent him for one year to Deerfield Academy in Massachusetts, then under the stewardship of Frank Boyden, a famous old-school headmaster who later became the subject of one of McPhee's profiles. From there, McPhee went to

*Princeton University, where he majored in English literature. He grad-
uated in 1953 and went to Cambridge University in England for graduate studies but apparently spent a great deal of time playing
basketball, an experience that became the subject of another essay.*

*When McPhee returned to New York City, he sold several plays to
television but took a job with* Time *magazine. He continued sending
articles to other magazines and finally, in 1965, sold a profile of Bill
Bradley, the basketball player, to the* New Yorker. *A short time later,
he was asked to be staff writer for the magazine, a position he has held
ever since. He is also Ferris Professor of Journalism at Princeton University where he teaches a course entitled "The Literature of Fact."*

*McPhee has always had a special interest in the environment and
natural history. His most recent writings, for example, have been on
the geological history of North America. Though a journalist at heart
and with the objectivity that craft requires, McPhee has never concealed his fascination for the outdoors and for those who work and
live in it. The excerpt here appeared as part of a profile of Carol Ruckdeschel, a biologist working for the state of Georgia who was assigned
to assess parcels of land for inclusion in a park system.*

As we moved east, pine trees kept giving us messages—small, hand-
painted signs nailed into the loblollies. "HAVE YOU WHAT IT TAKES TO MEET
JESUS WHEN HE RETURNS?" Sam said he was certain he did not. "JESUS WILL
NEVER FAIL YOU." City limits, Adrian, Georgia. Swainsboro, Georgia. Por-
tal, Georgia. Towns on the long, straight roads of the coastal plain.
White-painted, tin-roofed bungalows. Awnings shading the fronts of
stores—prepared for heat and glare. Red earth. Sand roads. Houses on
short stilts. Sloping verandas. Unpainted boards.

"D.O.R.," said Carol.

"What do you suppose that was?"

"I don't know. I didn't see. It could have been a squirrel."

Sam backed up to the D.O.R. It was a brown thrasher. Carol looked
it over, and felt it. Sam picked it up. "Throw him far off the road," Carol
said. "So a possum won't get killed while eating him." Sam threw the
bird far off the road. A stop for a D.O.R. always brought the landscape
into detailed focus. Pitch coming out of a pine. Clustered sows behind
a fence. An automobile wrapped in vines. A mailbox. "Donald Foskey."
His home. Beyond the mailbox, a set of cinder blocks and on the cinder blocks a mobile home. As Sam regathered speed, Carol turned on
the radio and moved the dial. If she could find some Johnny Cash, it
would elevate her day. Some Johnny Cash was not hard to find in the
airwaves of Georgia. There he was now, resonantly singing about his
Mississippi Delta land, where, on a sharecropping farm, he grew up.

Carol smiled and closed her eyes. In her ears—pierced ears—were gold maple leaves that seemed to move under the influence of the music.

"D.O.R. possum," Sam said, stopping again. "Two! A grown one and a baby." They had been killed probably ten minutes before. Carol carried the adult to the side of the road and left it there. She kept the baby. He was seven inches long. He was half tail. Although dead, he seemed virtually undamaged. We moved on. Carol had a clipboard she used for making occasional notes and sketches. She put the little possum on the clipboard and rested the clipboard on her knees. "Oh, you sweet little angel. How could anybody run over *you?*" she said. "Oh, I just love possums. I've raised so many of them. This is a great age. They are the neatest little animals. They love you so much. They crawl on your shoulder and hang in your hair. How people can dislike them I don't understand." Carol reached into the back seat and put the little opossum into a container of formaldehyde. After a while, she said, "What mystifies me is: that big possum back there was a male."

Bethel Primitive Baptist Church. Old Canoochee Primitive Baptist Church. "THE CHURCH HAS NO INDULGENCES." A town every ten miles, a church—so it seemed—every two. Carol said she frequently slept in church graveyards. They were, for one thing, quiet, and, for another, private. Graham Memorial Church of the Nazarene.

Sam and Carol both sat forward at the same moment, alert, excited. "D.O.R. Wow! That was something special. It had a long yellow belly and brown fur or feathers! Hurry, Sam. It's a good one." Sam backed up at forty miles an hour and strained the Chevrolet.

"What is it? What is it?"

"It's a piece of bark. Fell off a pulpwood truck."

The approach to Pembroke was made with a sense of infiltration—Pembroke, seat of Bryan County. "Remember, now, we're interested in frogs," Sam said, and we went up the steps of Bryan County Courthouse. "We understand there is a stream-channelization project going on near here. Could you tell us where? We're collecting frogs." It is hard to say what the clerks in the courthouse thought of this group—the spokesman with the black-and-white beard, the shoeless young woman, and their silent companion. They looked at us—they in their pumps and print dresses—from the other side of a distance. The last thing they might have imagined was that two of the three of us were representing the state government in Atlanta. The clerks did not know where the channelization was going on but they knew who might—a woman in town who knew everything. We went to see her. A chicken ran out of her house when she opened the screen door. No, she was not sure just where we should go, but try a man named Miller in Lanier. He'd know. He knew everything. Lanier was five miles down the track—literally so. The Seaboard Coast Line ran beside the road. Miller was a thickset man with unbelievably long, sharp fingernails, a driver of oil trucks. It seemed wonderful that he could get his hands around the wheel without cutting himself, that he could deliver oil without cutting the hose. He said, "Do you mind my asking why you're interested in stream channelization?"

"We're interested in frogs," Sam said. "Snakes and frogs. We thought the project might be stirring some up."

Miller said, "I don't mind the frog, but I want no part of the snake."

His directions were perfect—through pine forests, a right, two lefts, to where a dirt road crossed a tributary of the Ogeechee. A wooden bridge there had been replaced by a culvert. The stream now flowed through big pipes in the culvert. Upriver, far as the eye could see, a riparian swath had been cut by chain saws. Back from the banks, about fifty feet on each side, the overstory and the understory—every tree, bush, and sapling—had been cut down. The river was under revision. It had been freed of meanders. It was now two yards wide between vertical six-foot banks; and it was now as straight as a ditch. It had, in fact, become a ditch—in it a stream of thin mud, flowing. An immense yellow machine, slowly backing upstream, had in effect eaten this river. It was at work now, grunting and belching, two hundred yards from the culvert. We tried to walk toward it along the bank but sank to our shins in black ooze. The stumps of the cut trees were all but covered with mud from the bottom of the river. We crossed the ditch. The dredged mud was somewhat firmer on the other side. Sam and I walked there. Carol waded upcurrent in the stream. The machine was an American dragline crane. The word "American" stood out on its cab in letters more than a foot high. Its boom reached up a hundred feet. Its bucket took six-foot bites. As we approached, the bucket kept eating the riverbed, then swinging up and out of the channel and disgorging tons of mud to either side. Carol began to take pictures. She took more and more pictures as she waded on upstream. When she was fifty feet away from the dragline, its engine coughed down and stopped. The sudden serenity was oddly disturbing. The operator stepped out of the cab and onto the catwalk. One hand on the flank of his crane, he inclined his head somewhat forward and stared down at Carol. He was a stocky man with an open shirt and an open face, deeply tanned. He said, "Howdy."

"Howdy," said Carol.

"You're taking some pictures," he said.

"I sure am. I'm taking some pictures. I'm interested in the range extension of river frogs, and the places they live. I bet you turn up some interesting things."

"I see some frogs," the man said. "I see lots of frogs."

"You sure know what you're doing with that machine," Carol said. The man shifted his weight. "That's a *big* thing," she went on. "How much does it weigh?"

"Eighty-two tons."

"Eighty-two *tons?*"

"Eighty-two tons."

"Wow! How far can you dig in one day?"

"Five hundred feet."

"A mile every ten days," Sam said, shaking his head with awe.

"Sometimes I do better than that."

"You live around here?"

"No. My home's near Baxley. I go where I'm sent. All over the state."

"Well, sorry. Didn't mean to interrupt you."

"Not 't all. Take all the pictures you want."

"Thanks. What did you say your name was?"

"Chap," he said. "Chap Causey."

We walked around the dragline, went upstream a short way, and sat down on the trunk of a large oak, felled by the chain saws, to eat our lunch—sardines, chocolate, crackers, and wine. Causey at work was the entertainment, pulling his levers, swinging his bucket, having at the stream.

If he had been at first wary, he no doubt had had experience that made him so. All over the United States, but particularly in the Southeast, his occupation had become a raw issue. He was working for the Soil Conservation Service, a subdivision of the United States Department of Agriculture, making a "water-resource channel improvement"—generally known as stream channelization, or reaming a river. Behind his dragline, despite the clear-cutting of the riverine trees, was a free-flowing natural stream, descending toward the Ogeechee in bends and eddies, riffles and deeps—in appearance somewhere between a trout stream and a bass river, and still handsomely so, even though it was shaved and ready for its operation. At the dragline, the recognizable river disappeared, and below the big machine was a kind of reverse irrigation ditch, engineered to remove water rapidly from the immediate watershed. "How could anyone even conceive of this idea?" Sam said. "Not just to do it, but even to *conceive* of it?"

The purpose of such projects was to anticipate and eliminate floods, to drain swamps, to increase cropland, to channel water toward freshly created reservoirs serving and attracting new industries and new housing developments. Water sports would flourish on the new reservoirs, hatchery fish would proliferate below the surface: new pulsations in the life of the rural South. The Soil Conservation Service was annually spending about fifteen million dollars on stream-channelization projects, providing, among other things, newly arable land to farmers who already had land in the Soil Bank. The Department of Agriculture could not do enough for the Southern farmer, whose only problem was bookkeeping. He got money for keeping his front forty idle. His bottomland went up in value when the swamps were drained, and then more money came for not farming the drained land. Years earlier, when a conservationist had been someone who plowed land along natural contours, the Soil Conservation Service had been the epicenter of the conservation movement, decorated for its victories over erosion of the land. Now, to a new generation that had discovered ecology, the S.C.S. was the enemy. Its drainage programs tampered with river mechanics, upsetting the relationships between bass and otter, frog and owl. The Soil Conservation Service had grown over the years into a bureau of fifteen thousand people, and all the way down at the working point, the cutting edge of things, was Chap Causey, in the cab of his American dragline, hearing nothing but the pounding of his big Jimmy diesel while he eliminated a river, eradicated a swamp.

After heaving up a half-dozen buckets of mud, Causey moved backward several feet. The broad steel shoes of the crane were resting on oak beams that were bound together in pairs with cables. There were twelve beams in all. Collectively, they were called "mats." Under the crane, they made a temporary bridge over the river. As Causey moved backward and off the front pair of beams, he would reach down out of the sky with a hook from his boom and snare a loop of the cable that held the beams. He snatched them up—they weighed at least half a ton—and whipped them around to the back. The beams dropped perfectly into place, adding a yard to Causey's platform on the upstream side. Near the tree line beyond one bank, he had a fuel tank large enough to bury under a gas station, and every so often he would reach out with his hook and his hundred-foot arm and, without groping, lift the tank and move it on in the direction he was going. With his levers, his cables, his bucket, and hook, he handled his mats and his tank and his hunks of the riverbed as if he were dribbling a basketball through his legs and behind his back. He was deft. He was world class. "I bet he could put on a baby's diapers with that thing," Sam said.

Carol said, "See that three-foot stump? I sure would like to see him pull *that* out." She gestured toward the rooted remains of a tree that must have stood, a week earlier, a hundred and fifty feet high. Causey, out of the corner of his eye, must have seen the gesture. Perhaps he just read her mind. He was much aware that he was being watched, and now he reached around behind him, grabbed the stump in his bucket, and ripped it out of the earth like a molar. He set it at Carol's feet. It towered over her.

After a modest interval, a few more buckets of streambed, Causey shut off the dragline and stopped for an adulation break. Carol told him he was fabulous. And she meant it. He was. She asked him what the name of the stream was. He said, "To tell you the truth, Ma'am, I don't rightly know."

Questions for Thinking and Writing

1. Why do you think that Sam and Carol are so concerned about D.O.R.s? What point is McPhee trying to make? What do you think when you see a D.O.R.? What have you thought or how do you think you would react if you drove over an animal crossing the road?
2. How does McPhee characterize the dragline crane? What is ironic about the crane operator's inability to name the stream he is working on? What does this incident say about a person's tendency to generalize about nature?
3. What is stream channelization and how does it affect the surrounding environment? How does this complement the notion of mastering the natural environment? Relate this to David Lilienthal's argument for improving the natural environment in "One Valley—and a Thousand" (p. 170).

❦ N. Scott Momaday (b. 1934)
To the Singing, to the Drums (1975)

Navarre Scott Momaday is half Kiowa. His mother, Mayme Nat-achee, was from Kentucky, the daughter of a sheriff named Theodore Scotter. At some point, she adopted a Native American identity (Nat-achee is a Cherokee name) and called herself Little Moon. She was sent to school at the Haskell Institute, an Indian school in Kansas, where she met Momaday's father, a Kiowa.

Momaday was born in Lawton, Oklahoma, where he lived for a time on a farm before moving to New Mexico where his parents, both teach-ers, worked among the Jemez Indians in the mountains. He went to the University of New Mexico and then to Stanford where he received a doctorate in English literature. Momaday's first job was as an assis-tant professor of English at the University of California, Santa Bar-bara. He now teaches at the University of Arizona, Tucson.

If alienation, isolation, and separation are the most important con-flicts facing Native Americans today, then Momaday believes he has made a lifelong study of how these impositions affect individual lives. Though the traditional Native American world order is dominated by seeking harmony in the universe, Momaday points out that most Na-tive Americans live in a world without harmony.

Momaday began his first novel, House Made of Dawn, *when he was studying at Stanford. It was published in 1968 and won the Pulitzer Prize for literature. The story is about a Kiowa returning to his reser-vation after serving in the military and the difficulties in adjustment he encounters between Kiowa and white society. In the end, the hero accepts his heritage by participating in traditional rituals, thus ending his alienation from both his heritage and the world at large.*

Momaday's best known work is The Way to Rainy Mountain *(1969), about the Kiowa's migration from the Rockies down into the plains and their final defeat by the U.S. Cavalry. Other works by Momaday include two volumes of poetry,* Angle of Geese *(1973) and* The Gourd Dancer *(1976), and* The Names *(1976), a memoir.*

Momaday's grandmother took part in the last Sun Dance in 1987 before Kiowa traditions were wholly lost. The Gourd Dance is both a link to the past and the present. Those participating in it renew their sense of belonging to a tribe (the greater community) and family. The dance also links the celebrants with the harmony of the world and universe and is a way to enhance spiritual strength and a personal sense of dignity.

I t is a recurrent pilgrimage, and it is made with propriety, a certain sense of formality. I understand a little more of it each time. I see a little more deeply into the meaning of formality, the formality of meaning. It is a religious experience by and large, natural and appropriate. It is an expression of the spirit.

The Taimpe is an old society in the Kiowa tribe, dating back to the time of the Sun Dance. Not much is known of its origin; there are various accounts. An old woman, Ko-sahn, who knew many things and who is dead now, told me the following story:

"There was a young man who knew that he must go off by himself. It was necessary that he do this, for it was to be done for the people. He went out upon the prairie, where it was very dangerous, for there were enemies all around. He came to a high place, a kind of little mountain, which was overgrown with sagebrush and mesquite—and there was one tree. The young man heard something, a voice perhaps, but strange and troublesome, and he was afraid. He climbed the tree and hid among the branches. From there in the tree he watched the approach of his enemy. The enemy was outfitted in the regalia of the wolf clan of his people. He wore the hide of a wolf, and he carried a bow and arrows. The wolflike man crept among the bushes, moving strangely, crouching and peering all around.

"By and by he came beneath the tree, and there he stood still. The young man in the tree dropped down upon his enemy and killed him. Then the young man took up the enemy's arrows in his right hand and held them high and shook them. They rattled loudly like dry leaves in a hard wind, and to this music the young man danced around his dead enemy. The people heard the music and came to see what was going on. They were very happy for the young man, and they praised him."

This, said Ko-sahn, is how the Taimpe—the Gourd Dance—came to be, and she said it in the old, certain way, the way of the storyteller, nodding her head and speaking straightly, not to be in doubt or doubted.

Facets of the story flash upon me. I move toward the center with the others, dancing—yet not dancing, really—edging upon the music, that other, quicker element, fitting my motion to it slowly, waiting to enter wholly into it. The facets are the leaves of the solitary tree, glittering in the sky. I imagine the young, legendary man there, coiled. But I do not see him apart from the tree. His limbs are the limbs of the tree, his hair the splinters of light that pierce the shadows. His enemy is vaguely there in the mottled foreground, waiting.

The celebration of the Gourd Dance is performed on the Fourth of July at Carnegie, Oklahoma.

From the window of the plane I can see to the horizon. Even at 25,000 feet there is a sense of vastness in the landscape of the Great Plains. I wonder that it always takes me by surprise. It is a mood in the earth, I think, suffered here only, a deep, aboriginal intelligence in the soil, deeper than the intricate geometry that I see below, as deep as ever ran the roots of that single tree or the blood of the buffalo.

I anticipate the air. It is warm and heavy in July; you seem to move against it, to spend yourself upon it; it confirms you. I watch the ground rise up to the window, feel for the touch of it. Space becomes lateral and infinite, faintly distorted—I think of seeing through a glass of water.

At the Will Rogers World Airport at Oklahoma City my father and my three daughters are waiting for me; he spills the girls into my arms. Something now of the ritual proper has begun; generations have come together; the blood has begun to flow toward the center of time.

My children have an understanding of the occasion, rather a perception, not of what it is—that will likely come later in their lives—but *that* it is. It is a formality that gives shape to their lives.

From the time I was a small child I have heard stories from Kiowa tradition, and now so have my children, for I have seen to it. The stories are wonderful, engaging the imagination closely. They have a vitality that is peculiar to the spoken word; it does not exist in writing or it does not exist to the same degree. This vitality informs the Gourd Dance, too; it is as if the dance is told in a story, imagined, realized in the force and nuance of an ancient language; there is that character to it, that quality of invention, of proportion, of delight.

The songs are torrential. They work a flood upon the afternoon. The sound is full of energy. Little by little I take it in, appropriate it to my mind and body. The sun beats down harder as the afternoon goes on. The dance ring is full of dazzling light. Banners move softly against the vague backdrop of the trees. Perspiration runs in my hair; my skin and clothing are wet with it. It is as if I am suspended between the music and the heat. I feel good, strangely exhilarated and strong, as if I could dance on and on and on, so long as the songs are alive in the air.

We drive westward on the freeway. The little girls chatter in the back seat. My father's hands are dark, large-veined, laid lightly on the steering wheel of the rented car. I used to stand beside him when he painted, watching him touch the brush to the paper, wondering how he could make such fine lines of color, how it was that his hand was so sure, so true to him. It occurs to me now that his granddaughters, too, must wonder at the same thing in the same way. Cael, the oldest, has gone to school at his easel. Certainly, she see that his hand is an instrument that realizes the image in his mind's eye upon the picture plane. She will be a writer and a painter, she tells me. She will illustrate her own books.

At Chickasha we are on the edge of the old world that I knew as a child. We leave the freeway and proceed on Oklahoma 9, a more familiar and congenial way. At Anadarko we stop at the Southern Plains Museum to look at the arts and crafts exhibit there. This, too, we do each year, and always at the same time of day. It is where I complain that we are late, that the dance has already begun.

"How much farther?" asks Brit, the baby, who is six, when we are on the road again. "Oh, a few miles, not far," answers Jill, whose tenth birthday it is. "Oh, well, then." Brit thinks it will be too hot at the dance. Nevertheless, she is looking forward to it; there will be children she sees just this one time each year; she will observe how they have grown; and perhaps there will be presents.

The earth is red along the way. There are escarpments like great, gaping flesh wounds in the earth. Erosion is an important principle of geography here, something deep in the character of the plains. Nowhere else on earth, I suppose, is the weather so close at hand at it is here.

My father begins to recognize the landmarks of his growing up, and this excites the girls and me. "My dad and I used to come this way in a surrey," he says, pointing out a grove. "There we used to stop, every time, and eat. We ate watermelons. My dad loved watermelons." The girls look hard into the grove, trying to see the man and the boy who paused there in the other time.

Carnegie is a small, unremarkable town in the southern plains. It is like other towns thereabouts, essentially bland and tentative—seeming against the huge, burning landscape. In July the wide glass- and metal-bordered streets not only reflect the sun, they seem to intensify it. The light is flat and hard just now in the early afternoon; the day is at white heat. Later the light will soften and colors will emerge upon the scene; the town will melt into motion, but now it seems deserted. We drive through it.

The celebration is on the north side. We turn down into a dark depression, a large hollow among trees. It is full of camps and cars and people. At first there are children. According to some centrifugal social force, children function on the periphery. They run about, making festival noises. Firecrackers are snapping all around. We park and I make ready; the girls help me with my regalia. I am already wearing white trousers and moccasins. Now I tie the black velvet sash around my waist, placing the beaded tassels at my right leg. The bandoleer of red beans, which was my grandfather's, goes over my left shoulder, the V at my right hip. I decide to carry the blanket over my arm until I join the dancers; no sense in wrapping up in this heat. There is deep, brick-red dust on the ground. The grass is pale and brittle here and there. We make our way through the camps, stepping carefully to avoid the pegs and guy lines that reach about the tents. Old people, imperturbable, are lying down on cots and benches in the shadows. Smoke hangs in the air. We smell hamburgers, popcorn, gunpowder. Later there will be fried bread, boiled meat, Indian corn.

My father is a man of great presence, a certain figure in the world. He is tall in stature, substantial, good looking; there is a style to his attitudes, a quality most often called charm. Rather, I believe, it is good will. He simply enjoys society and is most closely realized in it. There is a deep-seated, native vanity to him, and ethnic confidence, and it is attractive. It is good to see him here among our kinsmen. He has sure, easy access to the tribal spheres of being. The old people recognize him: they are drawn to him; they are delighted to see him and call him by his Indian name.

Mammedaty was my grandfather's name; it means "sky walker," one who walks in the sky. In my mind's eye I see him in silhouette, at evening in the plain, walking against a copper sunset; so he lives for me in his name. Fifty years ago, more or less, he was given a horse on the occasion of the Gourd Dance. My father says: "Oh, it was a beautiful horse, black and shining. I was just a boy then, Jill's age or Brit's. His name, Mammedaty, was called out, and he was given that fine horse. Its mane was fixed in braids and ribbons. There was a beautiful blanket on its back."

We greet Taft Hainta, the leader of the Taimpe society. He embraces us. Jill gives him a hundred dollar bill. This, too, is traditional. Each year she has made the donation to the fund for the subsequent year's celebration. It is good that she gives a gift on her birthday. Taft sees that the girls are seated comfortably in view of the dance ground. It is not easy to find a good vantage point. There is a large crowd, and the shade is thickly populated.

Each year now it seems there are more and more young people in attendance. They come from far away, simply to be here, to be caught up in this returning, to enter into the presence of the old, original spirit that resides here.

For a time we stand on the edge of the crowd and watch, taking hold of the music and the motion. I see who is there, pick out friends and relatives. Fred Tsoodle is there always; he saw to my initiation five years ago. He counseled me, taught me how to take the steps, how to wear the regalia, how to hold the gourd and the fan properly. Now I look for him; it is a kind of orientation. My cousin, Marland Aitson, is across the circle. There is room next to him. I go there.

The sun descends upon the trees. There is a giveaway. People are standing in the circle, calling forth those to whom they will make gifts. I close my eyes, open them, close them again. There are so many points of color, like points of flame. The sun has drawn upon the place; it presses upon me. I feel the heat of it at my center. The heat is hypnotic—and the kaleidoscopic scene. It is as if I am asleep. Then the drums break, the voices of the singers gather to the beat, the rattles shake all around—mine among them. I stand and move again, slowly, toward the center of the universe in time, in time, more and more closely in time.

There have been times when I have wondered what the dance is and what it means—and what I am inside of it. And there have been times when I have known. Always, there comes a moment when the dance takes hold of me, becomes itself the most meaningful and appropriate expression of my being. And always, afterward, there is rejoicing among us. We have made our prayer, and we have made good our humanity in the process. There are lively feelings. There is much good talk and laughter—and much that goes without saying. Here and there the old people play at words with the children, telling stories of this and that, of Creation and of the good things and bad things in the world—and especially of that which is beautiful.

The eagle is my power,
And my fan is an eagle.
It is strong and beautiful
In my hand. And it is real.
My fingers hold upon it
As if the beaded handle
Were the twist of bristlecone.
The bones of my hand
    are fine
And hollow; the fan
    bears them.
My hand veers in the thin air
Of the summits. All morning
It scuds on the cold currents;
All afternoon it circles
To the singing, to the drums.

Questions for Thinking and Writing

1. Discuss the irony of these Native Americans traveling by jet and automobile to renew their tribal ties and celebrate the old ways. How does this blending of the new technology and the old tribal ways provide social and personal enrichment through festival, song, drums, and dance?
2. Though its origin is derived from an adventure of tribal hatred, war, and killing, what does the dance mean to Momaday? How does he link his participation in it to Kiowa cosmology? What rituals and festivals do you participate in that link you to the natural world?
3. Why is the dance called the gourd dance? What does the eagle symbolize? Explain how the Kiowa attempt to forge direct relationships with the natural environment. What common elements depicting the interaction of human and natural environments in "To the Singing . . . " are also evident in Tayo's experience in Leslie Marmon Silko's "Ceremony" (p. 338) and Chee's in Juanita Platero and Siyowin Miller's "Chee's Daughter" (p. 183)?

Thinking and Writing About Part 3

1. What attitudes toward machines and the natural environment are developed in O'Connor's "A View of the Woods" (p. 226) Gary Snyder's "Front Lines" (p. 307), and John McPhee's "Profiles: Carol Ruckdeschel" (p. 319)? How do these attitudes reflect the notion of mastering the landscape?
2. Take a position of either refuting or supporting the contention that the greatest good for the greatest number is bad for the natural environment.
3. If Rachel Carson's *Silent Spring* (p. 263) appeared today for the first time, how do you think the chemical industry would react? Try to explain why we are so surprised when we learn about some new abuse to the environment and why there always seems to be some interest group that supports the abuse.
4. In what ways does a journey express the notion that human beings are somehow not part of the natural environment? Explain the metaphors for spiritual journey used by Jack Kerouac in "Desolation Peak" (p. 248) and Annie Dillard in "Seeing" (p. 313), and Ernest Hemingway in "Big Two-Hearted River" (p. 127).
5. Do you sometimes find you have become a creature of habit and that by following the same routines you no longer notice the world around you? Try to describe the moment when you realize that you have suddenly seen something new, especially in the natural world. Compare Annie Dillard's "Seeing" (p. 313) with Henry David Thoreau's "Where I Lived, and What I Lived For" (p. 12) and Henry Beston's "Night on the Great Beach" (p. 135). Explain how each text reflects changes in attitudes toward the human and natural environments.
6. Consider whether or not strict controls should be enacted to protect national parks. At what point does protecting the environment overlap harming it?
7. Compare the biblical story of Adam and Eve's expulsion from the Garden of Eden (Genesis 2) with the story of the holocaust in Walter Miller's "Fiat Lux" (p. 259). How does this notion of environmental destruction compare with Leonard Crow Dog's story of recreation in "Remaking the World" (p. 309)? Consider how you would remake the world, if it were possible to start over again.

A train derailment in 1991 resulted in the spillage of 19,000 gallons of toxic weed killer into the Sacramento River in California. Emergency workers tried valiantly to plug the hole, but not before significant damage was done.

4 1976–1993: The Quandary of Achieving Individual and Social Harmony with the Environment

By the mid-1970s, an environmental ethic was growing in strength as assaults on the air, land, and sea increased. Our sensitivities sharpened. The American public learned definitively what had before been assumed: the extent of environmental degradation and the risks to all life. Rachel Carson had warned Americans that chemicals, especially DDT, were killing animals and plants and entering the human food chain. The dangers of nuclear holocaust were growing, and until 1990, it seemed that war between the superpowers might always be a threat. Nuclear threat remains with us, of course, but we are no longer sure where it will surface.

This period saw some Americans becoming angry and scared. They formed grass-roots protest groups in rural and urban areas alike to fight off the encroachment of polluters, whether from an incinerator, a proposed mall, or a highway. They met in kitchens and living rooms, in barns and town halls. The organizations they created came to be known as NIMBY (Not In My Back Yard) groups. The concern of their members focused on themselves, their families, their communities, and government. These groups won admiration for demonstrating the American spirit of standing up for the rights of the individual and not being afraid to fight huge bureaucracies. Activists found sympathizers in the established environmental organizations such as The Sierra Club, National Audubon Society, Defenders of Wildlife, the Wilderness Society, and others. These organizations now burgeoned with new members, who were no longer content to let others lobby for environmental reform and protection.

Some of the small groups learned guerrilla tactics, but their successes were limited. They had neither the organizational skills, the finances, nor the personnel to fight well-planned corporate and industrial development. Some grassroots organizers discovered a spiritual leader in Edward Abbey whose heroes in *The Monkey Wrench Gang* (1975) stopped bulldozers by pouring sugar into their fuel tanks and discussed the merits of cutting down power-line pylons and blowing up dams. Through the rebellious spirit inherent in Abbey's book, the radical environmental group Earth First! found a way to frustrate the cutting of old-growth forests in California—by driving spikes into trunks of trees destined to be logged. Other spontaneously formed grass-roots groups based their tactics on ferreting out legal loopholes, allying themselves with sympathetic politicians, or by practicing surveillance. The Hudson River Fisherman's Association hired a riverkeeper to report environmental abuses on the river and then to file lawsuits to halt and rectify the damage. A hefty settlement from Exxon was one of the organization's first successes following the discovery that Exxon tankers were cleaning their bilges in the lower Hudson River, and then taking on clean river water which was sold on the Caribbean Island of Aruba. Coincidentally, an Exxon supertanker, the *Exxon Valdez*, caused the largest U.S. oil spill in Prince William Sound, Alaska, in 1989.

As informal groups gained ground and respect, their focus and the interest of those watching them shifted from specific issues to broader political and economic considerations. Already in Europe, particularly Germany, so-called green political parties were making headway, gaining elected offices and garnering mainstream media attention. In the United States, the realization that environmental issues were far from locally based came from a variety of directions: from the gradual destruction of eastern forests by pollutants emitted by Midwest factories (acid rain, for example, was killing the hardwood trees in Vermont and New Hampshire, creating dead lakes in New York State, and decimating conifer forests in the Great Smokies); from the foreboding contamination of groundwater by chemicals; and from the ongoing loss of topsoil from the country's heartland due to inappropriate agriculture.

Among those who have raised the level of consciousness for a new environmentalism are the deep ecologists. They advocate a moratorium on developing any wilderness or virgin land, resistance to disturbing natural cycles, and thinking of nature first. They assert that fundamental social change is required to bring civilization into balance with nature, and not the other way around.

Many writers today try to come to grips with the dangers and devastation by airing the consequences. Christopher Hallowell's investigative report (1991) suggests that cancer rates on Cape Cod are linked with contamination of the water supply due to inefficient municipal plumbing, industrial negligence, and military waste. Don DeLillo's "Airborne Toxic Event" from *White Noise* (1984) is a fictional account of an environmental crisis caused by a chemical spill. Some people said such a thing was improbable, but the Three Mile Island nuclear reactor almost melted down (1979). As DeLillo's novel was being published, a Union Carbide plant in Bhopal, India, leaked toxic gas in December 1984, killing over 8,000 people and injuring 150,000. Two years later, a nuclear reactor in Chernobyl, Ukraine, exploded, causing a still unknown number of deaths and cancer cases in northwestern Europe. Anne Rivers Siddons based her novel, *King's Oak* (1990), on the environmental effects of nuclear waste dumping by the U.S. Department of Energy's Savannah River Site on the Georgia-South Carolina border.

The American electorate supported Ronald Reagan's presidency from 1981 to 1989, despite its lackadaisical attitude toward safeguarding the environment. Reagan's administration became known for its attack on environmentalism achieved by reducing funding, appointing industrial and antienvironmental lobbyists to government offices, underselling natural resources, increasing reliance on nuclear power, and discouraging grass-roots activists.

The threat of global environmental disaster galvanized the public and environmentalists to accept that we are passengers on "Spaceship Earth," a phrase coined decades earlier by the designer and visionary Buckminster Fuller (1895–1983). The interconnectedness of environmental degradation became predominant in the minds of many Americans. Rain forest destruction in the tropics, carbon dioxide release due to the consumption of fossil fuels in the Northern Hemisphere, and the release of chlorofluorocarbons everywhere were recognized as contributing to the destruction of the atmosphere and to a heating up of the earth—the greenhouse effect—which, if borne out, would spell economic, environmental, and social chaos. The degradation of the ozone layer in the upper atmosphere permits ultraviolet rays and high-energy radiation into the lower atmosphere. This phenomenon is harmful to all life and increases susceptibility to skin cancer. People are now being warned to take precautions from sun exposure to reduce their risk of skin cancer.

The first widespread publicity about the greenhouse effect appeared in 1988 while the population of the eastern half of the country simmered through the hottest summer on record. Whether or not this heat was a manifestation of global warming is debatable. Long-range documentation is required, but by then it may be too late to remedy the situation. So when the warning flag was hoisted that summer by the specter of melting ice caps and flooded coastlines, national sensitivity to environmental issues was keen. Talk of healing the environment swept the country. Over 80 percent of Americans said they thought pollution was worsening and over 70 percent said taxes should be raised to try to halt it. Mandates to recycle newspapers, plastics, and glass sailed through state and local governments. The automobile industry was pressured to decrease emissions and increase fuel efficiency, which it had resisted, claiming it would mean a loss of jobs. The ongoing protest against clear-cutting of Pacific-Northwest and western forests intensified when the Reagan and Bush administrations argued against federal regulation. In fact, the resurgence of environmentalism was strong enough for presidential candidate George Bush to make a campaign promise in 1988 that he would be the "environmental president." Four years later, Bush was voted out of office partially because he did not deliver on that promise.

The prospect of global warming had symbolic value, too. It was seen by some as the culmination of human distance from the environment and of greed to exploit it. Suddenly the question "Who do we think we are to have fostered such abuse?" surfaced with renewed urgency in developed countries. The term *environmental ethics,* called for by Aldo Leopold in the 1930s, sounded in lecture halls and on college campuses. The environmental crisis had inspired a new forum for thinking about our place in nature.

The fresh perspective inspired analysis. Both Bill McKibben's *The End of Nature* (1989) and Al Gore's *Earth in the Balance* (1992) are efforts to explain what we human beings have done to ourselves and the earth and how we must change our inner selves to regain an equilibrium and sense of unity with the environment. We may achieve harmony through a variety of means. In Ceremony (1977) Leslie Marmon Silko writes about renewing the deep relationship between an alienated Laguna Pueblo Indian and his people's ancient ceremonies, based on subtle rhythms of the land. Voices from the shape and texture of the land inform Wendell Berry's thoughts in *The Unsettling of America* (1977). He says we have imposed alien forms of agriculture on the land, and as a result, we no longer know it, or ourselves. Berry links the environmental crisis to a crisis of American character.

A suggestion of nostalgia prevails in some of the selections here. Being in awe of nature is embedded in Mary Oliver's "The Chance to Love Everything." Rick Bass's *Winter: Notes from Montana* (1991) reminds us that some of our old ways, such as lighting a fire because we like to hear the crackle of burning logs, are deeply lodged in our hearts and may not be worth giving up.

It does seem, though, that a fundamental change has come over us which will direct our future musings and calculations. We have finally realized that we can rearrange the environment to fit our needs only to a certain extent. We are still pioneers in learning those limits. The search to understand individual and social relationships between human beings and the planet is far from over, but it has been raised to a higher level of cognizance.

Yet there remains a quandary between humankind's drive for dominion over Earth and Nature's ultimate dominion over us. Ursula Le Guin's description of the eruption of Mount St. Helens (1980) renews our sense of awe before the imposing forces of nature. We may dominate only within bounds of responsibility, and we may have strayed from knowledge of those limits.

HISTORICAL CHRONOLOGY AND CONTEXT

1976:   Jimmy Carter elected president
United States celebrates the bicentennial of its independence
Viking II lands on Mars
Federal Land Policy and Management Act passed

Whale Conservation and Protective Study Act passed
National Forest Management Act passed

1977: First National Women's Rights Conference convenes
President Carter establishes U.S. Department of Energy
Soil and Water Conservation Act passed
Surface Mining and Reclamation Act passed

1978: Love Canal, New York State—toxic waste leaking into home basements causes neighborhood to be abandoned
Amoco Cadiz runs aground off France, spilling over 8 million gallons of crude oil
Antarctic Conservation Act passed
Endangered American Wilderness Act passed
National Energy Act passed

1979: Three Mile Island, Pennsylvania, nuclear power plant nearly melts down

1980: Comprehensive Environmental Response, Compensation, and Liability (Superfund) Act requires polluters to clean up major contamination sites
Alaskan National Interests Conservation Act passed
Mount St. Helens, Washington, erupts

1981: Ronald Reagan begins his presidency

1982: Coastal Barrier Resources Act passed
Nuclear Waste Policy Act passed

1983: International Environmental Protection Act passed

1986: Chernobyl, Ukraine, nuclear power plant explodes
AIDS reaches epidemic proportions

1987: Reagan and Gorbachev sign an Intermediate Nuclear Forces Reduction Treaty

1989: *Exxon Valdez,* supertanker, strikes a reef in Prince William Sound, Alaska, releasing 11 million gallons of oil
George Bush begins his presidency

1990: 20th anniversary of Earth Day—140 countries celebrate
Gallup Poll finds that 76 percent of Americans call themselves environmentalists

1991: The end of the Cold War; the breakup of the Soviet Union and its empire

1992: U.N. Earth Summit Conference meets in Rio de Janeiro
Bill Clinton elected president
Supertanker *Braer* runs aground in the Hebrides and leaks 26 million gallons of crude oil

1993: President Clinton takes steps to restrict logging in old-growth forests
Moratorium placed on toxic waste incineration

🌺 Leslie Marmon Silko (b. 1948)

Ceremony (1977)

Leslie Marmon Silko, a Pueblo Indian, writes from her heritage. She draws the oral traditions and myths of the past into a complex statement which, in Ceremony, suggests that dwelling on recriminations about white people's past abuses is not going to help Native Americans move forward. What will help heal, however, is adherence to the Pueblo's ancient tradition of ceremonies that bring them closer to the earth and to nature.

Silko was born on the Laguna Pueblo Reservation, New Mexico, to which she returned with her husband and their two sons when she was writing Ceremony. *She had left the reservation earlier to receive her education, which culminated with a bachelor's degree from the University of New Mexico. After teaching English at the University of New Mexico and University of Arizona, she settled into writing full time and now lives in Tucson.*

Silko's first published work was Laguna Woman: Poems *in 1974. That same year she received a grant from the National Endowment for the Arts as well as a poetry award from* The Chicago Review. *Her first widespread recognition came three years later with the publication of* Ceremony. *In that year she was also selected for a MacArthur Foundation Award whose generous stipend allowed her more time to write. In 1981, she published* Storyteller, *a collection of poems and short stories. In 1986, part of the correspondence she conducted with James Wright, the poet, was published as* The Delicacy and Strength of Lace. *Her latest novel is* Almanac of the Dead *(1991).*

Ceremony (1977) was the first novel ever published by a Native American woman. Influenced by N. Scott Momaday's House Made of Dawn *(1969), Ceremony examines the poverty and the effects of cultural decline, but points with pride to Native American traditions and their cultural healing power, which is so closely connected to the land. The plot of the book is about the return of a half-breed, Tayo, to a Navajo reservation after fighting in World War II. Tayo is haunted by demon memories of military violence and his mixed parentage, and attempts to reintegrate himself into reservation life. He meets an older half-breed, Betonie, who is a medicine man. Betonie conducts Tayo through the ritual of the white corn sand painting. Through it, he teaches Tayo the value of living one's life through and focusing on ceremonies that create a unified order linking humans to the cosmos.*

"There are some things I have to tell you," Betonie began softly. "The people nowadays have an idea about the ceremonies. They think the ceremonies must be performed exactly as they have always been done, maybe because one slip-up or mistake and the whole ceremony must be stopped and the sand painting destroyed. That much is true. They think that if a singer tampers with any part of the ritual, great harm can be done, great power unleashed." He was quiet for a while, looking up at the sky through the smoke hole. "That much can be true also. But long ago when the people were given these ceremonies, the changing began, if only in the aging of the yellow gourd rattle or the shrinking of the skin around the eagle's claw, if only in the different voices from generation to generation, singing the chants. You see, in many ways, the ceremonies have always been changing."

Tayo nodded; he looked at the medicine pouches hanging from the ceiling and tried to imagine the objects they contained.

"At one time, the ceremonies as they had been performed were enough for the way the world was then. But after the white people came, elements in this world began to shift; and it became necessary to create new ceremonies. I have made changes in the rituals. The people mistrust this greatly, but only this growth keeps the ceremonies strong.

"She[Betonie's grandmother] taught me this above all else: things which don't shift and grow are dead things. They are things the witchery people want. Witchery works to scare people, to make them fear growth. But it has always been necessary, and more than ever now, it is. Otherwise we won't make it. We won't survive. That's what the witchery is counting on: that we will cling to the ceremonies the way they were, and then their power will triumph, and the people will be no more."

He wanted to believe old Betonie. He wanted to keep the feeling of his words alive inside himself so that he could believe that he might get well. But when the old man left, he was suddenly aware of the old hogan: the red sand floor had been swept unevenly; the boxes were spilling out rags; the trunks were full of the junk and trash an old man saves—notebooks and whisker hairs. The shopping bags were torn, and the weeds and twigs stuck out of rips in the brown paper. The calendars Betonie got for free and the phone books that he picked up in his travels—all of it seemed suddenly so pitiful and small compared to the world he knew the white people had—a world of comfort in the sprawling houses he'd seen in California, a world of plenty in the food he had carried from the officers' mess to dump into garbage cans. The old man's clothes were dirty and old, probably collected like his calendars. The leftover things the whites didn't want. All Betonie owned in the world was in this room. What kind of healing power was in this?

Anger propelled him to his feet; his legs were stiff from sitting for so long. This was where the white people and their promises had left the Indians. All the promises they made to you, Rocky, they weren't any different than the other promises they made.

He walked into the evening air, which was cool and smelled like juniper smoke from the old man's fire. Betonie was sitting by the fire, watching the mutton ribs cook over a grill he had salvaged from the front end of a wrecked car in the dump below. The grill was balanced between two big sandrocks, where the hot coals were banked under the spattering meat. Tayo looked down at the valley, at the lights of the town and the headlights and taillights strung along Highway 66.

"They took almost everything, didn't they?"

The old man looked up from the fire. He shook his head slowly while he turned the meat with a forked stick. "We always come back to that, don't we? It was planned that way. For all the anger and the frustration. And for the guilt too. Indians wake up every morning of their lives to see the land which was stolen, still there, within reach, its theft being flaunted. And the desire is strong to make things right, to take back what was stolen and to stop them from destroying what they have taken. But you see, Tayo, we have done as much fighting as we can with the destroyers and the thieves: as much as we could do and still survive."

Tayo walked over and knelt in front of the ribs roasting over the white coals of the fire.

"Look," Betonie said, pointing east to Mount Taylor towering dark blue with the last twilight. "They only fool themselves when they think it is theirs. The deeds and papers don't mean anything. It is the people who belong to the mountain."

Tayo poked a stick into the coals and watched them lose shape and collapse into white ash. "I wonder sometimes," he said, "because my mother went with white men." He stopped there, unable to say any more. The birth had betrayed his mother and brought shame to the family and to the people.

Old Betonie sat back on his heels and looked off in the distance. "Nothing is that simple," he said, "you don't write off all the white people, just like you don't trust all the Indians." He pointed at the coffeepot in the sand at the edge of the coals, and then at the meat. "You better eat now," he said.

Tayo finished the meat on the mutton ribs and threw the bones to a skinny yellow dog that came out from behind the hogan. Behind the dog a boy about fifteen or sixteen came with an armload of firewood. He knelt by the fire with the kindling; Betonie spoke to him in Navajo and indicated Tayo with a nod of his head.

"This is my helper," he told Tayo. "They call him Shush. That means bear." It was dark, but in the light from the fire Tayo could see there was something strange about the boy, something remote in his eyes, as if he

were on a distant mountaintop alone and the fire and hogan and the
lights of the town below them did not exist.

He was a small child
learning to get around
by himself.
His family went by wagon
into the mountains near
Fluted Rock.

It was Fall and
they were picking piñons.
I guess he just wandered away
trying to follow his brothers and sisters
into the trees.
His aunt thought he was with his mother,
and she thought he was with her sister.

When they tracked him the next day
his tracks went into the canyon
near the place which belonged
to the bears. They went
as far as they could
to the place
where no human
could go beyond,
and his little footprints
were mixed in with bear tracks.

So they sent word for this medicine man
to come. He knew how
to call the child back again.

There wasn't much time.
The medicine man was running, and his
assistants followed behind him.

They all wore bearweed
tied at their wrists and ankles
and around their necks.

He grunted loudly and scratched on the ground in front of him
he kept watching the entrance of the bear cave.
He grunted and made a low growling sound.
Pretty soon the little bears came out
because he was making mother bear sounds.
He grunted and growled a little more
and then the child came out.
He was already walking like his sisters

he was already crawling on the ground.

They couldn't just grab the child
They couldn't simply take him back
because he would be in between forever
and probably he would die.

They had to call him
step by step the medicine man
brought the child back.

So, long time ago
they got him back again
but he wasn't quite the same
after that
not like the other children.

Tayo stood up and moved around the fire uneasily; the boy took some ribs and disappeared again behind the hogan. The old man put some wood on the fire. "You don't have to be afraid of him. Some people act like witchery is responsible for everything that happens, when actually witchery only manipulates a small portion." He pointed in the direction they boy had gone. "Accidents happen, and there's little we can do. But don't be so quick to call something good or bad. There are balances and harmonies always shifting, always necessary to maintain. It is very peaceful with the bears; the people say that's the reason human beings seldom return. It is a matter of transitions, you see; the changing, the becoming must be cared for closely. You would do as much for the seedlings as they become plants in the field."

. . .

They left on horseback before dawn. The old man rode a skinny pinto mare with hip bones and ribs poking against the hide like springs of an old car seat. But she was strong and moved nimbly up the narrow rocky path north of Betonie's hogan. The old man's helper rode a black pony, hunching low over its neck with his face in the mane. Maybe he rode like that for warmth, because it was cold in those foothills before dawn; the night air of the high mountains was chilled by the light of the stars and the shadows of the moon. The brown gelding stumbled with Tayo; he reined it in and walked it more slowly. Behind them in the valley, the highway was a faint dark vein through the yellow sand and red rock. He smelled piñon and sage in the wind that blew across the stony backbone of the ridge. They left the red sandstone and the valley and rode into the lava-rock foothills and pine of the Chuska Mountains.

"We'll have the second night here," Betonie said, indicating a stone hogan set back from the edge of the rimrock.

Tayo stood near the horses, looking down the path over the way they had come. The plateaus and canyons spread out below him like clouds falling into each other past the horizon. The world below was distant and small; it was dwarfed by a sky so blue and vast the clouds were lost in it. Far into the south there were smoky blue ridges of the mountain haze at Zuni. He smoothed his hand over the top of his head and felt the sun. The mountain wind was cool; it smelled like springs hidden deep in mossy black stone. He could see no signs of what had been set loose upon the earth: the highways, the towns, even the fences were gone. This was the highest point on the earth: he could feel it. It had nothing to do with measurements or height. It was a special place. He was smiling. He felt strong. He had to touch his own hand to remember what year it was: thick welted scars from the shattered bottle glass.

His mother-in-law suspected something.
She smelled coyote piss one morning.
She told her daughter.
She figured Coyote was doing this.
She knew her son-in-law was missing.

There was no telling what Coyote had done to him.
Four of them went to track the man.
They tracked him to the place he found deer tracks.
They found the place the deer was arrow-wounded
where the man started chasing it.
Then they found the place where Coyote got him.
Sure enough those coyote tracks went right along there
Right around the marks in the sand where the man lay.

The human tracks went off
toward the mountain
where the man must have crawled.
They followed the tracks to a hard oak tree
where he had spent a night.
From there he had crawled some distance farther
and slept under a scrub oak tree.
Then his tracks went to a piñon tree
and then under the juniper where he slept another night.

The tracks went on and on
but finally they caught up with him
sleeping under the wild rose bush.
"What happened? Are you the one
who left four days ago, my grandchild?"
A coyote whine was the only sound he made.

"Four days ago you left,
are you that one, my grandchild?"
The man tried to speak
but only a coyote sound was heard,
and the tail moved back and forth
sweeping ridges in the sand.
He was suffering from thirst and hunger
he was almost too weak to raise his head.
But he nodded his head "yes."

"This is him all right,
but what can we do to save him?"

They ran to the holy places
they asked what might be done.

"At the summit of Dark Mountain
ask the four old Bear People.
They are the only possible hope
they have the power to restore the mind.
Time and again
it has been done."

Big Fly went to tell them.
The old Bear People said they would come
They said
Prepare hard oak
scrub oak
piñon
juniper and wild rose twigs
Make hoops
tie bundles of weeds into hoops.
Make four bundles
tie them with yucca
spruce mixed with charcoal from burned weeds
snakeweed and gramma grass and rock sage.
Make four bundles.

The rainbows were crossed.
They had been his former means of travel.
Their purpose was
to restore this to him.

They made Pollen Boy right in the center of
the white corn painting.
His eyes were blue pollen
his mouth was blue pollen
his neck was too
There were pinches of blue pollen
at his joints.

He sat in the center of the white corn sand painting. The rainbows crossed were in the painting behind him. Betonie's helper scraped the sand away and buried the bottoms of the hoops in little trenches so that they were standing up and spaced apart, with the hard oak closest to him and the wild rose hoop in front of the door. The old man painted a dark mountain range beside the farthest hoop, the next, closer, he painted blue, and moving toward him, he knelt and made the yellow mountains; and in front of him, Betonie painted the white mountain range.

The helper worked in the shadows beyond the dark mountain range; he worked with the black sand, making bear prints side by side. Along the right side of the bear footprints, the old man painted paw prints in blue, and then yellow, and finally white. They finished it together, with a big rainbow arching wide above all the mountain ranges. Betonie gave him a basket with prayer sticks to hold.

> en-e-e-ya-a-a-a-a!
> en-e-e-ya-a-a-a-a!
> en-e-e-ya-a-a-a-a!
> en-e-e-ya-a-a-a-a!

> In dangerous places you traveled
> in danger you traveled
> to a dangerous place you traveled
> in danger e-hey-ya-ah-na!

> To the place
> where whirling darkness started its journey
> along the edges of the rocks
> along the places of the gentle wind
> along the edges of blue clouds
> along the edges of clear water.

> Whirling darkness came up from the North
> Whirling darkness moved along to the East
> It came along the South
> It arrived in the West
> Whirling darkness spiraled downward
> and it came up in the Middle.

The helper stepped out from the shadows; he was grunting like a bear. He raised his head as if it were heavy for him, and he sniffed the air. He stood up and walked to Tayo; he reached down for the prayer sticks and spoke the words distinctly, pressing the sticks close to his heart. The old man came forward then and cut Tayo across the top of his head; it happened suddenly. He hadn't expected it, but the dark flint was sharp and the cut was short. They both reached for him then; lifting him up by the shoulders, they guided his feet into the bear footprints, and Betonie prayed him through each of the five hoops.

e-hey-yah-ah-na!
e-hey-yah-ah-na
e-hey-yah-ah-na
e-hey-yah-ah-na!
e-hey-yah-ah-na!

Tayo could feel the blood ooze along his scalp; he could feel rivulets in his hair. It moved down his head slowly, onto his face and neck as he stooped through each hoop.

e-hey-yah-ah-na!
e-hey-yah-ah-na!
e-hey-yah-ah-na!
e-hey-yah-ah-na!

At the Dark Mountain
born from the mountain
walked along the mountain
I will bring you through my hoop,
I will bring you back.

Following my footprints
walk home
following my footprints
Come home, happily
return belonging to your home
return to long life and happiness again
return to long life and happiness
e-hey-yah-ah-na!
e-hey-yah-ah-na!
e-hey-yah-ah-na!
e-hey-yah-ah-na!

At the Dark Mountain
born from the mountain
moves his hand along the mountain
I have left the zigzag lightning behind
I have left the straight lightning behind

I have the dew,
a sunray falls from me,
I was born from the mountain
I leave a path of wildflowers
A raindrop falls from me
I'm walking home
I'm walking back to belonging
I'm walking home to happiness
I'm walking back to long life.

When he passed through the last hoop
it wasn't finished
They spun him around sunwise
and he recovered
he stood up
The rainbows returned him to his
home, but it wasn't over.
All kinds of evil were still on him.

From the last hoop they led him through the doorway. It was dark and the sky was bright with stars. The chill touched the blood on his head; his arms and legs were shaking. The helper brought him a blanket; they walked him to the edge of the rimrock, and the medicine man told him to sit down. Behind him he heard the sound of wood and brush being broken into kindling. He smelled a fire. They gave him Indian tea to drink and old Betonie told him to sleep.

He dreamed about the speckled cattle. They had seen him and they were scattering between juniper trees, through tall yellow grass, below the mesas near the dripping spring. Some of them had spotted calves who ran behind them, their bony rumps flashing white and disappearing into the trees. He tried to run after them, but it was no use without a horse. They were gone, running southwest again, toward the high, lone-standing mesa the people called Pa'to'ch.

He woke up and he was shivering. He stood up and the blanket covering him slid to the ground. He wanted to leave that night to find the cattle; there would be no peace until he did. He looked around for Betonie and his helper. The horses had been tied by a big piñon tree, but they were gone now. He felt the top of his head where the cut had been made; it wasn't swollen or hot. It didn't hurt. He stood on the edge of the rimrock and looked down below: the canyons and valleys were thick powdery black; their variations of height and depth were marked by a thinner black color. He remembered the black of the sand paintings on the floor of the hogan; the hills and mountains were the mountains and hills they had painted in sand. He took a deep breath of cold mountain air: there were no boundaries; the world below and the sand paintings inside became the same that night. The mountains from all the directions had been gathered there that night.

He heard someone come up from the west side of the ridge. He turned. Betonie looked even taller in the darkness. He motioned for Tayo to sit down. He sat down next to him and reached into his shirt pocket for the tobacco and wheat papers. He rolled a thin cigarette without looking down at his hands, still gazing up at the east sky. He lit it and took little puffs without inhaling the smoke.

Questions for Thinking and Writing

1. Why does Betonie assert that ceremonies are always changing? What happens if you try to make changes in ceremonies? What relationships can you find between Betonie's sense of ritual and Nick Adams' ritualization of camping and fishing in Ernest Hemingway's "Big Two-Hearted River" (p. 127)?
2. Who do you think the witch people are? Following Betonie's line of reasoning, who do you think the witch people of the environment are?
3. Why must Tayo sit in the center of the white corn sand painting? What is symbolic about painting with sand? Compare this episode with N. Scott Momaday's participation in a ceremony in "To the Singing, to the Drums" (p. 325).

 # Wendell Berry (b. 1934)

The Ecological Crisis as a Crisis of Character (1977)

Wendell Berry is descended from a family that has been farming the land for five generations, beginning with his great-grandfather who settled in Port Royal, Kentucky, in 1803. Berry was born in Henry County, Kentucky, the son of a lawyer who was a small farmer when he was not practicing law. Berry went to the University of Kentucky. He then taught writing at various colleges and universities, including Stanford and New York University. For a year, he lived in France and Italy on a Guggenheim fellowship.

In 1964, he returned to teach at the University of Kentucky and the following year moved with his wife and two children back to Port Royal, a little community on the banks of the Kentucky River. There, he began refurbishing a farm and joined the diminishing population of small farmers, renewing his acquaintance with people he had worked for during his youth. He knew he had come home to stay and that the writing he had begun years earlier would focus on this native community and his deep connection to it.

A poet, novelist, and essayist, Berry has consistently praised the merits of physical labor and working the land. That a man's merit is judged by his ability to be a steward of the land is one of his major themes. Berry has often been compared to William Faulkner (1897—1962) for the development of this theme of a historical relationship with the land through the members of the same farm families. There is also a quality to his writing that links him with the Native American tradition as evidenced by Platero and Miller in"Chee's Daughter" (p. 183).

*Berry is well respected for his firm views on maintaining a spiritual relationship with the land. Edward Abbey and Gary Snyder have praised him, though his opinions are less strident than theirs. The Un-*settling of America *(1977), from which this selection is taken, is a reiteration of Berry's belief that our "ecological crisis is a crisis of character." In a recent interview, he stated that many Americans "think the environment surrounds us. We don't have the idea that we eat it and breathe it and that it passes through our bodies." The "unsettling" of America that Berry refers to is our lack of a sense of place and community. The settlement, he notes, is a history of uprooting families and traditions and moving west. We are still wandering, he feels, alienated from the constancy that land can give us. For his entire adult life, he has exemplified this constancy by writing about the lost tradition of small farms.*

The disease of the modern character is specialization. Looked at from the standpoint of the social *system,* the aim of specialization may seem desirable enough. The aim is to see that the responsibilities of government, law, medicine, engineering, agriculture, education, etc., are given into the hands of the most skilled, best prepared people. The difficulties do not appear until we look at specialization from the opposite standpoint—that of individual persons. We then begin to see the grotesquery—indeed, the impossibility—of an idea of community wholeness that divorces itself from any idea of personal wholeness.

The first, and best known, hazard of the specialist system is that it produces specialists—people who are elaborately and expensively trained *to do one thing.* We get into absurdity very quickly here. There are, for instance, educators who have nothing to teach, communicators who have nothing to say, medical doctors skilled at expensive cures for diseases that they have no skill, and no interest, in preventing. More common, and more damaging, are the inventors, manufacturers, and salesmen of devices who have no concern for the possible effects of those devices. Specialization is thus seen to be a way of institutionalizing, justifying, and paying highly for a calamitous disintegration and scattering-out of the various functions of character: workmanship, care, conscience, responsibility.

Even worse, a system of specialization requires the abdication to specialists of various competences and responsibilities that were once personal and universal. Thus, the average—one is tempted to say, the ideal—American citizen now consigns the problem of food production to agriculturists and "agribusinessmen," the problems of health to doctors and sanitation experts, the problems of education to school teachers and educators, the problems of conservation to conservationists, and so on. This supposedly fortunate citizen is therefore left with only two concerns, making money and entertaining himself. He earns money, typically, as a specialist, working an eight-hour day at a job for the quality or consequences of which somebody else—or, perhaps more typically, nobody else—will be responsible. And not surprisingly, since he can do so little else for himself, he is even unable to entertain himself, for there exists an enormous industry of exorbitantly expensive specialists whose purpose is to entertain him.

The beneficiary of this regime of specialists ought to be the happiest of mortals—or so we are expected to believe. *All* of his vital concerns are in the hands of certified experts. He is a certified expert himself and as such he earns more money in a year than all his great-grandparents put together. Between stints at his job he has nothing to do but mow his lawn with a sit-down lawn mower, or watch other certified experts on television. At suppertime he may eat a tray of ready-prepared food, which he and his wife (also a certified expert) procure at the cost only of money, transportation, and the pushing of a button. For a few minutes between supper and sleep he may catch a glimpse of his children, who since breakfast have been in the care of education experts, basketball or marching-band experts, or perhaps legal experts.

The fact is, however, that this is probably the most unhappy average citizen in the history of the world. He has not the power to provide himself with anything but money, and his money is inflating like a balloon and drifting away, subject to historical circumstances and the power of other people. From morning to night he does not touch anything that he has produced himself, in which he can take pride. For all his leisure and recreation, he feels bad, he looks bad, he is overweight, his health is poor. His air, water, and food are all known to contain poisons. There is a fair chance that he will die of suffocation. He suspects that his love life is not as fulfilling as other people's. He wishes that he had been born sooner, or later. He does not know why his children are the way they are. He does not understand what they say. He does not care much and does not know why he does not care. He does not know what his wife wants or what he wants. Certain advertisements and pictures in magazines make him suspect that he is basically unattractive. He feels that all his possessions are under threat of pillage. He does not know what he would do if he lost his job, if the economy failed, if the utility companies failed, if the police went on strike, if the truckers went on strike, if his wife left him, if his children ran away, if he should be found to be incurably ill. And for these anxieties, of course, he consults certified experts, who in turn consult certified experts about *their* anxieties.

It is rarely considered that this average citizen is anxious because he *ought* to be—because he still has some gumption that he has not yet given up in deference to the experts. He ought to be anxious, because he is helpless. That he is dependent upon so many specialists, the beneficiary of so much expert help, can only mean that he is a captive, a potential victim. If he lives by the competence of so many other people, then he lives also by their indulgence, his own will and his own reasons to live are made subordinate to the mere tolerance of everybody else. He has *one* chance to live what he conceives to be his life: his own small specialty within a delicate, tense, everywhere-strained system of specialties.

From a public point of view, the specialist system is a failure because, though everything is done by an expert, very little is done well. Our typical industrial or professional product is both ingenious and shoddy. The specialist system fails from a personal point of view because a person who can do only one thing can do virtually nothing for himself. In living in the world by his own will and skill, the stupidest peasant or tribesman is more competent than the most intelligent worker or technician or intellectual in a society of specialists.

What happens under the rule of specialization is that, though society becomes more and more intricate, it has less and less structure. It becomes more and more organized, but less and less orderly. The community disintegrates because it loses the necessary understandings, forms, and enactments of the relations among materials and processes, principles and actions, ideals and realities, past and present, present and future, men and women, body and spirit, city and country, civilization and wilderness, growth and decay, life and death—just as the individual character loses the sense of a responsible involvement in these relations. No longer does human life rise from the earth like a pyramid, broadly and considerately founded upon its sources. Now, it scatters itself out in a reckless horizontal sprawl, like a disorderly city whose suburbs and pavements destroy the fields.

The concept of country, homeland, dwelling place becomes simplified as "the environment"—that is, what surrounds us. Once we see our place, our part of the world, as *surrounding* us, we have already made a profound division between it and ourselves. We have given up the understanding—dropped it out of our language and so out of our thought—that we and our country create one another, depend on one another, are literally part of one another; that our land passes in and out of our bodies just as our bodies pass in and out of our land; that as we and our land are part of one another, so all who are living as neighbors here, human and plant and animal, are part of one another, and so cannot possibly flourish alone; that, therefore, our culture must be our response to our place, our culture and our place are images of each other and inseparable from each other, and so neither can be better than the other.

Because by definition they lack any such sense of mutuality or wholeness, our specializations subsist on conflict with one another. The rule is never to cooperate, but rather to follow one's own interest as far as possible. Checks and balances are all applied externally, by opposition, never by self-restraint. Labor, management, the military, the government, etc., never forbear until their excesses arouse enough opposition to *force* them to do so. The good of the whole of Creation, the world and all its creatures together, is never a consideration because it is never thought of; our culture now simply lacks the means for thinking of it.

It is for this reason that none of our basic problems is ever solved. Indeed, it is for this reason that our basic problems are getting worse. The specialists are profiting too well from the symptoms, evidently, to be concerned about cures—just as the myth of imminent cure (by some "breakthrough" of science or technology) is so lucrative and all-justifying as to foreclose any possibility of an interest in prevention. The problems thus become the stock in trade of specialists. The so-called professions survive by endlessly "processing" and talking about problems that they have neither the will nor the competence to solve. The doctor who is interested in disease but not in health is clearly in the same category with the conservationist who invests in the destruction of what he otherwise intends to preserve. They both have the comfort of "job security," but at the cost of ultimate futility.

One of the most troubling characteristics of the specialist mentality is its use of money as a kind of proxy, its willingness to transmute the powers and functions of life into money. "Time is money" is one of its axioms and the source of many evils—among them the waste of both time and money. Akin to the idea that time is money is the concept, less spoken but as commonly assumed, that we may be adequately represented by money. The giving of money has thus become our characteristic virtue.

But to give is not to do. The money is given *in lieu* of action, thought, care, time. And it is no remedy for the fragmentation of character and consciousness that is the consequence of specialization. At the simplest, most practical level, it would be difficult for most of us to give enough in donations to good causes to compensate for, much less remedy, the damage done by the money that is taken from us and used destructively by various agencies of the government and by the corporations that hold us in captive dependence on their products. More important, even if we *could* give enough to overbalance the official and corporate misuse of our money, we would still not solve the problem: the willingness to be represented by money involves a submission to the modern divisions of character and community. The remedy safeguards the disease.

This has become, to some extent at least, an argument against institutional solutions. Such solutions necessarily fail to solve the problems to which they are addressed because, by definition, they cannot consider the real causes. The only real, practical, hope-giving way to remedy the fragmentation that is the disease of the modern spirit is a small and humble way—a way that a government or agency or organization or institution will never think of, though a *person* may think of it: one must begin in one's own life the private solutions that can only *in turn* become public solutions.

If, for instance, one is aware of the abuses and extortions to which one is subjected as a modern consumer, then one may join an organization of consumers to lobby for consumer-protection legislation. But in joining a consumer organization, one defines oneself as a consumer *merely*, and a mere consumer is by definition a dependent, at the mercy of the manufacturer and the salesman. If the organization secures the desired legislation, then the consumer becomes the dependent not only of the manufacturer and salesman, but of the agency that enforces the law, and is at its mercy as well. The law enacted may be a good one, and the enforcers all honest and effective; even so, the consumer will understand that one result of his effort has been to increase the number of people of whom he must beware.

The consumer may proceed to organization and even to legislation by considering only his "rights." And most of the recent talk about consumer protection has had to do with the consumer's rights. Very little indeed has been said about the consumer's responsibilities. It may be that whereas one's rights may be advocated and even "served" by an organization, one's responsibilities cannot. It may be that when one hands one's responsibilities to an organization, one becomes by that divestiture irresponsible. It may be that responsibility is intransigently a personal matter—that a responsibility can be fulfilled or failed, but cannot be got rid of.

If a consumer begins to think and act in consideration of his responsibilities, then he vastly increases his capacities as a person. And he begins to be effective in a different way—a way that is smaller perhaps, and certainly less dramatic, but sounder, and able sooner or later to assume the force of example.

A responsible consumer would be a critical consumer, would refuse to purchase the less good. And he would be a moderate consumer; he would know his needs and would not purchase what he did not need; he would sort among his needs and study to reduce them. These things, of course, have been often said, though in our time they have not been said very loudly and have not been much heeded. In our time the rule among consumers has been to spend money recklessly. People whose govering habit is the relinquishment of power, competence, and responsibilty, and whose characteristic suffering is the anxiety of futility, make excellent spenders. They are the ideal consumers. By inducing in them little panics of boredom, powerlessness, sexual failure, mortality, paranoia, they can be made to buy (or vote for) virtually anything that is "attractively packaged." The advertising industry is founded upon this principle.

What has not been often said, because it did not need to be said until fairly recent times, is that the responsible consumer must also be in some way a producer. Out of his own resources and skills, he must be equal to some of his own needs. The household that prepares its own meals in its own kitchen with some intelligent regard for nutritional value, and thus depends on the grocer only for selected raw materials, exercises an influence on the food industry that reaches from the store all the way back to the seedsman. The household that produces some or all of its own food will have a proportionately greater influence. The household that can provide some of its own pleasures will not be helplessly dependent on the entertainment industry, will influence it by not being helplessly dependent on it, and will not support it thoughtlessly out of boredom.

The responsible consumer thus escapes the limits of his own dissatisfaction. He can choose, and exert the influence of his choosing, because he has given himself choices. He is not confined to the negativity of his complaint. He influences the market by his freedom. This is no specialized act, but an act that is substantial and complex, both practically and morally. By making himself responsibly free, a person changes both his life and his surroundings.

It is possible, then, to perceive a critical difference between responsible consumers and consumers who are merely organized. The responsible consumer slips out of the consumer category altogether. He is a responsible consumer incidentally, almost inadvertently; he is a responsible consumer because he lives a responsible life.

The same distinction is to be perceived between organized conservationists and responsible conservationists. (A responsible consumer *is*, of course, a responsible conservationist.) The conservationists who are merely organized function as specialists who have lost sight of basic connections. Conservation organizations hold stock in exploitive industries because they have no clear perception of, and therefore fail to be responsible for, the connections between what they say and what they do, what they desire and how they live.

The Sierra Club, for instance, defines itself by a slogan which it prints on the flaps of its envelopes. Its aim, according to the slogan, is ". . . to explore, enjoy, and protect the nation's scenic resources . . . " To some extent, the Club's current concerns and attitudes belie this slogan. But there is also a sense in which the slogan defines the limits of organized conservation—some that have been self-imposed, others that are implicit in the nature of organization.

The key word in the slogan is "scenic." As used here, the word is a fossil. It is left over from a time when our comforts and luxuries were accepted simply as the rewards of progress to an ingenious, forward-looking people, when no threat was perceived in urbanization and industrialization, and when conservation was therefore an activity oriented toward vacations. It was "good to get out of the city" for a few weeks or weekends a year, and there was understandable concern that there should remain pleasant places to go. Some of the more adventurous vacationers were even aware of places of unique beauty that would be defaced if they were not set aside and protected. These people were effective in their way and within their limits, and they started the era of wilderness conservation. The results will give us abundant reasons for gratitude as long as we have sense enough to preserve them. But wilderness conservation did little to prepare us either to understand or to oppose the general mayhem of the all-outdoors that the industrial revolution has finally imposed upon us.

Wilderness conservation, we can now see, is specialized conservation. Its specialization is memorialized, in the Sierra Club's slogan, in the word "scenic." A scene is a place "as seen by a viewer." It is a "view." The appreciator of a place perceived as scenic is merely its observer, by implication both different and distant or detached from it. The connoisseur of the scenic has thus placed strict limitations both upon the sort of place he is interested in and upon his relation to it.

But even if the slogan were made to read " . . . to explore, enjoy, and protect the nation's resources . . . ," the most critical concern would still be left out. For while conservationists are exploring, enjoying, and protecting the nation's resources, they are also *using* them. They are drawing their lives from the nation's resources, scenic and unscenic. If the resolve to explore, enjoy, and protect does not create a moral energy that will define and enforce responsible use, then organized conservation will prove ultimately futile. And this, again, will be a failure of character.

Although responsible use may be defined, advocated, and to some extent required by organizations, it cannot be implemented or enacted by them. It cannot be effectively enforced by them. The use of the world is finally a personal matter, and the world can be preserved in health only by the forbearance and care of a multitude of persons. That is, the possibility of the world's health will have to be defined in the characters of persons as clearly and as urgently as the possibility of personal "success" is now so defined. Organizations may promote this sort of forbearance and care, but they cannot provide it.

Questions for Thinking and Writing

1. Explain whether or not you concur with the accuracy and validity of Berry's concept of the average American. Explain whether or not you think that Berry is using hyperbole to make a point. What is this point, and how is it linked to individual and social aspects of environmentalism?

2. How does Berry link the concept of natural ecology with spiritual ecology? Does Berry support his argument with factual citation or personal opinion? Does this weaken his argument or strengthen it (as in his complaint that the Sierra Club's use of the word *scenic* in its slogan represents a failure of character and a triumph of specialization)?

Joan Didion (b. 1934)
Holy Water (1979)

Joan Didion is something of an enigma. Her writing is so diverse and, at times, so personal that both reviewers and readers have felt frustrated by the impossibility of assigning her a slot in American literature. By her own admission, she is an extremely shy person. In a magazine interview she once said, "I don't talk much. I am not articulate. . . . I'm only myself in front of my typewriter."

Born in Sacramento, California, Didion attended the University of California at Berkeley. As a senior, she won a writing contest sponsored by Vogue *magazine, and after graduating in 1956, she moved to New York to work at* Vogue. *In 1963, her first novel,* River Run, *was published. The following year she married the writer John Gregory Dunne and moved back to California. The couple settled in Los Angeles. They have separate careers, but have collaborated on a number of screenplays.*

Following the publication of River Run, *Didion entered a tumultuous period in her life. She feared that she would never be able to write again. "I sat in front of my typewriter, and believed that another subject would never present itself. I believed that I would be forever dry," she recalled in an interview. By exerting enormous self-discipline, she managed to write three stories over the next 15 years, published in 1978 as* Three Stories. *In the interval, she also wrote many magazine articles, collected and published as* White Album *in 1979. The title is taken from a 1968 Beatles record album. Didion found the lyrics "ominous and disturbing," especially so, she said, because they were an apparent inspiration to Charles Manson and his followers in the brutal murder of actress Sharon Tate. Didion saw a symbolic connection between an emotional stress she suffered in the 1960s, Manson's cult, and the country's political and social upheavals. Many of the selections depict her intimate feelings regarding her own breakdown. Others are on the social tumult, student strikes, the Black Panthers, the disparity between wealth and poverty—all representing in her mind a sort of weakening of national tradition. Many of the pieces appear to be a quest to find order in the internal and external chaos she was experiencing. "Holy Water" is part of that search—to discover the order behind the water that is so important to our survival.*

Didion is not known as a writer with a particular interest in the environment. It is worth noting that this essay is inadvertently ecological in the sense that Didion is not advocating conservation or preservation. Yet "Holy Water" is a forceful commentary on human arrogance, both individual and social, in dealing with a crucial element of the environment.

Some of us who live in arid parts of the world think about water with a reverence others might find excessive. The water I will draw tomorrow from my tap in Malibu is today crossing the Mojave Desert from the Colorado River, and I like to think about exactly where that water is. The water I will drink tonight in a restaurant in Hollywood is by now well down the Los Angeles Aqueduct from the Owens River, and I also think about exactly where that water is: I particularly like to imagine it as it cascades down the 45-degree stone steps that aerate Owens water after its airless passage through the mountain pipes and siphons. As it happens my own reverence for water has always taken the form of this constant meditation upon where the water is, of an obsessive interest not in the politics of water but in the waterworks themselves, in the movement of water through aqueducts and siphons and pumps and forebays and afterbays and weirs and drains, in plumbing on the grand scale. I know the data on water projects I will never see. I know the difficulty Kaiser had closing the last two sluiceway gates on the Guri Dam in Venezuela. I keep watch on evaporation behind the Aswan in Egypt. I can put myself to sleep imagining the water dropping a thousand feet into the turbines at Churchill Falls in Labrador. If the Churchill Falls Project fails to materialize, I fall back on waterworks closer at hand: the tailrace at Hoover on the Colorado, the surge tank on the Tehachapi Mountains that receives California Aqueduct water pumped higher than water has ever been pumped before—and finally I replay a morning when I was seventeen years old and caught, in a military surplus life raft, in the construction of the Nimbus Atterbay Dam on the American River near Sacramento. I remember that at the moment it happened I was trying to open a tin of anchovies with capers. I recall the raft spinning into the narrow chute through which the river had been temporarily diverted. I recall being deliriously happy.

I suppose it was partly the memory of that delirium that led me to visit, one summer morning in Sacramento, the Operations Control Center for the California State Water Project. Actually so much water is moved around California by so many different agencies that maybe only the movers themselves know on any given day whose water is where, but to get a general picture it is necessary only to remember that Los Angeles moves some of it, San Francisco moves some of it, the Bureau of Reclamation's Central Valley Project moves some of it and the California State Water Project moves most of the rest of it, moves a vast amount of it, moves more water farther than has ever been moved anywhere. They collect this water up in the granite keeps of the Sierra Nevada and they store roughly a trillion gallons of it behind the Oroville Dam and every morning, down at the Project's headquarters in Sacramento, they decide how much of their water they want to move the next day. They make this morning decision according to supply and demand, which is simple in theory but rather more complicated in practice. In theory each of the Project's five field divisions—the Oroville, the Delta, the San Luis, the San Joaquin and the Southern divisions—places a call to headquarters before nine A.M. and tells the dispatchers how much water is needed by its local water contractors, who have in turn based their morning estimates on orders from growers and other big users. A schedule is made. The gates open and close according to schedule. The water flows south and the deliveries are made.

In practice this requires prodigious coordination, precision, and the best efforts of several human minds and that of a Univac 418. In practice it might be necessary to hold large flows of water for power production, or to flush out encroaching salinity in the Sacramento-San Joaquin Delta, the most ecologically sensitive point on the system. In practice a sudden rain might obviate the need for a delivery when that delivery is already on its way. In practice what is being delivered here is an enormous volume of water, not quarts of milk or spools of thread, and it takes two days to move such a delivery down through Oroville into the Delta, which is the great pooling place for California water and has been for some years alive with electronic sensors and telemetering equipment and men blocking channels and diverting flows and shoveling fish away from the pumps. It takes perhaps another six days to move this same water down the California Aqueduct from the Delta to the Tehachapi and put it over the hill to Southern California. "Putting some over the hill" is what they say around the Project Operations Control Center when they want to indicate that they are pumping Aqueduct water from the floor of the San Joaquin Valley up and over the Tehachapi Mountains. "Pulling it down" is what they say when they want to indicate that they are lowering a water level somewhere in the system. They can put some over the hill by remote control from this room in Sacramento with its Univac and its big board and its flashing lights.

They can pull down a pool in the San Joaquin by remote control from this room in Sacramento with its locked doors and its ringing alarms and its constant print-outs of data from sensors out there in the water itself. From this room in Sacramento the whole system takes on the aspect of a perfect three-billion-dollar hydraulic toy, and in certain ways it is. "LET'S START DRAINING QUAIL AT 12:00" was the 10:51 A.M. entry on the electronically recorded communications log the day I visited the Operations Control Center. "Quail" is a reservoir in Los Angeles County with a gross capacity of 1,636,018,000 gallons. "OK" was the response recorded in the log. I knew at that moment that I had missed the only vocation for which I had any instinctive affinity: I wanted to drain Quail myself.

Not many people I know carry their end of the conversation when I want to talk about water deliveries, even when I stress that these deliveries affect their lives, indirectly, every day. "Indirectly" is not quite enough for most people I know. This morning, however, several people I know were affected not "indirectly" but "directly" by the way the water moves. They had been in New Mexico shooting a picture, one sequence of which required a river deep enough to sink a truck, the kind with a cab and a trailer and fifty or sixty wheels. It so happened that no river near the New Mexico location was running that deep this year. The production was therefore moved today to Needles, California, where the Colorado River normally runs, depending upon releases from Davis Dam, eighteen to twenty-five feet deep. Now. Follow this closely: yesterday we had a freak tropical storm in Southern California, two inches of rain in a normally dry month, and because this rain flooded the fields and provided more irrigation than any grower could possibly want for several days, no water was ordered from Davis Dam.

No orders, no releases.

Supply and demand.

As a result the Colorado was running only seven feet deep past Needles today, Sam Peckinpah's desire for eighteen feet of water in which to sink a truck not being the kind of demand anyone at Davis Dam is geared to meet. The production closed down for the weekend. Shooting will resume Tuesday, providing some grower orders water and the agencies controlling the Colorado release it. Meanwhile many gaffers, best boys, cameramen, assistant directors, script supervisors, stunt drivers, and maybe even Sam Peckinpah are waiting out the weekend in Needles, where it is often 110 degrees at five P.M. and hard to get dinner after eight. This is a California parable, but a true one.

I have always wanted a swimming pool, and never had one. When it became generally known a year or so ago that California was suffering severe drought, many people in water-rich parts of the country seemed obscurely gratified, and made frequent reference to Californians having to brick up their swimming pools. In fact, a swimming pool requires, once it has been filled and the filter has begun its process of cleaning and recirculating the water, virtually no water, but the symbolic content of swimming pools has always been interesting; a pool is misapprehended as a trapping of affluence, real or pretended, and of a kind of hedonistic attention to the body. Actually a pool is, for many of us in the West, a symbol not of affluence but of order, of control over the uncontrollable. A pool is water, made available and useful, and is, as such, infinitely soothing to the western eye.

It is easy to forget that the only natural force over which we have any control out here is water, and that only recently. In my memory California summers were characterized by the coughing in the pipes that meant the well was dry, and California winters by all-night watches on rivers about to crest, by sandbagging, by dynamite on the levees and flooding on the first floor. Even now the place is not all that hospitable to extensive settlement. As I write a fire has been burning out of control for two weeks in the ranges behind the Big Sur coast. Flash floods last night wiped out all major roads into Imperial County. I noticed this morning a hairline crack in a living-room tile from last week's earthquake, a 4.4 I never felt. In the part of California where I now live aridity is the single most prominent feature of the climate, and I am not pleased to see, this year, cactus spreading wild to the sea. There will be days this winter when the humidity will drop to ten, seven, four. Tumbleweed will blow against my house and the sound of the rattlesnake will be duplicated a hundred times a day by dried bougainvillea drifting in my driveway. The apparent ease of California life is an illusion, and those who believe the illusion real live here in only the most temporary way. I know as well as the next person that there is considerable transcendent value in a river running wild and undammed, a river running free over granite, but I have also lived beneath such a river when it was running in flood, and gone, without showers when it was running dry.

"The West begins," Bernard DeVoto wrote, "where the average annual rainfall drops below twenty inches." This is maybe the best definition of the West I have ever read, and it goes a long way toward explaining my own passion for seeing the water under control, but many people I know persist in looking for psychoanalytical implications in this passion. As a matter of fact I have explored, in an amateur way, the more obvious of these implications, and come up with nothing interesting. A certain external reality remains, and resists interpretation. The West begins where the average annual rainfall drops below twenty inches. Water is important to people who do not have it, and the same is true of control. Some fifteen years ago I tore a poem by Karl Shapiro from a magazine and pinned it on my kitchen wall. This fragment of paper is now on the wall of a sixth kitchen, and crumbles a little whenever I touch it, but I keep it there for the last stanza, which has for me the power of a prayer:

> It is raining in California, a straight rain
> Cleaning the heavy oranges on the bough,
> Filling the gardens till the gardens flow,
> Shining the olives, tiling the gleaming tile,
> Waxing the dark camellia leaves more green,
> Flooding the daylong valleys like the Nile.

I thought of those lines almost constantly on the morning in Sacramento when I went to visit the California State Water Project Operations Control Center. If I had wanted to drain Quail at 10:51 that morning, I wanted, by early afternoon, to do a great deal more. I wanted to open and close the Clifton Court Forebay intake gate. I wanted to produce some power down at the San Luis Dam. I wanted to pick a pool at random on the Aqueduct and pull it down and then refill it, watching for the hydraulic jump. I wanted to put some water over the hill and I wanted to shut down all flow from the Aqueduct into the Bureau of Reclamation's Cross Valley Canal, just to see how long it would take somebody over at Reclamation to call up and complain. I stayed as long as I could and watched the system work on the big board with the lighted checkpoints. The Delta salinity report was coming in on one of the teletypes behind me. The Delta tidal report was coming in on another. The earthquake board, which has been desensitized to sound its alarm (a beeping tone for Southern California, a high-pitched tone for the north) only for those earthquakes which register at least 3.0 on the Richter Scale, was silent. I had no further business in this room and yet I wanted to stay the day. I wanted to be the one, that day, who was shining the olives, filling the gardens, and flooding the daylong valleys like the Nile. I want it still.

Questions for Thinking and Writing

1. What does Didion seem to suggest by her notion that she has a reverence for water? Why do you think she titles her essay "Holy Water"?
2. Discuss Didion's suggestion that water is no longer a natural free-flowing commodity in California. Why does Didion stress the public's lack of knowledge about how water gets to the tap or to an irrigation pipe?
3. Can you explain the connection between Didion's "Holy Water" and David Lilienthal's praise of the TVA in "One Valley—and a Thousand" (p. 170)? What does Didion value most, transcendent value or the control of the natural force of water? Do you believe Didion agrees with Lilienthal that water is best when it is humanized?

❦ Ursula K. Le Guin (b. 1929)

A Very Warm Mountain (1980)

Ursula K. Le Guin is a novelist whose milieu is science fiction. She was born in Berkeley, California, the youngest child of the famous anthropologist and authority on Native Americans, Alfred Kroeber, and Theodora Kroeber, an author of children's books.

Le Guin grew up in an intellectual environment where the differences between culture was family conversation. She wrote her first fantasy story when she was 9. "My father studied real cultures and I make them up," she once said. After graduating from Radcliffe College in 1951 where she was elected to Phi Beta Kappa, she received a master's degree from Columbia University in French and Italian Renaissance literature. She then went to France on a Fulbright fellowship where she met and married Charles A. Le Guin, a history professor, and settled in Portland, Oregon.

While she was raising her three children, Le Guin wrote five novels but could not find a publisher. Hoping to find a more welcoming market in science fiction, she wrote The Wizard of Earthsea *(1968) followed by* The Tombs of Atuan *(1971) and* The Farthest Shore *(1972) to make up what has become known as the Earthsea trilogy.* The Farthest Shore *won the National Book Award for children's literature.*

Le Guin has suggested that fantasy and science fiction are very un-American because they defy the Puritan-based work ethic. She takes issue with excessive attention to profit motive and expediency at the expense of the exercise of imagination to make sense of the world. Le Guin's science fiction is serious work and follows in the tradition of J. R. R. Tolkien, C. S. Lewis, and H. G. Wells. Major influences on her fiction are Carl Jung, Taoism, and cultural anthropology. Her major novels include The Left Hand of Darkness *(1969),* The Dispossessed *(1974), and* Malafrena *(1979).*

Le Guin is not well known as a nature writer, but her background as a writer of science fiction, fantasy, and children's stories enriches this personal attempt to deal with a force of nature directly rather than through fiction. In "A Very Warm Mountain," she makes St. Helens into a female of enormous personality and pride. The reader no longer sees the mountain as a culmination of geological events but as a reactive personality whose power is the power and spirit of nature.

An enormous region extending from north-central Washington to northeastern California and including most of Oregon east of the Cascades is covered by basalt lava flows. . . . The unending cliffs of basalt

along the Columbia River. . . . 74 volcanoes in the Portland area. . . . A blanket of pumice that averages about 50 feet thick . . .
                                            —Roadside Geology of Oregon
                                                Alt and Hyndman, 1978.

Everybody takes it personally. Some get mad. Damn stupid mountain went and dumped all that dirty gritty glassy gray ash that flies like flour and lies like cement all over their roofs, roads, and rhododendrons. Now they have to clean it up. And the scientists are a real big help, all they'll say is we don't know, we can't tell, she might dump another load of ash on you just when you've got it all cleaned up. It's an outrage.

Some take it ethically. She lay and watched her forests being cut and her elk being hunted and her lakes being fished and fouled and her ecology being tampered with and the smoky, snarling suburbs creeping closer to her skirts, until she saw it was time to teach the White Man's Children a lesson. And she did. In the process of the lesson, she blew her forests to matchsticks, fried her elk, boiled her fish, wrecked her ecosystem, and did very little damage to the cities; so that the lesson taught to the White Man's Children would seem, at best, equivocal.

But everybody takes it personally. We try to reduce it to human scale. To make a molehill out of the mountain.

Some got very anxious, especially during the dreary white weather that hung around the area after May 18 (the first great eruption, when she blew 1300 feet of her summit all over Washington, Idaho, and points east) and May 25 (the first considerable ashfall in the thickly populated Portland area west of the mountain). Farmers in Washington State who had the real fallout, six inches of ash smothering their crops, answered the reporters' questions with polite stoicism; but in town a lot of people were cross and dull and jumpy. Some erratic behavior, some really weird driving. "Everybody on my bus coming to work these days talks to everybody else, they never used to." "Everybody on my bus coming to work sits there like a stone instead of talking to each other like they used to." Some welcomed the mild sense of urgency and emergency as bringing people together in mutual support. Some—the old, the ill—were terrified beyond reassurance. Psychologists reported that psychotics had promptly incorporated the volcano into their private systems; some thought they were controlling her, and some thought she was controlling them. Businessmen, whom we know from the Dow Jones Reports to be an almost ethereally timid and emotional breed, read the scare stories in Eastern newspapers and cancelled all their conventions here; Portland hotels are having a long cool summer. A Chinese Cultural Attaché, evidently preferring earthquakes, wouldn't come father north than San Francisco. But many natives were irrationally exhilarated, secretly, heartlessly welcoming every steam-blast and earth-tremor: Go it, mountain!

Everybody read in the newspapers everywhere that the May 18 eruption was "five hundred times greater than the bomb dropped on Hiroshima." Some reflected that we have bombs much more than five hundred times more powerful than the 1945 bombs. But these are never mentioned in the comparisons. Perhaps it would upset people in Moscow, Idaho or Missoula, Montana, who got a lot of volcanic ash dumped on them, and don't want to have to think, what if that stuff had been radioactive? It really isn't nice to talk about, is it. I mean, what if something went off in New Jersey, say, and *was* radioactive—Oh, stop it. That volcano's way out west there somewhere anyhow.

Everybody takes it personally.

I had to go into hospital for some surgery in April, while the mountain was in her early phase—she jumped and rumbled, like the Uncles in *A Child's Christmas in Wales,* but she hadn't done anything spectacular. I was hoping she wouldn't perform while I couldn't watch. She obliged and held off for a month. On May 18 I was home, lying around with the cats, with a ringside view: bedroom and study look straight north about forty-five miles to the mountain.

I kept the radio tuned to a good country western station and listened to the reports as they came in, and wrote down some of the things they said. For the first couple of hours there was a lot of confusion and contradiction, but no panic, then or later. Late in the morning a man who had been about twenty miles from the blast described it: "Pumice-balls and mud-balls began falling for about a quarter of an hour, then the stuff got smaller, and by nine it was completely and totally black dark. You couldn't see ten foot in front of you!" He spoke with energy and admiration. Falling mud-balls, what next? The main West Coast artery, I-5, was soon closed because of the mud and wreckage rushing down the Toutle River toward the highway bridges. Walla Walla, 160 miles east, reported in to say their street lights had come on automatically at about ten in the morning. The Spokane-Seattle highway, far to the north, was closed, said an official expressionless voice, "on account of darkness."

At one-thirty that afternoon, I wrote:

It has been warm with a white high haze all morning, since six A.M., when I saw the top of the mountain floating dark against yellow-rose sunrise sky above the haze.

That was, of course, the last time I saw or will ever see that peak.

Now we can see the mountain from the base to near the summit. The mountain itself is whitish in the haze. All morning there has been this long, cobalt-bluish drift to the east from where the summit would be. And about ten o'clock there began to be visible clots, like cottage cheese curds, above the summit. Now the eruption cloud is visible from the summit of the mountain till obscured by a cloud layer at about twice the height of the mountain, i.e., 25–30,000 feet. The eruption cloud is very solid-looking, like sculptured marble, a beautiful blue in the deep relief of baroque curls, sworls, curled-cloud-shapes—darkening towards the top—a wonderful color. One is aware of motion, but (being shaky, and looking through shaky binoculars) I don't actually see the carven-blue-sworl-shapes move. Like the shadow on a sundial. It is enormous. *Forty-five miles away. It is so much bigger than the mountain itself. It is silent, from this distance. Enormous, silent. It looks not like anything earthy, from the earth, but it does not look like anything atmospheric, a natural cloud, either. The blue of it is stormcloud blue but the shapes are far more delicate, complex, and immense than stormcloud shapes, and it has this solid look; a weightiness, like the capital of some unimaginable column—which in a way indeed it is, the pillar of fire being underground.*

At four in the afternoon a reporter said cautiously, "Earthquakes are being felt in the metropolitan area," to which I added, with feeling, "I'll say they are!" I had decided not to panic unless the cats did. Animals are supposed to know about earthquakes, aren't they? I don't know what our cats know; they lay asleep in various restful and decorative poses on the swaying floor and the jiggling bed, and paid no attention to anything except dinner time. I was not allowed to panic.

At four-thirty a meteorologist, explaining the height of that massive, storm-blue pillar of cloud, said charmingly, "You must understand that the mountain is very warm. Warm enough to lift the air over it to 75,000 feet."

And a reporter: "Heavy mud flow on Shoestring Glacier, with continuous lightning." I tried to imagine that scene. I went to the television, and there it was. The radio and television coverage, right through, was splendid. One forgets the joyful courage of reporters and cameramen when there is something worth reporting, a real Watergate, a real volcano.

On the 19th, I wrote down from the radio, "A helicopter picked the logger up while he was sitting on a log surrounded by a mud flow." This rescue was filmed and shown on television: the tiny figure crouching hopeless in the huge abomination of ash and mud. I don't know if this man was one of the loggers who later died in the Emanuel Hospital burn center, or if he survived. They were already beginning to talk about the "killer eruption," as if the mountain had murdered with intent. Taking it personally . . . Of course she killed. Or did they kill themselves? Old Harry who wouldn't leave his lodge and his whiskey and his eighteen cats at Spirit Lake, and quite right too, at eighty-three; and the young cameraman and the young geologist, both up there on the north side on the job of their lives; and the loggers who went back to work because logging was their living; and the tourists who thought a volcano is like Channel Six, if you don't like the show you turn it off, and took their RVs and their kids up past the roadblocks and the reasonable warnings and the weary county sheriffs sick of arguing: they were all there to keep the appointment. Who made the appointment?

A firefighter pilot that day said to the radio interviewer, "We do what the mountain says. It's not ready for us to go in."

On the 21st I wrote:

Last night a long, strange, glowing twilight; but no ash has yet fallen west of the mountain. Today, fine, gray, mild, dense Oregon rain. Yesterday afternoon we could see her vaguely through the glasses. Looking appallingly lessened—short, flat— That is painful. She was so beautiful. She hurled her beauty in dust clear to the Atlantic shore, she made sunsets and sunrises of it, she gave it to the western wind. I hope she erupts magma and begins to build herself again. But I guess she is still unbuilding. The Pres. of the U.S. came today to see her. I wonder if he thinks he is on her level. Of course he could destroy much more than she has destroyed if he took a mind to.

On June 4 I wrote:

Could see her through the glasses for the first time in two weeks or so. It's been dreary white weather with a couple of hours sun in the afternoons.—Not the new summit, yet; that's always in the roil of cloud/plume. But both her long lovely flanks. A good deal of new snow has fallen on her (while we had rain), and her SW face is white, black, and gray, much seamed, in unfamiliar patterns.

"As changeless as the hills—"

Part of the glory of it is being included in an event on the geologic scale. Being enlarged. "I shall lift up mine eyes unto the hills," yes: "whence cometh my help."

In all the Indian legends dug out by newspaper writers for the occasion, the mountain is female. Told in the Dick-and-Jane style considered appropriate for popular reportage of Indian myth, with all the syllables hyphenated, the stories seem even more naive and trivial than myths out of context generally do. But the theme of the mountain as woman—first ugly, then beautiful, but always a woman—is consistent. The mapmaking whites of course named the peak after a man, an Englishman who took his title, Baron St. Helens, from a town in the North Country: but the name is obstinately feminine. The Baron is forgotten, Helen remains. The whites who lived on and near the mountain called it The Lady. Called her The Lady. It seems impossible not to take her personally. In twenty years of living through a window from her I guess I have never really thought of her as "it."

She made weather, like all single peaks. She put on hats of cloud, and took them off again, and tried a different shape, and sent them all skimming off across the sky. She wore veils: around the neck, across the breast: white, silver, silver-gray, gray-blue. Her taste was impeccable. She knew the weathers that became her, and how to wear the snow.

Dr. William Hamilton of Portland State University wrote a lovely piece for the college paper about "volcano anxiety," suggesting that the silver cone of St. Helens had been in human eyes a breast, and saying:

St. Helens' real damage to us is not . . . that we have witnessed a denial of the trustworthiness of God (such denials are our familiar friends). It is the perfection of the mother that has been spoiled, for part of her breast has been removed. Our metaphor has had a mastectomy.

   At some deep level, the eruption of Mt. St. Helens has become a new metaphor for the very opposite of stability—for that greatest of twentieth-century fears—cancer. Our uneasiness may well rest on more elusive levels than dirty windshields.

This comes far closer to home than anything else I've read about the "meaning" of the eruption, and yet for me it doesn't work. Maybe it would work better for men. The trouble is, I never saw St. Helens as a breast. Some mountains, yes: Twin Peaks in San Francisco, of course, and other round, sweet California hills—breasts, bellies, eggs, anything maternal, bounteous, yielding. But St. Helens in my eyes was never part of a woman; she is a woman. And not a mother but a sister.

These emotional perceptions and responses sound quite foolish when written out in rational prose, but the fact is that, to me, the eruption was all mixed up with the woman's movement. It may be silly but there it is; along the same lines, do you know any woman who wasn't rooting for Genuine Risk to take the Triple Crown? Part of my satisfaction and exultation at each eruption was unmistakably feminist solidarity. You men think you're the only ones can make a really nasty mess? You think you got all the firepower, and God's on your side? You think you run things? Watch this, gents. Watch the Lady act like a woman.

For that's what she did. The well-behaved, quiet, pretty, serene, domestic creature peaceably yielding herself to the uses of man all of a sudden said NO. And she spat dirt and smoke and steam. She blackened half her face, in those first March days, like an angry brat. She fouled herself like a mad old harridan. She swore and belched and farted, threatened and shook and swelled, and then she spoke. They heard her voice two hundred miles away. Here I go, she said. I'm doing my thing now. Old Nobodaddy you better JUMP!

Her thing turns out to be more like childbirth than anything else, to my way of thinking. But not on our scale, not in our terms. Why should she speak in our terms or stoop to our scale? Why should she bear any birth that we can recognize? To us it is cataclysm and destruction and deformity. To her—well, for the language for it one must go to the scientists or to the poets. To the geologists, St. Helens is doing exactly what she "ought" to do—playing her part in the great patterns of events perceived by that noble discipline. Geology provides the only time-scale large enough to include the behavior of a volcano without deforming it. Geology, or poetry, which can see a mountain and a cloud as, after all, very similar phenomena. Shelley's cloud can speak for St. Helens:

> I silently laugh
> At my own cenotaph . . .
> And arise, and unbuild it again.

So many mornings waking I have seen her from the window before any other thing: dark against red daybreak, silvery in summer light, faint above river-valley fog. So many times I have watched her at evening, the faintest outline in mist, immense, remote, serene: the center, the central stone. A self across the air, a sister self, a stone. "The stone is at the center," I wrote in a poem about her years ago. But the poem is impertinent. All I can say is impertinent.

When I was writing the first draft of this essay in California, on July 23, she erupted again, sending her plume to 60,000 feet. Yesterday, August 7, as I was typing the words "the 'meaning' of the eruption," I checked out the study window and there it was, the towering blue cloud against the quiet northern sky—the fifth major eruption. How long may her labor be? A year, ten years, ten thousand? We cannot predict what she may or might or will do, now, or next, or for the rest of our lives, or ever. A threat: a terror: a fulfillment. This is what serenity is built on. This unmakes the metaphors. This is beyond us, and we must take it personally. This is the ground we walk on.

Questions for Thinking and Writing

1. Why does Le Guin call a natural occurrence such as this eruption of Mount St. Helens an "outrage"? Is she being ironic when she calls the mountain "stupid"? Can a mountain or any natural object in the environment, such as a river, tree, or rock, be stupid?

2. Can a mountain teach a lesson? If so, in what sense? Does nature set out to do harm or good to humankind? Does nature have a morality, or do we give in to anthropomorphism when we attribute moral values to natural events?

3. Why does Le Guin take pleasure in calling the mountain by the pronoun *she*? Why is Le Guin so tentative about the meaning of the eruption of St. Helens? What is Le Guin suggesting about the usual concept of nature as a nurturing mother?

🌱 Eleanor Perenyi (b. 1918)

Compost (1981)

Eleanor Perenyi was born in Washington, D.C., and has worked as an editor and writer most of her adult life. Her first book was More Was Lost *(1946) followed by* The Bright Sword *(1955). In 1974, she wrote* Liszt: The Artist as Romantic Hero, *which was nominated for a National Book Award. She has also worked as an editor at Harper's magazine and was the managing editor of both* Charm *and* Mademoiselle.

Green Thoughts: A Writer in the Garden (*1981*), from which this selection is exerpted, *was well received by critics, who particularly com-
mented on the fact that the book is not only a practical guide to
gardening but an examination of the role of gardening in our society.
In fact,* Green Thoughts *is a collection of informal essays (pensées) designed to give pleasure. Though Perenyi's tone is friendly and chatty,
she appears to adhere to an iron will about plant culture and the practical art and design of gardens and gardening. Perenyi studied the field
as an amateur, but she gardens with the aplomb of a professional. Her
gardening text is a classic.*

*In her observations about composting, the evolution of an American
attitude can be discerned. Steadfastly concerned with cleanliness,
Americans until recently assumed that leftovers, whether lawn clippings or coffee grounds, were somehow tainted and had to be put out
of sight. The attitude, perhaps, had its beginnings in our Puritan heritage, the drive to dominate the earth, and the belief that nature is in-
domitable and without end. The idea of using refuse for our benefit, to
say nothing of nature's, would play no part in this thinking even though
most farmers are utilitarian and practice recycling.*

*Perenyi's tribute to J. I. Rodale not only takes into account his life
but also his commitment to environmentalism. Implicit is the notion
that renewing the land leads to a renewal of self. Over the past ten
years, the merits of composting espoused by Rodale and Perenyi have
become contagious. No suburban backyard is complete without a compost heap. Part of elementary school curricula includes composting
lunchroom leftovers. Newspapers and magazines run countless articles gloating over the good sense that composting makes, a sure sign
of a new attitude. It seems that we are trying to catch up and recover
all the years of throwing away our good waste.*

When fully 'cooked,' it looks like the blackest, richest soil in the
world—or a devil's food cake. But it isn't soil at all, and in the earlier
stages of decomposition you see, impacted like the layers of an archae-
ological site, what it is made of. This will vary from garden to garden. In
mine, leaves and grass clippings are the chief ingredients—then cabbage stumps, pea vines, hydrangea heads, apples, hedge clippings,
spent annuals, carrot tops, and I am sometimes afraid of coming on the
fragile skeleton of a bird or mouse, though I never have—all the debris,
in short, that the unconverted pay good money to have raked up,
bagged, and carted away to the dump or removed by the garbage men.
The compost heaps devour them all and return them in a form that is
priceless while costing nothing.

You can't buy compost. Neither can a healthy, well-conducted garden
do without it. Even if you can't bring yourself to believe in it as fertilizer
and use it only in conjunction with chemicals, you still can't do without

it, for the very life of the soil itself depends on it. Without the micro-organisms at work in compost, soil would literally be dead. Nature supplies the model in field and forest, whose base is in a perpetual cycle of decay and renewal—a vast program of soil building that a compost heap merely imitates. The process can be speeded up by the addition of animal manures, which will enrich the mixture as well; some materials also 'burn' faster than others; and shredding helps. But sooner or later any pile of organic matter will reduce itself to a rich dark humus that is the finest soil conditioner available. It imparts an incomparable tilth (sections of my flower and vegetable plots can be dug with bare hands), protects plants equally from drought and freezing, is the ideal environment for earthworms. . . . Together with cow manure—fresh when I can get it, dehydrated in 50-pound bags when I can't—seaweed and a little bonemeal, it is also the only fertilizer I have used for thirty years, and the results are impressive if I do say so.

All this has taken time, and faith. When I learned about composting after the war, it was a hobby for cranks, and neighbors refused to believe the heaps didn't attract rats. (They don't.) Today most gardeners have some idea of how to construct them, and composting machines are available—rotating drums said to produce the stuff in fourteen days. There are also shredders to break up branches and heavier materials like corn shucks, which in the ordinary way take years to decompose. Now that 'organic' has become a catch word, composting has even acquired a kind of mythical status. That is nonsense. It is a practice as old as agriculture, and no civilization has survived for long that hasn't found a way to recycle its vegetable and animal wastes.

The Mayas are a case in point. Yearly they burned over their corn-fields, grown in cleared spaces in the jungle, and yearly planted new ones because they had found no other way to enrich the old. When the distance between city and food source became too great, the cities were abandoned—or so goes the most plausible explanation for their swift decline. In Asia, on the other hand, the composting of vegetable, animal and even human wastes (China's famous 'night soil') has been practiced for thousands of years, making it possible to support populations many times greater than those of pre-Columbian America. Composting was, in fact, general throughout the world until the development of chemical fertilizers, which farmers were brought to believe were all that was necessary to replenish the soil. Especially was this true in advanced America, where some old-fashioned gardeners let their trash piles decay in order to acquire humus for a few favored plants but the vast majority relied on chemicals. I certainly did when I planted our wartime victory garden. Clearly though I remembered the smoking piles of straw and manure on our Hungarian estate, I supposed, rightly, that such methods were outmoded in America and knowing nothing of the virtues of mulch allowed the chemicals to be poured on. The family paid handsomely, too, to have the leaves raked up and removed each fall. It pains me now to think of it.

Not until 1945 or thereabouts did I learn that we were guilty of something like original sin. Someone sent me a copy of a magazine called *Organic Gardening & Farming*. It was and is (the *Farming* has since been dropped) an inelegant little publication printed on cheap stock, with photographs strictly of the hand-held Kodak variety and a down-home prose style. It changed my life nevertheless and is the only magazine I have continuously subscribed to for thirty-five years. The editor and publisher was J. I. Rodale, whose bearded countenance glared forth from the editorial page like that of an Old Testament prophet in those days (since his death it has been supplanted by the more benign one of his son), and his message was stamped on every page. Like all great messages, it was simple, and to those of us hearing it for the first time, a blinding revelation. Soil, he told us, isn't a substance to hold up plants in order that they may be fed with artificial fertilizers, and we who treated it as such were violating the cycle of nature. We must give back what we took away. Moreover we must stop using man-made poisons to deal with pests if toxic residues weren't to build up to intolerable heights. By relying on chemicals we were contaminating the food we ate, the air we breathed, the earth and the waters under the earth.

Any instantaneous conversion implies an already existing bias, even if one is unaware of it. To swallow Rodale without question, one had already to be indisposed toward the modern world and to have an instinctive mistrust of scientific progress. It didn't hurt either to have some experience of civilizations older than our own and thus not to feel the misplaced American contempt for the way things are done in 'backward' countries. Anyway, I was obviously prepared to accept him lock, stock and barrel—though this was a good fifteen years before the publication of Rachel Carson's *Silent Spring*, twenty before the banning of DDT, and thirty before the use of defoliants in Vietnam whose atrocious consequences we are hearing about for the first time. No American lake or river had yet been found deadly to wild or human life. No area of the country could then have been called, as parts of northern New Jersey now are, with gallows humor, 'cancer alley.' Rodale didn't just look like a Jeremiah. He was one, and for a long while he suffered the consequences, ridicule being the least, the threat of prosecution the worst. Both the Federal Trade Commission and the American Medical Association gave him trouble at various periods, and the chemical companies would have been glad to see him disappear. But time has been on his side. What they tried to condemn as quackery has too often turned out to be, literally, dead right, and today even the United States Department of Agriculture, for years anything but his friend, is sponsoring projects he pioneered.

This isn't to say that he didn't have in him a vein of nuttiness, which manifested itself in various ways—in crackpot theories about language; in his morality plays about health, which he put on at his own expense at a theater in New York's Bowery; and in a sense of humor that owed not a little to Baron Münchausen. But these, you felt, were the oddities of the self-taught and the self-made. Jerome Irving Rodale was a son of the old New York ghetto and by his own admission was plagued from childhood with its multiple neuroses. Thus the sickly boy became a fitness freak; the undereducated young man, a voracious but indiscriminate reader. He craved success, and achieved it, first as a chartered accountant, then as the manufacturer of electric-wiring devices, finally as a publisher. But the fanatic who would have gone down, guns blazing, in the service of a good cause can never have been far beneath the surface. He wasn't really a businessman, still less an intellectual. He was a visionary, and in 1940 he found his vision.

It came to him in a book called *An Agricultural Testament,* by Sir Albert Howard. Sir Albert had been an agronomist in British government service in India, and is now considered to have been the founder of modern organic farming—which could be described as a hybrid of western science and eastern agricultural wisdom based on poverty. For Sir Albert had what was rare in the early part of this century, a respect for 'native' methods and needs. He noticed, for example, that plant and animal diseases were more prevalent on chemically farmed government lands than on those of Indian peasants too poor to buy artificial fertilizer. On the other hand, the peasants' yields were low in spite of their intelligent rotation of crops, which helped to maintain a surprising degree of fertility. These observations came together in his decision to improve on local methods by devising a way to recycle the nutrients available in plant wastes on the spot. The result was the Indore system of composting, so called after the Indian state where he worked, and the original model for the scientifically layered heap we know. Sir Albert was of course primarily concerned with the economics of poverty in an undeveloped country, but he came to believe that the problems he encountered would soon have a world-wide application. Most important of all, he was convinced that chemical fertilizers, insecticides and drugs were the worst of all possible answers, the result of a dangerously mistaken view that animal, vegetable and human life are separable entities.

All this, which isn't as simple as I have made it, was set forth in *An Agricultural Testament,* and it seems to have sunk without a trace, at least in America, where Rodale may have been its only reader—and how he chanced to come upon it I never found out. He wasn't a farmer or even a gardener, though he had by that time migrated to the small Pennsylvania town where his electrical firm had its headquarters. Nevertheless, as he once told me, 'It hit me like a ton of brick. For the first time, I realized that food affects health, and that chemical fertilizers are dangerous to people, animals and the soil. I realized that our lives wouldn't be complete without a farm. No longer could I eat store-bought vegetables and meat. A powerful impetus surged over us, and within a few weeks my wife and I had become the proud owners of one of the worst pieces of land in the country.'

What followed was the prototype of countless similar stories told and retold in the pages of *Organic Gardening*—a sort of cross between the comic misadventures of S. J. Perelman on *his* Pennsylvania farm and morality tales with a happy ending. (I sometimes wished I could bring the two men together; they had more in common than might have been readily apparent to either.) Everything was wrong: the soil ruined by generations of chemical farmers, the animals sick, even the barn rats crazed from eating sprayed grain. But the Rodales (unlike the Perelmans) persevered and at least had their reward in a beautiful harvest of corn. Rodale has his second epiphany: 'If this was what a couple of amateurs could do, what could experienced soil men accomplish with the organic method? I felt I had to share this experience with the rest of the country. It wouldn't be fair to know this and say nothing about it.' *It wouldn't be fair.* . . . The essence of the man was in that endearing sentence. He had to share everything he knew, or believed, or that had happened to him. Like Freud, he was often his own case history. And so the experienced soil men were found, and the magazine that would expound the theory begun. As it happened, he already owned a small press, so there was no delay, and the first issue of the magazine appeared in 1942.

It was the preliminary trickle of a flood. Books, newsletters, other magazines (*Prevention* is the best known), brochures poured from the Rodale Press as his areas of concern broadened to include food additives, fluoridation, artificial vitamins, plastic, refined sugar, hormones in animal feed and God knows what else. I can't claim to have followed him down all these avenues. My favorites were and still are *Organic Gardening* and *The Encyclopedia of Organic Gardening*, my bible. I don't subscribe to *Prevention,* which is dedicated to health, mostly because I haven't the backbone to follow its precepts. I smoke, drink coffee and alcohol, use refined sugar to make jelly, buy eggs at the store, don't like most health foods, am perfectly aware that commercially raised chickens are death but eat them anyway because no local source supplies organically raised meats. And so on. I'm not a convert Rodale would take much pride in.

But I have been faithful in my fashion and look back on my visit to his farm as one of the more inspiriting events in my life. It happened in the early 1960's after my request for an interview. I had been commissioned to write an article about him, but that was an excuse. I had long wanted to set eyes on him and the farm, which I took to be a latter-day offshoot of those nineteenth-century experiments in living off the land, something like Bronson Alcott's Fruitlands, all unbolted bread and water and vegetarianism but without the metaphysics, and my first sight of Rodale seemed to confirm the impression that he belonged in another century. With his neatly trimmed beard, three-piece city suit and overcoat, he was an incongruously formal figure against the backdrop of rich Pennsylvania farmland. He might have been a visiting preacher, and one looked for the buggy he had just stepped out of. That impression, however, was incorrect. He may have been a visionary but he lived in the present, and he knew how things worked. The farm worked. You could see that at a glance. The compost piles, standing here and there in the fields like huge prehistoric structures, were awesome, obviously the last word in composting technology. The cattle were sleek; the chickens in the chicken houses, organically fed and living over specially designed pits of compost and topsoil, not only looked healthy, their premises were free of the usual chicken-house stink—and the one we had roasted for supper was the nearest thing to a *poulet de Bresse* I have eaten in this country, the breakfast egg the next morning was of a quality I had forgotten. No nonsense here about high thinking and bad food.

Still, it wouldn't have been the farm I was expecting if that had been all there was to it. There had to be a touch or two of fantasy, of magic, and sure enough . . Why, for instance, were the trees in the orchard twined with copper wires like bonsai in training? Why were cans of water buried among the cabbage heads? Well, that was part of an experiment with static electricity, which perhaps has a vivifying effect on plants. We had seen snapshots in the magazine of beans growing under wire and a control crop grown without, and manifestly the wired beans were taller and more productive. So the question was whether metal has the power to attract static electricity, which could then be expected to help the growth of trees and cabbages as well as beans. (This is my memory at least, and I find that as usual it has oversimplified. Electroculture is more fully if to me still bafflingly discussed in *The Encyclopedia of Organic Gardening.*)

Field trials were of course the farm's main business, for not only was Rodale curious to know all there was to know, he had much to prove to skeptics—about the superior food value of organically grown crops, about the non-toxic control of insects, and a lot else. Like his mentor Sir Albert Howard, he had his laboratory in the field and didn't believe in abstract research. That remains true of the Rodale operations, which have been enlarged in recent years. The Organic Gardening and Farming Research Center is now a 300-acre farm some distance from the old place and may not have the same charm (I haven't visited it), though the projects sound just as fascinating. In the last couple of years, for instance, they have been concentrating on the giant amaranth as a possible grain source for home gardens; and as you might expect the amaranth is an ancient food crop grown in remote and romantic parts of the world—Nepal, Mexico, Africa, whence seed has been fetched for trials. Today, the Research Center has 308 varieties of this plant, which is very beautiful, under cultivation. We readers are waiting to see how it all turns out, just as we followed the fortunes of electrocuted beans and are now learning how to construct solar green houses and wood-burning furnaces.

J. I. Rodale died of heart failure in 1971 as he was about to be interviewed by Dick Cavett. I had been worried about this appearance: Would he make a good impression, or come across as a bearded old crank? It was almost as though a member of one's family were suddenly going to be hauled into the spotlight, and one wasn't sure he could cope. Perhaps he wasn't sure either. At any rate, he collapsed. He was seventy-three. Adele Davis's death at a much earlier age caused considerable loss of faith in her theories and there were those who felt that Rodale should have lasted into his high nineties to prove his. Which of course is nonsense. Had he lived otherwise, he might have died much sooner.

Be that as it may, he was a loss. His son Robert, who bears a close physical resemblance to him even to the beard, is an able successor and professionally speaking does a better job than his father did. The magazines are far better edited than they were, and there are fewer detours into sheer zaniness. The younger Rodale is less likely than the old to cast doubt on the movement by his eccentricities, and if called into court would probably make a more convincing witness. But I miss the old boy who first laid it on the line for us all those years ago, who fought the good fight with Jewish jokes and mind-boggling schemes (one I recall was the use of playing cards to illustrate certain points about health)—and I know his son does too. But he has his memorial, a couple of million of them, surely, by now, in the form of all those compost heaps ripening on farms and in gardens where compost heaps never were before, where the very word 'compost' was unknown until he taught us what it meant.

Questions for Thinking and Writing

1. How does compost help improve the soil and nourish plants? How does the composting that humankind does mimic the natural order of growth and decay?
2. Why do you think that Perenyi is so dismissive of the word *organic* when it is used as a catchword? Why does she accept the usage of the word in J. I. Rodale's magazine and philosophy of gardening? Why should someone who advocates using nature be called a visionary?
3. Explain some of the obvious problems that deter urban dwellers from keeping compost piles. On the other hand, what seems to prevent communities and governments from insisting more on composting as a way to recycle waste products?

❧ Don DeLillo (b. 1936)

Airborne Toxic Event (1984)

In "Airborne Toxic Event," an environmental disaster produces a microcosm of comic, if not loony, characters trying their best to carry on and plan for the future while the massive toxic cloud above them takes on a ghoulish personality. The detached characters, their out-of-sync dialogue, the irreverence of bureaucracy, and the fast-moving pace are all typical of DeLillo's writing.

DeLillo was born and raised in the South Bronx, a part of New York City known for its street life, high crime rate, drug use, and violence. Fortunately, he was able to spend some of his childhood and teenage years living in Pennsylvania. He attended Fordham University in the Bronx and after graduating, lived in New York and in Canada. He knew he wanted to be a writer from an early age. His first novel, Americana *(1971), received a number of encouraging reviews, but critics were frustrated by the lack of originality in the loose plot—a young man wandering America in search of himself. They were dazzled, however, and continue to be fascinated by DeLillo's writing, his voice and style.*

DeLillo's other works include Ratner's Star *(1976),* The Day Room: A Play *(1986),* Libra *(1988), for which he won a National Book Award, and* Mao II *(1991).*

In "Airborne Toxic Event," which is exerpted from White Noise *(1984), DeLillo shows characters as "real" people. The pains they take to carry on their normal lives and thoughts in the face of the approaching horror, and the snarled evacuation effort, have the effect of reducing the severity of the toxic cloud. The message here goes far beyond this event; DeLillo implies that environmental disaster has the potential for catching us unawares, so suddenly that the only adjustment possible is to attempt to continue normal life. He suggests that the environment is so taken for granted that one forgets it is there except in times of disaster, natural or industrial. On the issue of culpability, DeLillo, rather slyly, lets the story's events speak for themselves. The reader is left to wonder why this accident happened, and why there seem to be no industrial safeguards and environmental policies.*

With great prescience, DeLillo combines fiction with real life. In this instance, the ecological event had not yet happened. But when it did in 1984, at Bhopal, India, as a result of incompetence at a Union Carbide chemical plant, thousands were killed and many more maimed by toxic gas. In this instance life imitates art, though DeLillo had a model in the events at Three Mile Island, Pennsylvania, where a nuclear power plant nearly melted down in 1979.

After a night of dream-lit snows the air turned clear and still. There was a taut blue quality in the January light, a hardness and confidence. The sound of boots on packed snow, the contrails streaked cleanly in the high sky. Weather was very much the point, although I didn't know it at first.

I turned into our street and walked past men bent over shovels in their driveways, breathing vapor. A squirrel moved along a limb in a flowing motion, a passage so continuous it seemed to be its own physical law, different from the ones we've learned to trust. When I was halfway down the street I saw Heinrich crouched on a small ledge outside our attic window. He wore his camouflage jacket and cap, an outfit with complex meaning for him, at fourteen, struggling to grow and to escape notice simultaneously, his secrets known to us all. He looked east through binoculars.

I went around back to the kitchen. In the entranceway the washer and dryer were vibrating nicely. I could tell from Babette's voice that the person she was talking to on the phone was her father. An impatience mixed with guilt and apprehension. I stood behind her, put my cold hands to her cheeks. A little thing I liked to do. She hung up the phone.

"Why is he on the roof?"

"Heinrich? Something about the train yards," she said. "It was on the radio."

"Shouldn't I get him down?"

"Why?"

"He could fall."

"Don't tell him that."

"Why not?"

"He thinks you underestimate him."

"He's on a ledge," I said. "There must be something I should be doing."

"The more you show concern, the closer he'll go to the edge."

"I know that but I still have to get him down."

"Coax him back in," she said. "Be sensitive and caring. Get him to talk about himself. Don't make sudden movements."

When I got to the attic he was already back inside, standing by the open window, still looking through the glasses. Abandoned possessions were everywhere, oppressive and soul-worrying, creating a weather of their own among the exposed beams and posts, the fiberglass insulation pads.

"What happened?"

"The radio said a tank car derailed. But I don't think it derailed from what I could see. I think it got rammed and something punched a hole in it. There's a lot of smoke and I don't like the looks of it."

"What does it look like?"

He handed me the binoculars and stepped aside. Without climbing onto the ledge I couldn't see the switching yard and the car or cars in question. But the smoke was plainly visible, a heavy black mass hanging in the air beyond the river, more or less shapeless.

"Did you see fire engines?"

"They're all over the place," he said. "But it looks to me like they're not getting too close. It must be pretty toxic or pretty explosive stuff, or both."

"It won't come this way."

"How do you know?"

"It just won't. The point is you shouldn't be standing on icy ledges. It worries Baba."

"You think if you tell me it worries her, I'll feel guilty and not do it. But if you tell me it worries you, I'll do it all the time."

"Shut the window," I told him.

We went down to the kitchen. Steffie was looking through the brightly colored mail for coupons, lotteries and contests. This was the last day of the holiday break for the grade school and high school. Classes on the Hill would resume in a week. I sent Heinrich outside to clear snow from the walk. I watched him stand out there, utterly still, his head turned slightly, a honed awareness in his stance. It took me a while to realize he was listening to the sirens beyond the river.

An hour later he was back in the attic, this time with a radio and highway map. I climbed the narrow stairs, borrowed the glasses and looked again. It was still there, a slightly larger accumulation, a towering mass in fact, maybe a little blacker now.

"The radio calls it a feathery plume," he said. "But it's not a plume."

"What is it?"

"Like a shapeless growing thing. A dark black breathing thing of smoke. Why do they call it a plume?"

"Air time is valuable. They can't go into long tortured descriptions. Have they said what kind of chemical it is?"

"It's called Nyodene Derivative or Nyodene D. It was in a movie we saw in school on toxic wastes. These videotaped rats."

"What does it cause?"

"The movie wasn't sure what it does to humans. Mainly it was rats growing urgent lumps."

"That's what the movie said. What does the radio say?"

"At first they said skin irritation and sweaty palms. But now they say nausea, vomiting, shortness of breath."

"This is human nausea we're talking about. Not rats."

"Not rats," he said.

I gave him the binoculars.

"Well it won't come this way."

"How do you know?" he said.

"I just know. It's perfectly calm and still today. And when there's a wind at this time of year, it blows that way, not this way."

"What if it blows this way?"

"It won't."

"Just this one time."

"It won't. Why should it?"

He paused a beat and said in a flat tone, "They just closed part of the interstate."

"They would want to do that, of course."

"Why?"

"They just would. A sensible precaution. A way to facilitate movement of service vehicles and such. Any number of reasons that have nothing to do with wind or wind direction."

Babette's head appeared at the top of the stairway. She said a neighbor had told her the spill from the tank car was thirty-five thousand gallons. People were being told to stay out of the area. A feathery plume hung over the site. She also said the girls were complaining of sweaty palms.

"There's been a correction," Heinrich told her. "Tell them they ought to be throwing up."

A helicopter flew over, headed in the direction of the accident. The voice on the radio said: "Available for a limited time only with optional megabyte hard disk."

Babette's head sank out of sight. I watched Heinrich tape the road map to two posts. Then I went down to the kitchen to pay some bills, aware of colored spots whirling atomically somewhere to the right and behind me.

Steffie said, "Can you see the feathery plume from the attic window?"

"It's not a plume."

"But will we have to leave our homes?"

"Of course not."

"How do you know?"

"I just know."

"Remember how we couldn't go to school?"

"That was inside. This is outside."

We heard police sirens blowing. I watched Steffie's lips form the sequence: *wow wow wow wow*. She smiled in a certain way when she saw me watching, as though gently startled out of some absent-minded pleasure.

Denise walked in, rubbing her hands on her jeans.

"They're using snow-blowers to blow stuff onto the spill," she said.

"What kind of stuff?"

"I don't know but it's supposed to make the spill harmless, which doesn't explain what they're doing about the actual plume."

"They're keeping it from getting bigger," I said. "When do we eat?"

"I don't know but it if gets any bigger it'll get here with or without a wind."

"It won't get here," I said.

"How do you know?"

"Because it won't."

She looked at her palms and went upstairs. The phone rang. Babette walked into the kitchen and picked it up. She looked at me as she listened. I wrote two checks, periodically glancing up to see if she was still looking at me. She seemed to study my face for the hidden meaning of the message she was receiving. I puckered my lips in a way I knew she disliked.

"That was the Stovers," she said. "They spoke directly with the weather center outside Glassboro. They're not calling it a feathery plume anymore."

"What are they calling it?"

"A black billowing cloud."

"That's a little more accurate, which means they're coming to grips with the thing. Good."

"There's more," she said. "It's expected that some sort of air mass may be moving down from Canada."

"There's always an air mass moving down from Canada."

"That's true," she said. "There's certainly nothing new in that. And since Canada is to the north, if the billowing cloud is blown due south, it will miss us by a comfortable margin."

"When do we eat?" I said.

We heard sirens again, a different set this time, a larger sound— not police, fire, ambulance. They were air-raid sirens, I realized, and they seemed to be blowing in Sawyersville, a small community to the northeast.

Steffie washed her hands at the kitchen sink and went upstairs. Babette started taking things out of the refrigerator. I grabbed her by the inside of the thigh as she passed the table. She squirmed deliciously, a package of frozen corn in her hand.

"Maybe we ought to be more concerned about the billowing cloud," she said. "It's because of the kids we keep saying nothing's going to happen. We don't want to scare them."

"Nothing *is* going to happen."

"I know nothing's going to happen, you know nothing's going to happen. But at some level we ought to think about it anyway, just in case."

"These things happen to poor people who live in exposed areas. Society is set up in such a way that it's the poor and the uneducated who suffer the main impact of natural and man-made disasters. People in low-lying areas get the floods, people in shanties get the hurricanes and tornados. I'm a college professor. Did you ever see a college professor rowing a boat down his own street in one of those TV floods? We live in a neat and pleasant town near a college with a quaint name. These things don't happen in places like Blacksmith."

She was sitting on my lap by now. The checks, bills, contest forms and coupons were scattered across the table.

"Why do you want dinner so early?" she said in a sexy whisper.

"I missed lunch."

"Shall I do some chili-fried chicken?"

"First-rate."

"Where is Wilder?" she said, thick-voiced, as I ran my hands over her breasts, trying with my teeth to undo her bra clip though the blouse.

"I don't know. Maybe Murray stole him."

"I ironed your gown," she said.

"Great, great."

"Did you pay the phone bill?"

"Can't find it."

We were both thick-voiced now. Her arms were crossed over my arms in such a way that I could read the serving suggestions on the box of corn niblets in her left hand.

"Let's think about the billowing cloud. Just a little bit, okay? It could be dangerous."

"Everything in tank cars is dangerous. But the effects are mainly long-range and all we have to do is stay out of the way."

"Let's just be sure to keep it in the back of our mind," she said, getting up to smash an ice tray repeatedly on the rim of the sink, dislodging the cubes in groups of two and three.

I puckered my lips at her. Then I climbed to the attic one more time. Wilder was up there with Heinrich, whose fast glance in my direction contained a certain practiced accusation.

"They're not calling it the feathery plume anymore," he said, not meeting my eyes, as if to spare himself the pain of my embarrassment.

"I already knew that."

"They're calling it the black billowing cloud."

"Good."

"Why is that good?"

"It means they're looking the thing more or less squarely in the eye. They're on top of the situation."

With an air of weary decisiveness, I opened the window, took the binoculars and climbed onto the ledge. I was wearing a heavy sweater and felt comfortable enough in the cold air but made certain to keep my weight tipped against the building, with my son's outstretched hand clutching my belt. I sensed his support for my little mission, even his hopeful conviction that I might be able to add the balanced weight of a mature and considered judgment to his pure observations. This is a parent's task, after all.

I put the glasses to my face and peered through the gathering dark. Beneath the cloud of vaporized chemicals, the scene was one of urgency and operatic chaos. Floodlights swept across the switching yard. Army helicopters hovered at various points, shining additional lights down on the scene. Colored lights from police cruisers crisscrossed these wider beams. The tank car sat solidly on tracks, fumes rising from what appeared to be a hole in one end. The coupling device from a second car had apparently pierced the tank car. Fire engines were deployed at a distance, ambulances and police vans at a greater distance. I could hear sirens, voices calling through bullhorns, a layer of radio static causing small warps in the frosty air. Men raced from one vehicle to another unpacked equipment, carried empty stretchers. Other men in bright yellow Mylex suits and respirator masks moved slowly through the luminous haze, carrying death-measuring instruments. Snow-blowers sprayed a pink substance toward the tank car and the surrounding landscape. This thick mist arched through the air like some grand confection at a concert of patriotic music. The snow-blowers were the type used on airport runways, the police vans were the type to transport riot casualties. Smoke drifted from red beams of light into darkness and then into the breadth of scenic white floods. The men in Mylex suits moved with a lunar caution. Each step was the exercise of some anxiety not provided for by instinct. Fire and explosion were not the inherent dangers here. This death would penetrate, seep into the genes, show itself in bodies not yet born. They moved as if across a swale of moon dust, bulky and wobbling, trapped in the idea of the nature of time.

I crawled back inside with some difficulty.

"What do you think?" he said.

"It's still hanging there. Looks rooted to the spot."

"So you're saying you don't think it'll come this way."

"I can tell by your voice that you know something I don't know."

"Do you think it'll come this way or not?"

"You want me to say it won't come this way in a million years. Then you'll attack with your little fistful of data. Come on, tell me what they said on the radio while I was out there."

"It doesn't cause nausea, vomiting, shortness of breath, like they said before."

"What does it cause?"

"Heart palpitations and a sense of *déjà vu.*"

"*Déjà vu?*"

"It affects the false part of the human memory or whatever. That's not all. They're not calling it the black billowing cloud anymore."

"What are they calling it?"

He looked at me carefully.

"The airborne toxic event."

He spoke these words in a clipped and foreboding manner, syllable by syllable, as if he sensed the threat in state-created terminology. He continued to watch me carefully, searching my face for some reassurance against the possibility of real danger—a reassurance he would immediately reject as phony. A favorite ploy of his.

"These things are not important. The important thing is location. It's there, we're here."

"A large air mass is moving down from Canada," he said evenly.

"I already knew that."

"That doesn't mean it's not important."

"Maybe it is, maybe it isn't. Depends."

"The weather's about to change," he practically cried out to me in a voice charged with the plaintive throb of his special time of life.

"I'm not just a college professor. I'm the head of a department. I don't see myself fleeing an airborne toxic event. That's for people who live in mobile homes out in the scrubby parts of the county, where the fish hatcheries are."

We watched Wilder climb backwards down the attic steps, which were higher than the steps elsewhere in the house. At dinner Denise kept getting up and walking in small stiff rapid strides to the toilet off the hall, a hand clapped to her mouth. We paused in odd moments of chewing or salt-sprinkling to hear her retch incompletely. Heinrich told her she was showing outdated symptoms. She gave him a slit-eyed look. It was a period of looks and glances, teeming interactions, part of the sensory array I ordinarily cherish. Heat, noise, lights, looks, words, gestures, personalities, appliances. A colloquial density that makes family life the one medium of sense knowledge in which an astonishment of heart is routinely contained.

I watched the girls communicate in hooded looks.

"Aren't we eating a little early tonight?" Denise said.

"What do you call early?" her mother said.

Denise looked at Steffie.

"Is it because we want to get it out of the way?" she said.

"Why do we want to get it out of the way?"

"In case something happens," Steffie said.

"What could happen?" Babette said.

The girls looked at each other again, a solemn and lingering exchange that indicated some dark suspicion was being confirmed. Air-raid sirens sounded again, this time so close to us that we were negatively affected, shaken to the point of avoiding each other's eyes as a way of denying that something unusual was going on. The sound came from our own red brick firehouse, sirens that hadn't been tested in a decade or more. They made a noise like some territorial squawk from out of the Mesozoic. A parrot carnivore with a DC-9 wingspan. What a raucousness of brute aggression filled the house, making it seem as though the walls would fly apart. So close to us, so surely upon us. Amazing to think this sonic monster lay hidden nearby for years.

We went on eating, quietly and neatly, reducing the size of our bites, asking politely for things to be passed. We became meticulous and terse, diminished the scope of our movements, buttered our bread in the manner of technicians restoring a fresco. Still the horrific squawk went on. We continued to avoid eye contact, were careful not to clink utensils. I believe there passed among us the sheepish hope that only in this way could we avoid being noticed. It was as though the sirens heralded the presence of some controlling mechanism—a thing we would do well not to provoke with our contentiousness and spilled food.

It wasn't until a second noise became audible in the pulse of the powerful sirens that we thought to effect a pause in our little episode of decorous hysteria. Heinrich ran to the front door and opened it. The night's combined sounds came washing in with a freshness and renewed immediacy. For the first time in minutes we looked at each other, knowing the new sound was an amplified voice but not sure what it was saying. Heinrich returned, walking in an over-deliberate and stylized manner, with elements of stealth. This seemed to mean he was frozen with significance.

"They want us to evacuate," he said, not meeting our eyes.

Babette said, "Did you get the impression they were only making a suggestion or was it a little more mandatory, do you think?"

"It was a fire captain's car with a loudspeaker and it was going pretty fast."

I said, "In other words you didn't have an opportunity to notice the subtle edges of intonation."

"The voice was screaming out."

"Due to the sirens," Babette said helpfully.

"It said something like, 'Evacuate all places of residence. Cloud of deadly chemicals, cloud of deadly chemicals.'"

We sat there over sponge cake and canned peaches.

"I'm sure there's plenty of time," Babette said, "or they would have made a point of telling us to hurry. How fast do air masses move, I wonder."

Steffie read a coupon for Baby Lux, crying softly. This brought Denise to life. She went upstairs to pack some things for all of us. Heinrich raced two steps at a time to the attic for his binoculars, highway map and radio. Babette went to the pantry and began gathering tins and jars with familiar life-enhancing labels.

Steffie helped me clear the table.

Twenty minutes later we were in the car. The voice on the radio said that people in the west end of town were to head for the abandoned Boy Scout camp, where Red Cross volunteers would dispense juice and coffee. People from the east end were to take the parkway to the fourth service area, where they would proceed to a restaurant called the Kung Fu Palace, a multiwing building with pagodas, lily ponds and live deer.

We were among the latecomers in the former group and joined the traffic flow into the main route out of town, a sordid gantlet of used cars, fast food, discount drugs and quad cinemas. As we waited our turn to edge onto the four-lane road we heard the amplified voice above and behind us calling out to darkened homes in a street of sycamores and tall hedges.

"Abandon all domiciles, Now, now. Toxic event, chemical cloud."

The voice grew louder, faded, grew loud again as the vehicle moved in and out of local streets. Toxic event, chemical cloud. When the words became faint, the cadence itself was still discernible, a recurring sequence in the distance. It seems that danger assigns to public voices the responsibility of a rhythm, as if in metrical units there is a coherence we can use to balance whatever senseless and furious event is about to come rushing around our heads.

We made it onto the road as snow began to fall. We had little to say to each other, our minds not yet adjusted to the actuality of things, the absurd fact of evacuation. Mainly we looked at people in other cars, trying to work out from their faces how frightened we should be. Traffic moved at a crawl but we thought the pace would pick up some miles down the road where there is a break in the barrier divide that would enable our westbound flow to utilize all four lanes. The two opposite lanes were empty, which meant police had already halted traffic coming this way. An encouraging sign. What people in an exodus fear most immediately is that those in positions of authority will long since have fled, leaving us in charge of our own chaos.

The snow came more thickly, the traffic moved in fits and starts. There was a life-style sale at a home furnishing mart. Well-lighted men and women stood by the huge window looking out at us and wondering. It made us feel like fools, like tourists doing all the wrong things. Why were they content to shop for furniture while we sat panicky in slowpoke traffic in a snowstorm? They knew something we didn't. In a crisis the true facts are whatever other people say they are. No one's knowledge is less secure than your own.

Air-raid sirens were still sounding in two or more towns. What could those shoppers know that would make them remain behind while a more or less clear path to safety lay before us all? I started pushing buttons on the radio. On a Glassboro station we learned there was new and important information. People already indoors were being asked to stay indoors. We were left to guess the meaning of this. Were the roads impossibly jammed? Was it snowing Nyodene D.?

I kept punching buttons, hoping to find someone with background information. A woman identified as a consumer affairs editor began a discussion of the medical problems that could result from personal contact with the airborne toxic event. Babette and I exchanged a wary glance. She immediately began talking to the girls while I turned the volume down to keep them from learning what they might imagine was in store for them.

"Convulsions, coma, miscarriage," said the well-informed and sprightly voice.

We passed a three-story motel. Every room was lighted, every window filled with people staring out at us. We were a parade of fools, open not only to the effects of chemical fallout but to the scornful judgment of other people. Why weren't they out here, sitting in heavy coats behind windshield wipers in the silent snow? It seemed imperative that we get to the Boy Scout camp, scramble into the main building, seal the doors, huddle on camp beds with our juice and coffee, wait for the all-clear.

Cars began to mount the grassy incline at the edge of the road, creating a third lane of severely tilted traffic. Situated in what had formerly been the righthand lane, we didn't have any choice but to watch these cars pass us at a slightly higher elevation and with a rakish thrust, deviated from the horizontal.

Slowly we approached an overpass, seeing people on foot up there. They carried boxes and suitcases, objects in blankets, a long line of people leaning into the blowing snow. People cradling pets and small children, an old man wearing a blanket over his pajamas, two women shouldering a rolled-up rug. There were people on bicycles, children being pulled on sleds and in wagons. People with supermarket carts, people clad in every kind of bulky outfit, peering out from deep hoods. There was a family wrapped completely in plastic, a single large sheet of transparent polyethylene. They walked beneath their shield in lock step, the man and woman each at one end, three kids between, all of them secondarily wrapped in shimmering rainwear. The whole affair had about it a well-rehearsed and self-satisfied look, as though they'd been waiting for months to strut their stuff. People kept appearing from behind a high rampart and trudging across the overpass, shoulders dusted with snow, hundreds of people moving with a kind of fated determination. A new round of sirens started up. The trudging people did not quicken their pace, did not look down at us or into the night sky for some sign of the wind-driven cloud. They just kept moving across the bridge through patches of snow-raging light. Out in the open, keeping their children near, carrying what they could, they seemed to be part of some ancient destiny, connected in doom and ruin to a whole history of people trekking across wasted landscapes. There was an epic quality about them that made me wonder for the first time at the scope of our predicament.

The radio said: "It's the rainbow hologram that gives this credit card a marketing intrigue."

We moved slowly beneath the overpass, hearing a flurry of automobile horns and the imploring wail of an ambulance stuck in traffic.
Fifty yards ahead the traffic narrowed to one lane and we soon saw why.
One of the cars had skidded off the incline and barreled into a vehicle
in our lane. Horns quacked up and down the line. A helicopter sat just
above us, shining a white beam down on the mass of collapsed metal.
People sat dazed on the grass, being tended to by a pair of bearded para-
medics. Two people were bloody. There was blood on a smashed window. Blood soaked upward through newly fallen snow. Drops of blood
speckled a tan handbag. The scene of injured people, medics, smoking
steel, all washed in a strong and eerie light, took on the eloquence of a
formal composition. We passed silently by, feeling curiously reverent,
even uplifted by the sight of the heaped cars and fallen people.

. . .

I turned off the radio, not to help me think but to keep me from
thinking. Vehicles lurched and skidded. Someone threw a gum wrapper
out a side window and Babette made an indignant speech about in-
considerate people littering the highways and countryside.

"I'll tell you something else that's happened before," Heinrich said.
"We're running out of gas."

The dial quivered on E.

"There's always extra," Babette said.

"How can there be always extra?"

"That's the way the tank is constructed. So you don't run out."

"There can't be *always* extra. If you keep going, you run out."

"You don't keep going forever."

"How do you know when to stop?" he said.

"When you pass a gas station," I told him, and there it was, a deserted and rain-swept plaza with proud pumps standing beneath an array of multicolored banners. I drove in, jumped out of the car, ran
around to the pumps with my head tucked under the raised collar of
my coat. They were not locked, which meant the attendants had fled
suddenly, leaving things intriguingly as they were, like the tools and
pottery of some pueblo civilization, bread in the oven, table set for
three, a mystery to haunt the generations. I seized the hose on the un-
leaded pump. The banners smacked in the wind.

A few minutes later, back on the road, we saw a remarkable and startling sight. It appeared in the sky ahead of us and to the left, prompt-
ing us to lower ourselves in our seats, bend our heads for a clearer view,
exclaim to each other in half finished phrases. It was the black billowing cloud, the airborne toxic event, lighted by the clear beams of seven

army helicopters. They were tracking its windborne movement, keeping it in view. In every car, heads shifted, drivers blew their horns to alert others, faces appeared in side windows, expressions set in tones of outlandish wonderment.

The enormous dark mass moved like some death ship in a Norse legend, escorted across the night by armored creatures with spiral wings. We weren't sure how to react. It was a terrible thing to see, so close, so low, packed with chlorides, benzines, phenols, hydrocarbons, or whatever the precise toxic content. But it was also spectacular, part of the grandness of a sweeping event, like the vivid scene in the switching yard or the people trudging across the snowy overpass with children, food, belongings, a tragic army of the dispossessed. Our fear was accompanied by a sense of awe that bordered on the religious. It is surely possible to be awed by the thing that threatens your life, to see it as a cosmic force, so much larger than yourself, more powerful, created by elemental and willful rhythms. This was a death made in the laboratory, defined and measurable, but we thought of it at the time in a simple and primitive way, as some seasonal perversity of the earth like a flood or tornado, something not subject to control. Our helplessness did not seem compatible with the idea of a man-made event.

In the back seat the kids fought for possession of the binoculars.

The whole thing was amazing. They seemed to be spotlighting the cloud for us as if it were part of a sound-and-light show, a bit of mood-setting mist drifting across a high battlement where a king had been slain. But this was not history we were witnessing. It was some secret festering thing, some dreamed emotion that accompanies the dreamer out of sleep. Flares came swooning from the helicopters, creamy bursts of red and white light. Drivers sounded their horns and children crowded all the windows, faces tilted, pink hands pressed against the glass.

The road curved away from the toxic cloud and traffic moved more freely for a while. At an intersection near the Boy Scout camp, two schoolbuses entered the mainstream traffic, both carrying the insane of Blacksmith. We recognized the drivers, spotted familiar faces in the windows, people we customarily saw sitting on lawn chairs behind the asylum's sparse hedges or walking in ever narrowing circles, with ever increasing speed, like spinning masses in a gyration device. We felt an odd affection for them and a sense of relief that they were being looked after in a diligent and professional manner. It seemed to mean the structure was intact.

We passed a sign for the most photographed barn in America.

It took an hour to funnel traffic into the single-lane approach to the camp. Mylex-suited men waved flashlights and set out Day-Glo pylons, directing us toward the parking lot and onto athletic fields and other open areas. People came out of the woods, some wearing headlamps, some carrying shopping bags, children, pets. We bumped along dirt paths, over ruts and mounds. Near the main buildings we saw a group of men and women carrying clipboards and walkie-talkies, non-Mylex-suited officials, experts in the new science and evacuation. Steffie joined Wilder in fitful sleep. The rain let up. People turned off their headlights, sat uncertainly in their cars. The long strange journey was over. We waited for a sense of satisfaction to reach us, some mood in the air of quiet accomplishment, the well-earned fatigue that promises a still and deep-lying sleep. But people sat in their dark cars staring out at each other through closed windows. Heinrich ate a candy bar. We listened to the sound of his teeth getting stuck in the caramel and glucose mass. Finally a family of five got out of a Datsun Maxima. They wore life jackets and carried flares.

Small crowds collected around certain men. Here were the sources of information and rumor. One person worked in a chemical plant, another had overheard a remark, a third was related to a clerk in a state agency. True, false and other kinds of news radiated through the dormitory from these dense clusters.

It was said that we would be allowed to go home first thing in the morning; that the government was engaged in a cover-up; that a helicopter had entered the toxic cloud and never reappeared; that the dogs had arrived from New Mexico, parachuting into a meadow in a daring night drop; that the town of Farmington would be uninhabitable for forty years.

Remarks existed in a state of permanent flotation. No one thing was either more or less plausible than any other thing. As people jolted out of reality, we were released from the need to distinguish.

Some families chose to sleep in their cars, others were forced to do so because there was no room for them in the seven or eight buildings on the grounds. We were in a large barracks, one of three such buildings at the camp, and with the generator now working we were fairly comfortable. The Red Cross had provided cots, portable heaters, sandwiches and coffee. There were kerosene lamps to supplement the existing overhead lights. Many people had radios, extra food to share with others, blankets, beach chairs, extra clothing. The place was crowded, still quite cold, but the sight of nurses and volunteer workers made us feel the children were safe, and the presence of other stranded souls, young women with infants, old and infirm people, gave us a certain staunchness and will, a selfless bent that was pronounced enough to function as a common identity. This large gray area, dank and bare and lost to history just a couple of hours ago, was an oddly agreeable place right now, filled with an eagerness of community and voice.

Seekers of news moved from one cluster of people to another, tending to linger at the larger groups. In this way I moved slowly through the barracks. There were nine evacuation centers, I learned, including this one and the Kung Fu Palace. Iron City had not been emptied out; nor had most of the other towns in the area. It was said that the governor was on his way from the capitol in an executive helicopter. It would probably set down in a bean field outside a deserted town, allowing the governor to emerge, square-jawed and confident, in a bush jacket, within camera range, for ten or fifteen seconds, as a demonstration of his imperishability.

What a surprise it was to ease my way between people at the outer edges of one of the largest clusters and discover that my own son was at the center of things, speaking in his new-found voice, his tone of enthusiasm for runaway calamity. He was talking about the airborne toxic event in a technical way, although his voice all but sang with prophetic disclosure. He pronounced the name itself, Nyodene Derivative, with an unseemly relish, taking morbid delight in the very sound. People listened attentively to this adolescent boy in a field jacket and cap, with binoculars strapped around his neck and an Instamatic fastened to his belt. No doubt his listeners were influenced by his age. He would be truthful and earnest, serving no special interest; he would have an awareness of the environment; his knowledge of chemistry would be fresh and up-to-date.

I heard him say, "The stuff they sprayed on the big spill at the train yard was probably soda ash. But it was a case of too little too late. My guess is they'll get some crop dusters up in the air at daybreak and bombard the toxic cloud with lots more soda ash, which could break it up and scatter it into a million harmless puffs. Soda ash is the common name for sodium carbonate, which is used in the manufacture of glass, ceramics, detergents and soaps. It's also what they use to make bicarbonate of soda, something a lot of you have probably guzzled after a night on the town."

People moved in closer, impressed by the boy's knowledgeability and wit. It was remarkable to hear him speak so easily to a crowd of strangers. Was he finding himself, learning how to determine his worth from the reactions of others? Was it possible that out of the turmoil and surge of this dreadful event he would learn to make his way in the world?

"What you're probably all wondering is what exactly is this Nyodene D. we keep hearing about? A good question. We studied it in school, we saw movies of rats having convulsions and so on. So, okay, it's basically simple. Nyodene D. is a whole bunch of things thrown together that are byproducts of the manufacture of insecticide. The original stuff kills roaches, the byproducts kill everything left over. A little joke our teacher made."

He snapped his fingers, let his left leg swing a bit.

"In powder form it's colorless, odorless and very dangerous, except no one seems to know exactly what it causes in humans or in the offspring of humans. They tested for years and either they don't know for sure or they know and aren't saying. Some things are too awful to publicize."

He arched his brows and began to twitch comically, his tongue lolling in a corner of his mouth. I was astonished to hear people laugh.

"Once it seeps into the soil, it has a life span of forty years. This is longer than a lot of people. After five years you'll notice various kinds of fungi appearing between your regular windows and storm windows as well as in your clothes and food. After ten years your screens will turn rusty and begin to pit and rot. Siding will warp. There will be glass breakage and trauma to pets. After twenty years you'll probably have to seal yourself in the attic and just wait and see. I guess there's a lesson in all this. Get to know your chemicals."

I didn't want him to see me there. It would make him self-conscious, remind him of his former life as a gloomy and fugitive boy. Let him bloom, if that's what he was doing, in the name of mischance, dread and random disaster. So I slipped away, passing a man who wore snow boots wrapped in plastic, and headed for the far end of the barracks, where we'd earlier made camp.

. . .

At the front of the hall a woman was saying something about exposure to toxic agents. Her small voice was almost lost in the shuffling roar of the barracks, the kind of low-level rumble that humans routinely make in large enclosed places. Denise had put down her reference work and was giving me a hard-eyed look. It was the look she usually saved for her father and his latest loss of foothold.

"What's wrong?" I said to her.

"Didn't you hear what the voice said?"

"Exposure."

"That's right," she said sharply.

"What's that got to do with us?"

"Not us," she said. "You."

"Why me?"

"Aren't you the one who got out of the car to fill the gas tank?"

"Where was the airborne event when I did that?"

"Just ahead of us. Don't you remember? You got back in the car and we went a little ways and then there it was in all those lights."

"You're saying when I got out of the car, the cloud may have been close enough to rain all over me."

"It's not your fault," she said impatiently, "but you were practically right in it for about two and a half minutes."

I made my way up front. Two lines were forming. A to M and N to Z. At the end of each line was a folding table with a microcomputer on it. Technicians milled about, men and women with lapel badges and color-coded armbands. I stood behind the life-jacket-wearing family. They looked bright, happy and well-drilled. The thick orange vests did not seem especially out of place even though we were on more or less dry land, well above sea level, many miles from the nearest ominous body of water. Stark upheavals bring out every sort of quaint aberrationby the very suddenness of their coming. Dashes of color and idiosyncrasy marked the scene from beginning to end.

The lines were not long. When I reached the A-to-M desk, the man seated there typed out data on his keyboard. My name, age, medical history, so on. He was a gaunt young man who seemed suspicious of conversation that strayed outside certain unspecified guidelines. Over the left sleeve of his khaki jacket he wore a green armband bearing the word SIMUVAC.

I related the circumstances of my presumed exposure.

"How long were you out there?"

"Two and a half minutes," I said. "Is that considered long or short?"

"Anything that puts you in contact with actual emissions means we have a situation."

"Why didn't the drifting cloud disperse in all that wind and rain?"

"This is not your everyday cirrus. This is a high-definition event. It is packed with dense concentrations of byproduct. You could almost toss a hook in there and tow it out to sea, which I'm exaggerating to make a point."

"What about people in the car? I had to open the door to get out and get back in."

"There are known degrees of exposure. I'd say their situation is they're minimal risks. It's the two and a half minutes standing right in it that makes me wince. Actual skin and orifice contact. This is Nyodene D. A whole new generation of toxic waste. What we call state of the art. One part per million million can send a rat into a permanent state."

He regarded me with the grimly superior air of a combat veteran. Obviously he didn't think much of people whose complacent and overprotected lives did not allow for encounters with brain-dead rats. I wanted this man on my side. He had access to data. I was prepared to be servile and fawning if it would keep him from dropping casually shattering remarks about my degree of exposure and chances for survival.

"That's quite an armband you've got there. What does SIMUVAC mean? Sounds important."

"Short for simulated evacuation. A new state program they're still battling over funds for."

"But this evacuation isn't simulated. It's real."

"We know that. But we thought we could use it as a model."

"A form of practice? Are you saying you saw a chance to use the real event in order to rehearse the simulation?"

"We took it right into the streets."

"How is it going?" I said.

"The insertion curve isn't as smooth as we would like. There's a probability excess. Plus which we don't have our victims laid out where we'd want them if this was an actual simulation. In other words we're forced to take our victims as we find them. We didn't get a jump on computer traffic. Suddenly it just spilled out, three-dimensionally, all over the landscape. You have to make allowances for the fact that everything we see tonight is real. There's a lot of polishing we still have to do. But that's what this exercise is all about."

"What about the computers? Is that real data you're running through the system or is it just practice stuff?"

"You watch," he said.

He spent a fair amount of time tapping on the keys and then studying coded responses on the data screen—a considerably longer time, it seemed to me, than he'd devoted to the people who'd preceded me in line. In fact I began to feel that others were watching me. I stood with my arms folded, trying to create a picture of an impassive man, someone in line at a hardware store waiting for the girl at the register to ring up his heavy-duty rope. It seemed the only way to neutralize events, to counteract the passage of computerized dots that registered my life and death. Look at no one, reveal nothing, remain still. The genius of the primitive mind is that it can render human helplessness in noble and beautiful ways.

"You're generating big numbers," he said, peering at the screen.

"I was out there only two and a half minutes. That's how many seconds?"

"It's not just you were out there so many seconds. It's your whole data profile. I tapped into your history. I'm getting bracketed numbers with pulsing stars."

"What does that mean?"

"You'd rather not know."

He made a silencing gesture as if something of particular morbid interest was appearing on the screen. I wondered what he meant when he said he'd tapped into my history. Where was it located exactly? Some state or federal agency, some insurance company or credit firm or medical clearinghouse? What history was he referring to? I'd told him some basic things. Height, weight, childhood diseases. What else did he know? Did he know about my wives, my involvement with Hitler, my dreams and fears?

He had a skinny neck and jug-handle ears to go with his starved skull—the innocent prewar look of a rural murderer.

"Am I going to die?"

"Not as such," he said.

"What do you mean?"

"Not in so many words."

"How many words does it take?"

"It's not a question of words. It's a question of years. We'll know more in fifteen years. In the meantime we definitely have a situation."

"What will we know in fifteen years?"

"If you're still alive at the time, we'll know that much more than we do now. Nyodene D. has a life span of thirty years. You'll have made it halfway through."

"I thought it was forty years."

"Forty years in the soil. Thirty years in the human body."

"So, to outlive this substance, I will have to make it into my eighties. Then I can begin to relax."

"Knowing what we know at this time."

"But the general consensus seems to be that we don't know enough at this time to be sure of anything."

"Let me answer like so. If I was a rat I wouldn't want to be anywhere within a two hundred mile radius of the airborne event."

"What if you were a human?"

He looked at me carefully. I stood with my arms folded, staring over his head toward the front door of the barracks. To look at him would be to declare my vulnerability.

"I wouldn't worry about what I can't see or feel," he said. "I'd go ahead and live my life. Get married, settle down, have kids. There's no reason you can't do these things, knowing what we know."

"But you said we have a situation."

"I didn't say it. The computer did. The whole system says it. It's what we call a massive data-base tally. Gladney, J. A. K. I punch in the name, the substance, the exposure time and then I tap into your computer history. Your genetics, your personals, your medicals, your psychologicals, your police-and-hospitals. It comes back pulsing stars. This doesn't mean anything is going to happen to you as such, at least not today or tomorrow. It just means you are the sum total of your data. No man escapes that."

"And this massive so-called tally is not a simulation despite that armband you're wearing. It is real."

"It is real," he said.

I stood absolutely still. If they thought I was already dead, they might be inclined to leave me alone. I think I felt as I would if a doctor had held an X-ray to the light showing a star-shaped hole at the center of one of my vital organs. Death has entered. It is inside you. You are said to be dying and yet are separate from the dying, can ponder it at your leisure, literally see on the X-ray photograph or computer screen the horrible alien logic of it all. It is when death is rendered graphically, is televised so to speak, that you sense an eerie separation between your condition and yourself. A network of symbols has been introduced, an entire awesome technology wrested from the gods. It makes you feel like a stranger in your own dying. . . .

Questions for Thinking and Writing

1. In the face of disaster why does Jack, the father, express the unfounded optimism of a parent? How does Babette, the mother, react? Suppose you were in a situation such as the one described here. Can you guess how your own feelings of impending doom might cause you to act? Might you act like Heinrich (the teenage son), Denise and Steffie (preteens), or Wilder (a toddler)?
2. Discuss why the family looks on the black cloud with a sense of awe bordering on the religious. What differentiates this sensibility to those described by the naturalists or natural observers?
3. Explain the irony of the family's passing by the sign advertising "the most photographed barn in America." How does this statement give you insight into DeLillo's point of view?

❧ Mary Oliver (b. 1935)

The Chance to Love Everything (1986)

Mary Oliver observes nature with simple precision and creates her poetry by employing images that have a reassuring sense of familiarity about them. Like Robert Frost, many of her poems include an inner querying of the connection between humanity and nature. She asks readers to look at nature with her and at the same time to look at themselves. Nature is a kind of religion to Oliver, which she worships in order to help secure her inner being. In a poem entitled "The Fawn" she writes, "Sunday morning and mellow as precious metal / the church bells rang, but I went / to the woods instead." Yet there is nothing entirely comprehensible about nature despite its obvious joys; rather, it has a mysterious side, perhaps "the dark heart of the story" in "The Chance to Love Everything."

Oliver was born in Cleveland, Ohio, the daughter of a teacher. She attended Ohio State University for one year before transferring to Vassar where she studied for another year. She then moved to Provincetown, Massachusetts, to live year round, joining the bohemian life of that artistic community. Her first collection of published poems was No Voyage and Other Poems (1965), which established her as a "nature poet." Since then, she has published a handful of other volumes culminating in 1986 with Dream Work, for which she received a Pulitzer Prize.

Most of Oliver's poems are set in the heartland, rural America. Many touch on our residual attraction to nature and our turning away from it. They strive to discover the meaning of nature in our lives through the themes of birth, death, decay, and dreams. Her images are of fleeting glimpses of animals, rich earth, dense forests, and humans trying to come to terms with loneliness and an inevitable sense of mortality.

"The Chance to Love Everything," from Dream Work *(1986), tells about spending a summer night in a tent. The night is pleasurable, but then the speaker is momentarily frightened. Quickly recovering her composure, she reaches out to the animal that made the sound, remembering that though she might be harmed, this is her chance to love everything.*

All summer I made friends
with the creatures nearby—
they flowed through the fields
and under the tent walls,
or padded through the door,
grinning through their many teeth,
looking for seeds,
suet, sugar; muttering and humming,
opening the breadbox, happiest when
there was milk and music. But once
in the night I heard a sound
outside the door, the canvas
bulged slightly—something
was pressing inward at eye level.
I watched, trembling, sure I had heard
the click of claws, the smack of lips
outside my gauzy house—
I imagined the red eyes,
the broad tongue, the enormous lap.
Would it be friendly too?
Fear defeated me. And yet,
not in faith and not in madness
but with the courage I thought
my dream deserved,
I stepped outside. It was gone.
Then I whirled at the sound of some
shambling tonnage.
Did I see a black haunch slipping
back through the trees? Did I see
the moonlight shining on it?
Did I actually reach out my arms
toward it, toward paradise falling, like

the fading of the dearest, wildest hope—
the dark heart of the story that is all
the reason for its telling?

Questions for Thinking and Writing

1. Discuss whether or not a human can really be in nature. Is there some gulf
   that separates humans from wilderness?
2. Why does the speaker say that the night she looks out on is "paradise
   falling," and what is "the dark heart of the story"? Does the speaker of this
   poem achieve the same transcendent experience as the couple who stare at
   the deer in Robert Frost's "Two Look at Two" (p. 124)?

🌿 Bill McKibben (b. 1961)

A New Atmosphere (1989)

When The End of Nature *first appeared, critics and environmentalists were struck by the simplicity and stark implications of the title. It
suggested a level to the environmental crisis that had not been previously explored. Alarm prevailed. Has it really gone this far? How could
there be no more nature? And if nature was no longer to exist, where
did that put human beings?*

McKibben wrote The End of Nature, *in which "A New Atmosphere"
appears, with a journalist's inquisitiveness, but he chose his subject for
personal reasons. His driving philosophy, he once said in answer to a
question, is that "environmental sanity and personal satisfaction lie in
the same direction." It is a philosophy that appears and reappears
throughout the book: There is no longer any escape from human influence, and while it is not always environmentally detrimental, it usually is. Harmful or not, constant human presence changes the way we
look at nature, removing its timelessness and independence. We are
now getting to the point, McKibben suggests, where nature and humankind cannot be thought of separately. We have come to dominate
nature in a different way than the early settlers did or even the manufacturers of pesticides. Our domination, he says, has taken over the
inner workings of nature. In believing this, McKibben allies himself
with Henry David Thoreau and John Muir and contrasts sharply with
Frederick Law Olmsted and Gifford Pinchot.*

*McKibben was born in California and now lives in the Adirondacks
in New York with his wife and dog. He says that he is an avid hiker*

and cross country skier there as well as a Sunday School teacher in a
Methodist church and the treasurer of a local fire department.

After graduating from Harvard in 1982, McKibben became a staff
writer for the New Yorker *where he wrote over 400 articles. In 1987,*
he became a free-lancer, writing for the New York Review of Books,
Rolling Stone, *and* The New Republic. The End of Nature *was his first*
book. It has been translated into 16 languages. The Age of Missing Information *(1992) is about the influence of television on American self-*
perception and historical outlook.

Though The End of Nature *(1989) has a wistful sense of loss to it be-*
cause human influence over nature is all-pervasive, it also suggests
that our best bet to reorient ourselves toward nature is to change our
value system. In this, McKibben shares some thoughts with Wendell
Berry (p. 348) and Al Gore (p. 452). Like Gore, McKibben sets our re-
lationship to nature in the context of global warming, a much larger,
albeit scientifically unproven, arena.

Nature, we believe, takes forever. It moves with infinite slowness
through the many periods of its history, whose names we dimly recall
from high school biology—the Devonian, the Triassic, the Cretaceous,
the Pleistocene. Ever since Darwin, nature writers have taken pains to
stress the incomprehensible length of this path. "So slowly, oh, so slowly
have the great changes been brought about," wrote John Burroughs at
the turn of the century. "The Orientals try to get a hint of eternity by
saying that when the Himalayas have been ground to powder by allowing a gauze veil to float against them once in a thousand years, eternity
will only just have begun. Our mountains have been pulverized by a
process almost as slow." We have been told that man's tenure is as a
minute to the earth's day, but it is that vast day which has lodged in our
minds. The age of the trilobites began some 600 million years ago. The
dinosaurs lived for nearly 140 million years. Since even a million years
is utterly unfathomable, the message is: Nothing happens quickly.
Change takes unimaginable—"geologic"—time.

This idea about time is essentially mistaken. Muddled though they
are scientifically, the creationists, believing in the sudden appearance
of the earth some seven thousand years ago, may intuitively understand
more about the progress of time than the rest of us. For the world as we
know it—that is, the world with human beings formed into some sort of
civilization, the world in which North America, Europe, and much of
the rest of the planet are warm enough to support large human populations—is of quite comprehensible duration. People began to collect
in a rudimentary society in the north of Mesopotamia some ten or
twelve thousand years ago. Using thirty years as a generation, that is
three hundred and thirty to four hundred generations ago. Sitting here
at my desk, I can think back five generations in my family—I have seen

photos of four. That is, I can think back nearly one-sixtieth of the way to the start of civilization. A skilled genealogist might get me one-thirtieth of the distance back. And I can conceive of how most of those forebears lived. From the work of archaeologists and from accounts like those in the Bible I have some sense of daily life at least as far back as the time of the pharaohs, which is more than a third of the way. Two hundred and sixty-five generations ago Jericho was a walled city of three thousand souls. Two hundred and sixty-five is a large number, but not in the way that six hundred million is a large number—not inscrutably large.

Or look at it this way: There are plants on this earth as old as civilization. Not species—individual plants. The General Sherman tree in California's Sequoia National Park may be a third as old, about four thousand years. Certain Antarctic lichens date back ten thousand years. A specific creosote plant in the Southwestern desert was estimated recently to be 11,700 years of age.

And within that ten or twelve thousand years of civilization, of course, time is not uniform. The world as we really know it dates back perhaps to the Renaissance. The world as we really, *really* know it dates back to the Industrial Revolution. The world we actually feel comfortable in dates back to perhaps 1945. It was not until after World War II, for instance, that plastics came into widespread use.

In other words, our reassuring sense of a timeless future, which is drawn from that apparently bottomless well of the past, is a delusion. True, evolution, grinding on ever so slowly, has taken billions of years to create us from slime, but that does not mean that time always moves so ponderously. Events, enormous events, can happen quickly. We've known this to be true since Hiroshima, of course, but I don't mean *that* quickly. I mean that over a year or a decade or a lifetime big and impersonal and dramatic changes can take place. We're now comfortable with the bizarre idea that continents can drift over eons, or that continents can die in an atomic second; even so, normal time seems to us immune from such huge changes. It isn't, though. In the last three decades, for example, the amount of carbon dioxide in the atmosphere has increased more than 10 percent, from about 315 to more than 350 parts per million. In the last decade, an immense "hole" in the ozone layer has opened above the South Pole. In the last half-decade, the percentage of West German forests damaged by acid rain has risen from less than 10 to more than 50. According to the Worldwatch Institute, in 1988—for perhaps the first time since that starved Pilgrim winter at Plymouth—America ate more food than it grew. Burroughs again: "One summer day, while I was walking along the country road on the farm where I was born, a section of the stone wall opposite me, and not more than three or four yards distant, suddenly fell down. Amid the general stillness and immobility about me the effect was quite startling. . . . It was the sudden summing up of half a century or more of atomic changes in the material of the wall. A grain or two of sand yielded to the pressure of long years, and gravity did the rest."

In much the same comforting way that we think of time as imponderably long, we consider the earth to be inconceivably large. Although with the advent of space flight it became fashionable to picture the planet as a small orb of life and light in a dark, cold vastness, that image never really sank in. To any one of us, the earth *is* enormous, "infinite to our senses." Or, at least, it is if we think about it in the usual horizontal dimensions: even the frequent flier with the most bonus miles has seen only a tiny fraction of the earth's terrain; even the most intrepid mariner cuts a single furrow across the ocean field. There are vast spaces between my house, in the Adirondack Mountains of upstate New York, and Manhattan—it's a five-hour drive through one state in one country of one continent. But from my house to the post office at the end of the road is a trip of six and a half miles. On a bicycle it takes about twenty-five minutes, in a car eight or nine. I've walked it in an hour and a half. If you turned that trip on its end, the twenty-five-minute pedal past Bateman's sandpit and the graveyard and the waterfall and Allen Hill would take me a mile beyond the height of Mt. Everest, past the point where the air is too thin to breathe without artificial assistance. Into that tight space, and the layer of ozone just above it, is crammed all that is life and all that maintains life.

This, I realize, is a far from novel observation. I repeat it only to make the same case I made with regard to time. The world is not so large as we intuitively believe—space can be as short as time. For instance, the average American car driven the average American distance—ten thousand miles—in an average American year releases its own weight in carbon into the atmosphere. Imagine each car on a busy freeway pumping a ton of carbon into the atmosphere, and the sky seems less infinitely blue.

Along with our optimistic perceptions of time and space, some comparatively minor misunderstandings distort our sense of the world. Consider the American failure to convert to the metric system. Like all schoolchildren of my vintage, I spent many days listening to teachers explain liters and meters and hectares and all the other logical units of measurement, and promptly forgot it all. We all did, except those of us who became scientists, who always use such units. As a result, if I read that there will be an 0.8-degree Celsius rise in the temperature between now and the year 2000, it sounds less ominous than a degree and a half Fahrenheit. Similarly, a ninety-centimeter rise in sea level sounds less ominous than a one-yard rise; and neither of them sounds so ominous until one stops to think that over a beach with a normal slope such a rise would bring the ocean ninety meters (that's 295 feet) above its current tide-line. In somewhat the same way, the logarithmic scale that we use to determine the overall composition of our soils or waters—pH—distorts reality like a fun-house mirror for anyone who doesn't use it on a daily basis. For instance, "normal" rainwater has a pH of 5.6. But the acidified rain that falls on the Adirondacks has a pH between 4.6 and 4.2—that is, it is ten to forty times as acid.

Of all such quirks, though, the most ephemeral may be the most significant. It is an accident of the calendar: we live too close to the year 2000. Forever we have read about the year 2000. It has become a symbol of the bright and distant future, when we will ride in air cars and talk on video phones. The year 2010 still sounds far off, almost unreachably far off, as though it were on the other side of a great body of water. If someone says to me that a very bad thing will happen in 2010, I may feign concern but subconsciously I file it away. So it always shocks me when I realize that 2010 is almost as close as 1970—closer than the breakup of the Beatles—and that the turn of the century is no further in front of us than Ronald Reagan's election to the presidency is behind. We live in the shadow of a number, and that makes it hard for us to see the future.

Our comforting sense of the permanence of our natural world, our confidence that it will change gradually and imperceptibly if at all, is, then, the result of a subtly warped perspective. Changes that can affect us can happen in our lifetime in our world—not just changes like wars but bigger and more sweeping events. I believe that without recognizing it we have already stepped over the threshold of such a change: that we are at the end of nature.

By the end of nature I do not mean the end of the world. The rain will still fall and the sun shine, though differently than before. When I say "nature," I mean a certain set of human ideas about the world and our place in it. But the death of those ideas begins with concrete changes in the reality around us—changes that scientists can measure and enumerate. More and more frequently, these changes will clash with our perceptions, until, finally, our sense of nature as eternal and separate is washed away, and we will see all too clearly what we have done.

. . .

And the changes—many of them, at least—are irrevocable. They are not possibilities. They cannot be wished away and they cannot be legislated away. To prevent them, we would have had to clean up our collective act many decades ago. Though scientists disagree about whether or not the warming has begun, they do not argue that carbon dioxide hasn't increased, or that the increase won't have an effect. The "thermal equilibrium"—the heat storage—of the oceans may be saving us at the moment. But if so it is only a sort of chemical budget deficit. Sooner or later our loans will be called in. The latest estimates predict that man's release *to date* of carbon dioxide and other gases will warm the atmosphere as little as 1 degree Fahrenheit or as much as 2.8. And we continue, of course, to burn oil and cut trees and grow rice.

We have done this ourselves, by driving our cars, building our factories, cutting down our forests, turning on our air conditioners. The exact physical effects of our alterations—even whether or not they will be for the worse—are for the moment beside the point. They will be dealt with in the second half of this book, which is about the future. For now, simply recognize the magnitude of what we have done. In the years since the Civil War, and mostly in the years since World War II, we have changed the atmosphere—changed it enough so that the climate will change dramatically. Most of the major events of human history have gradually lost their meaning: wars that seemed at the time all-important are now a series of dates that schoolchildren don't even try to remember; great feats of engineering now crumble in the desert. Man's efforts, even at their mightiest, were tiny compared with the size of the planet— the Roman Empire meant nothing to the Arctic or the Amazon. But now, the way of life of one part of the world in one half-century is altering every inch and every hour of the globe.

Questions for Thinking and Writing

1. What is McKibben's reason for contrasting the slowness of nature with the rapid development of human civilization? What illusion does he seek to dispel?
2. How does McKibben's sense of time and civilization compare with Cather's in "The Ancient People" (p. 109)?
3. Discuss any examples of environmental degradation you have experienced firsthand, or is your knowledge of environmental ills purely from hearsay and the media? Do you think environmentalists are alarmists?

❧ Anne Rivers Siddons

Chapter 15, King's Oak (1990)

King's Oak, *from which this selection is excerpted, is a blockbuster adventure-romance of mass market appeal set in the South. Its significance for this anthology lies in Siddons's decision to use an environmental disaster in the making as the setting for the book's climactic ending. The scenes described in this excerpt will certainly remind you of the horrors of the Savannah River Site where the U.S. Department of Energy manufactures nuclear weapons, the poisoning of suburban Love Canal, as well as any number of toxic waste dump sites suddenly revealed to the public through the media. Siddons has used an event formerly of only passing interest to the American consumer and positioned it as the crux of her novel, a telling entrance of environmental affairs into the marketplace.*

A professional writer of mass market books, Siddons has also written for magazines like House Beautiful, Reader's Digest, *and* Redbook *as well as having worked in advertising. Her first book,* John Chancellor Makes Me Cry *(1975), is a humorous reflection of a year in the author's life in Atlanta, Georgia, going about the daily business of family and social life. In* Heart Break Hotel *(1976), Siddons makes a conscious attempt to capture an audience by writing about situations that are on the forefront of the national conscience. The novel, set in the South, deals with a young woman trying to decide which suitor to choose. It dwells not only on recently emerged sexual and social mores but on the richness of southern history. The* House Next Door *(1978) picks up on a Hollywood-driven fascination with haunted houses. The novel is about sinister doings in a house neighboring one just purchased by an upwardly mobile young couple.*

King's Oak *combines the elements of a romantic love story with a consciousness of environmental disruption caused by greed. Siddons plays off the emotional fragility of her heroine against the fragility of the environment. Andy Calhoun's ability to keep up with Tom Dabney on their nighttime excursion into the swamp shows how she has developed a resourcefulness that will enable her to survive harsh realities. The degradation of the swamp, caused by illegal dumping of nuclear waste, requires remediation, and Siddons holds out the hope that concerned people like Andy and Tom can help make the positive change. This novel follows in the path of James Bridges's* The China Syndrome *(1979) and Mike Nichols's* Silkwood *(1984), two films that detail the effects of nuclear energy gone awry.*

I struggled to a sitting position and called out, my voice thick in my throat, "Who is it?"

"It's Tom," came the light, rich voice that was under every thought and at the edge of every dream that I had had that summer. "Can I come in? I need to talk to you."

I pulled myself to my feet. I could not feel them. I ran my hands through my wild hair; I could not feel my fingers on my scalp, either. There was an awful, metallic taste in my mouth, and the acid sweetness of old liquor, and a cottony unpleasantness . . . I had no idea on earth what time it was, and could not focus on my watch.

"Andy?" he called again.

"I'm coming."

I went on prickling, clumping feet to the door and unlocked it and stood looking at him through the screen. In the faint yellow light of the porch fixture, he looked as lunar and strange as if he had just come from another star. He was thin to bone, thinner even than on the night we had seen him at the convenience store, so thin that the ropes of his muscles and the long cords of the big veins stood out in his flesh like one of those plastic models that Charlie and Chris had used in med school. His thinness was shocking. But he was clean-shaven, and his black hair was cut short again, and the skin of his face and arms was its old deep walnut, the color of Clay Dabney's skin. Because of the dim light and the tan, I could not see the circles beneath his eyes, but the old eldritch blueness flashed at me out of the darkness of night and skin. There was the gleam of something wet on his face, and I thought it must be rain, but behind him, hanging low and swollen in the still, hot night, I could see the great, new-risen August moon.

He moved a little closer and I saw then that the wetness on his face was tears. My mind refused to compute, to deal with this fact. I simply stood still and stared at him. The thought occurred to me that we stood in a dream, Tom Dabney and I.

"Can I come in?" he said again, softly. His voice was thick and ragged in his throat. Silently I unhooked the screen door and stood aside, and he came into the room on his silent feet. I saw that he wore his soft, ragged old deerhide stalking moccasins, though he was dressed conventionally enough in fresh khaki pants and a faded old blue oxford cloth shirt with the sleeves rolled up. He smelled of soap and the woods, and the older, warmer, unknowable yet all-known smell of Tom.

We sat opposite each other in front of my dead fireplace, he on the edge of the chair Carter had favored, I on the rumpled sofa. I saw the half-empty Scotch bottle on the table, and the empty glass, and saw him see it, and was suddenly aware of how I must look, my face puffed and pale, my hair a snarl, my shorts and shirt corrugated like cardboard with the drenching sweat of terror.

"Are you all right?" he said, staring at me. "You look awful. Is Hilary all right? Scratch said she'd been sick."

"Hilary's fine," I said. "She's visiting her father. She'll be back in a week or so. She told me on the phone tonight to tell you hey. Did you . . . did you come to see her?"

"No," he said. "I came to see you. I . . . there wasn't anybody else who wouldn't throw me out. But if this isn't a good time for you . . . "

I shook my head to clear it. The room and Tom came into sharper focus. Some of the scum of the dream peeled away.

"I must look like I've been on a three-day drunk," I said. "But I've been asleep." The fact of his physical presence in my house hit me then, and my heart began to pound again. This time, though, it was not in fear. Not precisely.

"I think you look—" His voice thinned and broke, and he was silent, struggling for composure.

"What is it, Tom?" I said. Fear did come in then, over the other thing that had quickened my heart.

"It's Scratch," he said, and grief was heavy in his voice. I felt my own grief leap, freshening, to match his.

"Oh, God," I said, "Is he. . . ?"

"No," he said. "He's not dead. Not yet. But he's . . . Jesus, Andy, he's just eaten up. Just eaten up . . . "

I went over and sat on the arm of his chair and put my arms around him. I did it without thinking. My muscles did it, my hands and feet and arms. He pressed his head against my breast in silence, and then he sat up and took a deep breath, and I pulled away a bit, and looked at him.

"He came dragging up on the porch tonight about eight and col-lapsed," Tom said. "I had to carry him into the house, and put him on the sofa. I tried to call an ambulance, but he wouldn't let me. He kept trying to talk and choking, and choking, but finally he got it out that he'd come to tell me something—dragged himself all the way from up-swamp to the house to tell me—and then he had a hemorrhage. I never saw so much blood. Out of his mouth, and his nose, and his . . . rectum, and oh, Christ, Andy, on his neck and head . . . the tumors, the sores, like the deer."

I saw again, sickly, yet at a remove, the terrible sores on the belly of the dead doe, and the sly, slick blue of entrails. I remembered the muf-fler around Scratch's throat, and the stocking cap. It had not been cold, then, but the need to spare us, Hilary and me. . . .

"Oh, Scratch," I whispered, putting my hands over my face.

"I took him to the emergency room," Tom said, heavily, over the tears. "I thought the ER staff was going to throw up. They've got him in intensive care, with tubes and a respirator and God knows what else, but it isn't going to do any good. The doctor just shook his head when I asked."

"What is it?" I whispered. "What is it?"

"Cancer," he said. "I don't know what kind. They'll probably never know where it hit him first. I'd say lymphatic system, or liver. Lungs, maybe. That's where radioactive poison gets you, usually. I should have known all along. I've been seeing those animals all summer. It's the motherfucking, murdering water, of course; Scratch never would drink city water. They've got it, up there in the settlement, but he carried his own water from Goat Creek. He even kept jugs of Goat Creek water at my house to drink. . . . Andy, I need for you to come with me now. Can you come? Can you do that? I can't ask anybody else. . . . "

"Where?" I said. "Where?"

"Back up the creek to the lumber camp on King's Oak," he said. "Andy, he told me that the . . . whatever it is in the water, that's lighting it up and killing everything, is coming from the camp. Oh, God, when I think what it must have cost him to find that out . . . He went all the way back up there from his house; it must have taken him all day. Said he got the idea to look there in some kind of dream, or trance, and sick as he is, he went. And he went through that fence. You know how he hated that wire. You know he's never touched it, not in all the years since Clay put it up, but he took wire cutters with him and cut it and went in there and saw . . . whatever it is, and then came all the way down-creek to tell me. And it's killed him. He's dying now. And so I'm going up there. Tonight. I need you to come with me. Somebody . . . sane has to see it. Nobody else would go."

He stopped and looked at me. His eyes burned blue.

"Are you telling me that it's something Clay is doing?" I whispered, my voice shaking. "Are you telling me that, Tom? Because I don't believe you! My God, Clay Dabney has practically given up his life for you this summer!"

He shook his head.

"No. I don't know. I don't think so . . . but I don't know. But can't you see, I have to find out? Don't you see that I have to go and at least try to stop it? If you're afraid, I won't blame you, but don't you see why I need somebody else, somebody who isn't . . . suspect? Andy, Martin just plain won't go, and Reese is passed out drunk and can't. And I can't wait. Andy, please . . . "

His voice broke again, and tears ran down his brown face and dropped one by one onto the collar of the blue shirt. It was sodden on both sides, just above the small pearl buttons. I could see that one of them had been crushed in the laundry. One tear trembled, perfect like a diamond, in the hollow of his throat.

My thinking mind switched off and the old thing there, the old, deep, simple thing that had once called out to Tom, and been answered by him, lurched and ground and lumbered back to life.

"Fix yourself a drink," I said. "I'll just be a minute."

I went down the hall toward my bedroom and once again I heard him say, as he had said the night I had come to him in the jail, "Thank you, Andy."

I did not answer him this time, either.

We drove through the hot, moon-thick night mostly in silence. The truck was neat and swept out, and smelled as if he might have cleaned its interior with cleaning fluid. He had closed the windows against the heavy, breathless heat, and we jolted through the near-deserted town and out the highway toward King's Oak and the turnoff to Goat Creek in a humming capsule of stale-cold breath from the air conditioner. Just before we crossed the railroad tracks that marked the boundaries of Pemberton Over There, I caught a glimpse of the lighted time-and-temperature sign on the mellow brick First National Bank of Pemberton. It said 92 degrees, 10:10 P.M. Faint surprise scratched at the bubble of Xanax and fatigue and simple shock in which I floated. I had thought it must be the middle of the night.

Tom drove intently, bent slightly forward, his face cruelly and jovially underlit by the green dash glow, like a jack-o'-lantern. He did not look at me, did not seem to realize that I was with him in the truck. An occasional tear still slid down his face and dropped onto his collar, but the tears did not seem real; they had the illusory quality of the stigmatic tears on the face of a carved saint, bizarre miracles. Whatever part of him wept for Scratch, it was not his mind. I could feel that focused powerfully and singly on that burning point up the creek, like a palpable searchlight. Incredibly, I was almost comfortable, bowling through the night with this once-beloved madman on the way into what could scarcely escape being danger of one degree or another.

Once, he turned his head to look at me, and said, "I can't tell you this is not dangerous, but I don't know yet just how dangerous it is. When we get upcreek close to the wire, I'll know better. If it looks bad I'll leave you and go in alone. If you come in with me I'll take all precautions. I'm not going to let anything happen to you."

"I'm not afraid," I said serenely, and realized that I was not. Underneath the fatigue and the drug and the unreality of this night another feeling throbbed steadily, like an artery. It was a sense of ending, of impending settlement. One way or another, when this night was over, I would know something about Tom and myself and the water in Goat Creek; the obscene terror of it would have a name, and we could speak that name and find a way to defuse it of its menace. Perhaps Tom could end it; perhaps it would, even, end Tom. Either way, there was a finish to this foulness in the sunny silence of the Big Silver Swamp. Either way, Hilary would be safe and we could go on from this night. I was content to ride in silence toward whatever finish we would find. Frick Harper would, I suppose, have called the feeling the need for closure. It was a simpler and more powerful need than any fear of danger. And besides, I simply did not believe that Tom would let me be harmed. Even this new Tom, reviled and half mad with obsession, would keep me safe.

I turned my head to look through the rear window at the unwinding silver ribbon of road behind us and saw the gleam of dark metal. I looked more closely. On the ledge behind the seat lay two rifles, his old single-shot and my slim little Ruger. I caught the scent of fresh gun oil, and saw the sheen of newly cleaned barrels. I looked over at Tom.

"You're not taking your bow?" I said. And then, catching for the first time the significance of his ordinary dress, "You haven't done any kind of . . . ceremony, have you? I thought, for something like this . . . "

"The bow and the rituals and the songs and all that jazz haven't done any of us a whole hell of a lot of good, have they?" he said briefly and flatly. The flatness was more painful to hear than bitterness would have been, or grief. Pain flared in my chest like brushfire, but dully, like pain far down under morphine. I ached with the need to give his magic back to him, but the ache was far away.

"Maybe, when we get there, we could do one," I said clumsily. "I'll help."

The smile he gave me was brief and dead.

"Thanks, but it would be a sacrilege now," he said. "I can't do that anymore. I've lost the power. Maybe I never had it; I think it must have been Scratch all along, and what I felt was just spilling off him. All of it, everything, all that we learned and believed and loved . . . It couldn't help the woods. It couldn't heal the water. It couldn't save my goats. It couldn't keep Hilary safe. It couldn't get rid of one iota of the stink and pain and death out in the swamp. And Scratch . . . I couldn't even save Scratch."

"Tom . . . "

"No. Be quiet, Andy. I'm sorry, but we can't talk about that anymore. I can still stop it. I'm as good with a gun as I ever was with a bow and arrow. Or a fucking chant."

This time the bitterness was there, dark and old as the water at the core of the earth. I felt the tears begin to slide out of my eyes, even though the bubble in which I floated still held. I prayed silently that it would, for a little while yet. Enough to get me through this night.

After a space of silence we reached the turnoff for King's Oak, and he slowed the truck and turned in. We rattled down the close-grown, black dirt ribbon noisily, at a good clip, headlights on bright. I expected him to cut the lights and slow to a creep when we approached the clearing where the great lodge stood, but he didn't. He felt my question, and said, "There's not anybody at King's Oak. Chip gives the staff the last two weeks in August off, before hunting season opens. And besides, I rode by his house in town tonight. Having a dinner party, old Chip is. Looks like half the honchos from the Big Silver are there. I counted seven top-level security stickers. We don't need to worry about anybody seeing or hearing us until we get close to the lumber camp, and maybe not then. Scratch didn't see any sign of life this afternoon."

He laughed, an ugly laugh. "No sign of life at all."

As we had on that night, seemingly eons ago now, when we had come to King's Oak at the winter solstice—oh, that night of star-chipped magic!—we drove on past the great, sweet black bulk of the house, silvered now with thickly poured moonlight, and went on down the rutted lane through the black-green soybean fields, toward the blacker line of the river swamp. Tom did not speak again until he had parked the truck in the clearing on the bank of Goat Creek where he had parked it on that night. We got out of the truck in the same silence in which we had moved then; I remembered that silence, and the crunch of my high silver heels through ice-rimed brown grass stubble, and the sound of my breathing and my heart's deep, slow pounding. He had held my arm going down the bank to where the little skiff was tied that night, and over his other arm he had carried the mink throw. Now he carried the two rifles, and he did not take my arm. Now we went down the little bank, but we did not get into the waiting skiff. I remembered that on that other night crazy laughter had bubbled into my throat, irrepressibly, like champagne. Now what pressed there was grief and pain held back, and under that, the beginning again of fear.

"How far we've come," I said to myself. "What a long, terrible black way we've come."

I did not realize I had said it aloud until he said, softly, "A long way indeed."

We stood together in the moony white night, both looking across the summer-stunted creek to the island where the King's Oak stood, its great, beautiful, dark canopy clean and monstrous against the sky. I do not know what he saw under those cathedral branches. I saw leaping firelight, and the shimmer of joined naked flesh, and heard the caroling laughter of exuberance and joy. I turned away, so that my back was to the tree. He turned with me.

"We're going upcreek from here," he said. "You've never been up as far as we're going, and I don't go up there, either. But I have, when I was much younger, with Clay. Before he leased the land to the lumber company. I know the way. It's not a hard walk. There's a little ridge that parallels the creek most of the way, and the walking is firm and there's not much undergrowth. With the moonlight, it'll almost be like walking in your backyard. About three miles upcreek, we'll cut inland, up a little branch that forks off to the left. It runs right through the lumber company's main clearing, if I remember right, and on up to where the creek makes up. When we come to the branch, then we'll stalk, or maybe even go on our stomachs. I'll know by then. But it won't be far, and I'll lead the way. If I think I need to, that's where I'll leave you, at the cutoff of that branch. If I tell you to, I want you to go on back and take the truck into town and get Clay. But I probably won't have to do that."

"Tom, I can't get back through all those woods to the truck by myself," I said, the fear sharpening. "You can't leave me up there. . . . "

"You can track almost as well as any of us, and better than Martin," he said. "I've seen you do it. All you have to do is follow the creek to the King's Oak. Andy, don't let me down now. This is the end of it, this is where we start to stop it, if it can be stopped. This is for . . . this is for Hilary. Do this for Hilary if you can't do it for me. Do it for Hilary and yourself."

"Let's go, then," I said. And then, surprising myself by smiling, "If it's half the night you gave Tim Ford, I wouldn't miss it for the world."

His answering grin flashed out in the darkness, briefly. "That was some kind of night," he said.

We walked steadily for over an hour. He moved fast and quietly, and his feet in the soft, dry earth of the ridge were sure, but he was no longer totally silent, and I did not lose him into the immensity of the swamp forest, as I had on the other occasions when I had gone out into the night woods with him. At first, despite my thick-soled Nikes, I had trouble with my footing on the spongy, detritus-strewn floor of the forest, and was certain that I could be heard for miles around us, but it did not seem to bother him. He carried both guns and went steadily ahead, not turning back to look at me, as if certain I was not lagging behind. And I did not lag; even though, at first, my breath labored in my chest and sweat drenched through my jeans and long-sleeved shirt. I tramped grimly on behind him, hearing nothing but my own heart and feet, grimacing at my own noise. Occasionally he lifted his free hand to his face, and I thought that he was still weeping silently for his friend as he walked, but I heard no sound from him.

Gradually the noise of my clumsiness seemed to settle, and then dwindle, and my laboring heart found its rhythm, and the vivid silence of the Big Silver Swamp grew in my ears and slid into my mind, a living silence that seemed enhanced, not broken, by the night noises around me. I heard the thousands of tiny rustlings and splashings and snappings and whistlings and pipings and croakings and tickings that were the night music of the Big Silver. I heard, once, the faraway bellow of a big gator, hollow and ghostly over water, and an unseen stampede that was whitetails in flight from something, and the unearthly hunting call of a drifting owl, and the silver glissando of a whippoorwill. Under it all was the susurration of cicadas, a continual rhythm like a heartbeat, and under that, even, a kind of high, pulsing, dreaming hum that seemed to come from the very earth itself. Presently I felt myself begin to move in that rhythm, to swim through the dark, thick, murmurous air of the swamp as easily and naturally as through warm water. The night became, for a time, like those other nights that I had gone out into the woods with him. I forgot, as I had then, the essential incongruity of a forty-year-old divorced college public relations worker with a child and a leased house and a Toyota doing this. I forgot pain and fear. The night woods swallowed me and were, for a small space of time, all.

The pain and fear and the incongruity flooded back soon enough. We came at last to a place where Goat Creek doubled back upon itself, forming a dark, silent elbow. We had to cross it to go on. It was in thick, moonless shadow here, and looked deep. Tom stopped, and I stopped behind him. I waited for him to go through the creek and continue on the other side, but he did not. Instead, he ranged slowly up and down until he found a place he deemed narrow enough, and he pitched the rifles softly across and leaped himself, landing surefootedly and quietly in the leafy mold of the creek verge. Then he turned and held his hands out to me.

"Jump," he said. "Be sure and get a good start. Don't let the water touch you."

I remembered, then, why we had come. The woods, which had swallowed me, spat me back into reality. Coldness prickled the hairs on my arms and the back of my neck, even in the heat. The water flowed on between us, dark, unmarked by that devil's fire, but I would rather have died than gone into it at that moment. For the first time I feared the water as my daughter had, as Tom Dabney did now. I looked at him in terror, and then I backed off and got a running start and closed my eyes and flung myself into space. He caught my outstretched hands on the other side and pulled me up the bank, and we went on upstream. We did not speak again until we came to the tiny branch that cut off to the left through the woods. I thought that it must be well after midnight by then.

Tom stopped and looked ahead into the darkness. He signaled for me to be still. He stood motionless, hands relaxed at his sides, the guns laid at his feet, simply looking into the night and listening to it. I knew that the essence of him was ranging out in the night, a part of the water and wind and trees; I knew that when he moved again he would know what he wanted to do. Presently the stillness went out of him and he turned to me.

"It's okay," he said. "I don't think there's anybody up there. If there is, we're upwind of them. We can walk naturally until we're almost to the camp. But if I signal you then, I want you to drop. We'll have to go on our stomachs then."

He handed my rifle to me. "Don't use it unless I tell you. Or unless I can't help you anymore. Then use it instantly. You know how."

This time I did not argue. The fear in my stomach was not far from breaking free.

We turned and followed the little branch away into the deep heart of the Big Silver. This was country that I knew, country of deep, thick, wet woods floors and long, dark sloughs and standing black water, country of cypress and moss and tupelo and a thousand close-pressing hardwoods. The moon thrust through here only in sly, fitful fingers, and the wet heat thickened. Insects abound, keening in ears, swarming at mouth and nose. When we lifted our feet from the forest floor, they came away with a sucking sound. The calls of furred and feathered things dwindled, and the slither and cry of gilled and webbed things rose. Along the branch, ferns and reeds were black and lush. We saw no fire in this water, either, but I kept well away from it. I thought I would never again feel on my flesh the warm sweetness of the water of Goat Creek.

We came to a place where a fence of rusted wire, five barbed strands, bisected the branch and ran off into the darkness on either side. Tom stopped.

"Beyond that it's lumber company land," he said. "I don't know where Scratch cut the fence, but I don't have time to look for it. We'll have to go under it. Follow me. I'll hold it for you when I get through."

He dropped to his stomach, holding the rifle in the crook of both elbows, and wriggled under the wire on the creekbank, going like a snake, or a commando. Halfway under, he stopped, froze. A sound came from him, a gasp, a thick snort of revulsion. Then he wriggled on under and held the wire for me. It was only after I was under and up-right again that he parted the reeds on the creekbank with the barrel of the rifle and pointed at what he had seen. I leaned close, and then jumped back, my heart hammering with fear and disgust. Down at the very edge of the black water, at the roots of the ferns and the reeds, where the water kissed, a monstrous line of sickly white plants stretched, hidden in the dankness of the bank's curve. I did not know what they were, but knew in my hammering heart and heaving stom-ach that they were not natural. They were fleshy and pale, glowing white, damp and mottled and peeling and splotched, twisted and tu-morous and altogether grotesque. They might have been mushrooms, but were not; might have been twisted tree roots, but were not. They had never pushed through the soil of any other earth in any other time; you knew that. They gave off their own light, somehow; and they were truly terrible things. The line of them stretched off into the dark-ness upcreek and was lost in it. I looked at Tom, unable to speak. He looked back at me, impassively. We went on, keeping well away from the creekbank.

As we moved, the ferns and reeds themselves began to look strange, blighted and whitened and malformed. Soon they died, and then there were none at all, only wet black dirt, and standing slime, and the black roots of the trees. I became aware, gradually, that the sounds of the water creatures had stopped. No owls called, and no night birds. I could scarcely breathe around the fear in my chest. It was not the mindless fear of the early night, but an altogether and eons-older thing, some-thing atavistic, something that lifted my hair roots and drew my lips back over my teeth, just this side of a snarl. Ahead of me, Tom motioned to me to stop, and I did. Peering through the thick darkness, I could see, ahead of us in the forest, a thinning of the blackness and the faintest fitful frost of white light. We had come to a clearing, and I knew that we were at it now, the heart of the lumber camp, the dark thing we had come to find.

"Stay here," Tom whispered, and moved off toward the light. He moved quickly and soundlessly, in a running crouch. I stood hunched over, trying to will my hammering heart still, trying to think of nothing at all. Soon he had moved out of my sight.

In what seemed an eternity, but was more likely five minutes, I heard him call my name: "Andy." There was something wrong with his voice. I hesitated, and he called again. "Andy, Andy, come here."

And I broke into a trot, following the sound of his strangled voice, and ran into the clearing from the shelter of black woods.

It was large, perhaps the area of four football fields. In the middle of it, a jumble of rusted tin shacks stood, leaning in upon one another. Heavy machinery stood about, tire-deep in weeds, looking like the monstrous carapaces of prehistoric insects. There were one or two tanker trucks, tireless and obviously long useless, and a larger board shack, open on one side, where coiled wire and old tires and tools and sodden, disintegrated cardboard cartons were piled. The floor of the clearing was weed-choked white sand, and a spur rail line threaded through it, running out of sight into the trees on both sides. Only the rail line looked usable, or used; the rails were not rusted, but were the soft, buffed pewter that spoke of traffic. A staggering row of utility lights, white, so that I thought they must be mercury vapor, circled the clearing. There were no human beings in evidence, and no trace that any had been, for a long time. What tire tracks there were in the sand of the work yard had been diffused by months of rain and wind and sun.

At first I did not see Tom, and then I heard him call again and saw him, a small figure at the very end of the clearing on the far side, past the jumble of shacks and equipment, partially obscured by them. I followed the spur line to where he stood. It ended there. I saw what it ended in before I came near to it, and I could not make myself go further.

Four vast, square concrete pools lay there at the end of the spur, white-lit by another circle of work lights. Around them, the forest stretched away black and old and silent. Beyond them, the spur line picked up again and ran off into the forest to the east. Toward Goat Creek and the Big Silver River. The night was utterly still and quiet, but the pools were not. They were filled with a terrible, opaque, green-white liquid, and smoke and vapor lay so thickly over them that I could see their surfaces only intermittently. But I could make out that the surfaces were in motion of themselves; there was no wind. They writhed and bubbled and sucked. There was the sound of sibilant hissing, of boiling. When the vapors parted and the pool surfaces flashed clear for an instant, I could see that deep down, far down, the pools were an eerie, burning blue.

I went on numb, stumbling feet to where Tom stood.

"What is it?" I whispered, knowing that I was seeing horror, but unable to define it. "What in the name of God is it?"

"Seepage basins," he said. His voice was the high, eerie growl of an animal about to attack. "Seepage basins, cooling pools, whatever, for nuclear waste. I saw twenty-six others, just like them, over at the Big Silver plant last week; I've been over there for two weeks, scouting. Twenty-six just like these four, only they kept those cleaned up. They weren't . . . boiling. They weren't lit up. No wonder they test clean. This . . . this is where they put the worst of it, then. The really bad stuff. The stuff that tests out of sight with plutonium and strontium and God knows what else; the stuff that kills you. The stuff that spoils all your pretty PR. The stuff I took out of Goat Creek. They're dumping waste water up here on King's Oak, and more than water, I'll bet my life. I'll bet if we looked we'd find tank fields for sludge, and salts, and pools where they dump the radioactive hardware and tools and clothes, and maybe even the irradiated fuel and target rods. . . . Ford said that's what lights the water up blue, the rods."

He swung around to face me and I saw that his open eyes were totally mad, and blind. I knew that it was not me he saw with those eyes.

"They're not lumbering up here," he said, in the awful voice. "The spur, the turpentine trunks, the tank cars—they've been hauling it in here at night, maybe even in the daytime, for God knows how long. Look, see that second spur? That doesn't go out to the main line, you can bet your ass on it. That goes straight across the creek and the river onto the Big Silver. They can ship directly in here, in tank cars, and nobody even knows the hell they're doing it, because nobody ever comes in here. What do you want to bet there hasn't been a log or a drop of turpentine out of here in Christ knows how many years?"

He stopped, gasping for breath. A great, strangling, hopeless grief flooded me, a drowning, impotent outrage. I saw again the slender little goat, and the struggling death in the tender, perfect new morning.

"How dare they?" I said in a low, shaking voice. "Stupid, stupid, stupid . . . How *dare* they? How dare we? Look what we've all been given, and look what they've done to it, and what we've let them do. . . . Oh, how *dare* we? God should kill us all in our arrogant stupidity—"

"There isn't any God," Tom said. "We've killed sacredness, too."

We stood silent for a moment, and then he threw back his head and shouted, "They've been poisoning Goat Creek right out of King's Oak, Andy! *Right out of King's Oak!* Dear Christ in heaven . . . "

His voice rose, and rose, and I knew that I was about to hear once again that terrible, primal howl I heard the morning of the diseased deer, and that I could not, this time, bear it. I put my arms around him and held him close to me, and rocked him, or tried to. His body, under my arms, was as rigid as if in death.

"We have to go to Clay," I said. "Come on, Tom. Let's go tell Clay. Clay can help; Clay will know what to do about this."

"No," Tom said. "We don't have to go tell Clay. Clay knows." His voice was scarcely the voice of a living man. "He knows. He'd have to know. This is his land; there's no way he couldn't know. . . . "

Questions for Thinking and Writing

1. What is the implication inherent in the decaying plant life as Andy and Tom move deeper into the wilderness? Why does Siddons set this journey in the night? If Siddons is being theatrical, what point of view is she advocating? How different in environmental point of view and purpose is this night journey through the swamp from Annie Dillard's "Seeing" (p. 313) or Henry Beston's "Night on the Great Beach" (p. 135)?

2. Compare Siddons's environmental disaster with Don DeLillo's in "Airborne Toxic Event" (p. 376) from the standpoint of the notion that "it can't

happen here." Can you identify a potential environmental accident
waiting to happen in your neighborhood?

3. Write a report on the U.S. Department of Energy's Savannah River Site,
   the nuclear weapons matériels production facility that Siddons used as a resource for her novel.

❧ Michael Pollan (b. 1955)

The Idea of a Garden (1991)

*As editor and writer, Michael Pollan has made a career out of
questioning environmental and aesthetic considerations that many
people take for granted. In the essay reprinted here, "The Idea of a
Garden," from* Second Nature: A Gardener's Education *(1991), Pollan
examines the commonly held assumption that nature is what it
seems to be. When a grove of pine trees was destroyed by a storm,
the question arose of how it would be restored. When competing environmental groups and the local townspeople could not agree, the
question of nature's intent became an issue. In their arrogance, some
thought that they knew. Pollan is quick to point out that the grove of
pines was not an original forest but second growth, and that its debris is not necessarily unaesthetic or hazardous. The compromise
struck by the litigants is not satisfying to Pollan, who wonders if it is
ethical to influence the regrowth of the area. In an unobtrusive
manner, Pollan questions the assumptions of such defenders of nature as Henry David Thoreau, John Burroughs, and John Muir as
well as throwing the arguments of Gifford Pinchot and David Lilienthal into a new light.*

One of Pollan's most controversial essays from Second Nature,
"Why Mow?," was published in the New York Times Magazine *in 1989.
Here Pollan questions one of the basics of suburban contemporary
life: to mow or not to mow? Shrewdly, the essay unravels the American obsession with lawns, by pointing out that constant mowing is one
of the most unnatural and ecologically sterilizing uses of land possible. As in much of his writing, this essay also deliberates over our
naive relationship with nature. On the one hand we want to be in prox-
imity to nature; on the other hand, we make efforts to maintain that
relationship in our control.*

*Pollan was raised in Woodbury, Long Island, and attended Syosset
High School. He graduated from Bennington College, studied at
Oxford University, and received a master's degree in English from*

Columbia University. Since 1985, he has been executive editor of Harper's *magazine. His articles and essays have appeared in that magazine as well as in* The New York Times Book Review, Conde Nast Traveller, House Beautiful, *and* Organic Gardening.

His first book, Second Nature (*1991*), *received an award from the American Garden Writer's Association. He is currently at work on a book tentatively entitled* Habitations of the Heart, *about the history of a house. He divides his time between New York City and Cornwall Bridge, Connecticut, the site of the forest he writes about in "The Idea of a Garden."*

The biggest news to come out of my town in many years was the tornado, or tornadoes, that careened through here on July 10, 1989, a Monday. Shooting down the Housatonic River Valley from the Berkshires, it veered east over Coltsfoot Mountain and then, after smudging the sky a weird gray green, proceeded to pinball madly from hillside to hillside for about fifteen minutes before wheeling back up into the sky. This was part of the same storm that ripped open the bark of my ash tree. But the damage was much, much worse on the other side of town. Like a gigantic, skidding pencil eraser, the twister neatly erased whole patches of woods and roughly smeared many other ones, where it wiped out just the tops of the trees. Overnight, large parts of town were rendered unrecognizable.

One place where the eraser came down squarely was in the Cathedral Pines, a famous forest of old-growth white pine trees close to the center of town. A kind of local shrine, this forty-two-acre forest was one of the oldest stands of white pine in New England, the trees untouched since about 1800. To see it was to have some idea how the New World forest must have looked to the first settlers, and in 1985 the federal government designated it a "national natural landmark." To enter Cathedral Pines on a hot summer day was like stepping out of the sun into a dim cathedral, the sunlight cooled and sweetened by the trillions of pine needles as it worked its way down to soft, sprung ground that had been unacquainted with blue sky for the better part of two centuries. The storm came through at about five in the evening, and it took only a few minutes of wind before pines more than one hundred fifty feet tall and as wide around as missiles lay jackstrawed on the ground like a fistful of pencils dropped from a great height. The wind was so thunderous that people in houses at the forest's edge did not know trees had fallen until they ventured outside after the storm had passed. The following morning, the sky now clear, was the first in more than a century to bring sunlight crashing down onto this particular patch of earth.

"It is a terrible mess," the first selectman told the newspapers; "a tragedy," said another Cornwall resident, voicing the deep sense of loss shared by many in town. But in the days that followed, the selectman and the rest of us learned that our responses, though understandable, were shortsighted, unscientific, and, worst of all, anthropocentric. "It may be a calamity to us," a state environmental official told a reporter from the *Hartford Courant,* but "to biology it is not a travesty. It is just a natural occurrence." The Nature Conservancy, which owns Cathedral Pines, issued a press release explaining that "Monday's storm was just another link in the continuous chain of events that is responsible for shaping and changing this forest."

It wasn't long before the rub of these two perspectives set off a controversy heated enough to find its way into the pages of *The New York Times*. The Nature Conservancy, in keeping with its mandate to maintain its lands in a "state of nature," indicated that it would leave Cathedral Pines alone, allowing the forest to take its "natural course," whatever that might be. To town officials and neighbors of the forest this was completely unacceptable. The downed trees, besides constituting an eyesore right at the edge of town, also posed a fire hazard. A few summers of drought, and the timber might go up in a blaze that would threaten several nearby homes and possibly even the town itself. Many people in Cornwall wanted Cathedral Pines cleared and replanted, so that at least the next generation might live to see some semblance of the old forest. A few others had the poor taste to point out the waste of more than a million board-feet of valuable timber, stupendous lengths of unblemished, knot-free pine.

The newspapers depicted it as a classic environmental battle, pitting the interests of man against nature, and in a way it was that. On one side were the environmental purists, who felt that *any* intervention by man in the disposition of this forest would be unnatural. "If you're gong to clean it up," one purist declared in the local press, "you might as well put up condos." On the other side stood the putative interests of man, variously expressed in the vocabulary of safety (the first hazard), economics (the waste lumber), and aesthetics (the "terrible mess").

Everybody enjoys a good local fight, but I have to say I soon found the whole thing depressing. This was indeed a classic environmental battle, in that it seemed to exemplify just about everything that's wrong with the way we approach problems of this kind these days. Both sides began to caricature each other's positions: the selectman's "terrible mess" line earned him ridicule for his anthropocentrism in the letters page of *The New York Times;* he in turn charged a Yale scientist who argued for noninterference with "living in an ivory tower."

But as far apart as the two sides seemed to stand, they actually shared more common ground than they realized. Both started from the premise that man and nature were irreconcilably opposed, and that the victory of one necessarily entailed the loss of the other. Both sides, in other words, accepted the premises of what we might call the "wilderness ethic," which is based on the assumption that the relationship of man and nature resembles a zero-sum game. This idea, widely held and yet largely unexamined, has set the terms of most environmental battles in this country since the very first important one: the fight over the building of the Hetch Hetchy Dam in 1907, which pitted John Muir against Gifford Pinchot, whom Muir used to call a "temple destroyer." Watching my little local debate unfold over the course of the summer, and grow progressively more shrill and sterile, I began to wonder if perhaps the wilderness ethic itself, for all that it has accomplished in this country over the past century, had now become part of the problem. I also began to wonder if it might be possible to formulate a different ethic to guide us in our dealings with nature, at least in some places some of the time, an ethic that would be based not on the idea of wilderness but on the idea of a garden.

Foresters who have examined sections of fallen trees in Cathedral Pines think that the oldest trees in the forest date from 1780 or so, which suggests that the site was probably logged by the first generation of settlers. The Cathedral Pines are not, then "virgin growth." The rings of felled trees also reveal a significant growth spurt in 1840, which probably indicates that loggers removed hardwood trees in that year, leaving the pines to grow without competition. In 1883, the Calhouns, an old Cornwall family whose property borders the forest, bought the land to protect the trees from the threat of logging; in 1967 they deeded it to the Nature Conservancy, stipulating that it be maintained in its natural state. Since then, and up until the tornado made its paths impassable, the forest has been a popular place for hiking and Sunday outings. Over the years, more than a few Cornwall residents have come to the forest to be married.

Cathedral Pines is not in any meaningful sense a wilderness. The natural history of the forest intersects at many points with the social history of Cornwall. It is the product of early logging practices, which clear-cut the land once and then cut it again, this time selectively, a hundred years later. Other human factors almost certainly played a part in the forest's history; we can safely assume that any fires in the area were extinguished before they reached Cathedral Pines. (Though we don't ordinarily think of it in these terms, fire suppression is one of the more significant effects that the European has had on the American landscape.) Cathedral Pines, then, is in some part a man-made landscape, and it could reasonably be argued that to exclude man at this point in its history would constitute a break with its past.

But both parties to the dispute chose to disregard the actual history of Cathedral Pines, and instead to think of the forest as a wilderness in the commonly accepted sense of that term: a pristine place untouched by white men. Since the romantics, we've prized such places as refuges from the messiness of the human estate, vantages from which we might transcend the vagaries of that world and fix on what Thoreau called "higher laws." Certainly an afternoon in Cathedral Pines fostered such feelings, and its very name reflects the pantheism that lies behind them. Long before science coined the term *ecosystem* to describe it, we've had the sense that nature undisturbed displays a miraculous order and balance, something the human world can only dream about. When man leaves it alone, nature will tend toward a healthy and abiding state of equilibrium. Wilderness, the purest expression of this natural law, stands out beyond history.

These are powerful and in many ways wonderful ideas. The notion of wilderness is a kind of taboo in our culture, in many cases acting as a check on our inclination to dominate and spoil nature. It has inspired us to set aside such spectacular places as Yellowstone and Yosemite. But wilderness is also a profoundly alienating idea, for it drives a large wedge between man and nature. Set against the foil of nature's timeless cycles, human history appears linear and unpredictable, buffeted by time and chance as it drives blindly into the future. Natural history, by comparison, obeys fixed and legible laws, ones that make the "laws" of human history seem puny, second-rate things scarcely deserving of the label. We have little idea what the future holds for the town of Cornwall, but surely nature has a plan for Cathedral Pines; leave the forest alone and that plan—which science knows by the name of "forest succession"—will unfold inexorably, in strict accordance with natural law. A new climax forest will emerge as nature works to restore her equilibrium—or at least that's the idea.

The notion that nature has a plan for Cathedral Pines is a comforting one, and certainly it supplies a powerful argument for leaving the forest alone. Naturally I was curious to know what that plan was: what does nature do with an old pine forest blown down by a tornado? I consulted a few field guides and standard works of forest ecology hoping to find out.

According to the classical theory of forest succession, set out in the nineteenth century by, among others, Henry Thoreau, a pine forest that has been abruptly destroyed will usually be succeeded by hardwoods, typically oak. This is because squirrels commonly bury acorns in pine forests and neglect to retrieve many of them. The oaks sprout and, because shade doesn't greatly hinder young oaks, the seedlings frequently manage to survive beneath the dark canopy of a mature pine forest. Pine seedlings, on the other hand, require more sunlight than a mature pine forest admits; they won't sprout in shade. So by the time the pine forest comes down, the oak saplings will have had a head start in the race to dominate the new forest. Before any new pines have had a chance to sprout, the oaks will be well on their way to cornering the sunlight and inheriting the forest.

This is what I read, anyway, and I decided to ask around to confirm that Cathedral Pines was expected to behave as predicted. I spoke to a forest ecologist and an expert on the staff of the Nature Conservancy. They told me that the classical theory of pine-forest succession probably does describe the underlying tendency at work in Cathedral Pines. But it turns out that a lot can go, if not "wrong" exactly, then at least differently. For what if there are no oaks nearby? Squirrels will travel only so far in search of a hiding place for their acorns. Instead of oaks, there may be hickory nuts stashed all over Cathedral Pines. And then there's the composition of species planted by the forest's human neighbors to consider; one of these, possibly some exotic (that is, non-native), could conceivably race in and take over.

"It all depends," is the refrain I kept hearing as I tried to pin down nature's intentions for Cathedral Pines. Forest succession, it seems, is only a theory, a metaphor of our making, and almost as often as not nature makes a fool of it. The number of factors that will go into the determination of Cathedral Pines' future is almost beyond comprehension. Consider just this small sample of the things that could happen to alter irrevocably its future course:

A lightning storm—or a cigarette butt flicked from a passing car—ignites a fire next summer. Say it's a severe fire, hot enough to damage the fertility of the soil, thereby delaying recovery of the forest for decades. Or say it rains that night, making the fire a mild one, just hot enough to kill the oak saplings and allow the relatively fire-resistant pine seedlings to flourish without competition. A new pine forest after all? Perhaps. But what if the population of deer happens to soar the following year? Their browsing would wipe out the young pines and create an opening for spruce, the taste of which deer happen not to like.

Or say there is no fire. Without one, it could take hundreds of years for the downed pine trees to rot and return their nutrients to the soil. Trees grow poorly in the exhausted soil, but the seeds of brambles, which can lie dormant in the ground for fifty years, sprout and proliferate: we end up with a hundred years of brush. Or perhaps a breeze in, say, the summer of 1997 carries in seedpods from the Norway maple standing in a nearby front yard at the precise moment when conditions for their germination are perfect. Norway maple, you'll recall, is a European species, introduced here early in the nineteenth century and widely planted as a street tree. Should this exotic species happen to prevail, Cathedral Pines becomes one very odd-looking and awkwardly named wilderness area.

But the outcome could be much worse. Let's say the rains next spring are unusually heavy, washing all the topsoil away (the forest stood on a steep hillside). Only exotic weed species can survive now, and one of these happens to be Japanese honeysuckle, a nineteenth-century import of such rampant habit that it can choke out the growth of all trees indefinitely. We end up with no forest at all.

Nobody, in other words, can say what will happen in Cathedral Pines. And the reason is not that forest ecology is a young or imperfect science, but because *nature herself doesn't know what's going to happen here.* Nature has no grand design for this place. An incomprehensibly various and complex set of circumstances—some of human origin, but many not—will determine the future of Cathedral Pines. And whatever that future turns out to be, it would not unfold in precisely the same way twice. Nature may possess certain inherent tendencies, ones that theories such as forest succession can describe, but chance events can divert her course into an almost infinite number of different channels.

It's hard to square this fact with our strong sense that some kind of quasi-divine order inheres in nature's workings. But science lately has been finding that contingency plays nearly as big a role in natural history as it does in human history. Forest ecologists today will acknowledge that succession theories are little more than comforting narratives we impose on a surprisingly unpredictable process; even so-called climax forests are sometimes superseded. (In many places in the northern United States today, mature stands of oak are inexplicably being invaded by maples—skunks at the climax garden party.) Many ecologists will now freely admit that even the concept of an ecosystem is only a metaphor, a human construct imposed upon a much more variable and precarious reality. An ecosystem may be a useful concept, but no ecologist has ever succeeded in isolating one in nature. Nor is the process of evolution as logical or inexorable as we have thought. The current thinking in paleontology holds that the evolution of any given species, our own included, is not the necessary product of any natural laws, but rather the outcome of a concatenation of chance events—of "just history" in the words of Stephen Jay Gould. Add or remove any single happenstance—the asteroid fails to wipe out the dinosaurs; a little chordate worm called *Pikaia* succumbs in the Burgess extinction—and humankind never arrives.

Across several disciplines, in fact, scientists are coming to the conclusion that more "just history" is at work in nature than had previously been thought. Yet our metaphors still picture nature as logical, stable, and ahistorical—more like a watch than, say, an organism or a stock exchange, to name two metaphors that may well be more apt. Chance and contingency, it turns out, are everywhere in nature; she has no fixed goals, no unalterable pathways into the future, no inflexible rules that she herself can't bend or break at will. She is more like us (or we are more like her) than we ever imagined.

To learn this, for me at least, changes everything. I take it to be profoundly good news, though I can easily imagine how it might trouble some people. For many of us, nature is a last bastion of certainty; wilderness, as something beyond the reach of history and accident, is one of the last in our fast-dwindling supply of metaphysical absolutes, those comforting transcendental values by which we have traditionally taken

our measure and set our sights. To take away predictable, divinely ordered nature is to pull up one of our last remaining anchors. We are liable to float away on the trackless sea of our own subjectivity.

But the discovery that time and chance hold sway even in nature can
also be liberating. Because contingency is an invitation to participate in
history. Human choice is unnatural only if nature is deterministic; human change is unnatural only if she is changeless in our absence. If the
future of Cathedral Pines is up for grabs, if its history will always be the
product of myriad chance events, then why shouldn't we also claim our
place among all those deciding factors? For aren't we also one of nature's contingencies? And if our cigarette butts and Norway maples and
acid rain are going to shape the future of this place, then why not also
our hopes and desires?

Nature will condone an almost infinite number of possible futures for
Cathedral Pines. Some would be better than others. True, what we
would regard as "better" is probably not what the beetles would prefer.
But nature herself has no strong preference. That doesn't mean she will
countenance *any* outcome; she's already ruled out many possible futures (tropical rain forest, desert, etc.) and, all things being equal, she'd
probably lean toward the oak. But all things aren't equal (*her* idea) and
she is evidently happy to let the free play of numerous big and little
contingencies settle the matter. To exclude from these human desire
would be, at least in this place at this time, arbitrary, perverse and, yes,
unnatural.

Establishing that we should have a vote in the disposition of Cathedral
Pines is much easier than figuring out how we should cast it. The discovery of contingency in nature would seem to fling open a Pandora's
box. For if there's nothing fixed or inevitable about nature's course,
what's to stop us from concluding that anything goes? It's a whole lot
easier to assume that nature left to her own devices knows what's best
for a place, to let ourselves be guided by the wilderness ethic.

And maybe that's what we should do. Just because the wilderness
ethic is based on a picture of nature that is probably more mythical than
real doesn't necessarily mean we have to discard it. In the same way that
the Declaration of Independence begins with the useful fiction that "all
men are created equal," we could simply stipulate that Cathedral Pines
is wilderness, and proceed on that assumption. The test of the wilderness ethic is not how truthful it is, but how useful it is in doing what we
want to do—in protecting and improving the environment.

So how good a guide is the wilderness ethic in this particular case?
Certainly treating Cathedral Pines as a wilderness will keep us from
building condos there. When you don't trust yourself to do the right
thing, it helps to have an authority as wise and experienced as nature
to decide matters for you. But what if nature decides on Japanese honeysuckle—three hundred years of wall-to-wall brush? We would then

have a forest not only that we don't like, but that isn't even a wilderness, since it was man who brought Japanese honeysuckle to Cornwall. At this point in history, after humans have left their stamp on virtually every corner of the Earth, doing nothing is frequently a poor recipe for wilderness. In many cases it leads to a gradually deteriorating environment (as seems to be happening in Yellowstone), or to an environment shaped in large part by the acts and mistakes of previous human inhabitants.

If it's real wilderness we want in Cathedral Pines, and not merely an imagined innocence, we will have to restore it. This is the paradox faced by the Nature Conservancy and most other advocates of wilderness: at this point in history, creating a landscape that bears no marks of human intervention will require a certain amount of human intervention. At a minimum it would entail weeding the exotic species from Cathedral Pines, and that is something the Nature Conservancy's strict adherence to the wilderness ethic will not permit.

But what if the Conservancy *was* willing to intervene just enough to erase any evidence of man's presence? It would soon run up against some difficult questions for which its ethic leaves it ill-prepared. For what is the "real" state of nature in Cathedral Pines? Is it the way the forest looked before the settlers arrived? We could restore that condition by removing all traces of European man. Yet isn't that a rather Eurocentric (if not racist) notion of wilderness? We now know that the Indians were not the ecological eunuchs we once thought. They too left their mark on the land: fires set by Indians determined the composition of the New England forests and probably created that "wilderness" we call the Great Plains. For true untouched wilderness we have to go a lot further back than 1640 or 1492. And if we want to restore the landscape to its pre-Indian condition, then we're going to need a lot of heavy ice-making equipment (not to mention a few woolly mammoths) to make it look right.

But even that would be arbitrary. In fact there is no single moment in time that we can point to and say, *this* is the state of nature in Cathedral Pines. Just since the last ice age alone, that "state of nature" has undergone a thorough revolution every thousand years or so, as tree species forced south by the glaciers migrated back north (a process that is still going on), as the Indians arrived and set their fires, as the large mammals disappeared, as the climate fluctuated—as all the usual historical contingencies came on and off the stage. For several thousand years after the ice age, this part of Connecticut was a treeless tundra; is *that* the true state of nature in Cathedral Pines? The inescapable fact is that, if we want wilderness here, we will have to choose *which* wilderness we want—an idea that is inimical to the wilderness ethic. For wasn't the attraction of wilderness precisely the fact that it relieved us of having to make choices—wasn't nature going to decide, letting us off the hook of history and anthropocentrism?

No such luck, it seems. "Wilderness" is not nearly as straightforward or dependable a guide as we'd like to believe. If we do nothing, we may end up with an impoverished weed patch of our own (indirect) creation, which would hardly count as a victory for wilderness. And if we want to restore Cathedral Pines to some earlier condition, we're forced into making the kinds of inevitably anthropocentric choices and distinctions we turned to wilderness to escape. (Indeed, doing a decent job of wilderness restoration would take all the technology and scientific know-how humans can muster.) Either way, there appears to be no escape from history, not even in nature.

The reason that the wilderness ethic isn't very helpful in a place like Cathedral Pines is that it's an absolutist ethic: man or nature, it says, pick one. As soon as history or circumstance blurs that line, it gets us into trouble. There are times and places when man or nature is the right and necessary choice; back at Hetch Hetchy in 1907 that may well have been the case. But it seems to me that these days most of the environmental questions we face are more like the ambiguous ones posed by Cathedral Pines, and about these the wilderness ethic has less and less to say that is of much help.

The wilderness ethic doesn't tell us what to do when Yellowstone's ecosystem begins to deteriorate, as a result not of our interference but of our neglect. When a species threatens to overwhelm and ruin a habitat because history happened to kill off the predator that once kept its population in check, the ethic is mute. It is confounded, too, when the only hope for the survival of another species is the manipulation of its natural habitat by man. It has nothing to say in all those places where development is desirable or unavoidable except: Don't do it. When we're forced to choose between a hydroelectric power plant and a nuclear one, it refuses to help. That's because the wilderness ethic can't make distinctions between one kind of intervention in nature and another—between weeding Cathedral Pines and developing a theme park there. "You might as well put up condos" is its classic answer to any plan for human intervention in nature.

"All or nothing," says the wilderness ethic, and in fact we've ended up with a landscape in America that conforms to that injunction remarkably well. Thanks to exactly this kind of either/or thinking, Americans have done an admirable job of drawing lines around certain sacred areas (we did invent the wilderness area) and a terrible job of managing the rest of our land. The reason is not hard to find: the only environmental ethic we have has nothing useful to say about those areas outside the line. Once a landscape is no longer "virgin" it is typically written off as fallen, lost to nature, irredeemable. We hand it over to the jurisdiction of that other sacrosanct American ethic: laissez-faire economics. "You might as well put up condos." And so we do.

Indeed, the wilderness ethic and laissez-faire economics, antithetical as they might at first appear, are really mirror images of one another. Each proposes a quasi-divine force—Nature, the Market—that, left to its own devices, somehow knows what's best for a place. Nature and the market are both self-regulating, guided by an invisible hand. Worshippers of either share a deep, Puritan distrust of man, taking it on faith that human tinkering with the natural or economic order can only pervert it. Neither will acknowledge that their respective divinities can also err: that nature produces the AIDS virus as well as the rose, that the same markets that produce stupendous wealth can also crash. (Actually, worshippers of the market are a bit more realistic than worshippers of nature: they long ago stopped relying on the free market to supply us with such necessities as food and shelter. Though they don't like to talk about it much, they accept the need for society to "garden" the market.)

Essentially, we have divided our country in two, between the kingdom of wilderness, which rules about 8 percent of America's land, and the kingdom of the market, which rules the rest. Perhaps we should be grateful for secure borders. But what do those of us who care about nature do when we're on the market side, which is most of the time? How do we behave? What are our goals? We can't reasonably expect to change the borders, no matter how many power lines and dams Earth First! blows up. No, the wilderness ethic won't be of much help over here. Its politics are bound to be hopelessly romantic (consisting of impractical schemes to redraw the borders) or nihilistic. Faced with hard questions about how to confront global environmental problems such as the greenhouse effect or ozone depletion (problems that respect no borders), adherents of the wilderness ethic are apt to throw up their hands in despair and declare the "end of nature."

The only thing that's really in danger of ending is a romantic, pantheistic idea of nature that we invented in the first place, one whose passing might well turn out to be a blessing in disguise. Useful as it has been in helping us protect the sacred 8 percent, it nevertheless has failed to prevent us from doing a great deal of damage to the remaining 92 percent. This old idea may have taught us how to worship nature, but it didn't tell us how to live with her. It told us more than we needed to know about virginity and rape, and almost nothing about marriage. The metaphor of divine nature can admit only two roles for man: as worshipper (the naturalist's role) or temple destroyer (the developer's). But that drama is all played out now. The temple's been destroyed—if it ever was a temple. Nature *is* dead, if by nature we mean something that stands apart from man and messy history. And now that it is, perhaps we can begin to write some new parts for ourselves, ones that will show us how to start out from here, not from some imagined state of innocence, and let us get down to the work at hand.

Thoreau and Muir and their descendants went to the wilderness and returned with the makings of America's first environmental ethic. Today it still stands, though somewhat strained and tattered. What if now, instead of to the wilderness, we were to look to the garden for the makings of a new ethic? One that would not necessarily supplant the earlier one, but might give us something useful to say in those cases when it is silent or unhelpful?

It will take better thinkers than me to flesh out what such an ethic might look like. But even my limited experience in the garden has persuaded me that the materials needed to construct it—the fresh metaphors about nature we need—may be found there. For the garden is a place with long experience of questions having to do with man *in* nature. Below are some provisional notes, based on my own experiences and the experiences of other gardeners I've met or read, on the kinds of answers the garden is apt to give.

1. An ethic based on the garden would give local answers. Unlike the wilderness idea, it would propose different solutions in different places and times. This strikes me as both a strength and a weakness. It's a weakness because a garden ethic will never speak as clearly or univocally as the wilderness ethic does. In a country as large and geographically various as this, it is probably inevitable that we will favor ab ract landscape ideas—grids, lawns, monocultures, wildernesses—which can be applied across the board, even legislated nationally; such ideas have the power to simplify and unite. Yet isn't this power itself part of the problem? The health of a place generally suffers whenever we impose practices on it that are better suited to another place; a lawn in Virginia makes sense in a way that a lawn in Arizona does not.

So a garden ethic would begin with Alexander Pope's famous advice to landscape designers: "Consult the Genius of the Place in all." It's hard to imagine this slogan ever replacing Earth First!'s "No Compromise in Defense of Mother Earth" on American bumper stickers; nor should it, at least not everywhere. For Pope's dictum suggests that there are places whose "genius" will, if hearkened to, counsel "no compromise." Yet what is right for Yosemite is not necessarily right for Cathedral Pines.

2. The gardener starts out from here. By that I mean, he accepts contingency, his own and nature's. He doesn't spend a lot of time worrying about whether he has a god-given right to change nature. It's enough for him to know that, for some historical or biological reason, humankind finds itself living in places (six of the seven continents) where it must substantially alter the environment in order to survive. If we had remained on African savanna things might be different. And if I lived in zone six I could probably grow good tomatoes without the use of plastic. The gardener learns to play the hand he's been dealt.

3. A garden ethic would be frankly anthropocentric. As I began to understand when I planted my roses and my maple tree, we know nature only through the screen of our metaphors; to see her plain is probably impossible. (And not necessarily desirable, as George Eliot once suggested: "If we could hear the squirrel's heartbeat, the sound of the grass growing, we should die of that roar." Without the editing of our perceptions, nature might prove unbearable.) Melville was describing all of nature when he described the whiteness of the whale, its "dumb blankness, full of meaning." Even wilderness, in both its satanic and benevolent incarnations, is an historical, man-made idea. Every one of our various metaphors for nature—"wilderness," "ecosystem," "Gaia," "resource," "wasteland"—is already a kind of garden, an indissoluble mixture of our culture and whatever it is that's really out there. "Garden" may sound like a hopelessly anthropocentric concept, but it's probably one we can't get past.

The gardener doesn't waste much time on metaphysics—on figuring out what a "truer" perspective on nature (such as biocentrism or geocentrism) might look like. That's probably because he's noticed that most of the very long or wide perspectives we've recently been asked to adopt (including the one advanced by the Nature Conservancy in Cathedral Pines) are indifferent to our well-being and survival as a species. On this point he agrees with Wendell Berry—that "it is not natural to be disloyal to one's own kind."

4. That said, though, the gardener's conception of his self-interest is broad and enlightened. Anthropocentric as he may be, he recognizes that he is dependent for his health and survival on many other forms of life, so he is careful to take their interests into account in whatever he does. He is in fact a wilderness advocate of a certain kind. It is when he respects and nurtures the wilderness of his soil and his plants that his garden seems to flourish most. Wildness, he has found, resides not only out there, but right here: in his soil, in his plants, even in himself. Overcultivation tends to repress this quality, which experience tells him is necessary to health in all three realms. But wildness is more a quality than a place, and though humans can't manufacture it, they can nourish and husband it. That is precisely what I'm doing when I make compost and return it to the soil; it is what we could be doing in Cathedral Pines (and not necessarily by leaving the place alone). The gardener cultivates wildness, but he does so carefully and respectfully, in full recognition of its mystery.

5. The gardener tends not to be romantic about nature. What could be more natural than the storms and droughts and plagues that ruin his garden? Cruelty, aggression, suffering—these too are nature's offspring (and not, as Rousseau tried to convince us, culture's). Nature is probably a poor place to look for values. She was indifferent to humankind's arrival, and she is indifferent to our survival.

It's only in the last century or so that we seem to have forgotten this. Our romance of nature is a comparatively recent idea, the product of the industrial age's novel conceit that nature could be conquered, and probably also of the fact that few of us work with nature directly anymore. But should current weather forecasts prove to be accurate (a rapid, permanent warming trend accompanied by severe storms), our current romance will look like a brief historical anomaly, a momentary lapse of judgment. Nature may once again turn dangerous and capricious and unconquerable. When this happens, we will quickly lose our crush on her.

Compared to the naturalist, the gardener never fell head over heels for nature. He's seen her ruin his plans too many times for that. The gardener has learned, perforce, to live with her ambiguities—that she is neither all good nor all bad, that she gives as well as takes away. Nature's apt to pull the rug out from under us at any time, to make a grim joke of our noblest intention. Perhaps this explains why garden writing tends to be comic, rather than lyrical or elegiac in the way that nature writing usually is: the gardener can never quite forget about the rug underfoot, the possibility of the offstage hook.

6. The gardener feels he has a legitimate quarrel with nature—with her weeds and storms and plagues, her rot and death. What's more, that quarrel has produced much of value, not only in his own time here (this garden, these fruits), but over the whole course of Western history. Civilization itself, as Freud and Frazer and many others have observed, is the product of that quarrel. But at the same time, the gardener appreciates that it would probably not be in his interest, or in nature's, to push his side of this argument too hard. Many points of contention that humankind thought it had won—DDT's victory over insects, say, or medicine's conquest of infectious disease—turned out to be Pyrrhic or illusory triumphs. Better to keep the quarrel going, the good gardener reasons, than to reach for outright victory, which is dangerous in the attempt and probably impossible anyway.

7. The gardener doesn't take it for granted that man's impact on nature will always be negative. Perhaps he's observed how his own garden has made this patch of land a better place, even by nature's own standards. His gardening has greatly increased the diversity and abundance of life in this place. Besides the many exotic species of plants he's introduced, the mammal, rodent, and insect populations have burgeoned, and his soil supports a much richer community of microbes than it did before.

Judged strictly by these standards, nature occasionally makes mistakes. The climax forest could certainly be considered one (a place where the number and variety of living things have declined to a crisis point) and evolution teems with others. At the same time, it should be acknowledged that man occasionally creates new ecosystems much richer than the ones they replaced, and not merely on the scale of a garden: think of the tall-grass prairies of the Midwest, England's hedgerow landscape, the countryside of the Ile de France, the patchwork of fields and forests in this part of New England. Most of us would be happy to call such places "nature," but that does not do them (or us) justice; they are really a kind of garden, a second nature.

The gardener doesn't feel that by virtue of the fact that he changes nature he is somehow outside of it. He looks around and sees that human hopes and desires are by now part and parcel of the landscape. The "environment" is not, and has never been, a neutral, fixed backdrop; it is in fact alive, changing all the time in response to innumerable contingencies, one of these being the presence within it of the gardener. And that presence is neither inherently good nor bad.

8. The gardener firmly believes it is possible to make distinctions between kinds and degrees of human intervention in nature. Isn't the difference between the Ile de France and Love Canal, or a pine forest and a condo development, proof enough that the choice isn't really between "all or nothing"? The gardener doesn't doubt that it is possible to discriminate; it is through experience in the garden that he develops this faculty.

Because of his experience, the gardener is not likely to conclude from the fact that some intervention in nature is unavoidable, therefore "anything goes." This is precisely where his skill and interest lie: in determining what does and does not go in a particular place. How much is too much? What suits this land? How can we get what we want here while nature goes about getting what she wants? He has no doubt that good answers to these questions can be found.

9. The good gardener commonly borrows his methods, if not his goals, from nature herself. For though nature doesn't seem to dictate in advance what we can do in a place—we are free, in the same way evolution is, to try something completely new—in the end she will let us know what does and does not work. She is above all a pragmatist, and so is the successful gardener.

By studying nature's ways and means, the gardener can find answers to the questions, What is apt to work? What avails here? This seems to hold true at many levels of specificity. In one particular patch of my vegetable garden—a low, damp area—I failed with every crop I planted until I stopped to consider what nature grew in a similar area nearby: briars. So I planted raspberries, which are of course a cultivated kind of briar, and they have flourished. A trivial case, but it shows how attentiveness to nature can help us to attune our desires with her ways.

The imitation of nature is of course the principle underlying organic gardening. Organic gardeners have learned to mimic nature's own methods of building fertility in the soil, controlling insect populations and disease, recycling nutrients. But the practices we call "organic" are not themselves "natural," any more than the bird call of a hunter is natural. They are more like man-made analogues of natural processes. But they seem to work. And they at least suggest a way to approach other problems—from a town's decision on what to do with a blown-down pine forest, to society's choice among novel new technologies. In each case, there will be some alternatives that align our needs and desires with nature's ways more closely than others.

It does seem that we do best in nature when we imitate her—when we learn to think like running water, or a carrot, an aphid, a pine forest, or a compost pile. That's probably because nature, after almost four billion years of trial-and-error experience, has wider knowledge of what works in life. Surely we're better off learning how to draw on her experience than trying to repeat it, if only because we don't have that kind of time.

10. If nature is one necessary source of instruction for a garden ethic, culture is the other. Civilization may be part of our problem with respect to nature, but there will be no solution without it. As Wendell Berry has pointed out, it is culture, and certainly not nature, that teaches us to observe and remember, to learn from our mistakes, to share our experiences, and perhaps most important of all, to restrain ourselves. Nature does not teach its creatures to control their appetites except by the harshest of lessons—epidemics, mass death, extinctions. Nothing would be more natural than for humankind to burden the environment to the extent that it was rendered unfit for human life. Nature in that event would not be the loser, nor would it disturb her laws in the least—operating as it has always done, natural selection would unceremoniously do us in. Should this fate be averted, it will only be because our culture—*our* laws and metaphors, our science and technology, our ongoing conversation about nature and man's place in it—pointed us in the direction of a different future. Nature will not do this for us.

The gardener in nature is that most artificial of creatures, a civilized human being: in control of his appetites, solicitous of nature, self-conscious and responsible, mindful of the past and the future, and at ease with the fundamental ambiguity of his predicament—which is that though he lives in nature, he is no longer strictly *of* nature. Further, he knows that neither his success nor his failure in this place is ordained. Nature is apparently indifferent to his fate, and this leaves him free—indeed, obliges him—to make his own way here as best he can.

What would an ethic based on these ideas—based on the idea of the garden—advise us to do in Cathedral Pines? I don't know enough about the ecology of the place to say with certainty, but I think I have some sense of how we might proceed under its dispensation. We would start out, of course, by consulting "the Genius of the Place." This would tell us, among other things, that Cathedral Pines is not a wilderness, and so probably should not be treated as one. It is a cultural as well as a natural landscape, and to exclude the wishes of the townspeople from our plans for the place would be false. To treat it now as wilderness is to impose an abstract and alien idea on it.

Consulting the genius of the place also means inquiring as to what nature will allow us to do here—what this "locale permits, and what [it] denies," as Virgil wrote in *The Georgics*. We know right off, for instance, that this plot of land can support a magnificent forest of white pines. Nature would not object if we decided to replant the pine forest. Indeed, this would be a perfectly reasonable, environmentally sound thing to do.

If we chose to go this route, we would be undertaking a fairly simple act of what is called "ecological restoration." This relatively new school of environmentalism has its roots in Aldo Leopold's pioneering efforts to re-create a tall-grass prairie on the grounds of the University of Wisconsin Arboretum in the 1930s. Leopold and his followers (who continue to maintain the restored prairie today) believed that it is not always enough to conserve the land—that sometimes it is desirable, and possible, for man to intervene in nature in order to improve it. Specifically, man should intervene to re-create damaged ecosystems: polluted rivers, clear-cut forests, vanished prairies, dead lakes. The restorationists also believe, and in this they remind me of the green thumb, that the best way to learn about nature's ways is by trying to imitate them. (In fact much of what we know about the role of fire in creating and sustaining prairies comes from their efforts.) But the most important contribution of the restorationists has been to set forth a positive, active role for man in nature—in their conception, as equal parts gardener and healer. It seems to me that the idea of ecological restoration is consistent with a garden ethic, and perhaps with the Hippocratic Oath as well.

From the work of the ecological restorationists, we now know that it is possible to skip and manipulate the stages of forest succession. They would probably advise us to burn the fallen timber—an act that, though not strictly speaking "natural," would serve as an effective analogue of the natural process by which a forest is regenerated. The fires we set would reinvigorate the soil (thereby enhancing *that* wilderness) and at the same time clear out the weed species, hardwood saplings, and brush. By doing all this, we will have imitated the conditions under which a white pine forest is born, and the pines might then return on their own. Or else—it makes little difference—we could plant them. At that point, our work would be done, and the pine forest could take care of itself. It would take many decades, but restoring the Cathedral Pines would strain neither our capabilities nor nature's sufferance. And in doing so, we would also be restoring the congenial relationship between man and nature that prevailed in this place before the storm and the subsequent controversy. That would be no small thing.

Nature would not preclude more novel solutions for Cathedral Pines—other kinds of forest-gardens or even parks could probably flourish on this site. But since the town has traditionally regarded Cathedral Pines as a kind of local institution, one steeped in shared memories and historical significance, I would argue that the genius of the place rules out doing anything unprecedented here. The past is our best guide in this particular case, and not only on questions of ecology.

But replanting the pine forest is not the only good option for Cathedral Pines. There is another forest we might want to restore on this site, one that is also in keeping with its history and its meaning to the town.

Before the storm, we used to come to Cathedral Pines and imagine that this was how the New World forest looked to the first settlers. We now know that the precolonial forest probably looked somewhat different—for one thing, it was not exclusively pine. But it's conceivable that we could restore Cathedral Pines to something closely resembling its actual precolonial condition. By analyzing historical accounts, the rings of fallen trees, and fossilized pollen grains buried in the soil, we could reconstruct the variety and composition of species that flourished here in 1739, the year when the colonists first settled near this place and formed the town of Cornwall. We know that nature, having done so once before, would probably permit us to have such a forest here. And, using some of the more advanced techniques of ecological restoration, it is probably within our competence to re-create a precolonial forest on this site.

We would do this not because we'd decided to be faithful to the "state of nature" at Cathedral Pines, but very simply because the precolonial forest happens to mean a great deal to us. It is a touchstone in the history of this town, not to mention this nation. A walk in a restored version of the precolonial forest might recall us to our culture's first, fateful impressions of America, to our thoughts on coming upon what Fitzgerald called the "fresh green breast of the new world." In the contemplation of that scene we might be moved to reconsider what happened next—to us, to the Indians who once hunted here, to nature in this corner of America.

This is pretty much what I would have stood up and said if we'd had a town meeting to decide what to do in Cathedral Pines. Certainly a town meeting would have been a fitting way to decide the matter, nicely in keeping with the genius of *this* place, a small town in New England. I can easily imagine the speeches and the arguments. The people from the Nature Conservancy would have made their plea for leaving the place alone, for "letting nature take her course." Richard Dakin, the first selectman, and John Calhoun, the forest's nearest neighbor, would have warned about the dangers of fire. And then we might have heard some other points of view. I would have tried to make a pitch for restoration, talking about some of the ways we might "garden" the site. I can imagine Ian Ingersoll, a gifted cabinetmaker in town, speaking with feeling about the waste of such rare timbers, and the prospect of sitting down to a Thanksgiving dinner at a table in which you could see rings formed at the time of the American Revolution. Maybe somebody else would have talked about how much she missed her Sunday afternoon walks in the forest, and how very sad the place looked now. A scientist from the Yale School of Forestry might have patiently tried to explain, as indeed one Yale scientist did in the press, why "It's just as pretty to me now as it was then."

This is the same fellow who said, "If you're going to clean it up, you might as well put up condos." I can't imagine anyone actually proposing that, or any other kind of development in Cathedral Pines. But if someone did, he would probably get shouted down. Because we have too much respect for this place; and besides, our sympathies and interests are a lot more complicated than the economists or environmentalists always seem to think. Sooner than a developer, we'd be likely to hear from somebody speaking on behalf of the forest's fauna—the species who have lost out in the storm (like the owls), but also the ones for whom doing nothing would be a boon (the beetles). And so the various interests of the animals would be taken into account, too; indeed, I expect that "nature"—all *those* different (and contradictory) points of view—would be well represented at this town meeting. Perhaps it is naïve of me to think so, but I'm confident that in the course of a public, democratic conversation about the disposition of Cathedral Pines, we would eventually arrive at a solution that would have at once pleased us and not offended nature.

But unfortunately that's not what happened. The future of Cathedral Pines was decided in a closed-door meeting at the Nature Conservancy in September, after a series of negotiations with the selectmen and the owners of adjacent property. The result was a compromise that seems to have pleased no one. The fallen trees will remain untouched—except for a fifty-foot swath clear-cut around the perimeter of the forest, a firebreak intended to appease the owners of a few nearby houses. The sole human interest taken into account in the decision was the worry about fire.

I drove up there one day in late fall to have a look around, to see what the truce between the Conservancy and the town had wrought. What a sad sight it is. Unwittingly, and in spite of the good intentions on both sides, the Conservancy and the selectmen have conspired to create a landscape that is a perfect symbol of our perverted relation to nature. The firebreak looks like nothing so much as a no-man's-land in a war zone, a forbidding expanse of blistered ground impounding what little remains of the Cathedral Pines. The landscape we've made here is grotesque. And yet it is the logical outcome of a confrontation between, on the one side, an abstract and mistaken concept of nature's interests and, on the other, a pinched and demeaning notion of our own interests. We should probably not be surprised that the result of such a confrontation is not a wilderness, or a garden, but a DMZ.

Questions for Thinking and Writing

1. Comment on the irony of naming Cathedral PInes a "natural landmark." How is this incongruity reflected in the conflict between the town and the traditional naturalists? What is ironic about the cause of the destruction of the pine grove?
2. Discuss the possibility that our concept of how the ecosystem works might after all be a human construct that really does not explain how nature works at all.
3. If given the opportunity, how would you settle the dispute over Cathedral Pines? What line of reasoning would you take to mollify opposing sides?

❧ Christopher Hallowell (b. 1945)

Water Crisis on the Cape (1991)

Christopher Hallowell often writes about the awkward meeting of people and nature. He attributes this interest to his boyhood on a dairy farm in western Massachusetts. "A farm is a wonderful place to observe how nature reacts to being pushed around," he once said in an interview. "It is never destroyed in the sense of being paved over but it is manipulated through plowing and planting and through the rerouting of streams and the cutting of hay. Wildlife, domestic animals, and people all respond differently and tellingly."

The profound sense of loss in Hallowell's writing about the environment in this essay is an implicit acknowledgment of its degradation and need for renewal. His tone is poignant because the subject matter of "Water Crisis on the Cape" is so crucial to the character of a place he loves. Hallowell points out that while the people of Cape Cod have physically lost their water to contamination, they have lost much more in a spiritual sense, for they know that what had always been theirs for the taking, what had been given to them by nature, is no longer available.

Hallowell attended local schools near his family's farm and then Milton Academy in Milton, Massachusetts. In 1968, he graduated from Harvard College and spent the following year living in the Peruvian Andes on a Rockefeller fellowship administered by Harvard. There he began his professional career writing for the Christian Science Monitor. *Upon his return from Peru, he entered the Columbia University Graduate School of Journalism and graduated in 1971. Hallowell then worked as an editor and writer for a number of magazines, among them* Natural History. *His first book,* People of the Bayou *(1979), about the Cajuns in the marshes of south Louisiana, was inspired while on assignment for that magazine.*

In 1985, Hallowell published Growing Old, Staying Young, *a reportorial analysis of American gerontological research. He began the project while experiencing his parents aging in lonely and isolated ways. Two years later, he published* Father to the Man *(1987), a reflection on being a father to his two children and on being a son to his own father.*

Although Hallowell writes about subjects close to the heart, his main impetus for writing has always centered on environmental issues. He is a keen observer of how people living in a given environment learn to accommodate to it. In this regard, Hallowell shares a perception with Bill McKibben that there very well may be an end of nature.

Since 1988, he has divided his time between writing and teaching at Baruch College, City University of New York, where he is a professor of journalism. He still spends much time on Cape Cod, but brings his own supply of bottled water.

To the casual observer, the Massachusetts Military Reservation on Cape Cod looks asleep, incapable of rising to military might. Ranks of mostly empty barracks with shattered windows and peeling paint march on without a soldier to give them purpose. Untraveled networks of roads, crisscrossing the base's 21,000 acres in an irregular weave, are cracked and weed-streaked. Overgrown ballfields, shuttered recreation clubs, and rusting machine shops tell of dormancy.

Only occasionally, and far across the flatness, do squadrons of F-15 fighter jets on Air National Guard training missions rise from distant runways that are off limits to visitors. Helicopters fly sporadically and seemingly aimlessly over the scrubby pine cover.

Despite the present appearance of relative harmlessness, dangers lurk at this military base, familiarly known as Otis Air Force Base or Camp Edwards. It is horribly poisoned. The contamination here is among the worst of the 100-plus bases that the Environmental Protection Agency has assigned Superfund site status to (a classification that forces the responsible parties to clean up the mess). Millions of gallons of toxins—among them aviation fuel, emulsifiers, solvents, degreasers, photographic chemicals—seep beneath its runways, artillery ranges, and drill grounds.

Dumped during the base's various military heydays between the 1940s and 1970s, these contaminants are now percolating deep into the Cape's sandy soil beyond the base's boundaries. They are destined to poison much of the drinking water of the Upper Cape, which includes the towns of Barnstable, Bourne, Falmouth, Mashpee, and Sandwich.

Cape Cod's water is also being poisoned by other means—from the effluent flowing from the stampede construction of malls, from failing septic systems, from densely packed housing subdivisions, from leaking underground fuel tanks, from misplaced wells. The damage is exacerbated by the region's unique geological footing—a sand-filled aquifer from which virtually all the Cape's water is drawn.

This is a story about a tragedy unfolding and efforts to track its spread before too many people get hurt. It is a story of past mistakes and naive actions that are now merely bruising this famous gnarled arm that juts out into the Atlantic Ocean but that eventually could maim it.

"More and more portions of the aquifer are becoming contaminated; more and more places are unacceptable for wells," says Susan Nickerson, executive director of the Association for the Preservation of Cape Cod. "It's like a checkerboard; the empty spaces where there is no contamination are getting filled in with toxins."

Yet the poisoning of the Cape's water is no Love Canal or Minamata. Horrible birth defects, skin sores, and epilepsy are not part of the picture here. Even so, cancer is on an alarming rise. Between 1982 and 1988, its incidence was 22 percent greater in the five towns that make up the Upper Cape than in the rest of the state, according to the Massachusetts Cancer Registry. No one knows why, but almost everyone suspects pollution from the base.

"I am convinced intuitively that the base has caused a tremendous amount of cancer," says Joel Feigenbaum, a mathematics professor who lives in Sandwich and who founded the grass-roots organization called Upper Cape Concerned Citizens. "I am even more concerned about what will happen in the future when the mess is cleaned up. Plans mentioned to incinerate these contaminants really scare me."

Uncertainty is hard for people here to deal with, as it is for people in the other areas of the country suffering from the same relatively low-level but constant toxicity in water supplies.

"The average person on the Cape is scared to death to drink the water," says Al Orlando, an elementary school music teacher who lives in Mashpee, "but it's not bad enough to want to move. It's just a waiting game to see if anything happens to us."

Local geology makes the Cape's water crisis especially sinister. The region's attractions, from beaches and dunes to amusement parks, from tranquil marshes to Provincetown's tourist-clogged streets, rest on a pile of sand that is 300 to 900 feet thick and that was nudged into place by the last glacier and sculpted by time, current, and wind. Drop on this sand any liquid, whether it be rainfall, gasoline, or effluent from septic tanks or sewage treatment plants, and it vanishes as if into a sponge.

Almost every drop of water consumed on the Cape—save that which is imported from the mainland as bottled water and a portion of Falmouth's water supply that is pumped from a pond—comes from rain that has sunk into this gigantic aquifer.

The aquifer is segmented into six distinct, subterranean, sand-filled reservoirs called lenses. A longitudinal cross-section of the Cape would reveal the upward limit (what we think of as the water table) of these six bodies to conform in shape to the land above. The largest of these lenses lies under the Upper Cape, where 60 percent of the Cape's permanent population of around 190,000 lives. (During the summer months the population soars by an additional 300,000 people.) The highest point of this lens is located right under the military reservation, which is in turn the highest point on Cape Cod.

Rainwater, or any other fluid, flows along the underground contours of each lens just as surface runoff follows a hill's contours. Eventually it spreads outward from the steepest contour of the lens, moving at the average rate of one foot a day until it reaches the sea.

Raindrops that over a century ago splattered into the sand where the base's runways are located are just now entering Nantucket Sound. The contaminants, mixed with the water, will take as long a time before they can disperse in the sea.

Before the flow of water through the Cape's aquatic lenses was well understood, the assumption prevailed that what went into the ground sank straight down, disappearing as if by magic. From 1955 to 1969, Air Force Super Constellation early-warning radar planes testing their fuel-dump valves jettisoned between one and five million gallons of aviation fuel on the base's two runway turnarounds; workers at a former missile site nearby poured unknown quantities of waste chemicals into dry wells because it then seemed like the easiest means of disposal; the base's sewage treatment plant received not only sewage but solvents, degreasers, photographic chemicals, and anything else that was poured down drains.

No one elsewhere on the Cape gave much thought to the siting of municipal landfills and sewage treatment plants. They were generally located inland, away from valuable shorefront real estate. Inland, though, is where the land and consequently the water table are highest. Toxins leaching out of dumps seeped through the aquifer's lenses and flowed, it turned out in a number of instances, right into municipal water supply wells. Both Falmouth and Mashpee had to close wells located in the path of the creeping contamination. Effluent from the Barnstable sewage treatment plant is now inching towards that town's public water supply wells. It's just a matter of time. Recently, the Barnstable Water Company, which supplies water to Hyannis, initiated a water-cleansing process known as air-stripping, whereby toxins in water are removed by air forced through it.

On the Cape, homeowners have unwittingly contributed to the messy groundwater situation, too. Ninety percent of the homes here have their own septic systems. While sand is an excellent filter of bacterial contamination, it lets other household toxins—anything from bleach to paint thinner to pesticides—enter the water supply unaltered.

Every underground gas tank that springs a leak poses a threat, too. In Eastham, several years ago, gasoline spurted from the kitchen faucet in a house adjacent to a gas station. The station's underground tank had sprung a leak, and gas had trickled into the groundwater. In 1977, 60 percent of Provincetown's municipal water supply was cut off after two to three thousand gallons of gasoline leaked from a gas station's underground tank 600 feet from the well. The hole in the tank was the diameter of a pencil.

Today, more than thirteen years later, Provincetown has spent almost four million dollars trying to rectify the contamination by pumping the bad water out of the area through five wells especially drilled for that purpose, in hopes that increased filtering and aeration will remove the toxins.

The shallow waters that bathe the Cape's beaches and nurse its tidal ponds and mudflats are the end of the road, so to speak, for the contaminants from septic systems, treatment plants, landfills, the military base, and leaking storage tanks. Nitrates and fecal coliform bacteria from septic systems are the contaminants of the moment along the shore, but the chemical toxins from fuel spills and from the base are not far behind as they move through the aquifer to the ocean's edge. The effect on clamming has been drastic. By 1990, the pollution had closed almost 6,000 acres of clambeds; the clambed closures have increased annually since 1970, when only 400 acres were condemned.

Several summers ago, health authorities closed a public beach in the little Buzzards Bay community of Pocasset. High fecal coliform counts from cottages perched at the water's edge were to blame. For the first time, permanent residents and summer visitors were denied one of the season's most obvious pleasures, in the disbelief that the pollution associated with urban life had come to poison what many consider the sanctity of Cape life.

Problems with the Cape's drinking water first came to light in 1978 in an area of Falmouth known as Ashumet Valley. For several years, some residents had wondered about the suds that foamed from their taps. But this happened only occasionally and the water tasted okay. Then, in the early 1980s, a routine analysis in a nearby public supply well revealed the cause of the foaming. Oils, solvents, detergents, and nitrates were fouling this well and forty of 200 private wells nearby. The Massachusetts Department of Environmental Quality immediately closed the public well, and the state began delivering bottled water to residents.

The contamination was traced to the military base's sewage treatment plant, located since the 1930s a mere 600 feet from the Falmouth boundary line. Toxins tend to move through the aquifer in a swath, known as a plume, at varying depths depending on the type of substance. Solvents, for example, are heavy and sink down deep, while nitrates from a septic system remain closer to the surface.

The plume of poisoned water emanating from this site, and now moving under Ashumet Valley, is frighteningly large—two miles long, three-quarters of a mile wide, and more than fifty feet thick. Like the other eight plumes that have been identified as originating from the military base, this one is creeping southward at the rate of a foot a day. By the year 2000, its leading edge will be under the heart of Falmouth's commercial and residential district.

In a deserted part of the base, away from the artillery ranges, Daniel Santos, an intense young man, surveyed the progress of a monitoring well being drilled last winter. The drilling was taking place in response to contaminated water recently discerned in a well in the neighboring town of Sandwich. Santos suspected that the source is a leak in an old fuel line that snakes across the base's pine forests. To pinpoint the location, a string of monitoring wells has been sunk across the path of the groundwater's flow.

Santos was hired more than a year ago by the Air National Guard to be the liaison with a multitude of consulting firms trying to establish the extent of the contamination (the first step toward cleaning up), various state and federal environmental agencies, officials from the nearby towns, an increasingly frustrated public, and the press. He is constantly on the firing line, which is one reason he wanted to see the site. He wanted to be able to assure his detractors that something is being done.

A few evenings earlier, Santos had been taken to task for not doing enough. Angry residents of two neighborhoods in Mashpee had complained during a meeting that, while the National Guard has spent $15 million on studies on the pollution, virtually nothing had been done about cleaning up the mess.

"You spend more on studies, and we're the ones who suffer, with no results," William Martiros, a resident of Briarwood, a Mashpee subdivision, was quoted as saying in the Falmouth *Enterprise*. "What is your purpose? Aren't you trying to make it right for the people?"

"If someone tells me their water is leaking, or there's smoke coming into the house, I don't sit down and decide to do a study," accused Michael J. Forde, a resident of Johns Pond, another Mashpee neighborhood.

Accustomed as Santos is to such confrontation, indignation swelled in him. "We are doing exactly what we should be doing. These people are out of line. The average Superfund site cleanup time is ten years and we're going to come in under that," he exploded during an interview a few days later. "I'm sick of getting the blame. It only makes sense to find out the extent of the contamination before cleaning it up. After all, this is pretty low-level toxicity we are talking about here."

Finding out where the pollution is coming from, and the path it is taking, is only the first step in the cleaning-up process. The next step—what to do about it—is problematical. Santos listed the options. First, do nothing and let the toxins eventually seep into the ocean. Second, construct underground retaining walls to block the plumes, an option that would entail substantial physical disruption to the land. Third, attempt to clean the water by aerating it as it is pumped out of the ground, then running it through carbon filters, a course that would require literally decades to accomplish given the volume of water.

So far, more than seventy contamination sites have been identified, and many people think that this is only the beginning.

One of the most recent came to Santos rather informally. An anonymous caller who identified himself as an employee on the military reservation twenty years ago recalled having seen trucks dumping open barrels of a liquid in a deserted area. Santos went up in a helicopter to take a look. What he saw carved out of the pine forest below him was a grim acknowledgment of the unknown pollutant's toxicity: a splotch of sandy sterility the size of a baseball diamond. He knew he was looking down at the tip of another plume. Santos calls this kind of detective work "chasing a plume."

A mile from the drilling site, a fenced-off area with a large "Keep Out" sign warns trespassers away from an enormous, rusting building that is set back from the road. Just to the left of the structure—a former heating plant—Santos pointed out the location of three abandoned dry wells with cement block sides and gravel bottoms.

They had recently been cleaned out. Pride edged Santos' voice as he declared, "*There's* proof of something being done."

A report described the contents of one of the dry wells as "silty, black, tar-like, oily sediment." A more detailed analysis under a gas-chromato-graph screening revealed the organic compounds tetrachloroethylene (also called perchloroethylene or PCE), trichloroethylene (TCE), dichloroethylene (DCE), toluene, xylene, naphthalene, 2-methyl naph-thalene, phenanthrene, and a type of polychlorinated biphenyl (PCB). The gunk also included heavy metals such as aluminum, arsenic, bar-ium, cadmium, chromium, lead, mercury, and zinc.

All or some of these compounds and metals, sometimes in levels exceeding EPA guidelines by more than 100 times, are in the nine plumes so far discovered to be emanating from various points on the base. When ingested in sufficient quantities, they are known to cause a range of diseases and human tragedies including cancer, mutations, stillbirths, nervous disorders, and liver and kidney diseases.

Naturally, people like Michael J. Forde and Bill Martiros are con-cerned about these dangers. Martiros' well in Briarwood, a subdivision of wooded quarter-acre lots dotted with small ranch houses, split-levels, and modified saltboxes, was found to be contaminated in 1987. Since then the town of Mashpee has piped in water from a municipal well. Martiros had to pay $3,000 for a hookup.

He and his family have lived in their house since 1976. So, while the water that flows out of the home's faucets is now safe, the Martiros fam-ily may have been drinking water laced with contaminants for a decade. Martiros wonders if this is why he suffered from lightheadedness, dizzi-ness, balance difficulties, and a tendency to pronounce words backwards. He recalled that, after town water came in, these problems disappeared.

Michael Forde came to Johns Pond, a Mashpee subdivision adjacent to Briarwood, in the early 1980s, looking forward to the relative peace of Cape Cod. But he sensed something was wrong with the water.

"It smelled bad when you took a shower," he said. That worried him. Then one day, he recalled, some military people from the base rang his doorbell and told him that they wanted to talk to him about what they called "a problem."

"They told us that the odor was coming from sulphur in the water but that it was not dangerous," Forde said. "Then they said my well was con-taminated with toxins. It's funny. At first I was more worried about the smell. There was nothing tangible about the toxins. But then I won-dered if this was going to be another Love Canal."

Hoping to protect his family, Forde installed five water filters, three in his basement and two under his kitchen sink. The system cost him $2,800.

Almost everyone on the Cape, it seems, knows a friend or neigh-bor or colleague with some form of cancer. Until 1988, the link to contaminated water seemed obvious. But then the Massachusetts Department of Public Health released the results of a cancer study that left most people baffled. Though the study, the first one on the Cape, concluded that the lung cancer and leukemia mortality rates were significantly higher than in the rest of the state, there was no evidence that contaminated water was the culprit. In fact, there was no evidence that any single cause was to blame.

Yet the cancer rate is rapidly rising. In 1985, according to the Massachusetts Cancer Registry, 550 people on the Upper Cape were diagnosed with cancer; in 1986, 593 cases; in 1987, 641 cases; and in 1988, 752 cases.

Beginning in 1982, the Cancer Registry has calculated the number of cancer cases expected on the Upper Cape based on statewide averages. These expectations have taken into consideration such factors as the age, length of occupancy, occupation, race, and sex of the population. The expected cases on the Upper Cape based on this mathematical model have crept upwards annually from 450 per year in 1982 to around 500 in 1986, the last year for which a figure was calculated. (The state Cancer Registry is presently working on its calculations for 1987 and 1988, which will be released soon.)

When the actual number of diagnoses is compared to the expected number of cases and expressed as a percentage increase, the cancer picture on Cape Code becomes alarmingly dismal. Taking 1986 alone, the incidence rate for both males and females was 16.4 percent above the expected number. Although the state has not yet compiled expectation figures past 1986, Joel Feigenbaum, who has fought tirelessly to persuade the state to look more extensively at cancer on the Cape, has taken the state's mathematical model and calculated expectations for 1987 and 1988. His figures show that the actual diagnoses jumped to 26.1 percent over the expected number of cases for 1987, and preliminary estimates for 1988 suggest a 48 percent overage. For some unexplained reason, the rate among females is far greater than it is among males, particularly for lung cancer and leukemia.

"What really alarms me," Feigenbaum said recently, "is that, with all the people moving onto the Cape, the figures should become diluted and show a decreasing rate. So it may be that the situation is actually worse than these statistics imply." Between 1980 and 1990, the Cape's permanent, year-round population increased almost 15 percent to its present 190,000.

The contrast between the vague results of the 1988 study and the prevalence of cancer on the Cape prompted the state to contract with the Boston University School of Public Health for another study, this one on the incidence of nine different cancers (lung, breast, colon-rectal, bladder, kidney, brain, liver, and pancreatic cancers, and leukemia) found on the Cape. Though the results were still pending at the time of this article's preparation, the link between cancer and groundwater contamination, at least in the handful of plumes studied which emanated from the base and from several landfills, appears tenuous.

The B.U. study, which examined 1,042 cancer cases, "indicated that few study subjects had potential exposure from groundwater plumes emanating from various sites on or off the Massachusetts Military Reservation. These plumes, including the Ashumet Valley plume, do not appear to account for much if any of the cancer burden to the population at this time."

"Though it's unlikely that these plumes account for the increased cancer rate on the Upper Cape," said Dr. Ann Aschengrau, an associate professor of public health at Boston University who coordinated the study, "I wouldn't want to say it's safe to drink the water there."

The link between various cancers and many of the chemicals flowing from the base is well-established. Mice given oral doses of TCE, for example, have developed liver and lung cancers, lymphomas, and leukemia. Workers in the dry-cleaning industry, who tend to be exposed to high levels of PCE and TCE, suffer more deaths from leukemia and from bladder, kidney, and skin cancers than the norm. In Woburn, Massachusetts, drinking water contaminated with PCE and TCE is thought to be responsible for a high number of leukemia cases among children. And in areas of New Jersey, drinking water that is laced with up to 16 parts per billion of PCE and up to 46 parts per billion of TCE may be responsible for a high leukemia rate among females. For comparison's sake, these same contaminants in the water of the largest plume emanating from the base, the so-called CS-10 plume flowing from under the old BOMARC missile site, have been measured at 500 parts per billion.

Not only does water on the Cape, depending upon which part of the aquifer it is pumped from, contain PCE, but it may collect more of this carcinogen from the water pipes it travels through. In Massachusetts, some 700 miles of municipal water pipe, much of it on Cape Cod, is lined with vinyl which is supposed to maintain both the water's taste and appearance. In 1980, health officials discovered that the vinyl was leaching PCE, one of its components, because of a faulty manufacturing process. Though contaminant accumulations have been reduced through the installation of bleeder valves designed to keep the water moving through the pipes, the leaching is an ongoing process.

A lot of people on the Cape are drawing their own conclusions about the contamination. "I'm scared. We know so little about these chemicals," Ray Bowman, a Briarwood resident who now drinks town-supplied water, said. "My first thought when word got out was for my two young children. They're older now, but they still might come down with something. We all might."

The basement laboratory of the Barnstable County Health and Environmental Department fairly bristles with sophisticated new equipment. Five years ago, the lab's most sophisticated object was a device that measured coliform bacteria in water samples.

Stetson Hall, the department's director, was showing a visitor a gas-chromatograph mass spectrophotometer the state recently purchased for the lab. It has the capacity to measure what Hall says are "thousands of compounds" in water samples. His voice, his step, the sweep of his gestures, told of pride in this high-tech equipment. The spectrophotometer cost $100,000. It looks something like a very complicated photocopying machine.

Coliform is no longer a fail-safe measure of contaminated water; there are far subtler poisons. Besides, the sand underlying the Cape cleanses the groundwater of most of this bacteria. (The coliform that gets into marshes and the shallow ocean water off beaches comes from overflowing septic systems near the shore.) Of greater significance, and danger, are the increasing amounts of volatile organic compounds and nitrates that are being picked up by the spectrometers. Volatile organic compounds are not only coming from the base. They are also poured down drains by individuals and industries—cleansers, degreasers, bleaches, thinners, and solvents.

Then there are substances of more mysterious origin. The rising level of chloroform being detected in wells is a recent Cape water-contamination mystery. No one knows where it comes from. Perhaps, said Stetson Hall, bleaches in laundry soap are to blame.

Chloroform in trace levels is common in public drinking supplies. It usually occurs when chlorine, added to drinking water by some municipalities as a disinfectant, combines with surface runoff. In 1985 and 1986 all the public water supply wells on the Cape showed some chloroform, enough to be of concern but not enough to close down any wells. Last year a major well in Barnstable showed 39 parts per million of chloroform, a huge jump. The well, which has been closed, now shows 100 ppm of the substance.

"The mystery is that the water on the Cape is not chlorinated," says Dr. David Ozonoff, one of the principal scientists researching the cancer question on the Cape for the Boston University study. "So where does the chloroform come from? No one knows. What is known is that chloroform is carcinogenic and is particularly associated with colon and rectal cancers."

Nitrates, which are linked to stomach cancer and methemoglobinemia (blue baby syndrome), also occur in the water supply. The compound is formed when the ammonia in human and animal waste combines with microorganisms in septic systems. Nitrates also come from the tons of fertilizer annually dumped on golf courses and lawns.

Of the 90 percent of the homes on Cape Cod that have their own septic systems, many are on lots too small to have adequate leaching fields. Many systems are overused to the point of collapse, thus increasing nitrate levels.

Under usual conditions, groundwater contains from 0.5 to 1.0 part per million of nitrates. EPA guidelines specify no more than 10 ppm. Wells in some Cape subdivisions have measured 30 ppm, and wells with 15 to 20 ppm are not uncommon, particularly where lot sizes are between one-quarter and one-half acre.

Though the damage that nitrates are doing to Cape Codders is uncertain at best, these compounds are having a far more measurable effect on the countless estuaries and tidal ponds that form the shoreline's mottled edge. Scientists at the Woods Hole Oceanographic Institution have been witnessing the death of marine life in these shallow waters year after year. In warm weather, as the nutritious compounds trickle into ponds and marshes through leaking septic tanks and storm sewers, algae multiply in great blooms. As the bacteria population mushrooms, the available oxygen decreases and marine organisms begin to die off.

"Every coastal body of water around here shows some degree of oxygen depletion," says Brian Howes, a biogeochemist, from his cluttered office off his even more cluttered laboratory at Woods Hole. "What is happening in these ponds is an early warning system. They are the first interceptors of the toxins that may eventually affect life out in Buzzards Bay. Here is where the nurseries are."

Victims so far are the animals of the benthic, or bottom-dwelling, communities—marine worms, bivalves, and other invertebrates—the base of the carnivorous food chain. Though it is unknown the extent to which commercially valuable juvenile shell- and finfish species are affected by this hidden decimation, the assumptions are there. One example: During early spring, Woods Hole biologist George Hampson finds tiny shrimp in the ponds he studies. By midsummer, when algae levels are high and oxygen low, not a shrimp can be found. Entire local populations have been wiped out. Multiply this by the Cape's thousands of tidal basins, and you have a potentially serious adverse impact on fish and shellfish populations. The same may hold true for scallops, harvests of which have been declining for the past ten years; however, this may be due to normal, cyclical fluctuations.

"Even if a halt were put right now on the toxins going into the system," Hampson says, "you can't purge it overnight. It takes years for this stuff to weep out. We are doing everything wrong flushing into these ponds. There has to be an alternative system."

Such a system exists about twenty miles away. The Harwich Solar Aquatic Septage Treatment Plant has been in operation since March

1990. Designed to handle almost 5,000 gallons of septage (the "sewage" that is pumped out of septic tanks) per day, it generates two-thirds less sludge than a typical secondary sewage treatment plant, thus ameliorating the horrendous sludge disposal problem that plagues those operations. It also operates at a fraction of the cost. And the effluent that comes out of this innovative system is, technically speaking, potable. However, Bruce Strong, the plant's director of operations, says he would not tempt fate.

Strong talks about the facility as if it were *the* sewage solution. He could be right.

Raw sewage—after being aerated for several days in concrete basins where bacteria break down heavy particles which sink to the bottom—is pumped through three lines of six huge, transparent plastic tanks in a thirty-by-sixty-foot greenhouse that is made from struts and plastic sheeting. Duckweed and water hyacinths float in each tank, its liquid bubbling with air pumped up from the bottom. The hyacinths' dangling roots are home to myriad bacteria that forage on the nutrients in the sewage, breaking down the nitrates that have so much potential to do damage. The roots themselves absorb heavy metals. Strong lifts up a bunch of hyacinth and marvels at the plant's efficacy here in contrast to its destructive proliferation in the South, where it clogs streams, canals, and bayous.

Algae clinging to the interior wall of the tanks also feed on the nutrients, as do tiny worms that dwell in the algae. Golden shiners and tropical catfish inhabit the tanks but are lost to sight among the lush vegetation.

Effluent from these tanks nourishes two lovely, miniature marshes that sprout watercress, bulrushes, phragmites, and, in season, impatiens, and Johnny-jump-ups. "We'll try anything," Strong says. "If it works, great; if not, we just try something else."

If not yet sparkling, the water that comes out of these marshes and into a series of four additional plastic tanks for further cleansing is at least clear. From these, it gurgles into what Strong terms "polishing marshes." These sprout tiny prairies of canary grass bordered by banana plants, daffodils, and narcissus.

The greenhouse of the solar treatment plant is an entirely pleasant place. In winter, people come out to the Harwich town dump, a corner of which it occupies, to sit on benches in the balmy, 65-degree greenhouse to eat picnic lunches and be surrounded by the mini-marshes and all those plants thriving in sewage effluent. There is no foul odor here, just the feel of vibrant life being recycled. "It gladdens my heart to see folks enjoy this," says Bruce Strong. "We have taken everything nature has to offer us and we accelerate it."

Mind, this oasis is only a model. A decision will be made late this year whether to expand the project into a full-fledged treatment plant to handle all the septage of the 10,000 residents of Harwich. If this happens, and so far the project has been viewed with considerable respect as well as affection by Harwich residents, Strong has plans to expand his polishing marsh. "I see a lovely aquatic garden," he muses, "with walkways and paths and benches where people can come and relax and think about nature."

The development of Harwich's solar treatment plant suggests that a shift in perception is taking place among Cape Codders. There is increasing alarm here that the Cape is not bearing up well under the flood of people attracted to its shores. There is a sense that breaths are being held in hopes that worst fears will not be borne out—that the Cape will become so miserably crowded with malls and subdivisions and traffic jams and its water so horribly polluted that the place will lose its allure.

Tiring of looking around and seeing danger and damage, the residents of Barnstable County—which includes all of the Cape—decided to put into effect a plan that would attempt to assure a brighter future. In the spring of 1990, they voted in a referendum to form the Cape Cod Commission, whose purpose is to control development on the Cape. A unified body that has an influence over such a large geographic area is a new idea on the Cape, whose residents are noted for being as independent-minded as its commercial fishermen. By imposing housing-density restrictions, requiring the inclusion of open areas around developments, and preventing construction near public water supply wells, among other measures, the commission hopes to slow down, even rectify, the reckless building and thoughtless planning that have begun to change the Cape from peaceful refuge to garish sprawl.

Yet the formation of the commission is at best a catch-up effort. The damage has been done, particularly to the Cape's lifeblood—its water supply. Three generations from now, Cape Codders may finally see their drinking water clean. It will take that long for the pollutants to work through the aquifer and into the surrounding sea. Towards the middle of the next century, people on the Cape may be amazed at how *unthinking* their predecessors were to let pollution run rampant in the first place, and how *forward-thinking* they were to try to stop it before it was too late.

Questions for Thinking and Writing

1. How does Hallowell establish the connection between the present and future danger of the Cape's water supply with the pollution caused in the 1940s through the 1970s? Of the several kinds of effluent leaching into the Cape's aquifer, which of them may be leaching into a water supply in your community?

2. Compare the term *plume* as it is used to describe some negative aspect of the environment by Hallowell in "Water Crisis on the Cape" with Don DeLillo's use in "Airborne Toxic Event" (p. 376).
3. What are the basic steps in cleaning up the water pollution crisis as detailed by Hallowell? If the problem is so evident, why do you think it is taking so long for the cleanup to get into full swing? If you lived on Cape Cod, how would you feel about the risk of drinking the water? What would you do?

🌿 Rick Bass (b. 1958)

September 20 (1991)

Rick Bass maintains that isolation is essential to his ability to write. The sense of the isolation, in contrast to loneliness, he experiences in Montana calls out from the pages of this essay. The orientation is far different, however, than that of Henry David Thoreau (p. 12) or Henry Beston (p. 135). Survival in the Yaak Valley depends on preparation, and putting away a supply of wood is essential not only to heat the body but the spirit. In some ways, Bass is in the same situation as all life in this harsh environment. But the Dirty Shame, a bar that serves as the Yaak Valley's lone social center, shows how extraordinarily different humans are in their needs, and how they survive a cold climate.

Bass was born in Fort Worth, Texas, the son of a geologist. He graduated from Utah State University in 1979. Before settling in Montana, he lived in Texas, Mississippi, Vermont, and Arkansas. A prolific writer, his first book, a collection of natural history essays, The Deer Pasture, *was published in 1985. Two years later, another collection,* Wild to the Heart, *appeared followed by* Oil Notes, *followed by yet another collection of essays in 1988. This selection is from* Winter: Notes from Montana *(1991). Bass is now at work on several novels. He is also trying to save the Yaak Valley from degradation by logging.*

Winter is a meditation on living in a harsh environment and making do. Bass learns to adapt like the animals he carefully observes. But like all humans he plays out his options, making decisions that sometime fly in the face of good environmentalism. He is not without humor, though he is currently saddened by the prospect of congressional approval to permit extensive logging in his valley. Bass is lobbying Congress not to make any changes that will upset the balance of nature where he lives.

SEPTEMBER 20

We got four loads of wood yesterday, about one cord. It's hard getting used to talking and listening to someone else. I'm delighted to have her here, but am surprised at the adjustment I need to make.

We've been having hard frosts every night, twenty-five, twenty-six degrees; but we're in shirtsleeves and barefoot again during the day.

The dogs keep finding more bones. Things seem to die all the time around here.

Things to do: Clean chimney trap. Clean chicken coop and convert it to winter dog residence. Shovel ashes out of fireplace, wood stoves. Git wood.

Good things to know if you are a logger: wear high boots, of course, to protect your ankles against spike limbs, but also wear high-cuffed pants that are open around the cuffs, not unlike bell-bottoms. You want them stopping up high, around the ankle, so that when you are climbing around in a pile of slash, every little branch and limb doesn't go up your leg and trip you. You want baggy, flaring pants, so that if a branch does run up your cuff, then it won't wedge in there and trip you; you can just step out of it. Truman told me this over beers a few nights ago, and I'd forgotten it until yesterday, when I fell. Everyone's so helpful.

I introduced Elizabeth to the McGarys yesterday, up at the mercantile. Dick was talking about how wonderful winter can be; how it got down to eighty below (windchill) their first year up here; how on a cold, clear day in the heart of winter, with no one around, you can look up and see the sky swirling and sparkling with flashing ice crystals—above you the whole sky, crystals falling out of blue air, even though there is no wind.

Check the antifreeze. This is a simple, stupid thing that someone from easy times, from the warm, simple growth of Mississippi, might easily forget.

Everyone back east wants me to send them pictures, but very few of them sound serious about wanting to visit. This is fine with me. I will send them pictures.

A few nights ago, while getting wood, I saw some grouse. They are big, muscular, quail-chicken birds, runners and scooters, and they taste wonderful.

Haven't seen Tom and Nancy since Elizabeth got in. I think about Nancy a good bit. I want to ask both of them questions all day long, all winter—about dream hoops, about ravens, about trapping.

The consensus, unanimously so, is that this is going to be a fierce winter: fuzzy deer already, men's beards growing faster, old people feeling it in their bones, their hearts; the way stars flash and glimmer at night; the way trees stand dark against the sky. Driving back from the Shame late at night, I've already seen snowshoe hares turned completely white. They've staked their lives on the fact, or feeling, that it's going to be an early winter, and a hard one.

Great huge fat white rabbits, like magicians, rabbits the size of large cats, hide out in the darkness of the woods, waiting for the snow that will save them. Evolving all these thousands of years, tens of thousands: the foolish ones were long ago weeded out, the willy-nilly, turn-white-for-no-reason rabbits; those that turned white when there really wasn't any snow coming, or those that turned white too early, had nowhere to hide, and so were quickly consumed, visible prey to wolves, coyotes, hawks, owls, bobcats, lions, everything. And the hares that stayed brown, the ones that did not feel the hard winter coming and did not prepare for it, they got theirs.

So I figure these rabbits know. What a remarkable thing, to bet your life each year, twice a year actually, because they must know when to turn brown again. This year I have been seeing rabbits come out of hiding after the sun goes down, white rabbits hopping across the logging roads as I come down off the mountain with a load of wood—trying, with the windows rolled down, to listen and feel for myself, and to learn rather than always having to be told. I think that I can learn.

There are cars and trucks parked outside the Dirty Shame when I go past—mostly trucks—and it looks warm and inviting, a glow in the night woods. But I've got my window rolled down, I can feel it, feel what I *should* be feeling. What it tells me is that I have gotten up here late to this little valley, maybe too late; but once I'm home, unloading the wood from the truck, smelling the fresh cut of it and feeling the silence of the woods all around me, what I feel, like the rabbits, is this: surely better late than never. With a flashlight, after eleven o'clock, I go back into the night again, driving past the Dirty Shame once more and up onto the mountain for more wood, trying to beat what, like everyone else up here, I now know, rather than think, is coming.

What I feel is that I had better not stop, that I have lost time to make up for. Hard dreams, of the line-backed dun across the road, his face iced over with snow and sleet, his back to the wind, staring straight ahead as if seeing something far out in front of him; as if watching, through a looking glass, spring and its thaw, its greenness. Dreams of heavy axes hitting frozen wood, of steaming coffee from a thermos, of sitting inside the Dirty Shame, the whole valley—thirty or forty of us trapped by a blizzard—cheering at the football game on the little TV screen, yelling and making bets as to who will win.

What Edward Hoagland has called the courage of turtles, I can see now as the wisdom of rabbits. There is so much to learn. Everything I have learned so far has been wrong. I'm having to start all over. I want to find Nancy today and ask her one more time about those dream hoops, ask her again how they work, ask if there are life hoops as well, though already I know she will tell me that yes, there are.

It can be so wonderful, finding out you were wrong, that you are ignorant, that you know nothing, not squat. You get to start over. It's like snow falling that first time each year. It doesn't make any sound, but it's the strongest force you know of. Trees will crack and pop and split open later in the winter. Things opening up, learning. Learning the way it really is.

All through the forest, they say, you can hear the trees on the coldest of nights: cracking and popping like firecrackers, like cannons, like a parade, while rabbits, burrowed in the snow beneath them, sit quietly, warm and white, saved, having learned—having made the right bet.

Nancy, in the Shame, was telling me about how she hurt her wrist skiing one year. It wouldn't heal and it was all drawn up and forever cramping; a guy told her to stop drinking coffee, and she did, and two days later the wrist was supple again, strong.

I had bad dreams and a recurring headache all night, dreams of dying, murder, cancer, fires, traffic jams. I need a dream hoop.

Evening. I'm writing again, and throwing wood into the stove. Little wrist-size pieces, they burn almost as fast as you can look at them. Energy. Can't have too much wood. It makes the valley smell good. Of course, there are only thirty of us in this valley. This is the proper number. The Dirty Thirty. Next March I will be thirty. If everyone in the world burned as much wood as I am going to this winter, the planet would be obscured, one great wood-smoke cloud. I don't know what to think about that. We're all dirty, but we're all sweet!

I recycle my aluminum! I don't litter! I try to pee on the rocks, not on the soil, keep from killing things with too much nitrogen!

I remember now how my father pronounces the word "moron" when aiming it at me: "mo-ron." Maybe I am a mo-ron for using wood for fuel rather than the similarly priced propane (though I get my wood for free, with the saw, the ax, the biceps, the deltoids).

We all have dirt in us. Wood is better than coal, but not as good as gas.

No, that's hypocritical, rationalizing. Wood is bad, inefficient, dirty, but it smells good. It's fun to chop, and I like to watch the flames, watch the erratic, pulsing heat it gives, and I like the snaps and pops, and when I'm dead and gone, I'll be glad I used it.

"Mo-ron," the children of the centuries after me will cry. But there will be jealously as well as anger in their cries (and we are all the same, always have been), and there is wood lying all around, wood everywhere, and it is free, and I have a life to live. Me first, it feels like I am saying. It is my turn, and you may not even get yours.

You should hear my father say it—in traffic, or watching a baseball game, when the manager makes a bad move: "mo-ron." It's like a wave at sea, rolling high on the "mo" and cresting, rolling down into the curl and lick and wave of "ron," sliding softly to shore. The word of the nineties, I'm afraid, is environmental mo-ron, mo-ron, mo-ron . . .

I know I should be burning gas, not wood. I know I should.

Questions for Thinking and Writing

1. What practical advice does Bass offer for preparing to endure the severe winter environment of northern Montana?
2. How does Bass's observation of deer, and especially rabbits, suggest a rapid change of season? Compare the purpose of Bass's observations on the environment with Edward Beston's in "Night on the Great Beach" (p. 135) and Annie Dillard's in "Seeing" (p. 313). At what point do you think aesthetic observation and practical observation intersect? From your own experience, do you believe this happens often?
3. Comment on the notion that although wood is organic and pollutes the air when burned, there is something about a wood fire that seems to transcend the harm it might do.

❦ Al Gore (b. 1948)

Environmentalism of the Spirit (1992)

Albert (Al) Gore, Jr., is from Tennessee, the home of the TVA, described by David Lilienthal (p. 170), and the landscape described in Wallace Stevens's "Anecdote of the Jar" (p. 126). This irony is one of many in Gore's personal and professional life that led to Earth in the Balance, *from which this selection is excerpted. More than a political tract, Gore has undertaken a pilgrimage in search of a cause: global environmental preservation. As vice president of the United States, he exerts a strong influence on President Bill Clinton's environmental policies on a national and global scale.*

Gore, a scion of a southern political family, was born in Washington, D.C., where his father, Albert Gore, Sr., was a longtime congressman and, later, U.S. senator from Tennessee. His son, surrounded by Washington political life, was sent to prestigious St. Albans Episcopal School in Washington where he was captain of the football team as well as an honor student.

Though he was opposed to the Vietnam War when he graduated from Harvard College in 1969, Gore served as an army reporter in Vietnam for the 20th Engineering Battalion. During this time, he wrote articles for the Nashville Tennessean, *and after finishing his tour of duty, he took a job as a night reporter for the newspaper. Intellectually restless, Gore first studied philosophy at Vanderbilt University's Graduate School of Divinity. Later he studied law at Vanderbilt.*

In 1976, Gore ran for a congressional seat on the Democratic ticket and won a bitter primary campaign during which his father, then retired from politics, was impugned for being chairman of the Island Creek Coal Company. Gore easily won the election and served one term in the House. In 1984, he ran for the Senate and was overwhelmingly elected; in 1993, he began his term of office as vice president.

As a congressman and senator, Gore tackled complex issues, many of them health related. He held hearings on toxic waste dumping, helping to bring national attention to Love Canal, New York, a suburb so degraded by toxic waste that it had to be depopulated. He also participated in developing the Superfund Act (1980) to enforce the cleanup of toxic waste dumps.

Nuclear arms and disarmament were other issues he studied extensively, causing him to appreciate that the environment encircled the globe and could be damaged on a massive scale. With the Cold War over, global warming became the obvious threat. The escape of gases into the atmosphere, a concern first voiced to Gore by a professor when he was a student at Harvard, was the obvious catalyst for Earth in the Balance. *His study of global warming also led him to think about how humans relate to the environment, the subject of much of his book. "In the end," he writes, "we must restore a balance within ourselves between who we are and what we are doing."*

Gore's logic is closely tied to his study of politics, law, and religious philosophy. Earth in the Balance *is itself an attempt to balance competing forces of material and spiritual well-being. The argument is both personal and public, for this chapter—"Environmentalism of the Spirit"—shows how determined Gore is to harmonize the individual and the social quality of civic virtue and personal values.*

Twenty years ago, E F. Schumacher defined an important new issue arising from the relationship between a technology and the context—social, cultural, political, and ecological—in which it is used. For example, a nuclear power plant can certainly generate a lot of electricity, but it may not be an "appropriate" technology for an underdeveloped nation with an unstable government, a shortage of trained engineers, an absence of any power grid to distribute the electricity generated, and a megalomaniacal ruler anxious to acquire fissionable material with which to construct nuclear weapons. The appropriateness of a technology becomes increasingly important as its power grows and its potential for destroying the environment expands.

It is time we asked a similar question about ourselves and our relationship to the global environment: When giving us dominion over earth, did God choose an appropriate technology?

Knowing what we do about our new power as a species to interfere with and even overwhelm the earth's natural systems and recognizing that we are now doing so with reckless abandon, one is tempted to answer, the jury is still out.

Whether we believe that our dominion derives from God or from our own ambition, there is little doubt that the way we currently relate to the environment is wildly inappropriate. But in order to change, we have to address some fundamental questions about our purpose in life, our capacity to direct the powerful inner forces that have created this crisis, and who we are. These questions go beyond any discussion of whether the human species is an appropriate technology; these questions are not for the mind or the body but the spirit.

A change in our essential character is not possible without a realistic hope that we can make change happen. But hope itself is threatened by the realization that we are now capable of destroying ourselves and the earth's environment. Moreover, the stress of coping with the complicated artificial patterns of our lives and the flood of manufactured information creates a pervasive feeling of exhaustion just when we have an urgent need for creativity. Our economy is described as post-industrial; our architecture is called post-modern; our geopolitics are labeled post-Cold War. We know what we are not, but we don't seem to know what we are. The forces that shape and reshape our lives seem to have an immutable logic of their own; they seem so powerful that any effort to define ourselves creatively will probably be wasted, its results quickly erased by successive tidal waves of change. Inevitably, we resign ourselves to whatever fate these powerful forces are propelling us toward, a fate we have little role in choosing.

Perhaps because it is unprecedented, the environmental crisis seems completely beyond our understanding and outside of what we call common sense. We consign it to some seldom visited attic in our minds where we place ideas that we vaguely understand but rarely explore. We tag it with the same mental labels we might use for Antarctica: remote, alien, hopelessly distorted by the maps of the world we inhabit, too hard to get to and too unforgiving to stay very long. When we do visit this attic, when we learn about how intricately the causes of the crisis are woven into the fabric of industrial civilization, our hope of solving it seems chimerical. It seems so forbidding that we resist taking even the first steps toward positive change.

We turn by default to an imprudent hope that we can adapt to whatever changes are in store. We have grown accustomed to adapting; we are good at it. After all, we have long since adapted, with the help of technology, to every climate extreme on the surface of the earth, at the bottom of the sea and even in the vacuum of space. It is by adapting, in fact, that we have extended our dominion into every corner of the earth. And so it is tempting to conclude that this familiar strategy is the obvious response to our rapidly emerging dilemma.

But the magnitude of the change to which we must now consider adapting is so large that the proposals quickly trend toward the absurd. A study sponsored by the National Academy of Sciences, for example, suggested that as the earth warms, we might create huge corridors of wilderness as pathways to accommodate all of the species trying to migrate from south to north in search of a familiar climate. (Meanwhile, of course, we are laying siege to many of the wilderness areas that already exist—in the Pacific Northwest, for example—in search of timber and other resources.) Some even imagine that genetic engineering will soon magnify our power to adapt even our physical form. We might decide to extend our dominion of nature into the human gene pool, not just to cure terrible diseases, but to take from God and nature the selection of genetic variety and robustness that gives our species its resilience and aligns us with the natural rhythms in the web of life. Once again, we might dare to exercise godlike powers unaccompanied by godlike wisdom.

But our willingness to adapt is an important part of the underlying problem. Do we have so much faith in our own adaptability that we will risk destroying the integrity of the entire global ecological system? If we try to adapt to the changes we are causing rather than prevent them in the first place, have we made an appropriate choice? Can we understand how much destruction this choice might finally cause?

Believing that we can adapt to just about anything is ultimately a kind of laziness, an arrogant faith in our ability to react in time to save our skin. But in my view this confidence in our quick reflexes is badly misplaced; indeed, a laziness in our spirit has estranged us from our true selves and from the quickness and vitality of the world at large. We have been so seduced by industrial civilization's promise to make our lives comfortable that we allow the synthetic routines of modern life to soothe us in an inauthentic world of our own making. Life can be easy, we assure ourselves. We need not suffer the heat or the cold; we need not sow or reap or hunt and gather. We can heal the sick, fly through the air, light up the darkness, and be entertained in our living rooms by orchestras and clowns whenever we like. And as our needs and whims are sated, we watch electronic images of nature's destruction, distant famine, and apocalyptic warnings, all with the bone-weariness of the damned. "What can we do?" we ask ourselves, already convinced that the realistic answer is nothing.

With the future so open to doubt, we routinely choose to indulge our own generation at the expense of all who will follow. We enshrine the self as the unit of ethical account, separate and distinct not just from the natural world but even from a sense of obligation to others—not just others in future generations, but increasingly even to others in the same generation; and not just those in distant lands, but increasingly even in our own communities. We do this not because we don't care but because we don't really live in our lives. We are monumentally distracted by a pervasive technological culture that appears to have a life of its own, one that insists on our full attention, continually seducing us and pulling us away from the opportunity to experience directly the true meaning of our own lives.

How can we shake loose this distraction? How can we direct our attention to more important matters when our attention has become a commodity to be bought and sold? Whenever a new source of human interest and desire is found, prospectors flock to stake their claim. Using every available tool—newspapers, movies, television, magazines, billboards, blimps, buttons, designer labels, junk faxes—they assault our attention from every side. Advertisers strip-mine it; politicians covet it; pollsters measure it; terrorists steal it as a weapon of war. As the amounts close to the surface are exhausted, the search for fresh supplies leads onto primal paths that run deep into our being, back through our evolutionary heritage, past thought and beyond emotion, to instinct—and a rich vein of primal fears and passions that are also now exploited as raw material in the colossal enterprise of mass distraction. The prospectors of attention fragment our experience of the world, carry away the spoils, and then, in an ultimate irony, accuse us of having short attention spans.

The way we experience the world is governed by a kind of inner ecology that relates perception, emotions, thinking, and choices to forces outside ourselves. We interpret our experience through multiple lenses that focus—and distort—the information we receive through our senses. But this ecology now threatens to fall badly out of balance because the cumulative impact of the changes brought by the scientific and technological revolution are potentially devastating to our sense of who we are and what our purpose in life might be. Indeed, it may now be necessary to foster a new "environmentalism of the spirit." How do we, for example, conserve hope and minimize the quantity of corrosive fear we spill into our lives? How do we recycle the sense of wonder we felt as children, when the world was new? How do we use the power of technology without adapting to it so completely that we ourselves behave like machines, lost in the levers and cogs, lonesome for the love of life, hungry for the thrill of directly experiencing the vivid intensity of the ever-changing moment?

No wonder we have become disconnected from the natural world— indeed, it's remarkable we feel any connection to ourselves. And no wonder we have become resigned to the idea of a world without a future. The engines of distraction are gradually destroying the inner ecology of the human experience. Essential to that ecology is the balance between respect for the past and faith in the future, between a belief in the individual and a commitment to the community, between our love for the world and our fear of losing it—the balance, in other words, on which an environmentalism of the spirit depends.

To some, the global environment crisis is primarily a crisis of values. In this view, the basic cause of the problem is that we as a civilization base our decisions about how to relate to the environment on premises that are fundamentally unethical. And since religion has traditionally been the most powerful source of ethical guidance for our civilization, the search for villains has led to the doorstep of the major religious systems.

Here in the West, some have charged—inaccurately, I believe—that the Judeo-Christian tradition chartered the relentless march of civilization to dominate nature, beginning with the creation story of Genesis, in which humankind is granted "dominion" over the earth. In its basic form, the charge is that our tradition assigns divine purpose to our exercise of virtually complete power to work our will over nature. It is alleged that by endowing human beings with a completely unique relationship to God and then delegating God's authority over nature to human beings, the tradition sanctions as ethical all choices that put a higher priority on human needs and desires than on the rest of nature. Simply put, according to this view, it is "ethical" to make sure that whenever nature gets in the way of what we want, nature loses.

But this is a cartoon version of the Judeo-Christian tradition, one that bears little resemblance to the reality. Critics attack religion for inspiring an arrogant and reckless attitude toward nature, but they have not always read the relevant texts carefully enough. Although it is certainly true that our civilization is built on the premise that we can use nature for our own ends without regard to the impact we have on it, it is not fair to charge any of the major world religions with promoting this dangerous attitude. Indeed, all of them mandate an ethical responsibility to protect and care for the well-being of the natural world.

In the Judeo-Christian tradition, the biblical concept of dominion is quite different from the concept of domination, and the difference is crucial. Specifically, followers of this tradition are charged with the duty of stewardship, because the same biblical passage that grants them "dominion" also requires them to "care for" the earth even as they "work" it. The requirement of stewardship and its grant of dominion are not in conflict; in recognizing the sacredness of creation, believers are called upon to remember that even as they "till" the earth they must also "keep" it.

This has long been clear to those who have dedicated their lives to these duties. Richard Cartwright Austin, for example, a Presbyterian minister working among the poor in Appalachia, reports on his experience in trying to stop irresponsible strip mining: "I learned early on from my years as a pastor in Appalachia and from the days when I started fighting strip mining in southwest Virginia that the only defense those mountains have from exploitation by the energy conglomerates' bulldozers is the poor, isolated people who live in those hollows, who care so deeply that they would fight for that land. Take those people away and the mountains are totally defenseless. . . . From the biblical point of view, nature is only safe from pollution and brought into a secure moral relationship when it is united with people who love it and care for it."

All around the world, the efforts to stop the destruction of the environment have come mainly from people who recognize the damage being done in that part of the world in which they themselves have "dominion." Lois Gibbs and the other homeowners at Love Canal, Christine and Woodrow Sterling and their family, whose well water was poisoned in West Tennessee, "Harrison" Gnau and the indigenous peoples of the Sarawak rain forest in East Malaysia, Chico Mendes and his rubber tappers in the Amazon, the unemployed fishermen of the Aral Sea—all began their battles to save the environment because of the marriage of dominion and stewardship in their hearts. This is precisely the relationship between humankind and the earth called for in the Judeo-Christian ethic.

In my own religious experience and training—I am a Baptist—the duty to care for the earth is rooted in the fundamental relationship between God, creation, and humankind. In the Book of Genesis, Judaism first taught that after God created the earth, He "saw that it was good." In the Twenty-fourth Psalm, we learn that "the earth is the Lord's and the fullness thereof." In other words, God is pleased with his creation, and "dominion" does not mean that the earth belongs to humankind; on the contrary, whatever is done to the earth must be done with an awareness that it belongs to God.

My tradition also teaches that the purpose of life is "to glorify God." And there is a shared conviction within the Judeo-Christian tradition that believers are expected to "do justice, love mercy, and walk humbly with your God." But whatever verses are selected in an effort to lend precision to the Judeo-Christian definition of life's purpose, that purpose is clearly inconsistent with the reckless destruction of that which belongs to God and which God has seen as "good." How can one glorify the Creator while heaping contempt on the creation? How can one walk humbly with nature's God while wreaking havoc on nature?

The story of Noah and the ark offers further evidence of Judaism's concern for stewardship. Noah is commanded by God to take into his ark at least two of every living species in order to save them from the Flood—a commandment that might appear in modern form as: Thou shalt preserve biodiversity. Indeed, does God's instruction have new relevance for those who share Noah's faith in this time of another worldwide catastrophe, this time one of our own creation? Noah heeded this commandment, and after he and his family and a remnant of every living species on earth survived the Flood, God made a new covenant with him which affirmed His commitment to humankind. Often overlooked, however, is the second half of God's covenant, made not only with Noah but with "all living creatures," again affirming the sacredness of creation, which He pledged to safeguard in "seed time and harvest, cold and heat, summer and winter." It was the promise never again to destroy the earth by floods, which, according to Genesis, is the symbolic message of every rainbow.

In spite of the clear message from a careful reading of these and other Scriptures, critics have gained currency in part because of the prevailing silence with which most denominations have reacted to the growing evidence of an ecological holocaust. Nor does it help that some religious leaders have seemed to encourage environmental recklessness. I remember listening with closed eyes and bowed head to the invocation at the groundbreaking for a new construction project as the minister cited our "dominion over the earth" and then immediately went on to list with great relish every instrument of environmental mayhem he could name, from bulldozers and backhoes to chain saws and steamrollers, as though they were divinely furnished tools we should use with abandon in reshaping the earth for the sheer joy of doing so. Both behaviors—silence in the face of disaster and unthinking enthusiasm for further degradation—do nothing to counter the cartoon image of a faith bent on the domination of nature.

Happily, it has recently become clear that a great movement to protect the earth is stirring deeply within the faith, and many religious leaders are now sounding the alarm. But until now they have seemed reluctant to lend their moral authority to the effort to rescue the earth. Why?

In their defense, it should be said that religious leaders have faced the same difficulties as the rest of us in recognizing this unprecedented pattern of destruction, in comprehending the strategic nature of the threat, and in realizing the profound and sudden change in the relationship between the human species and the rest of the environment. But their failure to act is especially disturbing because the Christian Scriptures carry such a strong activist message. To me, it is best expressed in one of Jesus' parables, recounted in three of the four gospels, the Parable of the Unfaithful Servant. The master of a house, preparing to depart on a journey, leaves his servant in charge of the home and gives him strict instructions to remain alert in case vandals or thieves attempt to ransack the house while the master is away. The servant is explicitly warned that if the vandals come while he is asleep, he still has a duty to protect the house against them—and the fact that he was asleep will not be an acceptable excuse. A question raised by the parable is clear: If the earth is the Lord's and His servants are given the responsibility to care for it, then how are we to respond to the global vandalism now wreaking such unprecedented destruction on the earth? Are we asleep? Is that now an acceptable excuse?

But there is something else at work in organized religion as well. Many of those who might otherwise find themselves in the vanguard of the resistance to this onslaught are preoccupied with other serious matters. For example, Christian theologians and clergy who have traditionally supported a liberal political agenda have inherited a specific set of concerns defined early in this century as the Social Gospel. According to this humane view of the Church's role, followers of Christ should assign priority to the needs of the poor, the powerless, the sick and frail, the victims of discrimination and hatred, the forgotten human fodder chewed up by the cogs of industrial civilization. The moral imperative attached to this set of priorities leads many advocates of the Social Gospel to vigorously resist the introduction of competing concerns which they see as distractions from their appointed task, diluting their already over-taxed resources of money, time, moral authority, and emotional labor. After all, as an issue, "the environment" sometimes seems far from the more palpable sins of social injustice.

On the other hand, politically conservative theologians and clergy have inherited a different agenda, also defined early in this century. The "atheistic communism" against which they have properly inveighed for decades is, for them, only the most extreme manifestation of a statist impulse to divert precious resources—money, time, moral authority, and emotional labor—away from the mission of spiritual redemption and toward an idolatrous alternative: the search for salvation through a grand reordering of the material world. As a result, they are deeply suspicious of any effort to focus their moral attention on a crisis in the material world that might require as part of its remedy a new exercise of something resembling moral authority by the state. And the prospect of coordinated action by governments all over the world understandably heightens their fears and suspicions.

Thus, with activists of both the left and the right resisting the inclusion of the environment on their list of concerns, the issue has not received the attention from religious leaders one may have expected. This is unfortunate, because the underlying concern is theologically consistent with the perspectives of both sides; equally important, the issue provides a rare opportunity for them to meet on common ground.

As it happens, the idea of social justice is inextricably linked in the Scriptures with ecology. In passage after passage, environmental degradation and social injustice go hand in hand. Indeed, the first instance of "pollution" in the Bible occurs when Cain slays Abel and his blood falls on the ground, rendering it fallow. According to Genesis, after the murder, when Cain asks, "Am I my brother's keeper?" the Lord replies, "Your brother's blood calls out to me from the ground. What have you done?" God then tells Cain that his brother's blood has defiled the ground and that as a result, "no longer will it yield crops for you, even if you toil on it forever!"

In today's world, the links between social injustice and environmental degradation can be seen everywhere: the placement of toxic waste dumps in poor neighborhoods, the devastation of indigenous peoples and the extinction of their cultures when the rain forests are destroyed, disproportionate levels of lead and toxic air pollution in inner-city ghettos, the corruption of many government officials by people who seek to profit from the unsustainable exploitation of resources.

Meanwhile, religious conservatives might be surprised to find that many deeply committed environmentalists have become, if anything, even more hostile to overreaching statism than they are. The most serious examples of environmental degradation in the world today are tragedies that were created or actively encouraged by governments— usually in pursuit of some notion that a dramatic reordering of the material world would enhance the greater good. And it is no accident that the very worst environmental tragedies were created by communist governments, in which the power of the state completely overwhelms the capabilities of the individual steward. Chernobyl, the Aral Sea, the Yangtze River, the "black town" of Copsa Mica in Romania—these and many other disasters testify to the severe environmental threats posed by statist governments.

Both conservative and liberal theologians have every reason, scriptural as well as ideological, to define their spiritual mission in a way that prominently includes the defense of God's creation. Slowly and haltingly, both camps are beginning to do so. But most clergy are still reluctant to consider this cause worthy of their sustained attention; in my opinion, an important source of this reluctance is a philosophical assumption that humankind is separate from the rest of nature, an assumption shared by both liberals and conservatives. The basis for it deserves further attention, especially since the tendency to see human needs as essentially detached from the well-being of the earth's natural systems is not fundamentally Christian in origin. Even so, this tendency reflects a view of the world that was absorbed into the Christian tradition early on; specifically, it was part of the heritage of Greek philosophy, a heritage that had a powerful influence on early Christian thinking and behavior.

Questions for Thinking and Writing

1. Discuss Gore's version of ecological stewardship and the concept of dominion. How are these concepts complemented by the idea of inner ecology?

2. What is Gore's argument for linking environmental protection in the contemporary world with the Parable of the Unfaithful Servant (Luke)? How does he link social injustice and environmental degradation with the story of Cain and Abel (Genesis)? Comment on whether or not you agree with Gore's insistence that the Bible is relevant to today's environmental problems.

3. Discuss how Gore's argument for renewing personal values might build on Wendell Berry's "The Ecological Crisis as a Crisis of Character" (p. 348) and Aldo Leopold's "The Land Ethic" (p. 195).

❦ Charles C. Mann (b. 1955)

How Many Is Too Many? (1993)

Charles Cameron Mann is a free-lance journalist with wide-ranging interests in science and the environment. He was educated at Amherest College, Massachusetts, where he majored in mathematics and biology. This intellectual interest has led him to collaborate on two books: The Second Creation: Makers of the Revolution in 20th Century Physics *(1986) and* The Aspirin Wars: Money, Medicine, and 100 Years of Rampant Competition *(1991). Mann is currently at work on* Playing God: Hard Choices about Biodiversity, *a book about endangered species. In 1992 he was awarded the Alfred P. Sloan Foundation Science Writing Prize.*

Mann is a contributing editor to The Atlantic Monthly. *He has worked for the* International Daily News *(in* Rome*),* Attenzione, *and* Technology Illustrated. *His magazine articles have appeared in* Business Month, Geo, Mother Earth, *and* The New York Times.

"How Many Is Too Many?" questions whether recently reawakened fears of overpopulation should be debated in the environmental or the political arena. This question occurred to Mann several years ago as he roamed New York State's lower Hudson River Valley. He was looking for a country home to buy, having decided to leave New York City, where his office was saturated with Madonna's voice blaring from car radios on the street below, emblematic of the disarray of life in crowded New York City. Noting the extensive forests of the Catskill

Mountains within three hours' drive north of the city, he learned that the region's population is three times what it was a century ago, when the mountainsides were ravaged by farming and lumbering. In other words, more people do not have to lead to environmental degradation or to a lesser quality of life.

Mann suggests that compromised quality of life—often understood as a result of overpopulation—may stem less from environmental overload and more from "the human race's perennial inability to run its political affairs wisely." Even so, the dangers inherent in explosive population growth must be taken seriously. The issue has been clouded, Mann maintains, by domination of what he terms the Cassandras—the doomsayers—on the one side and the Polyannas—those who argue that everything will work out—on the other. Neither camp has produced a coherent argument about the effects of population growth, yet Mann's Hudson Valley experiences suggest that there can be coherent solutions to increased population, one that fast-growing centers like New York City, Texas, Florida, and California would be wise to deal with through clear thinking rather than political thinking.

Incidentally, Mann solved his Madonna problem by moving from New York City to pastoral Amherst, Massachusetts.

In 1980, when I was living in New York City, it came to my attention that the federal government was trying to count every inhabitant of the United States. In my building—subject, like many in New York, to incredibly complicated rent-control laws—a surprising number of apartments were occupied by illegal subtenants. Many went to elaborate lengths to conceal the fact of their existence. They put the legal tenant's name on the doorbell. They received their mail at a post-office box. They had unlisted telephone numbers. The most paranoid refused to reveal their names to strangers. How, I wondered, was the Census Bureau going to count these people?

I decided to find out. I answered an advertisement and attended a course. In a surprisingly short time I became an official enumerator. My job was to visit apartments that had not mailed back their census forms. As identification, I was given a black plastic briefcase with a big red, white, and blue sticker that said U.S. CENSUS. I am a gangling, six-foot-four-inch Caucasian; the government sent me to Chinatown.

Strangely enough, I was a failure. Some people took one look and slammed the door. One elderly woman burst into tears at the sight of me. I was twice offered money to go away. Few residents had time to fill out a long form.

Eventually I met an old census hand. "Why don't you just curbstone it?" he asked. "Curbstoning," I learned, was enumerator jargon for sitting on the curbstone and filling out forms with made-up information. I felt qualms about taking taxpayers' money to cheat. Instead, I asked to be assigned to another area.

Wall Street is not customarily thought of as residential, but people live there anyway. Some live in luxury, some in squalor. None were glad to see me, even though I had given away the damning U.S. CENSUS briefcase to my four-year-old stepson. The turning point came when I approached two small buildings. One was ruined and empty. The other, though scarcely in better condition, was obviously full of people, but not one of them would answer the bell. In a fit of zealotry I climbed through the ruin next door. Coated with grime and grit, I emerged on the roof and leaped onto the roof of my target. A man was living on it, in a big, dilapidated shack.

He flung open his door. Inside I dimly perceived several apparently naked people lying on gurneys. "Go away!" the man screamed. He was wearing a white coat. "I'm giving my wife a cancer treatment!"

My enthusiasm waned. I jumped back to the other roof. On the street I sat on the curbstone and filled out a dozen forms. When I was through, fifty men, women, and children had been added to the populace of New York City.

Professional demographers are not amused by this sort of story. This is not because they are stuffy but because they've heard it all before. Finding out how many people live in any particular place is strikingly difficult, no matter what the place is. In the countryside people are scattered through miles of real estate; in the city they occupy nooks and crannies often missed by official scrutiny. No accurate census has ever been taken in some parts of Africa, but even in the United States, the director of the Census Bureau has said, the last official count, in 1990, missed more than five million people—enough to fill Chicago twice over. If my experience means anything, that number is low.

It's too bad, because How many are we? is an interesting question. Indeed, to many people it is an alarming question. For them, thinking about population means thinking about *over*population—which is to say, thinking about poverty, hunger, despair, and social unrest. For me, the subject evokes the vague unease I felt toting around *The Population Bomb*, which I read in school. ("It's Still Not Too Late to Make the Choice," the cover proclaimed. "Population Control or Race to Oblivion.") In other people it evokes the desire to put fences on our borders and stop the most wretched from breeding.

The Population Bomb appeared twenty-five years ago, in 1968. Written by the biologist Paul Ehrlich, of Stanford University, it was a gloomy book for a gloomy time. India was still undergoing a dreadful famine, Latin American exports of grain and meat had dropped to pre-war levels, and global food production was lagging behind births. More than half the world's people were malnourished. Nobel laureates were telling Congress that unless population growth stopped, a new Dark Age would cloud the world and "men will have to kill and eat one another." A well-regarded book, *Famine 1975!*, predicted that hunger would begin to wipe out the Third World that year. (Fortunately, the book pointed out, there was a bright side: the United States could increase its influence by playing triage among the victims.) In 1972 a group of researchers at MIT would issue *The Limits to Growth,* which used advanced computer models to project that the world would run out of gold in 1981, oil in 1992, and arable land in 2000. Civilization itself would collapse by 2070.

The projections failed to materialize. Birth rates dropped; food production soared; the real price of oil sank to a record low. Demographers were not surprised. Few had given much credence to the projections in the first place. Nonetheless, a certain disarray appeared in the work of what Ansley Coale, of Princeton's Office of Population Research, calls the "scribbling classes." Doubts emerged about the wisdom and effectiveness of the billion-dollar population-control schemes established by the United Nations and others in the 1960s. Right-wingers attacked them as bureaucratic intrusions into private life. Critics on the left observed that once again rich whites were trying to order around poor people of color. Less ideological commentators pointed out that the intellectual justification for spending billions on international family-planning programs was shaky—it tacitly depended on the notion that couples in the Third World are somehow too stupid to know that having lots of babies is bad. Ehrlich dismissed the carpers as "imbeciles."

Population has become the subject of a furious intellectual battle, complete with mutually contradictory charts, graphs, and statistics. The cloud of facts and factoids often seems impenetrable, but after peering through it for a time I came to suspect that the fighters had become distracted. Locked in conflict, they had barely begun to address the real nature of the challenge posed by population growth. *Homo sapiens* will keep growing in number, as everyone agrees, and that growth may have disagreeable consequences. But those consequences seem less likely to stem from the environmental collapse the apocalyptists predict than from the human race's perennial inability to run its political affairs wisely. The distinction is quite important, and dismaying.

CASSANDRAS AND POLLYANNAS

How many people is too many? Over time, the debate has spread between two poles. On one side, according to Garrett Hardin, an ecologist at the University of California at Santa Barbara, are the Cassandras, who believe that continued population growth at the current rate will inevitably lead to catastrophe. On the other are the Pollyannas, who believe that humanity faces problems but has a good shot at coming out okay in the end. Cassandras, who tend to be biologists, look at each new birth as the arrival on the planet of another hungry mouth. Pollyannas, who tend to be economists, point out that along with each new mouth comes a pair of hands. Biologist or economist—is either one right? It is hard to think of a question more fundamental to our crowded world.

Cassandras and Pollyannas have spoken up throughout history. Philosophers in ancient China fretted about the need to shift the masses to underpopulated areas; meanwhile, in the Mideast, the Bible urged humanity to be fruitful and multiply. Plato said that cities with more than 5,040 landholders were too large; Martin Luther believed that it was impossible to breed too much, because God would always provide. And so on.

Early economists tended to be Pollyannas. People, they thought, are a resource—"the chiefest, most fundamental, and precious commodity" on earth, as William Petyt put it in 1680. Without a healthy population base, societies cannot afford to have their members specialize. In small villages almost everyone is involved with producing food; only as numbers grow can communities afford luxuries like surgeons, scientists, and stand-up comedians. The same increase lowers the cost of labor, and hence the cost of production—a notion that led at least one Enlightenment-era writer, J. F. Melon, to endorse slavery as an excellent source of a cheap work force.

As proof of their theory, seventeenth-century Pollyannas pointed to the Netherlands, which was strong, prosperous, and thickly settled, and claimed that only such a populous place could be so rich. In contrast, the poor, sparsely inhabited British colonies in the New World were begging immigrants to come and swell the work force. One of the chief duties of a ruler, these savants thought, was to ensure population growth. A high birth rate, the scholar Bernard Mandeville wrote in 1732, is "the never-failing Nursery of Fleets and Armies."

Mandeville wrote when the Industrial Revolution was beginning to foster widespread urban unemployment and European cities swarmed with beggars. Hit by one bad harvest after another, Britain tottered through a series of economic crises, which led to food shortages and poverty on a frightful scale. By 1803 local parishes were handing out relief to about one out of every seven people in England and Wales. In such a climate it is unsurprising that the most famous Cassandra of them all should appear: the Reverend Thomas Robert Malthus.

"Right from the publication of the *Essay on Population* to this day," the great economic historian Joseph Schumpeter wrote in 1954, "Malthus has had the good fortune—for this *is* good fortune—to be the subject of equally unreasonable, contradictory appraisals." John Maynard Keynes regarded Malthus as the "beginning of systematic economic thinking." Percy Bysshe Shelley, on the other hand, derided him as "a eunuch and a tyrant." John Stuart Mill viewed Malthus as a great thinker. To Karl Marx he was a "plagiarist" and a "shameless sycophant of the ruling classes." "He was a benefactor of humanity," Schumpeter wrote. "He was a fiend. He was a profound thinker. He was a dunce."

The subject of the controversy was a shy, kindly fellow with a slight harelip. He was also the first person to hold a university position in economics—that is, the first professional economist—in Britain, and probably the world. Married late, he had few children, and he was never overburdened with money. He was impelled to write his treatise on population by a disagreement with his father, a well-heeled eccentric in the English style. The argument was over whether the human race could transform the world into a paradise. Malthus thought not, and said so at length—55,000 words, published as an unsigned broadside in 1798. Several longer, signed versions followed, as Malthus became more confident.

"The power of population," Malthus proclaimed, "is indefinitely greater than the power in the earth to produce subsistence for man." In modern textbooks this notion is often explained with a graph. One line on the graph represents the land's capacity to produce food; it slowly rises from left to right as people clear more land and learn to farm more efficiently. Another line starts out low, quickly climbs to meet the first, and then soars above it; that line represents human population. Eventually the gap between the two lines cannot be bridged and the Horsemen of the Apocalypse pay a call. Others had anticipated this idea. Giovanni Botero, an Italian scholar, described the basic relationship of population and resources in 1589, two centuries before Malthus. But few read Malthus's predecessors, and nobody today seems inclined to replace the term "Malthusian" with "Boterian."

The *Essay* was a jolt. Simple and remorselessly logical, blessed with a perverse emotional appeal, it seemed to overturn centuries of Pollyanna-dom at a stroke. Forget Utopia, Malthus said. Humanity is doomed to exist, now and forever, at the edge of starvation. Forget charity, too: helping the poor only leads to more babies, which in turn produces increased hardship down the road. Little wonder that the essayist Thomas Carlyle found this theory so gloomy that he coined the phrase "dismal science" to describe it. Others were more vituperative, especially those who thought that the *Essay* implied that God would not provide for His children. "Is there no law in this kingdom for punishing a man for publishing a libel against the Almighty himself?" demanded one anonymous feuilleton. In all the tumult hardly anyone took the trouble to note that logical counter-arguments were available.

The most important derived from the work of Marie-Jean-Antoine-Nicolas Caritat, Marquis de Condorcet, a French *philosophe* who is best known for his worship of Reason. Four years before Malthus, Condorcet observed that France was finite, the potential supply of French infinite.

Unlike Malthus, though, Condorcet believed that technology could solve the problem. When hunger threatens, he wrote, "new instruments, machines, and looms" will continue to appear, and "a very small amount of ground will be able to produce a great quantity of supplies." Society changes so fast, in other words, that Malthusian scenarios are useless. Given the level of productivity of our distant ancestors, in other words, we should already have run out of food. But we know more than they, and are more prosperous, despite our greater numbers.

Malthus and Condorcet fixed the two extremes of a quarrel that endures today. The language has changed, to be sure. Modern Cassandras speak of "ecology," a concept that did not exist in Malthus's day, and worry about exceeding the world's "carrying capacity," the ecological ceiling beyond which the land cannot support life. Having seen the abrupt collapses that occur when populations of squirrels, gypsy moths, or Lapland reindeer exceed local carrying capacities, they foresee the same fate awaiting another species: *Homo sapiens*. Pollyannas note that no such collapse has occurred in recorded history. Evoking the "demographic transition"—the observed propensity for families in prosperous societies to have fewer children—they say that continued economic growth can both feed the world's billions and enrich the world enough to end the population boom. No! The Cassandras cry. Growth is the *problem*. We're growing by 100 million people every year! We can't keep doing that forever!

True, Pollyannas concede. If present-day trends continue for centuries, the earth will turn into a massive ball of human flesh. A few millennia more, Ansley Coale, of Princeton, calculates, and that ball of flesh will be expanding outward at the speed of light. But he sees little point in the exercise of projecting lines on a graph out to their absurdly horrible conclusion. "If you had asked someone in 1890 about today's population," Coale explains, "he'd say, 'There's no way the United States can support two hundred and fifty million people. Where are they going to pasture all their horses?' "

Just as the doomsayers feared, the world's population has risen by more than half since Paul Ehrlich wrote *The Population Bomb*. Twenty-five years ago 3.4 billion people lived on earth. Now the United Nations estimates that 5.3 billion do—the biggest, fastest increase in history. But food production increased faster still. According to the Food and Agricultural Organization of the UN, not only did farmers keep pace but per capita global food production actually rose more than 10 percent from 1968 to 1990. The number of chronically malnourished people fell by more than 16 percent. (All figures on global agriculture and population in the 1990s, including those in this article, mix empirical data with projections, because not enough time has elapsed to get hard numbers.)

"Much of the world *is* better fed than it was in 1950," concedes Lester R. Brown, the president of the World-watch Institute, an environmental-research group in Washington, D.C. "But that period of improvement is ending rather abruptly." Since 1984, he says, world grain production per capita has fallen one percent a year. In 1990, eighty-six nations grew less food per head than they had a decade before. Improvements are unlikely, in Brown's view. Our past success has brought us alarmingly close to the ecological ceiling. "There's a growing sense in the scientific community that it will be difficult to restore the rapid rise in agricultural yields we saw between 1950 and 1984," he says. "In agriculturally advanced nations there just isn't much more that farmers can do." Meanwhile, the number of mouths keeps up its frantic rate of increase. "My sense," Brown says, "is that we're going to be in trouble on the food front before this decade is out."

Social scientists disagree. An FAO study published in 1982 concluded that by using modern agricultural methods the Third World could support more than 30 billion people. Other technophiles see genetic engineering as a route to growth that is almost without end. Biologists greet such pronouncements with loud scoffs. One widely touted analysis by Ehrlich and others maintains that humanity already uses, destroys, or "co-opts" almost 40 percent of the potential output from terrestrial photosynthesis. Doubling the world's population will reduce us to fighting with insects over the last scraps of grass.

Neither side seems willing to listen to the other; indeed, the two are barely on speaking terms. The economist Julian Simon, of the University of Maryland, asserts that there is no evidence that the increase in land use associated with rising population has led to any increase in extinction rates—despite hundreds of biological reports to the contrary. The biologist Edward O. Wilson, of Harvard University, argues that contemporary economics is "bankrupt" and does not accommodate environmental calculations—despite the existence of a literature on the subject dating back to the First World War. A National Academy of Sciences panel dominated by economists argues in 1986 that the problems of population growth have been exaggerated. Six years later the academy issues a statement, dominated by biologists, claiming that continued population growth will lead to a global environmental catastrophe that "science and technology may not be able to prevent." Told in an exchange of academic gossip that an eminent ecologist has had himself sterilized, an equally eminent demographer says, "That's the best news I've heard all week!" Asking himself what "deep insights" professional demographers have contributed, Garrett Hardin answers, "None."

The difference in the forecasts—prosperity or penury, boundless increase or zero-sum game, a triumphant world with 30 billion or a despairing one with 10—is so extreme that one is tempted to dismiss the whole contretemps as foolish. If the experts can't even discuss the matter civilly, why should the average citizen try to figure it out? Ignoring the fracas might be the right thing to do if it weren't about the future of the human race.

TWO NATIONS

Population questions are fuzzy. Even an apparently simple term like "overpopulation" is hard to define exactly. Part of the reason is that evaluating the consequences of rapid population growth falls in the odd academic space where ecology, economics, anthropology, and demography overlap. Another part of the reason is that attempts to isolate specific social or environmental consequences of rapid population growth tend to sink into ideological quicksand.

By way of example, consider two nations. One is about the size of Maryland and has a population of 7.2 million; the other is as big as Montana but has a population of 123.5 million. The first has a population density of 703 people per square mile, a lot by most standards; the second has a density of 860 per square mile, among the highest on the planet. Country No. 1 has tracts of untouched forest and reserves of gold, tin, tungsten, and natural gas. Country No. 2 has few natural resources and little arable land. Life there is so crowded that the subways hire special guards to mash people onto the trains. Is it, therefore, overpopulated?

Most economists would say no. Country No. 2 is Japan. Paul Demeny, a demographer at the Population Council, in New York City, notes that Japan is where the Malthusian nightmare has come true. Population has long since overtaken agricultural capacity. "Japan would be in great trouble if it had to feed itself," Demeny says. "They can't eat VCRs. But they don't worry, because they can exchange them for food." Demeny is less sanguine about Country No. 1—Rwanda, the place with the highest fertility rate in the world. There, too, the production of food lags behind the production of people. But Rwanda, alas, has little to trade. "If something goes wrong," Demeny says, "they will have to beg."

Some economists might therefore attach to this crowded land the label "overpopulated." Others, though, might say that Rwanda has not yet reached the kind of critical mass necessary to develop its rich natural endowment. Fewer than 200,000 souls inhabit Kigali, its capital and biggest city, hardly enough to be the hub of a modern nation. In this case, a cure for having too many children to feed might be to have more children— the approach embraced by the Rwandan government until 1983.

Rwanda's leaders may well have been bowing to the popular will. By and large, people in the developing world have big families because they want them. "The notion that people desperately want to have fewer children but can't quite figure out how to do it is a bit simple," Demeny says. "If you picture an Indian who sees his children as capital because at the age of nine they can be sent to work in a carpet factory, his interest in family planning will not be keen." If the hypothetical impoverished Indian father does not today desperately need the money that his children can earn, he will need it in his dotage. Offspring are the Social Security of traditional cultures everywhere, a form of savings that few can afford to forgo. In such cases the costs of big families (mass illiteracy, crowded hiring halls, overused public services) are spread across society, whereas the benefits (income, old-age insurance) are felt at home. Economists call such phenomena "market failure." The outcome, entirely predictable, is a rapidly growing population.

Equally predictable is the proposed solution: bringing home the cost to those who experience the benefits. Enforcing child-labor and truancy laws, for example, drives up the price of raising children, and may improve their lives as well. Reducing price controls on grain raises farmers' incomes, allowing them to hire adults rather than put their children to work. Increasing opportunities for women lets them choose between earning income and having children. In the short term such modifications can hurt. In the long term, Demeny believes, they are "a piece of social engineering that any modern society should aspire to." Rwanda, like many poor countries, now has a population-control program. But pills and propaganda will be ineffective if having many children continues to be the rational choice of parents.

To ecologists, this seems like madness. Rational, indeed! More people in Rwanda would mean ransacking its remaining tropical forest—an abhorrent thought. The real problem is that Rwandans receive an insufficient share of the world's feast. The West should help them rise as they are, by forgiving their debts, investing in their industries, providing technology, increasing foreign aid—and insisting that they cut birth rates. As for the claim that Japan is not overpopulated, the Japanese are shipping out their polluting industries to neighboring countries—the same countries, environmentalists charge, that they are denuding with rapacious logging. "If all nations held the same number of people per square kilometer," Edward O. Wilson has written about Japan, "they would converge in quality of life to Bangladesh. . . . " To argue that Tokyo is a model of populousness with prosperity is, Wilson thinks, "sophistic."

Wait, one hears the economists cry, that's not predation, that's trade! Insisting on total self-sufficiency veers toward autarky. Japan logs other people's forests because its own abundant forests are too mountainous to sustain a full program of—*and wait a minute*, haven't we been here before? The competing statistics, the endless back-and-forth argument? Isn't there some better way to think about this?

GOOD NEWS, BAD NEWS

In 1968, when *The Population Bomb* was first published, the United Nations Population Division surveyed the world's demographic prospects. Its researchers projected future trends in the world's total fertility rate, a figure so common in demographic circles that it is often referred to, without definition, as the TFR. The TFR is the answer to the question "If women keep having babies at the present rate, how many will each have, on average, in her lifetime?" If a nation's women have two children apiece, exactly replacing themselves and the fathers of their children, the TFR will be 2.0 and the population will eventually stop growing. (Actually, replacement level is around 2.1, because some children die.) In the United States the present TFR is about 2.0, which means that, not counting immigration, the number of Americans will ultimately hit a plateau. (Immigration, of course, may alter this picture.) But the researchers in the division were not principally concerned with the United States. They were looking at poorer countries, and they didn't like what they saw.

As is customary, the division published three sets of population projections: high, medium, and low, reflecting different assumptions behind them. The medium projection, usually what the demographer regards as the most likely alternative, was that the TFR for developing nations would fall 15 percent from 1965–1970 to 1980–1985. At the time, Ronald Freedman recalls, this view was regarded as optimistic. "There was a lot of skepticism that anything could happen," he says. He was working on family-planning programs in Asia, and he received letters from colleagues telling him how hopeless the whole endeavor was.

Now a professor emeritus of sociology at the University of Michigan, Freedman is on the scientific advisory committee of Demographic and Health Surveys, a private organization in Columbia, Maryland, which is funded by the U.S. government to assess births and deaths in Third World nations. Its data, painstakingly gathered from surveys, are among the best available. From 1965–1970 to 1980–1985 fertility in poor countries dropped 30 percent, from a TFR of 6.0 to one of 4.2. In that period, Freedman and his colleague Ann K. Blanc have pointed out, the poor countries of the world moved almost halfway to a TFR of 2.1: replacement level. (By 1995, Blanc says, they might be two thirds of the way there.) If the decrease continues, it will surely be the most astonishing demographic shift in history. (The second most astonishing will be the rise that preceded it.) The world went halfway to replacement level in the twenty years from 1965 to 1985; arithmetic suggests that if this trend continues we will arrive at replacement level in the subsequent twenty years—that is, by 2005.

That's the good news. The bad news is that since the late 1960s, 1.9 billion more people have arrived on the planet than have left. Even if future rates of fertility are the lowest in history, as is likely, the children of today's children, and their children's children, will keep replacing themselves, and the population will increase vastly. Nothing will stop that increase, not even AIDS. Pessimists estimate that by the end of the decade another 100 million people will be infected by HIV. Almost ten times that number will have been born. Barring unprecedented catastrophe, the year 2100 will see 10 to 12 billion people on the planet.

Nobody will have to wait that long to feel the consequences. In a few years today's children will be clamoring to take their place in the adult world. Jobs, homes, cars, a few occasional treats—these are things they will want. And though economists are surely right when they say the lesson of history is that the great majority of these men and women will make their way, it is hard not to be awed by the magnitude of the task facing the global economy. A billion jobs. A billion homes. A billion cars. Billions and billions of occasional treats.

TREES AND SOIL

Few places in the United States better illustrate the unforeseen consequences of population growth than the lower valley of the Hudson River, which runs south from Albany to New York City. The river is wide and placid in appearance, and its banks sparkle with towns that were young when the nation was young. To the west rise the Catskills, blue at sunset and blanketed by trees. Interstate 87 makes a ribbon between the water and the mountains. A while ago I spent some time driving on that road, and down long miles of its length the forest stretched out so far and so dark and so empty that I imagined I was looking at the America of a hundred years ago, before there were millions of people like me around. How wonderful, I thought, that so close to Manhattan is a huge piece of real estate that we never trashed.

I was wrong. If I had traveled through the Hudson Valley at the end of the last century, I would have passed through an utterly different landscape. I would have been surrounded by small hardscrabble farms, fields of wheat and corn, and pastures ringed by stone walls. It might have looked picturesque—certainly guidebook writers of the day thought so. But I wouldn't have seen many trees, because long before, almost every scrap of land that wasn't vertical had been clear-cut or burned.

The forest was stripped to make way for agriculture and to supply New York's army of charcoal-burners (who needed lumber to make charcoal), tanners (who extracted tannin from bark), and salt-makers (who used wood fuel to boil down seawater). Loggers played a role too: Albany, the northernmost deepwater port on the Hudson, was the biggest timber town in the nation and possibly the world. When the first Europeans came to New York, the region was almost entirely covered by trees; by the end of the nineteenth century less than a quarter of the state was wooded, and most of what was left had been picked through, or was inaccessible, or was being kept by farmers as private fuel reserves. During the epoch that I, swooping along the tarmac in my minivan, was nostalgically picturing as a paradise, newspaper editorials were warning that deforestation would drive the valley toward ecological disaster.

Since then the collapse of small farming has allowed millions of acres to return to nature. When New York State surveyed itself in 1875, the six counties that make up the lower Hudson Valley—Columbia, Dutchess, Greene, Orange, Putnam, and Ulster—contained 573,003 acres of timberland, covering about 21 percent of their total area, In 1980, the date of the most recent survey, trees covered almost 1.8 million acres, more than three times as much. (This is no scrubby growth, mind you. Michael Greason, an associate forester in the state's Department of Environmental Conservation, calls today's Hudson and Catskill forest a "beautiful, diverse ecosystem.")

I was driving around the Hudson Valley partly because I was looking for a house in the country. My method of looking, insofar as one could call it a method, was to hunt in the counties with the lowest populations, figuring that they would be the least spoiled. I was trying to get away from people, and from the unpleasantness I associated with urban life. The more crowded an area, I thought, the more degraded its environment. I wanted natural beauty, and that meant "uninhabited."

Learning some local history gave me pause. Back in 1875 my six counties had a collective population of 345,679. The U.S. Census says the figure for 1990 was 924,075. In other words, the number of people living there almost tripled in the same period that the local ecosystem climbed out of its sickbed and threw away its crutches. This wasn't just some odd thing that happened in New York. As a whole, American forests are bigger and healthier than they were at the turn of the century, when the country's population was below 100 million. Massachusetts and some other states have as many trees as they had in the days of Paul Revere. Nor was this growth restricted to North America: Europe's forest resources increased by 25 or 30 percent from 1970 to 1990, a time in which its population grew from 462 million to 502 million. Presumably the forest figure would have been yet higher without the continent's damaging acid rain.

People pollute. But more people does not always mean more pollution. Eco-critics can claim, with some justification, that the forests of the Hudson Valley recuperated because farmers abandoned them in order to wipe out the native grasslands of the Great Plains. But they can't explain away all the good news. Salmon are reintroduced to the Thames. White-tailed deer, almost extinct in 1900, plague New England gardens. Air quality in Tokyo improves remarkably. Wild turkeys have a greater range than they did when they were first seen by white settlers. If all this occurred during the population boom, why the belief, now frequently voiced, that overpopulation will lead to an eco-catastrophe?

"You can look at Lake Erie or Detroit and see it's gotten better," says Dennis L. Meadows, the leader of the research group that produced *The Limits to Growth*. "But to leap from that to the conclusion that there has been overall improvement is to look at one person getting rich and say that everybody is better off." Now at the helm of the Institute for Policy and Social Science Research at the University of New Hampshire, Meadows, with two co-authors, has recently published a sequel, *Beyond the Limits,* which is even more pessimistic than the first book. "When a rich country becomes concerned about environmental problems," Meadows says, "then it can typically develop effective responses." Lead additives in gasoline became a subject of American worries. The nation forced petroleum companies to phase out leaded gas, and lead levels diminished. Similar fears have led twenty-three industrialized countries since 1987 to halve the rate of release of the worst ozone-eating compounds. In Meadow's view, rich countries have the wealth to buy their way out of many such difficulties. But other difficulties remain, and their number grows. Soil erodes; draining ruins wetlands; contaminants infiltrate groundwater; toxic wastes keep accumulating. The situation is much worse in poor countries that cannot pay to clean themselves up. Behind all the concerns is the specter of growing numbers, of insatiable human wants, of continually increasing demand. "We're trying to sustain physical growth on a finite planet," he says. "Growth will stop in our lifetime." Meadows, who is fifty, confidently expects to see the end of population growth in his lifetime—probably through ecological breakdown.

Cassandras like Meadows, Ehrlich, and Lester Brown, of Worldwatch, regard land degradation as one of the worst and most obvious ecological consequences of crowding too many people into too little space. "Land degradation" is a catchall term covering such problems as wind and water erosion, soil pollution by urban wastes or pesticides, and the buildup of mineral salts caused by improper irrigation. The term may bring to mind newspaper photographs of faraway African husbandmen in terrain nibbled to exhaustion by cattle. But environmentalists say the problem is bigger than that—"virtually a world-wide epidemic," in the words of Anne Ehrlich, a research associate at Stanford University, a veteran Cassandra, and the wife of Paul Ehrlich. The International Soil Reference and Information Centre (ISRIC), in the Netherlands, estimates that since 1945 *Homo sapiens* has degraded 17 percent of the world's land, not counting wastelands like Antarctica and the Gobi Desert. Two thirds of the devastated area will require major restoration.

Every year, Brown warns, erosion steals 24 billion tons of soil from the world's farmers—a figure that the ecology-minded cite as plain evidence that humanity is exceeding the carrying capacity of the planet.

The economics-minded see rhetoric and hand-waving. "Those figures Lester Brown is going on are based on really wild assumptions," says Pierre Crosson, a senior fellow at Resources for the Future, a nonprofit research group in Washington, D.C. "He's taking poorly understood sedimentation figures from big river deltas and extrapolating them to get a figure for productivity loss for the whole world." As for the ISRIC study, Crosson points out that it classifies most of Illinois, Iowa, Kansas, Nebraska, and the Dakotas as degraded enough to "greatly reduce" productivity. "The problem with this," he says, "is that in those six states yields have risen steadily over the last forty years."

The United States has the most carefully measured soil in the world. Every five years the U.S. Department of Agriculture evaluates the nation's land, county by county, in terms of something called "the universal soil loss equation," which assesses the soil movement in a given area. Because the equation measures movement rather than absolute disappearance, the results are hard to evaluate; they don't distinguish between soil that ends up on the bottom of the ocean and soil that is merely shifted to a neighbor's property, enriching yields there. (Sometimes the neighbors are far away: according to measurements by atmospheric scientists at the University of Virginia, more than 13 million tons of rich African soil are blown every year onto the Amazon forest floor.) In the 1980s three independent studies, one by Crosson, used the data to estimate actual soil loss. All concluded that the peril to U.S. agriculture from erosion is negligible. "The Soil Conservation Service is doing its job," Crosson says.

It is hard to be as sanguine about the developing world. Sub-Saharan Africa, for instance, is often described as a place where overpopulation has led to a terrible destruction of land. The region has high birth rates; per capita food production has consistently fallen in the past ten years. Rainless years in the same period led to overgrazing, deforestation, wide-scale erosion, and the hunger shown in sad televised images. Civil strife and famine have driven at least two million people from their homes. The desert is said to be marching south at a rate of five to six miles a year, a scary prospect that Cassandras regard as dramatic evidence of Africa's population quandary.

No one doubts that Africa is in a dire position, but the Pollyannas think that the problem is bad luck, bad weather, and bad planning. Traditionally, African villagers often held land in common, with access regulated by unwritten cultural rules. "In those circumstances," Crosson says, "the people responsible for the management of the land take overuse into account, so they enforce rules of access that limit the use of the land." When modern crops and agricultural techniques appear, the system comes apart, because yields shoot high enough to give people a greater incentive to cheat. If they break the rules, they can make a bundle and skip town with the profit; those who play fair are left with the ruins. (Garrett Hardin calls this the "tragedy of the commons.") Population pressures exacerbate the problem, most economists concede, by shrinking everyone's share of the common land. Add drought or ethnic conflict and the result is disaster. But, they say, African nations without drought or conflict have done increasingly well. Given half a chance, people in Africa, like people anyplace else, seem to make their own way.

The Cassandras base their case "on intuitively powerful hypotheses that slide over the need for empirical verification," says Michael Mortimore, a senior research associate at Cambridge University, England. "Unfortunately, the only way to test them is to collect a large amount of empirical data." Mortimore has spent years gathering information on farms in Nigeria and Kenya. His comparison of contemporary and thirteen-year-old dirt samples in Nigeria, one of Africa's most heavily populated nations, shows that increasing population has, if anything, *raised* land productivity. In decades past, farmers could exhaust an area and then move on. Now rising numbers have made land more expensive, and people have greater incentives to take care of what they have. "You're not going to pass on a desert to your children," Mortimore says. Claiming that Africans are otherwise inclined is, to his mind, "straightforward cultural prejudice." The agricultural systems that he studies are "economically, socially, and ecologically sustainable." In Nigeria, he says, the 1992 harvest was the biggest in twenty years.

As for other parts of sub-Saharan Africa, no one denies the famine there. Yet recent independent studies have found no *long-term* environmental consequences of the recent and devastating drought; the southern border of the desert, one study shows, is in about the same place it was eighty years ago, suggesting that the desert expands and contracts with little regard for its human inhabitants. The drought may have led to temporary overuse of common property, economists concede, but the proper response would be to adjust land-use rules—change the zoning, so to speak—as societies did in other parts of Africa. That response's alleged failure to occur in sub-Saharan Africa says more about the pervasive corruption, inefficiency, and civil turmoil there than about the inherent evils of breeding.

"You always can blame any particular difficulty on something that is not overpopulation," Dennis Meadows says. "Nobody ever dies of overpopulation. They die of famine, pestilence, and war. There's always some proximate cause." Adjusting land-use rules is desirable in his view, but it does nothing to eliminate the fundamental problem. At bottom, more people means more resource use and more loss of biodiversity, all of which must eventually stop. We can't go on forever, because the world is finite. No matter how smart we are, Cassandras say, we can't avoid being part of the web of life, governed by its laws. True enough, the Pollyannas say. But our part in that web is to be different. Other species die when they breed enough to wreck their environments, as they sometimes do. Human beings don't wait to be overwhelmed. When problems arise, we solve them—that's our nature. This argument makes Cassandras smite their collective brow and deride, as Ehrlich did recently, the "imbeciles running around today saying not to worry, that with the aid of science and technology we can take good care of many billions more."

THINKING DIFFERENTLY

In Nathan Keyfitz's view, the argument amounts to a classic academic standoff. Keyfitz leads a group of demographers at the International Institute for Applied Systems Analysis (IIASA), a research group in Austria, and is one of the few people I heard praised by both sides in the dispute. Keyfitz recalls attending a meeting at Brandeis University convened with the noble intention of reconciling biologists and economists. For three days speakers from each side stated their points of view, completely ignoring everything the other side had said. Then, apparently satisfied, everyone went home. "Here," Keyfitz has written, "is a nightmare for democratic politics: what action to take on vital questions where the experts disagree violently."

A first step away from the impasse, Keyfitz suggests, might be for each side to accept the validity of the other's arguments, as long as they pertain to that side's discipline. Give the biologists their due, and agree that an increased human presence poses a huge threat to the environment, even if some of the biologists' claims are exaggerated. Then agree with economists that the problems are not due to population growth per se. Instead, population growth changes social and economic systems, which inevitably creates environmental problems: more food must be grown, so that once-adequate agricultural methods now overuse land.

But Keyfitz is hesitant to embrace the next step in the economists' logic. "I think we all know the idea," he says. "As you catch up with these problems one by one, you turn the power of science on them and produce solutions." Sometimes the correction is expensive, Cassandras admit, but thoughtful government policies can minimize the pinch. Here we step outside the boundaries of economics into political science, into arguments nobody has promised to accept. The picture, Keyfitz says, has governments responding wisely—and, as everyone knows, they often don't. Indeed, an outside observer might find it curious that economists—disdainful of government in other matters—exhibit such touching faith in the power of their elected representatives to resolve the troubles exacerbated by rising population.

Even if governments try to respond, they are often unable to anticipate the consequences of their actions. As a means of fostering international communication, Keyfitz says, "the worldwide air-transport network does nothing but good. But it's responsible for the spread of AIDS. Otherwise it would be an unrecognized, unnamed disease in a corner of Africa." With the instant contact possible today, a local problem became a global catastrophe. "You'd like more chance to breathe," Keyfitz says. "I'm not saying that any of these problems are inherently unresolvable by themselves, but we wouldn't be running so fast if the world had half its present population."

As the human presence increasingly dominates the earth, new difficulties emerge at ever greater speed: The ozone layer. The exhaustion of fisheries. The greenhouse effect. The overuse of aquifers. The need to increase yields of tropical foodstuffs. Each must be evaluated, absorbed, treated, even as the next problem appears. The loss of biodiversity. The collapse of the infrastructure. The destruction of rain forests. And on and on. Maybe people can keep up; certainly Keyfitz's colleagues, the computer modelers at IIASA, think so. But in a world where every citizen is surrounded by examples of governmental incompetence, it is hard to imagine that nations will keep coming through, time after time. There'll be so much *juggling*. So many things will have to be fixed all at once. Societies will find themselves in the position of the antic ninjas in video arcades, hordes of enemies to every side. Whack! Bam! Pow! Eventually, as any adolescent knows, the ninja slips up, and the game is over.

MY MADONNA PROBLEM

For many years I had an office on the fourteenth floor of a building in Manhattan, overlooking a busy avenue. During that time I never had air-conditioning, because it does something to the air that makes my nose run. In hot weather I opened the window. A breeze came in, reducing the temperature to a range I found tolerable. The problem was that it was hard to speak on the phone with the window open. People drove around the city with their car stereo systems cranked up to medically unsafe levels. Abrupt blasts of noise filled the room.

A debacle occurred when I interviewed Mario Cuomo, the governor of New York. Arranging the call involved considerable negotiation with his office in Albany. Two minutes into the conversation Madonna arrived. I had to shout over her moans. The governor did not immediately believe my explanation of the sound's origin. The light changed; the noise went away. I asked him a question. Suddenly Madonna showed up again. I realized that she was circling the block, looking for a parking space. I slammed the window shut, raising the room's temperature by ten degrees. The song was still devastatingly loud. The third time the song came round, I draped my jacket over the window. The fourth time, the governor hung up.

Soon after, I began looking for a house in the country.

The noise, and my response to it, illustrate what social scientists might regard as typical population-related feedback. Congestion grows in a city; it becomes impossible to avoid Madonna indoors; people move; the city becomes less congested. Or, perhaps, the city enforces noise ordinances. In either case the problem is resolved after temporary conflict.

"Temporary"—note the hedge word. The window of my old office looked out over the remains of the West Side Highway, part of which was closed as unsafe in the 1970s. I began using the office after a lengthy squabble had broken out over the best way to repair the road. Some wanted to do the job cheaply, shifting the money to mass transit; others said that the city needed the highway to revitalize its waterfront. Politicians, environmentalists, neighborhood groups, and construction unions attacked one another. Reconstructing the West Side Highway became a legal imbroglio of dizzying complexity. Charges and countercharges, suits and countersuits—I couldn't begin to follow it. Meanwhile, huge rush-hour lines built up twice a day on the partially closed road. Not wanting to sit in traffic, people took the exit near my office and continued their journeys on my street. They've been doing that in one form or another for more than a decade—which is part of the reason there was so much congestion on the street, and part of the reason Madonna was in my office for so long.

Move to the country, buy extra-thick insulated windows—middle-class Americans like me are unlikely to face the extreme choices that will confront people in developing nations. As Meadows says, we will be able to buy our way out of some problems. But that does not mean that Americans will escape the repercussions of population growth. In 1990 the United States had 249 million inhabitants. Current Census Bureau projections foresee that births and immigration will drive that number to 345 million by 2030. Ninety-six million more Americans! Imagine everything that local, state, and federal governments will have to do to accommodate them. Think of all the thoughtful planning that will be required to make life pleasant. Whether it will happen "is an absolutely open question, in my judgment," says Allen Kelley, an economist at Duke University. "We're talking about political theory, and there just *is* no theory for this."

The future is not completely opaque. Demographers know roughly where those 96 million new Americans will live, who they will be, and what they will do. The Census Bureau projects that the extra people will not distribute themselves in an even blanket over the country. About half will choose to live in just three states: California, Texas, and Florida. Not one of these can absorb its share easily. California has too little water. Texas an unsteady economy, Florida a particularly troubled set of ecosystems. All three will also need many new roads, bridges, sewers, and schools—an expensive proposition.

Relatively few of the newcomers will be white. By 2030 about 40 percent of Americans will have ancestral roots in Africa, Asia, or Latin America. Few would disagree that people of color have long been at the bottom of the American pyramid. If that continues, many of the 96 million will be poor, and in the twenty-first century a bigger percentage of the U.S. population will be below the poverty level than is now. If that does not continue, white Americans will for the first time face nonwhite power centers. California, Texas, and Florida will have three of the four biggest voting blocs in the House of Representatives (the fourth will be New York's). All three could be dominated by Hispanics and African-Americans. If history is any guide, either alternative will put white Americans' moral grace sorely to the test.

The United States has a long border with Mexico, and thousands of miles of coastline. Migrants want to come in, and Americans seem increasingly diffident about putting out the welcome mat. (In 1991 Argentina's president publicly toyed with the idea of resettling skilled refugees at a price of about $50,000 a head.) Meanwhile, rising numbers will thrust together the blacks, whites, yellows, browns, and reds who are already here in ways they have not been before. Political turmoil is increasing in Europe—especially in France and Germany—as migrants from Africa, the Middle East, and the former Soviet bloc demand a piece of the better life. Population growth did not cause ethnic conflicts, but it could sharpen them.

At the same time, the United States will have to address its age shift. Census Bureau projections tell a sobering story. By 2030, one out of five Americans will be sixty-five or older. The ratio of elderly people to people of working age will have tripled since 1950, meaning that, on average, workers will have to support three times as many older people. (The figure may be offset somewhat by the smaller number of children there will be to support. But the problem will be amplified by the growing number of people in their sixties and seventies who will be taking care of still more elderly people, in their eighties and nineties.) Workers, meanwhile, will be facing gloomier prospects. Nowadays fewer older people are alive than younger people, which means that there is an approximate match between the small number of older workers and the small number of important jobs. As the population ages, this will change. "In a stationary population," Ansley Coale, the Princeton demographer, has written, "there would no longer be a reasonable expectation of advancement as a person moves through life." More and more people will find themselves trapped in dead-end jobs. In some ways, Coale suggests, we may end up looking back with envy at the days of rapid population growth.

People will have to deal with the frustration—at the same time that they seek politicians able to resolve all the other problems. An optimist can say that the American people are kind, clever, and adaptable. An optimist can say that Americans can resolve the difficulties described, and the others these will inspire. But even an optimist must conclude that the government will have its hands full, and might well wonder what it will be like to live in a future America that must balance so much so artfully. My guess is that it will be something like living in New York City today.

Because I had nothing else to do, I walked along the last remaining section of the West Side Highway one recent Friday afternoon—a masochistic act. The road is officially under construction, and so its shoulders have not been cleaned up. Heaps of trash lie in windblown aggregations. The walls are gray and peeling. Cars move slowly and impatiently, in billows of exhaust. It is like an evocation of an unpleasant future. New York City took a hit in the recession, and the familiar assortment of urban evils got worse. Unemployment and crack use went up; real estate values, tax revenues, and bond ratings went down. The city fabric sprang a hundred big leaks. Like so many Dutch boys, the city fathers raced to plug them. Meanwhile, a thousand interest groups scrabbled to protect themselves. Understandably, fixing the highway seems not to have assumed pressing importance.

That day on the West Side Highway, I heard many radios played at high volume. I could see the point. License plates came from Connecticut, New Jersey, and Pennsylvania; drivers were commuting for hours to sit in traffic. Only part of their daily grind was due to the sheer size of New York; traffic jams afflict much smaller cities. But a three-hour commute is what some architects call a "disamenity." The waiting, the ugly walls, the blaring horns, the inability to get away from it all: these are the disamenities of overpopulation in rich societies. None is directly attributable to population growth. Each is an emblem of bureaucratic overload—overload caused by the hundred predicaments that population growth aggravates. The city could have fixed the West Side Highway long ago. So could the state, or the federal government. But they didn't. There are too many other, bigger concerns, and there will be for a long time. My Madonna problem is not going to vanish.

Population growth forces nations to confront problems that they could finesse in less crowded times. The inefficiencies of New York's highways surely mattered less when the metropolitan area held eight million people rather than fifteen. Governments may, as economists hope, avoid the major, life-threatening disasters. "Even Congress isn't stupid enough to avoid dealing with the ozone layer," one economist told me. Americans may create a society that can hold an older, darker-colored population. But while they are doing that, the disamenities accrue, making the future a grayer, grimier place. Per capita GNP may go up and up, but life will be less pleasant. How much less pleasant? The answer depends on the strength of the citizenry's desire to have a government that works much more flexibly and wisely than government does now. New Yorkers to date have shown little such inclination.

Down by Wall Street the West Side Highway has been demolished. The reconstructed roadway passes a few blocks to the west of the building where I saw those people on the gurneys. My guess is that most of its inhabitants—the real ones, I mean—have moved on. More have moved in, though. We're marching into the future together. Curtains are visible from the highway. There's some lawn furniture on the roof. It makes me wonder who owns it, and what they do, and whether, like me, they have children.

Questions for Thinking and Writing

1. Explain the distinctions between Cassandras and Pollyannas. Who are the proponents and which position do you support? How would you attempt to bridge the communication gap between contemporary biologists and economists?
2. What is the paradox of American forests? How can some ecological problems dissipate while the environment degrades and population increases?
3. What is Mann's point of view in this essay? How does he resolve his "Madonna Problem"?

Questions for Thinking and Writing About Part 4

1. Suppose you were in a debate and had to take a stand on this statement: "I believe humankind can achieve a working, sustainable relationship with the environment." How would you present your response (either pro or con) and support your thesis?

2. Does the idea of individual ownership of land make sense from an environmental viewpoint? Discuss your answer in light of the Native American concept of land ownership given in Leslie Marmon Silko's "Ceremony" (p. 338). How does this sense of intangible ownership compare with Henry David Thoreau's "Where I Lived, and What I Lived For" (p. 12) and Mary Hunter Austin's "My Neighbor's Field" (p. 61)?

3. Consider whether or not our uses of and attitudes toward nature need to change with the times and contexts of historical necessity. In what ways does Michael Pollan examine the conflict of the environmentalist's reverence for natural nature and the desire to make nature what we think it ought to be?

4. Explain the similarities and dissimilarities concerning the spiritual efficacy of place and humankind's situation in the natural environment in Leslie Marmon Silko's "Ceremony" (p. 338) and Jack Kerouac's "Desolation Peak" (p. 248).

5. How can Wendell Berry in "The Ecological Crisis as a Crisis of Character" (p. 348) defend his notion that "The good of the whole of Creation . . . is never a consideration because it is never thought of" when there is a considerable body of evidence to the contrary? What reading selections in Part 4 can be used to refute Barry's assertion?

6. How do you contradict the argument of the health official who says that the high rates of cancer on the Upper Cape may not be caused by the plumes and contamination, but maintains that "I wouldn't want to say it's safe to drink the water there"?

7. When factories and communities exist side by side, who is responsible for public safety? To what extent is anyone ready to save lives? What is the government's role? What is industry's role?

8. What keeps us from destroying ourselves? Do you think there is something about our instinct for survival that acts as a safeguard against massive destruction?

Credits

Index